Digital Media Tools

Third Edition

Nigel Chapman and Jenny Chapman

Copyright © 2007   Nigel Chapman and Jenny Chapman
Published by   John Wiley & Sons Ltd, The Atrium, Southern Gate, Chichester,
                       West Sussex PO19 8SQ, England

                       Telephone   (+44) 1243 779777

Email (for orders and customer service enquiries): cs-books@wiley.co.uk
Visit our Home Page on www.wiley.com

First edition © 2002 by John Wiley & Sons, Ltd. Second edition © 2003 by John Wiley & Sons, Ltd
Cover illustration: Fernand Léger: Study for Constructions: The Team at Rest, 1950
© ADAGP, Paris and DACS, London 2007

Other Wiley Editorial Offices

John Wiley & Sons Inc., 111 River Street, Hoboken, NJ 07030, USA

Jossey-Bass, 989 Market Street, San Francisco, CA 94103-1741, USA

Wiley-VCH Verlag GmbH, Boschstr. 12, D-69469 Weinheim, Germany

John Wiley & Sons Australia Ltd, 33 Park Road, Milton, Queensland 4064, Australia

John Wiley & Sons (Asia) Pte Ltd, 2 Clementi Loop #02-01, Jin Xing Distripark, Singapore 129809

John Wiley & Sons Canada Ltd, 22 Worcester Road, Etobicoke, Ontario, Canada, M9W 1LI

Wiley also publishes its books in a variety of electronic formats. Some content that appears in print may not be
available in electronic books.

British Library Cataloguing in Publication Data

A catalogue record for this book is available from the British Library

ISBN 978-0-470-01227-7 (PB)

Produced from the authors' own PDF files
Printed and bound in Great Britain by Bell & Bain, Glasgow
This book is printed on acid-free paper responsibly manufactured from sustainable forestry
in which at least two trees are planted for each one used for paper production.

Contents

Welcome

This book is intended primarily as a lab work text for use in college courses on Web design, digital media, multimedia and Web graphics, though it will be of equal value to anyone wishing to learn on their own. Most courses in these subjects deal with the preparation and manipulation of individual media, as well as with the bringing of media together into Web pages or some other sort of multimedia presentation. Several quite different tools are involved in the practical side of these studies. This presents an unprecedented learning and teaching challenge to students and tutors. Students typically require a fast way in to a basic mastery of the complex tools which put their more intellectual studies into practice, and which are used in the industry. Tutors are expected to provide instruction on a collection of rapidly developing programs. Most texts, however, concentrate on a single program, typically contain far more information than is required by students who are not intending to specialize in that program, and tend to lack pedagogical features suited to learning in a college environment.

In contrast, this book brings together in one volume several of the major software tools for preparing and combining digital media, and addresses the particular needs of Web design and digital media students at an appropriate level of detail. It provides a thorough, well-guided, and clearly focused introduction to each tool, with the acquisition of essential skills made as straight-forward as possible, without unnecessary embellishments or over-refinement. Explanation of principles and underlying theory is provided throughout, in order to ensure that practice-based learning is properly supported by a genuine understanding of what is actually going on when each feature of these tools is used. Our approach is to encourage learning by doing, but not just by slavishly copying the steps of some exercise or project that we have set up as an example to follow. Instead, throughout each chapter, we provide numerous exercises intended to systematically develop the physical and mental skills which are needed to use the tools effectively. These exercises are staged so that they only require an understanding of the features that have already been described in each chapter, and they typically focus on the particular feature which has just been discussed in the preceding section.

We should stress that we are addressing people whose primary interest is in combining media into Web pages and multimedia, not potential specialists in any single program. This book is not intended to create expert users, and it doesn't describe every single command and operation you can use in each program, but it should provide the basic skills necessary to perform everyday tasks, together with an understanding of what is actually going on when these tasks are carried out. This may serve as a springboard for later specialization, but should be adequate in itself for generalists to be able to make work using a combination of tools. The experience gained from using tools in this way should also provide an understanding of the potential of each tool, an appreciation of the skills of specialists and a basis for communicating with colleagues in professional contexts.

The book was written both to provide a practical complement to our theoretical course texts *Web Design: A Complete Introduction* and *Digital Multimedia* (published by John Wiley & Sons, Ltd.), and to serve as a stand-alone text for individuals or courses with a wholly practical orientation. It has no pre-requisite in computer science, and will be of value to anyone undertaking practical work in digital media, Web design and Web graphics. We do assume that readers have some experience of using a desktop computer system and know how to use menu commands, dialogue boxes, and so on. The book has been written from experience in teaching software tools to undergraduates at all levels.

The book is arranged as follows. The Introduction expands on our view of the skills demanded by digital media tools, and the best way to acquire them. Chapter 2 provides a general description of the user interface elements that are found in all or most of the programs we cover. Chapters 3 to 7 are each devoted to a single program. Chapter 8 describes a number of features which appear in almost identical form in two or more of the programs. Unlike Chapter 2, Chapter 8 will not make much sense until you have started working with the programs. One way of reading the book would be to start with the Introduction, skim through Chapter 2 to make sure you are familiar with the standard interface elements, and then read the chapters for specific applications you are interested in, turning to Chapter 8 when you find forward references. Alternatively, you could read all of Chapters 2 and 8 before you move on to any specific application.

All the programs we describe in this book are available in both Adobe Creative Suite 3 Design Premium and Adobe Creative Suite 3 Web Premium. They are all clear leaders in their field and are treated as industry standards, which anybody working professionally with digital media will be expected to know. Tools for video and audio editing have not been included in this volume.

We gratefully acknowledge Adobe's support and assistance with this project. The fact that this book focuses on Adobe software should not be taken as an endorsement of this text by Adobe, nor as an endorsement of Adobe's software by the authors.

There are, of course, many digital media tools in existence besides the few we have been able to accommodate in this book. Many of them have a thriving community of enthusiastic users, but do not have the status of an industry standard. For students and institutions that cannot afford the steep prices commanded by the professional tools, there are Open Source alternatives to Photoshop, Illustrator and Dreamweaver, in the form of The Gimp, Inkscape and NVu. These are not generally used in the industry, however, and we do not cover them in this book; if you wish to learn about these alternative tools you will need to look elsewhere.

Teaching and Learning Features

- The most important aspect of learning to use digital media tools is personal practice. To assist you we have suggested numerous practice exercises throughout the book. They are presented in distinctive "Try This" boxes, at the end of each sub-section or topic in every chapter.

- To help you memorize the most important features of each program, key points are presented in tinted "Don't Forget" boxes at appropriate points throughout the text. These key points are also available as slides which you may download from the supporting Web site.

- Important terms, marked in *bold italics* on their first occurrence in each chapter, are defined in a glossary which can be found on the supporting Web site.

Supporting Web Site

Further resources to support teaching and learning can be found at the book's own Web site, www.digitalmediatools.org. Here you will find a wide range of material, including working versions of some of the examples in the book, files to download for your own practical exercises, slides of the "Don't Forget" key points, teaching notes, practical hints and tips, suggestions for projects, information about updates to the software and the interactive glossary. Any corrections to errors that are discovered after the book is printed are also posted on the support site.

Much life of the hands is a form of knowledge: not a linguistic or symbolic knowledge such as you might use to read this book or write a computer program, but something based more on concrete action, such as sculpting plaster or clay.

Malcolm McCullough, *Abstracting Craft: The Practiced Digital Hand, p2.*

If your experience of using software has been confined to word processors, text editors, spreadsheets, database systems or compilers, Malcolm McCullough's words might seem, at first sight, to have little relevance to computer programs and their users. However, if you think for a moment about your experience of using the programs that you work with every day, you will see that many actions that contribute to your task have been internalized to such an extent that you don't have to think about what movements to make in order to pull down a menu and select a command to save a file, for example: you decide to save the file and your hands move to do so.

There's nothing scientific about ascribing knowledge to your hands – to the extent that we understand anything about knowledge, we know that it is the province of the brain. But the "knowledge of the hands" is more than a metaphor for the absorption of knowledge so that actions become apparently automatic. It's what it feels like. This sort of knowledge is best appreciated when we consider highly refined physical actions. The playing of a musical instrument, for example, requires that the hands "know" what to do. A significant stage in the learning of an instrument comes when your fingers start to move to the next note in a scale apparently on their own. In a more mundane sphere, knocking in a nail or chopping vegetables are tasks that we do not think about in any detail, although they require continuous fine judgements of position, force and movement. In fact, if you try to think about what you are doing while performing some of these tasks – where to place the knife, how hard to swing the hammer – you will become confused and clumsy, and will probably hurt yourself. Not only can you let your hands apparently work on their own, you have to in order to do the job well. It's only when the knowledge has been acquired in the hands – or if you prefer, when the actions have become automatic and the decisions subliminal – that you really know how to do the job. In the context of actions in the physical world, we might say that you had then become "skilful" at the particular task.

In everyday computing, typing on a keyboard is the action that most obviously exemplifies the difference between the hands knowing and not knowing. Even though many computer users cannot touch-type in the sense that trained typists can, experienced users can move their fingers without the laborious searching and poking that characterizes newcomers and occasional users. People who are experienced with a system with a command line interface, such as Unix, will be able to type common commands (such as ls -l) as if each were a single action, not a sequence of key presses: you want to find out what files are in the current directory, and your fingers just

Much life of the hands is a form of knowledge: not a linguistic or symbolic knowledge such as you might use to read this book or write a computer program, but something based more on concrete action, such as sculpting plaster or clay.

Malcolm McCullough, Abstracting Craft: The Practiced Digital Hand, p2.

If your experience of using software has been confined to word processors, text editors, spreadsheets, database systems or compilers, Malcolm McCullough's words might seem, at first sight, to have little relevance to computer programs and their users. However, if you think for a moment about your experience of using the programs that you work with every day, you will see that many actions that contribute to your task have been internalized to such an extent that you don't have to think about what movements to make in order to pull down a menu and select a command to save a file, for example: you decide to save the file and your hands move to do so.

There's nothing scientific about ascribing knowledge to your hands – to the extent that we understand anything about knowledge, we know that it is the province of the brain. But the "knowledge of the hands" is more than a metaphor for the absorption of knowledge so that actions become apparently automatic. It's what it feels like. This sort of knowledge is best appreciated when we consider highly refined physical actions. The playing of a musical instrument, for example, requires that the hands "know" what to do. A significant stage in the learning of an instrument comes when your fingers start to move to the next note in a scale apparently on their own. In a more mundane sphere, knocking in a nail or chopping vegetables are tasks that we do not think about in any detail, although they require continuous fine judgements of position, force and movement. In fact, if you try to think about what you are doing while performing some of these tasks – where to place the knife, how hard to swing the hammer – you will become confused and clumsy, and will probably hurt yourself. Not only can you let your hands apparently work on their own, you have to in order to do the job well. It's only when the knowledge has been acquired in the hands – or if you prefer, when the actions have become automatic and the decisions subliminal – that you really know how to do the job. In the context of actions in the physical world, we might say that you had then become "skilful" at the particular task.

In everyday computing, typing on a keyboard is the action that most obviously exemplifies the difference between the hands knowing and not knowing. Even though many computer users cannot touch-type in the sense that trained typists can, experienced users can move their fingers without the laborious searching and poking that characterizes newcomers and occasional users. People who are experienced with a system with a command line interface, such as Unix, will be able to type common commands (such as ls -l) as if each were a single action, not a sequence of key presses: you want to find out what files are in the current directory, and your fingers just

Introduction

are treated as industry standards, which anybody working professionally with digital media will be expected to know. Tools for video and audio editing have not been included in this volume.

We gratefully acknowledge Adobe's support and assistance with this project. The fact that this book focuses on Adobe software should not be taken as an endorsement of this text by Adobe, nor as an endorsement of Adobe's software by the authors.

There are, of course, many digital media tools in existence besides the few we have been able to accommodate in this book. Many of them have a thriving community of enthusiastic users, but do not have the status of an industry standard. For students and institutions that cannot afford the steep prices commanded by the professional tools, there are Open Source alternatives to Photoshop, Illustrator and Dreamweaver, in the form of The Gimp, Inkscape and NVu. These are not generally used in the industry, however, and we do not cover them in this book; if you wish to learn about these alternative tools you will need to look elsewhere.

Teaching and Learning Features

- The most important aspect of learning to use digital media tools is personal practice. To assist you we have suggested numerous practice exercises throughout the book. They are presented in distinctive "Try This" boxes, at the end of each sub-section or topic in every chapter.

- To help you memorize the most important features of each program, key points are presented in tinted "Don't Forget" boxes at appropriate points throughout the text. These key points are also available as slides which you may download from the supporting Web site.

- Important terms, marked in **bold italics** on their first occurrence in each chapter, are defined in a glossary which can be found on the supporting Web site.

Supporting Web Site

Further resources to support teaching and learning can be found at the book's own Web site, www.digitalmediatools.org. Here you will find a wide range of material, including working versions of some of the examples in the book, files to download for your own practical exercises, slides of the "Don't Forget" key points, teaching notes, practical hints and tips, suggestions for projects, information about updates to the software and the interactive glossary. Any corrections to errors that are discovered after the book is printed are also posted on the support site.

type the command. With command lines largely superseded by graphical user interfaces, control of the system is even more obviously in your hands, since it is the movements of the mouse that make most things happen. Although the graphical interface is supposedly more user-friendly and appealing to novices than the old-fashioned command line, to watch somebody who has never used a mouse before – even an experienced computer user – try to do something as simple as open an application program from the desktop can be a painful experience. The mouse runs away, the pointer moves slowly in jerks and misses the icon, a second click follows the first too slowly to be accepted as a double-click, and so on. Using a graphical user interface to a desktop operating system requires a non-trivial level of coordination. It is an acquired skill.

If this is so on the desktop, consider how much more skill is needed when we are using programs to create images or manipulate other digital media. Although applications such as the ones we describe in this book are computer programs and work with digital representations composed of bits, they provide interfaces to these digital representations that bear more resemblance to the use of physical tools for the manipulation of physical media than they do to the use of symbolic notations for the manipulation of bit patterns. If the only way to make an image on a computer was to write a program to set the values of all the pixels making up the picture, there would be very little computer graphics in the world. It is only because programs like Photoshop and Illustrator provide a means of manipulating pictures directly on the screen using your hands that designers, illustrators and artists and domestic consumers are able to work with computers.

It has become common to refer to computer programs that perform a single job as software tools, but our use of *Digital Media Tools* as the title of this book is also intended to draw your attention to the similarities between the applications used to create work in digital media and the tools used to create work in physical media. Digital media tools are devices to shape bits into images, animation, Web pages and other forms. And although present-day computers cannot provide us with the same contact with the medium we are working with as we are used to when working with real tools and real materials, they are largely controlled by the hand, using an input device such as a mouse or a graphics pen with a pressure-sensitive tablet, and they provide visual, if not tactile, feedback. They are tools in the sense that they extend our capabilities to let us do jobs that would be difficult or impossible without them, in the way that a screwdriver does. They are also tools in the sense that, in order to use them effectively, we need to learn them with our hands.

It is not just the hands that need to learn; the eyes, too, need training. When experienced users look at the screen of a computer running a program they know well, they will see something utterly different from what a novice will see. It's almost like the difference between what somebody who can read will see when they look at this page, and what someone who can't read will see. Almost every element of a program's user interface can tell you something, once you know what each one means. It may tell you something about the state of the document you are working on, or something about what you can do next. Part of the skill of using a program lies in being able to see the whole situation at a glance, without having to look at each individual icon or palette, in the way that chess grandmasters are said to be able to see the patterns of a game's possible evolution when they look at a chessboard, instead of an arrangement of pieces.

It's as well to remember, however, that there are important differences between using physical tools and digital tools. Malcolm McCullough once again succinctly expresses the differences in the physical relationship. "...consider the example of a skilled computer graphics artisan – if we may use this word. His or her hands are performing a sophisticated and unprecedented set of actions. These motions are quick, small, and repetitive, as in much traditional handwork, but somehow they differ. For one thing, they are faster – in fact, their rates matter quite a bit. They do not rely on pressure so much as position, velocity, or acceleration. The artisan's eye is not on the hand but elsewhere, on a screen."

There are other differences, too. Media tools programs are much more like a whole workshop than a single tool. Indeed, many of the operations you can perform in Photoshop, for example, are done by clicking on one of a set of icons that resembles an individual tool, such as a paint brush or a rubber stamp, and then dragging that tool over the image you are working on. In terms of the muscular actions you are carrying out, and the nature of the result achieved, it is these individual tools that are similar to a craftsman's tools, rather than the program considered as a whole.

However, the analogy should not be pursued too far. Photoshop, and all the other programs we describe, are just that: computer programs. We cannot always control them using movements; often, it is necessary to interact through menus and dialogue boxes. We can set a wide range of options for some tools and operations, so that it becomes necessary to think about parameters. There is a good deal of intellectual and symbolic activity involved in using any program, but these are programs of a special sort, whose interfaces need approaching in a different way from those of word processors and other office software or development tools.

Above all, to learn anything useful about a media tool, you must use it, and practise its use. We can tell you what the various commands and tools do, and an instructor can demonstrate them to you, but if you don't try for yourself, you won't know anything. It would be as if you tried to learn to play the guitar by reading a book or watching an instructional video without picking up the instrument. Perhaps, if you had a good enough memory, you might be able to memorize the fingering for chords and scales, but you would not be able to play them.

More than that, you still don't really know, in the way that someone who habitually uses these programs knows, until you have practised, and repeated the actions many times. Learning, and hence teaching, of this sort requires a different approach from more conventional academic learning. If this was a book about programming or the theory of multimedia, we would probably try to stretch your understanding by asking you to think about difficult things. Here, though, what we want to try and make you do is practise basic operations until you can feel them and know them for yourself. To this end, we have included simple practice exercises throughout the main chapters of the book. These are not in any sense intellectually demanding; you don't have to figure anything out. They don't have right answers, or even any answers at all. They may make you feel impatient or bored and want to get on to something more substantial (in the same way that it can be boring practising scales…). You may even feel that your intelligence is being insulted. Most of the time, though, these exercises are not concerned with intellect; we are trying to help you make your hands learn to move, your eyes learn to see and your brain learn how to coordinate.

We have made two assumptions. One is that you actually want to learn how to use the programs we are describing to you. We expect the learning to be a voluntary and an active process, and we assume that you will explore for yourself: try clicking on things to see what happens, move the mouse around and see what tool tips pop up, and so on. Our second assumption is that you will be able to figure some things out for yourself. If a preferences dialogue has a checkbox with the words Show tooltips next to it (as Flash's does), we aren't going to tell you that selecting the box will cause Flash to show tool tips. But we will tell you what tool tips are.

Even if you assiduously practise everything we suggest, this book is not likely to make you an expert in any of the programs it describes. It is only intended to provide the level of knowledge needed for somebody working in multimedia or Web design. This means enough working knowledge to be able to turn your hand to any of the tools when you have to, and enough knowledge to be able to understand what specialists and experts are talking about and to make informed decisions about what the tools are capable of and which might be best for any particular job. We stress again, though, that even the knowledge you need to make managerial decisions about the use of media tools cannot be an abstract knowledge, it must be based on experience. If you have read that it is possible to draw round an object with a tool called the background eraser in Photoshop, in order to extract it from its background, you know that extraction with the background eraser is an operation that a Photoshop user can perform. Thinking about that, you might see when it would be a useful thing to do, and how someone could go on to put the extracted object into another image, and so on. But until you've actually tried to use the background eraser yourself, you have no idea how hard or easy it is to use, or how well it works, and therefore no idea what you are actually asking of somebody when you tell them to use it. Try it yourself once, and you'll have some idea. Try it lots of times, and you'll know.

There is one other thing about the effective use of media tools. Like someone without artistic judgement who has learned how to use a paintbrush, or someone with no ear for music who has learned how to play a guitar, you could become highly proficient at using a digital media tool and still produce a terrible result. We have stressed the role of the hands and eyes, but as well as dexterity and coordination you need a sense of judgement, often based on observation, a clear idea of what you are trying to achieve, and the ability to recognize when you have – or have not – successfully achieved it. You also need the intelligence to choose the right tool for the job. We can't give you these things, we can only advise you to look at a lot of work that has been made with digital media tools, and learn what is good and bad about it. Follow links from the Showcase pages on Adobe's Web site, for example, and links on other sites that seek to highlight excellence in multimedia and Web design. Discover – or guess, if you can't find out – what tools have been used to create Web sites, animations and images. On the basis of what you have learned from using the tools yourself, observe how the tools have shaped the work, and always be on the lookout for original ways of applying tools.

Safe Working with Digital Media Tools

Using a computer for any purpose for extended periods of time carries with it certain health risks, the best-known of which is the risk of repetitive strain injuries (RSI), more properly called Cumulative Trauma Disorder. Users of media tools software are particularly at risk from such injuries, because these programs' interfaces are based on direct manipulation, which means that you will be making lots of small precise movements with an input device such as a mouse or graphics pen. Additionally, tasks such as image retouching are inherently fiddly and slow, but at the same time they can be quite absorbing, so you can easily find yourself spending extended periods of time at the computer, making repetitive movements with the mouse or pen. There is also a real risk of eye strain and possibly of damage to the eyes for anyone who stares at the screen for long periods, no matter what their age. You should rest your eyes by looking away from the screen and looking round the room at regular intervals. You should be especially careful if you experience headaches after computer use. All computer users should see an optician regularly, even if they are young or believe that they have perfect sight.

RSI from using computer input devices is usually first felt in the hands, particularly the thumb joints, wrists, forearm or neck. If you feel a burning pain in any of these areas, be sensible and stop work at once. If you don't, and it is RSI, it will only get worse, and the longer you persist despite the pain – which may be tempting if you are trying to finish a job or an assignment – the longer it will take to heal, and the more trouble you will be building for yourself in the future. Repetitive strain injuries are no joke and should not be taken lightly. They can render you unable to work for months at a time; severe cases may require years of rest or even surgery, which is not always effective. Even if you recover from an acute repetitive strain injury, the affected parts may be permanently weakened and thus susceptible to further injury, even after modest amounts of work. RSI can develop into a permanent disability.

We are not experts in RSI, but from personal experience we are painfully aware of the effects and their consequences. Anyone who suspects they may be suffering from RSI should consult a physiotherapist or doctor without delay, and anyone who is responsible for setting up equipment or supervising laboratory work should find out as much as they can about ergonomics and the prevention of injury. We can, however, pass on some simple advice for general use. We also provide links to useful Web sites on this book's support site **www.digitalmediatools.org**.

- If your fingers, thumb, wrist, arm, shoulder or neck start hurting when you are working, especially if you feel a sort of burning, tingling or shooting pain that repeats when you repeat a movement, *stop work at once*.

- Take frequent breaks.

- When working try to change position often, don't get locked into one position.

- Take your hand off the mouse or put down the pen whenever you are not using it. If you have more than one type of input device, try switching between them to avoid using the same one all the time.

- It is very important to maintain blood flow to the hands, so let your hands hang down loosely and shake them from time to time to improve circulation.

- Set up your equipment, desk and chair or stool so that you are comfortable, and don't have to stretch to use the keyboard and other input devices. You should never have to work with your hands higher than your elbow; your wrists should be straight. Having your arm extended while working at a desk can be an unnecessary strain. Try working on your lap instead (on a laptop or with a graphics tablet).

- Avoid putting pressure on your wrist as this restricts blood flow. (Some so-called ergonomic wrist wrests actually do more harm than good in this respect, so be wary.)

- Many injuries are the indirect result of poor back posture, so sit upright, and periodically roll your shoulders to ease any strain. Try to be aware of your posture and correct it if necessary.

- Some people find it helpful to alternate between using their right and left hands for the mouse or pen, but it takes a bit of practice to get used to using your less dominant hand.

Unfortunately, by the time you start to feel pain, it is too late to avoid injury entirely; the pain is telling you that some damage has already been done. But even at this point it lies within your power to limit the damage. So we cannot stress strongly enough that you should never carry on working if it is causing you pain – not even if you are half an hour away from a project deadline. Although you might make your deadline you could be risking your working life for years ahead. Many millions of people have sought medical attention for RSI of the hand, and the number is growing all the time. It is up to you to ensure that you are not among that number.

Interface Basics

The burden of trying to cope with many different applications when you're working in multimedia is substantially reduced by the fact that most of them have a large number of interface features in common. To begin with, all of the media tools which we describe in this book follow the standard model for a desktop application program. That is, each one opens documents – of a type appropriate to the particular application – in separate document windows, where they are displayed so that you can work on them. In each program, menus provide commands, many of which have keyboard shortcuts, for making changes to the document and performing other operations. Dialogue boxes containing controls such as buttons, scrolling lists and pop-up menus are used to enter parameters. Standard file navigation dialogues are used to open and save files. Documents that are saved by an application become associated with it, so in future you can open them in the application that created them just by double-clicking on the icon representing the saved file.

All the programs described in this book are produced by Adobe, but Flash and Dreamweaver were developed by a different company, Macromedia, which has recently been acquired by Adobe. The different origins of these programs is apparent in numerous differences in their user interface. Although Flash mostly uses the standard interface elements that are also found in Photoshop, Illustrator and Bridge, there are some detailed differences in some aspects of how they work. At present, Dreamweaver retains its original Macromedia interface, which we will therefore describe separately for the most part.

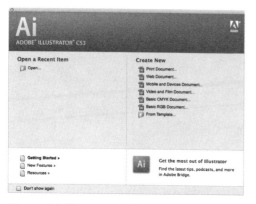

Figure 2.1 *Illustrator's welcome screen*

The very first time you start up one of these applications after you have installed it, you will have to go through the business of entering serial numbers, activating and perhaps registering it. After that, the first thing you will see after the splash screen disappears – except in Photoshop – is a *welcome screen*, like the one for Illustrator, shown in Figure 2.1. This is intended to provide quick access to the tasks you might want to perform when you start the program, and to serve as an entry point for the built-in documentation. It behaves much like a Web page: the items are highlighted when you roll over them and you click to activate them. If the program has been used before, a list of recently opened files appears in the column on the left. The welcome screen may help you orient yourself when you begin using a new program, but once you know what you are doing you will probably find that it just gets in your way. We recommend that you tick the checkbox in the bottom left corner, so that you will not be bothered with it again.

Platforms

There are, of course, differences between the appearance and functionality of applications on the two platforms – Mac OS X and Windows – on which these digital media tools programs run. (None of these programs is available for Linux or any version of Unix other than Mac OS X. Older versions ran on the Classic Mac OS, but we consider this to be an obsolete system.) Figure 2.2 shows the appearance of Photoshop's workspace on these two platforms. Despite the heated emotions the differences sometimes excite, they are largely concerned with cosmetic features, such as the system fonts and the appearance of buttons and dialogue boxes. The most significant difference between the Windows and Mac workspaces is that on Windows there is an enclosing window, with a menu bar at the top, and the document window and all the other interface elements within it. Closing this outermost window will quit the application. On the Mac there is no such container. Each window is an independent entity and closing the document window does not quit the program. (Habitual Windows users often make the mistake of assuming

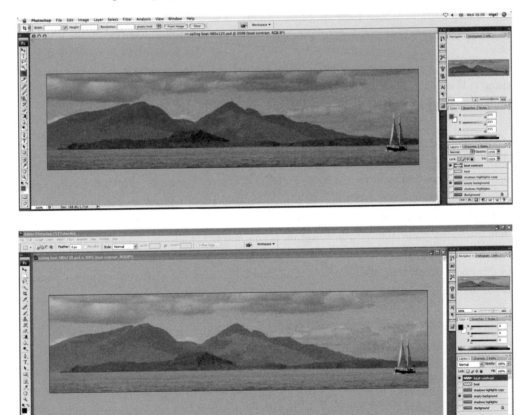

Figure 2.2 *Photoshop's default workspace in Mac OS X (top) and Windows XP (bottom)*

that closing a document is sufficient to quit the program, and forget to use the explicit Quit command when they find themselves using a Mac.) The Mac's menu bar is always at the top of the screen, no matter where the other windows are moved. However, since most Windows users will put Photoshop and the other media tools into full-screen mode to get the most use out of the space on their screens, there is little practical significance in this difference.

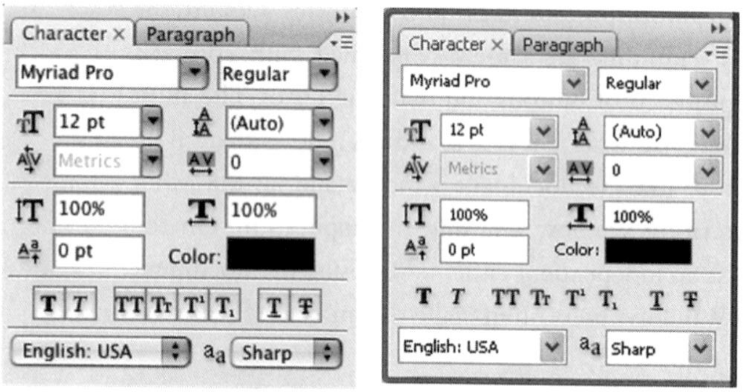

Figure 2.3 *Panels on Mac OS X (left) and Windows XP (right)*

Adobe have gone to some lengths to produce interfaces to their programs which are not only platform-independent but are also consistent between programs. In particular, dockable panels (described below) have become a standard way of organizing the often large number of functions provided by these programs. As Figure 2.3 shows, the appearance of these panels is almost identical on the Windows and Mac versions. Only the font and the appearance of drop-down menus differs. Sadly, Dreamweaver does not yet use the same panels as those in Photoshop, Illustrator and Flash, but the appearance of the panels it does use is the same on both platforms.

If you delve further into the interfaces, you find that dialogue boxes are not unified, but use the controls that belong to each platform, although the layout within any particular dialogue matches between platforms, as you see in Figure 2.4. The combo-boxes, checkboxes and buttons are platform-specific, and so is the system font used for labels and values, but functionally the dialogues are identical on the two systems. This means that users do not have to get used to a new interface for interacting with dialogues; as Java desktop applications demonstrate, diverging from the standard system controls is rarely popular. The result, though, is that some screenshots in this book, which were taken on a Mac, will not look quite like what you see on your screen if you are using Windows.

Input devices – keyboards, mice and graphics tablets – behave in nearly the same way on both systems. Whereas formerly the Mac only used a single-button mouse, multi-button mice are now standard. For anyone still using a single-button mouse on a Mac, the function of the second button is simulated by using a modifier key (ctl). There are differences in the names of the modifier keys and the way they are used. In particular, the ctl (Control) key is used differently on the two platforms, and the keys that correspond to ctl and alt on Windows are called cmd and opt on the Mac. Throughout this book we will use shorthands such as [opt/alt] to mean the key called opt on a Mac and alt on a PC.

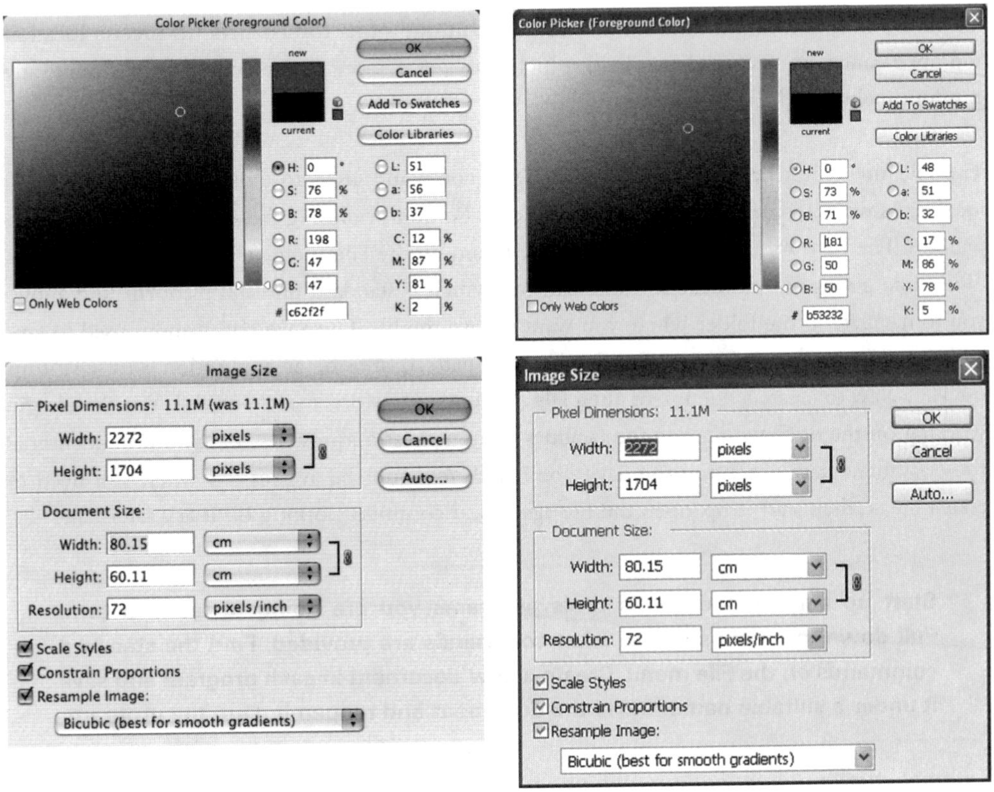

Figure 2.4 *Dialogue boxes on Mac OS X (left) and Windows XP (right)*

Menus and Commands

File Menu

You are probably used to applications that behave in the way described at the beginning of this chapter. If so, you will know that commands grouped together on a File menu provide operations on files stored on disk. The File menu will invariably provide a New command to create documents associated with the application.

The File menu will also have an Open... command, to reopen files you have saved previously, using a system-dependent standard file opening dialogue, which allows you to navigate through the directory structure to find the file you wish to open. Most programs nowadays (including all those described in this book) provide a means of opening files you have worked on recently that by-passes the Open dialogue, in the form of an Open Recent or (in Illustrator) Open Recent Files sub-menu on the File menu, which contains a list of a dozen or so files you have worked on most recently. This feature is an invaluable one. There is always a Close command on the File menu, which is used to close the current document window without saving it (although usually you are asked to confirm that that is what you want to do if there are any unsaved changes).

However, every window comes with a close box in one of its top corners (its precise location and appearance are system-dependent) which provides a more convenient way of closing any window, including document windows.

The File menu is where the all-important Quit command, used to exit from the program, is located. As we noted earlier, on Windows you can also quit by closing the application's containing window. The Save As... command can also be found on the File menu; it is used to save a file to disk while giving it a new name via a dialogue which is standard on each platform, and allows you to navigate to the folder where you want to save the file. The Save command is used to save a file to disk under its existing name. So, the usual pattern of using an application is to start it up, use File>New to create a document, then File>Save As... to store it safely on disk. You then begin working on the document, using the facilities your application provides, and save it frequently as the document develops, using the Save command. You quit the application when you need to take a break, then start it up, open the file again, and continue working on it at a later date.

┌─ TRY THIS ───┐

Start up each of the media tools programs you are going to learn in turn. Pull down the menus to see what commands are provided. Find the standard commands on the File menu. Create a new document in each program and save it under a suitable name. Close the document and reopen it. Quit the program.

└───┘

Many media tools create more than one type of file. For example, Flash creates Flash documents, which are the files that record the structure of a project so that you can edit it, but it also creates Flash movies, which are the real end-product, being the files that can be played in Web browsers. In a different vein, Photoshop can create images in many different image file formats, as well as its own native format in which documents are saved by default. As a result, when you have finished working on a document, you may need to export the document in a different format for its ultimate use.

Several mechanisms are employed for saving files in different formats. The File>Save As... command causes an extended version of the standard dialogue to be displayed, which not only lets you choose the name under which to save your file and the location to save it in, as described already, but also lets you choose a file type. For example, in Photoshop a pop-up menu is used to select a file type; the type you select determines which options are available for the saved file.

The other mechanism is to provide an explicit Export sub-menu or command on the File menu. The resulting dialogue is similar. For the special case of saving image files for use on the Web, Photoshop and Illustrator provide a Save for Web & Devices... command, which we describe in detail in Chapter 8, and Flash has a Publish command for rapidly generating all the required files for making a movie and a Web page in a single command. Whichever mechanism the application employs, we will refer to saving in this way as exporting a file in a certain format. Quite often the actual outcome of your work with a media tool will be an exported file, not the main document you have been using to create the piece of work.

As well as exporting different types of files, media tools often import them, too. Again, there are two cases. Most applications allow you to use the File>Open... command to open files in formats other than their own. For instance, Photoshop will open image files in a host of different formats. It is also possible to import a file of some type so as to incorporate it into another document that is already open, rather than open the file in its own document window. For instance, Flash provides an Import... command on its File menu, which is used to bring data from different types of file into a movie. Among other things, you can import a series of still image files, and they will be added to the Flash document as consecutive frames in the timeline.

Edit Menu

The File menu is a standard interface component of every desktop application. The other standard menu that all such applications are supposed to provide is the Edit menu. At the very least, this menu should always provide three commands: Cut, Copy and Paste, which are used to transfer data between a document and the clipboard. Again, this should be familiar to you from using word processors and similar applications.

The Edit menu commands operate on the current selection in a document. In a word processor, you often select a word, a sentence or a paragraph by clicking or dragging with the mouse. When we are dealing with media data, selection may not be such a straightforward process and usually requires the use of specialist tools. However, every application allows you to make selections somehow, whether you are selecting characters in text, pixels in an image, frames in an animation, or whatever, and having made the selection you can use the Edit menu commands on the selected data. Deselect is also commonly provided, though it is not quite universal; it cancels any selections already made, ensuring that nothing remains selected. (It can be quite important to be certain that nothing is selected sometimes.)

Edit>Cut removes the current selection from the document and places it on the clipboard – a temporary storage space provided for the purpose – from which it can subsequently be retrieved using Edit>Paste, which copies the contents of the clipboard into the document. Edit>Copy copies the current selection to the clipboard without removing it from the document. Precisely where pasted data is placed in a document depends on the application. The Cut, Copy and Paste commands are therefore used to move and duplicate elements of a document. Most applications also allow you to use drag-and-drop for this purpose, though sometimes the nature of the data makes this more complicated than it is in simple text applications.

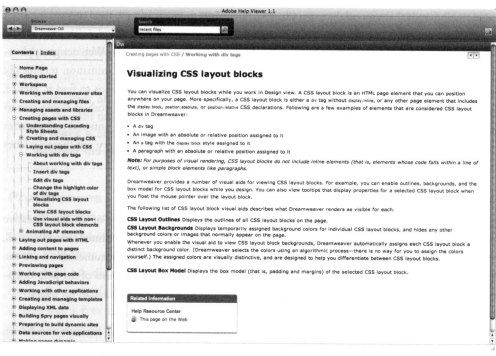

Figure 2.6 *The Help Viewer*

Flash does not use the Help Viewer, but displays its help pages in a panel inside the program itself (which tends to get in the way of what you are doing). As you should be able to see from Figure 2.7, it is functionally equivalent to the Help Viewer, although it lacks some of its features. (There is a link to a LiveDocs version at the bottom of each page, though you can't see it in this screenshot.) In particular, you can increase the font size in the Help Viewer, just as you can in a Web browser, but not in the Flash Help panel.

The Help menu is also the unlikely location of the Deactivate… command. You need to use this command if you wish to transfer your copy of the program to a different machine.

—TRY THIS—

In each application, examine the available preference settings. See how many of them have obvious meanings. Change any that don't suit you.

Open the help pages for several applications. Practise using the navigation controls. Search for "opening files" and some other terms you would expect to be defined in the particular manual.

Go to the LiveDocs version of some pages. Is the help text the same there? Are there any useful comments from other users?

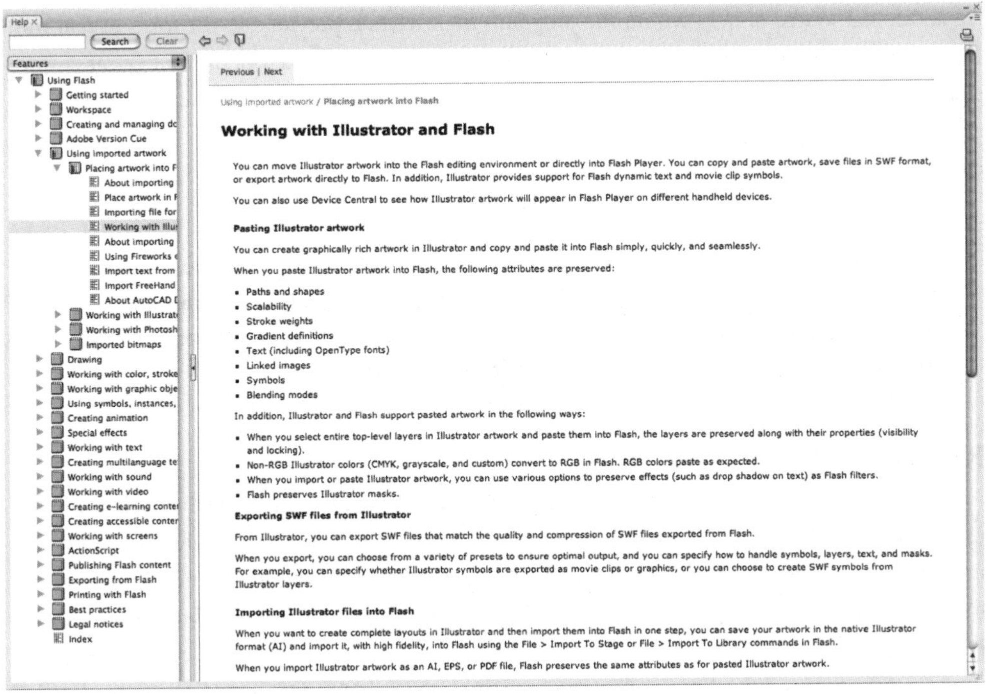

Figure 2.7 *Flash help*

The support section of Adobe's Web site includes technical notes for each application. These are among the most valuable sources of information, since they often cover techniques that are not obvious from simply reading the manual, and provide news of updates and work rounds for bugs (for it must be admitted that media tools are not exempt from bugs). Revisions to operating systems also lead to incompatibilities, so it is necessary for patches and updates to be applied from time to time, between version releases. The Web is used to distribute such updates. It pays to keep an eye on the support sites for your media tools, and ensure that you have the latest versions.

The Adobe support site also hosts forums, where users, and sometimes the people who write the programs, can exchange ideas, ask questions and complain. The quality of these forums is variable – users of some programs seem to be more polite and helpful than users of others – but they are worth looking at when you are experiencing difficulties. There are facilities to search within the forums to see whether anybody else is having the same problem as you are.

---TRY THIS---

Visit the areas of Adobe's support site for each application and investigate the resources that are provided. If you maintain your own system, download any updates necessary to ensure that your programs are up to date. (If you have a system administrator, try to persuade them to do this for you.)

An additional source of help within the programs themselves is provided in the form of *tool tips*. A tool tip is a small label which pops up when the cursor is held over a tool or some other control element for a few moments, to tell you what it does. In most media tool applications, moving the cursor over almost any object in the interface which would make something happen if you clicked on it will cause a tool tip to be displayed. This can be an invaluable aid.

┌─TRY THIS──┐
│   │
│   **Move the cursor around the workspace of each application and hover over the** │
│   **various icons for tools etc. Notice where tool tips appear. Become familiar with** │
│   **their appearance, and practise making them pop up. (If they don't appear, check** │
│   **that some preference has not been set to turn them off.)**   │
│   │
└──┘

Keyboard Shortcuts

Another universal feature of desktop applications that is implemented by media tools is the use of keyboard shortcuts as an alternative to menu commands. Once you know what you are doing, it is quicker and less likely to lead to repetitive strain injuries to type [cmd/ctl]-O, for example, than to use the mouse to move across the screen, pull down the File menu and select the Open... command. For the standard menu commands, there are standard shortcuts, which, apart from the use of a different modifier key, are the same on Windows and Mac OS: [cmd/ctl]-X, [cmd/ctl]-C and [cmd/ctl]-V for the standard clipboard commands on the Edit menu, for example.

In many media tools the use of keyboard shortcuts is taken much further, with shortcuts being provided for many operations besides menu commands. In particular, in programs that provide tools for drawing and painting, including Photoshop, Illustrator and Flash, it is possible to switch between tools by typing a single letter instead of clicking on the tool's icon. This is much faster and allows you to leave the cursor where it was when you switch tools. To a large extent, the same shortcuts are used in all the programs wherever the same function is provided. For example, typing t will switch to the type tool in Photoshop, Illustrator and Flash.

If you are not happy with the default keyboard shortcuts, you can assign your own. In Photoshop and Illustrator on both platforms, and in Flash and Dreamweaver on Windows, use the Edit>Keyboard Shortcuts command for this. On Mac OS X, Flash and Dreamweaver put the command on the application menu.

Although you may eventually use keyboard shortcuts all the time if you become proficient in any of the media tools described in this book, in our descriptions we have generally omitted them, since beginners will find it easier to use the menus and Tools panels (see below) most of the time. We certainly would not advise you to start customizing the keyboard shortcuts until you have gained some experience with the programs.

Context Menus

One of the few user interface innovations made by the Windows operating system is the use of menus which pop up when the right button on the mouse is clicked, providing immediate access to commands which are relevant to the object or window being clicked on. Such context-sensitive menus, usually simply called **context menus**, also became available on the Mac with the introduction of Mac OS 8, using the ctl modifier key with the standard single-button Mac mouse. With the arrival of Mac OS X and support for multi-button mice on the Mac, context menus have become a more prominent feature of the user interface. Figure 2.8 shows some of the context menus that pop up in different parts of the workspace in Flash. (Of course, you can only

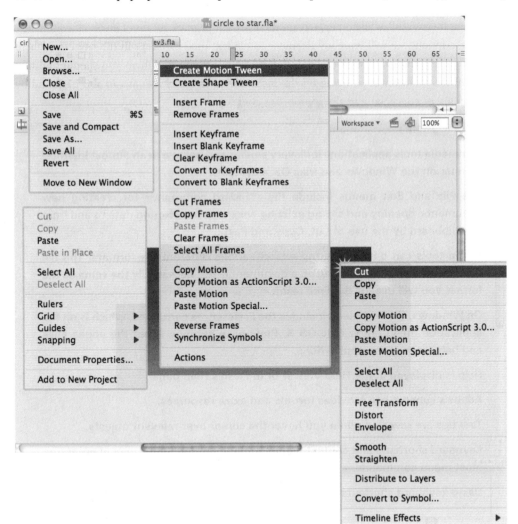

Figure 2.8 *Some context menus in Flash*

have one context menu popped up at a time in reality; we have just shown a selection together to give you an idea of what is available.) Fairly fine distinctions between contexts are drawn: the two menus shown in the main window at the bottom are different, because in one case the click occurred in an empty space, and in the other, it was over the artwork. In a program that provides tools the context menu displayed will take account of the currently selected tool. If the system of context menus is well designed, it should be the case that the commands that pop up in a particular part of the screen are those that you are most likely to want to use in that context.

All the applications described in this book provide context menus. However, it is almost never the case that a context menu is the only place you can find a certain command. Some users never use context menus at all, while others rely on them as their primary means of invoking commands. In our descriptions, we will omit any reference to context menus, except in the rare cases where there is no alternative way of invoking an operation, but if you like them you should find that the commands we describe as being on the menu bar or in panel menus can also be found by right-clicking or ctl-clicking in the appropriate context.

DON'T FORGET

The media tools applications look very similar and behave in an almost identical manner on the Windows and Mac OS X systems.

The File and Edit menus include the standard commands for creating new documents, opening and saving existing ones, and transferring data to and from the clipboard by the use of Cut, Copy and Paste.

Media tools can open, save and export various different file formats. The file format you use while working on a document is not necessarily the same as the format you will use for the final result.

On Windows, the Edit menu includes the Preferences command, which is on the application menu under Mac OS X. Preference settings affect the appearance and behaviour of the applications.

Help is displayed in the Help Viewer or in Flash's Help panel.

Adobe's support site provides forums and extra resources.

Tool tips are revealed when you hover the cursor over relevant objects.

Keyboard shortcuts and context menus provide an alternative way of accessing most menu commands.

Using keyboard shortcuts can help you avoid repetitive strain injuries.

Panels

Many operations that you carry out in a program require *parameters* – values that affect how the operation is carried out. For instance, if you want to add some text to a document, you must choose a font to set it in: the font name is a parameter. Parameter values may be entered in text boxes, chosen from pop-up menus, or turned on or off using checkboxes and radio buttons.

There are two broadly different ways of allowing a user to enter parameters. The first is to use a *modal dialogue box*. A modal dialogue box will have a button, usually labelled something like OK, which you must click to dismiss the box and apply the values you have entered in it. Figure 2.4 showed some examples. Until you click OK, you cannot do anything except change the values in the box. While you are interacting with a modal dialogue, the program is in a different mode (entering parameters) from its normal mode when you interact with the document.

The alternative to modal dialogues is to use some *modeless* element. This may be a dialogue box, but it is distinguished from a modal one by the fact that you can leave it open while you are working on the document, and return to it when you need to. There may or may not be a button that causes values you have entered to be applied, but even if there is, clicking on it will not close the box, as it would with a modal dialogue. If there isn't such a button, it is usually sufficient to make a choice from a menu or set of checkboxes or radio buttons, or to move the cursor out of a text field, by pressing tab or return, to cause any value just entered to be applied.

There is evidence from studies in the field of human-computer interaction (HCI) to suggest that users, especially novices, find modal dialogues confusing. The trouble with modeless alternatives is that they quickly clutter up the screen. Various broadly similar devices have been adopted in many programs to manage modeless dialogues and keep them under control. Photoshop, Illustrator and Flash use an identical system of tabbed *panels* for this purpose. Dreamweaver, as is often the case, is different, using an alternative design of panel, which we will describe separately in Chapter 7.

If you consult the help pages for Photoshop, you will find that panels are referred to using the older term *palettes*, even though they are identical to the panels in Illustrator and Flash (and InDesign). This inconsistency appears to be an oversight, and we will use the name "panel" throughout, even in Chapter 4, to avoid adding to the confusion. "Panel" has the added advantage of not being ambiguous in the context of colour, where "palette" has a separate meaning.

Panels offer great flexibility in the way they can be organized on the screen. The description may sound complicated, but the necessary manipulations are easily mastered in a short time.

Panel Groups and Docks

Panels are usually combined into *panel groups*. For instance, Figure 2.9 shows a panel group containing three panels. The group as a whole can be treated more or less like an ordinary

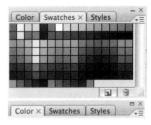

window. You can drag the grey area surrounding the tabs to move it around the screen, minimize it (as shown at the bottom of Figure 2.9) or close it using the – and x controls in the top right-hand corner, or resize it by dragging out its bottom right corner. Note that these are not the standard system window controls, but are specific to Adobe's user interface. The individual panels are revealed by clicking on the tabs along the top of the window to bring them to the front of the group.

Figure 2.9 *A panel group*

The arrangement of panels into groups is not fixed. You can customize your workspace in any of the applications in this book by dragging panels out of their groups by their tabs. If you drag a panel so that it is over the grey area at the top of a different group, a blue outline appears around the new group; if you then drop the panel it joins the group. If you drop the panel in an empty space away from any group, it appears in a group of its own. In this way you can organize your panels so that their grouping reflects the way you like to work with them.

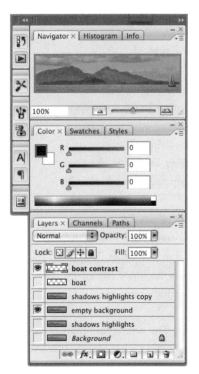

You can close individual panels that you are not using by clicking the x control in the panel's tab; you can also control their visibility using the **Window** menu, which is available in all the applications in this book. This menu has an entry for each panel and for any open document windows. If a panel is currently visible, there will be a tick next to it in the **Window** menu. Selecting a ticked entry closes the panel and removes the tick. Selecting a panel without a tick opens it. However, you should note that if you close or open a panel using a menu command, its entire group will close or open, contrary to what you might expect. Selecting any currently closed panel from the **Window** menu will therefore open the whole panel group that it was last a part of.

In Photoshop and Illustrator you can hide all the open panels at once – including the **Tools** panel – by pressing the **tab** key, and then bring them all back by pressing **tab** again. Pressing **shift-tab** hides (or reveals) all open panels except the **Tools** and **Options/Control** bar; this can be very useful if you need some extra screen space but also need to retain the tools and controls for working on a document.

Figure 2.10 *Panel groups in docks*

Panel groups are further organized into **docks** and **stacks**.

A dock is a set of panel groups that are arranged vertically; docks themselves are arranged next to each other, usually with the rightmost fixed at the right-hand edge of your screen. Any other docks are placed up against their neighbour. If you refer back to Figure 2.2 you will see two docks to the right of the main image; Figure 2.10 shows them in greater detail. The dock on the right consists of three panel groups. The dock to its left only shows as a set of icons. This is because it has been **collapsed**, which simply means that it has been reduced to this minimal form to save screen space. In fact, there is an intermediate collapsed form, shown in Figure 2.11, where the palettes in the dock are reduced to icons with their names beside them. For beginners, this collapsed form may be the best option for docks, since it makes finding a particular panel easy, while not taking up much space. When

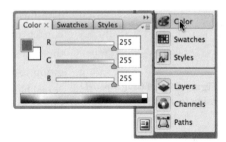

Figure 2.11 *Docks as icons and names*

you are familiar with the panels' icons, you may prefer to collapse right down to just the icons, freeing up a little more screen space. In either of the collapsed forms, broad horizontal dividers separate groups within the dock, as, for instance, above the Brushes panel in Figure 2.11.

But how do you collapse a dock? If it is in its expanded form, like the right-hand dock in Figure 2.10, there will be a pair of arrowheads pointing right in the top right corner. Clicking on these will collapse the dock to icons and names. To collapse it fully, drag the pair of vertical lines in the top left corner. The names' area will shrink as you do so, the names becoming abbreviated, until there is no room for even the first letter, at which point the dock will snap down to a set of icons. (This may sound awkward, but is straightforward in practice.)

Figure 2.12 *Temporarily expanding a collapsed panel*

If a dock is collapsed, you reveal a panel by clicking on its icon. It will fly out from the dock, as shown in Figure 2.12. To put it back, click on the icon again, or click on any other panel's icon. In a collapsed dock, the arrows in the top right corner point to the left, and clicking on them expands the whole dock.

In all three programs that use the standard panels there is a checkbox somewhere in the preference settings labelled Auto-Collapse Icon Panels (Auto-Collapse Icon Palettes in Photoshop). If you tick this checkbox, panels will always revert to their collapsed form as soon as you click away from them, for example, when you select a tool or place a cursor on your document.

Figure 2.13 *Creating a new dock*

Figure 2.14 *Adding a panel group to a dock*

Figure 2.15 *Adding a panel group to a stack*

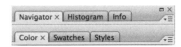

Figure 2.16 *A minimized stack*

Reorganizing entire docks is conceptually simple but may take practice. If you drag an undocked panel group or a single panel to one edge of the screen or to the edge of another dock, you will see a bright blue vertical line appear down that edge, as in Figure 2.13. If you now drop the panel group, it will become a new dock next to the existing one. Note, though, that the left edge of the screen is usually occupied by the Tools panel, described later. Placing a dock on the left of the screen will push the Tools panel out of the way, but it is possible to add a dock to its right, even though the Tools panel is not a dock itself and cannot be grouped with other panels.

If, instead of dragging a panel group to the edge of a dock, you drag it right over an existing dock, a blue outline will appear around the panel group your cursor is over, as in Figure 2.14, and dropping the panel group at that point will add all its panels to the outlined group. If you drop the group between groups in the dock, or at the top or bottom of the dock, it will be added as a group. You can remove groups or individual panels from a dock just by dragging them out.

The final possibility for organizing panels is as a stack, which, like a dock, consists of several panel groups arranged vertically, but it is not attached to the edge of the screen and, importantly, it cannot be collapsed. To add a panel group to an existing stack, drag it to the bottom of the stack. When a horizontal blue line appears at the bottom, as it does under the Histogram panel in Figure 2.15, drop the panel group. You can make a new stack from two panel groups. Stacks behave as if the panel groups in them are glued together, so you can drag the whole stack about the screen as a unit and close all the panels in it at once using the stack's x control. If you minimize the stack, all the panel groups are minimized, as shown in Figure 2.16.

---TRY THIS---

Practise using and organizing panels. In any application, bring each panel in a group to the front. Drag one panel out of a group and drop it into a different group. See what happens if you drag a panel out of a group and then back in.

Hide and reveal individual panels and note what happens to the groups. Hide all the panels, noting which interface elements remain.

Collapse the dock to icons and names, then just to icons. Practise revealing individual panels that are in the collapsed dock.

Remove several panels from the dock and combine them into a stack. Practise minimizing the stack.

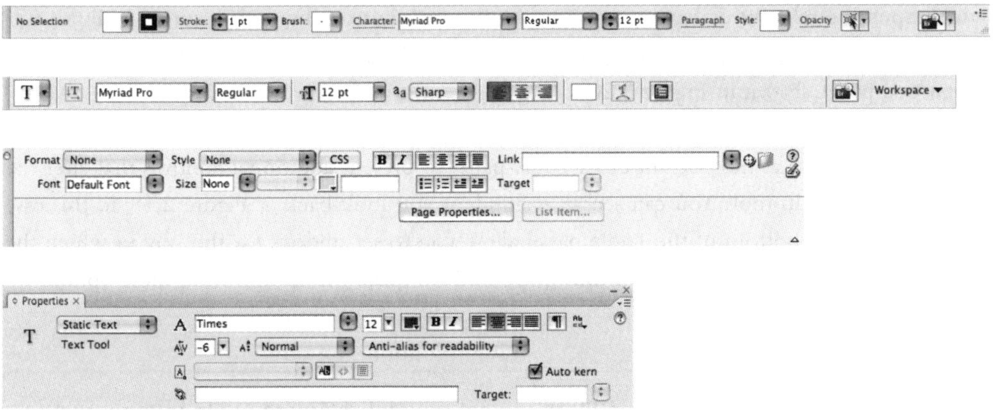

Figure 2.20 *The* Control *panel (Illustrator),* Options *bar (Photoshop) and* Properties *panel (Dreamweaver and Flash)*

the same: they are a place where you can set most of the parameters you commonly need without using other panels; their content depends on the currently selected tool or object.

In effect, the **Options** bar and so on serve the same function as the individual dedicated panels which are associated with the current tool. For example, the type tool's options can be set on the **Character** and **Paragraph** panels; when you select the type tool, all the most commonly used typographic parameters can be set on the **Options** bar (or **Control** or **Properties** panel) instead. When you switch to a different tool, the available options change to those that are appropriate to the new tool, as shown in Figure 2.21. This means that most of the time you can leave all the panels in their collapsed state and just use the bar.

Where there are options on the panels that don't fit on the bar, as in the case of text tools shown in Figure 2.20, various means are provided to show the necessary panels. Illustrator offers the most elaborate solution: the names of related panels are shown on the **Control** panel, in blue, with underlines, as if they were links on a Web page. Clicking one of these "links" makes the corresponding panel pop up below the **Control** panel. In Photoshop, a single icon appears on the **Options** bar when there are related panels available, and clicking this icon opens them. Flash and Dreamweaver don't provide such a feature, but in some contexts the **Properties** panel has buttons

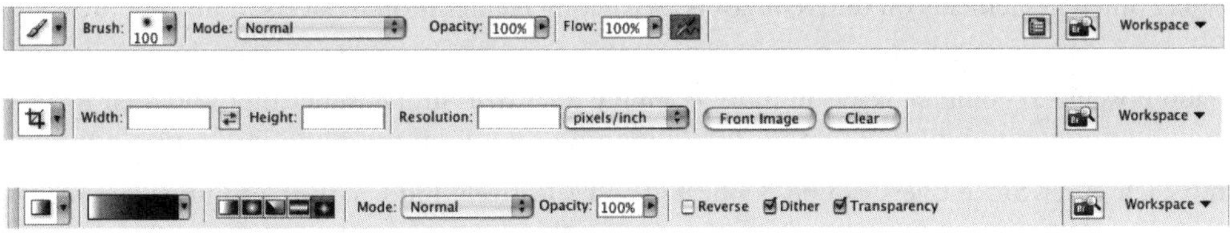

Figure 2.21 *The* Options *bar in Photoshop with different tools selected*

which open the relevant dialogues. You can identify such buttons by their having an ellipsis (...) at the end of their label, as in the case of the **Page Properties**... button in Dreamweaver's **Properties** panel, shown in Figure 2.20.

Flash uses the space at the bottom of its **Tools** panel to present additional controls that alter the behaviour of certain tools. You can see an example if you look back at Figure 2.18; in this case the buttons at the bottom of the **Tools** panel allow you to set options for the way in which the selection tool behaves. The use of buttons in a restricted space means that what these options do can sometimes be rather unclear.

┌─ TRY THIS ──┐

In Photoshop, Illustrator and Flash, select several different tools in turn and note how the Options bar/Control panel/Properties panel changes. Where appropriate, open the related panels and note which controls are duplicated and which provide extra options.

└──┘

In Photoshop, there is a pop-up menu of workspaces at the extreme right of the **Options** bar. The button to its left, which can also be found at the right-hand end of the **Control** panel in Illustrator, launches Bridge (see Chapter 3). This is in keeping with the idea that the panel should provide a single convenient place for performing common actions, although, as you can see, it is not implemented in a consistent way across all programs.

Layers Panel

The concept of layers originally appeared in Photoshop in 1994, and it has now become all-pervasive. Layers are popular because they are intuitively easy to understand and yet allow you to perform complex operations, in particular compositing, by separating different elements of a composition in such a way that you can alter one without altering the rest.

Layers are pure metaphor: a layer is like a sheet of transparent acetate, on which an image has been placed. (Anyone who knows how traditional cel animation is made will understand this at once.) Layers can be stacked on top of each other and, where there are transparent areas, the images on the layers beneath them show through. You can build up a complicated composition by superimposing different elements on different layers. Separating elements on to layers in this way makes it easier to isolate them when necessary – for example, to make changes to certain elements only. It is also possible to combine layers in more complex ways than simply superimposing their images on top of each other. For example, in Photoshop you can make images on two layers dissolve into each other. Since layers can be duplicated and selectively hidden, they also provide a means of experimenting by making different changes to different copies of the same layer.

The metaphor of layers has been so successful that it has been applied even in areas where it is not really an accurate model of what is going on. HTML documents are not composed of separate superimposed layers, for example, but Web design software, including Dreamweaver, allows you to deal with absolutely positioned (AP) elements in a document as if they were independent layers. (For many years, such elements were even called "layers" in Dreamweaver, but that has been corrected now.) Photoshop has extended the layer metaphor in another direction, by allowing you to create "adjustment layers", which behave like a special sort of acetate that applies transformations to everything underneath it. (See Chapter 4.) Flash presents movies as layers, even though they are built on a timeline.

We describe the detailed use of layers in each of our applications in the appropriate chapter, since each program uses them in distinctive ways, but some features are common to them all. In particular, facilities to manage a collection of layers are fairly uniform across all the programs.

The **Layers** panel is used to show you the layered structure of a document, and to allow you to add new layers, copy or delete layers or rearrange them in a new stacking order. Figure 2.22 shows the **Layers** panels in Photoshop and Illustrator. They are basically the same, although there are detailed differences resulting from the different types of image these programs work with. Note that Illustrator's panel tells you how many layers you have in your document (at the bottom left), which is particularly useful when working on animation, but Photoshop's panel does not.

Dreamweaver's **AP Elements** panel, shown at the top of Figure 2.23, is quite a lot simpler, because of the underlying simplicity of the HTML constructs that it presents as layers, but it does provide some of the same functions as the **Layers** panel. At the bottom of Figure 2.23 you see how layers are represented in Flash's timeline window, here performing essentially the same function of managing layers as the **Layers** panel does in the programs that have one.

In layered documents you always have at least one layer, of course. To add layers you can just click the **New** button at the bottom of the **Layers** panel. It is a good idea to give each layer a name that indicates what it contains, because in a document with a hundred or so layers (by no means an uncommon sort of document) it isn't very helpful to have the layers just called Layer1, Layer2,... as they are by default. In every program we are describing, you double-click the layer name in the panel (make sure you double-click on the name itself, not on some other part of the layer). Illustrator then presents you with a dialogue box, while the other programs let you type the new name *in situ*.

Figure 2.22 Layers *panel in Illustrator (top) and Photoshop*

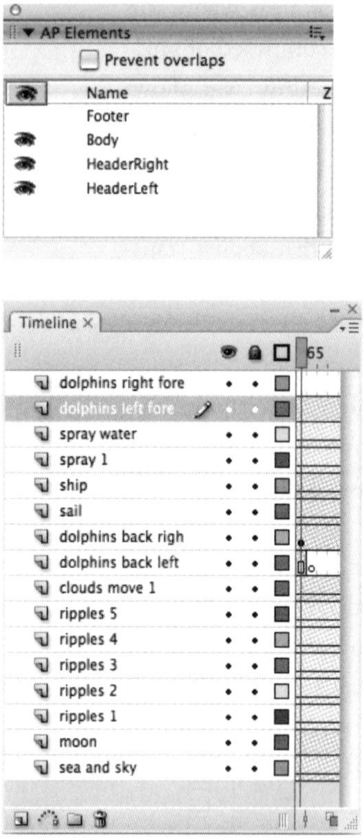

Figure 2.23 *AP elements in Dreamweaver (top) and timeline layers in Flash*

At any particular time, only one layer will be the current, or active, layer – this is the layer on which you can draw or paint, apply transformations, and so on. In Illustrator, Flash and Dreamweaver, any new elements that you add to your document will be added to the current layer. Photoshop, however, will automatically create additional layers for certain kinds of new elements, including text, vector objects and pasted objects (see Chapter 4). In programs that provide a **Duplicate Layer** command, usually in the **Layers** panel menu, it is always the current layer that is copied to make a new one. If you click on the dustbin icon, it is the current layer that is deleted.

The current layer is usually highlighted, as you can see in Figures 2.22 and 2.23. (The Dreamweaver example shows no highlighted layer, since none is selected.) You can make any layer current – or select it, as it is more usual to say – by clicking on its entry in the panel. If you make a selection of some element in the document window, the layer it is on automatically becomes selected too. Beware of accidentally making a layer current in this way, and then forgetting to switch back to the layer you next want to work on; check the **Layers** panel to make sure that you are working on the layer you think you are.

The order in which layers are stacked – their *z-ordering* – naturally makes a difference to the composite image, movie or Web page that is produced. You can rearrange layers by simply dragging them up and down in the panel.

All applications that use layers allow you to hide them. In Figures 2.22 and 2.23 you can see an icon representing an eye in a column next to some or all of the layers in each of the panels, except for the Flash timeline, where the eye is at the top of the column and dots are placed next to the layers. The presence of an eye icon (or a dot in Flash) in a layer shows that it is visible. It can be made invisible by clicking on that icon. Invisible layers can be made visible again by clicking in the same place, that is, at the point where the eye appears.

Hiding layers serves many purposes. The first, which may seem slightly frivolous until you have got lost in a document with dozens of layers, is to find out exactly what is on a particular layer, by observing what disappears when you hide it. Layers can also be hidden to get things out of the way so that you can see clearly what is on the layer or layers you are currently working on, and be sure that you are working on the right thing. Hidden layers allow you to experiment, by producing different versions of a layer and then making each one visible in turn to see which looks best, or by choosing different combinations of layers to try different compositions. Some users like to duplicate a layer when it reaches a certain stage of development, then hide it and go on working on the duplicate, keeping the hidden layer as a record of an earlier stage. (This is particularly useful when you are about to make changes to a layer that cannot be undone at a later stage in the work.) Finally, a layer may be used during the creation of an image – as a tracing image or the source of a pasted element – without appearing in the finished result. It is sensible to hide such a layer instead of deleting it, in case you need to go back to it later.

> ┌─TRY THIS─
> **In every program that you are using, practise creating layers and placing objects or artwork on them. Try hiding individual layers, or hiding all the layers but one. Duplicate a layer and make some changes to it, then try hiding each of the versions in turn to see how the changes affect the result. Experiment with moving layers up and down in the Layers panel to change their z-ordering.**

You can usually *lock* layers, which prevents you from making any further changes to them until they are unlocked again. This is a good thing to do once you are satisfied with a layer, because it is only too easy to select a layer accidentally. A padlock icon is used to show that a layer is locked. In Flash and Illustrator, the padlock works to denote a locked layer the same way as the eye denotes a visible one, and it can be locked and unlocked simply by clicking in the lock icon position, in the same way that the layer can be made visible and invisible by clicking in the eye icon position. Photoshop provides a slightly more elaborate locking system: each of three aspects of a layer can be locked separately, by selecting from the checkboxes along the top of the Layers panel. Checking the last box, with the padlock, locks every aspect of the layer, in the more conventional way. (But note that the Background layer in Photoshop, which is always locked by default, is an exception: you are able to make a range of changes to it, despite the lock icon, and it can never be unlocked.) In these programs, the padlock denoting a locked layer appears to the right of the layer's thumbnail. The padlock may be black, to indicate a fully locked layer, or grey, to indicate a partially locked one.

Navigator Panel

Beginners sometimes overlook the fact that media tools let you work on a document at different magnifications. If you need to make precise adjustments to an image by eye, it is easier to work accurately if you blow the image up so you can see exactly what you are doing. (In fact, trying to make adjustments visually without blowing up the image is one of the most common ways of producing a sloppy result.) Since the size of your monitor is fixed, zooming in like this necessarily means that you can only see a smaller part of the document. Sometimes you therefore need to zoom out and work at a lower magnification so that you can fit an entire document into the window and see it all at once.

All the programs we describe except Bridge provide Zoom In and Zoom Out commands on a View menu to increase or decrease magnification in fixed steps. The keyboard shortcuts [cmd/ ctl]+ and [cmd/ctl]– are used by all programs. It is convenient to think of it in this way: + to make things bigger, – to make them smaller. However, + is actually a shifted = key on standard keyboards, but you don't have to hold down shift to zoom in. Flash and Dreamweaver, therefore, correctly, but not necessarily helpfully, show the shortcut for Zoom In as [cmd/ctl]=.

You can also enter magnification factors, in a variety of ways. In Photoshop and Illustrator, you can enter exact values numerically by typing a percentage in a field at the bottom left corner of the document window, which always shows the current magnification. In Illustrator, there is a pop-up menu attached to this field, from which you can choose one of a number of fixed magnifications; Flash and Dreamweaver have a View>Magnification sub-menu for the same purpose. Each application also gives you some way of choosing a magnification that makes best use of the available screen space: View>Fit On Screen in Photoshop, View>Fit In Window in Illustrator, View>Magnification>Show Frame in Flash, and View>Fit All in Dreamweaver. Flash and Dreamweaver have other fitting commands, whose effect you can discover by experimentation.

┌─ TRY THIS ───┐

Open a document in an application that supports zooming and practise zooming in and out. Make changes at different magnification levels – for example, try erasing a small area of a photo in Photoshop, or moving an arrowhead until it exactly touches the edge of a circle in Illustrator, at several different zoom levels. Try to get a feel for the appropriate magnification for different purposes.

└───┘

It's possible to get lost in a document. For example, the screenshot on the right of Figure 2.24 shows what you would see if you blew up the photograph on the left to four times its actual size, perhaps to make a precise selection of part of the gate. Could you be entirely sure which part of the photograph you were working on? Alternatively, suppose you are working on a drawing in Illustrator and the objects that you are drawing only occupy a small part of the artboard (the notional piece of paper on which you are drawing). If you zoom in to work on part of the image at very high magnification, it is perfectly possible to find yourself looking at a blank window, because all the objects are on parts of the artboard that isn't displayed. (It is harder than you might think to ensure that the area of interest is always in the middle of your window when you zoom.) You can then spend many fruitless moments scrolling back and forth vertically and horizontally in an increasingly desperate attempt to find some recognizable shape.

Illustrator and Photoshop therefore provide a Navigator panel (but Flash and Dreamweaver do not). Figure 2.25 shows Photoshop's Navigator, as it appears in the situation shown in Figure 2.24. The panel displays a thumbnail of the full image, no matter how much of that image is visible in

Figure 2.24 *Zooming in*

the document window – you can increase or decrease the thumbnail's size just by resizing the panel. The small area of the thumbnail in the **Navigator** panel which is outlined by a bright red rectangle (a part of the paved path in Figure 2.24) is called the ***proxy preview area***; it identifies which part of the image is visible in the document window at the current magnification.

You can change which part of the image is displayed in the document window in two ways from within the **Navigator** panel. Either drag the proxy preview area so that it encloses the part of the picture you want to display, or just click on the point in the thumbnail image which you would like to appear in the centre of the document window: the proxy preview area will jump so that it is centred on the point where you clicked.

Figure 2.25 *The* Navigator *panel*

The controls at the bottom of the **Navigator** panel provide an alternative way of zooming in and out. The two buttons with double triangle icons duplicate the **Zoom In** and **Zoom Out** commands on the **View** menu. The slider between them allows you to zoom continuously in either direction – the document window updates in real time as you do so. Alternatively, you can enter a percentage value in the field in the bottom left-hand corner, just as you can in the document window.

History Panel

Media tools provide considerable scope for making mistakes. As well as the usual slips of the hand, it is possible to make aesthetic misjudgements which need to be put right. The simplest method of making corrections is the Undo command. This is so well established that, like Cut, Copy and Paste it has a standard place in the Edit menu in all conventional programs, and a universal keyboard shortcut: [cmd/ctl]-Z. It does not have a universal semantics, though.

To be more precise, using the Undo command twice in a row does not have a universal interpretation. The question is, does the second Undo undo the first one, or does it undo the command before the one that the first Undo undid? In other words, do two Undo commands in a row have the effect of taking one step back and then one forward, or two steps back? The first option means that you can only ever undo one command. A single level of Undo like this, while it is popular with programmers because it is easy to implement, is unpopular with users, who usually want unlimited Undo levels. The second alternative, which provides this, is now more widespread, at least in media tools, and its absence is usually a source of users' grievance. Truly unlimited Undo is not possible, because of the finite size of even the biggest computer's memory, but in practice a hundred or so is usually enough. Notice that if you have unlimited Undos you need a Redo command to undo an Undo (or step forward again). This also appears in the Edit menu, but there is no universally agreed keyboard shortcut; [cmd/ctl]-Y and shift-[cmd/ctl]-Z are both popular.

In carefully written programs, the menu entry for the Undo command will change to show what will be undone if you use the command. (By this criterion, Dreamweaver is not a carefully written program, since it only provides the bare Undo and Redo commands, without any indication of what you would undo.) For example, in Illustrator, if you rotate an object, the menu will change to Undo Rotate. If you had scaled the object before you rotated it, it will change to Undo Scale if you undo the rotation. At the same time, the command Redo Rotate will appear, to show you what will happen if you want to undo the Undo. When you have gone so far back in undoing that there is nothing left to undo – which usually means as far as the last time you saved the document – the Undo command is greyed out in the conventional way.

As well as allowing you to correct mistakes, Undo can be used as a way of judging the effect of some change you have made: make the change, then repeatedly undo and redo it, to get a quick impression of the state of the document before and after the change.

> ─TRY THIS─
>
> **Go through your applications and check how the Undo and Redo commands operate in each one. Practise making some changes (it doesn't matter if you don't know what you're doing yet, just choose some menu commands) and then using Undo and Redo to judge their effect.**

As a sort of emergency fall-back, programs also provide a Revert command on the File menu. Selecting this command causes any changes you have made since the last time you saved the file to be discarded (after you have confirmed that that is what you want to do).

History

It may have come as something of a surprise when you did the previous exercise to find that Photoshop only provides a single level Undo. It does, however, provide an alternative mechanism for "stepping backwards" and reversing the effect of changes to an image: the History panel. This is an innovation originally pioneered by Photoshop that has proved so popular and successful that it is being incorporated in some form into nearly every other media tool. (Illustrator and Bridge are currently the only exceptions among those we cover here.)

The idea behind the History panel is simple: it provides a record of each of the commands that you have executed, in chronological order. Figure 2.26 shows examples from Photoshop and Flash. The History panels in Flash and Dreamweaver are similar, although there are some cosmetic differences. History runs from top to bottom of the panel: the first thing that was done after opening the Photoshop document whose History panel is shown in Figure 2.26 was to make a new layer. Next, a selection was made with the rectangular marquee, which was transformed before some levels adjustments were made, and so on. The latest operation shown is the application of an Image Size command. To the left of the entry for this command you can see a small cursor; by dragging the cursor you can, as it were, turn back time, and revert to any of the previous states. Alternatively, just clicking on any entry in the History panel will return the image to the state it was in when the corresponding command was executed. In the example in Figure 2.26, clicking on the entry for Rectangular Marquee would take you back to the point where you had just made the selection with that tool, undoing the free transformation of the selection and everything that followed after. You can also step backwards and forwards one state at a time using the Edit>Step Backward and Edit>Step Forward commands. If you redefine the keyboard shortcuts so that [cmd/ctl]-Z is Step Backward, and [cmd/ctl]-Y is Step Forward, Photoshop will behave as if it had multiple levels of undo.

Figure 2.26 *The* History *panel in Flash (top) and Photoshop*

Usually, when you go back to an earlier state, it is because you wish to do something different instead of what is shown in the History panel. It is important to realize that as soon as you make any change after returning to an earlier state, all the later states that were previously shown in the panel are destroyed, and you cannot then step forward to them again. (As in tales of time travel, if you go back and change history, the nature of the present will change. In the History panel, though, this does not lead to a paradox.) For as long as you make no changes, however, you can run forwards and backwards through the history, reviewing all the steps you have taken.

The History panel as described merely provides a shortcut for a series of Undo or Redo commands in a program that supports multiple undos. This is actually more useful than it may sound, since each time you pick up a tool or perform a single operation with it, a new history state is created. For example, if you are erasing pixels in Photoshop, each time you release the mouse button you have, as far as Photoshop is concerned, carried out a new operation. Usually, erasing a detailed area is done using many such small operations, so if you wanted to reverse the effect of all your erasing, it would take many undos. With the History panel, you can go back to the situation before you picked up the eraser with a single click. (Some operations, though, such as zooming in or rearranging the panels are not added to the history, but you can't use Undo to reverse them, either.)

The number of steps that are remembered in the History panel is limited, however. It is surprisingly easy to exceed its capacity simply by a series of erase or paint actions, and then you can't get all the way back to the point before you started. You can increase the number of steps the History panel will remember using a preference – the default in Photoshop is only 20 – but you should realize that the more states you save in the history, the more memory will be needed.

When you close a document, all the states in the History panel are lost and do not reappear when you re-open the document, so once a document has been closed you cannot undo any changes you have made. However, simply saving a document without closing does not lose the history.

Figure 2.27 *Snapshots in Photoshop's* History *panel*

Photoshop's History panel – the original of the concept – is actually more sophisticated than the imitators which have followed it. At any time, you can create a snapshot of the state of a document, using the New Snapshot... command on the panel menu. A snapshot is like a History panel entry except that it does not get destroyed if you return to an earlier state and make some changes. So, for instance, you might crop an image, adjust its levels, take a snapshot, return to the state where you resized it and have another go at adjusting the levels. If you decide that your first attempt was more successful, you just click on the snapshot to return to it. If you had not taken the snapshot, the state of the image after the first set of adjustments would have been permanently lost when you tried the second set of adjustments. You can also use snapshots when you are making lot of detailed changes to an image, to preserve states which would otherwise be lost when the history overflowed. In this case, you take a snapshot whenever you think the image is in a state to which you might want to return later. As Figure 2.27 shows, snapshots appear at the top of the panel, separated from the history proper. A snapshot corresponding to the state of the image when it was first opened is automatically created by default.

TRY THIS

Open an image in Photoshop and make several random changes to it. Look at the History panel and see how your actions have been recorded. Experiment with moving up and down the history to review different states of the image, then go back several steps and make some new change to your image, noting what happens to the History panel then. Carry out a similar exercise in Flash and Dreamweaver.

Practise taking snapshots in Photoshop and using them to remember history states which you feel it might be useful to return to.

DON'T FORGET

The Tools panel holds a set of icons representing tools that you use to work on documents by direct manipulation.

Photoshop's Options bar, Illustrator's Control panel and the Properties panel in Flash and Dreamweaver are context-sensitive panels that provide a convenient way of entering values relevant to the tool you are currently using or the objects that you have selected.

The layer metaphor provides a way of organizing documents so that elements can be separated and superimposed on each other.

Layers work like stacks of transparent acetate; you can see the layers underneath through any part of a layer which does not have an object on it.

The Layers panel lets you create, delete, hide, lock and reorder layers.

Zoom in and out of documents quickly by using keyboard shortcuts [cmd/ctl]+ (plus) and [cmd/ctl]- (minus).

The Navigator panel helps you find your way around a document when you are zoomed in to high magnification.

The History panel records changes you have made to a document in chronological order, and lets you step backwards and forwards through those changes.

At any time you can take a snapshot of the current state of a Photoshop document, to provide a record to return to later, even if the history overflows.

Automating Repetitive Tasks

You will sometimes find yourself performing the same task over and over again. This may just be the simple job of downsampling an image to 72 dpi from some higher resolution, which you might need to carry out on a large collection of files, or it may be a more complex sequence of operations, such as the alignments needed to centre a box around some text or draw a standard shape, which will be required many times in the course of a single project, such as the production of a set of technical diagrams. It can get very tedious going through the same dialogues and typing the same values again and again. Computers are well known to be good at performing repetitive tasks. All the media tools in this book (except Bridge) provide some way of recording a sequence of operations, saving the recording and playing it back.

The remainder of this section will make more sense to you once you have started to use the programs and have learned something about what they can do. You may therefore prefer to omit this material for now and return to it after you have gained some experience using Photoshop, Illustrator, Flash and Dreamweaver.

Replaying History

The most elegant solution – although it is limited in what it can do – is found in Dreamweaver and Flash. The History panel has a button at the bottom labelled Replay, which executes any commands that are selected in the history. Figure 2.28 shows an example from Dreamweaver: the sequence of commands that is highlighted has the effect of inserting a horizontal rule (line) with default attributes in a document, then setting its Width and Height to new values, left aligning it and adding a paragraph break after it. Taken all together, these commands insert a hairline rule into the Dreamweaver document. With the whole sequence selected as shown, clicking on the Replay button will have the effect of adding another hairline rule. Each time you do so, a Replay Steps entry is added to the history, as you can see in the lower part of Figure 2.28. Undoing the Replay Steps entry undoes all the commands contained in it, in a single step.

Figure 2.28 *Replaying history in Dreamweaver*

However, since the history is lost when you close the document, you cannot replay this sequence of commands after you reopen it, nor can you use it with a different document. If you want to be able to reuse some operations over a period of time, or in many different documents, you can save a sequence of history states as a single command, by selecting them all and choosing Save As Command... from the History panel menu. You can give your command a meaningful name, such as Insert Hairline Rule in this example, and subsequently it will appear in the Commands menu. It stays there permanently, even after you quit the program. (If at a later stage you find that you no longer need the command, you can use Commands>Edit Command List... to remove it.)

Commands which are applied to the current selection, such as **Set Alignment**, can be applied to different objects by selecting the object and using the **Replay** button. For instance, if you wanted to set the **Height** of a rule to 1pt, but leave its **Width** as it was, you could insert the rule in the normal way, select it, and then select the **Set Attribute** and **Set Alignment** steps in the **History** panel and replay them. There is, however, no other way of parameterizing a recorded action. That is, when you play steps back they are performed exactly the same way as they were when you first recorded them, with all the same settings. There is, for example, no way of making a command that inserts a rule, then asks you for the **Width** value before setting its **Height** and **Alignment**.

Flash's **History** panel works in the same way as Dreamweaver's and allows you to replay steps and save commands in the same way. However, at the time of writing, Flash's implementation of this feature can only be described as unreliable – sometimes it works as it should, sometimes it doesn't – so you should use this feature with caution for now.

TRY THIS

When you are familiar with using Dreamweaver, create a document and type a paragraph of text. Replay the commands from the History panel to make a copy of the paragraph. Select some words in your paragraph and set them in a different font at a larger size. Select some different words and replay commands in the History panel to set these to the same font and size as your first selection. Save the commands to set words in that font at that size as a new command, and use it to set the characteristics of some more text. Experiment further with replaying history to carry out different sequences of commands, paying particular attention to how the current selection interacts with the replay.

Create and test a similar command in Flash.

Actions

Photoshop and Illustrator use a more elaborate method of recording actions, which does accommodate the use of new parameters when the action is replayed. The basic operation is not really different from that in Dreamweaver and Flash, except that a separate **Actions** panel is used to record the steps to be replayed, and you must explicitly start and stop recording.

Figure 2.29 shows the **Actions** panel in Illustrator. Within the panel, actions are grouped into sets, which makes it easier to manage large numbers of them. Each application that provides an **Actions** panel comes with a set of default actions, which perform tasks that are widely used but not available as primitive commands on the menus. In Illustrator, for instance, the **Default Actions** set includes actions to export an image for the Web using various optimization settings, set the transparency of a selected object to several useful values, and so on.

Figure 2.29 *The* Actions *panel in Illustrator*

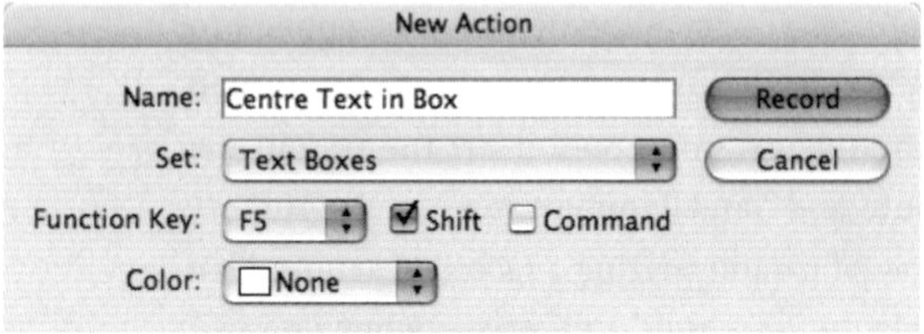

Figure 2.30 *Creating a new action*

You create new sets of actions by clicking on the **New Set** icon at the bottom of the **Actions** panel. When you click on the standard **New** button, the dialogue shown in Figure 2.30 lets you give your new action a name and optionally assign a function key (with modifiers, if you wish) to it, so that you can replay the action later with a single keystroke. Otherwise, actions can be replayed from the panel, as we will describe shortly. In this example, we chose to use **shift-F5** to trigger the command called **Centre Text in Box**.

After you click the **Record** button in the **New Action** dialogue, everything you do is recorded in the **Actions** panel, in the same way as it is in the **History** panel, under the heading for your new action. The **Record** button turns red to show that an action is being recorded. Figure 2.31 shows that two alignment commands followed by a **Group** command were recorded as the **Centre Text in Box** action. When you have reached the end of the sequence that performs the desired action, you must explicitly stop recording by clicking on the **Stop** button at the left of the row of buttons at the bottom of the panel. You can then replay the action by selecting it by clicking its name in the **Actions** panel, and then clicking on the **Play** button. You can modify the behaviour of an action by leaving out some steps: the tick marks in the boxes in the column at the left edge of the panel indicate the steps that will be included, by default all of them. To omit some steps, just untick the relevant boxes before you play back the action.

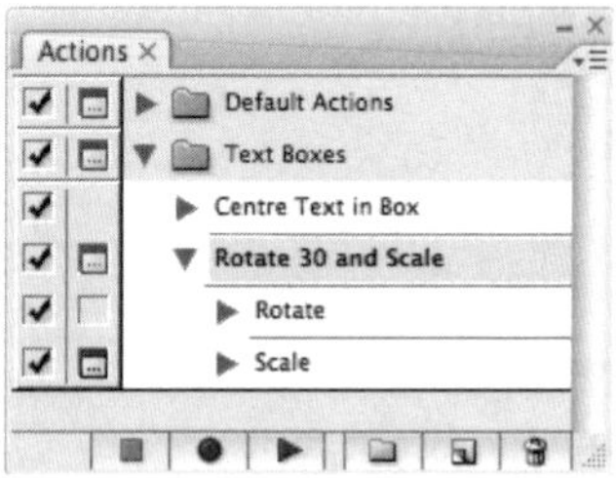

Figure 2.31 *An action with a dialogue*

So far, then, the **Actions** panel is little different from the replayable **History** panel in Dreamweaver and Flash. The difference comes when you include commands in your action that bring up dialogue boxes. Suppose we record an action which rotates an object by 30° and scales it down to 70% of its original size. By default, if we select another object and play back the action, it will be rotated and scaled by the same amount. However, if we click on the checkbox in the second column, to the right of the tick boxes, an icon resembling a dialogue box appears in it, as shown next to the **Scale** operation in Figure 2.31 for example. This indicates that when the action is played back, the dialogue box associated with scaling will be displayed, so that we can enter a new factor to scale by. The rotation will be left at 30°, since the box is not checked for the **Rotate** step. In this way, you can create actions that have parameters, for which dialogue boxes will be displayed. If you have enabled a dialogue in this way for any step in an action, a version of the dialogue box icon appears both next to the action's name and next to the name of the action set containing it. This means that even if you are just looking at the list of action names, without the details of the actions revealed, you can tell which actions are using dialogues.

The little triangles next to the entries in the Actions panel can be used to hide or show members of a set, hide or show the individual steps of an action, and hide or show the details of each step, such as the values of any parameters that you set for it. You can delete individual steps, whole actions or complete sets of actions, using the dustbin icon.

Photoshop takes automation a stage further, by allowing you to apply the same action to a whole collection of files. The File>Automate>Batch… command lets you choose an action and apply it to all the files in a folder, or all the files you have open in Photoshop, either saving the changed documents or saving new versions to a new folder under new names, whose form you can specify. You can also apply a batch action to image files selected in Bridge, as described in Chapter 3. This facility is invaluable to serious Photoshop users, but it has the potential to permanently corrupt or overwrite a lot of files at once if you fail to set the Destination for the results of applying the action correctly, so it should only be used with caution. We do not advise its use for beginners.

It would not be appropriate to go into details in this book, but you should also be aware that all the programs can be controlled by scripts, written in various scripting languages, which can provide further automation.

---TRY THIS---

When you feel confident about using the programs, record an action in Illustrator by drawing a hexagon and setting its fill colour and stroke weight and colour. (Make a bright pink shape with a thick green outline, for example.) Play back the action to make another hexagon. Now, check the dialogue box option for the step where you drew the polygon. Play back the action, entering a new value for the number of sides, to make a triangle with the same fill and stroke.

Practise creating different actions that include operations that take parameters (such as scale, rotation, flip) in both Illustrator and Photoshop.

DON'T FORGET

In Dreamweaver and Flash, replay selected steps from the History panel using the Replay button, but only for as long as the document remains open.

To be able to replay the same steps again in the future, save the selected steps as a command and replay them from the Commands menu.

In Photoshop and Illustrator, use the Record and Stop buttons at the bottom of the Actions panel to record a series of operations. Use the Play button to replay a selected action.

Display dialogues at specific steps in an action if you want to set parameters.

In Photoshop, use File>Automate>Batch… to apply an action to a set of files.

Layout Aids

Computer programs are generally better than people at doing things with great precision. By entering numerical values in various panels, it is possible to position anything in a document arbitrarily precisely – but first you have to work out which numbers to enter. Most designers will find it easier and more natural to position and align objects by eye, but unless you are very careful and have unusually good coordination and judgement, the result will not be precise. Various layout aids are available to help you make a better job of positioning things on the screen.

Figure 2.32 *Illustrator's* Info *panel*

Photoshop, Illustrator and Flash all provide an Info panel (Illustrator's panel is shown in Figure 2.32), which gives a constantly updated summary of some important values. Usually, it tells you the width and height of any current selection, the colour of the pixel or object beneath the cursor, and the current *x*- and *y*-coordinates of the cursor. You can therefore drag things and make selections to exact positions and sizes by watching the Info palette as you drag. This is not very efficient, though.

Rulers and Grids

Rulers along the edges of a document window provide a basis for measurement. The only program described in this book that doesn't provide such rulers is Bridge. In all the other programs, a command on the View menu is used to show the rulers, which appear along the top and left sides of the document, as shown in Figure 2.33. The precise command varies: View>Rulers in Photoshop and Flash, View>Show Rulers in Illustrator. In Dreamweaver, the command is on a sub-menu as View>Rulers>Show. With the exception of Illustrator, if the rulers are visible, a tick appears beside the menu entry, indicating that if you select it again, the rulers will be hidden. In Illustrator, the command changes to Hide Rulers when the rulers are visible.

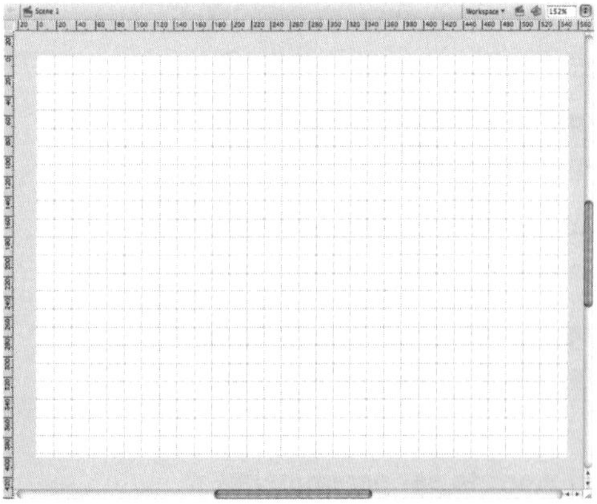

Figure 2.33 *Rulers and a grid in Flash*

If rulers are visible, a small cursor appears in each of them as you move the mouse, so that you can read off the current position of the main cursor. Except in Flash, you can move the origin of the rulers by dragging the top left corner, at the point where the vertical and horizontal rulers intersect, to the point in the document you want to measure from. For instance, you could drag the origin to one corner of an object in an image, so that you could read off distances from that object using the rulers. To reset the origin to the top left of the document, double-click the top left corner. Rulers are not very easy to make immediate use of, because of the distance between the ruler and the objects or spacings you are measuring in the document window. The main reason for showing the rulers is that it enables you to drag out guides, as we will describe below.

Graphic designers have traditionally used a grid to assist with the layout of documents and designs. When working with physical media, the simplest way of doing this is by using squared paper. The elements of the document are placed so that their edges lie on grid lines – or not, where irregularity is required. Objects with their edges on the same grid lines will be aligned, giving the arrangement an orderly appearance. To enable designers to work with digital media in this traditional way, our media tools programs provide a *layout grid*, which can be revealed or hidden at any time using commands on the View menu, or the View>Grid sub-menu, if there is one. The precise command varies slightly between programs, as with rulers.

To make it easier to use a layout grid, programs can be instructed to force objects to snap to it. That is, if Snap to Grid is turned on, when you drag something and drop it within a small distance of a grid line, the position of the object you dragged will automatically be adjusted so that its edge aligns precisely with the grid. Again, the command for setting this snapping option can always be found on the View menu, but its precise form differs: View>Snap To>Grid in Photoshop, View>Snap to Grid in Illustrator, View>Grid>Snap to Grid in Dreamweaver and View>Snapping>Snap to Grid in Flash. If you keep "grid" and "snap" in mind, you should be able to find the command in any program. Even when the grid is showing, you can turn snapping on and off as you require; you may not always want everything you move to snap to the grid.

The units for the divisions on rulers and the spacing and colour of the grid can be set in each program, either as a preference or using commands on the View menu, according to which program you are using. (Note that the spacing on grids is always uniform.)

---TRY THIS---

In each program, make the rulers visible. Find out how to change the ruler units in the program you are using, and switch between the available options. Observe how the position of the cursor over the document is tracked in the rulers. How easy is it to use the rulers for measurements and spacings?

Display and hide a grid in each program. Experiment with changing the spacing and colour of the grid. When would a widely spaced grid be more useful than a tight one, and vice versa?

Turn on Snap to Grid in any of the media tools programs (except Flash) and try moving an object so that its edge is close to a grid line. How easy is it to make it snap to the grid?

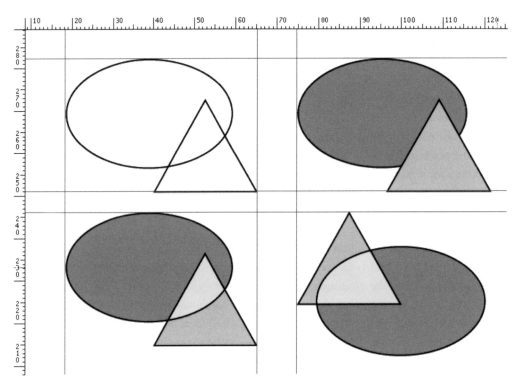

Figure 2.34 *Guides*

Guides

For lining things up by hand, *guides* are invaluable. A guide is just a horizontal or vertical line, which is displayed in the document window. You must have the rulers displayed before you can add guides. To add a horizontal guide, move the cursor to the top of the document, over the ruler, press the mouse button, and drag downwards. You will see the guide follow the cursor as you drag. When it is in the right place, release the mouse button. Add a vertical guide in a similar way, by dragging it out from the ruler at the left edge. If you don't position the guide correctly in the first instance, or if you change your mind about where you want it, it can be moved later.

If you want to place a guide at a precise distance from the top or left edge of your document, you can read its position from the rulers or Info panel, and drop it at the correct point. More often, though, you may want to place the guide along the edge of an object, or line it up with some feature of an image, as in Figure 2.34, where the guides ensure that the different versions of the design are properly aligned, despite their confusing shapes which would make aligning them by eye difficult. In this case it is necessary to position them by hand. (All the vertical and horizontal lines in Figure 2.34 are guides.) Any guides that you set are always available when a document is reopened in the program that created it, though they may be hidden, but they can only be seen if the file is being viewed with its creator program. For example, if you add guides to a Photoshop file, they will be available every time you reopen the file in Photoshop, but they will not be available if you place the Photoshop file in an Illustrator document, and they will not be present in any other image file that you may export from Photoshop, such as a JPEG.

You can show and hide guides, and snap objects to them, just as you can with the layout grid. You can also lock guides, which means you cannot move them by accident. This is often worth doing, since the guides may form the framework on which you are composing an image or layout, and moving a guide could cause chaos. If the guides are not locked, you can move them. In Illustrator and Flash, use the arrow tool to move guides; in Photoshop and Dreamweaver, just hold the cursor over a guide, and it will turn into a pair of arrows, showing that you can drag the guide.

You can snap to guides in the same way that you can snap to a grid. Snapping things to guides is a good way of making them line up. An alternative way of doing so is to use the Align panel, which can be used to align the horizontal and vertical edges or centres of objects, and also to equalize the spacing between them. This is another feature that, while common to all the programs (except Bridge) differs in important respects – including what you can align – from one program to another, so we will describe alignment in detail in the chapter for each program.

┌─ TRY THIS ───

In each program, practise dragging out vertical and horizontal guides. (If you can't see the guides, make sure that they have not been hidden.) Hide and reveal the guides. Find the commands for locking and unlocking guides.

Open a document in Photoshop or Illustrator and add guides to it so that they align with the edges of features of the image.

Find all the preference settings that affect guides, grids and rulers, and experiment with changing them.

└──

DON'T FORGET

Use the Info panel to see the precise coordinates of the cursor.

Show rulers to measure horizontal and vertical distances, and to make it possible to drag out guides.

Show the grid and make objects snap to it when you want a regularly spaced layout. Turn snapping off when you do not require it.

Drag guides out from the rulers to assist with horizontal and vertical layout. Hide the guides when you don't want them cluttering up the document.

Snap things to guides to line them up.

Bridge

Bridge is a key component of Adobe's Creative Suites; it is also included with each of the individual applications described in this book. In essence, it is just a file browser, which duplicates the functions of the Mac OS Finder or Windows Explorer in allowing you to navigate your folders, examine their contents and perform some simple operations. However, Bridge provides more flexible ways of displaying images, which makes it especially valuable to digital photographers. It also communicates with the other CS3 applications, which facilitates sharing of resources between them. Bridge may be particularly useful if you are working with several CS3 programs, but it can still be valuable on its own or in conjunction with Photoshop or Illustrator.

Choosing Browse... from the File menu in Photoshop, Illustrator or Flash, or File>Browse in Bridge... in Dreamweaver launches Bridge. Alternatively, Bridge can be started up on its own like any other program on your computer, using whatever means your operating system provides.

The Browser Window

Bridge's main purpose is to provide a means of looking at a collection of images in a convenient and efficient manner. The browser window provides the basic facilities for doing this. One of the first things you will probably notice when you start Bridge up is that the background is a dark

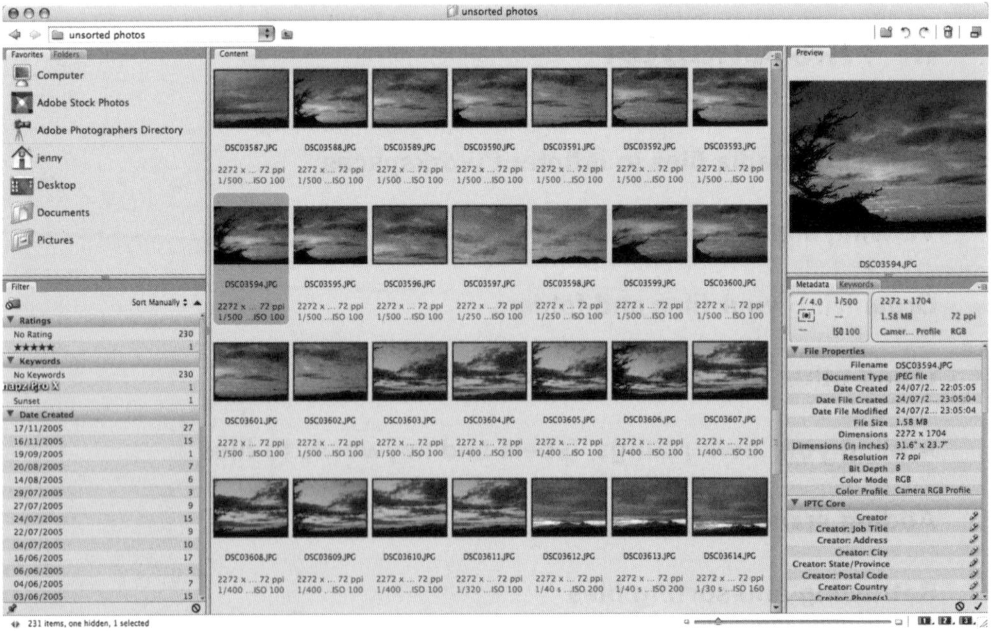

Figure 3.1 *The default workspace*

grey colour, unlike most other programs. This is intended to provide a better environment for looking at images, but if you find it too gloomy you can use the User Interface Brightness and Image Backdrop sliders in the General tab of the Preferences dialogue to lighten it up. (We have done this for the screenshots in this chapter to improve their contrast.)

The Default View

By default, when Bridge is started up it opens a window divided into three vertical panes, as shown in Figure 3.1. The main part of the window, in the middle, shows all the files in a selected folder on your disk. Images are shown as thumbnails; sub-folders and files that do not contain images are usually displayed as generic folder icons, but if you click on the Flatten View button, which you will find at the top left of the panel labelled Filter in the left pane, sub-folders will be expanded, so you can see all the images in a folder and its sub-folders together. (Thinking of the Flatten View button as a "no sub-folders" icon might help to explain its appearance.) The View>Show Thumbnails Only command on the menu bar has the effect of hiding the minimal information about each image that is normally displayed below each thumbnail, leaving nothing but the images themselves in the main browser window.

Files and folders can be selected in this central pane in the way you probably expect: click on a thumbnail to select it, [cmd/ctl]-click on additional thumbnails to add them to the selection or to remove them from it if they are already selected, shift-click to add or remove a contiguous set of thumbnails.

Typically, you will navigate to a folder of images, using the various navigation options provided, in order to view them in the browser window. The simplest way to move around the folder hierarchy is to double-click on a folder's icon in the main part of the window, which opens it and displays its contents. The icon to the right of the pop-up at the top of the window can be used to go up a level in the folder hierarchy. By combining these methods of moving down and up among folders you can reach any folder on your disk. Other navigation facilities, which may be more efficient, will be described later.

To the left and right sides of the main pane of the window in its default state are several tabbed panels, arranged in groups. At the top of the right-hand column is a *preview panel*. If one of the thumbnails is selected a larger version of the image is displayed in this preview area, as you can see in Figure 3.1. If you select a thumbnail of a file in some time-based format that Bridge recognizes, the preview will play. In particular, Flash movies (SWF files) and any video or audio format that can be displayed using QuickTime will be played in the preview panel. For QuickTime formats, if you hover the cursor in the space below the movie, a simple controller will appear, as shown in Figure 3.2, allowing you to stop and start the movie or the sound and adjust the sound level.

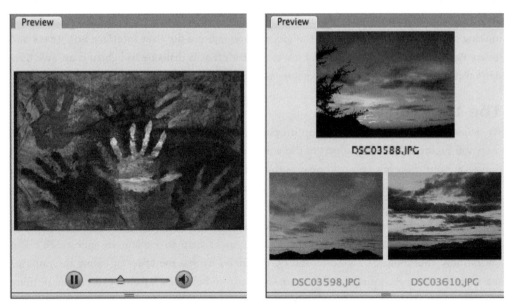

Figure 3.2 *Previewing video*   Figure 3.3 *Previewing several images at once*

Bridge does not display this controller for Flash movies, but any interactive controls embedded in the movie itself will operate in the preview in Bridge.

If several thumbnails are selected, larger versions of all of them are shown in the preview panel, as in Figure 3.3. The main intended purpose of this feature is to allow you to compare different versions of the same photograph.

Figure 3.4 *A loupe*

Even the previews of images are quite small. To see a part of the image magnified, click on the preview. A sub-window resembling a magnifying glass, known as a *loupe*, will pop up, as shown in Figure 3.4. You can use your mouse's scroll wheel, if it has one, or the + and − keys, to increase or decrease the magnification, and you can drag the loupe around the preview to see different parts of the image magnified.

The panels at the top of the left-hand pane are used for navigation, and the one at the bottom for restricting the images displayed to ones that satisfy specified criteria, as we will describe later. The panels on the right, below the preview area, are used for adding annotations to files and also for displaying any metadata which may be embedded in the file. (Metadata is data about the image, including information which is added to the image file automatically by most digital cameras when the photograph is taken, such as a record of the date and time a photograph was taken and the camera settings that were used to take it.)

Other Workspaces

Many other ways of displaying the images in a folder are possible in addition to the default workspace. You can select different preset arrangements from the Window>Workspace sub-menu, shown in Figure 3.5. Experimentation will quickly show you what each one represents, so we will only describe these workspaces briefly.

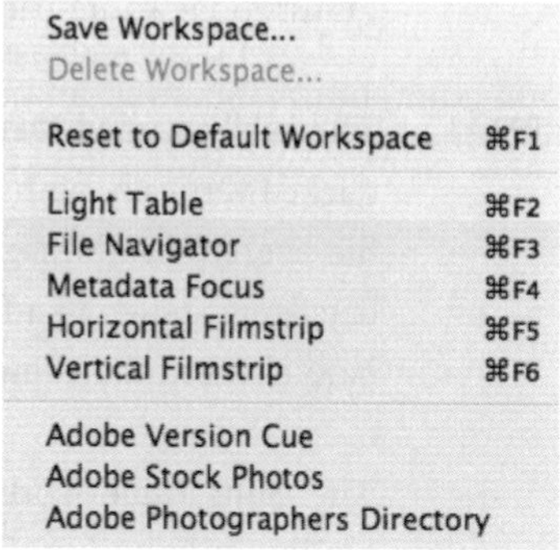

The Horizontal Filmstrip view, illustrated in Figure 3.6, shows the thumbnails in a horizontal strip along the bottom of the window, with the selected image shown larger above it. The scroll bar below the main image allows you to scrub through the thumbnails. The scroll bar arrows function as "next" and "previous" buttons, selecting the images following and preceding the current one, which allows you to look through the images sequentially. (Incidentally, notice that the scroll bars in Bridge are not the standard system controls, but are drawn by Bridge itself and don't respect any interface preferences you might have set, such as placing both arrows together at one end.) By adjusting the size of the filmstrip thumbnails, using

Save Workspace...	
Delete Workspace...	
Reset to Default Workspace	⌘F1
Light Table	⌘F2
File Navigator	⌘F3
Metadata Focus	⌘F4
Horizontal Filmstrip	⌘F5
Vertical Filmstrip	⌘F6
Adobe Version Cue	
Adobe Stock Photos	
Adobe Photographers Directory	

Figure 3.5 *Preset workspaces*

Figure 3.6 *Horizontal filmstrip view*

the slider at the bottom right of the window, you also adjust the size of the large preview image: the smaller the thumbnails, the larger the preview.

The Vertical Filmstrip workspace is similar to the Horizontal Filmstrip, but displays the thumbnails vertically down the right-hand side of the window, and is controlled by a vertical scroll bar. Filmstrip views are particularly useful when you need to see large previews of your images.

The oddly-named Metadata Focus workspace, illustrated in Figure 3.7, shows the thumbnails stacked vertically, with a summary of their properties – filename, creation and modification dates, file size, type and image size in pixels, by default – beside them. (In the other workspaces, these details are shown in a floating window that pops up when the cursor is over a thumbnail, if you have checked the Show Tooltips box in the Thumbnails pane of the Preferences dialogue.)

The Light Table workspace is a minimal workspace in which all panels are removed and the entire window is devoted to the display of the thumbnails.

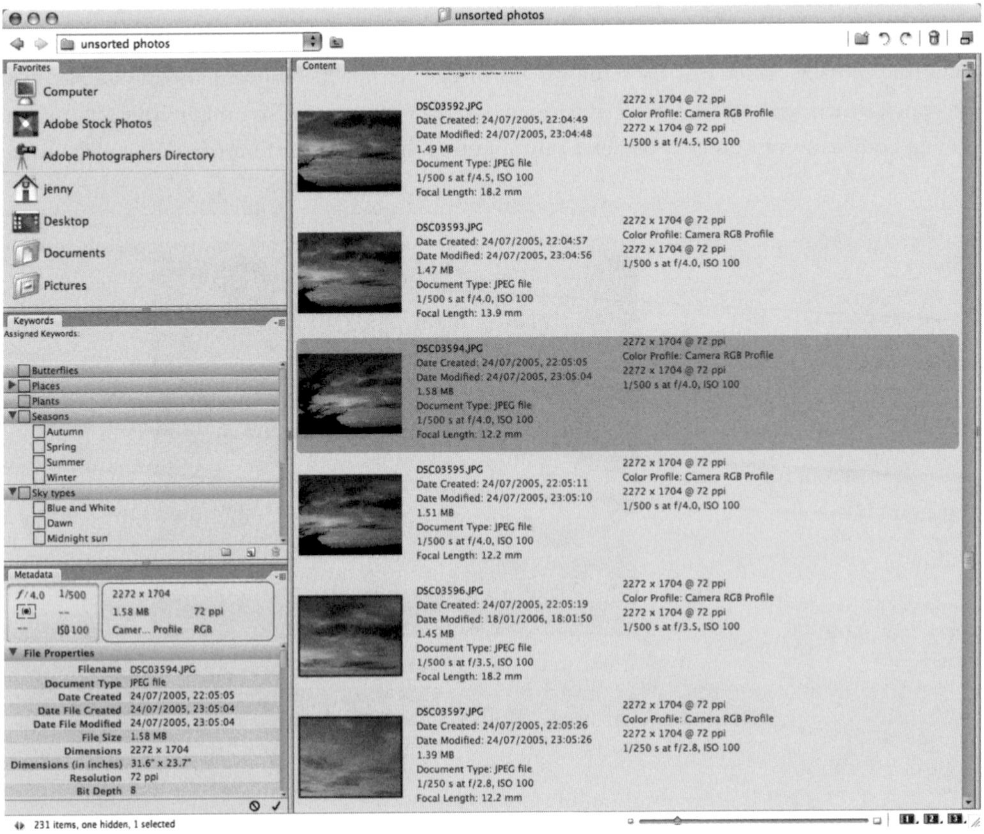

Figure 3.7 *Metadata focus*

The File Navigator workspace displays the thumbnails in the same way as the default workspace, but removes the right-hand pane of the window, and devotes the left to the panels for moving around in the file system which we will describe in a later section.

In all workspaces, you can change the size of the thumbnails by dragging the slider at the bottom of the window on the right-hand side, to make them bigger or smaller.

You don't have to restrict yourself to the preset workspaces. There is an entry in the Window menu for each of the panels; selecting one of these toggles the panel open or closed. Thus, you can modify any view so that only the panels of interest to you are displayed. All the panels can be dragged from their original positions and docked with others, like the true dockable panels described in Chapter 2, but they can't be minimized to icons, and you must use the Window menu to close and open them. The relative sizes of the various areas of the window can be adjusted by dragging the separators between them.

With all the options for displaying, there are many possible ways of configuring the browser window. The Window>Workspace>Save Workspace... command can be used to save a configuration as a custom workspace that can be used again subsequently, as described in Chapter 2. In Bridge, there is an alternative method for saving workspaces and switching between them. In the bottom right corner of the window there are three buttons with numbers on. If you hold down the mouse button while the cursor is over one of these, a menu that is almost identical to the Window>Workspace sub-menu will pop up. There will be a tick mark against one of the workspaces listed on the menu, which indicates that clicking the button will switch to that workspace. You can associate a different workspace with any button by selecting a new workspace from the pop-up list, or by choosing the Save Workspace... command to save the current workspace and associate it with the button. Thus, you can set up the buttons so that the three workspaces you use most frequently are associated with them and you can swap rapidly between your favourite workspaces just by clicking the buttons.

TRY THIS

Open Bridge and navigate through the folders on your hard disk looking for images and movies. Experiment with all the options for displaying a folder of images. Try out each of the ready-made workspaces. What sort of tasks do you think you would find each workspace useful for?

Arrange the panels in a way you like and save that arrangement as a workspace. Attach the three workspaces you think you will use most often to the workspace buttons in the bottom right-hand corner of the window.

Rotating

When taking photographs, you will sometimes turn the camera on its side to take a picture in portrait orientation. When Bridge displays such a picture, it shows it on its side, in landscape orientation. You can rotate images in JPEG, TIFF and Photoshop formats clockwise or anti-clockwise, in 90° increments, using the buttons at the top right of the browser window, or the rotate commands on the Edit menu. Rotating an image only affects the way thumbnails and previews are displayed in Bridge, it doesn't actually change the data in the image file. It does, however, cause the image to be displayed in its rotated state if you open it in Photoshop.

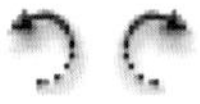

Slide Shows

Instead of looking at all the images in a folder at once, you can choose Slideshow from the View menu. This causes the images in the current folder to be displayed as a slide show, which takes over the entire screen. Everything else is hidden, including the menu bar. Various keys can be used as slide show controls. For basic operation, press the space bar to start and pause the show, and press the escape key to stop the show and return to the browser window.

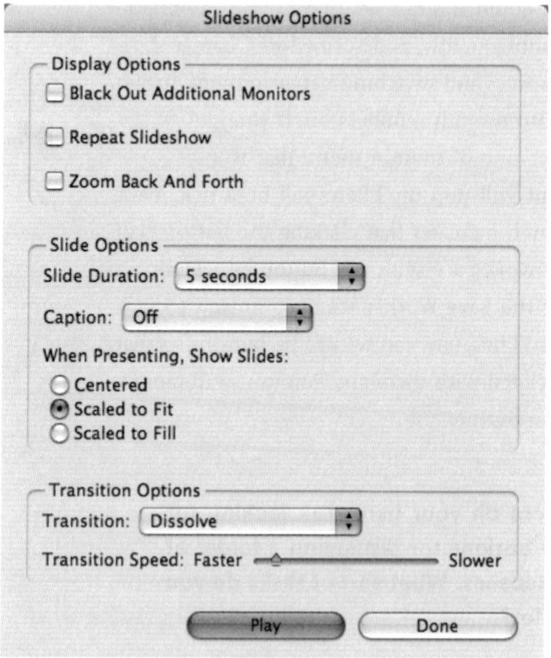

Figure 3.8 *Slide show options*

The slide show can be displayed in several different ways. Pressing L while it is playing, or choosing Slideshow Options... from the View menu, brings up the dialogue shown in Figure 3.8, which allows you to change some aspects of the display. There are three possibilities for the way in which the image is fitted to the screen: the image can be centred, with a border on all sides, it can be scaled to fill as much of the screen or window as possible while maintaining its aspect ratio, or it can be scaled to fill the whole screen area – this may cause some of the image to be cut off.

By default, each image is displayed for five seconds. You can choose a different duration or select Manual from the Slide Duration pop-up menu. In the latter case, you move on to the next slide by pressing the space bar or right-arrow key. By default, the slide shows stops after the last image has been displayed. If the Repeat Slideshow checkbox is ticked, it will go back to the first and repeat indefinitely until you explicitly stop it. The transition used to move from one slide to the next can also be changed using the pop-up menu at the bottom of the Slideshow Options dialogue. The default Dissolve is probably the easiest on the eye, while None is more austere. The other transitions are probably best avoided, as is the Zoom Back And Forth option, which seems designed to make you feel seasick. The speed of transitions is set using the Transition Speed slider in the Slideshow Options dialogue.

If the currently selected folder includes PDF files comprising more than one page, the slide show will display the pages of each file in order. Some additional navigation keys are available for such files. Pressing h during a slide show will show you a list of these, together with one or two additional options, which should be self-explanatory. Among these you will see some commands for simple editing and annotating from within a slide show. We will return to these later in the context of Bridge's annotation features.

---TRY THIS---

Run a slide show of all the images in one of your folders. Try altering the duration of each slide until you find a suitable speed for the show. Experiment with the different display options, noting any cropping that occurs when the slides fill the screen or window.

Compact Mode

A final option for displaying the browser window is Bridge's *compact mode*. In this mode, which can be selected from the View menu or by clicking on the icon in the top right corner of the

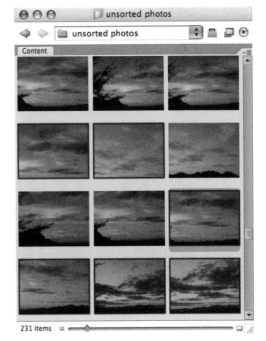

browser window, everything except the thumbnails and basic navigation controls is hidden, as shown in Figure 3.9 (irrespective of which workspace is being used in the full browser window). The compact window can be resized by dragging out the bottom right-hand corner in the usual way. A panel menu with some useful commands is added at the top right corner.

By default, in compact mode, the Bridge window floats over any other open windows on your computer screen. This is convenient (if you have a big enough screen): it ensures that the browser is visible all the time, no matter which program you are actively working on. Photoshop and Illustrator users may find it useful to have a floating browser window to select files from, instead of relying on the normal file open dialogues. If you prefer the compact view to behave like an ordinary window, so that it is obscured when another program is at the front, deselect Compact Window Always On Top in the panel menu.

Figure 3.9 *Compact mode*

Some commands on the View menu still work in compact mode. For instance, the View>Show Thumbnails Only command has been used in Figure 3.9 to hide file information and display only the image thumbnails. A subset of the relevant View menu commands appears in the View sub-menu of the panel menu. You can also sort the displayed files, and use the slider at the bottom of the compact mode window to change the size of thumbnails. Filter settings are respected in compact mode, so only files that would be displayed in full mode are visible.

To return to the full browser view, select Full Mode from the View menu or sub-menu, or click on the icon at the top right of the compact mode window, next to the panel menu control. To toggle quickly between full and compact mode, use the keyboard shortcut [cmd/ctl]-return. If you are short of screen space, there is also an *ultra-compact mode*, in which the thumbnails are hidden, leaving just the controls, as shown in Figure 3.10. You can toggle between compact and ultra-compact modes using the other icon at the top right of the compact mode window, thus hiding or revealing the thumbnails with a single click. It can be convenient to leave the ultra-compact window floating at the top of your screen until you need an image, then switch to compact or full mode when you want to browse. (Note that if you return to full view and later select compact mode again, you will get the ultra-compact window if that is the view you last used in compact mode.)

Figure 3.10 *Ultra-compact mode*

Stacks

A large collection of files or folders will overflow the main content window. To help you manage large numbers of files more easily, you can group them into *stacks*. These are just virtual collections, although usually you would only group files in a stack if they had something in common.

To group a set of images or other files or folders together into a stack, select them all (they do not need to be contiguous thumbnails) and then choose Group as Stack from the Stacks menu.

Figure 3.11 *A collapsed stack*

The thumbnails will collapse, with only the first one displayed, as shown in Figure 3.11. The number in the top left corner of the stack tells you how many files it contains. If you click on this number, the stack expands so that you can see all the thumbnails in it. The files still remain stacked, though, which is indicated by an outline around them all, and the number, which now appears by the first file in the stack. Clicking the number again collapses the stack once more.

The slider and play button that you can see at the top of the stack in Figure 3.11 appear when you hover the cursor over a collapsed stack, providing there are ten or more items in it and the thumbnails are big enough to accommodate the controls. You use these controls to scrub or play through all the files in the stack – each one comes to the top in turn as you drag the slider or click the play button. The rate at which the files in the stack are played is set in the Thumbnails pane of the Preferences dialogue. However, the available values are all typical film and video playback speeds, suggesting that the play button is intended to be used for previewing sequences of video or animation frames. These speeds certainly don't give you enough time to look at individual images or other files, so if you just want to look through a stack quickly, use the slider instead.

You can add more files to a stack by dragging and dropping them onto it, or remove files by dragging them out; you can only drag individual files out if the stack is expanded, of course. To dismantle a stack, use the Stacks>Ungroup from Stack command. This conveniently leaves all the unstacked files selected. If you click on a collapsed stack, only the top file is selected, but you can select the entire stack by clicking on its border, allowing you to apply commands to all the files in the stack at once. In particular, you can attach keywords, labels and ratings, as we describe later.

---TRY THIS---

Familiarize yourself with the use of stacks by selecting several files within a folder and grouping them into a stack. Expand and collapse the stack, add some extra files and remove some others. Group a selection of image files into a stack (try an image sequence if you can) and experiment with the playback controls.

DON'T FORGET

Use Bridge to navigate and display collections of images and media files.

Choose between the default, filmstrip, metadata focus, file navigator and light table workspaces. Assign your favourite workspaces to the numbered buttons at the bottom right of the window, for quick switching between them.

Use a slide show to display selected images in sequence at a large size.

Use compact mode to keep a floating window of files available.

Group files into stacks to save space and organize them better.

Navigation and File Operations

Bridge allows you to navigate the file system and perform many of the tasks that are normally done at the desktop using the Mac OS Finder or Windows Explorer, without leaving the file browsing environment. It also interacts in various ways with other Creative Suite programs.

Navigation

Navigation in Bridge shares many characteristics with the File>Open dialogues in Windows Explorer, so experienced users of Windows should be able to move around using Bridge easily. Mac OS X users may be a little disoriented at first, but the navigational concepts used in Bridge should be familiar to anyone who has used a computer with a graphical user interface.

As we described earlier, you can double-click folders in the browser window to open them, just as you can in a desktop window.

Figure 3.12 *The* Look In *menu*

The drop-down menu (sometimes called the Look In menu) found at the top left of the browser window can be used for quick navigation. Dropping the menu down, as shown in Figure 3.12, displays all the ancestors of the current folder, allowing you to move up several steps at once. It also shows you a list of folders that you have designated as *favourites*, which are like Web browser bookmarks. (You can add the current folder to your list of favourites using the File>Add To Favorites command.) At the bottom of the menu is a list of the folders you have recently visited in Bridge. This is not shown in Figure 3.12 as the Clear Recent Folders Menu command, also at the bottom of the menu, has been used.

As we mentioned earlier, the button to the right of the Look In menu takes you up one level in the file system hierarchy. The left and right arrows to the left of the menu allow you to step back to the folder you visited most recently, and then forwards again, like the back and forward buttons on a Web browser.

To browse the hierarchy and go directly to a folder, you can use the Folders panel, which is in the top left of the window in the default workspace. This shows the file system as a tree structure, very much like a file browser in Windows. Clicking on the disclosure triangles (plus signs in Windows) reveals or hides the next level of detail. Clicking on a file or folder selects it.

In the default workspaces, the Folders panel is docked with the Favorites panel (which you can see in the top left corner of Figures 3.1, 3.6 and 3.7). This shows all your favourite folders and documents (plus, by default, some folders which Adobe would like you to have as favourites). Clicking on a folder in the Favorites panel selects it as the current folder; clicking on a document opens it in its default application (usually the one that created it). As well as using the File>Add to Favorites command, you can also create favourites by dragging them from the main browser window in to the Favorites panel. To remove a folder from your list of favourites, you can select it in the main browser window or the Favorites panel, and use the File>Remove From Favorites command. You cannot remove a file from the favourites by selecting it in the Favorites panel, however; you must select the file in the main browser window before using the command.

TRY THIS

Experiment with the different ways of navigating around your hard disk in Bridge. Decide which ways suit you best.

Create some favourite folders and files using the different possible methods. Use the Favorites panel to return to your favourite folders.

File and Folder Operations

If you prefer to stay within Bridge all the time you are working with image files, you can perform all of the usual file management operations inside it. You can delete files and folders by selecting them and clicking on the dustbin icon, which is situated in the top right corner of the browser window. You can rename an item by clicking on its name in the browser window and typing a new name. You can create new folders with the File>New Folder command. All these operations affect the actual files and folders on your disk and are not in any sense restricted to Bridge's view; all other applications will see any changes you make. In particular, if you delete an item, it will be moved to the system Trash (recycle bin) and will be permanently deleted once you empty the Trash, just as if you had deleted it on the desktop. File management operations cannot be undone inside Bridge, so they must be used with caution.

You can move files by dragging them to another folder. You can drag to a folder in the browser window, the Folders panel, the Favorites panel or a new Bridge window. Holding down [opt/alt] while dragging causes the item to be copied. The File menu includes Move To and Copy To sub-menus, with entries for your recent folders, allowing you to copy files directly to them. There are also context-menu items for this and for other file-handling operations.

If you prefer to stick with the operating system's normal interface for performing file management, you will find that any changes you make in the Finder or Explorer are not immediately reflected in Bridge. To update Bridge's view of your disk, use the View>Refresh command.

─TRY THIS─

Try using Bridge to create and delete folders, rename, move and copy files, but be careful! Decide whether you find the convenience of performing these operations without leaving the browsing environment preferable to using your operating system's normal interface.

Interacting with Other Programs

One of Bridge's main strengths is its ability to interact with other programs. You can open any type of file from inside Bridge: if you double-click a thumbnail, the corresponding image is opened in its default application – even if this is not an Adobe program. Alternatively, the File>Open With sub-menu lists all the programs installed on your system which are capable of opening the selected file. Choose any one of these to open the file in the program you wish to use.

Integration with the other components of Creative Suite is more complete. You can place images using Bridge's File>Place sub-menu, which lists any other CS applications you have installed. (For Flash, there are two entries, Place>In Flash and Place>In Flash Library. See Chapter 6 for an explanation of the difference between these.) By selecting one of them, you place the image selected in Bridge into a document in the chosen application, as if you had used that application's own File>Place command. It is also possible to drag images from a Bridge window and drop them into another application. The effect is the same as if you had placed it. For example, you can drag an image into an Illustrator window and it will be added to the document as if you had used Illustrator's Place command. The compact mode is convenient if you work in this way.

On the Tools menu, there are sub-menus for each of the other Creative Suite programs you have installed. These list the operations that can be performed from inside Bridge. For instance, the Illustrator sub-menu includes the Live Trace command, so you could select some bitmapped images in Bridge and by choosing this command have all of them vectorized using Illustrator's Live Trace operation, which is described in Chapter 5. A simplified version of the Live Trace dialogue opens, from which you can choose a preset for the command's parameters, and choose where the processed images are to be saved, and how they are to be named.

The Tools>Photoshop sub-menu provides the largest list of commands, which essentially provide Bridge with all the facilities of Photoshop's File>Automate sub-menu, described in Chapter 2. In particular, the Photoshop>Batch… command allows you to apply any action you have already defined in Photoshop to a set of images selected in Bridge. When used from Bridge, Photoshop's File>Automate>Batch… command offers Bridge as the default option for the source images. When you use the Tools>Photoshop>Batch… command from Bridge, it starts up Photoshop and opens the Batch dialogue. From there on, you can proceed exactly as you would if you were applying a batch action from inside Photoshop.

—TRY THIS—

> **Define a Photoshop action to perform some simple operation, such as resizing or changing the resolution of an image. (If you don't know how to define a Photoshop action you can use one of the default actions supplied with the program.) Apply the action from within Bridge to images you have selected by hand. (Take care to specify a new folder under Destination for the results of the batch processing, to avoid overwriting your original images.)**

File Organization

If you deal with large collections of images, it is important to keep them organized or it will become difficult to find the ones you want. Simply filing them in different, meaningfully named folders is often not sufficient. Bridge allows you to annotate images with keywords, apply different coloured labels to them and give them a star rating. It also provides support for attaching metadata describing a wide range of properties to images. All these different forms of annotation can be used as the basis for displaying only certain files, or for searching among collections of files.

Ratings, Labels and Keywords

Often, when working on a project that uses photographs, you will start out with a set of pictures, perhaps from a photo shoot, and need to choose the best to work with. Bridge allows you to apply a *star rating* to each image. Simply select the image and click on the dot below the thumbnail that corresponds to the required number of stars (you may need to increase the size of the thumbnails to see the dots), or choose a number of stars from the Label menu. You can also use this menu to apply coloured labels to your images, another rough and ready way of classifying them, as shown in Figure 3.13, which also shows how ratings are displayed. The default names for the labels, and the entries in the Label menu, suggest their use for choosing or rejecting shots from a photo shoot, but you can use your own labelling system, setting the names of your coloured labels in the Labels pane of the Preferences dialogue. Note that labels and ratings are applied independently. For example, setting a rating to five stars would not automatically label a photo as Approved. The keyboard shortcuts for ratings and labels consist of the usual system modifier (cmd or ctl) with digits. For star ratings, the mapping is intuitive, [cmd/ctl]-1 gives an image one star, [cmd/ctl]-2 gives it two, and so on.

It is possible to set and alter ratings and attach labels while viewing a slide show. The keys 1 to 5 apply the corresponding number of stars to the current slide, while period and comma add and subtract one from an existing rating, respectively. 0 deletes any rating. The keys 6 to 9 apply a label to the current slide, using the same mapping as the keyboard shortcuts in the Label menu. (Hence, you cannot apply purple labels during a slide show.) The possibility of assigning labels

Figure 3.13 *Ratings and labels*

and ratings this way means that you can, for example, upload a large set of images off your camera and perform a preliminary rough classification while you run a slide show to look at them all.

Figure 3.14 *Keywords*

Adding **keywords** to a file effectively allows you to classify the same image in different ways. For instance, a picture of a sunset taken in spring could have the keywords Sunset and Spring attached to it, so that it could be found when you were looking for spring pictures or pictures of sunsets. If you have visited any photo-sharing or social bookmarking Web sites that use tagging, the idea of using keywords in this way should be familiar to you.

The Keywords panel (to the right of the browser window), shown in Figure 3.14, displays a collection of keyword categories, within each of which is a set of individual keywords. You can create and delete your own categories and keywords using the conventional buttons at the bottom of the panel. Bridge comes with a few ready-made categories containing keywords supplied by Adobe, but these are of little or no general use.

To assign a keyword to a file, select the file in the browser window and tick the checkbox next to the keyword in the Keywords panel. You can assign multiple keywords to a single file, which allows you to retrieve that file by any one of the keywords attached to it, as we describe later. To assign all of the keywords in a category to a file, just tick the checkbox next to that category.

As we mentioned earlier, if you select all the images in a stack you can rate, label or tag them all at once, providing you wish to add the same labels, ratings or keywords to all of them

---TRY THIS---

Try assigning labels and ratings to individual images in the browser, then try adding labels and ratings while viewing a set of images as a slide show.

Navigate to a folder of images, such as a set of photographs you have uploaded from a digital camera. Decide upon a suitable set of keywords for classifying these images, define each keyword (assigning them to categories if this makes sense), and then add keywords to each of your images.

Metadata

Keywords allow you to classify images in an *ad hoc* way. Systematic metadata, which is organized according to international standards, can also be attached to images. Any metadata attached to a file is displayed in the Metadata panel, shown in Figure 3.15.

All images come with some metadata (data about the image file), such as their file names and sizes, dimensions and creation and modification dates. Images uploaded from digital cameras also usually have so-called *Exif* metadata, which records details about how the picture was taken: exposure time, focal length and so on, and some information about when it was taken. Some cameras will also add GPS metadata to images too.

A trade standard known as the **IPTC core specification** provides a uniform way of recording information about an image's creator, its copyright status, and various pieces of information that help to classify the image. **DICOM** is a standard used in hospitals, which provides a set of metadata for describing medical images. Although we have concentrated on using Bridge with image files, you can also preview and organize audio and video files; a set of metadata is provided for these types of media, too.

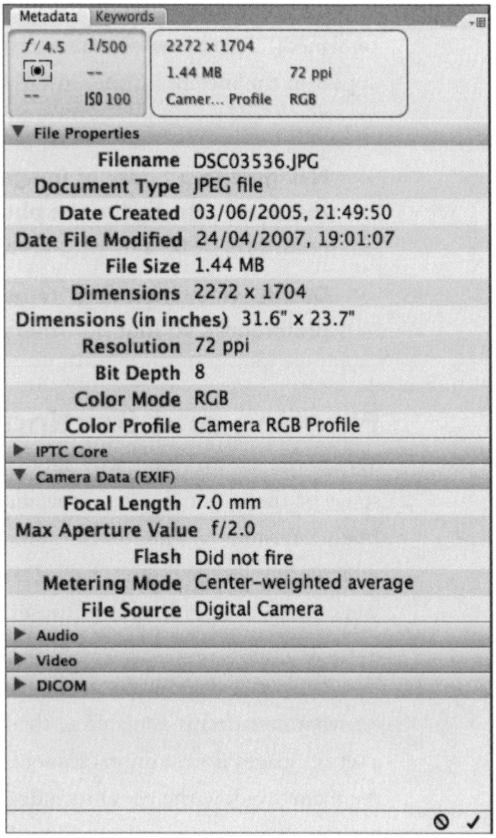

Figure 3.15 *The* Metadata *panel*

The Metadata panel is divided into sections, each corresponding to a particular metadata standard. You can hide or disclose the items within each section by clicking on the triangle next to its name. At the top of the panel is a little summary, known as the **metadata placard**. Here, the important Exif data values are shown in a way that resembles the display on the screen of a digital camera. A photographer can easily see what exposure and other settings were used to take the image. Other metadata, about the image's size, resolution and colour profile, is shown on the right of the metadata placard.

The Metadata panel also allows you to enter your own metadata about the selected image in addition to any that is automatically attached to the file. (You cannot edit the metadata which has been automatically attached to a file.) Any item that can be edited has a pencil icon to the right of it. Clicking this icon allows you to enter a value for the item. As well as entering metadata directly into the panel, you can use the File>File Info... command to open a dialogue with fields for every possible metadata item.

Few users will want to see all the metadata that can possibly be attached to an image. For example, only medical personnel will have any use for DICOM metadata. You can specify which items will appear in the metadata panel in the Metadata pane of the Preferences dialogue.

┌─TRY THIS───
│
│ **Navigate to a folder of images uploaded from a digital camera and look at the metadata attached to the photographs. Add IPTC metadata to some of the files, recording details of who created them, where they were taken and so on.**
│
│ **Decide which metadata items you are likely to find useful and set your metadata preferences so that no others are displayed in the Metadata panel.**
│
└──

Filtering and Sorting

When you are working with any large collection of images, you may often want to see only some of them, which satisfy specific criteria. In particular, you might want to use the ratings, labels, keywords and metadata to determine which images Bridge should display. The Filter panel, which occupies the bottom half of the left pane of the Bridge window in the default and filmstrip workspaces, is used for this purpose.

The categories that appear in the Filter panel are determined dynamically by Bridge depending on what metadata is available in the files and how you have annotated them. For instance, when a set of images from a digital camera, which had already been labelled and rated, was displayed in the main window, the panel included the categories shown in Figure 3.16. The modification and creation dates are known from the file system and the ISO rating and orientation are obtained from the images' metadata; only labels and star ratings that have actually been used are shown.

In the example shown in Figure 3.16 there were no keywords, but if any were added, they would appear under the **Keywords** heading.

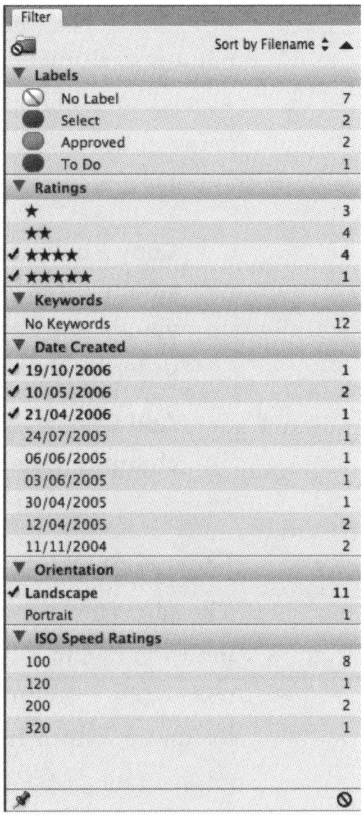

Under each of the category headings there appears a list of the particular values which Bridge encountered in this collection of images. (In the example in Figure 3.16, therefore, you can see that there were no images assigned a rating of three stars.) If you click on a value, a tick appears next to it, and only images with that value for the attribute will then be displayed. However, the way in which the filter operates across different categories is not intuitive. If only a single category is used for filtering, images that satisfy any of the values selected will be displayed. So, for example, if there had been no ticks under any category except **Ratings** in Figure 3.16, all images that had been assigned four or five stars would have been displayed, regardless of any other criteria. But if values are selected across more than one category in the **Filter** panel, images must then satisfy at least one of the values selected in every category that has ticks in it. Thus, the only images actually displayed using the configuration of the **Filter** panel shown in Figure 3.16 were landscape-oriented files that also had a four or five star rating and, in addition, were created on one of the three selected dates in 2006. A landscape format image with a four star rating that was created in 2004, for example, would not be displayed using these filter settings.

Figure 3.16 *The* Filter *panel*

Normally, when you move to a different folder, the filter settings are cleared, and all the files in the new folder will be displayed. Clicking on the pin icon at the bottom left of the **Filter** panel makes the settings stay on as you browse. Clicking on the icon in the bottom right corner of the panel clears all filters.

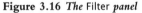

A different way of finding files that satisfy some simple criterion is by sorting them according to one of their attributes. For instance, if you wanted to see the best images in a folder, you could sort according to their star ratings, so that the ones with the highest rating would be shown first in the window. The **View** menu has a **Sort** sub-menu, shown in Figure 3.17. From this you can select an attribute to be used as a sort key; the files in the browser will be displayed in the sequence that is created by sorting them according to the values of the selected attribute. The **Ascending Order** entry in the sub-menu toggles between sorting in increasing and decreasing order of the key. For instance, if you have selected **By Date Created** and deselected **Ascending Order**, your files will be displayed in reverse chronological order. The current sort key is shown at the top right of the

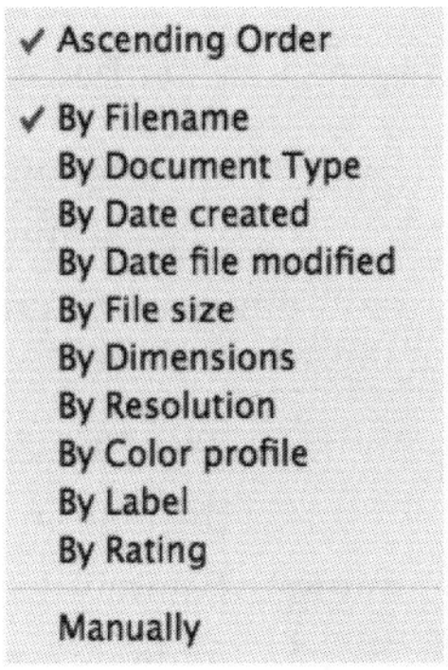

Figure 3.17 View>Sort

Filter panel, with another copy of the View>Sort sub-menu available to the right of it, under a pop-up, so that you can control the sorting of filtered files directly from the panel. (Instead of an Ascending Order option in this menu there is a triangle to the right of the pop-up, used to toggle between ascending and descending order.) The default sort key is Sort by Filename.

TRY THIS

Copy a collection of bitmapped images and vector graphics into a folder. Observe which categories and values are displayed in the Filter panel. Choose some values and see how the images are filtered. Sort the images into chronological order by their creation date, and by decreasing file size.

Add keywords and ratings to some or all of the images. See how the Filter panel changes. Select certain keywords as a filter, and sort the results by rating.

Retrieval

The Edit>Find... command is provided for more sophisticated retrieval. It opens the dialogue box shown in Figure 3.18. Here you can set precise criteria for retrieval, using the pop-up menus and text box. In the example shown in Figure 3.18, we were looking only in a folder called "Photos", for images which had been assigned any keyword containing the word "flowers" or had been given a rating of not less than three stars.

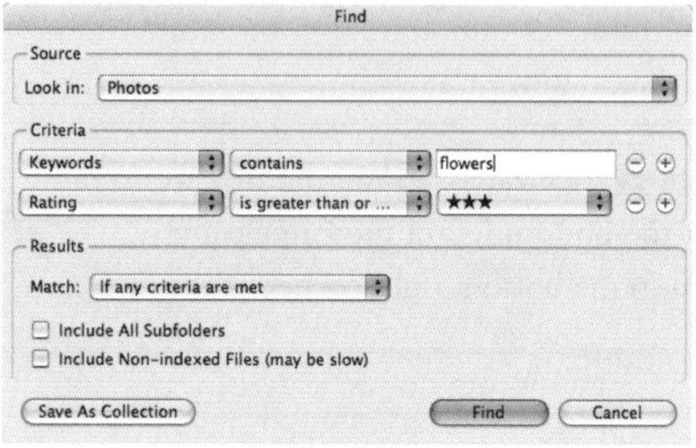

A long list of possible search criteria is provided under the left-hand Criteria pop-up menu. Files can be retrieved according to a wide range of criteria based on metadata and any annotations that you may have attached to a file. Once you have made a selection from this list, the middle pop-up menu changes to present a list of relevant comparison operations, and a suitable input control is shown at the right for you to enter an appropriate value. The + button on the far right-hand side of the dialogue allows you to add extra criteria; the – button removes the criterion it is placed next to. If you use more than one criterion in the Find dialogue, the Match pop-up menu allows you to choose whether to retrieve only those images that match all your specified criteria or images that match any one of them.

Figure 3.18 *The* Find *dialogue*

The Find dialogue also offers the option of saving the results of your search as a **collection**, using the button labelled Save As Collection that appears in the bottom left corner, as shown in Figure 3.18. You will be prompted for a location to save the collection in. When you browse the folder in which you saved it, you will see the collection denoted by a special icon. If you double-click this icon to open the collection, the results of your saved search are displayed. The search is run again each time you open the collection, so it reflects the state of the disk at that time. It follows that if you delete any of the files that used to be in a collection, they will not appear in Bridge next time you try to open that collection. (Collections are similar to Mac OS X's smart folders, Apple Mail's smart mailboxes, iTunes' smart playlists and Windows Vista's search folders.)

TRY THIS

Practise using the Find dialogue to retrieve images you previously classified and rated, according to their rating, label, keywords and any other criteria that apply to your files. Combine different search criteria to find images with a combination of properties and save these as a collection.

DON'T FORGET

Browse the file system in the Folders panel.

Use the Favorites panel to access frequently-used folders.

Move, copy and rename files and folders within the browser window.

Place files in other documents using the File>Place sub-menu or drag and drop; run automated operations in other Adobe programs using the Tools menu.

Add star ratings and labels to help classify or organize your files.

Tag images with your own keywords for *ad hoc* classification.

Add metadata to describe images and media files systematically.

Use the Filter panel to restrict the display to files with specific ratings, labels, keywords and metadata; sort files in order, according to a chosen attribute.

Retrieve files by specifying more sophisticated criteria using Edit>Find... and save the results as a collection.

WHAT ELSE?

Bridge has some extra facilities that provide access to Adobe's online collection of stock photos and a directory of photographers, so you can buy images and hire a photographer from within the program.

Bridge is the preferred interface to the Version Cue version management system. You can check files in and out of a repository using Bridge. We do not describe Version Cue as it is only of use for certain types of project, generally large collaborative ones.

Bridge can be used to start an online meeting in Acrobat Connect, a Web-based collaboration service (with a subscription fee). You could share your Bridge browser window and discuss its contents in real time with other people.

Photoshop

Photoshop is the leading program for retouching, editing and compositing bitmapped images. It is so well established that it could justifiably be called the standard program for these tasks. It is not difficult to get started in Photoshop, but it takes time and practice to fully master all that it offers. This is not just because of the sheer number of features it provides, although there are many, but because of the ways in which these features interact and must be used in combination to achieve the results that Photoshop is capable of. This is a program that offers little in the way of instant gratification. In fact, the newcomer to Photoshop may not understand what all the fuss is about. It is only through experience coupled with a certain amount of understanding of how bitmapped images can be manipulated that you come to realize why so many graphic designers and other visual artists working in digital media rely on Photoshop and rate it so highly.

There is a popular belief that computers make life easier by automating tasks that must otherwise be performed by hand. While there are programs that take that approach, Photoshop is not one of them. It is not its business to provide shortcuts and quick solutions. Instead, it provides powerful tools for the manipulation of digital images that are equal to, or exceed in power, traditional darkroom tools used for photography, and in many ways they have made the altering of photographs and other bitmapped images very much easier than physical methods. However, Photoshop's tools still require a considerable amount of patience, skill and visual sense to obtain good results, and can be just as frustrating as darkroom work if you approach them casually. Above all, remember that Photoshop is a professionals' tool. Use it professionally and you will get professional results.

Photoshop was originally designed at a time when the majority of images were ultimately destined to be printed. Print design and pre-press work remain important areas in which it is used today, and many of the things you can do in Photoshop only make sense if your images are eventually going to be printed using ink on paper. For multimedia and Web work, where images are only ever going to be displayed on a monitor, features which are specifically oriented towards print can be ignored, so we will omit these print-specific features from this chapter.

There are now two versions of Photoshop: Standard and Extended. The Extended version is included in the Premium Creative Suites, while the Standard version is part of the Standard Design Suite. The additional features in Photoshop CS3 Extended (as it is properly called) are aimed at specialist areas of application, including video, animation and scientific visualization. In this chapter, we will confine ourselves to describing Photoshop CS3 Standard, which is powerful enough for most users' needs. If you have Photoshop Extended, you will find that there are a few menu commands that we do not describe, but when you are starting out with Photoshop you do not need to know about them.

Fundamentals

A digital image displayed on a monitor is made up of small coloured dots called *pixels*. Each pixel is too small to be seen by the naked eye, so when you look at an image, you see what appears to be continuous areas of colour. A *bitmapped image* is a representation of an image that can be stored as a file on disk or edited, using a program such as Photoshop. The representation is simple: each pixel's colour is recorded as a number (see Chapter 8), and the collection of pixel values is arranged in rows and columns. The image is displayed by setting the colour of each pixel on the screen to the value stored in the corresponding position in the bitmapped image.

Making changes to the stored values changes the appearance of the image when it is displayed. Putting that the other way round, if you want to make changes to the appearance of the image, you must change the stored values. Many images contain millions of pixels, so making such changes is easier said than done. It is usually far from clear exactly which pixels must be changed and to what value in order to achieve a desired visual result. If editing bitmapped images is to be feasible, we need some way of translating intelligible operations – such as removing overhead telephone lines from a photograph of an otherwise picturesque landscape – into changes to stored pixel values. This is what Photoshop does.

The following are just a few examples of tasks that you might use Photoshop for: removing a colour cast (that is, an unnatural predominance of one colour) from a photograph or scanned image; sharpening up a blurry or badly focused image; compensating for bad exposure in an original photograph; removing unwanted background objects from a photograph; superimposing type on a picture and altering its appearance, for example to give it a 3D bevelled look; creating a collage from a mixture of scanned images, graphics created in some other program and still images taken from digitized video footage; increasing the contrast of a screenshot to make the text more legible; changing the resolution of a scanned image from 600 dpi to 72 dpi for display on a monitor; optimizing an image for display on a Web site, where you need to compromise between image quality and file size; or even creating animation. Almost always, to achieve a complex result, a combination of tools and commands is required. Often, you will combine many operations on an image in order to obtain the effects you want.

Opening and Importing Images

Photoshop has painting and drawing tools for creating images from scratch – we will describe these tools later, after we have explained some properties of bitmapped images that you need to understand first – but it is more commonly used to alter and correct existing images. There are two ways of getting an image into Photoshop, depending on whether it already exists in a digital file or is only available in some external physical medium.

Opening Files

The File>Open... command can be used to open files in many bitmapped and some vector graphics formats, including, of course, native Photoshop files. You can also open files in Photoshop from Bridge, as we described in Chapter 3. The formats which you can open include those used for Web images: GIF, JPEG and PNG. TIFF files, which are a common choice as an interchange format for bitmapped images, can also be opened and so can the platform-dependent formats which are used under Mac OS and Windows: PICT and BMP. For users of high-end digital cameras, Photoshop is able to open *Camera Raw* files, and provides some special facilities for working with them. Other, less commonly used, formats are also supported, although Photoshop is by no means able to open all of the hundreds of image file formats in existence. For this you need to use a specialized format conversion utility such as GraphicConverter or DeBabelizer.

---TRY THIS---

Experiment with opening images in Photoshop in as many different file formats as you can find. Make a note of which file formats the program can and cannot open. See what happens if you try to open an Illustrator (.ai) or a PDF file.

You can only open an image in Photoshop if it has been stored in a file that already exists. You may have downloaded an image file from a digital camera or a Web site, or found it on a CD-ROM image library. It may have got there by being exported from some other application – perhaps it was an image of a scene rendered in a 3D program or a frame exported from a video application. Photoshop can also import images directly from an external device, such as a scanner. In this case the scanner digitizes the image and the file is immediately opened in Photoshop.

Importing from External Devices

Importing from external devices directly into Photoshop is done using *plug-ins*. These are not supplied as part of Photoshop, but must be obtained from the device's manufacturer and installed according to their instructions. The name of any plug-in of this sort that has been installed will appear in the File>Import sub-menu. Usually, selecting a plug-in for a scanner causes an elaborate dialogue box to be displayed, which is basically the interface to a scanning sub-application. Depending on the scanner's manufacturer and its quality, a range of facilities may be available from within the plug-in interface. There will certainly be a means of previewing the scan, and you can usually select just part of the image to import. Some method of making colour adjustments and sharpening is generally provided, too. If you are using a low-cost desktop scanner then these adjustments are usually better made in Photoshop itself, after you have imported the scanned image, but high-end scanners may offer reliable colour management systems, tuned to the particular model of scanner. When you are satisfied with the preview and any adjustments you have made, clicking the OK button is usually all that is required to start the scanning process. When it is complete, the scanned image appears in a new Photoshop window.

Scanners do vary considerably in quality, and obtaining the best results from them, particularly from high-end models, requires some specialized skill and experience. For images that are going to be used on Web pages, cheap scanners often produce acceptable results and do not require much by way of skilled operation, so they may actually be more appropriate for capturing Web images than more expensive models intended for the pre-press industry.

Saving and Exporting

Although Photoshop is not an image file conversion utility, it can save images, using the File>Save As… command, in the same range of formats that it can import, so it can be used to translate between any of the formats it supports. There are a few options in the Save As… dialogue that control some properties of the saved file, but you can ignore these at first, except for the checkbox labelled As A Copy. Normally, when you save a file, the open document becomes associated with that file and if you continue working on it you will be changing the new file. If you save as a copy, the open document remains associated with the file you originally opened, and any changes will not affect the file you saved as a copy. For some file formats, and in order to set options in some others, the As A Copy option must be selected. Where it is compulsory in this way, it is selected by default, so you do not usually have to worry about it, but you may be confused by the warning message that appears in the Save As… dialogue, shown in Figure 4.1.

You should use Photoshop's own *PSD* format for saving working versions of your files, only using a different format at the end of a project if you need to, when delivering the final version of the image. If you work with very large or very high resolution images, or are working on a file with a very large number of layers, you may need to use *Large Document Format (PSB)* files, since PSD files cannot be more than 2GB in size. Most people are rarely inconvenienced by this limit.

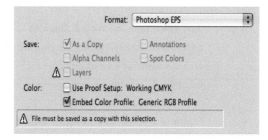

Figure 4.1 *Saving an image in a different file format*

─TRY THIS─

If there is a scanner attached to your computer, practise importing scans into Photoshop. Experiment with the different options provided by your scanner's plug-in. Try scanning some unusual objects, such as some clothing or your hand, as well as flat images such as photographs and magazine pages. (Never look at the scanner bed while it scans because that can damage your eyes.)

Practise saving your scanned images in several of the different file formats that Photoshop supports. Reopen each saved file and note whether there are any differences from your original scanned image.

Saving for the Web

For Web formats, elaborate facilities for optimizing images are provided through the File>Save for Web & Devices… command. To get the most out of this command, you need to understand some of the characteristics of the Web image file formats. These are described in detail in Chapter 8, where you can also find an account of the command's more advanced options. Using it for routine tasks is simple, though, and does not require much knowledge.

The two file types most commonly used on the Web are JPEG and GIF. A third type, PNG, is available but has failed to achieve much popularity so far.

JPEG files are the best choice for photographic material and scanned art work in natural media. They are efficiently compressed by discarding information that is not readily perceptible. High quality settings produce bigger files; low quality settings result in much smaller files but use high levels of compression, so some noticeable loss of visual quality can occur.

GIF files are usually more appropriate for computer-generated images, because they only allow a restricted number of colours (256 at most). This often leads to an unacceptable distortion in photographic images or elaborate art work. However, for images that include text at a small size, GIF is better than JPEG because it preserves sharp edges, making the text easier to read.

The File>Save for Web & Devices… command opens a dialogue box in which you can experiment with various settings, including the file type, the amount of compression applied (for JPEG) and the number of colours (for GIF). The dialogue also allows you to open Device Central (see Chapter 8), where you can preview images intended for mobile devices.

Figure 4.2 shows the **Save for Web & Devices** dialogue. The interface is modal, that is, until you dismiss it using the **Done**, **OK** or **Cancel** button you cannot do anything else in the main document window. The **OK** and **Cancel** buttons have the expected effect. **Done** allows you to save the settings you have chosen, which will be remembered next time you use the command, and close the dialogue without actually saving a new file.

GIF 128 Dithered
GIF 128 No Dither
GIF 32 Dithered
GIF 32 No Dither
GIF 64 Dithered
GIF 64 No Dither
GIF Restrictive
JPEG High
✓ JPEG Low
JPEG Medium
PNG-24
PNG-8 128 Dithered

Original

Most of the time, all you need to do in this dialogue is choose one of the options from the Preset pop-up menu and examine the preview of the optimized image, as we will describe shortly, to see whether it is acceptable. If it is not, try another preset; if it is, save it. When you click on OK, you are presented with a file save dialogue, but the options below the file browser are different from those you usually see in Photoshop. You should always select Images Only for the format and ignore the other options: they are used if you are creating entire Web pages in Photoshop, which we do not recommend.

Figure 4.2 *Saving for the Web: 2-up view (top) and 4-up view (bottom)*

The window is dominated by a large tabbed pane that displays the image you are optimizing. The tabs at the top left are used to choose between four different views. The Original tab shows the image as you made it; the Optimized tab shows it as it will appear if you save it with the settings that are currently selected. You can gauge the effect of compression and dithering by switching between these two tabs. More conveniently, if you don't need the full window size, the 2-Up tab allows you to see the original and optimized versions (or two different optimized versions) side by side, as we have shown them at the top of Figure 4.2. The 4-up tab splits the preview window into four, allowing you to compare the original with three different optimized versions. This is shown in the bottom screenshot in Figure 4.2. In both 2-up and 4-up views, any settings you choose from the controls on the right of the window are applied to the version of the image you most recently clicked on. This is identified by a yellow border, which you may be able to see if you look carefully at Figure 4.2. Use the Zoom and Hand tools to magnify the preview and move around the image when you want to check the quality carefully. Don't be surprised if you cannot really see any difference between a JPEG, even at medium quality, and an original photograph. JPEG compression can produce surprisingly good results, and you should not automatically set the quality to High without first checking versions with lower quality settings applied to them. Lower quality settings offer significant savings in file size, and are often of good enough quality.

Below any optimized image you will see a summary of its characteristics, including the chosen format, main optimization settings, file size and an estimate of the time it will take to download. Using the dialogue's main pop-up menu (above and to the right of the previews) you can choose a bandwidth on which to base this estimate.

For a final check before saving, you can preview an optimized image in any Web browser installed on your system. Clicking on the browser icon below the bottom right-hand corner of the previews will launch your default browser and show you how the image would appear on a Web page. (Some information about the optimization settings and the HTML used to embed it are also shown on the page. A temporary file is created for this previewing operation.) If you have more than one browser installed – and most Web professionals do – a pop-up menu attached to the browser icon can be used to select among them. For important Web images, it is considered good practice to preview on as many browsers as possible. However, to be sure of knowing what any user may see, you also need to preview it on as many different platforms as possible, and this cannot be done from within a single application.

---TRY THIS---

**Open a photograph in Photoshop, and select File>Save for Web & Devices....
Switch to 4-up view and apply different JPEG and GIF settings. Examine the
previews carefully. Choose the version you think is the best (considering quality
and file size) and save it.**

DON'T FORGET

Photoshop is a program for editing bitmapped images.

Use File>Open to open an image held on disk in PSD, TIFF, GIF, JPG, PNG or most other common bitmapped formats.

Use a plug-in from the File>Import sub-menu to import from an external device such as a scanner.

Use File>Save As... to save in any of the formats Photoshop can open.

Keep a file in PSD format for as long as you are working on it in Photoshop.

Use File>Save for Web & Devices... to optimize images for the Web.

Save in JPEG or GIF format for the Web; PNG is rarely used in practice.

Resolution

A bitmapped image is a rectangular array of values, each one representing the colour of a pixel – that is, a coloured dot on a screen or a dot of ink on paper. When it is stored in a computer system, such an image has no intrinsic physical dimensions. Its width and height are recorded as a number of pixels, but unless you know how many pixels are displayed in an inch or centimetre – the display *resolution* – this tells you nothing about how much space it will occupy on your screen or on paper. There was a brief moment, many years ago, when monitors and printers all used pixels 1/72 inch square – which, as we will explain shortly, is what we still pretend screen resolution is. At that time, what you saw really was what you got, but printers now use much higher resolutions, monitors usually support several different resolutions, and scanners have their own, sometimes very high, resolutions. There is considerable scope for confusion.

The confusion arises from two sources. First, the resolution of different sorts of device is quoted in different ways. For printers and scanners, the resolution is usually given as the number of dots printed or sampled per inch (or other unit of length). For digital cameras, video screens and monitors, though, it is more often given in the form of pixel dimensions. Digital cameras offer very high resolutions, usually quoted in megapixels. A 5-megapixel camera can take a photograph of 2592 by 1944 pixels. A VGA monitor is usually said to have a resolution of 800 by 600, while Apple's 23-inch widescreen display has a resolution of 1920 by 1200. PAL televisions are always 768 by 576. Obviously, a 20-inch monitor set to 800 by 600 is actually displaying fewer dots per inch than a 13-inch screen on a laptop which is set to the same resolution. However, the 20-inch monitor can be set to higher resolutions. When we choose a higher resolution we don't expect the quality of images to improve, we expect to be able to fit more of them on to the screen. Hence, it isn't actually much use to quote monitor resolutions in dots per inch (dpi), the way printers' resolutions are quoted. Instead, when it is necessary, it is (nearly) always assumed that monitors have a resolution of 72 dpi – even though very few actually do, nowadays.

The second source of confusion about resolutions arises from the fact we stated earlier: images in files and computer programs do not have any inherent resolution, they just have pixel dimensions. Nevertheless, most original images have a natural physical size. For instance, if you were to scan a 6 by 4 inch photograph, irrespective of the scanner's resolution, you would only consider it to be the "right" size if it was shown 6 inches wide and 4 inches tall. So a scanned image file does have a resolution associated with it: the resolution that the scanner used to create it. If a photograph is scanned in Photoshop using a plug-in, the image file will by default have a resolution associated with it – the resolution chosen for scanning. For example, if you choose to scan at 600 dpi, that resolution will remain associated with the resulting image file unless you choose to change it. But note that this resolution is an added piece of information about the number of pixels per inch you must use to reproduce the size of the original image: the digital image is still just a rectangular array of pixels with no intrinsic resolution.

When images are created by programs, they can also have a resolution associated with them. This will not necessarily be the resolution of the monitor being used at the time, and there is no reason why it should be. If an image is being prepared for printing, it will normally be created at a resolution appropriate to the device on which it will be printed. The size that an image appears to be on your screen when it is being worked on in Photoshop is determined by a combination of three factors: the resolution settings associated with the file (for example, from the scanner), the display resolution, and the amount of zooming in or out you have selected. The size displayed on screen can therefore vary considerably, and it will only sometimes look like the size you originally scanned, or the size it will be if you print the image.

Changing Image Size and Resolution

It is often necessary to change an image's resolution, for example to prepare it for printing, to send it as an email attachment, to display it on a mobile phone, or to prepare it for the Web. (All scanners will offer much higher resolutions than you require for the Web.) It is sometimes useful to change an image's resolution just to make it easier to work with. However, there are two interpretations of what it means to change an image's resolution. You can simply change the resolution associated with the image, which is a value stored in the file. For instance, if you had scanned a photograph at 300 dpi, you could change its resolution to 72 dpi, to see what it would look like in a Web browser. Since you haven't changed the pixel dimensions, just the associated resolution, the image would look much larger on your screen than it did as a photograph: exactly the same pixels are being displayed, but each one is occupying more space. Quite often, however, you will want to store only 72 pixel values for each linear inch of image. The image will then appear the same size on screen but fewer pixels will be used. This is usually necessary when you are preparing an image imported from a scanner or digital camera for the Web, for example, and it can only be done by throwing some of the original pixels away, a process known as ***downsampling***. In this process, the file size (the number of bytes) will also change, sometimes quite dramatically.

In principle, changing an image's size can be achieved with or without changing the pixel dimensions. But if you want to keep all of the pixels, changing the size can only be done by changing the resolution, and the resolution setting required to make the image look the right size will often not be suitable for your final output. For instance, if you had a 6 inch by 4 inch image at 72 dpi and you resized it to 120 mm by 80 mm without changing the number of pixels, your image would have a resolution of 91.44 pixels per inch. No output device has such a resolution.

If your image does not look the right size at the resolution you require – for example, if it looks too big or too small at 72 dpi when you are preparing an image for the Web – you must either downsample (to make your image smaller) or *upsample*, that is, add extra pixels to make the image bigger. Downsampling and upsampling are collectively referred to as *resampling*.

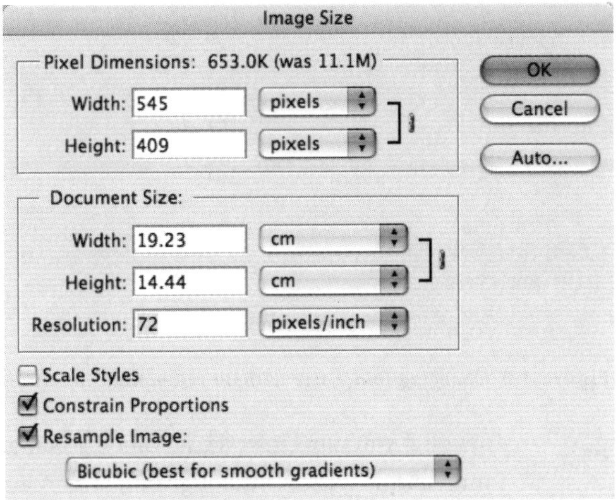

Because of the relationship between an image's size and its resolution, changing either of them (or both) is done in Photoshop in a unified dialogue box, which is shown in Figure 4.3. It is invoked by the Image>Image Size… menu command. The easiest thing to do is change the resolution, which is done by entering a new value in the field labelled Resolution, towards the bottom of the box. (You can use the pop-up menu next to the Resolution field to choose between imperial and metric units.) At the bottom left of the dialogue, you will see a checkbox labelled Resample Image. When this is ticked, which it is by default, the image's apparent size is left unaltered when the resolu-

Figure 4.3 *Changing resolution*

tion is changed. However, this means that the image must be resampled, and its pixel dimensions, which are shown at the top of the dialogue box, will change, which will affect the quality of the image. The pop-up menu at the bottom allows you to select one of three resampling algorithms, which we will describe shortly. If you un-tick Resample Image, the pixel dimensions will not change, but the document size – its physical dimensions – will. Changing the resolution without resampling is a non-destructive operation: it does not make any real changes to your image file.

If it is the image's size that you are changing, rather than the resolution, you can again either tick Resample Image or not. If you do tick this checkbox, you can enter new values in the Width and Height fields for either the pixel dimensions (at the top of the dialogue) or the document size (in the middle), according to which you need to change. Use the pop-up menu to the right of the Width and Height boxes to choose the units for these dimensions. Choosing percent allows you to change the size proportionally, instead of setting it to an absolute value. If you tick the checkbox labelled **Constrain Proportions**, near the bottom of the dialogue box, you only need to enter a value for one dimension (either one) and the other will automatically be set to preserve the image's aspect ratio (the ratio of its width to its height). This is indicated by the chain links connecting the height and width boxes. If you un-tick **Constrain Proportions**, you can enter separate values for height and width, but this will generally result in a distortion of the image, which is rarely what you want to do.

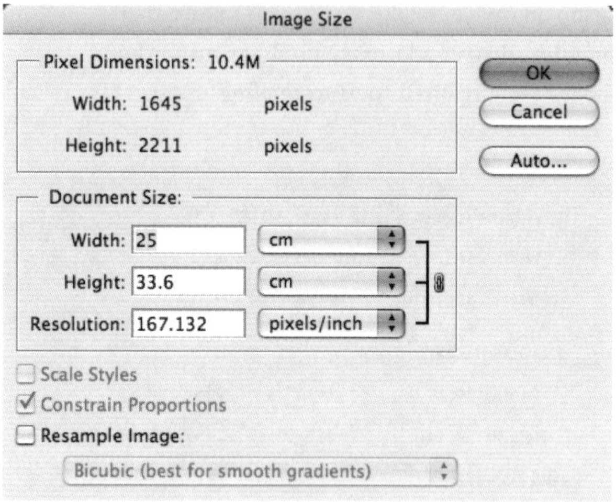

Figure 4.4 *Changing image size without resampling*

If you don't tick **Resample Image**, however, the pixel dimensions text fields change to a read-only display of the values, shown in Figure 4.4, and you cannot alter them. If you don't want to resample your image then your only option is to change the values given under **Document Size**. These are always linked, so if you enter new values for **Width** and **Height** you will find that **Resolution** changes automatically, usually to an awkward value, as seen in the illustration. If you enter a new value for **Resolution**, then the values for **Width** and **Height** will be adjusted accordingly. As the quality of an image is always going to be better if it is not resampled, it is worth using this option if you can. However, it will only be possible if you don't mind changing the size at which your image appears. Although this may sound complicated in explanation, it becomes much clearer when you actually try it and experiment with the various possibilities.

---TRY THIS---

Open any image file and experiment with changing its resolution and size, both together and independently. Try upsampling and downsampling the image by a large amount, changing the resolution to a value many times higher or lower than it was, with the Resample Image checkbox ticked. Use View>Actual Pixels to examine the image before and after resampling and observe the changes.

When you are preparing images for the Web, you will always need to set the resolution to 72 dpi. This will usually entail downsampling: typical scanned images and digital photographs appear huge at 72 dpi. If you intend to make alterations to the image before saving it for the Web, it is better either to work on it at its original size until your alterations are complete, or, if necessary, to resize it to about twice its final size, as you will get better results from any filters, effects or adjustments that you apply. Only reduce an image to its final output size when you have finished work on it, and even then, always keep a copy of the original at full size.

Resampling nearly always involves discarding some information. (The exception is upsampling to a resolution that is an exact multiple of the original.) The amount of information that is lost depends both on the value you set when resampling and on the way in which the new pixel values are computed from the old ones. This may be done in a naive way, that only takes account of one pixel at a time, or by using more complicated algorithms that use information from neighbouring pixels. The methods supported by Photoshop are *nearest neighbour* (the naive method just referred to, which tends to produce poor results), *bilinear* and *bicubic*, which are progressively better methods. Three different options for bicubic resampling are supplied: Bicubic Smoother and Bicubic Sharper apply extra processing intended to improve enlarging and reducing the size of your image, respectively. If you wish to apply this extra processing, you will need to take account of the image's characteristics, to get the best results by choosing appropriate parameters. However, you will gain better control over the result if you use the simple Bicubic option and do any smoothing or sharpening by hand, as we will describe later.

As you might expect, the more complex methods of resampling require more computation, and so they take longer, but modern machines are so fast that you are unlikely to notice the difference, so there is no real reason to settle for anything less than bicubic resampling. It is the default option in Photoshop, so generally you will not even need to think about this.

If you downsample you always lose image information. The larger pixels corresponding to lower resolutions give images a blocky quality, as illustrated in Figure 4.5. At this magnification, the effect of downsampling (by a factor of 20, in this example) are clear. However, if the image is displayed at its natural size, the quality appears acceptable, although the picture is small.

Figure 4.5 *Downsampling*

┌─ TRY THIS ───

Repeat the previous exercise, but try each of the different resampling methods in turn for each resizing and resolution-changing operation. Compare the image before and after resampling, and see whether you can spot any differences in the actual pixels when you choose different resampling methods.

└──

It is always a good idea to use Photoshop to resample an image that was not originally made at screen resolution or is the wrong size, especially if you are going to use it on a Web page. In fact, for many images this may be the only thing you use Photoshop for. If you embed an image at a resolution other than 72 dpi in a Web page, or set its width and height using HTML attributes to some other values than those stored in the file, the Web browser will have to resample when it displays the page, and you can be sure that it will make a mess of it – and of your image. However, resampling is something you should leave until you have made any other alterations to your image, because you can never regain the information that is lost in the resampling process. Furthermore, you should always keep a safe copy of the original image file.

Having said that, you should remember that very large and high resolution images use up a lot of memory, and, because of the way Photoshop works, a lot of scratch space on disk. Working on very large images can slow the program down, too, especially if you do not have a lot of memory (1GB is about the minimum for fast processing of Photoshop images). If you have opened an image that is very big, such as a photograph from a high-end digital camera, or one that was made at a very high resolution, for example a large image scanned at high resolution or a picture provided by an image library for professional design work, you may find it expedient to down-sample it straight away (but always keep a safe copy of the original if possible, just in case). We would still recommend that you do not go immediately to 72 dpi, but work on the image at no less than twice that resolution.

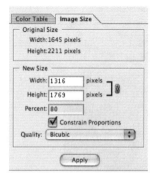

Figure 4.6 *Resizing while optimizing for the Web*

If you use **File>Save for Web & Devices**… to save an image for the Web, you can resize it during the optimization process – perhaps the only way you can make it small enough is by shrinking it. The **Image Size** tab in the lower right of the dialogue box is attached to a simplified version of the image resizing dialogue, as Figure 4.6 shows, in which you can set a new size, either using absolute dimensions for the height and width, or as a percentage. (It is concealed by the **Color Table** tab in Figure 4.2.) You can choose the interpolation method from the same five options as are available in the full **Image Size** dialogue. Click on the **Apply** button to actually change the size. If all you are doing is preparing a file for embedding on a Web page without altering it in any way, you can just open it, then go straight into the **Save for Web & Devices** dialogue to set its size and optimize it.

---TRY THIS---

Open any high resolution image, such as a photo from a good digital camera or a large scanned image. Just using the Save for Web & Devices dialogue, save it as a JPEG image 240 pixels wide and assess the result.

Observe how the memory required by the image changes as you resample it.

DON'T FORGET

In Photoshop, the resolution of an image is the number of pixels per unit length (pixels/inch or pixels/cm).

Changing either resolution or size without resampling will cause the other to change, leaving the total number of pixels the same.

To change the size without changing the resolution, or vice versa, you must tick Resample Image in the Image Size dialogue.

Downsampling always results in loss of image information.

Images for the Web should always be saved at 72 dpi.

You can change the size of an image while optimizing it for the Web.

Modes and Colour Spaces

We stated earlier that the colour of a pixel is represented by three numbers, but we didn't say anything about how the numbers are related to the colours. There are several different ways in which this is done, and you need to understand a little about colour representations to avoid making mistakes that can lead to colours not being displayed correctly. For more information on this subject, consult *Digital Multimedia*.

The different ways in which colours are represented are referred to as *colour modes*. In Photoshop's default mode, *RGB colour*, each pixel will be represented by three values, representing the intensity of red, green and blue light which, when mixed together, produce that pixel's colour. This corresponds to the way in which colour is produced on a monitor, and so it is the natural choice for images intended for multimedia and the Web. Most of the time, if you are working for these media, you should make sure that the colour mode is RGB, and then forget about it.

The other modes supported by Photoshop are mostly used in print, with the exception of *greyscale*, which is used for black and white images generally, for which it affords a considerable saving in file size, and *indexed colour*, which we will describe shortly. Greyscale is not, however, supported by Web browsers, so it is less useful in that respect than it might have been. Discarding colour may be done for aesthetic reasons, though, and is sometimes a useful form of pre-processing before further manipulations of an image (for example, before vectorizing it in Flash). Note that changing an image's mode is a one-way process: if you change it back, you won't get the same image you started with. In particular, if you change an RGB image to greyscale, you completely lose the colour information. (You can undo the change, though, for as long as the history permits, or until you close the document, whichever is the sooner.)

Indexed colour is a means employed to reduce the file size of colour images. We describe it in more detail in Chapter 8. For now, all you really need to know is that images using indexed colour can only have a restricted number of colours in them. Usually, this number is 256. Whether or not this is an acceptable limitation depends on the nature of the image. Some images created on a computer use very few colours, but most photographs of the real world use a great many. The most important application of indexed colour nowadays is in GIF images for the Web: GIF images can only use up to 256 colours. Normally, therefore, you will work in RGB colour and only convert to indexed colour if and when you export your image to GIF. This happens automatically if you choose one of the GIF presets in the **Save For Web & Devices...** dialogue.

You should be aware that there are colours that can be perceived by people but cannot be represented in RGB colour, or any of the other commonly encountered colour modes.

Changing Colour Mode

Every image has a colour mode associated with it. As we will describe in the next section, you must specify a colour mode whenever you create an image from scratch. Digital photographs and scanned images have their colour mode set by the device that created them, almost always to RGB. Sometimes, though, if you open a file in Photoshop that you have not created yourself, you will find that its mode is something other than RGB. In particular, stock art collections that are intended for use in print will usually be in **CMYK** colour, which is a colour mode based on the inks used in most printing processes. For high quality images you may sometimes see an esoteric mode called **Lab** colour. To change the mode of an image to RGB, select **RGB Color** from the **Image>Mode** sub-menu, as shown in Figure 4.7. (Note that Photoshop uses North American spelling on its menus, so we have not only **RGB Color** and so on, but also **Grayscale**.) The number of colours that can be represented in RGB is greater than that which can be represented in CMYK, but there are nevertheless some colours that can be represented in CMYK but not in RGB, so changing

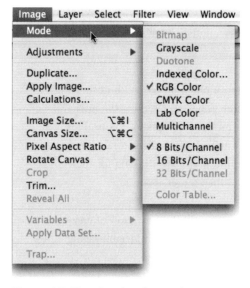

Figure 4.7 *Changing the colour mode*

modes may cause some noticeable colour shifts. It is best to trust Photoshop to take care of this, unless you know a great deal about colour. If you are working for the Web, RGB is the only colour mode you will usually be interested in.

Creating Images

You need to think about an image's colour mode, size and resolution when you create a brand new image using the File>New... command. This brings up the dialogue shown in Figure 4.8, where you can set the width, height and resolution by entering numbers in the appropriate boxes. Photoshop provides ready-made combinations of values for common types of document. If you choose one of the classes of document from the pop-up labelled Preset, a suitable value is entered in the Resolution field for you, and the pop-up menu labelled Size becomes active. This menu lists some common or standard sizes for the class of document you have chosen. For instance, if you choose Web, the resolution is set to 72 dpi and the size menu includes common monitor resolutions and the dimensions of some of the standard Web advertisement formats.

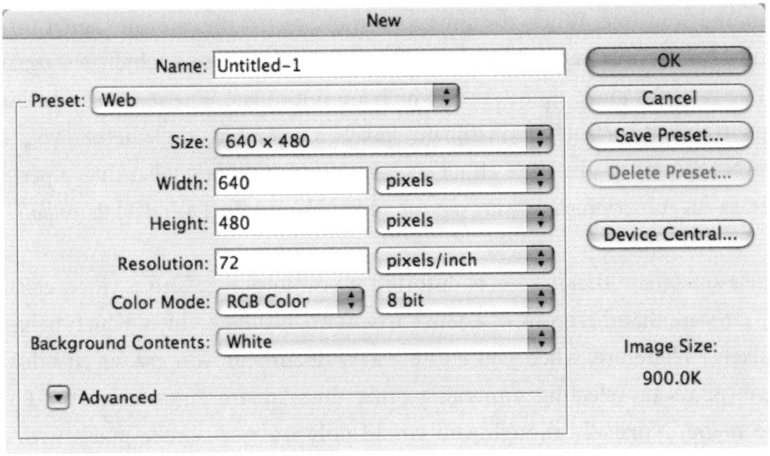

New		
Name: Untitled-1		OK
Preset: Web		Cancel
Size: 640 x 480		Save Preset...
Width: 640	pixels	Delete Preset...
Height: 480	pixels	
Resolution: 72	pixels/inch	Device Central...
Color Mode: RGB Color	8 bit	
Background Contents: White		Image Size: 900.0K
Advanced		

Figure 4.8 *Creating a new image*

As well as listing commonly used image types, the Preset pop-up has entries for any images that are open when you create a new document, which makes it easy to make a new image the same size and resolution as another you are working on.

The dialogue also allows you to choose a colour mode, and to specify whether the image should start out with a white background, use another colour for the background (as set on the background colour swatch in the toolbox) or use a transparent background. Transparent areas are displayed as a chequer board pattern in the document window. They allow the colour of the paper or Web page background to show through when they are printed or saved in a suitable format and displayed on a Web page.

Non-Square Pixels

At the bottom of the File > New...dialogue is a turn-down arrow labelled **Advanced**, which reveals some additional options if you click on it. Unless you fully understand colour management, do not change the **Color Profile** setting. However, you may need to select an option from the **Pixel Aspect Ratio** pop-up if you are making an image for incorporation into a digital video (DV) clip. (If you never intend to do this, you can leave the **Pixel Aspect Ratio** set to **Square Pixels** and skip

the rest of this section.) It is safest to choose one of the presets in the **Film & Video** class, which sets the pixel aspect ratio correctly for the chosen standard, but it is useful to understand what you have done by doing so.

Television screens aren't actually divided up into discrete pixels. The phosphors are effectively continuous, and activated by an analogue signal which can be switched on and off at arbitrary points on each horizontal scan line. When the image on the screen originates in digital form, pixels in the image file can be mapped to rectangles, instead of the squares which we usually assume them to be. The image is made up of pixels which are not square. The standards defining digital video formats are based on such "non-square" pixels. Depending on whether you are working with PAL or NTSC, video pixels are either slightly wider or slightly taller than a perfect square. (For more details on this confusing issue, see the video chapter in *Digital Multimedia*.)

An image whose pixels are square therefore gets distorted if you import it into a video editing program for use in DV. (Note that the problem doesn't arise with analogue video, which behaves as if it used square pixels.) Therefore, when you create a new document, you can specify that it should use non-square pixels by selecting something other than **Square Pixels** from the **Pixel Aspect Ratio** pop-up menu. Normally, though, you would only use non-square pixels with an image destined for a particular digital video format. The **Preset** pop-up menu includes presets for most digital video formats, including HD, in both PAL and NTSC standards. When you choose one of these, the pixel aspect ratio is set accordingly; at the same time, the image dimensions are set to match the frame size, and guides are added to the image to show the safe and title-safe areas. (These guides are not part of the image and will not appear when it is displayed.)

Normally, if you are working with an image whose pixels are not square, you will want to see it in Photoshop as it would appear when displayed on a video monitor. The **View > Pixel Aspect Ratio Correction** command causes the image to be displayed in this way. When you create a new image with non-square pixels, this correction is turned on automatically. If you want to see the image's pixels displayed square, you can turn it off. If you import a still frame from a DV movie, you will have to turn pixel aspect ratio correction on to see the frame as it would appear in the movie.

┌─ TRY THIS ───┐

Create a new document, suitable for using as an imported still in a video editing project using NTSC or PAL DV. Paste a digital image of a suitable size into the document. Experiment with turning pixel aspect ratio correction on and off. Import a still from a DV video clip into Photoshop and observe the effect of turning pixel aspect ratio correction off and on.

└──┘

DON'T FORGET

An image's colour mode determines how colour values are stored, and may limit the range of colours in the image.

Images intended for display on a computer monitor and for use on the Web should be in RGB colour. Use the Image>Mode sub-menu to change the colour mode if necessary.

Use one of the video presets if you need to create an image with non-square pixels to incorporate into digital video.

Layers

As we explained in Chapter 2, layers can be thought of as sheets of transparent material which can have images on them, like the sheets of acetate used on overhead projectors, or cels in traditional animation. Layers are overlaid; in the places where a layer is transparent, the layers below it show through. If you are used to painting on paper or canvas, this may seem like an unnecessarily elaborate and artificial way of organizing a picture, but it allows you to manipulate digital images in ways that are not possible in physical media. By providing layers, which are a natural expression of the digital nature of bitmapped images, Photoshop can be more than just a poor substitute for natural media; layers open up possibilities that belong to the new digital medium.

In addition to ordinary layers, which contain actual content, Photoshop also offers **Adjustment Layers**, which contain no image content but allow certain types of changes to the image, such as adjustments to contrast or colour, to be made without altering the pixels of the image itself. Because these layers work in a different way from ordinary layers, and cannot be created through the menu on the Layers panel, we describe them in the section on *Adjustments and Retouching,* a little later on in this chapter.

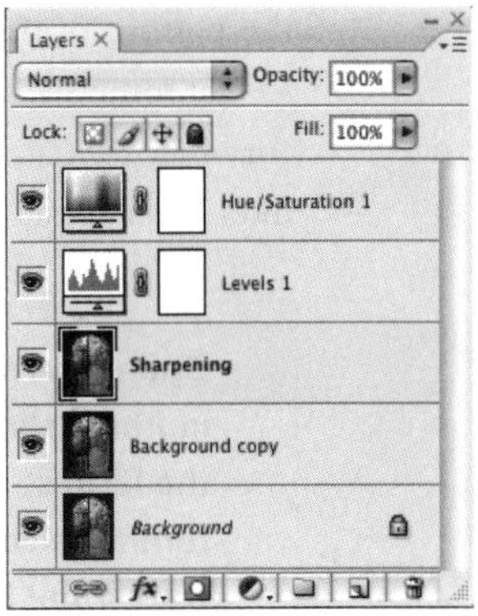

Figure 4.9 *The Layers panel*

Layers are created in the Layers panel – or palette – which is described in general terms in Chapter 2. A typical Layers panel is shown in Figure 4.9. Here, there are three ordinary layers with image content, and two adjustment layers (Hue/Saturation and Levels). A new layer can be explicitly created by duplicating an existing layer, or by using the panel menu or Layer>New>Layer… from the menu bar to create a new empty layer. New layers are also created automatically whenever you paste something into an image from elsewhere, or when you use the type tool to add some text. As in other layer-based applications, the Layers panel can be used to hide layers, allowing experimentation, and to lock them to prevent accidental changes. Layer order can be changed by dragging layers up and down in the panel, and layers can be hidden and revealed again by clicking on the eye icon to the left of each layer.

When an image is created in Photoshop, it consists of a single layer, designated the Background layer. As you add layers, they are stacked on top of the background. A common way of putting together a composite image is by using several different source image files. You start by creating a new empty image file for the composite. Next, for each of the other images in turn, you open them, make a selection and copy and paste it into the new image. A new layer will automatically be created each time you do this. You now have all the original images safely untouched in their own files (which should be closed without saving at this point), and a new image with copies of the originals on separate layers, so that you can alter them independently and then combine them into your final composition, possibly adding layers on which you have painted or set some text.

Figure 4.10 shows a simple composite image composed of two layers, a sunset photograph and a lighthouse which has been extracted from another photo. In Figure 4.11 you can see the original lighthouse photo on the left. The sky in a copy of this original photograph was deleted – using a method we will describe later – to get an image of a lighthouse with a transparent background (the transparency is indicated by the chequerboard pattern in the lighthouse layer), shown in the centre in Figure 4.11. A new document was created, and a sunset photograph (far right in Figure 4.11) was copied from another file and pasted onto a new layer. The lighthouse was then copied from its source, and pasted onto a second layer in the new document, above the sunset layer, to create the composite. There was no need to worry about the bit of landscape showing at the bottom of the sunset photograph as the lighthouse was big enough to simply cover it over, so that someone seeing only the composite would never know that the landscape had been there. (In order to match the colour of the lighthouse a little better to its new background, a warming filter was applied to the lighthouse layer. We describe how to do this later in this chapter.)

---TRY THIS---

Open several different image files, including some small ones. Create a new file in Photoshop, making sure that you set its dimensions to be at least as big as the largest of the images you have just opened. Copy the contents of each file in turn (use cmd/ctl-A to select all) and paste into separate layers in your new file. Note what happens if not all your source files have the same resolution. Practise hiding and showing each of the layers. Save this file for further exercises.

Figure 4.10 *An image composed from two layers*

Figure 4.11 *A source photograph (left) and the two layers of the new composite image*

Layer Opacity and Blending Modes

Apart from the background layer, each layer has its own ***transparency setting*** and ***blending mode***, which you can set by selecting the layer and using the controls at the top of the Layers panel, as shown in Figure 4.12. These settings govern the way in which pixels on the layer interact with those on layers beneath it. You can enter any value in the Opacity field between 0% (entirely transparent) and 100% (entirely opaque). Intermediate values allow you to make the layer partially transparent, so you can build up an image out of translucent layers. If you hold down the mouse over the triangle to the right of the Opacity field, a slider appears as shown, which allows you to

Figure 4.12 *Changing layer opacity*

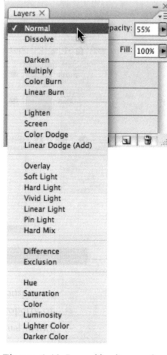

Figure 4.13 *Layer blending modes*

change the opacity by dragging the slider to the left or right. The image in the document window changes as you do this, allowing you to assess the results of adjusting the opacity interactively.

Photoshop goes rather further than this however, by allowing you to set the blending mode of your layers. The drop-down menu at the top left of the Layers panel shown in Figure 4.13 allows you to choose between 25 different ways of combining the selected layer with the layer underneath it. The default Normal mode is what you expect: the underlying layer is obscured in proportion to the Opacity setting. If the opacity has been set to 100%, the layer beneath is entirely obscured (except where the selected layer is transparent in any case, as in Figure 4.10 for example, where part of the lighthouse layer is transparent). The other modes perform calculations which allow Photoshop to blend the selected layer with the layer beneath it in various different ways, some of them relatively straightforward, but some of them rather counter-intuitive if you are used to thinking in terms of physical media. For example, in the Luminosity mode, the hue of each pixel on the layer is ignored, but the brightness of the pixel beneath it is set to its luminosity. The Hard Light mode is described as producing an effect similar to shining a harsh spotlight on the image. It is not easy to convey the effects of different blending modes; you should try to judge them for yourself by experimenting. Modes other than Normal are used by experts to achieve effects that cannot easily be achieved in any other way, but using these modes well requires a lot of practice, and some can seem obscure and confusing, even to professionals.

When you set the opacity of a layer, the value is applied to every pixel on it that is not transparent, and to everything that you subsequently paint on that layer. That is, the opacity is a property of the layer (the whole sheet of acetate, if you like) and not just a property of the individual marks that are on it at the time you set the opacity value. In a similar way, you can apply certain types of special effect, called *Layer Styles*, to an entire layer and the effects will be treated as a property of the layer and not just a property of the image that happens to be on that layer at that time. They are applied to any material already on the layer, and to anything added to it subsequently. The image on the layer is not actually changed by the effect. This means that if the layer style is later removed from the layer, the image is left behind without it. Layer styles are used for effects like glowing edges and drop shadows, and we describe these in more detail later in the chapter. They are an essential part of the way in which rollovers and certain types of Web animation are created in Photoshop.

TRY THIS

Using your layered image from the previous exercise, experiment with transparency settings to see how lower layers can show through the one on top. Experiment with different blending modes to see how the layers can interact in more complex ways.

Selecting and Linking Layers

You can select several layers at once in the Layers panel. You can make a multiple selection in the obvious way. To select contiguous layers, click on the first layer that you want, then shift-click on the last. The first and last layer and all those in between will be selected. To select non-contiguous layers, click on one layer, then cmd/ctl-click on each of the others that you wish to select; cmd/ctl-clicking on a layer which is already selected will remove it from the selection. A multiple layer selection, such as that shown in Figure 4.14, only lasts until a new layer selection is made.

Figure 4.14 *Layer selection*

In images whose layers have transparent areas, you can select a layer directly by clicking in the document with the move tool (described in the next section). All you need to do is check the Auto-Select box in the Options bar when the move tool is selected.

If you need to associate layers together in a more persistent way, you should first select all the layers you want to link, and then either click the chain link icon at the bottom left of the Layers panel or choose Link Layers from the Layers panel drop-down menu. Layers stay linked even when they are not selected, until such time as you explicitly unlink them. (To unlink linked layers you simply click on the chain link icon at the bottom of the Layers panel once again, or select Unlink Layers from the panel's fly-out menu.)

Having selected or linked several layers, you can move, align and transform them together. The commands on the Layer>Align and Layer>Distribute sub-menus apply to the currently selected or linked layers – there must be more than one layer selected or at least two linked together for aligning, and more than two for distributing. Similarly, the commands on the Edit>Transform menu and the Edit>Free Transform command are applied to all the selected or linked layers, and dragging with the move tool moves them all together. If you are using linked layers then at least one of the linked layers must be selected in the panel for these movements or transformations to be applied to those layers. These various methods of moving and transforming layers will be described in the next section.

Figure 4.15 *Linked layers*

Moving and Transforming Layers

If you think about a layer as a sheet of acetate, then you can see that it makes sense to move layers about, each sliding across the one above or below it. By using the *move tool*, you can move any layer except the background layer. Make sure you have selected the layer you wish to move by clicking on it in the Layers panel, select the move tool from the toolbox, and then you can drag the selected layer around in the document window. You can move several layers together by using multiple selections or linking, as described in the previous section. Moving layers in this way is most likely to be useful if they contain text or separate objects with transparent backgrounds. For instance, in the example in Figure 4.10, the lighthouse layer could be moved down to reduce the amount of building showing at the bottom of the image and increase the amount of sky.

Figure 4.16 *A* Free Transform *bounding box*

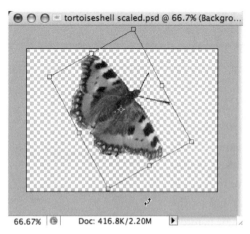

Figure 4.17 *Layer rotation using* Free Transform

The move tool only allows you to move layers vertically and horizontally – you can't drag them round to change their orientation. The Free Transform command, which is on the Edit menu, is used to rotate layers and to apply other geometrical transformations. (As we will see later, you can apply transforms just to selected parts of a layer.) When you choose the Free Transform command, a bounding box is displayed, which surrounds the coloured pixels on the layer. Figure 4.16 shows a bounding box, which, as you can see, has small squares at each corner and in the middle of each side. These are called *handles* and are used to carry out transformations. In the middle of the bounding box you will see a symbol that looks like the cross-hairs in a gun sight. This marks the centre of the layer for the purposes of free transformation.

If you position the cursor outside the bounding box, it changes appearance to a curved two-headed arrow, which indicates that you can use it to rotate the image, which you do just by dragging round, as illustrated in Figure 4.17. This works like a lever: the further away the cursor is from the bounding box, the further you have to drag to get the same amount of rotation, so if you want precise control you should move the cursor well outside the bounding box. If you want to rotate the contents of the layer around a point other than its geometrical centre, you can drag the centre symbol to a different place.

Figure 4.18 *The* Free Transform *options bar*

Whenever you use the **Free Transform** command, two things happen. First, the **Options** bar changes as shown in Figure 4.18. You can apply precise transformations numerically by entering values in the boxes. Figure 4.19 shows the butterfly scaled up in size by entering a scaling factor (as a percentage) in the width (**W**) and height (**H**) boxes of the **Free Transform Options** bar. Second, the menu bar changes, with most commands being disabled. This is because a sequence of transformations must be finished and confirmed (or cancelled) before you can do anything else – working with free transformations is like using a modal dialogue box. When you have finished the transformation, you can press the return key or click on the tick mark (the **commit button**) at the right-hand end

Figure 4.19 *A scaled layer*

of the **Options** bar to confirm the operation if you have achieved the result you wanted, or press escape or click on the **cancel button** to abandon the transformation if you don't like it.

There are various ways to distort images using **Free Transform**, but many of these distortions are more likely to be useful in vector graphics work (and so should be carried out in Illustrator) than when working with typical bitmaps. For example, you can scale the image disproportionally by hand: pulling one of the handles in a vertical side will scale in a horizontal direction only; pulling a handle in the top or the bottom will scale vertically, and pulling one of the corner handles scales in both directions. (You can also scale proportionally by hand if you hold down the **shift** key while pulling a corner handle.) You can reflect the image by pulling a handle all the way through an image and out of the other side of the bounding box, but unless you get the distance exactly right the image will also be distorted. For a precise reflection of the original image it is better to use **Edit>Transform>Flip Horizontal** (or **Flip Vertical**). More esoteric transformations are performed by holding down modifier keys while dragging the handles of the bounding box. If you press [**cmd/ctl**] while dragging a corner handle the corner will move independently of the other points, causing distortion. If the **shift** key is held down at the same time as [**cmd/ctl**], and a handle in the middle of one side is dragged, the image will be skewed.

When you use free transformation on a bitmapped image you should also bear in mind that, in general, changing the geometry of a bitmap will necessarily result in it being resampled and this may cause some loss of quality in addition to the distortion.

Layer Alignment and Distribution

A collection of layers can be arranged in various ways using the Layer>Align and Layer>Distribute sub-menus, or by using the alignment and distribution icons which appear in the Options bar when the move tool is selected. The icons for alignment only have one line running beside or through the pairs of tiny rectangles, whereas the icons for distribution have two. (If you are in doubt, hovering over an icon with the cursor will bring up a tool tip which identifies that particular icon.) Linked layers can be lined up horizontally along their top edges, centre lines or bottom edges, or vertically along their left edges, horizontal centre lines or right edges, as indicated graphically by the icons on the buttons (reading left to right). These operations align the areas of the layer which are not transparent, that is, those areas that you have painted on or pasted an image into. In effect, the objects on the layer are being aligned. Distribution equalizes the space between layers' edges or centres in the same sense, and the same options – top, vertical centre, bottom, left, horizontal centre and right (reading from left to right) – are available as for alignment.

Layer alignment and distribution can be used to produce compositions with a grid-like layout. In the simple example shown in Figure 4.20, five small images were roughly pasted onto separate layers in a document, as shown in the upper

Figure 4.20 *Aligned and distributed layers*

illustration. The result shown at the bottom was achieved by selecting those five layers and then 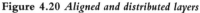 clicking on two icons: Align bottom edges and Distribute horizontal centers. While this could have been done by eye, with the aid of some guides or a grid, it is much quicker to do, and more likely to be accurate, if you use the Align and Distribute commands.

Flattening and Merging Layers

Photoshop experts working on complex graphics often use a large number of layers – a hundred is not uncommon. Many of these may be hidden, having been used as experiments or interim stages. Because each layer can occupy as much space as a single image of the same size, using this many layers requires a machine with a lot of memory and a large scratch disk. Before saving a final version of an image for display, it is common to *flatten* the layers, that is, combine them all into a single layer. (Be sure to save a safe copy of the image file in its layered form before you do this. You'd be surprised how often you need to go back to an image after it is supposedly finished.) If you save the image in certain formats, including the common Web image formats, layers will be flattened automatically, because those formats do not support layers. However, there will be other times when you need to flatten explicitly. This is done by selecting Flatten Image from either the Layers panel drop-down menu or the main Layer menu. You can also selectively merge layers: the Merge Layers command (which also appears on both the Layers panel menu and the Layer menu) merges all the currently selected layers. (Note that it does not merge all linked layers automatically if only one of them is actually selected.) If no more than one layer is currently selected, the available merge options change to Merge Down, which merges the selected layer with the one below it, and Merge Visible, which merges all currently visible layers into one layer.

Layer Groups and Layer Comps

Although the examples in this chapter only feature a few layers, Photoshop images often comprise tens or even hundreds of layers. To help you organize large numbers of layers and reduce the Layers panel to a manageable size, you can collect layers together into *layer groups*. A layer group resembles a folder on your hard disk, in that it provides a container for a collection of related items. Indeed, the icon at the bottom of the Layers panel for creating new layer groups looks like a folder. It works in the usual way: clicking creates a new group with a default name; alt/opt-clicking brings up a dialogue in which you can name the group and set some options. You can group layers by selecting them in the Layers panel and dragging and dropping them on to the group's entry. To create a group and populate it in one go, you can drag selected layers on to the new group icon. Transparency and blending mode can be set for a layer group. They are applied to the group as a whole, on top of any settings that have been applied to the individual layers.

Layer comps help you work with layers in another way. Comp is an abbreviation of composition; a layer comp is a composition formed by a combination of layers. Professional designers often create different versions of an image to show to a client by combining different sets of layers. For instance, Figure 4.21 shows two different versions of our composite lighthouse image. Each is made by combining two layers, as we explained earlier. All four layers are kept in the same Photoshop file (together with some invisible layers used as the basis for the final ones). Each of the two images is made by making two of the four layers visible, as you can see from the Layers panels shown beside each one.

A layer comp is a record of the state of the Layers panel. It records which layers are visible, their position and any layer styles that have been applied to them. Here, we changed the visibility of some layers, so we can create a layer comp for each state. This is done using the Layer Comps panel. Clicking on the New button opens the simple dialogue shown in Figure 4.22, where you can give the comp a name and specify which properties of the layers it should record. If you then change the state of some layers, in this case by altering their visibility, you can make a new layer comp corresponding to the changed state. You can then show the image in one of its states by applying the corresponding layer comp. This is done by clicking in the box next to it in the panel. A small icon identifies the comp that is currently applied. At the right of the composite images in Figure 4.21 we have shown how a layer comp was applied to obtain each of the two images. You can also cycle through a collection of layer comps using the arrows at the bottom of the panel. There is always a layer comp called *Last Document State* at the top of the panel. Applying this restores the image to the state it was in before you applied any of the named comps.

Layer comps are only useful for images, such as collages, which are made by combining several layers. You will also come across a very similar concept later in this chapter when we describe how to create Web animations in Photoshop.

---TRY THIS---

Create a large document and paste half a dozen small images into it, leaving them on separate layers. Make several different arrangements of the small images, using only some each time, and create layer comps to record the position and visibility of the layers in each arrangement. (Hide the layers containing the images you are not using in each case.) Show each layer comp in turn as if you were presenting the alternative compositions to a client.

DON'T FORGET

Hide or show layers by clicking the eye icon in the Layers panel.

Pasting creates a new layer.

Set opacity and blending mode to control how layers interact.

Select multiple layers by shift-clicking or cmd/ctl-clicking in the Layers panel.

Use the move tool and Free Transform command to move and transform layers. Enter numerical values in the options bar for precise transformations.

Use the Align and Distribute menus or option bar controls to produce regular arrangements of linked or selected layers.

Flatten or merge layers to save space, but always keep a layered version.

Use layer comps to create different versions of a composition in a single file.

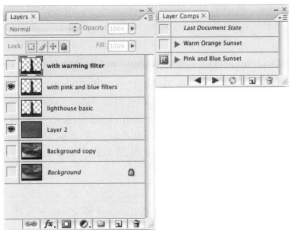

Figure 4.21 *Layer comps*

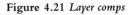

Figure 4.22 *Creating a new layer comp*

Making and Using Selections

You frequently need to select part of an image so that you can move it to another position or copy and paste it into another image, delete it, make changes or apply a free transform only to the selected part. You also make a selection to protect the selected part from changes, or to create a mask to conceal parts of another image or layer.

You are probably accustomed to the idea of selecting some text in a word processor and applying a style, such as italicization, to it. In a broadly similar way, if you have made a selection in Photoshop, just about anything you can do will be applied only to selected pixels. For instance, if part of an image is selected and you paint with a brush tool, brush strokes will only appear in the selected area. Similarly, if you use the image correction and retouching tools described in a later section, your changes will only be applied to the selection. In other respects, selections in Photoshop are like selections in a word processor: you can delete, cut, copy and paste selected pixels in just the same way.

There are several different tools and methods of making selections, but conceptually there are really just three kinds of selection: selecting areas with a particular shape (for example, a rectangular piece of the image), selecting distinct objects (for example, a dog) and selecting parts of the image with common optical characteristics (for example, all the red bits). As we will explain later, in Photoshop it can make sense to describe pixels as being partially selected, and selections as having soft (or feathered) edges, where the degree of "selectedness" tapers off at the boundary of the selected area.

You need to bear in mind that visual processing in the human brain is a complex and sophisticated activity, one that a computer program cannot readily simulate. This means that where you might be able to look at an image of a plant, for instance, and immediately identify each flower and leaf as separate objects, Photoshop cannot do the same thing. It can try to determine where the boundaries of objects are, but is not always successful. Hence, most of the time, it is necessary to select pixels using properties that Photoshop can easily determine, or to provide the program with some help in finding regions and edges.

Before we describe ways of selecting parts of an image, we should point out that sometimes you need to select all of it, or at least all of one layer. For this, use the Select>All command. This selects everything on the currently active layer. (If you switch layers, the selection moves to the new current layer. This is also the case with other more complicated selections.) You also often need to deselect whatever you have selected. The command to achieve this is Select>Deselect. Once you have done so, the menu command Select>Reselect becomes available, which is useful on those occasions when you deselect a complicated selection and then discover you still need it.

Figure 4.23 *A typical case requiring inversion of the selection*

Another generally useful command is Select>Inverse, which has the effect of deselecting every-thing that has been selected and selecting instead everything that was not previously selected. Figure 4.23 shows a typical use of an inverted selection. What we wanted to do was remove the background to get a picture of the butterfly on its own, so that it could be placed on another background. Selected pixels can be removed from an image just by pressing the delete key, or by using the Edit>Clear command. The outline of the butterfly could be (painstakingly) selected by hand with some accuracy, but the result is a selection consisting of the pixels we wanted to keep. By selecting the inverse we were able to deselect those pixels and select all the other pixels in the image, which are the ones we wanted to remove. Deletion of those pixels (that is, the background) was then simple, producing the cut-out butterfly image on the right of Figure 4.23.

Marquee Selection and Cropping

The simplest of Photoshop's selection tools are the *marquee* tools, with which you can select areas of pixels that lie within a geometrical shape. Photoshop has four such tools: the rectangle, ellipse, single-pixel row and single-pixel column marquee tools.

To make a rectangular or elliptical selection with a marquee tool, select the tool of your choice – they all share the same location in the toolbox – and drag across the image diagonally. The shape of the selection is pulled out across the image. (Making selections by dragging out a marquee is probably familiar to you.) When you release the mouse button, the edges of the selected area are shown as a dashed outline, which appears to move round slowly. The movement makes it much easier to see the selection. This moving dashed outline is often referred to as "the marching ants". If you select either of the single-pixel marquee tools, you just need to click once, and every pixel in the row or column in which you have clicked is selected. This is useful for removing borders that may have been inadvertently introduced by a misaligned scan. Once you've made a selection you can move it by dragging with the selection tool inside the selected area. The area will remain selected until you make a new selection or explicitly deselect it.

A common reason for making rectangular selections is to crop an image, for example a photograph, such as the one on the left of Figure 4.24, whose subject has been badly framed. This picture shows a common problem with photographing wildlife. The photo had to be taken from indoors, to avoid frightening the animal, and in a hurry, in case it ran away. In the absence of a zoom lens, the result, shown on the left, has a lot of dull extraneous background. Hence, we wanted to remove everything outside a rectangle around the pine marten, to get a smaller image showing just the subject, without the unwanted background elements. In other cases, you might want to perform a similar operation just to improve the proportions of a picture. Making a selection, inverting it and deleting everything outside the rectangle doesn't actually crop the picture down to a smaller size – it just erases the unwanted parts to the background colour, but leaves the image the same size it was originally. To completely remove the extraneous parts of the image, use the Crop command from the Image menu. (You can use this command even if the selection is not rectangular; the effect is to crop the image to the smallest rectangle which encloses the selection, whatever shape it may be.) By selecting the subject and then cropping, we obtained the much better image shown on the right of Figure 4.24. (Some additional corrections were made after cropping to improve the quality of the image. We will describe these later.)

Figure 4.24 *Cropping an image*

 You may prefer to use the ***crop tool***, which combines selection with a cropping operation, and at the same time gives you extra control over the shape of the selected area. To begin with, you use the crop tool in the same way as a rectangular marquee, that is, you select it and drag out a rectangle. When you let go of the mouse button, though, you don't see a selection outlined by marching ants, but a bounding box, which looks the same as when you are using a free transform. (See Figure 4.16.) The area of the image outside this bounding box is dimmed, so you can more easily see the effect that will be achieved by cropping. You can pull the bounding box's handles to alter it and position the edges of your rectangle precisely. You can also rotate the bounding box by dragging outside it. (As we will describe later, you can transform any selection in a similar way, but using the crop tool avoids an intermediate step.) When you are satisfied with the position of the box, press return or click on the commit button in the Options bar and the image will be cropped to the rectangle you have made.

TRY THIS

Select a suitable image – one that is badly framed or includes extraneous objects – and crop it to leave only the parts that you want. Try using both a selection tool followed by the Image>Crop command and the crop tool.

Another way of cropping an image is based on its content. If you select Image>Trim, the dialogue box shown in Figure 4.25 is displayed. If you select the default option Top Left Pixel Color, then rows and columns of pixels around the edges of the image which are the same colour as the top left-hand corner will be removed from the sides you have selected in the checkboxes in the lower half of the dialogue box. What this means is that if your image is an object on a plain background, empty background margins will be cropped off, leaving the object in the smallest rectangle that can contain it. You can base the trimming on the colour of the bottom right corner or trim off transparent borders, as appropriate. Because there is no tolerance in the trim settings, only pixels which match exactly will be trimmed. This means that trimming works best with computer-generated images or ones which have been given a background of a single colour. It is unlikely to work on photographic images, which will have natural colour variations even in an apparently plain background. Figure 4.26 shows an example: the butterfly had been extracted from its original background, but was surrounded by unwanted space, which was trimmed using a single command.

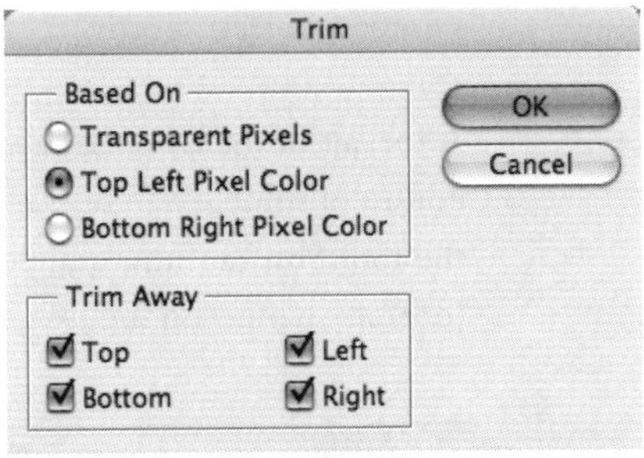

Figure 4.25 *The* Trim *dialogue*

Figure 4.26 *Trimming an image*

TRY THIS

Practise using the Trim command to remove unwanted border pixels. Try it with both computer-generated images – such as screenshots or images made in a 3D application – and photographs. Try applying the command repeatedly to the same image.

Lasso Selections

It is rarely the case that the part of an image that you want to select is a convenient geometrical shape that you can draw round with a marquee tool. Freeform selections can be made in several ways, the most direct being by drawing round an object using the **lasso tool**. This sounds easy: you select the tool, position the cursor somewhere on the border of the area you want to select, and drag round to draw the outline of the selection. When you let go of the mouse button, the selection will be joined up in the most direct line possible, so usually you will draw all round the object you want to select, only releasing the button when you get back to where you started.

Whether this operation actually is easy depends on how good you are at precise freehand drawing. Most people find it difficult to achieve accurate control using a mouse: a graphics tablet and pen are easier to use for this job. It may be obvious, but it helps to zoom in on the image so that you can see exactly what you are doing. Because of the difficulty of achieving a precise result, the lasso tool is best used for the digital equivalent of rapidly cutting out an object from a picture in a magazine with scissors, so that you can discard most of its background, and if necessary, refine the selection later using more precise methods. (We will return to the subject of selecting objects shortly.)

A variant of the lasso tool is the **polygonal lasso**, which is used to draw selections whose outlines consist of straight line segments. These are made by simply clicking at a succession of points with the tool. You can mix straight lines and freeform segments in the same selection: holding down [opt/alt] while you are using the lasso or the polygonal lasso temporarily switches to the other.

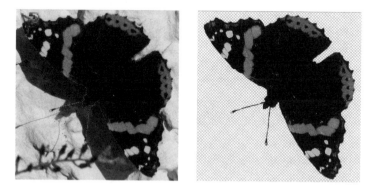

Figure 4.27 *Selecting with the magnetic lasso*

A second variant is the **magnetic lasso**. It is used in a similar way to the ordinary lasso tool; that is, you draw around the object you are trying to select but, as you draw, the selection boundary snaps to the nearest clearly defined edge. If you're lucky, Photoshop's interpretation of a clearly defined edge will match yours. Figure 4.27 shows an example where the edge of the subject was sufficiently well defined in terms of contrast for the magnetic lasso to make a good job of the selection. The magnetic lasso can often be the best choice for this type of selection.

In more detail, the magnetic lasso works as follows. The selection boundary is built up as a series of segments between what are called **fastening points**. You can imagine the fastening points as being like pins that fix the selection boundary in place. In between the fastening points the boundary of the selection is like some flexible material that clings to the edges of objects – a sort of two-dimensional cling film. You select the magnetic lasso tool from the toolbox in the usual way and click to place the first fastening point. You then drag the cursor (you don't need to keep the mouse button pressed down or click) around the edge of the object you wish to select. Fastening points will be added automatically as you drag, at a frequency you specify in the **Options** bar. If the selection boundary strays too far from where you want it, you can explicitly add fastening points by clicking. You can also delete fastening points by pressing the delete key.

There are two options which control the precise behaviour of the magnetic lasso. **Width** is the maximum distance from the actual path you draw at which pixels are examined for an edge. **Contrast** defines what should be considered to be an edge, in terms of the minimum brightness variation it exhibits. Both of these values can be set in the **Options** bar when the magnetic lasso is selected. Experimenting with different values may produce better results for particular images.

┌─ TRY THIS ───┐

    Choose an image that includes a prominent object that is simple enough to be drawn round. Experiment with using each of the three lasso tools to select this object. (Invert the selection, delete and deselect to see how successful you have been.) Try different settings for Width and Contrast with the magnetic lasso.

└──┘

Selecting by Colour

If you want to select a region of pixels that have roughly the same colour value, you can use the *magic wand*. With this tool you just click somewhere in the image; all pixels with a similar colour value to the one you have clicked on are selected. The magic wand takes several important options, which are set in the **Options** bar, as shown in Figure 4.28. A value can be entered in the **Tolerance** field to specify how closely a colour must match the one under the wand to qualify for selection. The checkbox labelled **Contiguous** is used to specify whether or not the selection should be contiguous. If this box is checked, only pixels that are both within the specified tolerance and adjacent to selected ones are added to the selection; that is, the selection comprises a single region of similar colour around the point where the magic wand was clicked. Another checkbox is used to specify whether the selection should be anti-aliased, that is, whether its edges should be softened. (We will look at anti-aliased selections in more detail near the end of this section.) The final checkbox, **Sample All Layers**, allows you to choose whether the selection should be restricted to pixels on the active layer only (do not tick the checkbox) or should be extended to every layer (tick the checkbox).

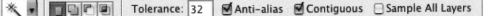

Figure 4.28 *Magic wand options*

Figure 4.29 *Selecting with the magic wand*

Figure 4.29 shows an example of the sort of selection that the magic wand can perform effectively and easily. Because the plant is silhouetted against the sky, it is of a fairly uniform colour, which does not occur in the rest of the image. By using the magic wand, all of the plant was selected just by clicking within the dark area.

The idea behind the magic wand is simple, but, like most of Photoshop's tools, using it effectively takes a bit of effort and practice. Once again, the problem is that Photoshop is dealing purely with numbers that represent colour values, whereas when we look at a picture we see it as a representation of something, or at least as a composition with some structure to it. For example, you might think that if you clicked somewhere on one of the stripes in a picture of a zebra, you would be able to select all of the animal's stripes. In fact you wouldn't, unless you used a high tolerance, which might well select other parts of the picture too. The reason is that, because of the differences in shading caused by the way light falls on the curved surface of a body, the actual colour values in a stripe vary quite widely. The situation is made worse by the fact that Photoshop does not always consider two colours to be close when we do, and vice versa. Again, this is because the computer program uses purely numerical calculations to determine the distance between two colours, but human colour perception is much more complicated, owing to the structure of the eye and brain, and we distinguish more finely between shades in some parts of the spectrum than in others. It is usually necessary to experiment with the tolerance settings for each image individually to get the magic wand to make the selections you want. Nevertheless, with a bit of practice, the magic wand can be a valuable selection tool, not only for selecting objects according to their colour, but for choosing ranges of colour for making tonal and other adjustments.

┌─TRY THIS───

Practise using the magic wand tool on different images with a range of visual characteristics, adjusting the tolerance to enable you to make the selections you want. Try greyscale images, portraits, landscapes, night scenes, and so on.

└──

There is an alternative way of selecting colours in Photoshop, which works in a slightly different way from the magic wand. The Select>Color Range... command brings up a dialogue box containing a preview of a selection (which is blank to begin with) and some controls, as shown

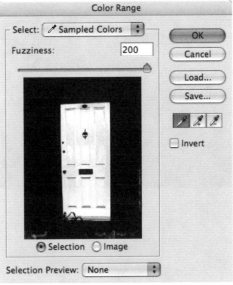

Figure 4.30 *Selecting a colour range*

on the right in Figure 4.30. The pop-up menu at the top allows you to select a pre-defined range of colours – all the reds, greens, or blues, for example – which you might want to select if you needed to compensate for problems with a scanner. Most of the other options are directed towards printed material, apart from **Highlights**, **Midtones** and **Shadows**, although these only select a brightness range, which appears to approximate the sort of area indicated by the name. The most usual option to use is **Sampled Colors**, which lets you choose the colours to select.

When **Sampled Colors** is chosen, the eyedropper tool is used to sample a colour from the main image, and colours similar to the sampled colour are then selected. In Figure 4.30, the colour of the door was sampled, leading to the selection shown on the right. (We will show how to change the colour in a selected area later in this chapter.) You can add extra colours to your selection by sampling again with the eyedropper with a + sign attached to it, or remove colours from the selection by sampling with the eyedropper with a - sign. The **Fuzziness** slider is an essential part of the process; it is used to control how colours which are close to the sampled one are added to the selection.

The **Fuzziness** slider appears to behave somewhat like the tolerance value for the magic wand, adding more colours as the value is increased, but actually it works in a different way, which introduces a new idea. With the magic wand, pixels are either selected or they are not. With a colour range selection, some pixels can be partially selected, a concept that we will examine in

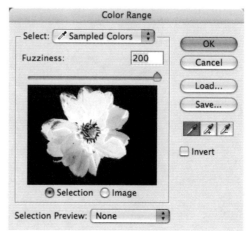

Figure 4.31 *Partial selection using colour range*

more detail later. Increasing the fuzziness value increases the extent to which colours that do not exactly match the sampled ones are selected. The dialogue box provides an immediate preview of the selection – fully selected pixels are shown in white, with shades of grey showing which pixels are partially selected and the degree of partial selection – so it is possible to adjust the fuzziness interactively to obtain the desired selection.

Figure 4.31 shows an example of how this partial selection works. The original photograph (top left) has a strong image of the central flower, but the background is fussy and uninteresting. We wanted a simple but sophisticated graphic suitable for a Web page. This was easily achieved using Select>Color Range... because the flower is of a striking red colour that does not occur in the background of the photo. Clicking on the bright red area below the centre of the flower with the eyedropper, and adjusting the fuzziness slider, was enough to select the flower. The extent and degree of the selection are shown in the preview in the dialogue box. The selected area could then easily be copied and pasted into a new image with a plain coloured background. The partially selected pixels allow some of the new background colour to show through, whereas the fully selected pixels remain opaque, giving an interesting variation and effect to the final graphic.

┌─ TRY THIS ───┐

Practise using the Select>Color Range... command on different images, as you did with the magic wand. Observe the effect of adjusting the Fuzziness slider.

Select part of an image using Select>Color Range..., then copy and paste the selection into a new image with a coloured background. Observe how the background shows through the areas that were partially selected.

Paths

If you are used to working with vector graphics applications such as Illustrator, you may find that the best way of making precise selections is by using the vector drawing tools that Photoshop provides. (On the other hand, if you dislike vector drawing tools, you should skip this section.)

Using vector drawing tools in Photoshop, you can construct a ***path***, a slightly confusing name for a collection of curves and lines. You do this by clicking the Paths button in the Options bar when you select a vector drawing tool. This path can then be used in several different ways. In particular, it can be converted to a selection.

The most flexible way of creating paths is by using the pen tool, which is a standard vector drawing tool, to construct Bézier curves, as described in Chapter 8. That chapter also describes how you can use the vector selection tools to alter paths after you have constructed them.

The other vector drawing tools provided include several for drawing simple geometrical shapes: rectangles (with or without rounded corners), ellipses and regular polygons. These are all used in the same way: select the tool and drag in the image. The shape is pulled out as you drag. Where appropriate you can set parameters, such as the number of sides of a polygon, in the Options bar. When used to make selections, these tools either duplicate the effect of a marquee tool, or create such specialized shapes that they are unlikely to be useful in this context.

Figure 4.32 *Selecting with the pen tool*

Figure 4.32 shows a situation where the pen tool can be used profitably to make a selection. Because the fish is camouflaged and was photographed through water, there is little differentiation between the pixels on the fish's body and those in the background, making a magic wand selection impractical. Instead, the pen tool was used to draw round the fish, following the outline that is visible to the eye, even though Photoshop cannot easily discern it from pixel values.

Drawing with the pen or any other vector tool creates a path, but what we wanted here is a selection. It is simple to convert between the two.

Paths are manipulated in the Paths panel. Most of the time, if you are creating paths to use as selections, you just work with a single path, known as the ***work path***. (If you find yourself using paths a lot, you can create named paths using the New button at the bottom of the panel.) The work path and any named paths are displayed in the panel; as Figure 4.33 shows, a thumbnail of the path's shape is displayed in the panel. Once you have drawn a work path and adjusted it so that it encloses the area of the image you want to select, choose Make Selection... from the Paths panel menu. (For named paths, you must first select the one you want to use in the panel.) The dialogue box shown in Figure 4.34 is displayed. By choosing an appropriate radio button you can turn the path into a new selection on its own, or combine the selection made from the work path with any existing selection. (See the following section for a description of the different options for combining selections.) You can also choose whether or not to anti-alias the selection, which has the effect of smoothing its edges. It is also possible to convert an existing selection into a path, using the Make Work Path command from the Paths panel menu. You might do this, for example, so that you could use the direct selection tool to refine a lasso selection; after you had done so, you could turn the path back into a selection.

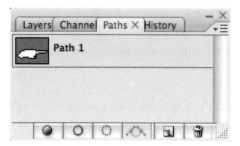

Figure 4.33 *The* Paths *panel*

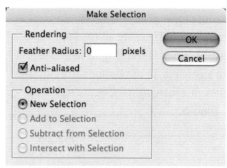

Figure 4.34 *Converting a path into a selection*

Combining and Transforming Selections

Sometimes the best way of making a complicated selection is by building it up in pieces. For instance, you might select a coloured area with the magic wand, and then extend the selection by adding a differently coloured area. Alternatively, to make an L-shaped selection, you might select a square with the marquee tool and then remove a smaller square from the selection. If you look at the Options bar when you are using any of the selection tools we have described so far, you will see a set of four small icons at the left-hand end. These are used to control the way in which any selection you make interacts with any pixels that are already selected. Normally, the leftmost of the four buttons is selected. This default option causes a new selection to replace any previous one. If you click on one of the other three buttons before making a new selection, this behaviour is altered.

The second button causes the new selection to be added to any existing selection. If you prefer to use a keyboard modifier, holding down the shift key while making a selection has the same effect. When you are adding to a selection, the cursor has a small + sign attached to it. You can use this facility in two ways: either to build up a complicated shape by combining simpler shapes, or to select several different parts of an image, depending on whether your new selection is separate from any existing selection.

The third button causes a new selection to be subtracted from the existing selection. That is, it allows you to deselect some pixels that you have already selected. If you prefer to use a keyboard modifier, hold down [opt/alt] while making a selection if you want to subtract it from an existing selection. When you are subtracting from a selection, the cursor has a small − sign attached to it. Sometimes, this is the only way to make selections of a certain shape. For instance, the image on the left of Figure 4.35 shows a framed painting photographed against a coloured background. Suppose you want to select just the frame, perhaps in order to put a different picture in it. You can easily do so by making a rectangular marquee selection that encloses the entire frame and picture, choosing the subtraction button from the Options bar, and making a new selection that includes everything inside the frame. Because the subtraction option has been used, this leaves only the frame selected; if this selection is now inverted, all the rest of the image can be deleted, leaving just the frame, as shown on the right of Figure 4.35. (You could also leave both frame and mount by selecting just the painting itself when using the subtraction button, which would give a better result if you wanted to use this example to create a new framed picture.)

Figure 4.35 *Subtracting selections*

The final option for these selection tools (on the far right of the four) causes a new selection to be intersected with the existing one. That is, only those pixels that lie within both the originally selected area and the new one will be selected. Hold down both shift and [opt/alt] to create an intersected selection using keyboard modifiers. The cursor acquires a small x when the intersection option is being used.

Because it is frequently necessary to refine magic wand selections, it is particularly useful to be able to use the add and subtract modifiers with the magic wand. You will often make an initial selection and then add pixels by shift-clicking with the wand, or subtract them by holding down [opt/alt] when clicking, until you achieve the selection you require. You can also profitably use the intersection modifier: make a rough selection of the part of the image that you are interested in with a marquee tool, and then intersect that with a magic wand selection to pick out areas of a certain colour from within the selected region only. The add and subtract modifiers are also valuable for refining lasso selections.

As we mentioned previously, a selection made in the Select>Color Range... dialogue can be extended or reduced by using the eyedropper tools with + and – by them. Using this command when you already have a selection restricts its effect to the area that is already selected, so it acts to reduce the selection. In effect, the colour range selection intersects with the existing selection.

Any selection can be transformed using the Select>Transform Selection command. This causes a bounding box to appear around the selection's outline, which you can manipulate in just the same way as when you use the free transform command on the image to scale, rotate, skew or distort the selection. Although the method is identical, in this case it is the selection that is being transformed, not the selected pixels. When you have finished adjusting the bounding box, you click in the tick or the cross in the Options bar and the transformed selection will be shown in the usual way, by marching ants.

┌─TRY THIS───

Make a rectangular selection in an image, then make a second, elliptical selection, using each of the modifiers in turn when you create the second selection. Do this with selections that overlap, ones that are completely separate and ones that are enclosed in each other. Make sure you understand why the resulting selection is what it is in each case.

Open a photograph of a landscape with a cloudy sky and use the magic wand to select all the clouds.

Make a diamond-shaped selection in any image, by transforming a selection made by the rectangular marquee.

DON'T FORGET

Use the marquee tools to select simple geometric shapes.

Use the crop tool, or the Image>Crop or Image>Trim commands to remove superfluous areas round the outside of an image.

The lasso tools can be used to make irregularly shaped selections.

The magic wand tool and the Select>Color Range command select pixels with similar colours. Tolerance and fuzziness can be set respectively.

Paths drawn with the pen and other vector tools can be converted into selections. If you are skilled at vector drawing, precise shapes can be selected.

New selections can be added to, subtracted from or intersected with an existing selection by using buttons on the options bar or keyboard modifiers.

Selections can be moved, scaled, rotated, skewed and distorted.

Selecting and Extracting Objects

In our examples so far, we have typically selected an object within an image. Although this is not the only sort of selection you will ever need, selecting an object is something you often need to do, in order to separate it cleanly from its background — so that you can place it against a different background, for example. You can use any of the selection methods we have described so far, and then either copy the selection to a new document, or invert the selection and delete, to remove the background. Sometimes, this requires you to make a painfully fiddly selection with the lasso or pen tools. For instance, loose strands of hair, fur, fuzzy twigs, and so on, can make accurate selection extremely difficult. Photoshop provides some specialized tools that attempt to automate the extraction of objects from their backgrounds.

The task is quite difficult, since in effect you are expecting Photoshop to perform some of the same processing tasks that go on in your brain when you look at an image and recognize certain regions of it as being an identifiable person, creature, plant and so on. There is nothing recorded in the array of pixels in which the image information is stored to identify any such object; it is only by looking at how colours and brightness change that it is possible to identify edges, and these changes can be subtle. Our brains make use of knowledge of the world to help interpret image information, but Photoshop knows nothing about the world. In other words, you should not expect extraction tools to work miracles, and sometimes it will only be possible to extract an object from its background by painstaking use of the manual selection tools.

The oldest and simplest of Photoshop's tools for extracting objects is the magnetic lasso, which we described earlier. It can perform quite impressively on certain types of image, but notoriously difficult objects, such as a person's head with loose strands of hair, usually defy it.

Figure 4.36 *Making a quick selection*

The **Quick Selection** tool provides an alternative way of selecting objects – or more precisely, regions with well-defined edges – in a semi-automatic fashion. You simply drag the tool over the region you want to select. As you drag, the selection expands until it reaches what Photoshop considers to be the edge of the region. This may or may not agree with your own idea of where the edge should be.

Figure 4.36 shows the sort of result that can be achieved swiftly with the **Quick Select** tool. The rocks form a coherent mass that is well distinguished from the background, so dragging the tool a few times within the rocky area makes a selection whose boundary isolates the rocks from the surrounding water. Because of the variations in colour and shading on the rocks, the magic wand would not have selected this region so completely. The central image in Figure 4.36 shows the selected region more clearly than the marching ants in the screenshot on the left. On the right, we have shown what happens if the background is erased. If you look closely, you will see that the selection is not perfect: some dark-coloured water in front of the rocks has been included. We will describe how the edge can be refined to make a better selection shortly.

If you stop dragging, then click or drag again nearby, the selection will automatically extend to take in the new area; there is no need to hold down **shift**. If you don't want this to happen, click on the leftmost of the three icons that appear in the **Options** bar; this forces the tool to make a new selection every time. The icon at the right is used to subtract areas from a quick selection, while the one in the middle causes the default behaviour, of always adding to a selection. Note that the default option is different from that for the other selection tools.

The **Quick Select** tool is rather hit-and-miss in its results. It has a tendency to make the selection jump across indentations in outlines, such as the little inlet at the bottom left of the rocks in Figure 4.36, instead of following the edge of an object. It's pretty hopeless at dealing with fussy outlines, such as the bushes in the foreground. To deal with such difficult subjects, you need to do some extra work, using a better tool.

The most intelligent facility for extracting objects from their backgrounds in Photoshop is a complete mini-application within Photoshop, which is invoked by the **Filter>Extract**... command. Figure 4.37 shows the sort of result that can be achieved, and Figure 4.38 shows the interface to the **Extract** filter. The mode of operation is quite simple. You begin by using the edge highlighter tool to draw fairly roughly round the edge of your object; the highlight is shown in a lurid green. You must highlight the entire edge. In other words, you must keep dragging until you get back to where you started. The eraser tool within this dialogue can be used to erase the highlighting if necessary. You need to ensure that all of the actual outline of your object lies within the highlighted area, but otherwise you don't need to be too accurate. If your object has a well-defined edge, you can select the **Smart Highlighting** checkbox. The highlighter will then snap to edges as you drag it around the object. Its width will automatically be set to the narrowest size that covers the edge. If you aren't using smart highlighting, you can vary the size of the highlighter by setting a value in the **Brush Size** box under **Tool Options** at the right of the dialogue box: it should be big enough to cover all the boundary region of your object, including any wisps and strands, but no bigger than necessary, otherwise unwanted pixels may be included in the extracted object. (In Figure 4.38 we used a wide highlighter to help you see what was going on. For Figure 4.37 we used smart highlighting, which gave a much narrower highlighted region and a better result.)

Once the edge is highlighted you use the fill tool (paint bucket) to fill in the inside of the object – you just click with the tool inside any areas you wish to retain. The filled region turns purple, as shown on the right of Figure 4.38. To see the result, click the button labelled **Preview**. It will almost certainly not be perfect. You can try again, using the highlighter on the preview, or, if the

Figure 4.37 *Extracting an object from its background*

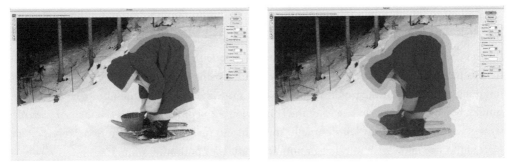

Figure 4.38 *The interface to the* Extract *filter*

result is nearly right, you can touch it up using the cleanup and edge touchup tools. The former behaves like an eraser; you drag it to remove extra pixels. If you hold down [opt/alt] while you drag it, it behaves in the opposite fashion, putting back pixels that have been excluded. You would normally use the cleanup tool to remove any extraneous pixels that had been left in the background after the basic extraction. The edge touchup tool is used to define edges more clearly. Like the highlighter it is dragged along an edge, and sharpens it as you go. Once you are satisfied with the preview, you click OK to apply the extraction to the image itself.

For suitable images, this process can produce impressive results, as Figure 4.37 demonstrates. Note how the white trim on the robe was extracted cleanly from the white snow. Where there is little contrast or extraneous details surround the object, the result may be less satisfactory. It pays to be selective about the extraction tasks you attempt.

The Extract filter works on the currently selected layer, but its typical use is to extract objects from photographs, which will only have a single layer when they are imported. For safety's sake, though, it is advisable to copy the original layer, hide it, and apply the filter to the copy.

TRY THIS

Open an image containing an object with a poorly defined outline and experiment with different methods for extracting the object from its background. Try all the methods we have described so far and assess how easy and effective each one is. Repeat the experiment on different images with varying amounts of contrast between an object and its surroundings.

Masks

We remarked at the beginning of this section that once you have made a selection, any changes you make are applied only to the selected pixels and not to the rest of the image. Looking at this another way, the area of the image outside the selection is protected from any such changes. The situation is analogous to the use of a stencil in conjunction with a paint spray. You place the stencil – typically a piece of card with some shapes cut out of it – on top of the picture you are creating and spray your paint. Where the paint strikes the card, it can't reach the paper to leave a mark. A similar technique is used by photographers, who place shapes on top of the paper onto which they are making a print, to protect parts of the print from the light projected by an enlarger. This way, unwanted parts of the image on the negative won't be printed. In this context the protective stencils are called **masks**. Unlike the masks used with a paint spray, which either completely stop the paint or let it all hit the paper, a photographic mask does not limit the photographer to the simple choice between excluding all of the light or letting all of it through; it can include partially transparent areas which just let some light through, and such masks are used to achieve certain sorts of special effects, such as placing a soft edge around a portrait.

Thinking about these analogies, you can see that when we make a selection in Photoshop we are, in effect, defining a mask comprised of the pixels which are not selected. Like the photographer's masks, Photoshop masks can be partially transparent. This is what it means for some pixels to be partially selected – the areas of the mask corresponding to those pixels are partially transparent.

Photoshop allows you to work directly with masks, providing several ways of creating them and editing them, as well as a range of different ways of using them. We will only describe some of the simpler aspects of masking, which is a complex subject.

If you think of a mask as something that allows light to pass through it in some places, and blocks light or allows it through partially in others, you can imagine something like a sheet of acetate (like a Photoshop layer, in fact) that has been blackened in some places to stop light passing through, left clear in other places to allow it to pass, and painted in shades of grey where light is to pass partly through. In other words, it is a greyscale image, and that is how Photoshop actually represents masks: as greyscale images which it uses in special ways to modify the associated layer. Since a mask is just an image, you can modify it in the same way as you can any other image.

Thinking about masks makes it easier to understand the effect of the **Refine Edge** button, which appears in the **Options** bar whenever you have just made a selection. (The same function is available from the **Select>Refine Edge...** menu command whenever a selection is active.) This button opens a dialogue box, in which you can alter the edge of the selection in various ways.

A nice use of this facility is to place a selected part of an image in a soft frame, in a manner made popular by Victorian photographers. Figure 4.39 shows an example. To create the vignette, an elliptical selection was made from the full photograph, as shown in Figure 4.40. However, this selection has a hard edge, so deleting the background does not produce the desired effect, which is characterized by the subject fading into the background without a definite border. To soften the edge, the **Refine Edge** dialogue was invoked.

Figure 4.39 *A vignette*

On the left of Figure 4.41 is the dialogue as it first appears, with default settings. The five sliders can be used to alter the mask's edge in different ways. When you hover over one of them, the area labelled **Description** at the bottom of the dialogue tells you what effect it has, and illustrates

Figure 4.40 *A hard-edged selection*

Figure 4.41 *Refining the edge of a selection*

it on a little icon. Experimentation is the best way to find out how the various refinements work. The screenshot on the right of Figure 4.41 shows the actual combination of settings used for Figure 4.39. The row of buttons across the bottom of the dialogue box is used to select how the refined selection is displayed in the main document window, so you can see whether the mask is as you want it. Showing the mask in reverse, as a white image on a black background, as we have done in Figure 4.42, is often the best way to see the edge clearly. (In this case black areas are fully transparent, so the image will show through them, white areas are fully opaque, blocking the image, and grey areas are partially transparent, providing the feathered edge in this example.)

Figure 4.42 *The mask in white on black*

TRY THIS

Choose a photograph with a clear central subject (a portrait would work well) and try to reproduce the vignette effect we have just described. Experiment with different settings in the Refine Edge dialogue. Try viewing the mask using the different options available, and see which ones allow you to see the edge of your mask and judge its visual effect best.

A selection is lost once you have created another one. You sometimes want a mask to persist for longer. One way of making it do so is by associating it with a layer. Each layer of an image except the background layer can have a mask – called its *layer mask* – associated with it. This lets you create transparent areas in a layer so that parts of the layers below show through it. There are several ways of creating a layer mask. The easiest to understand in the context of our discussion of the relationship between masks and selections is by converting a selection into a mask. Once you have made a selection, this can be done (on any layer except the background layer) by clicking on the mask icon at the bottom of the Layers panel. When you create a mask in this way,

it shows up as a thumbnail in the panel's entry for the corresponding layer. If you click on the layer mask's thumbnail, any painting, erasing or other changes you make affect the mask, not the image. When working on the mask you can even use the selection tools; they will select areas of the mask, not the image. For example, if you select part of the mask and delete it, this alters the shape of the layer mask, not the image itself.

As well as preserving a mask after a new selection has been made, a layer mask has the advantage of allowing you to make non-destructive changes to an image. If we had saved the selection in our vignette as a layer mask instead of deleting the background, the appearance would have been the same, but the background could have been restored at any time by simply deleting the mask. The Layer>Layer Mask>Delete command does this.

Layer masks can be used to combine parts of different layers, since they allow you to mask out the parts you don't want without actually deleting them, so you can return to the layer and alter the mask or restore all its contents at a later time. By using masks with soft edges or gradients, you can make images fade into each other. For instance, you could put a textured background behind the vignette, by putting it on a layer beneath the original photograph.

TRY THIS

Scan a piece of wallpaper, wrapping paper or textured paper, crop the image to match the size of the photograph you used in the previous exercise and paste it into a layer underneath the photo. Make a vignette again, but this time use a layer mask so that the pattern shows through as the background.

We have stressed the link between selections and masks, but we should emphasize that, although you can convert between them, they are not the same thing. A selection, in itself, makes no difference to an image. A mask is more permanent than a selection and, depending on the sort of mask it is, it will affect the appearance of an image in different ways. In particular, when you turn a selection into a layer mask, all the masked pixels (the ones outside the original selection) become transparent.

The last way of working with masks and selections which we will describe is the method of saving them as *alpha channels*. (Don't worry about the origin of the name.) The command Select>Save Selection... (which is only available if there is a current selection) causes the dialogue shown on the left of Figure 4.43 to be displayed, where you can give the selection a name, so that you can easily identify it later. To reload the selection, you use Select>Load Selection..., which leads to the dialogue shown on the right of Figure 4.43. Any saved selections will be listed in the Channel pop-up menu. When you choose a menu entry, the selection you saved with that name is reselected or combined with any current selection, depending on which of the radio buttons at the bottom of the dialogue box you choose. You can also use the buttons at the bottom of the Channels panel to save the current selection as an alpha channel, or to load a selected channel as a selection, providing you only want to load it into the current document.

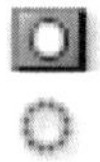

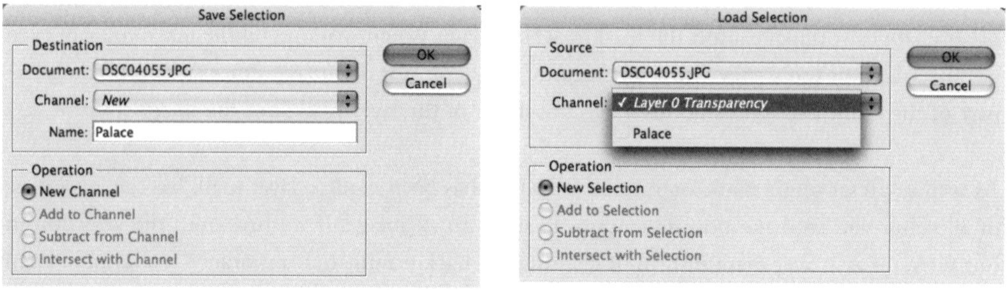

Figure 4.43 *Saving and loading selections*

You can use alpha channels in the obvious way, just to remember selections so that you don't have to go through the mechanics of selecting again later if you need to. You can also modify saved selections: they are displayed in the Channels panel, from which they can be selected and edited as greyscale images. It is especially useful to be able to load an alpha channel from one image into another, though you can only do so if both images are the same size. You do it by opening both images at once and using the Document pop-up menu in the Load Selection dialogue (shown in Figure 4.43) to choose a document to load the alpha channel from. If you have a set of images which are all the same size – for example, frames of an animation – you can quickly select the same part of each of them by making the selection in one file and saving it as an alpha channel which you load into each of the others in turn. (When you combine this facility with the automation features described in Chapter 2, you can apply a common process to selected parts of a set of images with relative ease.)

Alpha channels can also be used in more imaginative ways. For instance, you can make a selection based on an image on one layer, perhaps using the magic wand, save it and delete the layer, then reload it as a selection on a different layer, and turn it into a layer mask. The outline of the mask will be the shape derived from the deleted layer, so a "knockout effect" will be created, with any lower layer showing through the knocked-out shape.

┌─ TRY THIS ───

Practise saving selections as alpha channels and then reloading them, both into the document they were made in and into other documents (of the same size).

Try using saved selections to produce knockout effects. For example, make a picture of the place where you work shown through the logo of your college or company, or make a picture of the environment in which you would expect to find a certain animal shown through the outline of that animal.

└──

┌─ DON'T FORGET ───

The Quick Select tool can be used to select regions with well-defined edges just by dragging, but is not always successful.

The Filter>Extract... command opens a mini-application for extracting objects from their background, which can achieve excellent results.

A selection defines a mask, which protects the pixels that have not been selected from alteration.

The Refine Edge button allows you to change the edge of a mask, incorporating semi-transparent areas, for example to make a vignette with a fading edge.

A mask can be attached to a layer, as a layer mask, or saved as an alpha channel.

└──

Adjustments and Retouching

Photoshop's name draws our attention to its role as a digital image retouching application, which incorporates many of the tools and techniques that are traditionally employed in a photographic darkroom for altering and improving the quality of prints. Photoshop provides a host of ways of making adjustments to brightness and colour in an image. Any adjustment you make is applied only to selected pixels if you have made a selection; otherwise, it is applied to all of the current layer. Some of the adjustments which you can make, such as **Selective Color...**, are intended only for use by professional technicians who understand about process and spot colours, and other such esoterica of printing technology; they are much too specialized for novices and have no use in multimedia, so we will omit them from our descriptions. We will also ignore some of the options in the adjustments we do describe, for similar reasons.

Commands for making adjustments can be found in the **Image>Adjustments** sub-menu, but for many (though not all) of them there is also an entry in the **Layer>New Adjustment Layer** sub-menu. As we mentioned briefly when describing layers, adjustment layers are an extension of the layer concept; you can think of them as being layers that you look through and see an adjusted version of what lies beneath. An adjustment layer carries just one kind of adjustment, as if you had applied one command. The dialogue boxes used to apply the adjustment are the same in both cases, but there are important differences between the two methods of application. When you add an adjustment layer, you are first offered the option of setting a blending mode and opacity setting for it, as you are with a normal layer, which affects how the adjustment is applied to the pixels on underlying layers. The adjustments associated with an adjustment layer affect any layers beneath it. By moving the adjustment layer up or down in the **Layers** panel, you can affect different layers. But most significantly, the adjustment is attached to the layer and is not actually applied to any pixels in the image (unlike the **Image>Adjustments** commands). This means that when you use adjustment layers you are free to experiment with adjustments, without having to worry about irreparably changing the image itself. You can always go back to an adjustment layer to change the parameter values. If you decide not to apply the changes, you can just delete the adjustment layer, or you can hide it and add another to try a different set of alterations.

Adjustment layers appear in the **Layers** panel, as we saw in Figure 4.9, with **Control** panel icons suggesting each adjustment's effect instead of the image thumbnails used for normal layers. By double-clicking this icon you can bring up the dialogue box for that adjustment and change its parameters. Like any layer, an adjustment layer can have a layer mask, which prevents the adjustments being applied to parts of the image. If a selection is active when you add an adjustment layer, the selection is automatically converted into a layer mask attached to the adjustment layer.

We recommend using adjustment layers rather than **Image>Adjustments** whenever possible.

Tonal Adjustments

It's only a slight exaggeration to say that most of Photoshop's tonal adjustment commands fall into one of two categories: powerful and difficult or simple and useless. For example, the Levels and Curves adjustments, which we will describe shortly, allow you considerable control over the tonal balance of an image, but getting the right result requires patience, experience and a good eye. The Brightness/Contrast, Auto Levels and Auto Contrast adjustments, on the other hand, can be made just by selecting the command or dragging a couple of sliders, but the results are usually poor, and can often be worse than the original. As a general rule, the best results are achieved in Photoshop by avoiding automatic features, and relying on your skill and judgement.

Shadows and Highlights

There is one tonal adjustment that is easier to master than Levels and Curves, and which can still produce good results. The Shadow/Highlight... command is found on the Image>Adjustments sub-menu. It is designed to correct poorly exposed photographs with uneven lighting. If you are a digital photographer, this command may be all you need to correct most exposure problems.

Despite what we said earlier about adjustment layers, the Shadows/Highlights adjustment is not available as an adjustment layer, it must be applied destructively to the image layer (or, preferably, to a copy) or as a smart filter, which we will describe in the *Effects and Filters* section.

The simple dialogue which opens when you first select the Shadow/Highlight... command is shown in Figure 4.44. It allows you to adjust two values: the amount of correction applied to shadows (i.e. dark areas) and highlights (light areas). The default values are intended to deal with backlit subjects, such as a person photographed with their back to a window, and the effect is to bring up the dark areas, which will have been underexposed. To bring down the lighter areas, slide the Highlights slider to the right.

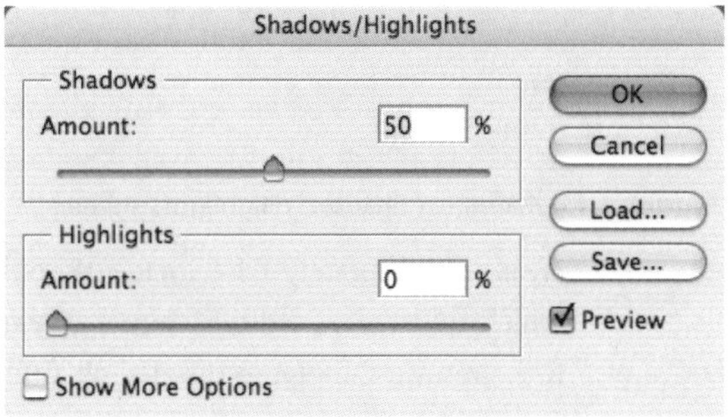

Figure 4.44 *Basic* Shadows/Highlights *adjustment*

These adjustments may be enough to correct a photograph, but finer control is available: by ticking the checkbox labelled Show More Options, you can expand the dialogue box, as shown in Figure 4.45. The top two sets of three sliders allow you to adjust not only the amount of correction applied to the shadows and highlights, but the degree of tonal variation that determines what constitutes a shadow and a highlight: the tonal width specifies the range of values (a narrower width applies the correction to only the darkest and brightest areas) while the radius specifies how many values adjacent to each pixel are examined to determine whether it belongs to a shadow or highlight area. The Adjustments sliders at the bottom control how the pixel

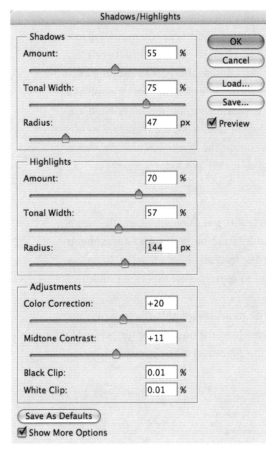

Figure 4.45 *Additional* Shadows/Highlights *options*

values in the shadows and highlights are altered. (Note that the contrast is always altered according to the **Amount** values you set for each of **Shadows** and **Highlights**; the **Color Correction** and **Midtone Contrast** adjustments are additional.) The **Black Clip** and **White Clip** settings allow you to force pixels to the extreme black and white values.

Figure 4.46 shows the sort of result that can be achieved using **Shadows/Highlights** adjustments. The original photograph on the left was taken indoors on a sunny day, resulting in an image with a washed out exterior seen through a window and a dark foreground lacking in detail. Applying the settings shown in Figure 4.45 produced the adjusted image on the right: the extreme contrasts have been evened out and much more detail has been brought out, especially from the shadows. Little effort was needed to obtain this result. You may feel that this is cheating: the adjusted picture is not exactly true to life. However, the original photograph wasn't either, and the adjustment has created a better picture, which conveys more of the reality of the scene.

You can use shadows and highlights adjustments to create a deliberately false image, though. At the left of Figure 4.47 is an original photograph, which once again exhibits some exposure problems, owing to the deep shadows. On its right is the result of applying the default values in the **Shadows/Highlights** dialogue: the contrast has

Figure 4.46 *Adjusting shadows and highlights*

Figure 4.47 *Using* Shadows/Highlights *for exposure correction*

Figure 4.48 *Using* Shadows/Highlights *to create an artificial moonlight effect*

Shadows/Highlights

Shadows
Amount: 84 %
Tonal Width: 30 %
Radius: 40 px

Highlights
Amount: 77 %
Tonal Width: 89 %
Radius: 50 px

Adjustments
Color Correction: −89
Midtone Contrast: +65
Black Clip: 1 %
White Clip: 0.01 %

OK
Cancel
Load...
Save...
☑ Preview

Save As Defaults
☑ Show More Options

been reduced and more detail has emerged from the shadows. Figure 4.48 shows another version of the photograph, made by using the settings shown in the Shadows/Highlights dialogue on the right. The result here is an artificially lit picture that looks as though it was taken by moonlight – a sort of "day for night" effect has been achieved.

The Shadows/Highlights dialogue is not a panacea for all exposure problems, but it can be effective and is often worth trying before you start using more advanced techniques. (You might have thought that the Exposure adjustment was intended for making the type of exposure corrections we have made with Shadows/Highlights, but in fact its main purpose is different: adjusting the exposure of "High Dynamic Range" photographs. This is a specialized topic which we will not discuss. Using Exposure on an ordinary image produces disappointing results.)

Levels and Curves

The most basic adjustments you can make alter the distribution of light and dark tones in selected areas of an image. The crudest adjustments of all are made with the brightness and contrast sliders, shown in Figure 4.49, which are displayed when you add a Brightness/Contrast adjustment layer,

Figure 4.49 Brightness *and* Constrast *sliders*

or select Brightness/Contrast... from the Image>Adjustments sub-menu. The sliders work like the corresponding controls on a monitor or television set. Brightness adjusts the value of each pixel up or down uniformly, so increasing the brightness makes every pixel lighter and decreasing it makes every pixel darker. Contrast is a little more subtle: it adjusts the range of values, either enhancing or reducing the difference between the lightest and darkest areas of the image. Increasing contrast makes the light areas very light and the dark areas very dark, decreasing it moves all values towards an intermediate grey. As with all the adjustment controls, if you tick the checkbox labelled Preview any adjustments you make are shown in the image window as you move the sliders, so you can assess your settings as you work.

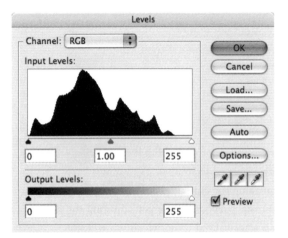

More precise control over the tonal balance of an image is provided by the Levels dialogue, shown in Figure 4.50. It can be opened either from the Image>Adjustments sub-menu or by using a Levels adjustment layer. This allows you to set the white and black levels in the image and adjust the mid-point. In terms of the content of the image, you are adjusting the tones of the shadows, highlights and mid-tones.

The little graph that occupies most of the dialogue box is called the ***image histogram***. It shows how

Figure 4.50 *The* Levels *dialogue*

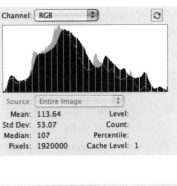

Channel: RGB

Source: Entire Image

Mean:	113.64	Level:
Std Dev:	53.07	Count:
Median:	107	Percentile:
Pixels:	1920000	Cache Level: 1

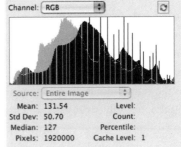

Channel: RGB

Source: Entire Image

Mean:	131.54	Level:
Std Dev:	50.70	Count:
Median:	127	Percentile:
Pixels:	1920000	Cache Level: 1

Figure 4.51 *Levels adjustment and image histograms*

the different brightness levels are distributed among the pixels of the image (or selection). The horizontal axis represents the different possible brightness levels, with black (zero) at the left, and white (255) at the right. The height of the graph at each point indicates the number of pixels with that brightness, so in Figure 4.50 you can see that most of the pixels fall below the middle brightness value, with a distinct peak. There are secondary peaks above and below the main one.

If you look at the photograph on the left of Figure 4.51 you may be able to see where these peaks come from: the bulk of dark pixels is a result of the area of dark sky at the top of the picture, the shadows on the rocks, and the top of the lighthouse, while the upper peaks are probably due to light areas in the rocks and the white-ish building below the lighthouse. (The histogram shows that there are no pure white pixels, so we can tell that the building isn't actually white.) Don't worry if you can't see how the photograph relates to the histogram, you will be able to interpret histograms with practice. Once you have learned to use them, image histograms are a useful aid in judging the tonal make-up of an image. An image's histogram is not only visible in the Levels dialogue; you can see it at any time, with some additional details, in the Histogram panel, shown on the right of Figure 4.51. (You may need to select Expanded View from the panel menu to see the numerical data.) Sometimes Photoshop speeds up the display of the histogram by using only a sample of the pixels in the image. If it is doing this, a warning triangle appears in the panel. Click on the refresh icon at the top right to obtain an up-to-date and accurate histogram.

In the Levels dialogue, the sliders immediately below the histogram control the range of input values. The slider at the left controls the pixel value that will be mapped to black. If you drag this slider to the right, say to 10, any pixels whose value is less than or equal to 10 will be displayed as black (that is, as 0). The slider at the right controls the pixel value that is mapped to white, so if you drag it to the left, say to 245, any pixels with value greater than or equal to 245 will be displayed as white (that is, as 255). In order to spread the range of tonal values evenly across the image, the input sliders are moved so that they line up with the lowest and highest values that have a non-zero number of pixels shown in the histogram. (This will be done for you – unless your image has an unusual tonal distribution – if you click the Auto button or select Auto Levels from Image>Adjustments. Most people prefer to adjust levels by eye, though, using the preview to judge the result instead of trusting Photoshop's mechanical adjustments.) Moving beyond these points will expand the dynamic range artificially. As you move the sliders, the Histogram panel (not the histogram in the dialogue box) shows a ghost image of the histogram before the adjustment. The screenshot at the top right of Figure 4.51 demonstrates how the histogram changes as the right slider is dragged down to the original maximum value. Adjustment of the white and black input values can have a dramatic effect on badly exposed photos or dull images.

The values of pixels in between the black and white extremes are normally mapped linearly to intermediate shades. By dragging the middle slider, which represents the mid-point in the tonal range, you can affect the distribution of these intermediate pixels. If an image's brightness is concentrated in a particular range, you can move the mid-point slider under the corresponding point on the histogram, so that the brightness values are adjusted to put this range in the centre of the available scale of values. The screenshot at the lower right of Figure 4.51 shows how the histogram changes as this is done on our example image. The result is a brighter and more detailed image, but the effect is too subtle to reproduce well, so we have not shown the adjusted photo in this instance. Adjustment of the mid-point slider can often restore some detail to images, but it needs to be used with care.

The pair of sliders at the bottom of the Levels dialogue is used to control the range of displayed brightness. That is, they determine the appearance of the pixels that have been mapped by the input sliders to black and white. If, for instance, you drag the left (black) slider up to a value of 15, then any black pixels will actually be shown as a dark grey – the tone that would otherwise be used for pixels whose stored value was 15. Similarly, if you drag the right slider down to 240, white pixels will be displayed as a pale grey. These output adjustments can be used to compress the dynamic range of your image and to avoid extreme blacks and whites in the final image.

The pop-up menu at the top of the Levels dialogue can be used to select whether to apply the adjustments to the complete image, as tonal adjustments, or to one of the red, green or blue channels of the image independently. Adjusting the levels in a single channel is likely to alter the colour balance of the image substantially. For beginners, this offers too much control and you will be better off using some of the more specialized colour adjustments to be described shortly.

┌─TRY THIS───┐

Use a Levels adjustment layer to correct the image whose brightness and contrast you adjusted in the previous exercise. Experiment with both sets of sliders to see the effect on the image and how this relates to the histogram.

└──┘

As we have described it, a Levels adjustment is applied to an entire layer – or to the entire image, if it only has a single layer, like a photograph you have just imported into Photoshop, for example. This is appropriate for correcting problems, such as a mis-calibrated scanner, that affect an entire image, but does not always do a good job on images with exposure problems such as we considered earlier, where some parts of the picture are too dark but others are too bright. One way of dealing with such images – if Shadows/Highlights fails – is by creating a mask that exposes only the shadows, and applying a Levels adjustment to lighten them up. You can then create another mask that exposes only the bright highlights, and apply a different Levels adjustment to tone those down. In fact, you can create a whole collection of masks and apply different adjustments to different parts of the image through them. This gives you great control over where your adjustments are applied, but requires you to make precise selections to create the masks in the first place, and problems can arise at the boundaries of masks. The Shadows/Highlights adjustment does something similar automatically, so you should try it first. It often does a good job.

┌─TRY THIS───┐

Take the poorly exposed photograph that you corrected with the Shadow/ Highlight... command earlier. Try to reproduce or improve on the correction by using a combination of masks and Levels. As before, try the same experiment with some images that have less extreme contrast problems.

└──┘

If you are used to thinking about relationships as functions and to visualizing functions as curves, you will find the Curves dialogue provides a powerful way of manipulating the relationship between stored pixel values and displayed tones. (If you are not familiar with these things, you may prefer to stick with Levels.) The dialogue is displayed when you create a Curves adjustment layer or select the Curves... command from the Image>Adjustments sub-menu.

To begin with, let's just consider greyscale images, where each pixel is represented by a single byte containing a value between 0 and 255. Normally, we consider 0 (no light) to be black and 255 to be white, with the values in between representing shades of grey. But we don't have to map those stored values to displayed shades in that way – they're just numbers. When we use the Levels dialogue to make adjustments, we alter the mapping function from stored to displayed values.

At first, when stored values are used directly to set the displayed brightness, the function is represented by a straight line, with a gradient of 1. In the Levels dialogue, the input slider at the left controls the pixel value that will be mapped to black, so, in graphical terms, it moves the bottom end of the mapping function's line along the horizontal axis. The input slider at the right controls the pixel value that is mapped to white, so it moves the top end of the line along the horizontal line corresponding to the maximum pixel value. In a similar way, the output slider controls move the end points of the line up and down.

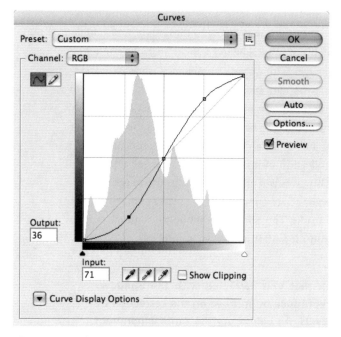

Figure 4.52 *The* Curves *dialogue*

The Curves dialogue, which is illustrated in Figure 4.52, allows you to take detailed control of this graph. Manipulating the curve is straightforward. If you drag a point on the curve it is pulled out as if it was a piece of elastic. To fix a point in place, you click on it. If you wish, you can make arbitrary changes by completely redrawing the curve with a pencil tool: just click on the pencil icon to the left of the curve and draw freely with it. To return to reshaping the curve by dragging, click on the curve icon next to the pencil. The histogram of the original image is shown behind the curve, to give you some idea of how many pixels will be affected by adjustments in different parts of the curve. Whichever method of reshaping you choose, the curve does not have to be kept as a straight line, but can be any shape you like. The almost complete freedom to map grey levels to new values that this provides permits some strange effects – for example, turning the curve upside down, as the Negative preset does, creates the effect of a photographic negative – but it also makes it possible to apply subtle corrections to incorrectly exposed photographs, or to compensate for wrongly calibrated scanners. However, this requires considerable skill.

An S-shaped curve such as the one illustrated in Figure 4.52 is often used to increase the contrast of an image: the mid-point is fixed and the shadows are darkened by pulling down the quarter-point, while the highlights are lightened by pulling up the three-quarter-point. The gentle curvature means that, while the overall contrast is increased, the total tonal range is maintained and there are no abrupt changes in brightness. In the image, the curvature is somewhat exaggerated: several of the presets produce a gentler curve with a similar shape.

---TRY THIS---

Repeat the previous exercise, using a Curves adjustment layer. Try the preset curves, to see how they alter the image. Create a second Curves adjustment layer and use it to experiment with the effect of making wild alterations to the shape of the curve by dragging or drawing.

DON'T FORGET

Use adjustment layers whenever possible, as they are non-destructive.

Try using a Shadows/Highlights adjustment first for exposure problems. It often corrects them with little effort and is simple to use, but the adjustment is destructive, so remember to keep a copy of the original layer.

Levels adjustments allow you to adjust the brightness distribution and dynamic range of an image or a selected area of it.

Curves adjustments give you maximum control over the distribution, but can be difficult to use well and require some experience to master.

Colour Adjustments

Normally, curve adjustments are applied to all three colour components combined, which has the effect of altering the brightness levels without changing any colours. Like the Levels dialogue, the Curves dialogue has a pop-up menu that allows you to select one of the colour components to apply the adjustment to. This is probably the most flexible means of making colour adjustment that there is, but it is not easy to see in advance what the effect of any adjustment will be. The non-linear way in which colours are perceived and combined makes judging how any adjustment will affect the appearance of the image extremely difficult. Adjusting colours in this way needs a great deal of trial and error, and can lead to considerable frustration: it is therefore not recommended for novices. If you need to make changes to colour balance, it is easier to use one of the dialogues that provide a higher-level interface to the colours of the image. Photoshop provides many of these, and we have only described a few of them, which we have found to be most useful. However, once you have mastered these, you should experiment with all the other colour adjustments, to see which work best for you. (Don't expect much from Auto Color, though.)

The simplest possible colour adjustment you can make is to remove all colour, using the Image>Adjustments>Desaturate command. Note that this does not change the colour mode.

To appreciate how the colour adjustments work, it is necessary to understand a little bit about colour theory. If concepts such as hue and saturation, the RGB and HSB colour models and the use of colour pickers are not familiar to you, you should read the short section on colour in Chapter 8 before proceeding with this section.

Since this book has been printed in black and white, illustrating colour adjustments is very difficult. To see the illustrations properly and understand the examples, you will have to download the colour versions from www.digitalmediatools.org. Better still, experiment with the adjustments we describe on your own images.

Like the tonal adjustments described in the previous section, colour adjustments are applied only to selected pixels if a selection is active, or to the whole layer if no selection has been made. Many colour problems do affect the entire image, so a selection is often unnecessary.

The use of the word "filter" in the context of image manipulation arises from the practice in photography of placing coloured semi-transparent filters in front of the camera lens, to alter the colour balance of the light striking the film. For users who are familiar with this way of changing images, Photoshop now provides a **Photo Filter...** command on the **Image>Adjustments** sub-menu. This command brings up a simple dialogue box in which you can choose one of an extensive range of filters, mostly corresponding to standard photographic filters, or select your own colour to use as a photo filter. A slider is provided for you to adjust the density – the amount of filtering, in effect. (See Figure 4.53.) Filtering light tends to darken the image. Ticking the checkbox labelled **Preserve Luminosity** causes Photoshop to compensate for this, leaving the image as bright as it was originally.

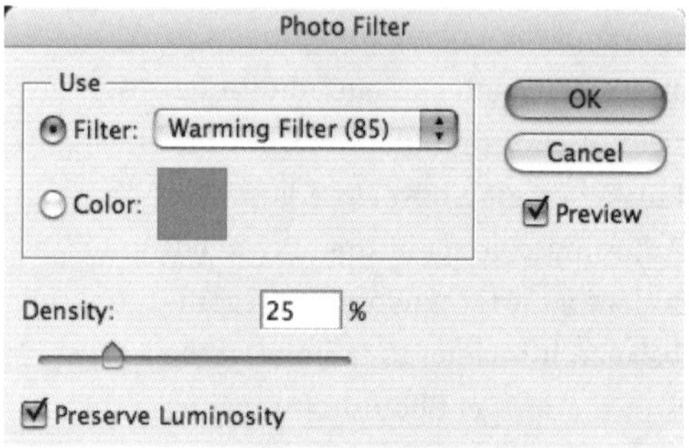

Figure 4.53 *Applying a photo filter*

If you are used to working with photographic filters, the **Photo Filter...** command will provide you with a familiar way of making quick adjustments. Even if you are not, the effect is simple to understand, and although you may not know in advance what a **Warming Filter (85)** will do, for example, you will see the effect straight away if you try it, and soon learn which filters are appropriate to particular colour problems. The effect of applying many of the filters is intuitively obvious.

One situation in which photo filters are particularly useful is for compensating for colour casts. A picture taken indoors under electric light will normally appear too orange or yellow compared to one taken in sunlight; applying one of the blue photo filters will compensate for this. Filters can also be used to intensify or correct certain colours in an image; a photo of pale blue flowers on green foliage was improved by applying the **Deep Blue** filter, for example.

Photo filters are applied to make fairly subtle changes to colour temperature, but such subtle changes can make all the difference to the finished result. More radical colour temperature changes can be made using the **Hue/Saturation** dialogue, which we will describe shortly.

If you are new to colour adjustments, the most appealing interface may be that provided by the Image>Adjust>Variations... command, which allows you to change hue, saturation and brightness by selecting new versions of your image from a gallery of thumbnails that illustrates possible variations. An example is shown in Figure 4.54 (though some of the variations are not clear in this black and white reproduction, of course). The two thumbnail images at the top of the box show the original image (on the left) and the "current pick", that is, the image with your currently chosen set of adjustments made to it. These adjustments are made by picking one of the thumbnails in the lower part of the dialogue box. The seven images on the left are used to adjust colour.

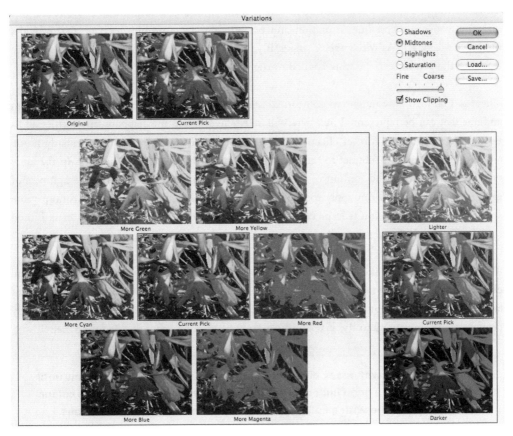

Figure 4.54 *Variations*

With a little imagination, you can see these as comprising six variations arranged around the rim of a colour wheel at the positions occupied by the primary and secondary colours, with a seventh image in the centre, which is another copy of the current pick. To add more of a primary colour, click on the corresponding peripheral image: for instance, to add more red, click on the one at the right. To subtract some of a primary colour, click on the secondary opposite it; so to remove some red, click on the image at the left, labelled **More Cyan**. The slider at the top right of the dialogue is used to determine how much is more, that is, how big a step each of the thumbnails represents. (We set the value to its highest for Figure 4.54, to make the differences more apparent in reproduction. Normally, you are more likely to work with finer variations.) When you click on one of these small images, the current pick at the top is replaced by the variation you have chosen, which is in turn replaced by a new variation with still more red, or whatever.

The three images on the right are used to adjust brightness in the same way. The radio buttons at the top right of the dialogue apply the variations to the darkest (**Shadows**), lightest (**Highlights**) or mid-range (**Midtones**) tones of the image. If you select the last radio button, labelled **Saturation**, the display changes to show just three thumbnails which are used to adjust the saturation in the same way as the ones originally at the right are used to adjust brightness. Thus, in this one dialogue, you can adjust hue, saturation and brightness using a simple interface that provides immediate feedback. As with other changes, if you had made a selection before bringing up the dialogue, the adjustments are only applied to the selected pixels.

There is a limit to how much red you can add to any particular pixel: eventually the maximum amount that can be represented in a byte will be reached. When this happens, any further addition of red will have no further effect on that pixel, though it may affect others. Similarly, if you add too much cyan (i.e. subtract too much red), eventually there will be no red left. In the same way, there is a limit to the amount of green or blue you can add or subtract, or the lightness or extent of saturation you can apply to any pixel. Pixels that have reached their maximum value are said to be clipped. If you tick the checkbox labelled **Show Clipping** a fluorescent mask is used to show the pixels that are clipped.

The **Variations** dialogue is easy to use, but it only provides a crude interface to colour adjustment, even with the slider set to **Fine**. It also has the drawback that it cannot be used on an adjustment layer. The **Variations…** command is only available in the **Image>Adjustments** sub-menu and any changes made are applied to the pixels and can only be undone using the **History** panel.

---TRY THIS---

Choose an image with many different colours and practise using Variations until you feel you have a good understanding of how each variation affects the colour. Now take an image with a colour cast and try to correct it using variations.

If you want to use an adjustment layer or you feel that the Variations dialogue does not offer you sufficient control, you can use the Color Balance dialogue, which can be brought up either from an adjustment layer or from the Image>Adjustments sub-menu. It is shown in Figure 4.55. In effect, this performs the same job as the hue adjustments in the Variations dialogue. By dragging each slider towards either the primary or complementary secondary colour labelling its ends, you

Figure 4.55 *Adjusting the colour balance*

can add or subtract the corresponding colour component from the selected pixels in the image. Like Variations, Color Balance can be applied separately to shadows, midtones and highlights. A potential pitfall with this arrangement is that applying separate adjustments to these three sets of pixels can easily lead to discontinuities in the adjusted image.

Like other adjustments, checking the Preview box causes the effect to be shown live in the document window. This allows you to experiment, which for most people is a better way of arriving at the desired result than trying to predict the effect of any particular setting.

As with the photo filters, if you tick the Preserve Luminosity checkbox, Photoshop will compensate for these colour adjustments so that the brightness is unaffected. (If you don't do this, since colour adjustment adds or subtracts light, the brightness will normally change as well as the colours.) Making small adjustments to the colour balance of an entire image is one way of compensating for colour casts introduced by a scanner.

TRY THIS

Use the same images you chose for the previous exercise and experiment with using the Colour Balance dialogue, both to see the effect of adjusting the sliders and to try to correct a fault or colour cast in the image.

For even greater control over colour adjustments, you can use the Hue/Saturation dialogue shown in Figure 4.56, which is also available both as an adjustment layer and as an adjustment from the Image>Adjustments sub-menu. When it first opens, the Hue/Saturation dialogue provides a similar facility to Color Balance, but in terms of the HSB model of the colours in the image instead of the RGB model. This is in itself an advance if you find it easier to think about colour in terms of its hue, saturation and brightness

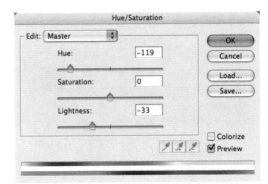

Figure 4.56 *Adjusting hue and saturation*

instead of its red, green and blue components. The interface to hue and saturation adjustments provides three sliders, one for each of the three HSB components (although the brightness slider is labelled **Lightness**). Dragging the top one moves colours around the colour wheel (the value shown is a rotation in degrees). The other two sliders change saturation and brightness, adding or removing white or black; in their case, the numerical values are percentages. As you move the sliders, the effect is shown in the colour ramps at the bottom of the dialogue: the top one shows the standard range of colours, the lower one changes to show how each is altered by the adjustments. (It's worthwhile just playing with the sliders and watching the effect on the lower colour ramp to get a feel for how these adjustments in the HSB space work.)

In conjunction with selecting a colour range, the **Hue/Saturation** adjustment can be used to change the colours of objects in an image. Look back at Figure 4.30, where we selected the door on the basis of the colour it was painted. Having made that selection, the hue and lightness of the selected pixels could be changed, to paint the door in different colours, as shown (within the limits of greyscale reproduction) in Figure 4.58. The door is shown its original red (left), blue (centre) and ochre (right). The settings shown in Figure 4.56 and Figure 4.57 correspond to the blue door.

The Image>Adjust>Replace Color... command combines a colour range selection with a hue and saturation adjustment in a single dialogue, as shown in Figure 4.57. This is convenient, but it has two disadvantages compared to performing the selection and adjustment separately. First, it can only be used destructively, not as an adjustment layer. Second, you have no opportunity to refine your selection using some other tool or command before applying the adjustment.

The Hue/Saturation dialogue offers much more flexibility. The pop-up menu labelled **Edit** at the top lets you choose to apply changes to any one of the primary or secondary colours. The default choice of **Master** applies your changes to all colours, but it is often the case that you only need to adjust a limited range. When you select another value from the pop-up menu, some extra controls appear in the dialogue box, as shown in various states at the bottom of Figure 4.59. The grey bar that appears between the colour ramps shows the range of colours that will be affected by the changes you make. The two light grey bars around the

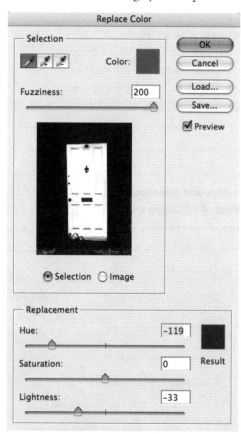

Figure 4.57 *Replacing colour*

Figure 4.58 *Changing the colour of a selected colour range*

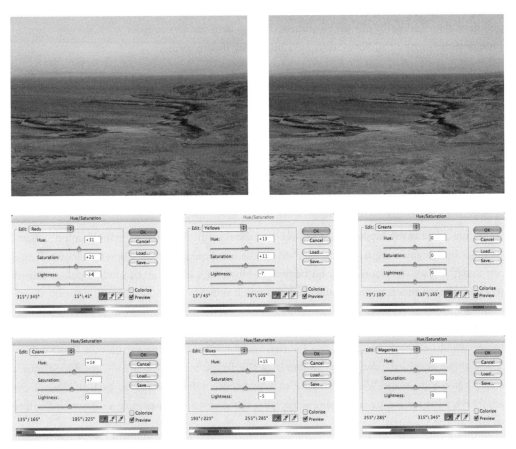

Figure 4.59 *Turning winter into spring with hue and saturation adjustments*

central dark grey bar indicate a fuzzy area, where changes will be partially applied. (Compare this behaviour with the fuzziness in the Select>Color Range dialogue.) You can stretch or shrink the colour range by dragging the small vertical bars between the central dark grey band and the fuzzy bands, or change the extent of the fuzzy area by dragging the outermost triangular slider controls. Alternatively, you can use the eye droppers to set the colour range by sampling colours from the image: the plain eyedropper sets the centre of the range, the eyedropper with a plus sign extends it and the one with a minus sign shrinks it. You can make changes to each of six ranges without leaving the dialogue. Clicking OK will apply the whole lot at once.

Figure 4.59 is actually a dramatic example of the changes that can be made by applying hue and saturation adjustments to different colour ranges. The small screenshots at the bottom show the several adjustments that were applied. Their combined effect is to turn a winter image into a spring one: the image on the left was an original photograph, taken in mid-winter, where the landscape is dominated by shades of brown from dead foliage and dry grass, and the pale light from the low winter sun gives a cyan hue to the sea. In the altered version on the right, the foliage and grass have turned bright green and the light is brighter and sunnier, with the sea a strong blue, as if the picture had been taken on a sunny day in late spring.

---TRY THIS---

Practise making hue and saturation adjustments to the two images you used in the previous two exercises. Try to simulate the effect of colour balance adjustments using hue and saturation.

Take a photograph of a landscape or building in the middle of a sunny day. Using whichever colour adjustments you find most effective, change the lighting so it looks as if the picture was taken in the early evening or during a sunset.

As we remarked at the beginning of this section, the most flexible way of making colour adjustments is by manipulating the three separate colour components in the Curves dialogue. This is not something we can recommend for beginners. However, Curves can be used on colour images to create special effects without calling for too much skill.

It may help to know that the pixel values for the colour components are stored as if there were three separate greyscale images – one for red, one for green and one for blue in RGB colour. These three images are the colour *channels* of the image, which are usually combined into a single full-colour image. When we apply an adjustment, such as Curves, to each of the colours separately, what we are actually doing is applying the greyscale adjustments we described before to each of the channels.

Figure 4.60 *Changing colours using* Curves

Figure 4.60 illustrates a particular application of this approach. The original image on the left is a black and white sketch. The dramatic colouring on the right was applied by selecting the Color Negative (RGB) preset from the curves dialogue, with all three channels selected. (That is, with the channel pop-up set to RGB.) After this, each of the channels was selected in turn and its curve was adjusted further by hand to create the desired highlights. The values are shown below the images. (Note that, in order for this to work, the mode of the image must be RGB Color, even though we are starting with a picture that has no colour in it.)

It's easy enough to find your way around the colour adjustment dialogues, but quite another thing to know how to achieve any particular visual adjustment using them. That takes practice.

TRY THIS

Open any photograph and use Image>Adjustments>Desaturate to take the colour out. Try to reproduce the effect in Figure 4.58 by adjusting curves.

Using any photograph, experiment further with curve adjustments on the three channels to see what other special effects you can achieve easily.

Retouching by Hand

Making selections and then applying adjustments through the various dialogues we have described will suffice to improve or alter many images, but there are some jobs that are better done by working directly on the image using retouching tools. Some examples of the sort of jobs that are best done that way include removing marks, blemishes or unwanted elements from an image, or reducing shadows, for instance from under a person's chin in a badly lit portrait.

In a later section we will describe how Photoshop's brushes and erasers can be used to paint pixels directly on an image or remove them from it. Erasing, in particular, is a good way of removing unwanted elements from certain sorts of image – usually those that do not have a background. Suppose, though, that you have scanned a watercolour painting on coarse paper with a visible grain and that there was a speck of dust or a scratch on the glass of the scanner. If you try to remove the resulting mark from the scanned image by painting or erasing, the corrected area will still show up because, no matter how careful you are, you will not be able to capture the texture of the paper that you have erased where you have made your changes. The *clone stamp* tool is a very useful hand retouching tool, which is used to repair problems such as this. It paints a copy of part of an image onto a different part, so in this case, you could find an area of the image that was the same colour as the damaged area and remove the unwanted mark by cloning.

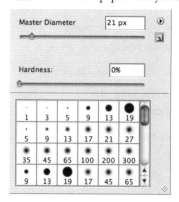

The clone stamp is one of Photoshop's brush tools, which we will describe in detail later in the chapter. As you will discover, when you select any brush, you can set a host of options that govern the way it makes marks. For now, though, it is adequate to set a brush size, which determines how large an area is cloned at once. You do this by clicking on the control labelled Brush, which appears in the Options bar when

Figure 4.61 *Setting the brush size*

the clone stamp is selected. This will cause a panel to drop down, as shown in Figure 4.61. Drag the slider at the top, labelled **Master Diameter**, to set the brush's size. Unless you have changed any settings, the clone stamp will use a soft round brush by default, as indicated by the icon displayed in the **Options** bar. This is often the best choice. If you want to experiment with using other types of brush for cloning, consult the section headed *Brushes*.

Having set the diameter, the next step is to [opt/alt]-click at the point from which you want to start cloning. Once you have established this starting point you can paint with the stamp by dragging it in the image where you want the cloned pixels to appear. As you do so, a cross-hair shows the point from which you are cloning; the cloned pixels are copied to the area over which you drag the tool. Figure 4.62 shows the clone stamp tool in action. The original photograph on the left has a single fan on the wall. The clone source was set on the fan, and then the clone tool was dragged in the blank area of wall above it, causing a second fan to appear there – an exact copy of the first one. As the final result on the right clearly shows, simply waving the clone stamp so that the cross hairs cover the object you want to clone is not usually going to create a workable result. By not being precise in the cloning, we have brought part of the wall with the fan, creating a clearly visible discontinuity. To avoid such problems, it is necessary to use a smaller brush and follow the edges of the object to be cloned more carefully, or to make further corrections later.

Sometimes, though, if the background is uniform or has a clear pattern, objects can be duplicated or removed fairly easily. Figure 4.63 shows an example: we removed the peculiar object from the sideboard on the right side of this Victorian photograph by cloning the wallpaper.

The clone stamp actually copies pixels from its source to the area you drag over, without altering them. If the image is not uniformly lit, this can make the cloning apparent. The cloned pixels bring their lighting with them, as it were, so they do not match the surrounding area. The ***healing brush*** is a refined version of the clone stamp, which can overcome this shortcoming.

Figure 4.62 *Duplicating an object with the clone stamp tool*

Figure 4.63 *Removing an object with the clone stamp tool*

The healing brush is used in just the same way as the clone stamp: [opt/alt]-click to set a source, then drag in the image to copy pixels. While you are dragging across the image, it may well look as if the healing brush is making a paticularly poor job of matching the surrounding area, but when you stop dragging, Photoshop does some extra processing, and after a short pause (or a long one if you are using an older computer) the texture, lighting, transparency and shading of the newly cloned area will change to match its context. Sometimes, the result is spectacularly good; other times, it is less impressive.

Certain repairs can be made to images very quickly using the ***spot healing brush***. (This brush's toolbox icon is very similar to the ordinary healing brush, so watch the tooltip when you select either of them.) With this tool you don't need to select a source before you start work. Just scribble over an unwanted part of the image, and the spot healing brush will clone surrounding pixels to remove it. The brightness will be matched, as with the healing brush. It is generally recommended that this tool only be used for removing small blemishes, as its name suggests. In such a case, you can set the brush size slightly larger than the defect and just click. However, for suitable subjects, the spot healing brush can perform larger repairs, as Figure 4.64 illustrates.

Figure 4.64 *Using the spot healing brush*

The original photograph on the left has prominent rusty water stains on the wall. These were removed just by dragging the spot healing brush over them. (As the central illustration shows, when you use this brush, the area you drag over is initially blacked out. As with the healing brush, once you stop dragging the pixels are matched to the surroundings.) The surrounding pixels provide a source, so after the lighting has been matched up, the wall appears nice and clean and no longer detracts from the main subject of the photo. You may not be able to see this clearly in the illustration, but the healing process has preserved the pebble-dash texture of the underlying wall in the retouched area.

The final retouching tool in this group is the **patch tool**. This enables you to clone a region of an image by drawing round it, as you would with the lasso tool. Having made a selection, you then indicate in the **Options** bar whether you want to select a source or destination for the cloning operation. If you select source, you can drag the selection to somewhere else in the image, and the pixels will be transferred to the originally selected area. Alternatively, if you select destination, the pixels in the original selection will be copied to wherever you drag the patch. In either case, the lighting and so on are adjusted to match the destination, as with the healing brush and spot healing brush. The patch tool provides immediate visual feedback – you can see the pixels that will be cloned as you move the stamp around. It is a difficult tool to obtain good results with, however, not least because of the difficulty of making an accurate selection, and we would advise you to use the healing brush in preference for most tasks.

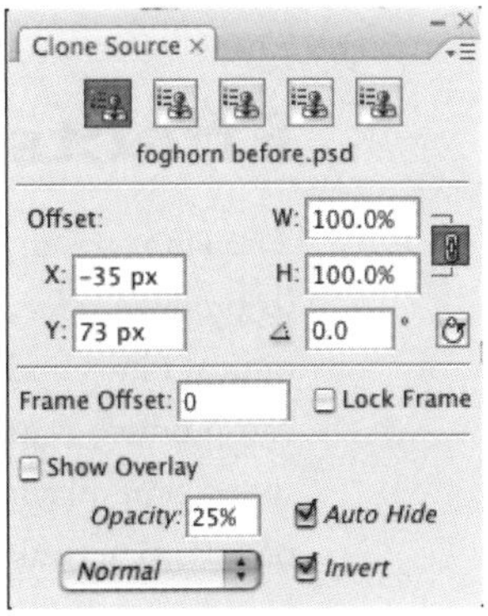

For complicated retouching jobs, Photoshop provides the **Clone Source** panel, shown in Figure 4.65. Here you can store up to five different clone sources and switch between them, and you can also scale or rotate the cloning. For example, if you rotate by 90°, when you drag the tool horizontally the sample point will move vertically. Such refinements are advanced and require practice to use confidently; we advise you to master the basic operation of these tools before you try to use the **Clone Source** panel.

Figure 4.65 *The* Clone Source *panel*

As well as correcting defects in an image, the clone stamp tool and its relatives are often used for artificially improving images – faking, in other words. The clone stamp is the secret of some models' perfect complexions, as illustrated in magazines. Like all the other retouching tools, it takes skill and a good visual sense to make a convincing job of such subtle alterations.

---TRY THIS---

Find an image with a clearly-defined subject, a background and some other objects and use the clone stamp tool to remove some of the extraneous objects. Repeat the exercise using the healing brush, and compare the different results.

Experiment with using the spot healing brush to remove blemishes of different types from several photographs. See which it handles well and which badly.

Try drawing round an object with the patch tool and replacing it with a patch of the background.

DON'T FORGET

Use the clone stamp tool to copy areas of an image or to remove objects or blemishes by cloning their surroundings. Any part of the image may be used as the clone source: [opt/alt]-click to specify the starting point of the source.

The healing brush performs the same function as the clone stamp but retains the texture, lighting, transparency and shading of the area being repaired.

Use the spot healing brush to repair small blemishes. It uses neighbouring pixels as the clone source – it does not have to be specified explicitly for this tool.

Use the patch tool to clone whole regions; select a region by drawing around it and set source or destination in the options bar before dragging the selection.

The Clone Source panel provides advanced cloning options.

Effects and Filters

The Filter menu provides commands for systematically changing the values of pixels in an image to produce effects reminiscent of natural art media and of special effects produced by the use of optical filters and other techniques in a traditional photographic darkroom. Many of these filters can produce immediate and striking results with little effort, so newcomers to Photoshop often spend time playing with filters. There is no harm in that, but the results can easily be crude and of little practical use, so filters should generally be used judiciously. Some are vital – the better blurring and sharpening filters, for example – but many of them are just gimmicks. A filter can potentially alter every pixel in an image, and some filters perform fairly complex calculations using the values of several neighbouring pixels. As a result, applying a filter may take some time.

In all cases, filters are applied to selected pixels, unless no selection has been made, in which case they are applied to the entire contents of the currently active layer. So, having made a selection if necessary, you choose a filter from one of the sub-menus of the Filter menu. The next step depends on which filter you have chosen.

Some filters are always applied in the same way, with no variable parameters, so there is no need to set any values. The filter is applied immediately. Such filters can be identified by the absence of an ellipsis (...) after their name in the menu. Examples include Facet and Fragment on the Filter>Pixelate sub-menu, and Blur and Blur More on the Filter>Blur sub-menu. All filters that lack parameters are crude and are rarely of much use.

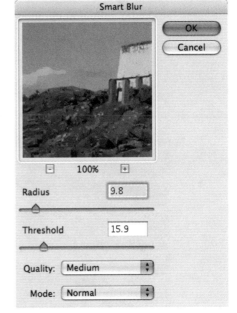

Many more useful filters have their own dialogue boxes, which allow you to alter various parameters controlling the extent of the alterations which the filter produces. Figure 4.66 shows a typical example. Nearly all of these parameters are controlled by sliders or rotating dials (for setting angles), and although it is the case that each one really controls a clearly defined aspect of the particular filter it relates to, you don't need to understand in any detail what is being controlled; you can just fiddle with the controls and see what happens. The effect of all filters with parameters can be previewed – they have a detailed preview within the dialogue box itself. The + and – signs underneath the preview box are used to zoom in and out, so you can see both the overall effect on a large area of the image and the detailed effect on a few pixels.

Many filters may be applied by way of the *filter gallery*. This is invoked either directly by choosing Filter Gallery... from the

Figure 4.66 *A filter dialogue*

Filter menu, or indirectly by selecting one of the filters available in the gallery from the Filter menu. Figure 4.67 shows a filter being applied using the filter gallery. Controls for changing the values of any parameters for the chosen filter are displayed in the upper part of the right-hand side of the filter gallery window. The two screenshots show how different parameter values can be set and how the large preview pane on the left shows their effect on the image.

The filters which may be applied are shown in the middle pane, in the form of thumbnails showing their effect on a standard sample image. The filters are grouped into related sets, whose members can be hidden or revealed using the disclosure triangles next to the folder symbols. To apply a filter, select its thumbnail. (If you opened the filter gallery by choosing a filter from the Filter menu, the filter you chose will be applied straight away, as you would probably expect.)

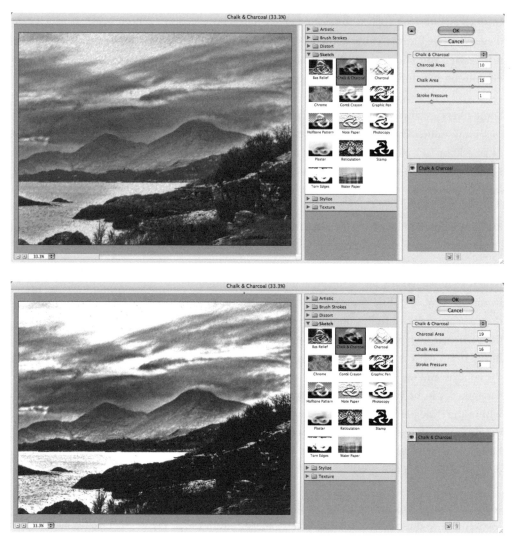

Figure 4.67 *The filter gallery*

Using the filter gallery, you can apply several filters in combination. You can think of them as filter layers, which are stacked on top of each other. To add a new filter, click on the standard **New** icon below the filter list at the bottom right of the window. This will initially add a second copy of the current filter, but if you then select the thumbnail for the additional filter you want to apply it will replace the duplicate of the previous filter. Note, though, that in general the order in which you apply filters alters their combined effect, and it may radically affect the final result. That is, if you apply a filter *A* followed by a filter *B*, the result will not usually be the same as if you had applied *B* first and followed it with *A*. You can reorder the filters by dragging their entries in the filter list at the lower right of the filter gallery window.

Finally, a few filters (those at the top of the Filter menu, above the sub-menus) cause elaborate dialogues, which constitute specialized mini-applications, to open. We have already described one of these, the Extract filter, and we will look at the Vanishing Point filter later in this section, and the Pattern Maker briefly later on. The Liquify filter is used for a specialized type of distortion, and is only very occasionally useful, so we will not devote any space to it.

Despite their name, the photo filters are actually adjustments, as we described earlier.

Irrespective of the method you used to apply a filter, after you have applied it an entry will appear right at the top of the Filter menu, with the name of the filter you used. Choosing this menu entry will cause the filter to be reapplied, with the same parameters, without displaying the filter gallery or a dialogue box. This is simply a time-saving device for repeating the filtering operation. (If you applied a combination of filters in the gallery, the menu entry will read Filter Gallery, and the whole combination will be reapplied, even if you originally invoked the gallery by choosing a specific filter.)

TRY THIS

Go ahead. Spend a couple of hours playing with filters. Use a range of different source images and experiment with the full range of available filters. Try using extreme values for the parameters, then experiment with more subtle effects. Try to get a feel for what each adjustment does, and how the visual result is altered by changing parameters.

Try using several filters in combination. Which combinations work and which don't?

When you have finished experimenting, look at the results critically and assess whether any of them could be useful in an actual project. Which ones, if any, would you feel happy showing to a client?

Smart Filters

When you apply filters in the ways we have described so far, they are applied destructively. That is, they alter the pixels of the image permanently, and can only be undone using the History panel or Undo command, while the document is still open. Once applied, the values of parameters cannot be altered, so if you discover later that you should have used a higher value for a filter's intensity, for example, you will have to go all the way back in the history to remove the filter and apply it again, which will mean losing all the changes you made to the document subsequently.

Nearly all filters, and some adjustments, can also be applied non-destructively, as *smart filters*. These are similar to adjustment layers, in that they allow you to apply a filter without actually altering the image pixels, so that you can turn it off again or alter its parameters later.

Smart filters are applied to *smart objects*. Smart objects can be transformed (scaled, rotated, and so on) without the loss of quality that normally occurs when you use the **Free Transform** commands, as we described earlier.

There are several ways of creating smart objects, including the use of the **File>Place...** command, which embeds another image in a document, and allows you to edit its original contents at any time. This is particularly valuable in the case of placed vector images, such as Illustrator files. These retain their vector character, and can be scaled and otherwise transformed inside Photoshop without the loss of quality that occurs when these operations are carried out on bitmapped images. Including vector graphics in Photoshop documents was originally the primary reason for smart objects, but it isn't something you will necessarily want to do very often. However, you can also turn layers into smart objects within an image, and not only transform them, but apply filters to them non-destructively.

To turn a layer into a smart object, make sure it is selected in the **Layers** panel, and choose the **Filter>Convert for Smart Filters** command. A warning will appear. Once you have dismissed the

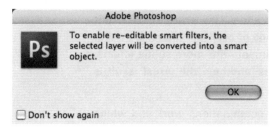

dialogue, your layer will have become a smart object, to which you can apply smart filters. You can apply any filter to a smart object except the four special ones listed near the top of the **Filter** menu – **Extract, Liquify, Pattern Maker** and **Vanishing Point**. You can also apply the **Shadows/Highlights** adjustment to a smart object.

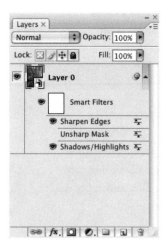

Figure 4.68 *Smart filters in the* Layers *panel*

Smart filters are applied in just the same way as ordinary filters, through the filter gallery or a dialogue box. They are only "smart" because of what they are applied to.

If any smart filters have been applied to a layer, they appear below it in the **Layers** panel, as shown in Figure 4.68. Beside each filter's name is an eye icon; clicking this turns off the filter, clicking again in the same column turns it back on again. In this example, we have applied two different sharpening filters (described in the following section), and turned one of them off. This arrangement can be used for experimenting, to determine which form of sharpening works best on an image. Notice that we have also applied **Shadows/Highlights** as a smart filter. Using the eye icon next to the **Smart Filters** heading in the **Layers** panel, you can turn all the smart filters applied to a layer on and off at once.

To change the values of a filter's parameters, double-click the small icon consisting of a pair of sliders to the right of its name. This will cause a dialogue box to open, in which you can adjust the parameters. In this context, every filter's parameters are adjusted in a dialogue resembling the one shown in Figure 4.66, even if the filter is normally applied through the filter gallery. You can remove a smart filter permanently by dragging it to the dustbin icon in the Layers panel.

The advantages of applying filters non-destructively should be evident, so why would you ever apply them the other way? The drawback of smart objects is that you can't do much to them, except transform them or apply filters, so if you need to do any retouching after applying a smart filter, you can't. You can turn the smart object back into a layer, by selecting it and using the Layer>Rasterize>Smart Object command, but this applies the filters permanently – they are no longer smart and cannot be altered later. Alternatively, you can edit the contents of the smart object, using the Layer>Smart Objects>Edit Contents command, or by double-clicking the smart object's thumbnail in the Layers panel. This opens a new document window, with an image comprising the pixels of the smart object, but without any filters or transformations applied. (If you had created a smart object by placing a file, editing the contents would mean editing the original file. In the case of a smart object made from a layer, what actually happens is that the layer is saved to a temporary file, which is what you edit.) You can only see the combined effect when you save and close the temporary document: the changes you have made to the smart object's contents will be taken back to the document containing it, where any smart filters will be applied. Clearly, this is an awkward way to work, so applying filters destructively still has its place. (Remember to make a copy of any layer which you intend to alter destructively.)

> ─TRY THIS──────────────────────────────────
>
> **Open a suitable image with just a single layer, convert the layer to a smart object and apply two or more filters. See how the image changes as you turn the smart filters on and off. Try changing some parameter values.**
>
> **With the filters applied, try editing the contents of the smart object. How easy is it to judge the effect of editing the contents on the original document?**

Blurring and Sharpening

Among the wealth of special effects and distortions that are only occasionally required, there are two filters which are more or less essential: Gaussian Blur and Unsharp Mask, which are on the Blur and Sharpen sub-menus of the Filter menu, respectively.

Normally, you would not want a blurred picture, but when you are working with digital images, a slight amount of blur is often just what you need to remove characteristic digital artefacts, such as jagged edges caused by too low a resolution, Moiré patterns, which occur when a regular pattern interacts with the array of pixels, and, for Web images, the visible blocks that can result from excessive JPEG compression (see Chapter 8). When we talk about blurring in this context, we mean an operation that combines the value of a pixel with those of some of its neighbours, rather as if we were able to rub together the colour values of the pixels, in the same way as you blur edges in a pastel drawing by rubbing them with your finger. Taken to extremes, such an operation will produce a completely blurred image, but done more gently it will remove the undesirable features just mentioned.

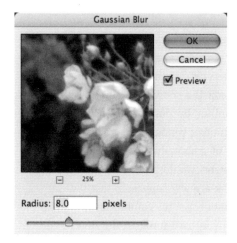

Figure 4.69 *Applying Gaussian blur*

When you apply a Gaussian blur, each pixel is combined with several of its neighbours for some distance, the extent of the contribution of each neighbour falling off with radius. The falling off follows a "bell curve", so that most of the contributions come from adjacent pixels, but those further away still contribute to some extent. (In theory, every pixel in the image will contribute something, but in practice the finite nature of computation means that only those within a radius of a few pixels will have any measurable influence.) Because of this spread-out influence, Gaussian blurring has a natural effect that is not visually intrusive.

The dialogue box for the Gaussian Blur filter, shown in Figure 4.69, lets you set the radius of the curve – a value which determines the width of the curve, although its exact relationship to the extent of the blurring is complicated. All you need to know is that higher values produce more blurring. A radius of 0.1 pixels produces a very subtle effect; values between 0.2 and 0.8 pixels are good for removing artefacts from low resolution scans, and so on. Higher values are used to produce a deliberately blurred effect. Figure 4.70 shows the effect of a Gaussian blur with an 8 pixel radius. A radius of 100 pixels or more blurs the entire image into incoherence; one of 250 pixels (the maximum)

Figure 4.70 *The effect of a fairly large amount of Gaussian blur*

just averages all the pixels in the area the filter is applied to. The Gaussian Blur dialogue also has a Preview checkbox. If you tick this box, the effect is previewed in the main image window, as well as in the small preview in the dialogue box.

Gaussian Blur is not the only filter on the Filter>Blur sub-menu. The simple Blur and Blur More filters apply a much more crude blur, which cannot be controlled by parameter settings and usually produce too coarse an effect. (They are more efficient than Gaussian Blur, which is notoriously demanding of processing time, but this is less of a problem than it used to be, because of the increased power of modern computers.) Smart Blur can be used to remove certain sorts of noise, such as film grain, from an image. It only blurs similar colours, while preserving edges. It is worth experimenting with Smart Blur, because it can sometimes do a more intelligent job of disguising artefacts than Gaussian Blur. The remaining blur filters use different algorithms to apply blurring to the image. They can produce special effects which are only occasionally useful.

TRY THIS

Practise applying Gaussian Blur to an image. Observe how the settings alter the appearance. Find values which (a) make no visible difference and (b) reduce the picture to incoherence. Try with another image with different visual characteristics, and see whether the same values have the same effect.

Try the effect of the other blur filters on your images. (If you can't see what some of them do, consult the Blur Effects page in the Filter Effects Reference section of Photoshop Help.)

Sharpening up an image is a more obviously desirable thing to be able to do than blurring it. It is perhaps surprising that it is possible to sharpen an image just by applying some algorithm to it, but it works quite well. Like the Filter>Blur sub-menu, the Filter>Sharpen sub-menu offers several filters for performing this operation, but only one of them is generally considered to be really effective at producing pleasing results and that is Unsharp Mask. This filter's curious name is derived from a photographic process, in which a positive image is masked with its blurred (unsharp) negative. The effect of adding a blurred negative is to subtract blurriness from the positive. Photoshop's digital equivalent works by creating a copy of the image, applying Gaussian blur, and then subtracting it from the original. Figure 4.71 shows an example of the change in appearance that unsharp masking produces. Although this filter enhances features of an image, it should be understood that it can add no information to it. On the contrary, information is actually lost whenever you use unsharp masking, although, if the sharpening is successful, the lost information will have been irrelevant, distracting or positively unwanted.

The parameters dialogue for Unsharp Mask is shown in Figure 4.72. The radius controls the amount of Gaussian blur applied to the mask; the amount determines by how much the contrast

Figure 4.71 *Sharpening with* Unsharp Mask

of edge pixels is increased. A threshold can also be specified: no sharpening is performed where the difference between the original pixel and the mask is less than the threshold value. This prevents the operation from enhancing noise by sharpening it – a risk in any sharpening operation, especially if the image you are sharpening has been JPEG-compressed. If the image is over-sharpened – that is, if too much sharpening is used – the result will have a characteristic sparkly appearance. If you see this, try again, with a smaller amount of sharpening and a smaller radius.

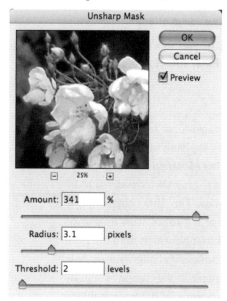

Figure 4.72 *Applying unsharp masking*

If you need to print from a scan, or display an image made by a cheap scanner or a low resolution photograph on a Web page, you will probably have to sharpen it. Unsharp masking can also be used for (apparently) restoring detail that has been lost by applying a Gaussian blur. If you apply a Gaussian blur followed by an unsharp masking you don't end up back where you started. The blur will remove unwanted artefacts and then the sharpening will restore detail at edges, but the picture will be permanently altered. Scanned images are often improved by this blurring and sharpening sequence, but it is not infallible and you should not apply it blindly every time you scan something. High resolution images from good digital cameras may not need sharpening, especially if the camera can create uncompressed images, in TIFF or RAW format.

TRY THIS

> **Start with a scan or some other image lacking in sharpness. Practise using unsharp masking to create the sharpest possible on-screen image. Try both with and without a preliminary Gaussian blur. Try over-applying the unsharp masking and describe the resulting side-effects.**

Figure 4.73 *Using blurring and sharpening to compensate for poor focusing*

Unsharp masking can be used for enhancing detail in a poorly focused photograph or one that has been blown up, but it can't perform miracles, as a close inspection of Figure 4.73 shows. The photograph on the left was taking using auto-focus, and, as often happens, the camera's idea of what it should focus on did not agree with the photographer's. The subject of the picture should have been the flowers, but the camera focussed on the foliage behind them. Ideally, you would discard such a picture, since no amount of processing is going to focus it correctly, but supposing it was all you had and you had to make the best of it, then you could improve it by blurring the foliage, to make it look out of focus as it would have been if the camera was correctly focused, and sharpening the flowers.

This is easier said than done, since, in order to sharpen just part of the image, it is necessary to select only the area that should have been in focus: the flowers together with the details of buds and stems among them. This was done by making an initial colour range selection and then refining it by adding and subtracting using the magic wand, until it was judged that the appropriate parts of the image were selected. (This isn't the only way the selection could have been done.) The selection was saved as an alpha channel, then the layer was copied (as always when performing destructive editing) and the selection was reloaded and inverted. The edges were feathered, using **Refine Edges**, to avoid too harsh a transition between the blurred and sharpened parts of the photo in the end result. Gaussian blur was applied to the inverted selection, using the settings in Figure 4.69, to knock back the leaves so you no longer see the details.

Rather than simply inverting the selection again to return to the flowers, the leafy background was deselected after blurring and the alpha channel was reloaded and feathered again, since the sharpening seemed to work better falling off at the edges of the selected area (the flowers) in a slightly different way from the blurring. Because the flowers were so blurry in the original, quite a high amount of unsharp masking (shown in Figure 4.72) was applied to this part of the image. Normally, you would be more likely to use an **Amount** of between 100% and 200%.

This example is typical of much serious Photoshop work in requiring the combination of several techniques and a certain amount of judging by eye. The final result is a fairly subtle change from the original, but succeeds in shifting the focus from the background leaves to the foreground flowers. However, as the details in Figures 4.70 and 4.71 show, the altered image does not stand up to close scrutiny. It is, however, adequate to use at small size, possibly on a Web page.

TRY THIS

Try to repeat the example just described. Take a photograph with a clear main subject, but focus on the background. If you have a camera with manual focus, you can do this deliberately. If your camera only has auto-focus, it will probably focus on the wrong thing if you place the "subject" at the edge of the picture instead of the centre. Now use a combination of blurring and sharpening of different areas to improve the picture and bring the intended subject into prominence. (You will need to make careful selections to do this.)

Like other filters – in fact, like almost everything in Photoshop – obtaining good results with blurring and sharpening requires practice and a good eye. Every image will need slightly different treatment and it is not possible to come up with a set of infallible rules and formulas that will tell you which settings to use.

Artistic Filters and Distortion

The majority of the filters that are available in Photoshop could be classified under this heading. The filters you can find on the Artistic, Brush Strokes, Pixelate, Render, Sketch, Stylize and Texture sub-menus are all attempts to add the appearance of art materials or techniques of one sort or another – or traditional photographic effects – to an image. We will refer to these filters collectively as artistic filters, although we use the term in a broad sense. Artistic filters have evocative names such as Colored Pencil, Dry Brush, Palette Knife, Crosshatch, Spatter, Mezzotint, Pointillize, Lens Flare, Chalk & Charcoal (as seen in Figure 4.67), Conté Crayon, Water Paper, Solarize, Craquelure and Stained Glass. Some – mostly the ones based on photographic effects – produce an effect that does resemble their name, others are not so successful. Most of them work by identifying edges in the image and altering them in some way. Generally speaking, it's worth asking yourself whether it's really a good idea to try and make an image look like something it isn't before you apply one of these filters. This isn't to say you can't have fun with artistic effects, and everyone ought to spend some time experimenting with them.

The filters on the Distort sub-menu work in a different way from the artistic filters. Distortions are achieved by moving pixels to new positions, which makes it possible to apply ripples and waves, for example, to selected parts of an image. Again, you might well find that this isn't really something with any value in practice, although it can be entertaining.

┌─TRY THIS───┐

Choose several images of different types (e.g. a landscape, a portrait, a graphic design) and experiment with applying different artistic filters to them. Which – if any – of these filters produces results that resemble the physical media they claim to simulate? Do any of the filters improve the images?

Repeat the exercise, using distortion filters on the same images.

Try creating background textures by applying filters to a layer containing a plain colour. (Note that only some filters will have any effect on a plain layer.)

└──┘

The Liquify filter provides another type of distortion. It opens a large window in which you can use brush tools to freely distort your image as if you were actually picking up its pixels and smearing them around. The effect is somewhat like smearing wet oil paint with your fingers. (It is easier to appreciate what this filter does if you try it; a description does not convey a very clear impression.) This filter can permit quite subtle and sophisticated distortions to be applied interactively to an image, but it is of very limited use in professional work.

Layer Effects and Layer Styles

Photoshop provides an alternative to applying filters to produce special effects in the form of *layer effects*. These are applied to a layer – to the layer itself, not the pixels it contains. This means, among other things, that the effect is not only applied to the pixels that are on the layer at the time, it is also applied to any marks you make on the layer, by painting, pasting or applying an ordinary filter, at a later time.

You can combine several layer effects into a *layer style*, which you can store and then apply to other layers to achieve a consistent appearance. Several prefabricated layer styles are supplied. While layer styles are fairly restricted in their creative possibilities, they provide a quick and easy way of creating stylized artwork to be used as furniture on Web pages.

The range of layer effects is much more limited than the range of filters. The basic effects can be found on the Layer>Layer Style sub-menu, which is shown in Figure 4.74. (This sub-menu contains some other commands that affect layer style, hence its name.) Most of these effects can be characterized as simulating light, textured surfaces and three-dimensionality. Figure 4.75 shows examples of the Bevel and Emboss effect. Layer effects are well suited to creating buttons for use on Web pages and user interfaces. Mostly they create a slight three-dimensional illusion; changing some parameter (e.g. from a raised embossing to a depressed one) is often a good way of creating visually related images for rollover effects.

Blending Options...

✓ Drop Shadow...
Inner Shadow...
Outer Glow...
Inner Glow...
Bevel and Emboss...
Satin...
Color Overlay...
Gradient Overlay...
Pattern Overlay...
Stroke...

Copy Layer Style
Paste Layer Style
Clear Layer Style

Global Light...
Create Layer
Hide All Effects
Scale Effects...

Figure 4.74 *The* Layer Styles *sub-menu*

Nearly all layer effects work on edges between transparent and painted pixels. If you apply them to a layer containing no transparent areas, you won't see much happening, except at the very edge of the image.

No matter which layer effect you apply, an elaborate dialogue box will open when you do so, giving you access to the full range of styles and, initially, the parameters for the style you selected. Figure 4.76 shows the dialogue as it opens when you apply a drop shadow effect. The main central area of the box is occupied by controls that allow you to alter various properties of the drop shadow, such as the angle from which it appears to be lit and the distance the shadow should be separated from the object throwing it. Every layer effect has its own parameters; as with filters, there is little point providing an exhaustive description of all of these and their results, since a little experimentation will soon show you how they work.

Figure 4.75 *Using* Bevel and Emboss *as a layer effect*

On the left of the dialogue is a list of all the layer effects, each with a checkbox. By selecting effects in this list, you can combine them. Ticking its checkbox adds an effect to the layer; selecting it in the list, by clicking the name, brings up its parameter controls so that you can make detailed adjustments to the appearance. If you come up with a combination of layer effects that you think you are likely to want to use again, clicking on the **New Style**... button allows you to name it and save it as a layer style. Whenever you are in the dialogue box of Figure 4.76, you can

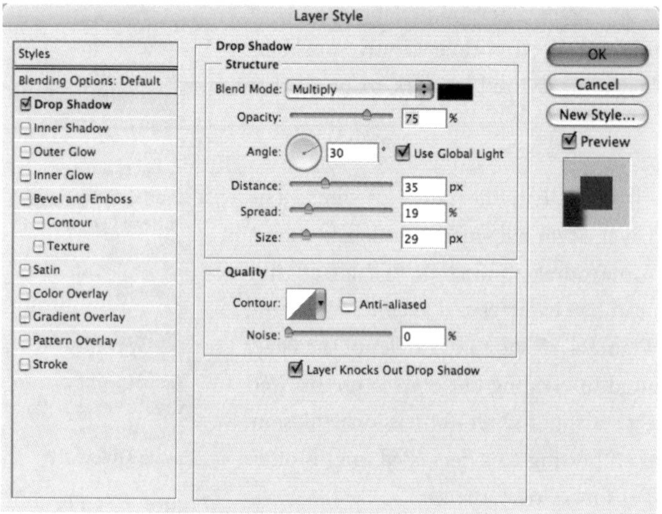

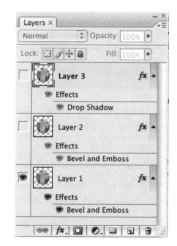

Figure 4.77 *Layer styles in the* Layers *panel*

Figure 4.76 *The* Layer Style *dialogue*

click on the word **Styles** at the top of the list on the left to see any styles you have saved, together with a small collection that come with Photoshop, displayed as small buttons. You may need to hover over each button and read the tool tip to identify the style it represents. To apply a style, just click its button. (Actually, the Photoshop manual offers no fewer than eight different ways of applying a style to a layer, but this way should suffice to start with.)

If a layer has one or more layer effects applied to it, these are shown in the **Layers** panel, in the manner illustrated in Figure 4.77. You can hide the effects by clicking the disclosure triangle by the *fx* symbol next to the layer's thumbnail. With the effects visible, though, you can double-click the name of one of them to bring back the **Layer Style** dialogue box of Figure 4.76 and change any of its parameters you are not satisfied with. You can also temporarily remove a layer effect by clicking its eye icon, as though you were making a layer invisible.

TRY THIS

Select part of a layer and delete the rest, so you end up with a layer having a clear boundary. Practise applying layer effects to it, singly (varying the parameters of each effect to see what they do) and in combination.

Choose several combinations of layer effects that you like, save them as layer styles, and try them out on different layers. (You might want to try applying layer styles to type layers. Refer to Chapter 8 to find out how to create these.)

Vanishing Point

One of the most spectacular and elaborate effects in Photoshop is the **Vanishing Point** filter, which helps you alter images while preserving their perspective. This is best illustrated by an example: the large picture on the left of Figure 4.78 appears to be a photograph of the front of two houses, the one on the left having a cleaner and more elaborately tiled path than the one on the right. In fact, the two houses have similar paths, as the original photograph at the upper right of Figure 4.78 shows. The tiled pattern at the lower right of Figure 4.78 was added and fitted to the perspective plane of the picture with the aid of the **Vanishing Point** filter.

Because the **Vanishing Point** filter relies on perspective, it will only work on images that have well-defined planes in perspective. Features such as the sides of buildings and receding straight paths or roads will work well. The image does not need to have a single classical vanishing point, but there must be straight lines defining areas that are really rectangular in shape and which recede into the distance if using the filter is to be at all simple.

Like the **Extract** and **Liquify** filters described previously, **Vanishing Point** is a mini-application within Photoshop, which opens in its own window with its own special set of tools. With a suitable image open, the **Filter>Vanishing Point...** command opens the **Vanishing Point** dialogue,

Figure 4.78 *Altering a photograph with the* Vanishing Point *filter*

which initially just shows a copy of the image; a small toolbox appears in the top left of the window. The **Create Plane** tool is used to draw a plane. That is, it is used to mark out (by clicking) the four corners of a quadrilateral grid that identifies an area of the image which corresponds to a rectangular plane in the real world. For instance, Figure 4.79 shows the plane drawn out for our example; it corresponds to the plane of the house's front path.

The grid has to define a geometrically feasible plane. If it succeeds, the grid will be shown in blue. If it fails, the grid lines will be drawn in either red or yellow, indicating that Photoshop is having severe (red) or less severe (yellow) problems resolving the geometry. In those cases the **Create Plane** tool turns into the **Edit Plane** tool, and you can drag one or more corners of the plane until it turns blue. You can use this tool in any case to adjust the shape of the plane: when it is selected, drag handles appear at each corner and half way along each side of the grid. The handles can be used to transform the grid, in the same way as you would apply a free transform, by dragging the handles of its bounding box.

When you are happy with your perspective plane, you are ready to use it to alter the image. If you don't want to perform the editing straight away, you can click the **OK** button in the **Vanishing Point** dialogue box at this point and your plane will be saved so that you can return to the dialogue later, and continue working where you left off.

Figure 4.79 *Defining a perspective plane*

Figure 4.80 *Adjusting the perspective plane*

In our example, another image (the bright tiled pattern) was pasted into the photograph and fitted to the perspective plane. To do this, the image for pasting must first be copied onto the clipboard. It can be part of the main image or taken from another source. Within the Vanishing Point dialogue, pasting causes the contents of the clipboard to be pasted as a "floating selection". That is, it is pasted into the window in such a way that you can drag it around with the Edit Plane tool. When you drag the floating selection onto the perspective plane, it distorts itself to fit the plane. As the screenshot on the left of Figure 4.80 shows, the pasted image initally retains its original aspect ratio (but in perspective), so in order to fit it to the plane it will usually be necessary to transform it before trying to drag it into place. This is done using the Transform tool from the Vanishing Point toolbox. Once the pasted image is fitted to the perspective plane, clicking OK causes it to be added to the image – it does not occupy its own layer, so if you want to isolate it, you should create and select a new layer before applying the Vanishing Point filter. (You will still see the whole image in the Vanishing Point dialogue.)

Simply pasting an image into the perspective plane in this way will ensure that it is geometrically correct, but this will not necessarily be enough to blend it into the original image, as you can see from the screenshot on the right of Figure 4.80. In our example, when the tiled pattern was pasted in place and fitted to the shape of the path, it overlaid part of the gate and the leaves that were originally on the path, so it was necessary to select parts of the original layer and paste them back on top of the tiled pattern, to restore these details. We also added a Hue and Saturation adjustment layer to alter the colours of the bright tiled pattern so that they were consistent with the lighting and tone of the original photo.

The Vanishing Point dialogue features a clone tool, which works like the conventional clone stamp: you first [opt/alt]-click to set a source point and then click and drag to add copies. With the Vanishing Point clone tool, however, both the source and the cloning must be within a perspective plane. The cloning then respects the perspective. For instance, we could have set a clone source among the leaves lying on the path, and cloned them along its length; they would then have got smaller towards the house. Alternatively, the marquee tool can be used to make a selection inside a plane. The shape of the selection automatically conforms to the geometry of the plane. You can then [opt/alt]-drag the selection to copy its contents to a different part of the plane and it will be scaled appropriately.

You can create several perspective planes in the same image, but to maintain consistency it is recommended that you do not create them independently. If you [cmd/ctl]-drag an edge handle of a plane with the Edit Plane tool, it drags out a new plane perpendicular (in perspective) to the first one. This way you can, for instance, create planes defining the ground and a wall.

The Vanishing Point filter does not always behave in an intuitive way. In particular, a pasted image may not fill a plane in the way you expect: the attenuation caused by perspective is quite severe.

---TRY THIS---

Take or find a photograph of a straight road receding into the distance. Create a yellow brick pattern and use it to turn the road in your photograph into the Yellow Brick Road. Don't worry if your first attempt is not a great success – the Vanishing Point tool requires more practice than most of Photoshop's features.

Take a photograph along the length of an advertising hoarding. Use some other image to replace the advertisement in perspective. Copy this altered hoarding and make a line of hoardings receding into the distance.

DON'T FORGET

Apply filters to a selection or a layer by selecting them from the Filter menu's sub-menus.

Some filters have no parameters or their own special dialogue, but most can be applied through the filter gallery.

You can apply a filter non-destructively by converting a layer to a smart object and applying it as a smart filter.

Blurring and sharpening are useful filters for improving images. Gaussian Blur and Unsharp Mask are the most effective of these tools.

Artistic filters and distortion are only occasionally useful for special effects.

Layer effects work on the edges of layers; mostly they create pseudo-3D effects suitable for buttons and their rollover states.

The Vanishing Point filter is used to alter images while preserving perspective.

Painting Pixels

Photoshop provides tools for colouring pixels directly, as if you were painting on the image with a brush. This allows you to achieve a range of "natural media" effects, which are supposed to simulate the appearance of physical art materials. This may not be something you wish to do, especially if you mostly work with photographs. However, the principles behind the painting tools are applied to other tools, including the healing brush and the quick select tool. Various erasers behave as "negative brushes", removing colour from pixels in the same way that brushes apply it. If you want to take full advantage of these tools, it helps to understand how brushes work, and what options they provide. Furthermore, brushes are not only used for painting pixels. They can be used to create selections, by painting a mask, as we will describe later.

The Paintbrush and Pencil

There are two different painting tools, which share the same location in Photoshop's toolbox: the paintbrush and the pencil. Both of these are used in the same way. You select a tool by clicking its icon in the toolbox, and then make marks by dragging in the image or, if you want to make a straight line, clicking at the start point, then shift-clicking where you want it to end. Before making any marks, however, you must set the colour using the Color panel or eyedropper tool, or by clicking on the foreground colour swatch in the toolbox and choosing a colour from the colour picker. These methods of setting colours are described in Chapter 8.

The names of these two tools give a broad indication of the nature of the marks they make. The pencil makes hard-edged lines and the paintbrush makes softer strokes. Apart from this, though, both tools can be used in the same way, with almost the same set of options. (In fact, you can, if you like, set the paintbrush's options so that it produces the same marks as the pencil.) From now on, when we are describing features common to the pencil and the paintbrush, we will use the term "brush" to include both tools.

A brush can have many variants, differing in size, hardness, shape and the angle between the simulated brush head and the orientation of the image. You can also specify how a brush will react to pressure when you are using a graphics tablet, set semi-random variations in certain properties of the brush marks, or associate a texture with the brush to simulate different types of support (paper, canvas, parchment, and so on). You can even specify a second tip for a brush. Several libraries of preset brushes come with Photoshop, and the easiest way to start working with painting tools is by using some of these presets.

Figure 4.81 shows the active part of the Options bar as it appears when each of the brush tools has been selected. In both cases, at the left, next to the tool presets drop-down palette, is a swatch representing the tip of the currently selected brush, with a number indicating its size in pixels.

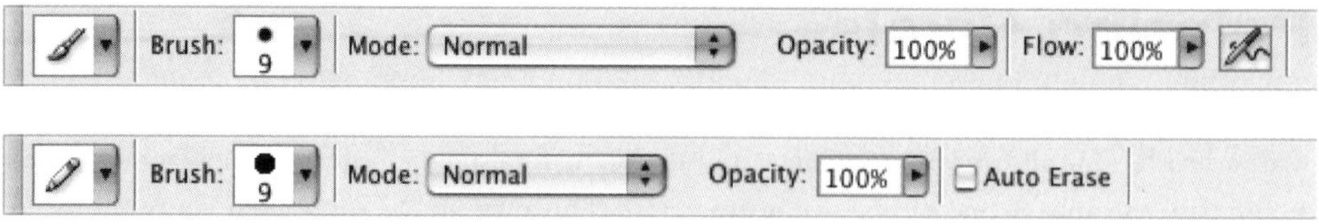

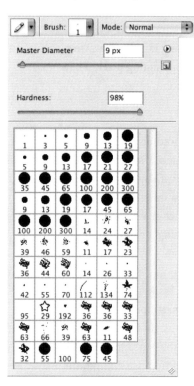

Figure 4.81 *Options for the paintbrush (top) and pencil (bottom)*

Clicking on this causes a palette to drop down, on which you can find swatches indicating the type of mark made by the tip of each of the currently loaded brushes. By default, the set of brushes shown in Figure 4.82 is available; this includes simple round brushes, varying only in diameter, and some brushes with more elaborately shaped tips, which produce more complex marks.

The two sliders at the top of the palette are used to set the brush's diameter, which controls the width of the marks it makes, and its hardness, which controls how the edges fade out. For many brush-like tools, such as the Quick Select tool, choosing one of the round presets and setting these values may be all you need to do by way of setting options. You can enter numerical values in the fields above the sliders. The diameter can be any number of pixels between 1 and 2500; the hardness is a percentage between 0 and 100. Changes only affect the tool while it is selected, like other options. If you want to keep a brush of a non-standard size for future use, you can click on the New Preset icon, and it will be added to the set of preset brushes after you have provided a name for it in the dialogue box that appears.

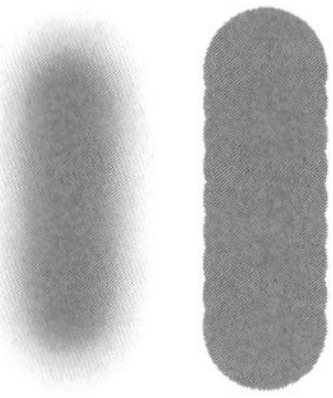

Figure 4.82 *The default set of brushes*

You can use the menu on this drop-down palette to load different libraries of brushes, including calligraphics and natural media brushes. Figure 4.84 shows the complete collection of brush presets that come with Photoshop. Figure 4.85 gives some indication of the range of marks that can be made with the brushes.

Figure 4.83
Paintbrush (left) and pencil (right) marks

Note that each preset can be applied to either the paintbrush or the pencil tool, to produce either a hard or a soft mark with the same characteristics. Figure 4.83 shows the different strokes produced by the paintbrush and pencil with the same preset selected (Soft Round 100px). This illustration demonstrates that the diameter of the brush tip is not necessarily equal to the width of the stroke for the soft-edged brushes.

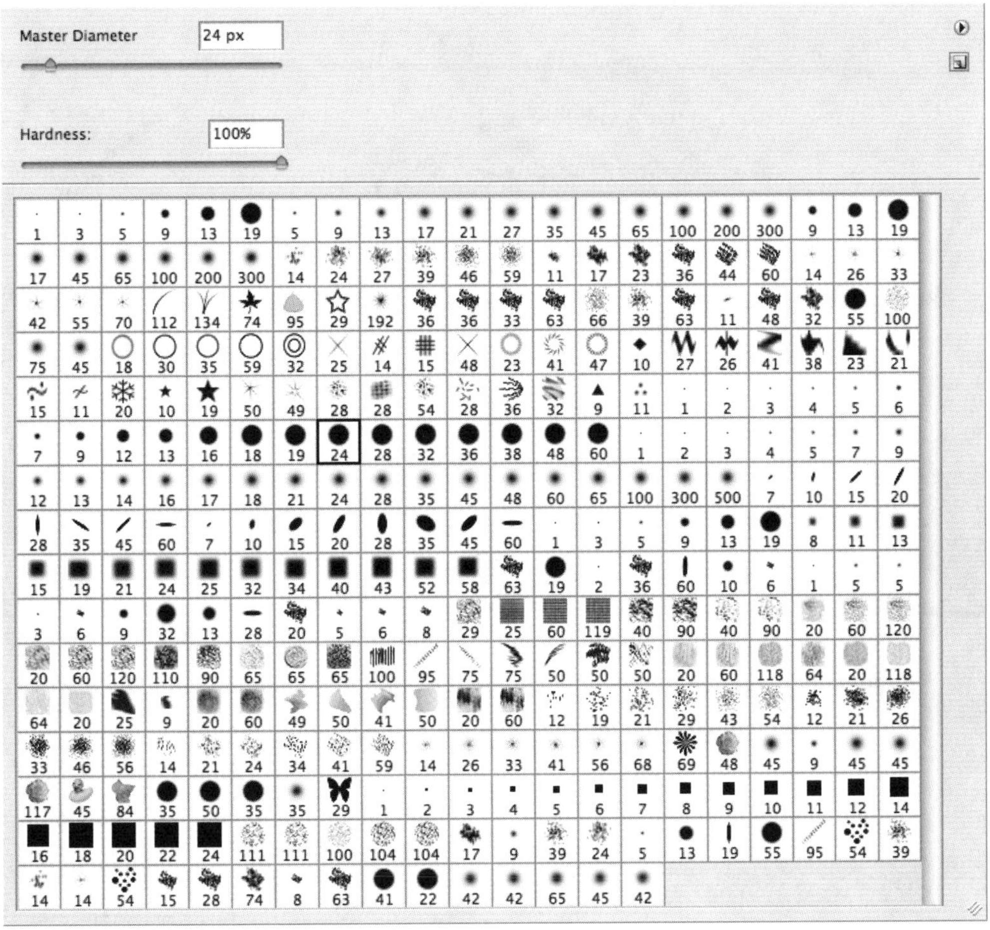

Figure 4.84 *All the preset brushes*

As you can see from Figure 4.81, the options for the two painting tools are not quite identical. For both of them, as well as choosing a preset, you can set the blending mode and the opacity, which work for brushes in the same way as they do for layers. The default Normal mode is what you expect: underlying colour is obscured or allowed to partially show through depending on the opacity, while the other modes allow your brush strokes to interact with the pixels below them in more complicated ways. Setting the opacity to less than 100% allows you to make semi-transparent brush strokes which allow the underlying colour to show through.

─ TRY THIS ─

Practise using the paintbrush and the pencil with several different preset brushes in a range of different colours, until you get a feel for which tool is suited to which type of job. Experiment with using different settings for opacity and blending mode, and assess the results.

Figure 4.85 *Painting with some of Photoshop's brushes*

The paintbrush has two useful options that the pencil lacks. You can set the **Flow** to values between 1% and 100% to simulate different rates of application of paint. You can also make the paintbrush behave somewhat like an airbrush, by clicking on the airbrush icon in the **Options** bar. With this option selected, if you hold the brush still (with the mouse button depressed, if you are using a mouse, or the pen in contact with the tablet if you are using one) paint will continue to build up around the cursor, as if you were spraying it from an airbrush or paint spraycan. This can be used to simulate an airbrushed style of painting or graffiti art.

TRY THIS

Use a large brush to paint an area of colour. Try this both with and without the airbrush option, to judge the relative ease and the different results you obtain each way. Try different blending modes and opacity settings with the airbrush option turned on, and observe the results.

The Brushes Panel

You can do a lot of work just using the preset brushes supplied with Photoshop, possibly changing their diameter or hardness, but if you are interested in simulating different sorts of brush strokes, you may want to customize some aspects of the preset brushes, or even build your own from scratch. This is quite advanced and most users will probably never need to do such things, but it is interesting to see what options are available, as this gives you some insight into how brushes work.

Elaborate changes to brushes are made in the **Brushes** panel, which you also use to create a brand new brush. A brush is just a metaphor for a set of values that, in conjunction with Photoshop's painting algorithm, define which pixels' colours will be changed in the region of the cursor when the brush is dragged across an image. This is determined by, among other things, the brush's size, shape and hardness, the angle it makes with the path of the cursor, and the spacing between the individual strokes that make up a line. All of these values can be changed.

Figure 4.86 shows the **Brushes** panel, as it might appear when you first open it. (You must have a brush tool selected first, or all the controls on the panel will be greyed out.) As you can see, it largely duplicates the function of the preset brushes drop-down palette from the **Options** bar, with the same list of previews of the strokes of the available presets, and a master diameter slider. At the bottom is an enlarged preview of the stroke of the brush currently selected in the panel. There is, however, much more to the **Brushes** panel. You can select any of the headings down the left-hand side of the panel in order to change different aspects of the brush.

The options below the dividing line in this list of headings are the easiest to understand. Each of these can be switched on or off to control whether random noise is added to the brush stroke, whether it behaves like an airbrush, and so on. The stroke preview at the bottom of the panel changes to show you the effect of setting each of these options, so it is easy to see what is going on.

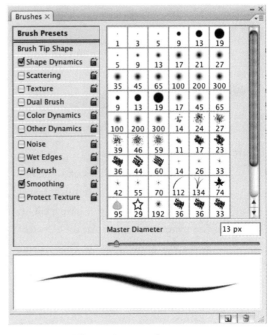

Figure 4.86 *The* Brushes *panel*

The options above the divider are much more complex. Most of them are intended to compensate for the fact that the marks which Photoshop's brushes make do not resemble those made with physical paintbrushes very closely; they tend to have an artificial or mechanical character.

To try to produce more realistic brush effects, the Brushes panel provides ways of introducing variations into brush strokes, either randomly or under the control of a pressure- and tilt-sensitive pen used with a graphics tablet. These options are set by selecting the headings Shape Dynamics, Scattering, Color Dynamics and Other Dynamics. Note that to set options for one of these categories, you need to click on the name, which will then be highlighted. Clicking on the checkbox next to the name just activates the dynamic option with the current values.

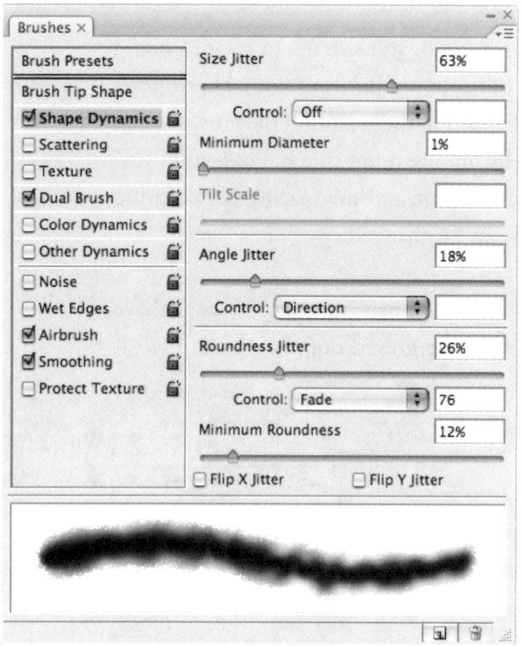

Figure 4.87 *Adding shape dynamics*

The controls that appear when you select one of these options are sliders that allow you to set the amount of *jitter* – random variation – of one or more aspects of the brush stroke. For instance, Figure 4.87 shows how varying amounts of jitter can be added to different aspects of the shape of the mark produced by the brush. In this screenshot you can also see a pop-up menu (in the upper right of the palette) labelled Control. You can choose the method by which jitter is controlled from this menu. If you set it to Off, the jitter is random; more interestingly, if you set it to Pen Pressure, the amount of jitter is determined by the pressure you apply to the pen. (You can only use this type of control if you are drawing on a graphics tablet; if you don't have a tablet connected to your computer, a warning symbol will be displayed when you select any option that requires one.) Within this pressure-sensitive variation, there is also some randomness, so that the resulting brush stroke

has some of the qualities of a real brush wielded by a human hand. This is the principle behind all the brush dynamics settings. Instead of pen pressure, you can choose to have jitter controlled by the pen's angle, if you have a tilt-sensitive pen, or by a stylus wheel. You can also select Fade as the control value; this has the effect of fading out the jittered value along the length of the stroke, perhaps as though the amount of paint left on the brush was reducing as the stroke is painted.

Selecting Brush Tip Shape allows you to change the geometry and hardness of the brush tip. You can also add jitter to these values, using Shape Dynamics.

There are two other sets of controls available in the Brushes panel. The Dual Brush facility lets you create a brush with two tips, one of which paints in the foreground colour, the other in the background. The tips don't have to be the same shape, so you can create some highly elaborate patterns of paint in your brush strokes this way, if you have the patience and skill to do so.

The final brush parameter you can select is a texture. This is a rather odd concept, at first sight – brushes don't tend to have textures in the sense meant here. What is really being simulated is the texture of the surface to which the paint is being applied. It would be more logical to associate this texture with the layer on which you are painting, but in Photoshop it is associated with the brush instead. The effect is the same, at least where brush strokes are actually made on the image: the way in which pixels are coloured as you drag the brush over them is modified as if there was a textured surface, such as canvas, beneath the paint. When **Texture** is selected a swatch of the currently chosen texture is displayed at the top of the **Brushes** panel. A drop-down palette is attached to this swatch, as shown in Figure 4.88, from which you can choose a different texture. This palette of textures has its own fly-out menu, from which you can load different libraries of textures. Several of these libraries

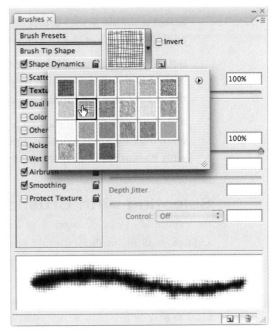

Figure 4.88 *Choosing a texture*

are included with Photoshop, including many textures intended to model real supports, such as watercolour paper or canvas, which are shown in Figure 4.88, and some other, more whimsical textures, for achieving special effects. To see textured effects, it may be necessary to reduce the flow rate of your brush in the **Options** bar, otherwise the texture can get overwhelmed.

If you are trying to create something that looks like a painting, it is obviously necessary to make sure that the whole image has the same texture. In other words, you will need to use the same texture with all your tools, so it looks as if the background is textured, even though it is not in fact. To do this, choose **Copy Texture To Other Tools** from the **Brushes** panel menu. All the painting tools will then have a consistent texture. Even then you will need to ensure that the whole surface is covered. If you started with a white background layer, for example, any part of it which you do not make marks on will remain untextured.

With brush dynamics and textures, Photoshop's brushes can resemble real art materials, which means that using them effectively requires a similar set of skills. If you have such skills, you are almost certainly familiar with using real materials, in which case – if you want to create an image with the visual characteristics of a piece of artwork in natural media – the best way to do so is usually to use real media and scan the result (unless you have developed an allergy to art materials). It only makes sense to use digital art materials if you need to combine the look of real media with other sorts of digital image – for example, if you want to paint on to a video frame.

Selecting with Brushes

We explained in our description of masks that an alpha channel is just a greyscale image. In addition to all the methods for performing selections that we have already described, Photoshop provides a means of painting an alpha channel directly, using brush tools. An alpha channel created in this way can be loaded as a selection, so in effect, you are able to select or mask out parts of an image by painting on them. Because painting masks can be a painstaking and fiddly process, it is usual to make a less accurate selection first and then edit it with a brush.

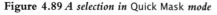

But how do you create masks and edit them separately from the image? There are several ways. The easiest way is to make an initial rough selection, and then click on the Quick Mask button in the toolbox. Two things happen when you do this. First, the mask becomes visible as a partially transparent red overlay, sometimes referred to as a *rubylith*, covering the area outside the original selection, as shown in Figure 4.89. (Note that this is not part of the image, it just shows you where the mask is, the same way the marching ants show you where a selection is.) Second, any painting you do affects the mask, not the image.

Figure 4.89 *A selection in* Quick Mask *mode*

The most common way of modifying a mask is by painting on it. By convention, if you paint on a mask in white, it allows the image to show through (in other words, it extends the selection to which the mask corresponds), and if you paint in black, it masks more of the image, with greys being treated as intermediate values. (Since the mask is greyscale, if you use colours to paint on it, they are mapped to a shade of grey, according to their tonal values.) The eraser tools (see below) can be used to delete parts of the mask, which may be more intuitive than painting with white. When you are in Quick Mask mode, any selection you make affects the painting of the mask, not the image itself.

It is common to use brushes with a soft edge to paint in new areas of mask, in order to create masks which also have soft edges. In the example shown in Figure 4.89, you might, for example, modify the shape of the mask by painting round the edge to give it a less regular shape. In more complex situations, by zooming in and using small brushes, you can create extremely accurate selections to extract objects that are not well handled by the semi-automatic tools we described previously. (You will need a steady hand and a graphics tablet – a mouse cannot be controlled sufficiently accurately.)

When you have finished altering the mask, you return to ordinary image editing mode by clicking on the **Standard Mode** button, which the **Quick Mask** button will have turned into while you were editing the mask. Now, the mask you created in **Quick Mask** mode will be treated as a selection, so it will modify any paint or effects you apply to the layer. If, for example, you created a mask with soft edges, any effects you apply to the image will fade gradually over the edge.

TRY THIS

Choose a suitable photograph – a landscape will probably work best – and use a fairly wide brush to create a mask with soft jagged edges so that, when you return to standard mode and delete the selected area, it looks as if the picture was a watercolour painting, where the artist had not painted right out to the edges of the paper.

Try applying one or more artistic filters to the result, to see if you can make the picture actually look like a watercolour.

Erasing

The *eraser* tool is used for removing colour from an image. You don't need this for correcting mistakes – you can use the **History** panel for that. The eraser is used either to remove areas from an imported image that are not wanted, or to produce an effect similar to that made by rubbing out part of a drawing, or using a scalpel or spatula to scrape paint off a painting to reveal the paper or canvas beneath. When you select the eraser, a pop-up menu labelled **Mode** appears in the **Options** bar, from which you choose **Brush**, **Pencil** or **Block**. These different modes determine which pixels are erased when you drag the eraser. In **Block** mode, a square block of pixels is erased, so this mode is rather like a conventional eraser. It is a crude tool, but useful for removing large areas of an image. The other two modes behave just like the corresponding brush tools, except that they remove colour instead of applying it. In these modes, you can set the eraser's opacity and its size, just as you can with the painting tools, and if you select **Brush** you can use the airbrush option. An eraser set to less than 100% opacity only removes some of the colour when you drag it over the image, so that it increases transparency of the part you erase, or thins down previously painted strokes rather than removing them. (Remember that it is much easier to perform precise erasing if you blow up the image to a high magnification on the screen.)

We have been rather vague about what it means to erase colour from an image. Pixels that have been erased from a layer other than the background become transparent – or semi-transparent if the opacity of the eraser is set to less than 100%. Hence, in a layered image, erasing lets parts of the layers underneath show through. If you erase on the background layer, erased pixels are set to the current background colour (which you can set by clicking on the background colour swatch in the toolbox) unless you specified a transparent background when you created the image, in which case pixels are erased to transparency.

TRY THIS

Choose a fairly complex image and practise using the different modes of the eraser to remove just the parts of it that you want to. Practise erasing both large areas and small fine details.

Use the eraser on a multi-layered image and observe how it affects the interaction of the layers, and how it works on the background layer. Experiment with the eraser's opacity settings to create semi-transparent effects.

If you know that you want to erase only pixels of a particular colour, you can use the *magic eraser*. When you click with this tool, all pixels of the same colour as the one you clicked on are erased. It combines a magic wand selection with erasing. As with the magic wand, you can specify whether only a contiguous area of colour around the pixel you have clicked on should be removed, or all pixels of that colour anywhere in the layer. You can also set a tolerance, which determines how closely a pixel's colour must match before it gets erased. Choosing to anti-alias the erasure produces a smooth-looking edge to the erased area; if you don't do this, the edges may look jagged at low resolution. Like the other erasers, the magic eraser can be set to an opacity less than 100% for partial erasing. All of these options are set on the Options bar.

TRY THIS

Try using the magic eraser on any photographic image. You will probably need to adjust the tolerance in order to erase just the pixels you want to.

Compare the ease of using the magic eraser with making a magic wand selection and deleting.

There is one other eraser tool. The *background eraser* tool is similar to the ordinary eraser, being a negative brush, which can be set to different shapes and hardness, but it is designed to help with extracting objects. It does not actually recognize backgrounds and erase them. What it does is erase all pixels within the area of the brush which are the same colour as the pixel under its centre, within a tolerance value you set in the Options bar. This can be used to erase uniform backgrounds. If you drag the eraser so its centre, which is shown by a cross hair, is in the background but the brush intersects the edge of an object which is a different colour, all the background pixels under the brush will be erased, but the object will be left intact. For complicated backgrounds and objects with complicated edges – most realistic images, in other words – the Extract filter will do a better job, so the background eraser is only of limited utility.

---TRY THIS---

Try using the background eraser to isolate an object from its background. Experiment with different tolerance values, which you can set in the options bar. Try to get as clean a result as possible.

Compare the ease of use and the quality of the results you get with the background eraser and the Extract filter.

DON'T FORGET

The paintbrush and pencil tools are used to paint pixels directly on an image.

You can choose a brush preset from a palette that drops down from the options bar, and change its diameter and hardness, if necessary.

The Brushes panel lets you customize all aspects of a brush. Natural media effects may be better simulated by controlling jitter and setting a texture.

You can use brushes to paint masks in Quick Mask mode.

Erasers are negative brushes that remove colour from pixels.

Fills

You can fill whole layers or selected areas with solid colour, a colour gradient or a pattern. This can be useful if you need to create plain-coloured background layers, but fills may also be combined with other elements to make more interesting compositions, or be used as an intermediate stage in a more complex set of operations.

The Edit>Fill... command provides an easy way to fill areas. When you select this command, the dialogue shown in Figure 4.90 appears. The pop-up menu at the top is used to choose between the foreground and background colours, a custom colour, black, white or a 50% grey, a pattern, or a value chosen from the image's history (an option we will not describe). If you wish to fill with a custom colour, selecting Color... will bring up a standard colour picker. Opacity and blending mode for the fill are set in the bottom part of the dialogue (which is partially concealed here) as if you were using a painting tool.

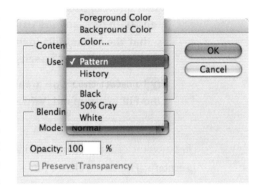

Figure 4.90 *Choosing a fill*

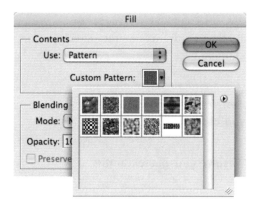

Figure 4.91 *Using a pattern fill*

If you select **Pattern** from the **Use** pop-up menu, the swatch below it becomes active, displaying a thumbnail of the current pattern. Clicking on the triangle to its right reveals a palette of patterns. The default patterns are shown in Figure 4.91. You can load additional patterns using the drop-down palette's menu, but the selection provided with Photoshop is fairly limited. Making your own patterns is quite easy, as we will describe shortly.

Immediately after you have applied a plain colour or pattern fill (and at no other time) you can use the **Edit>Fade Fill...** command to alter the opacity and blending mode of the fill you have just applied. The **Fade** dialogue – unlike the **Fill** dialogue – allows you to preview the effects of any adjustments you make interactively, so you can experiment with the settings.

The *paint bucket* tool can also be used to fill areas with colour or patterns, but it doesn't behave in the way you might expect. What it does is apply colour to pixels that are adjacent to and the same colour as the one you click on with the bucket. The **Options** bar for the paint bucket has a **Tolerance** field, which works in the same way as that for the magic eraser. Setting a very low value will cause the paint bucket to fill in a highly selective manner. Setting a high tolerance will allow it to fill larger areas. Getting the tolerance right to make the bucket fill an area that looks to you as if it is all the same colour can be tricky – you may find the **Edit>Fill** command easier to work with for most filling jobs. The paint bucket can be used to fill with either the current foreground colour or a pattern, which you select from the drop-down palette on the **Options** bar. The mode and opacity can also be set on the **Options** bar. The remaining options resemble those for the magic eraser or magic wand, including the **Contiguous** pixels checkbox.

┌─**TRY THIS**───

Open a photographic image, such as a landscape, and practise filling different areas with new colours using the paint bucket. See if you can set the tolerance so that the bucket fills identifiable areas of colour, such as the sky. Experiment with using different opacity settings and blending modes for the paint bucket.

Try to select the same areas using any selection method, and fill them with the Edit>Fill... command. Which method is easier? Compare the results.

└───

Just as you can apply colour with a paintbrush, you can use the *pattern stamp tool* to paint with a pattern. This tool behaves just like a brush. You can select a preset for it, and it has the same options for mode, opacity and flow, and an airbrush mode, but instead of painting with a colour, it paints patterns. When you select the pattern stamp, a pop-up menu of available patterns appears on the Options bar, and you can use it to select the pattern you wish to brush onto your image. You might use the pattern stamp tool to remove unwanted elements of a picture that were in front of a regular background. For instance, you might be able to remove some graffiti from a brick wall in this way.

---TRY THIS---

Practise using the pattern stamp tool to paint with patterns from the default set. Experiment with using different options for the tool.

Try using some of the less conventional preset brushes with the pattern stamp. Observe how the pattern interacts with the shape of the marks made by the brush. How might you use this combination?

It is sometimes useful to fill areas with gradients, where colours blend gradually into each other (as described in Chapter 8). You use the gradient tool to add gradient fills to an image.

If all you want to do is create a layer entirely filled with a colour, gradient or pattern, the quickest thing to do is create a fill layer of the appropriate type. The Layer>New Fill Layer sub-menu has entries at the top for each of the three types of fill. When you select Solid Colour..., after you have dealt with the usual dialogue for a new layer you are presented with the colour picker, from which you select the layer's colour, as described in Chapter 8. Similarly, if you select Pattern... or Gradient... you can select a pattern or gradient in a dialogue box which includes the appropriate drop-down palette. You may often want to set the opacity or blending mode of a fill layer to some value other than the defaults in order to combine it with other, more interesting, layers.

Once you have made a fill layer, you can't paint in it with other colours. If you select the layer, you will find that you can only paint on it with shades of grey and that doing so does not have the effect you expect: painting with black removes parts of the layer, painting with grey makes semi-transparent marks, and erasing has no effect on the fill colour, only on painted marks. This is because you can't actually edit a fill layer, you can only edit its associated layer mask. When you paint in a fill layer, you are therefore effectively changing the shape of the visible fill, letting whatever is beneath it show through in some places.

Patterns

If you need a pattern fill – for example, to use as a background texture – but none of the default patterns will serve, it is relatively easy to create your own patterns to use as fills.

A pattern consists of a small image, called a *tile*, which is repeated in a regular grid layout to fill an area, in the way that ceramic tiles are arranged to fill a wall. You can make any rectangular area of an image into a tile that can be used as a pattern, by selecting the area with the rectangular marquee tool (the feather must be set to 0 px) and choosing the Edit>Define Pattern... command. A dialogue appears, in which you can give your pattern a name. After that, it can be used like the built-in patterns. For instance, you can use the Layer>New Fill Layer>Pattern... command to create a fill layer containing your pattern, or you can select it for use with the pattern stamp tool.

---TRY THIS---

Open any image file and practise turning areas of it into patterns. Create fill layers filled with your patterns. Try this exercise using both big and small selections to make the pattern tiles.

When you tried the practice exercise above, you probably found that most parts of an image don't make very good patterns – you can see the edges of the tiles and the repetition is obvious. The *Pattern Maker* filter is provided to help you make more pleasing tiles.

In the simplest case, the pattern maker can be used to replace a layer in an image with a pattern constructed from tiles which are created by rearranging the pixels in a selected area of the layer's original content. This rearrangement is performed in such a way that the resulting pattern has the general textural characteristics of the original selection. For example, if you select an area of wool in a picture of a sheep, you can create a woolly pattern, as shown in Figure 4.92.

To use the pattern maker in this way, first select a layer containing an object from which the pattern is to be generated, and then choose Pattern Maker... from the Filter menu. A window opens, showing a copy of the chosen layer, together with some controls, shown in Figure 4.93 for making the pattern. In the top left corner are three tools; the topmost of these is a rectangular

Figure 4.92 *A woolly texture made from a sheep*

selection tool. You use this in just the same way as the rectangular marquee tool in the main Photoshop application, to drag out a rectangular area on the image which will be used as the basis for the pattern. (The other two are a zoom tool and a moving tool, which allow you to adjust the visible part of the image to help you make a selection. These tools are also used like the normal move and zoom tools.) When you have selected a suitable area, click on the **Generate** button and a pattern will be created and used to tile the image area in the dialogue box.

As the example in Figure 4.92 shows, the tile used as the basis of the pattern is not simply a copy of the selected area, but it does retain its qualities, in terms of colour and contrast. (In fact, in this example, you could just about believe that the pattern had been created by knitting the wool.) The tile clearly repeats, but there are none of the harsh discontinuities at the boundaries between tiles that you would see if you just took an arbitrary selection and tiled the image with it.

There is an element of randomness in the pattern-making process, which means that different patterns can be generated from the same selection, as Figure 4.94 demonstrates. If you don't like the first pattern that is produced, you can click on the button now labelled **Generate Again** and another attempt will be made. You can also vary some parameters of the generation process, using the controls shown in Figure 4.93. By increasing the **Smoothness** value, you can make edges in the generated pattern (within the tile, not between tiles) less prominent. The **Sample Detail** value controls the size of the elements that are rearranged to make the tile;

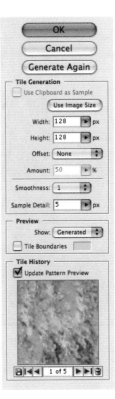

Figure 4.93 *Controls in the* Pattern Maker

increase this value if you want to preserve details of the original sample. You can change the size of the tile used for the generated pattern, using the **Width** and **Height** controls, and apply offsets to the generated tiles. The resulting pattern is not always as you might expect. Use of the **Pattern Maker** and the effects of changing the various parameters are best understood by experiment.

┌─ TRY THIS ───

Use the Pattern Maker filter to make a range of patterns from different kinds of images. Try it on pictures with natural textures (e.g. animals or plants) and artificial ones (e.g. machinery or household objects). Experiment with all the controls in the Pattern Maker dialogue.

──

When trying the **Pattern Maker**, you will probably have seen that generating patterns with this filter is a rather unpredictable operation. Typically, you fiddle with the parameters and then click on **Generate Again** a few times in the hope of coming up with something good. It can often be the case that you end up generating worse patterns than the one you started with, and therefore want to go back to an earlier one. For this reason, a method of reviewing patterns is provided.

Figure 4.94 *More patterns generated from the same sample*

In the bottom right corner of the Pattern Maker dialogue, you will see a small representation of the tile of the current pattern. (You can see it at the bottom of Figure 4.93.) Beneath this are some controls for navigating through the list of patterns you have generated so far. The left and right triangles are the familiar previous and next buttons; the triangles with a vertical line at the end take you to the first and last pattern. When you use these controls, the preview of the entire pattern changes, not just the tile. You can also delete patterns that are no use at all, by clicking on the dustbin icon, and save particularly good ones, by clicking on the disk icon. A pattern saved in this way can be used in the same way as patterns created using the Edit>Define Pattern... command, as described earlier.

When you have made a pattern you are satisfied with, click the OK button, and the active layer in your document will be filled with the pattern. It is important to note that this destroys the original contents of the layer, so unless you are just making a background texture, you should always copy a layer before using the pattern maker to generate a pattern from it. If you want to make a new layer or a new image and fill it with a pattern, then you should select the area you want to use as the basis for the pattern from an existing layer and copy that area to the clipboard. Then create an empty layer or a new document, invoke the pattern maker and tick the checkbox labelled Use Clipboard As Sample.

TRY THIS

Generate a series of patterns. Practise reviewing the patterns in the Pattern Maker dialogue, deleting ones that you do not like and saving the good ones. Use your saved patterns to fill layers and selections in a new image.

DON'T FORGET

Layers or selected areas can be filled with solid colour, gradients or patterns.

The Edit>Fill... command applies a solid colour or a pattern fill to a selection or layer. Opacity and blending mode for the fill can be set in the dialogue.

The Edit>Fade Fill... command allows you to interactively edit the opacity and blending mode of a fill, but only immediately after the fill has been applied.

The Layer>New Fill Layer command creates a new layer containing a specified fill, which can be a solid colour, a pattern or a gradient.

The paintbucket applies a colour or pattern to areas of pixels of a similar colour. Tolerance and other settings can be set in the options bar.

The Pattern Maker filter creates patterns from selected areas of an image.

Animation

Photoshop is usually thought of as a program for editing still images, but it has some facilities for creating animation too. Their main use is in creating animated GIFs for the Web, but animations can also be exported as QuickTime movies, or as numbered image sequences that can be imported into other programs, such as Flash. (You cannot save animations as Flash movies from Photoshop.) We will only describe animation in the standard version of Photoshop, but animators should be aware that Photoshop Extended has some extra animation facilities, including the ability to import frames of video and paint on them, to combine animation with live action.

Animated GIFs

The GIF file format provides for animation. A single GIF file can contain many images. Most Web browsers, when they find a GIF with more than one image, show each one in turn. When images are shown in succession sufficiently rapidly, persistence of vision leads to an illusion of movement, or animation. GIFs thus provide a simple means of adding animated elements to a Web page, without the use of a plug-in. GIFs containing several images are called *animated GIFs*.

An animated GIF can include a specification of how many times the animation is to be played (including an infinite number) and the delay that the browser should allow to elapse between frames. This delay sets the frame rate for the animation, though there is no guarantee that any browser will consistently maintain the specified rate, and in fact they often do not. A value of zero is used to mean that the frames should be played as fast as possible.

There is an added complication in the case of images that include transparent areas. Usually, when a frame is displayed, you will want the page background to show through in the transparent areas. For this to happen, the previous frame must be discarded when a new frame is displayed. Sometimes, though, it is advantageous to have the previous frame showing through. This can be used deliberately as the basis of an animation in which a picture is built up incrementally over the course of several frames. In a less specialized way, not disposing of frames can be used to reduce the size of animated GIF files. If each image in the file contains, instead of a complete frame, just the difference between one frame and the one preceding it, then overlaying these successive images (which will usually be smaller, and possibly much smaller, than a complete frame) will produce the same animation as showing the complete frames in turn and disposing of each one before showing the next. Photoshop provides an option to perform this optimization for you.

The Animation Panel

An animation in Photoshop is a sequence of frames, which can be manipulated in the **Animation** panel. Each frame in an animation is associated with a layer comp (although these comps are not stored in the **Layer Comps** panel, they can only be accessed as frames in the **Animation** panel). That is, a frame records the visibility, transparency, blending mode and any styles applied to each layer; it also records each layer's position. By varying these properties, for instance, by hiding some layers and making others visible, or by moving a layer, each frame can be made to differ from the one before it, so that when the frames are played back the illusion of motion or change is created. While this approach supports a variety of animation styles and techniques, it is best suited to techniques which are based on layers, effects and compositing – the concepts which underlie Photoshop's approach to image manipulation.

One traditional animation technique consists of drawing each frame on a separate sheet of paper, photographing each sheet in turn with a camera, then playing back the resulting sequence of frames. This technique can be simulated in Photoshop, by identifying each frame with its own layer, which is only visible in that frame. By drawing, painting, importing an image from a scanner, or otherwise creating an image on that layer, a frame can be created as if it was being drawn on its own sheet of paper. The mechanics of making this sort of animation in Photoshop are fairly straightforward, although it must be admitted the technique is labour-intensive. Later we will describe animation techniques in which the program does more of the work for you.

Frames can be created in the **Animation** panel, part of which can be seen along the bottom of Figure 4.95. This panel has the standard **New** button at the bottom and it is by clicking on this that you add frames. It does not, however, behave in quite the standard way. Every time you click

Figure 4.95 *Creating animation a frame at a time*

on the icon, it duplicates any frames you may have selected in the Animation panel, so if you have the latest frame selected, it will add a copy of it as the new frame. So, to make animation in the fashion outlined in the preceding paragraph, you could proceed as follows: first, make a new layer in the first frame and create the first image on it. Next, add a new frame. The new frame will be selected when you create it. In the Layers panel add a new layer and make the layer on which the first frame was drawn invisible. Now create the image for the second frame on your new layer. You could continue in this way, adding new frames on new layers while making all other layers invisible except for the one for the frame you are working on. For each frame, one layer will be visible; the rest will be hidden. Fortunately, however, Photoshop gives you some help if you want to animate in this fashion. If you select Create New Layer For Each New Frame from the Animation panel menu, whenever you create a frame a new layer will automatically be created at the same time which, by default, will be invisible in all preceding frames. So now, when you add a frame you just need to make the preceding frame's layer invisible and create the new image in the new frame, on the layer that has been created for it.

Instead of putting each frame on its own layer, it may be more efficient to share some layers between frames. For instance, a background could be kept visible in every frame, and characters could be drawn over it on layers with transparent areas for the background to show through, as in traditional cel animation or its digital equivalent in programs like Flash. Many layers can be combined in this way, with different amounts of change occurring on each layer. Figure 4.95 shows part of an animation made in this way. Down the right-hand side you can see the Layers panel corresponding to the frame in the document window. Note that two image layers, one of them containing a background image, and an adjustment layer are visible in this frame, but all the other layers are invisible. Other frames of the animation have different configurations of the many layers in the panel.

Photoshop is not the best tool to use for painted animations, but it can profitably be used for other ways of making animation – or, at least, motion graphics. For instance, you can perform a sequence of adjustments to a single image to make its appearance change over time. Figure 4.96 shows some of the frames of two versions of an animation created in such a way. (Unfortunately, since it is the colour that changes, the effect does not show at its best in greyscale reproduction.) In the top row, only the flower changes against a constant background, showing how you can make an effective animation by altering just part of an image. In the bottom row the background has been deleted, giving an animation with a transparent background, suitable for a Web page.

The starting point for these animations was a digital photograph of a flower, taken fairly close up. The flower was well distinguished by colour from its background, so, after the original image had been cropped and downsampled to be suitable for Web use, it was possible to select just the flower, using Select>Color Range..., with just a little cleaning up by hand with the eraser. The selection was saved as an alpha channel, because it had to be used repeatedly in the subsequent process.

The background layer was copied over and over again, with the layers being labelled f1, f2, and so on, until there were 30 layers to work on. These would be used for the frames of the animation, in the order indicated by the names they were given. All of the layers except the first were then

Figure 4.96 *Animating hue*

turned off (i.e. made invisible) to start with, giving the content of the first frame of the animation. Note that at this stage we have 30 layers but only one frame of animation.

The remaining frames were created using a laboriously repetitive process. First, a new frame was added in the Animation panel, then, in the Layers panel, the visible layer was turned off, and the layer corresponding to the current frame was turned on. (So, for instance, in frame 12, only the layer labelled f12 would be visible.) With the correct layer selected in the Layers panel, the saved alpha channel was loaded, so that the flower was selected on that layer, and the Image>Adjustments>Hue/Saturation command was used to change its colour: hue values were set numerically, changing by positive increments of five for each new frame.

The version with a transparent background was then created from this animation, by reloading the saved selection, inverting and deleting, in each frame in turn.

Frames can be selected, copied and pasted in the Animation panel in the obvious way. A sequence of selected frames can be reversed using the Reverse Frames command on the panel menu. To make this animation loop, the 30 frames were copied and pasted after frame 30. Frames 31 to 60 were then selected and reversed, so the colour pulsates from its original value, to an altered hue and back again. The new frame 31 was then deleted, to avoid holding that state for two frames in the middle – that may not sound like a discernible difference, but the hold was noticeable.

An alternative way of creating the frames of an animation is by placing each image on a separate layer to begin with, using the Layers panel, as if you were working on a single layered image. You can then select Make Frames from Layers from the Animation panel menu. Each layer will be sent to its own frame. The animation and its properties can be edited in the same way as an animation created a frame at a time using the Animation panel in the way we described before.

You can use the Animation panel to set various properties of your animation. In particular, you can specify the delay between successive frames, which determines the speed at which the animation will play back. You do this by choosing a value from the pop-up menu displayed beneath the thumbnail on the panel. You can in fact set a different delay for each frame, but normally you will want the animation to play back at a constant rate. The easiest way to ensure this is by first choosing Select All Frames from the panel menu; if you then choose a delay for any frame it will be applied to all of them, and to any frames that you add subsequently.

You can also specify how many times the animation will play (or loop) in a browser, by using the pop-up menu in the bottom left corner of the Animation panel. This offers three choices: Once, Forever and Other.... If you choose the last option you can set a specific number of times for the animation to loop, in a simple dialogue box that is displayed.

At the bottom of the Animation panel there is a set of playback controls for previewing the animation in Photoshop. However, animations will often not play back at the correct frame rate when you do so; it is usually better to save them (using File>Save for Web & Devices...) and preview the animation in a browser. Note that GIF is the only single file format that Photoshop can save in which supports animation, so you must choose this format when you're saving animations. If you select GIF as the file format in the Save for Web & Devices dialogue and there is more than one frame in the Animation panel, an animated GIF is saved automatically. Player controls appear in the dialogue, so you can preview the optimized version of the animation.

You can also export animations as still image sequences or as video in any format that QuickTime can generate, by using the File>Export>Render Video... command. A dialogue is used to choose between QuickTime Export or Image Sequence, and to select a specific format for each choice, such as MPEG-4 or JPEG sequence. Further options can be set for the chosen format by clicking the Settings... button, for those who understand about video and image compression. Note that here is a potential pitfall in exporting image sequences. If you have set a delay for the frames in your animation, Photoshop will create enough copies of each frame to match the delay at the chosen frame rate. For instance, suppose you had set the delay to 0.1 seconds, and the frame rate in the export dialogue to 30 frames per second. Then three copies of each frame would be created. If you are saving a QuickTime movie at this rate, you would expect each frame from your animation to be held for three video frames, but it is more surprising to find multiple images being created when you export an image sequence. The way to avoid this is to set the delay to 0 for all frames if you are intending to export an image sequence.

As we mentioned earlier, animated GIFs can be optimized so that only the differences between successive frames are stored in the file. Select Optimize Animation... from the Animation panel menu if you wish to do this. (Leave both options selected in the dialogue box that appears.) Effective optimization depends upon not disposing of each frame before the next one is displayed. Unusually, the only way in which you can set the disposal method for frames is by using a contextual menu. If you right-click/ctl-click on a frame, the disposal menu pops up; you can choose Automatic, Do Not Dispose or Dispose. For optimized images you should choose Automatic.

─TRY THIS─────────────────────────────────

> **Try animating your signature. Write your name using a suitable brush – or scan in your signature – and use this as the first frame of the animation. Then make a new frame in which you erase a small part of the writing from the end. Continue making new frames and erasing more of your signature until all the letters have gone, giving you an animation in which your name disappears. Now select all the frames and choose Reverse Frames from the Animation panel menu, to produce an animation in which your signature appears as if an invisible hand were writing it. Experiment with the frame delay to get a smooth effect.**

Animating Layer Properties

Making animations one frame at a time offers the greatest range of possibilities to the animator, but it is hard work and if you're going to animate in that way you'll probably prefer a more powerful animation tool. If you're animating in Photoshop, it is much simpler to produce animations by changing layer attributes over time, instead of laboriously changing the image content frame by frame. Unlike frame-at-a-time animation, such animations are relatively easy to produce.

The simplest sort of animation that you can produce in Photoshop is made by moving the contents of a layer over successive frames. For this you do not want to create a new layer for every frame, so you must deselect **Create New Layer for Each New Frame** in the **Animation** panel menu before you start. You then create a single layer and draw or paste the image you wish to animate onto it. If necessary, use the move tool to move the layer to the position you want it to occupy in the first frame of your animation. You can now add frames to the animation; each time you do so, use the move tool to reposition the layer for the new frame. To take a simple, silly case as an example, if you place an image of a single object – say, a teapot – on your layer so that in the first frame it is positioned at the left, and then move the layer a small amount to the right every time you add a new frame, when you preview the animation your teapot will appear to move across the screen from left to right. (Remember that with this method you only move the layer, as you are only working with a single layer in this case. If you were to try to move the teapot itself, by redrawing it, its new position would be the one used in every frame of the animation.) Clearly the business of moving the layer by hand for each new frame is still fairly laborious, but this process can be easily automated using *tweening*, as we will describe shortly.

You can animate other attributes of a layer besides its position. For example, images can be made to fade out (grow dim and disappear) by steadily decreasing the opacity of a layer over the course of an animation. Conversely, they can be made to appear and grow brighter by steadily increasing it. A very simple fade-out could be made by creating a new layer (this won't work on the background layer) and placing an image on it, then, in the **Animation** panel, adding a second frame and setting the opacity to 90%, adding a third frame with the opacity set to 80%, and so on. Again, you only need one layer, whose properties are altered to give it a different appearance in each frame. Compare this case with the animation of hue in the flower example. In that case, an adjustment was made that affected the pixels, so a new layer was needed for each frame. Here, we are just changing a layer property, so only require a single layer. You can use a similar method to animate layer effects, by setting different values for their parameters in each frame.

┌─ TRY THIS ───┐

Make a frame-by-frame animation consisting of an object extracted from its background with a drop shadow whose direction and intensity vary, as if the object was illuminated by the sun moving around the sky from dawn to dusk.

└──┘

Animating layer attributes depends on the fact that any changes you make to the **Layers** panel are only applied to the frame you have currently selected in the **Animation** panel. If you want to make changes that apply to all frames, or apply some settings you have made in one frame to all of them, you should select **Match Layer Across Frames...** from the **Animation** panel menu and select all the appropriate properties.

Varying parameters in a simple linear way, as in the suggested fade-out, is tedious; it is also just the sort of thing that computer programs are good at doing for you. In Web animation, the automatic interpolation of frames is called *tweening*. Photoshop provides primitive tweening facilities for layers. It can automatically calculate intermediate properties for a layer's position, its opacity and the parameters to any effects applied to it, on the basis of their starting and ending values.

Returning to our example of a fading image, then, a much quicker way of creating this animation would be to use tweening. We would begin as before by creating a layer and placing the image we wish to fade on it, but then, after switching to the **Animation** panel, we would just make a single copy of this initial frame. We would select the copied frame – that is to say, frame 2 of the animation – in the **Animation** panel and set its opacity to zero in the **Layers** panel. Next, we would select the frame 1 and click on the tweening button at the bottom of the panel. The dialogue box shown in Figure 4.97 would be displayed. The options here are self-explanatory. The pop-up menu labelled **Tween With** lets us choose which frame is going to be the other end of the tweened sequence; in our case we want the next frame (that is, the current second frame) to be the end of the sequence. (We could have selected frame 2, and set the pop-up to **Previous Frame** if that had been more convenient for some reason.) The field below this pop-up menu lets us specify how many new frames should be inserted between the first and last of the tweened sequence. Clearly, the number of frames we specify here, in conjunction with the inter-frame delay set for the animation, determines the speed at which the fading occurs. The two options in the middle of this dialogue box give you a choice of interpolating just one selected layer (in which case the other layers become invisible during the tweening, except for the background, which is held static) or all of them. The checkboxes at the bottom of the dialogue box let you choose which attributes (**Parameters**) of the layer are going to be tweened. These are the same attributes that you can vary in a handmade animation.

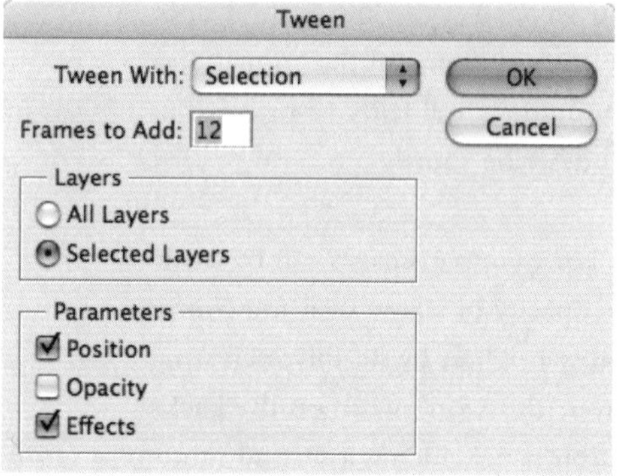

Figure 4.97 *Tweening*

Tweening in Photoshop has the effect of inserting new frames, for which the parameters that you have specified are given values in between those that you set in the start and end frames.

(It doesn't just store some instructions about how to compute the intermediate frames, in the way that Flash does, however. Each frame is actually there. This is very inefficient in terms of storage, but can result in smoother playback.) The intermediate values are equally spaced; if you want them to change over time in more sophisticated ways you must add extra frames explicitly, to build up the effect you want as a series of linearly tweened sequences.

A consequence of the way in which Photoshop implements tweening is that once you have completed the operation you are left with a sequence of frames which are in no way distinguished from any you might create explicitly yourself. You can therefore edit these frames. On the other hand, if you change the value of a parameter that you have already tweened, in the first or last frame of a tweened sequence, the intermediate values are not recalculated. For instance, you might make a fade by tweening as we described above, but then decide that you didn't want your image to fade down to nothing after all, but only to fade down to half its original brightness. If you then selected the last frame and set its opacity to 50%, instead of achieving a less pronounced fade you will end up with an animation in which the image fades to almost nothing and then suddenly brightens up again. If you wish to change the start or end values in this way, you must redo the whole tweening process. You don't have to delete all the tweened frames, though. Instead, you only need to select them all before you click the tweening button. When you do that, the tweening dialogue is by-passed. The interpolated frames replace the selection, using the values in the first and last selected frames as the new start and end values.

> ┌─ TRY THIS ─
> **Repeat the previous exercise, but instead of creating every frame manually use tweening of the layer effect's parameters. Vary the speed at which the drop shadow moves, so that it is slow at the beginning and end of the sequence, but fast in the middle.**

There is one very useful refinement to the tweening process. If you select the last frame in an animation, you can then choose, when the dialogue box is displayed, to tween it with the first frame. The effect is to add frames after the last one which interpolate whatever value it is you are tweening to the corresponding values in the first frame. What this means is that, if your animation is played in a continuous loop, there will be no discontinuities between the last frame and the first frame when the loop completes itself.

In making animation of this sort you are not restricted to a single layer, of course. You can place different images on separate layers and move each layer independently to create complicated motions and interactions. Simply combining images from different sources is unlikely to produce a good result. A better way to proceed may be to base the elements of your animation on a single original image, so that lighting, scale and so on, will match.

Figure 4.98 *Animating part of a photograph*

Figure 4.98 illustrates this point. We started with the photograph shown on the left, and cropped it to a size suitable for an animated banner. The background layer was duplicated, leaving a safe copy of the original, which was locked and hidden, in case anything went wrong. The difficult part of creating this animation was selecting the boat, owing to the similarity between the pixels of the boat's sails and parts of the background, as shown in Figure 4.99. The selection was done

(on the duplicate layer) with the magic wand, set to its minimum tolerance of 1, without anti-aliasing; the selection needs to be clean for the animation to work. (Other techniques would be possible, depending on what you feel most comfortable with.) The selection was saved frequently as an alpha channel, as a precaution against accidentally deselecting, and to allow rests. (This sort of fiddly selection is the type of operation that can easily lead to repetitive strain injuries.) The selected boat was cut and pasted on to a new layer, leaving a hole in the

Figure 4.99 *The selection problem*   background, which was filled in by cloning the surrounding area. To help make the motion look more convincing, a wake was drawn behind the boat, on the boat's layer, using a dark tone picked up from the sea. So, at this point, we had a boat with wake on its own layer, and beneath it a layer with sea and landscape, but no boat, and beneath that a hidden and unaltered original layer for reference and backup.

The animation was simply tweened, with the boat and the wake being placed just outside the frame on the right side in the first frame (using the move tool) and just outside the frame on the left side in the final frame. A large number of tweened frames were required to get a vaguely realistic motion. The completed animation has 600 frames, played at a rate of 5 frames per second. Despite the fact that the sea and clouds do not move, and the boat just moves in a straight line, when the animation is played back, the effect is fairly convincing.

---TRY THIS---

Try making an animation by moving the contents of a single layer in successive frames. Start just by making an abstract shape on a layer and experiment with making it move, with and without the use of tweening.

Find a photograph containing a suitable object, perhaps a car or train, and make the object move across the background, in a manner similar to the boat in the example just described.

DON'T FORGET

Animated GIFs can be used to add animation to a Web page.

Frames are layer comps that are manipulated in the Animation panel.

Animations can be created one frame at a time by drawing or making adjustments to an image on separate layers.

Inter-frame delays, looping counts and disposal methods can all be set in the Animation panel. Sequences of frames can be reversed using Reverse Frames.

Animations can be exported as animated GIFs using File>Save for Web & Devices..., or as QuickTime movies or sequences of still image files using File>Export>Render Video....

Instead of creating separate images for each frame, you can animate layer properties: position, visibility, transparency, blending mode and the parameter values of any layer styles.

Use tweening to create intermediate frames automatically, by interpolating the values of layer properties.

WHAT ELSE?

We have by no means described all of Photoshop. Once you have mastered the basics of making selections, performing adjustments, applying filters and using brushes, you should be able to pick up most of the other features quite easily.

The Premium version of Photoshop includes some specialized features that will be of interest to people using the program for certain types of work. It allows you to import video footage and edit the frames. It also has some support for 3D, allowing you to import 3D models and combine them with images. For scientific users, there are tools for measuring and counting features of images, as well as support for radiological images in DICOM format, and a means of combining sequences of images in order to eliminate noise. Finally, Photoshop can communicate with the popular MATLAB environment, allowing them to cooperate on image processing tasks.

Illustrator

In This Chapter

Technical drawing: strokes, fills and shape tools

Freehand drawing: pencil tool and brushes

Selection, transformation and reshaping

Complex fills and strokes, Live Paint, styles, effects and 3D

Symbols and instances, symbol sets and symbolism tools

Combining bitmaps and vector artwork

Live Color, guides and alignment, layers and type

Exporting Web graphics

Illustrator is one of the leading programs for producing vector graphics. It is the oldest of the programs described in this book, originating in 1987, and is now in its thirteenth version. As you would hope from such a mature program, Illustrator's core features are stable: the way in which you perform the basic drawing operations has remained the same for many versions. Over the years, additional capabilities have been added to the program, which allow you to create visually rich images with it, and to work in more flexible and intuitive ways than the original vector drawing tools permit. Recent versions even have support for simple three-dimensional graphics.

Although all Illustrator can really do is create shapes made out of straight lines and simple curves, it is not limited to drawing technical diagrams and other mundane illustrations. Shapes can be filled with complex gradients, where colours blend into each other, and lines may be given the appearance of marks made by various sorts of natural drawing materials, including ink, charcoal and watercolour. Patterns, varying from classical geometrical designs to whimsical lines of ants and paw prints, can be used to fill shapes or follow lines. Work made by Illustrator always has a graphic, drawn quality, but within this limitation a great deal of variety can be achieved.

Vector graphics have been overshadowed by bitmapped images for Web and multimedia work until recently, but the substantial growth in the use of Flash has led to a renewed interest in vector-based formats. Flash's SWF format has been made freely available so that other programs, including Illustrator, now generate it. The WWW Consortium has developed an alternative vector format SVG (Scalable Vector Graphics) for use in Web pages, and this too is supported by Illustrator. Additionally, Illustrator allows you to export finished pictures in any of the bitmapped formats used on the Web (JPEG, GIF and PNG), so you can make use of the precise drawing tools and flexible editing facilities it provides to prepare images, even if they are ultimately destined to appear as bitmaps.

Illustrator is now part of both the CS3 Design Suites and the CS3 Web Suite Premium, and has been integrated with the other programs in the suites. It has the usual File>Browse... command for opening Bridge, and files can be placed or dragged from Bridge to Illustrator. Some automated tasks can be initiated in Bridge and performed in Illustrator. Photoshop files can be imported into Illustrator and turned into vector graphics, while Illustrator files can be incorporated into Photoshop images as smart objects. (See Chapter 4.)

Photoshop and Flash are integrated with Illustrator in another way, too. Some of the functions of these two programs are available within Illustrator. For instance, Photoshop filters can be applied to objects inside Illustrator, and objects in Illustrator can be converted into symbols, which can then function as Flash movie clips when the document is exported to SWF.

For people creating images for print, Illustrator provides many options for controlling aspects of the printing process. For Web and multimedia work, it provides facilities for optimizing and saving images for the Web, making image maps and creating Web animations.

For people accustomed to working with physical media or with bitmapped images, Illustrator may appear unintuitive and daunting at first, but it is worth mastering because it can be used to create some types of image easily which can only be made with difficulty in Photoshop.

Fundamentals

Vector Graphics

Vector graphics are images made up of shapes which can be described in mathematical terms. As we explained in Chapter 4, the more familiar bitmapped images are stored as arrays of colour values, one for each pixel. Displaying the image just means setting the colour of each pixel according to the colour value recorded in the corresponding element of the array.

In vector graphics, we don't record every pixel's value explicitly. Instead, we record information about the objects that make up the image. Consider Figure 5.1. Suppose we record somehow in our image the fact that the object on the left is a rectangle, and we also record the position of its top left and bottom right corners, and its colour. Then to display the rectangle, all we need to do is apply the specified colour to any pixel that lies to the right of the top left corner but to the left of the bottom right, and below the top left corner but above the bottom right. As you probably know, the location of a point can be specified by just two numbers, and as we explain in Chapter 8, a colour may be specified by three numbers, so to describe this rectangle all we need is seven numbers, together with some value, which could just be a single letter, that identifies the shape as a rectangle. This rectangle is 133 pixels wide by 64 pixels high, so, unless compression was applied, it would require 133×64×3, which is just over 25000, values to describe it as a bitmap.

Not all vector images can be described quite so compactly. The rectangle on the right of Figure 5.1, for example, has a coloured outline. Instead of just recording the colour it has been filled in with, we would need to record both the colour and the thickness of this outline too. Other, more complicated shapes, which we will see later in this chapter, require more values still.

Figure 5.1 *Shapes in vector graphics*

Nevertheless, you should be able to see that, for simple shapes – and even moderately complex ones – vector graphics provide a much more compact way of representing images than bitmaps do. Don't be misled into thinking that vector graphics are always smaller than bitmaps, though.

There are other advantages to vector representations. Suppose we just added 10 to all the numbers recording the position of the corners of one of our rectangles. Then the whole shape would move down and to the right by ten pixels. (In vector graphics, vertical coordinates increase downwards, not upwards as in conventional coordinate geometry.) In order to move a shape to a new position in a bitmapped image, it is necessary to change the values of all the pixels affected by the movement. We can change the size of a vector shape and transform it in some other ways with equal ease. Generally, vector graphics allow us to deal with shapes as individual objects, which can be selected and manipulated in various ways.

The final advantage of using vector graphics is that images do not have any resolution. Since the shapes are turned into pixels by using the mathematical description to work out which pixels must be coloured, the same description can be used to draw an image at screen resolution or on a high-resolution phototypesetter or any other device. It will appear just as smooth in every case. This is totally different from bitmapped images. A screen resolution image will be blocky if you print it on a high-resolution output device.

Although its use of vector graphics limits the expressive possibilities offered by Illustrator, it provides great flexibility in working, since shapes retain their identity and can be freely edited and transformed. Vectors provide a relatively compact representation of images and they can be scaled and rendered at arbitrary resolutions without any loss of quality.

Creating Documents

When you create a new document using the File>New... command, you are presented with the dialogue box shown in Figure 5.2. You can give the document a title, by entering it in the text box at the top of the dialogue. You can also choose the colour mode (use RGB for images destined for a screen, CMYK is for printing) and set the size of the *artboard*. This defines the notional area of your image. The quickest way to set these values is to choose one of the *document profiles* from the pop-up menu below the document name. This lists several common

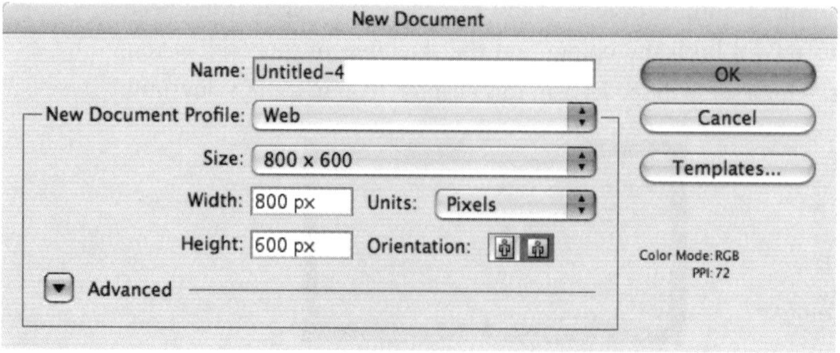

Figure 5.2 *Creating a new document*

types of document. If you choose one of the profiles, the colour mode is set to an appropriate value for that sort of document, and a pop-up menu offering some suitable preset sizes appears, from which you may choose one. For instance, if you choose the **Web** profile, the colour mode is set to RGB and the size options are 640×480, 800×600 and 1024×768 pixels. (These are intended to be typical screen sizes, appropriate for designing entire Web pages, not the sizes of images to be included on a page.) If you are not happy with any of the preset sizes, you can enter your own values in the **Width** and **Height** fields. The colour mode should always be correct for the chosen profile, but if you need to change it, you can click on the triangle labelled **Advanced**, which reveals some extra controls, including a pop-up menu for choosing the colour mode.

| Print |
| ✓ Web |
| Mobile and Devices |
| Video and Film |
| Basic CMYK |
| Basic RGB |
| [Custom] |
| Browse... |

When you dismiss the dialogue, a window appears with the document's title in its title bar and a rectangle representing the artboard centred within an effectively infinite white area. (It's actually just under nineteen feet, or nearly six metres, square when displayed at full size. Scroll bars are provided.) For images that are only going to be displayed on a screen, the artboard is somewhat irrelevant. When you save an image to any format except PDF, all the objects you have drawn are included anyway, and the rest of the artboard is discarded. The artboard does give you a frame of reference, though, if you have an image size in mind, and if you export to PDF the artboard defines the extent of the page. For printing, the artboard is usually set to the page size and the rest of the window is used as scratch space. If you select **Show Page Tiling** from the **View** menu, you will see a dotted rectangle which shows the printable area of your currently selected printer. (This is usually smaller than the paper.) This is only relevant if you intend to print your document. You can remove it using the **View>Hide Page Tiling** command.

TRY THIS

Create new Illustrator documents using each of the available profiles. Do you think that the range of preset sizes and the chosen colour mode are appropriate for the purpose each is intended for? Create a document suitable for drawing a diagram to be embedded in a Web page, setting the size and colour mode explicitly yourself.

Technical Drawing

Illustrator provides an entirely conventional interface, as described in Chapter 2, with menus and many panels, including a **Tools** panel, from which you can select tools for performing the major drawing tasks, and a **Control** panel, which is equivalent to Photoshop's **Options** bar. Because of the nature of creating vector graphics – which is basically a drawing activity – the **Tools** panel plays a more prominent role in Illustrator than it does in most other digital media tools programs.

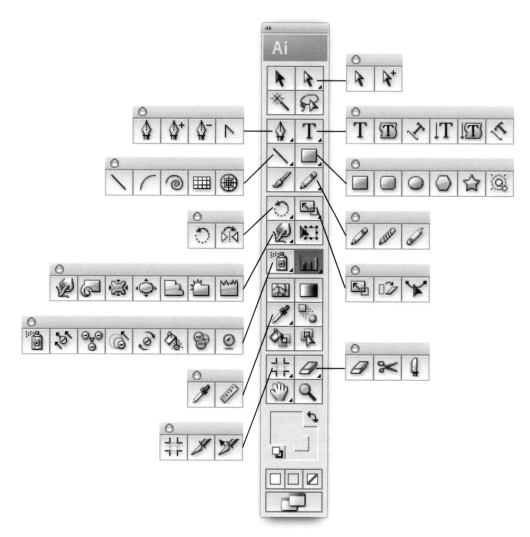

Figure 5.3 *The* Tools *panel and tear-off sub-panels*

In some cases, less commonly used tools are concealed in "sub-panels" beneath other tools. As well as being revealed if you hold down the mouse button when the cursor is over the tool that hides it, a concealed sub-panel can be torn off by clicking on a small triangle that appears at the end of it when it pops up (an interface feature unique to Illustrator among the programs in this book). Figure 5.3 shows the Tools panel and most of the tear-off sub-panels. (To keep the illustration clearer we have arranged the Tools panel in two columns, as described in Chapter 2, and omitted some tear-off panels, which contain tools we will not describe.) The torn-off panels cannot be docked, grouped or stacked, and are closed using the control in the top left corner.

Drawings made in Illustrator consist of a collection of objects: lines, curves and filled shapes. Depending on whether you can draw or not, you will either find it easiest to start working with Illustrator by doing freehand drawing with the pencil or pen tools, or by creating basic shapes with the special tools provided for the purpose. We will begin with the second option, which we refer to as technical drawing, to emphasize the way it uses constrained devices to create drawings, in the same way that a draughtsman uses rulers, set squares, French curves, and so on. We do not wish to imply that these tools can only be used for engineering drawing, though. In the course of describing Illustrator's technical drawing tools, we will introduce some basic concepts which are also applicable when you come to freehand drawing.

Stroke and Fill

We will start by considering the most basic shapes: squares and rectangles, which can be drawn with the ***rectangle tool***. Drawing a rectangle could hardly be easier. Select the rectangle tool from the Tools panel, move the cursor, which will have changed to a cross-hair, to the point where you want one corner of the rectangle, then hold the mouse button while you drag to where you want the diagonally opposite corner. (Most right-handed people tend to drag from the top left to the bottom right, but you can start at any corner.) As you drag, you will see the rectangle being pulled out. When it reaches the correct size, simply let go of the mouse button. This simple operation can be used to introduce several important features of drawing with Illustrator.

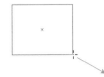

When you have completed a rectangle as just described, it will be shown (by default) as a thin blue shape. This indicates that it is ***selected***. Objects that are selected can be manipulated and transformed in several ways, as we will describe later, but if you don't want to do anything of that sort, you should ***deselect*** the rectangle you have just drawn. The quickest way to do so is by [cmd/ctl]-clicking anywhere away from the shape. It will then (again, by default) change to a black outline, made of straight lines one point wide.

Any shape has two important properties, its ***stroke*** and its ***fill***. The stroke specifies the colour, width and other characteristics of its outline; the fill specifies the colour or gradient to be used to colour it in. Illustrator keeps track of a current stroke and fill, which are used by default when you draw any object. You can draw rectangles with a different appearance by changing the stroke and fill before you select the rectangle tool. (We will describe later how to change these attributes of an object after you have drawn it.)

Stroke

To change the stroke's colour, you must click on the stroke swatch at the bottom of the Tools panel. The stroke swatch is the one with a hollow middle. If it is behind the other swatch, clicking it will bring it to the front. You can then use the Swatches or Color panel to choose a new colour, as described in Chapter 8. The square with a red diagonal stripe through it, below the swatches and at one end of the ramp in the Color panel, denotes no stroke. Click this for invisible outlines. At the opposite end of the ramp in the panel you can select black or white. Note that white and no stroke are different. On a white background, both will be invisible, but a white stroke is opaque and hides anything underneath it, whereas no stroke, since it is a complete absence of stroke, lets objects underneath show through. The difference becomes much more evident when we consider filling objects with colour. For greater precision in choosing colours, double-click the stroke swatch, either in the Color panel or the Tools panel, to access the Adobe colour picker, as described in Chapter 8. To reset the stroke (and fill) to the default value, black (and white), click on the tiny pair of swatches above and to the left of the larger ones.

┌─TRY THIS───

Make sure that the stroke and fill are set to their default values and then draw four rectangles of different sizes. Draw another four, each using a different colour for the stroke. What happens if you set the stroke to None and draw a rectangle? Reset the stroke and fill to their default values.

└──

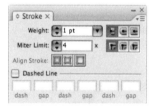

Figure 5.4 *The* Stroke *panel*

Other attributes of the stroke are set in the Stroke panel, shown in Figure 5.4. (You may have to choose Show Options from the panel menu to see all of its controls.) The *weight* – that is, the width of the stroke – is usually specified in printer's *points* (written pt), which are units equal to 1/72 of an inch. Since monitors are usually considered to have a nominal resolution of 72 dots per inch (whether or not they actually do in physical units), points are equivalent to pixels for screen display. The up and down arrows to the left of the Weight field can be used to increase or decrease the line weight (thickness) in increments of one point. The arrow to the right of the field hides a pop-up menu from which you can choose among a range of popular weights between 0.25 pt and 100 pt, or type your own value in the field.

The icons on the two rows of buttons in the top right-hand corner are illustrations of the different ways in which the ends of lines (top row) and intersections between lines (lower row) can be finished off. Ends of lines can be capped flush with the end point, projected with a rounded end, or projected with a square end. In the projected cases, the stroke projects beyond the end point of the drawn line by half the stroke width; this is a sigificant amount for heavier strokes. Lines can be joined using one of three styles. The Miter Limit value is used only in conjunction with the mitred joining style: if a mitred join (like the corner of a picture frame) is chosen by selecting the first join button and the lines join at an acute angle, the point will stick out. After a certain distance this begins to look ridiculous, so a limit can be set on the size of protrusion, above which a bevel join will be used instead, as if the third button had been selected. However, the default Miter Limit value is usually all right.

If you select the checkbox labelled Dashed Line, you can set a pattern of dash and gap lengths in the boxes below it. For a simple dashed line, just setting a suitable value in the first dash box provides a pattern of uniformly spaced dashes, separated by spaces equal in length to the dash. Entering a value in the first gap box has the obvious effect of setting the size of the interval between dashes. This is normally adequate.

TRY THIS

Draw four more rectangles, each with a different stroke weight. Use a range of values from very fine to quite heavy. What do you notice about the size of rectangles with different stroke widths? Experiment with the effect of using different joining styles.

Try drawing rectangles with dashed lines with different dash lengths. Experiment with the effect of setting different values in each of the dash and gap boxes.

Fill

The simplest fill is a solid colour. To set the fill, you click on the Fill swatch at the bottom of the Tools panel and then choose a colour in any of the ways described in Chapter 8. As with the stroke, you can select no colour, to make transparent objects. You can also use gradient as fills (also described in Chapter 8), and make objects partially transparent, simply by setting a value for their opacity, ranging from 0% (totally transparent) to 100% (totally opaque) in the Transparency panel. In this panel you can also choose between 16 different methods of combining the colour of a transparent object with its background. Unless you intend to become an Illustrator expert, we advise you to stick with Normal at first, which corresponds to the way we expect partially transparent objects to behave.

TRY THIS

Practise drawing rectangles with different combinations of stroke and fill colours. Include some with no stroke and others with no fill.

Set the fill to any colour and draw a large rectangle. Draw a smaller rectangle overlapping it, with the fill set to white, and another with the fill set to None. Observe the difference. Try changing the transparency of the white rectangle.

Shape Tools

The rectangle tool as just described demonstrates the pattern of usage for drawing shapes with specialized tools. There are some refinements to the basic mode of drawing by dragging. Many people prefer to set the size of objects by eye, but sometimes precise values are needed. To create a rectangle of an exact size, select the rectangle tool and then just click where you want the top left corner to be, instead of dragging out the rectangle. A dialogue box will appear, with fields for you to enter the width and height of the rectangle. You may use most commonly employed units to specify the dimensions. For multimedia work, pixels (abbreviated px) are often useful. You can set your preferred default units in the dialogue displayed in the Units & Display Performance section of the Preferences. (Note that separate defaults may be used for stroke weights and type sizes.) Most of the tools for creating shapes can be used in this way to set dimensions and other parameters numerically.

Another feature that the rectangle tool shares with the other shape tools is that its behaviour can be altered using modifier keys. Holding down shift while dragging out the rectangle constrains it to be a square – there is no separate tool for drawing squares. Holding down [opt/alt] produces a centred rectangle: the point from which you start to drag becomes the centre of the shape, which grows outward from it in all directions as you drag. Sometimes, this is an easier way to position the shape. You can also move the rectangle while you are drawing it: press the space bar while you still have the mouse button depressed. The partly drawn shape will follow the movement of the cursor for as long as the space bar is held down.

TRY THIS

Draw a rectangle exactly 81 pixels wide and 43 pixels tall.

Practise using modifier keys while you draw rectangles: draw some squares and some centred rectangles. Try drawing a centred square. Can you move it while you draw? (Don't hurt yourself trying this if you find it hard to hold down that many things at once.)

If you hold down the mouse button with the cursor over the rectangle tool, a hidden tool for drawing rectangles with rounded corners is revealed. This can be used in exactly the same way as the rectangle tool, either by dragging or by clicking and entering values in a dialogue box. For rounded rectangles, the dialogue has an extra field in which you can enter a radius for the corners. Figure 5.5 shows a series of rectangles with corners of increasing radii. (If you increase the radius much further you will end up with a circle.) You can alter the corner radius as you draw by pressing the up and down arrow keys, while the mouse button is held down. The outline of the partly drawn shape changes as you do so. Since corners with the same curvature look different with different length sides, it is useful to be able to adjust the curvature dynamically in this way.

Figure 5.5 *Rectangles with round corners*

The shift and [opt/alt] modifiers work in the same way as they do with ordinary rectangles, to produce rounded squares and centred shapes, respectively. Stroke and fill attributes can be set in the same way as for rectangles, too.

Rounded rectangles can be particularly attractive when filled with text, as we will describe later in this chapter.

> ┌─ TRY THIS ───
> **Practise drawing rounded rectangles. Use different colours for the stroke and fill, and try both fine and heavy strokes. Try using a dashed stroke. Practise changing the corner radius, both numerically and on the fly. Try drawing some centred rounded rectangles.**

Regular Shapes

You will go far with rectangles if you are using Illustrator for UML diagrams and similar technical figures, but once you have exhausted their possibilities there are tools for making other shapes. They can be found on a sub-panel, originally hidden underneath the ellipse tool. The *ellipse tool* is used for drawing ovals and circles, and behaves very much like the rectangle tool. You can draw by dragging in just the same way. An ellipse is fitted into an invisible rectangle whose corners are the start and end of the drag. You are not really aware that this is what happens, though, because you just see the ellipse being pulled out as you drag. If you prefer to set the size numerically, click instead of dragging, as before, and enter values for the height and width. Since the top left-hand corner of the rectangle enclosing it is not actually a point on the ellipse, positioning ellipses precisely is more difficult than positioning rectangles. It may be easier to position the centre, which is done by holding down [opt/alt] while dragging with the ellipse tool. Alternatively, you can use the space bar to move the ellipse as you draw. (Later, we will show how to position objects precisely after you have drawn them.) As you might guess, holding down shift while using the ellipse tool forces it to draw a circle. Both modifiers can be used at the same time if you want to draw a centred circle.

> ┌─ TRY THIS ───
> **Practise drawing ellipses and circles. Use different colours for the stroke and fill, and both fine and heavy strokes. See whether you prefer to drag out from the centre or from the top left corner.**
>
> **Try to draw a rectangle and then an ellipse that fits inside it perfectly.**

A *polygon tool* is provided for drawing shapes with straight edges that are all the same length: equilateral triangles, squares (again), regular pentagons, dodecagons, and so on. With this tool, the shape you draw is always centred on the point where you start to drag. As you drag, you can rotate

Figure 5.6 *Regular polygons and stars*

the polygon, just by dragging round: one point of the object always follows the cursor. You can also use the up and down arrow keys to add or remove sides while you are drawing; the space bar lets you move the shape during the drawing, as with the other tools. If you click with the polygon tool, the dialogue lets you set the number of sides and the radius, which is the distance from the centre to each corner. (This poses a diverting trigonometrical problem if you only know how long you want each side to be.) The values you type are remembered for the next time you use the tool without going through the dialogue so if, for example, you needed to draw a lot of penta-gons, you would use the dialogue to set the number of sides of the first one to five and then just drag out the rest with the tool. Figure 5.6 shows the kind of shapes you can draw with the polygon tool and with the *star tool*, which is also on the same sub-panel. Once you have mastered the polygon tool it should be easy to learn how to make stars. They are of limited use, though, so we will not dwell on this tool. The final tool you will find with the five we have described is a highly specialized tool for adding flare effects to images. This may occasionally be just what you need, but not very often, so we will leave you to experiment with it for yourself.

---TRY THIS---

Fill a page with regular polygons, stars and spirals, using a full range of colours, stroke weights, and so on. Experiment with setting the parameters in each tool's dialogue box and with rotating and positioning shapes as you draw them.

Try using the flare tool to add some exciting effects to the page.

A second sub-panel, usually hidden under the line segment tool, contains another set of simple drawing tools. (The logic determining how these tools are grouped together is obscure.)

The *line segment tool* is redundant in fact, since you can draw straight lines by clicking with the pen tool, as we explain in Chapter 8. However, you may well find the line segment tool more convenient. Having selected it, you hold down the mouse button where you want your straight line to begin, then drag. As you do so, you see the line apparently being pulled out by the cursor; when it is the length and direction you want, you let go of the button. The immediate advantage of this over using the pen is that you can see the line being drawn before you commit yourself to its end point. As you might expect, holding shift while you drag constrains the drawing; in the case of the line tool, it restricts the direction to multiples of 45°. Holding down [opt/alt] makes the line grow in opposite directions from the start point, which thus becomes the centre of the finished line. If you click with the line tool instead of dragging with it, a simple dialogue lets you specify the length and direction of the line numerically, which is something you cannot do with the pen tool. To draw a polygon, or any kind of sequence of connected lines, drag out the first side, then release the mouse button to finish the line and immediately press it again and start dragging the next side.

The *arc segment* tool is also more of a convenience than a necessity: it allows you to draw parts of ellipses and circles. To be precise, it is used to draw quarters of ellipses, such as those making up the little design at the top of Figure 5.7. This is done by dragging diagonally from one end point to the other, holding down shift as you do so if you want a quarter-circle. As with other drawing tools, clicking instead of dragging brings up an options dialogue. This is shown at the bottom of Figure 5.7. As you can see, you can set the length along each of the horizontal and vertical axes numerically. By clicking one of the four tiny squares to the left of the OK button, you can determine which quadrant the arc will be in. You can also choose which axis will form the base of the arc, and whether it should be closed, with the horizontal and vertical radii drawn in, or open, without these lines, like the arcs shown in Figure 5.7. Selecting the Fill Arc checkbox causes the current fill to be applied to the area the arc defines. (If the arc is not closed, a line will automatically be drawn directly between the two ends of the arc to define the filled area, as you can see in our illustration.) Finally, you can use the slider at the bottom of the dialogue to adjust the bulge of the arc, relative to the chosen base.

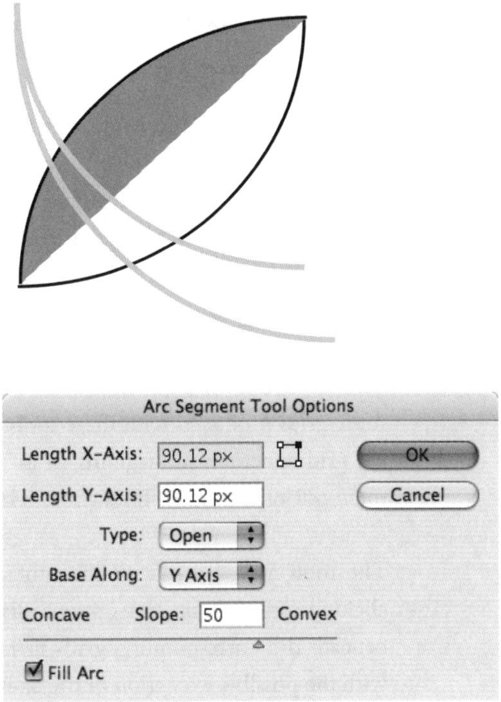

Figure 5.7 *Using the arc segment tool*

─TRY THIS─

Practise using the line and arc segment tools to draw geometrical shapes.

Try making a plan of the room you are in, showing the position of doors and windows using conventional architectural symbols.

The *spiral tool* is another one that is only useful on rare occasions, but when you need to draw spirals there is no other easy way. By now, you should be able to predict how this tool works. You can drag out a spiral or click and set some parameters. The default settings produce a dull little spiral, so you will probably want to use some values of your own. Figure 5.8 shows the options. It is important to understand that each turn of the spiral consists of four segments, so the value

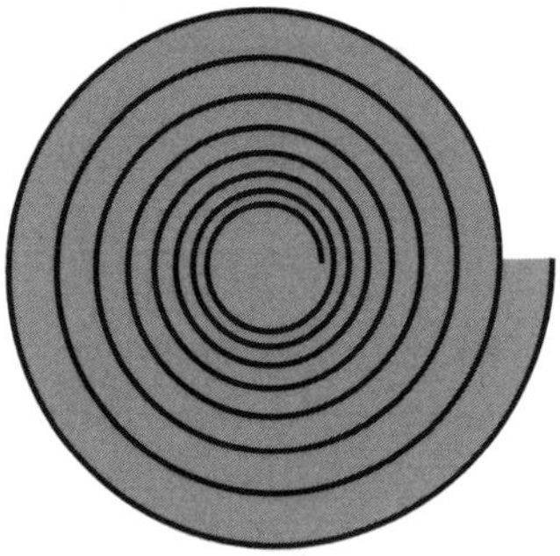

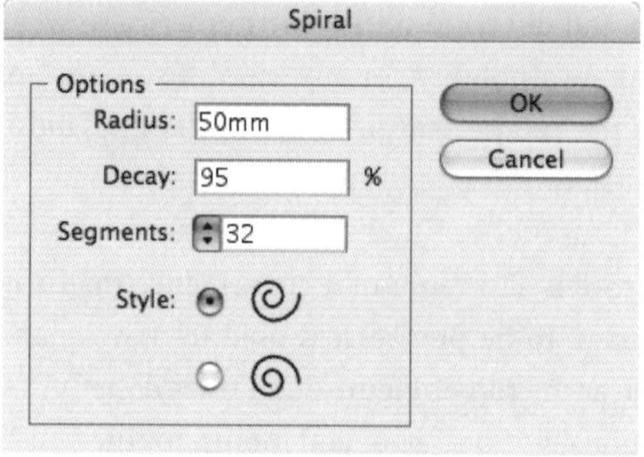

Figure 5.8 *Drawing a spiral*

you enter into the Segments box is four times the number of turns you will end up with. The value for the Radius is the radius of the first turn, where the spiral starts. The Decay is the ratio of successive turns, as a percentage. If you set this to a value greater than 100, the spiral will grow outwards from the initial turn; if you set it to a value less than 100, it will grow inwards. The value must lie between 5 and 150. The radio buttons at the bottom of the dialogue are used to set the direction of the turns, which they indicate in an obvious way.

The remaining shape tools are used for creating rectangular and polar *grids*. Figure 5.9 shows some grids produced with these tools. These are hardly exciting, but it is quite often necessary to use grid structures in diagrams, or as a starting point for illustrations or layouts, and constructing them out of individual lines and circles is tedious, so these tools can be a great convenience.

The tools are used like all the other drawing tools by dragging, with the usual modifiers, or clicking to bring up the options dialogue. The two grid tools' options dialogues are shown beneath the corresponding grids in Figure 5.9. Most of the options should be self-explanatory, with the possible exception of the Skew sliders. This is a misleading name: these sliders don't skew the angles of the lines, but skew the size of the gaps between them according to a logarithmic scale. In other words, they squash the grid lines (of a rectangular grid) or the radii and ellipses (of a polar grid) together, as shown in the third example of each type of grid in Figure 5.9.

By default, grids are not filled, but the current stroke values are applied. If you select the Fill Grid checkbox, the current fill is applied to the gaps in the grid, as shown in the lower right examples of Figure 5.9. For polar grids you can also choose to Create Compound Paths From Ellipses, the visible effect of which is to create shapes from the gaps between the rings. If you have elected to fill the grid, alternate rings are coloured in, as shown in the filled polar grid in Figure 5.9.

-TRY THIS-

Practise drawing spirals and grids of both types. Try various options settings until you feel able to predict what their effect on the result will be.

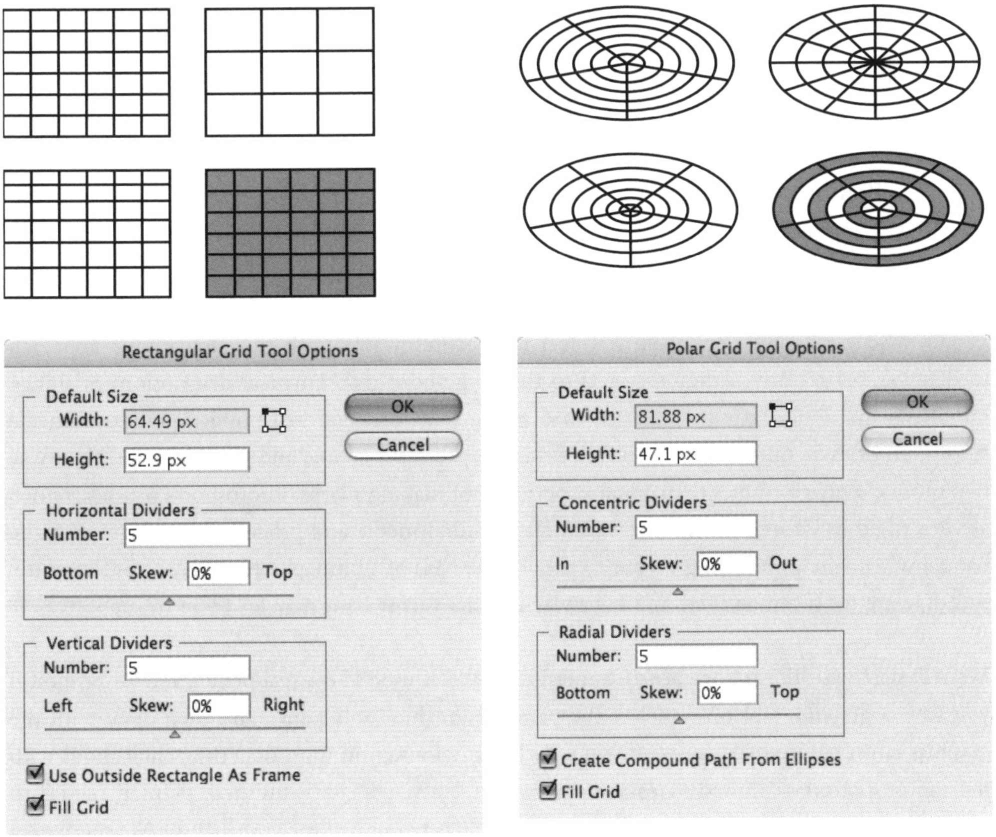

Rectangular Grid Tool Options

Default Size
Width: 64.49 px
Height: 52.9 px

OK
Cancel

Horizontal Dividers
Number: 5
Bottom   Skew: 0%   Top

Vertical Dividers
Number: 5
Left   Skew: 0%   Right

☑ Use Outside Rectangle As Frame
☑ Fill Grid

Polar Grid Tool Options

Default Size
Width: 81.88 px
Height: 47.1 px

OK
Cancel

Concentric Dividers
Number: 5
In   Skew: 0%   Out

Radial Dividers
Number: 5
Bottom   Skew: 0%   Top

☑ Create Compound Path From Ellipses
☑ Fill Grid

Figure 5.9 *Rectangular and polar grids*

DON'T FORGET

Use profiles to create new documents with standard characteristics.

The stroke specifies the weight, colour and other characteristics of a line.

The fill specifies the colour or gradient to be used to colour in an object.

Set the stroke and fill colours by clicking on the swatches at the bottom of the Tools panel and selecting a colour or gradient.

Set other stroke properties in the Stroke panel. Set opacity in the Transparency panel.

Drag out rectangles, ellipses, polygons and other shapes using the special tools, or click with a tool and set values for a shape's size and other properties.

Hold down the shift key while dragging to constrain the shape.

Hold down [opt/alt] to drag the shape out from the centre.

Freehand Drawing

Some sorts of drawing, particularly technical diagrams, require the precision of the shape tools described in the previous section. You could think of this style of drawing as being essentially *algorithmic*: the objects are created by entering numerical values or from simple gestures that have the effect of setting values. The pen tool, which is described in Chapter 8, uses a similar algorithmic approach to creating smooth curves. When you draw with the pen, you drag lines that relate to the mathematical parameters of the curve; you don't actually draw the curve itself.

People who can't draw very well may feel more comfortable with this algorithmic approach to drawing, particularly if they are used to thinking about mathematical descriptions of things, but artists and designers who are used to drawing with conventional physical tools and media usually find this a completely alien way of thinking about drawing, and prefer to work in a way that more closely resembles their usual experience of making marks. Photoshop's brushes, which are described in Chapter 4, attempt to simulate natural media and processes, which seems quite natural when you are applying colour to the actual pixels of a bitmapped image, but in Illustrator, too, drawing tools can be used in a freer way than its vector basis may lead you to suppose.

We will start with Illustrator's *pencil*. Superficially this is used like a real pencil, and works best if you have a graphics tablet. You select the pencil from the **Tools** panel, and then draw with the graphics tablet pen to make a line. If you only have a mouse, you must drag the pencil about with the mouse button depressed, releasing the button when you have finished. (This is harder to control than a graphics pen, as well as being bad for your hand.) As you draw, a dotted line follows the cursor, as shown on the left of Figure 5.10; when you stop drawing, this is converted to a finished line using the current stroke, as you can see on the right of the figure. Hence you can draw pencil lines of any colour and weight (thickness).

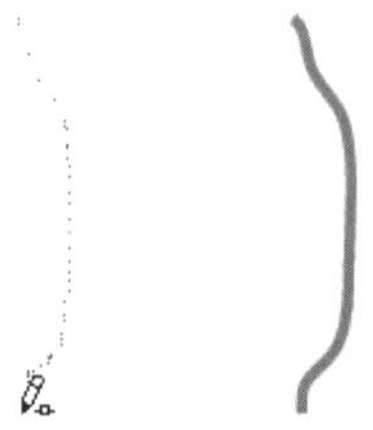

If you play with the pencil, just scribbling some lines, you will probably see that it really behaves differently from a real pencil: the finished line does not exactly follow the track of the graphics pen or mouse. Small irregularities are levelled out and the final line is a continuous smooth curve of uniform thickness.

Figure 5.10 *Drawing a pencil line*

There is also a difference between the pencil and the shape tools we previously described. Whenever you finish drawing a line with the pencil, you will find that, whatever you may have set it to before, the fill has been set to none. As we will see later, when you draw any path, it is treated as if its ends were joined with a single straight line, of width zero. If the fill was not set to none, the path would be filled in, which is rarely what you want to do when making marks with this tool. If you do want paths filled as you draw, you can set an option to make this happen.

Beware, though, that if you do this and inadvertantly set the fill to white instead of none, you may find parts of your lines mysteriously disappearing.

If you want to draw a closed shape without having to return the pencil to its exact starting point, you can hold down the [opt/alt] key while drawing (not before you start) and keep it held down until after you have let go of the mouse button or lifted your graphics pen. The start and end of the line you have drawn will be joined up with a straight line in the current stroke.

---TRY THIS---

Try scribbling some lines with the pencil tool, using different stroke weights and colours. Experiment with holding down [opt/alt] while you draw, to make closed shapes with the pencil.

Make a simple drawing composed entirely from pencil lines.

Since Illustrator is a vector-based program, the marks you make with the pencil tool must be converted to some mathematically representable form. Bézier curves, which are described in Chapter 8, are used for this purpose. The precision with which the curve approximates the movement of the pencil is determined by the tolerances specified in the pencil options dialogue, shown in Figure 5.11, which is invoked by double-clicking the pencil in the Tools panel. Two values control the tolerance. The Fidelity might be better called the infidelity: it is the number of pixels by which the approximation may deviate from the path followed by the pencil. The Smoothness is a measure of the extent to which the bumps in the path are smoothed out. If the smoothness is set to zero or a low value, a curve that reflects any jaggedness in the drawing motion is produced. High values smooth this jaggedness out, so if you want smooth curves (especially if you are trying to draw with a mouse) you should set the Smoothness value quite high. Ticking the checkbox labelled Fill new pencil strokes causes the filling behaviour we described earlier. We will explain the significance of the other checkboxes in the Options section later.

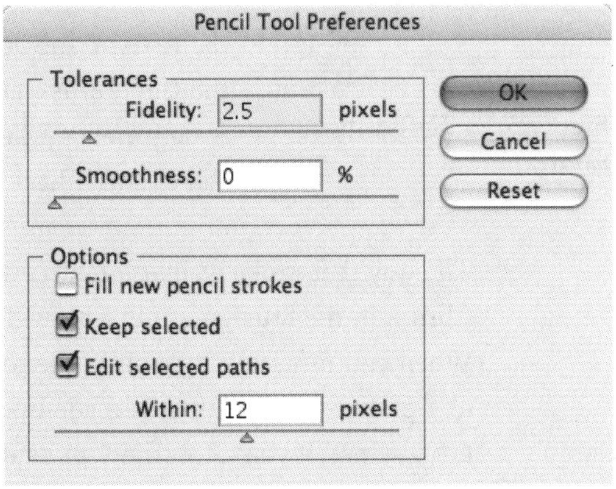

Figure 5.11 *Options for the pencil*

---TRY THIS---

Scribble a line with the pencil tool, making a zig-zag movement with your graphics pen or mouse. Change the fidelity and smoothness of the pencil tool a few times, making a similar scribble each time and noting the different appearance of the resulting curves.

The closest Illustrator comes to natural media drawing is in the use of its **paintbrush tool**. Again, this is best used with a graphics tablet and a pressure-sensitive pen if possible. In use it is similar to the pencil: you drag the tool around and a path that approximates your movements is built out of Bézier curves. Double-clicking the paintbrush in the **Tools** panel brings up an options dialogue identical to that for the pencil. The difference is that instead of a uniform stroke being applied to produce lines that look as if they have been drawn with a technical draughtsman's round-nibbed pen, a variable stroke is used. The exact appearance of the stroke depends on the particular type of brush you have chosen to use. Illustrator provides four broad categories of brush. To begin with, we will consider its **calligraphic brushes**, which produce marks that look as if they have been applied with some sort of calligraphic pen or an italic nib. Figure 5.12 shows some examples of the different strokes that are available from among Illustrator's default calligraphic brushes.

Figure 5.12 *Marks made by calligraphic brushes*

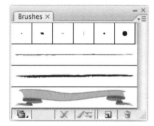

Figure 5.13 *The* Brushes *panel*

You need to set the stroke colour before using the paintbrush (usually you won't want to use a fill), and then select a brush from the **Brushes** panel. In the default configuration of the panel, shown in Figure 5.13, only the top row contains calligraphic brushes; we will come to the other types shortly. You can access several more designs by choosing Artistic_Calligraphic from the **Artistic** sub-menu of either the **Window>Brush Libraries** sub-menu, or the **Open Brush Library** sub-menu on the **Brushes** panel menu, to display an extra panel of calligraphic brushes. With a brush chosen, you can set tolerance values and other options by double-clicking the brush in the **Tools** panel.

The way that stroke weight interacts with brushes is quite confusing. If you hover the cursor over a brush in the **Brushes** panel, you will see that each brush has a stroke weight as part of its name. When you first select a brush in the panel, the stroke weight, as shown in the **Control** panel, is set to 1 pt, but the mark that is made by the paintbrush will have the weight indicated by its name. For instance, if you select the **5 pt oval** brush, you will get a brush stroke roughly 5 pt wide. (The width of the stroke won't be uniform.) If you set the stroke weight after you choose the brush but before making any marks, the width of the stroke will be multiplied by the value you set. For example, if you set the stroke weight to 2 pt, you will get a stroke twice as wide as if you had left it at 1 pt. So, in the example just given, using a **5 pt oval** brush with the stroke weight set to 2 pt, the marks actually made by the brush would be roughly 10 pt wide.

When the paintbrush is selected, its style and stroke weight can be set from the **Control** panel.

Rather than setting the stroke every time you use a brush, you may find it more convenient to create a new brush that incorporates your preferred weight. For calligraphic brushes this is fairly easy. Since the other parameters that control the marks made by such a brush are easy to understand, you can create your own brushes if you find that you use calligraphic brushes frequently.

In the **Brushes** panel menu, select **New Brush...**. Then, in the simple dialogue that is displayed, select the **New Calligraphic Brush** radio button and click OK to get the dialogue shown in Figure 5.14, in which you can set the characteristics of your brush, starting with its name. The other characteristics are the diameter, angle and roundness. All of these can either be

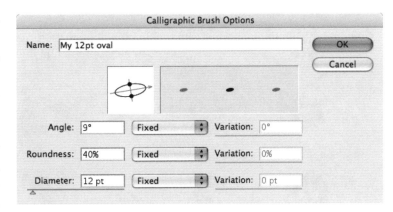

Figure 5.14 *Defining a calligraphic brush*

set numerically or by direct manipulation: the diameter with a slider, the other two values using the iconic representation in the middle of the dialogue. To adjust the angle, pull the arrowhead round; to change the roundness of the brush (the eccentricity of the ellipse, technically speaking) pull one of the black dots in or out. The preview on the right shows the resulting shape of the brush tip. Brush strokes are made to look as if that shape was being pulled across the paper at the specified angle, hence, if the shape is a pronounced oval, vertical and horizontal strokes will be different widths, as though you were using a pen with an italic nib. Using the pop-up menus next to the value of each parameter, you can choose to make that parameter respond to pressure when a graphics tablet is used, or you can add random variation, to avoid the mechanical look that tends to result from applying exactly the same brush stroke to different paths.

Creating a good brush that makes the marks you want requires plenty of practice. If you wish to create custom brushes it is worth taking the time to experiment extensively.

TRY THIS

Make some marks with each of the calligraphic brushes, using different colours. When you feel that you understand what sort of marks you can make, create a picture using the brushes.

Make a new calligraphic brush that is wide and nearly flat. Practise altering each of its characteristics. Draw some lines and curves with your modified brush each time you change a value, until you can see how changing the parameters affects the marks you make.

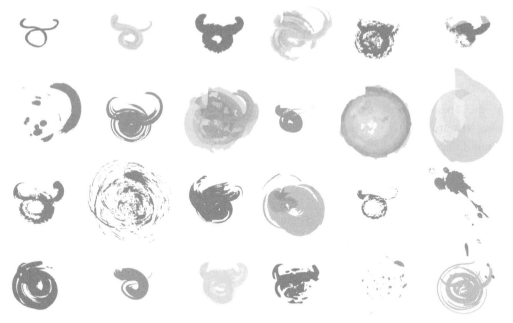

Figure 5.15 *Some* Artistic *brush strokes*

Besides calligraphic brushes, Illustrator provides three other types of brush. *Scatter brushes* place copies of an object along a path, with some randomness. This allows you to make lines of foot-prints, for example, or to place a cloud of butterflies around a shape. *Art brushes* are also based on an object, but when you use one of these, the object is stretched out along the line you draw. Some of the art brushes in the libraries that are provided with Illustrator are built from objects that, when stretched in this way, result in strokes that look as if they were made with different sorts of real art materials. Others produce more stylized strokes, such as ribbons and arrows. *Pattern brushes* provide a quick way of applying tiled patterns.

Libraries of all these types of brush are supplied with Illustrator, although some are rather juvenile. The brush libraries in the **Artistic** category, however, enable you to make a wide range of marks, as Figure 5.15 shows. The mark shaped like a roughly simplified bull's head with curly horns, shown in the top left-hand corner of Figure 5.15, is a single path drawn with a basic brush; all the other marks in the figure are exact copies of the same path, but they were made using different artistic brush strokes, giving a very wide range of results. As you can see, some of them – like the ink splash – retain little obvious connection to the original path.

The mechanics of creating your own art and scatter brushes is simple: create an object, select it (see below) and then choose **New Brush...** from the **Brushes** panel menu. You can then set some parameters, which are fairly self-explanatory. Making useful brushes is much harder, though, and should be left until you have quite a lot of experience using Illustrator.

TRY THIS

Open all the available brush libraries and inspect the brushes that they supply. Make some marks with each brush to see how it works.

Make a picture using just the paintbrush tool and whichever of the brushes you find useful. If necessary, define your own brushes.

DON'T FORGET

Draw freehand lines using the pencil tool. They will be converted to Bézier curves automatically.

Adjust Smoothness and Fidelity in the Pencil Tool Preferences.

Use the paintbrush in a similar freehand way, to draw lines with strokes that are not uniform.

Calligraphic brushes produce marks like calligraphic or italic pens.

Art brushes work by stretching an object along the stroke, usually to make marks that look like real art media.

Scatter brushes are used to place copies of an object along a stroke.

Pattern brushes are used to apply tiled patterns.

Several libraries of all four types of brush are provided.

You can define your own brushes to incorporate your preferred settings for width, shape, angle and so on.

Manipulating Objects

One of the things that makes the process of creating artwork in a vector graphics program different from using a bitmapped images application is the ease with which objects can be modified after you have drawn them. If you draw a square, it remains an identifiable entity, whose attributes, such as its position, the length of its sides, its stroke and fill, can be changed at any time. It does not become just a collection of pixels of a particular colour that just happen to lie along the sides of a square.

Selection

Before you can do anything to an object it must be *selected*. The solid arrow tool in the top left corner of the Tools panel is used for making selections. You will probably need this so often that it is worth using the keyboard shortcut v habitually. In addition, you can switch to the selection tool temporarily by holding down the [cmd/ctl] key. When you hold down that key and click away from a shape when you have finished drawing it, as we recommended when we introduced you to the rectangle tool, you are actually using the selection tool to select nothing, and hence to deselect the shape. (You can do so explicitly with the Select>Deselect command.)

By default, clicking anywhere within an object with the arrow tool – that is, anywhere on its outline or within its filled area – selects the entire object. Illustrator provides some visual feedback: when the cursor is over an object, a small black square appears next to the arrow to indicate that clicking will make a selection. To select more than one object at a time, you can click to select the first and then shift-click to select additional ones. If you shift-click on an already selected object, it is deselected. You can also select multiple objects by dragging out a rectangular marquee with the arrow tool. Any object that intersects the marquee is added to the selection.

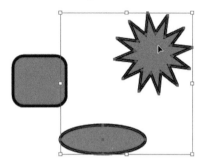

Figure 5.16 *Selected objects*

Selected objects are highlighted in a colour associated with the layer they are on. A *bounding box* is drawn around any selection, as shown in Figure 5.16, where the ellipse and star have been selected. The bounding box is the smallest rectangle that can enclose all the selected objects. The square "handles" at the corners and in the middle of the sides of the bounding box can be used for transforming the selected objects, as we will describe shortly. The highlighted dots that appear on selected objects are their *anchor points*. You can use the direct selection tool to change the shape of curves by moving and otherwise adjusting these anchor points. A description of how this is done, and how it works, can be found in Chapter 8. Illustrator provides a lasso tool for selecting several anchor points at once: just draw around part of a curve with the lasso, and any anchor points inside the area you draw will be selected. You will probably find it easier to make precise selections of anchor points by shift-clicking with the direct selection tool, though.

If an object is selected, pressing the delete key will remove it from the artwork. It can also be cut or copied to the clipboard in the usual way. Changing the fill or stroke attributes will change the fill and stroke of all selected objects. (So make sure nothing is selected when you change these values unless you mean to do so.)

─TRY THIS──────────────────

Draw a circle, an oval, a square, a rectangle, a triangle, a star and a spiral. Practise selecting each shape, any pair of shapes, any three, and so on, using the arrow tool.

Practise deselecting, first with all your objects selected, then reselect them and deselect each one, any pair, any three, and so on.

Copy a selected object to the clipboard and then paste it back into the document.

You will sometimes want to treat several objects as a single entity, at least temporarily. For instance, if you have nine objects arranged in a 3 by 3 grid, you might want to be able to treat each row as a single object, so you could move all the objects in it at once. You can combine several objects into a group by selecting them and using the Object>Group command. After you have done so, the entire group can be selected with a single click, using the arrow tool.

When you wish to select individual objects within a group, you can break the group apart again, using Object>Ungroup. All the objects that were grouped beforehand will still be selected after you ungroup them, so you will need to deselect them and then select the ones you are interested in. Since you often have to regroup a collection of objects after you have done something to just one of them, it is often more convenient to use the *group select tool*, to select a member of a group without ungrouping. This tool is usually to be found underneath the direct selection tool, which it resembles, being represented as a hollow arrow with a small + sign attached to it. Clicking on an object within a group with this tool selects it. Clicking again selects the whole group; clicking yet again selects the group containing the group, if there is one, and so on.

TRY THIS

With the objects from the previous exercise, select all the shapes with sharp corners and group them together, and select all the curved shapes and group them together.

Practise selecting individual shapes within each group. Break the groups apart and regroup the shapes according to some other criteria of your own.

Sometimes, Illustrator makes groups for you. For instance, grids drawn with the rectangular and polar grid tools are groups. If you select a rectangular grid and ungroup it, you will be able to select the vertical and horizontal lines individually. If you ungroup a polar grid, it will become two separate groups, the radial lines and the rings. You can ungroup each of these in turn to access the individual radii and ellipses.

TRY THIS

Draw a circular grid with the polar grid tool and then, by ungrouping it, try to turn it into an archery target by removing the radial lines and colouring in alternate rings in different colours.

Transforming Objects

You can transform selected objects in various ways with the arrow tool, using the handles (the small hollow squares) which appear at the corners and mid-way along each side of the bounding box. When you hover over a handle, the cursor changes shape to indicate what operations the arrow tool will perform at its current position.

When you are using the select tool and the cursor is anywhere within a selected object, the arrow loses its shaft, changing to a bare arrowhead, to indicate that you can move the selected objects by dragging. You can see this in Figure 5.16, but you'll see it more clearly if you try it for yourself. Note that all the objects within a selection are dragged, not just the one beneath the cursor, so in Figure 5.16 both the ellipse and the star would move if you held down the mouse button and dragged. If you hold down [opt/alt] while dragging, a copy of the selected objects is made and dragged to a new position. A second, hollow, arrowhead appears near the cursor to show you that you can make a copy. For precise positioning, instead of dragging use the arrow keys to nudge a selected object left, right, up or down – the distance is set in the Keyboard Increment field of the General category of the Preferences dialogue.

When the cursor is right over any of the handles, it turns into a pair of arrows, indicating that you can stretch or shrink the object by dragging. If you drag in or out of the middle of any side, the object shrinks or stretches in the direction you drag, with the opposite side of the bounding box staying where it is. The object stays the same size in the direction perpendicular to the drag, so it will end up distorted. If you drag one side right across the object and through the opposite side, the object will be reflected, or flipped, in the appropriate axis. If you drag a corner, you can alter the object's height and width, both at the same time; the opposite corner stays fixed. By holding down shift while you drag a corner you can force the same scaling to be applied to both dimensions, so the object shrinks or grows while retaining its proportions. By holding down [opt/alt] you can scale the object while keeping its centre fixed instead of the opposite corner or edge. This can also be used to flip objects about their centre lines.

If you hold the cursor just outside the bounding box, near one of the handles but not over it, it turns into a small arc with arrowheads at each end. This means that you can rotate the selected objects by dragging the cursor in a circular motion. Whichever handle you use, the rotation is always performed about the centre of the selection. If the selection contains just a single object, the bounding box will rotate with it. (To return the bounding box to a vertical orientation, use the Object > Transform > Reset Bounding Box command.) If several objects are selected when you rotate, the bounding box always remains vertical, so it changes shape in a rather disturbing way when you finish rotating. The objects are still rotated about their common centre, however. If you hold down shift while you rotate, the rotation is constrained to multiples of 45°.

TRY THIS

Draw several objects of any shape. Practise moving them to new positions, scaling, reflecting and rotating them with the arrow tool. Practise transforming objects one at a time and several at a time. Use the shift key to constrain the different transformations.

Illustrator provides very many different ways of transforming objects. We have described how the arrow tool can perform movement, scaling and rotation. The *free transform tool* can also be used to perform these transformations and to reflect, shear and distort objects. Additionally, there are special-purpose tools for scaling, rotation, reflection and shearing, which provide additional control over the transformations. The Object>Transform sub-menu provides commands which partially duplicate the functions of the specialized tools. Finally, values can be entered in the Transform or Control panels to apply some transformations numerically. This array of different ways of achieving the same results may appear redundant and confusing, but it supports different methods of working, with differing emphasis on hand and eye or numerical precision, which will suit different people and tasks.

The free transform tool provides an extension of the purely visual and manipulative way of working that we have already seen with the arrow tool. In fact, at first sight it seems just to duplicate its functions, other than selection. To use the free transform tool you must first select one or more objects, then pick up the tool from the Tools panel. You can then move, scale and rotate the selection in more or less the same way as you can with the arrow tool, with a couple of significant differences. The free transform tool will move selected objects if you drag anywhere within the bounding box, not just if you drag within one of the selected objects. (The cursor changes shape as it does with the arrow tool, to show you when dragging will move objects.) You can't copy an object by holding down [opt/alt] while you drag with the free transform tool, but you can use the modifier keys to scale about the centre and constrain objects' proportions.

Scaling and reflection are performed by dragging the handles of a bounding box, as with the arrow tool. Rotation is also done in a similar way, but with the free transform tool the cursor does not need to be near a handle: dragging anywhere outside the selection causes a rotation. Dragging further away from objects gives you more precise control over the amount of rotation.

Additional transformations can be achieved by using modifier keys with the free transform tool. In general, to achieve these extra distortions, you first start to drag a handle and then hold down one or more keys on the keyboard. The cursor must be positioned right over the handle when you start to drag, otherwise the operation will be treated as a rotation. If you hold down both

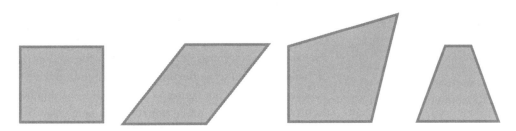

Figure 5.17 *Skewing and distortion using the free transform tool*

[cmd/ctl] and [opt/alt] the object is sheared (or skewed). The second shape in Figure 5.17 shows the horizontal shearing effect produced by dragging the handle in the middle of the top edge of the bounding box; dragging the handles on the vertical edges produces vertical shearing, while dragging the corner handles shears in both axes. Holding [cmd/ctl] while dragging a corner distorts the object by just pulling that corner, as shown in the third shape in Figure 5.17. The fourth shape shows what happens if you hold down all of shift, [cmd/ctl] and [opt/alt] while dragging a corner handle with the free transform tool (a feat requiring a certain amount of dexterity): the object is distorted in perspective, at least in a simple-minded way. The corners are moved symmetrically in opposite directions to approximate classical perspective.

TRY THIS

Repeat the previous exercise, but use the free transform tool instead of the arrow. Practise using the modifier keys while dragging to perform the additional transformations that this tool permits.

The main difference between using the free transform tool and the specialized tools for each transformation is that the latter allow you to specify the point or axis relative to which the transformation is performed. For example, after choosing the ***rotation tool***, you can click anywhere – not necessarily in or on the object – to set the centre of rotation, and then drag the selected objects around this point. Similarly, for the ***scaling*** and ***shearing tools***, you click to define the point which stays fixed while the object is transformed. With the ***reflection tool***, you click twice to define a line – once at each end – and the object is reflected in that axis.

TRY THIS

Practise using the specialized transformation tools. Try rotating an irregular polygon around one of its corners, reflect it horizontally and vertically, scale it while keeping the top left corner fixed, and so on.

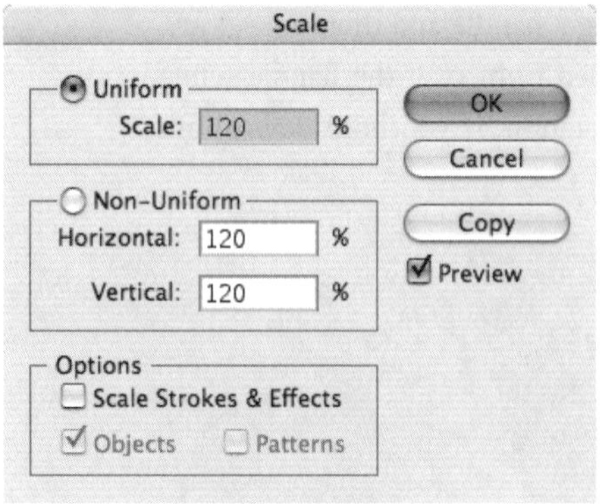

Figure 5.18 *The scaling dialogue*

These specialized tools also permit a different way of performing transformations. If you double-click a tool in the Tools panel, a dialogue box is displayed, in which you can enter values for that transformation's parameters. For example, Figure 5.18 shows the dialogue for the scaling transformation, which allows you to specify the amount to scale in each direction as a percentage. To scale by the same amount in each direction, you select the Uniform radio button and enter a single factor, as in the figure; to scale by different amounts in the two directions, select Non-Uniform and enter two different percentages. The Scale Strokes & Effects checkbox causes the weight of strokes (and other effects that can be applied to objects, as we will see later) to be scaled by the same amount, so that the scaled object retains the same proportion between its area and the width of its outlines. If you uncheck this box, the line weights are left as they are. This will change the appearance of the objects, but is often the more appropriate option. If, for example, you are drawing a diagram, you will usually want all the line weights to be the same, so if you resize a box or an arrow, you should not scale the stroke.

Ticking the Preview checkbox causes the transformation to be shown in the document window before the dialogue is dismissed, so that you can see whether the value you have chosen is right. As well as the conventional OK and Cancel buttons, the dialogue can also be dismissed using a third option, Copy. This causes a new copy of the selected object to be created and scaled, instead of applying the scaling to the selection.

Double-clicking the other tools which perform a single transformation brings up similar dialogue boxes. These specialized dialogues can be accessed from the Object>Transform sub-menu too. This sub-menu also includes a useful Transform Again command, which can be used to repeat the most recent transformation (no matter how it was applied). Transformations specified in dialogues are always applied to the current selection.

─TRY THIS─────────────────────────────────────

Draw a freehand shape with the pencil tool and practise scaling it numerically. Try uniform and non-uniform scaling, with and without scaling the stroke weight. Make similar experiments with the other specialized transformation tools, using their dialogues to enter values to define transformations.

If you like to use numerical values for transformations, but you don't care for modal dialogue boxes, you can use the Transform panel, shown in Figure 5.19. You can enter values in the X and Y fields to position the selected object at a specific point, and in the W and H fields to set its width and height. Note the chain link icon between the W and H fields. If it has little bracketing lines above and below it, as in Figure 5.19, when you enter a value for either

Figure 5.19 *The* Transform *panel*

dimension, the other is set automatically to maintain the aspect ratio. In other words, the object is scaled uniformly. If you click the chain link icon the bracketing lines disappear, allowing you to set the width and height independently, to scale the object non-uniformly. Clicking toggles the state of the link, so to go back to uniform scaling, you just click again.

The units that appear in the fields originally are those you set as the default in the Units & Display category of the Preferences dialogue, but you can use any units you like, including % to scale by a percentage. You can also enter these values in the Control panel, which has the same fields.

The Transform panel (but not the Control panel) can also be used to apply rotation and shearing by entering angles in the boxes at the bottom of the panel. The pop-up menus next to these boxes let you select from a range of common angles.

Any transformation set in the panel can be applied relative to any of the corner points of the object (that is, of its bounding box), its centre, or the mid-point of any of its sides. You choose which by clicking on one of the small squares in the grid to the left of the X and Y fields. In Figure 5.19, the coordinates of the top left-hand corner are being set. Any changes to the width and height would therefore leave that corner in place, with the object growing or shrinking only to the right of the corner or below it, and the corner would be used as the centre of any rotation that was applied. The chosen point does not affect any transformations applied with other tools, however: dragging outside the object with the free transform tool will still rotate it about its centre point, for example.

TRY THIS

Draw a shape, select it, and experiment with transforming it by entering values in the fields of the Transform and Control panels.

Make nine copies of your shape and scale each one 150%, each time relative to a different point on the bounding box, by clicking a different square in the grid on your preferred panel. Repeat the exercise for all the other transformations.

Reshaping

The transformations described so far only change the shape of objects in a few formally defined ways – that is, ways that can be easily described as mathematical operations on the vectors used to represent objects. Less organized changes in shape can be achieved by moving, adding or deleting the anchor points of the lines and curves (paths) making up the objects. This can be done using the direct selection and pen tools, as described in Chapter 8. Illustrator makes it easy to find anchor points: if the option Highlight anchors on mouse over is selected in the Selection & Anchor Display Preferences, a prominent square appears whenever the cursor is near an anchor point, so you just have to follow the path with the cursor to see the anchor points pop up.

If you don't find it easy to reshape paths by manipulating their anchor points, you can reshape them indirectly using the pencil and smoothing tools.

We described earlier how you can draw an apparently freehand curve with the pencil tool, which Illustrator automatically approximates by Bézier curves. In a similar way, you can apparently reshape a curve by redrawing it with the pencil and Illustrator will automatically approximate your changes by moving, adding and deleting anchor points. This is surprisingly easy to do, but not so easy to achieve smooth curves in this way.

The procedure for reshaping is simple. Select an object (which may just be an open path) and then pick up the pencil tool. Move the cursor over the selected path or the outline of the selected object. When it gets close to the path, the small x near the pencil cursor disappears. This signifies that if you now drag, instead of a new line being drawn, the existing line will be reshaped to follow the track of the pencil. You can start anywhere on an existing line, but you must finish on or near the same line in order to reshape it.

Using the pencil for reshaping is not restricted to lines and shapes that were originally pencil-drawn. Any path can be reshaped in this way. You can, for instance, take a square drawn with the rectangle tool and give it wavy edges by selecting it and then dragging the pencil tool around it with an undulating motion, or reshape a curve drawn with the pen tool.

TRY THIS

> **Draw any geometrical shape and practise reshaping it with the pencil tool by making its edges wavy in the manner just described. It helps to zoom in and to use a stroke heavier than the default 1 pt when you first draw the shape.**
>
> **See if you can reshape a square, one side at a time, into something that approximates a circle. (Note: this is difficult; don't hurt yourself trying it.)**

The *smooth tool*, which is normally hidden underneath the pencil in the Tools panel, does what its name implies, smoothing out irregularities in a curve. It does this by removing anchor points. Like the pencil tool, it provides a more intuitive interface to operations that can also be performed directly on the anchor points using the pen tool. All you need to do with the smooth tool is drag it over part of a selected curve, which will be smoothed out. Fidelity and smoothness can be set in a dialogue displayed by double-clicking the smooth tool in the Tools panel. In the case of lines drawn with the pencil, the smooth tool effectively gives you a second chance to determine how closely Illustrator's curves should approximate the track you followed when drawing. The best way to understand what it does is by experiment. It can do quite a good job of smoothing.

TRY THIS

> **Scribble a line with the pencil tool, using low values for the Fidelity and Smoothness, and then smooth it out with the smooth tool using high values for these parameters. What happens if you go over your smoothed line again with the smooth tool?**

A more drastic way of changing shapes is by removing parts of them. There are two approaches to doing this, corresponding to the technical and freehand methods of drawing that we described earlier. The freehand methods of erasing, which we will describe first, are more intuitive, but the technical approach allows for greater precision and flexibility.

The *eraser tool* is perhaps the most intuitive tool of all. You simply select it in the Tools panel and drag it over any parts of your drawing that you want to erase. You will see the erased parts disappear, and when you stop dragging, what remains will be reconstituted into closed paths. (See Figure 5.20.) If anything is selected when you use the eraser, only parts of the selected objects will be removed, otherwise it will erase anything you drag it over. You can therefore protect objects from accidental erasure by selecting only those that you want to erase. If you drag the eraser over an object that isn't selected, you will see parts of it being removed, but as soon as you stop dragging they reappear. This can be confusing, and may convey the impression that the eraser isn't working.

Figure 5.20 *Erasing*

The eraser is like a negative calligraphic brush. That is, it has a notional shape, size and angle, and what it removes is determined by these settings. If you double-click the eraser tool a dialogue identical to that shown in Figure 5.14 appears, so that you can enter values and choose settings for the brush-like options for the eraser.

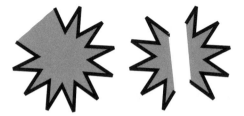

Just as the paintbrush has an erasing equivalent in the eraser, so the pencil has its own erasing equivalent in the *path eraser* tool (found in the pencil's concealed sub-menu). You'll notice that this tool's icon is the pencil turned upside down, like a real eraser on the end of a school pencil. That's just how this tool is used: drag it over a selected path and the path is deleted. You must, though, remember to select the path first. Because the path eraser is removing whole pieces of path and does not have a shape itself, the result is cleaner than that achieved by the eraser. Any gaps that result from erasing a path are automatically closed with a straight line. In Figure 5.21, the same pieces of the star were removed as in the two right-hand examples shown in Figure 5.20, but since only the path was being erased, the resulting shapes are quite different. As with the smooth tool, you don't have to be exact in tracing the path you are erasing; just drag over it roughly. Again, this is unlike the eraser, which has to be used with precision.

Figure 5.21 *Erasing paths*

A different way of removing part of an object is by separating it into pieces and then selecting and deleting one of them. This can be done with the *knife tool*, which is on the concealed sub-menu underneath the eraser tool. With this tool you can draw a freehand line, as with the pencil, and any shapes it intersects are cut into separate pieces on each side of the line. It is as if the tool were a craft knife or scalpel cutting through cardboard shapes, which can then be separated, as in Figure 5.22. Holding down [opt/alt] while you drag the knife forces it to cut in a straight line, as if you were holding it against a straight edge. If any objects are selected when you use this tool, the knife cuts only the selected objects; if there is no selection, it cuts everything it intersects.

Figure 5.22 *Cutting with the knife*

The knife tool is not only used when you want to delete something. Its role is to split an object into multiple objects. You can then move or transform each piece you have cut off individually, or apply different strokes and fills to them. Every piece which you cut off with the knife becomes a complete object in itself.

If you prefer to work with anchor points and the structure of paths, instead of using the knife tool you can split curves at selected anchor points to produce separate pieces. Simply select several anchor points, with the direct selection tool or the lasso, and click the icon on the Control panel for splitting a path at selected

Figure 5.23 *A path split at anchor points*

anchor points. For instance, we took the star in Figure 5.23 to pieces just by drawing roughly round the top right quadrant with the lasso, splitting the path at the anchor points that we had selected by doing so, and then pulling the pieces of path apart. You could delete parts of a path by splitting it in this way and then selecting and deleting pieces, but you can also click the icon for removing selected anchor points on the Control panel, which achieves the same result.

You can split a path between anchor points using the *scissors tool*. After selecting the tool (which is found concealed under the eraser tool), when you click anywhere on an open, unfilled path it will be split into two paths, which can be selected separately. Clicking again with the scissors tool splits it into more pieces. You can then select each new path individually and move or delete it or apply different strokes. If you want to split a closed path, it is necessary to cut it in two places. After cutting you will find that one of the two resulting paths is left selected. It is almost always not the one you want to select.

---TRY THIS---

Draw some filled shapes and some open paths, and practise deleting parts of them using the eraser tool and the knife tool.

Try splitting a path both at selected anchor points and between anchor points (without using the knife tool), using the methods we have just described.

Using the scissors and knife tools, separate some filled shapes into pieces and alter the separated pieces by means of different transformations and by changing their fills and strokes. Move some pieces to new positions.

Appearance

You will often want to change objects in other ways besides altering their geometry. You might, for instance, want to change their stroke and fill. This can be done, as we mentioned already, by selecting the object and then changing values in the Stroke and Color panels, or by clicking a swatch. When changing colours, you must first indicate whether you are changing the stroke or fill by clicking on the corresponding swatch at the bottom of the Tools panel or in the Color panel, just as you would if you were setting the values before starting to draw a shape.

There is an analogy here that will be familiar if you use a word processor, where you can apply different styles, such as italicization or underlining, to words in a document. Whenever you have some words selected, choosing a style from the toolbar or a menu causes that style to be applied to the selected words. If nothing is selected, choosing a style causes anything you type subsequently to be displayed in that style. Similarly, in Illustrator, if you have already selected some objects, any settings you choose for stroke and fill will be applied to the selected objects, but if nothing is selected, the values will be used for the next object you draw.

Complex Fills and Strokes

We have said that you can change the fill and stroke of objects, but we have not yet described all the different sorts of fill and stroke that Illustrator provides, nor all the ways of applying them.

Gradient Fills

The flat areas of solid colour that result from choosing a single colour to apply as a fill are only suitable for certain styles of illustration. Sometimes, more realistic and subtle effects rely on continuous tonal variation. While vector drawings cannot easily achieve the tonal subtlety of photographs and other bitmapped images, the use of *gradient fills* extends their expressive range considerably, at least into the realm of airbrushed painting. Gradient fills are often more effective when they are applied to objects whose stroke has no colour.

We describe how to create and apply gradient fills using the Gradient panel in Chapter 8.

TRY THIS

Draw several different shapes, both with the shape tools and using the pen or pencil. Select each shape in turn and practise changing its stroke and fill.

Apply linear and radial gradients to each shape (refer to Chapter 8).

What happens if you select several objects and change the stroke and fill?

When you apply a gradient fill, it extends to the edges of the object you apply it to, and at the angle specified. If you want to set different end points or change the angle of a linear gradient while looking at it in context and without defining a new gradient, you

Figure 5.24 *Using the gradient tool*

can do so using the *gradient tool*. You must start by filling an object with a linear gradient fill in the usual way, as shown on the left of Figure 5.24. You then select the object and pick up the gradient tool, which you position at the point where you want the gradient to begin. Next, drag in the direction you want the gradient to fade, letting go of the mouse button at the point you want the gradient to end at. Figure 5.24 illustrates the whole process.

The gradient tool can also be used to do something that you can't do in any other way: apply a gradient so that it fades across several different objects. If you select more than one object and apply a gradient fill, each object will be filled with its own gradient, as shown in the top row of Figure 5.25. If you then select all the objects and drag the gradient tool through them, the gradient will be spread across the whole set of objects, as in the lower row of Figure 5.25.

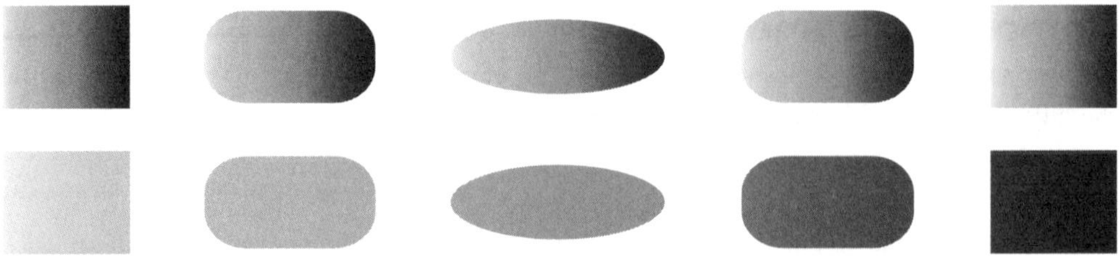

Figure 5.25 *Applying a gradient to several selected objects (top) and across them all (bottom)*

Figure 5.26 *A mesh*

The most elaborate and the most natural-looking fills are produced using Illustrator's *mesh tool*. When you click inside an object with this tool, a net-like **mesh** is created, which divides the object into four segments, with curves that meet at the point where you clicked. If you select one of the anchor points on this mesh, again by clicking with the mesh tool, you can set a colour in the usual way. A two-dimensional blend of colours is produced around the point. You can set the colours of as many points on the mesh as you like in this way. If you click within one of the sub-regions of the mesh with the tool, it will be sub-divided into its own mesh, and you can then set colours at the points of the sub-mesh. (See Figure 5.26.) You can reshape the mesh at any time by moving its anchor points and their direction lines. (You use the mesh tool like the direct selection tool for this purpose, as described in Chapter 8.) It is much easier to appreciate the mesh tool by experimenting with it than by reading about it. The drawing on the left of Figure 5.27 shows a complex example of the mesh tool in action; a detail of part of the mesh is shown on the right.

---TRY THIS---

Draw a large, simple shape, such as an ellipse. Practise using the mesh tool to add a complex fill to it. (You may want to set the stroke to nothing.) Experiment with reshaping the mesh and adding extra mesh points. When you think you can see what the tool is doing, try to use it deliberately to fill your shape with a specific blend of coloured areas that you have imagined.

Strokes

We have seen that strokes can be made with calligraphic brushes. Brush strokes can also be applied to existing objects. By now, you can probably guess how to do so: you select an object and then click a brush in the **Brushes** panel. Thus, you can easily draw one of the geometrical shapes, such as a circle, and stroke it with a calligraphic or an art brush to make it appear to be drawn with ink or some other natural medium. You don't have to draw it by hand with brush strokes.

As we remarked earlier, the stroke weight of brushes is a part of their definition, and the marks you make with a brush are scaled up by any weight you set explicitly. Once you have applied a brush stroke you can alter its weight using the **Stroke** panel, as you do for other, uniform strokes.

Figure 5.27 *A complex mesh fill*

The value in the panel will be used to scale the brush stroke in the same way. Figure 5.28 shows a square that has been stroked with a palette knife art brush. The version at the top uses the weight as it comes, which is treated as a default 1 pt stroke; the one below has had its weight reduced to 0.5 pt. You can also apply colour to a brush stroke in the usual way.

Remember that, if after you have applied some special strokes and fills you want to revert to the default of a black 1 pt stroke and a plain white fill, you can just click the small black and white squares to the left of the stroke and fill swatches at the bottom of the Tools panel.

Although art brushes permit you to create strokes with many different sorts of apppearance, you can only achieve certain effects by their use. To make an even greater range of marks, you can convert strokes into filled shapes. With an object selected, choose Object>Expand..., and accept the defaults in the dialogue box that is displayed. The single object will be replaced by a group, consisting of two objects: the original fill and the original stroke. Neither of these is stroked, each has its fill set to its original colour. If you ungroup them, you can separate them, and apply a fill, such as a gradient, to the original stroke. You will recall that it is not possible to build an art brush from a shape filled with a gradient, so gradient strokes cannot be achieved directly. Figure 5.29 shows a simple example. A rectangle with a relatively wide stroke was expanded and ungrouped. The former stroke, now a filled object the shape of an empty picture frame, was filled with a linear gradient, and the fill was dragged away from it.

Figure 5.28 *Brush strokes applied to a shape*

Figure 5.29 *An expanded object*

Live Paint

People who are accustomed to working with natural media or with bitmapped images in Photoshop can find it difficult to get used to working with vector images made out of discrete objects. For instance, consider Figure 5.30. The underlying design, shown at the top left, consists of a triangle on top of an ellipse – two objects. If you select and fill each one in turn, you will end up with something like the design in the top right. However, suppose you had drawn this in pencil and wanted to paint it: you would see three distinct regions and it would be quite natural to colour them in like the version at the bottom left.

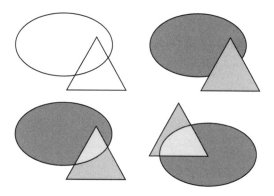

Figure 5.30 *Colouring overlapping objects*

Illustrator's **Pathfinder** panel, shown in Figure 5.31, provides a long-established way of dealing with such situations. Its purpose is to create one or more new objects out of two existing ones. To use it, you select a pair of overlapping objects, and then click on one of the buttons in the panel; the icons indicate how the two objects will be combined. The result isn't always quite what you expect, but usually you can quite quickly find the right way of combining a pair of shapes to obtain a result that – as in this example – would be hard to draw from scratch.

Figure 5.31 *The* Pathfinder *panel*

The top row of buttons in the **Pathfinder** panel actually apply **Shape Modes**, or *effects*, which we will discuss shortly. In brief, when you apply an effect, the original shapes are still available, but they look as though they have been combined. Clicking the **Expand** button actually changes the objects that you have combined in this way. If the combination produces two or more objects, they are grouped; to get at the individual objects you must ungroup them.

Returning to Figure 5.30, to colour the two shapes in the way shown at the bottom left, you would have had to split the ellipse into two objects using the **Pathfinder** panel's divide button, ungroup the result, and apply a fill to each of the three objects thus produced. This is tedious, but it does work. However, if you wanted to move the triangle, as shown at the bottom right of the figure, you would have had to undo everything and start all over again.

┌─TRY THIS───┐

Draw any two shapes, making sure that they overlap. Select them, then combine them in all the ways that the Pathfinder panel provides. Try expanding the top-row combinations, and see what happens. Where a group of objects is created, ungroup them and move them apart so you can see exactly what shapes have been produced and how they relate to the function of the buttons.

└──┘

Live Paint is provided to make colouring areas of a vector graphics image much easier. It lets you apply fills and strokes to an image in a natural way that corresponds to the shapes you actually see in front of you, rather than the vector objects they are made from.

To start using Live Paint you must first select some objects (it doesn't make much sense to use Live Paint with a single object) and turn them into a *Live Paint group*. There are two ways of doing this. Either select *Make* from the *Object>Live Paint* sub-menu, or just pick up the *Live Paint bucket* from the Tools panel and click in the selection. (A helpful note will pop up to tell you that you can do this when the tool is in the selected area.) Once you have created your Live Paint group, the Live Paint bucket is the tool you use to colour it in.

When you move the Live Paint bucket over a Live Paint group, red outlines are drawn to show you the edges of the region that you can fill, as illustrated in Figure 5.32. (The red outlines in the figure define an area in the centre of the plant; this is not very clear in this greyscale reproduction.) Clicking within the region causes it to be filled with the current fill colour, gradient or pattern. It is quite easy to colour a picture made from many overlapping shapes in this way, as Figure 5.33 illustrates.

Figure 5.32 *Regions in a Live Paint group*

By default, the Live Paint bucket only applies fills. If you want to apply strokes to the edges of the regions making up a Live Paint group, just shift-click an edge. The current settings for stroke colour, width and dashes are used. (Pattern and art brushes cannot be applied in this way.)

┌─TRY THIS───┐

Draw four rectangles, positioned so that they overlap with an area common to all four (which means that there will also be overlaps between pairs of rectangles). Convert them into a Live Paint group and practise using the Live Paint bucket to fill and stroke the regions and edges.

If you are practised at freehand drawing, draw a simple illustration in outline, and colour it in using Live Paint.

└──┘

Figure 5.33 *A suitable job for Live Paint*

A Live Paint group is a special sort of object, but it and its component objects can be manipulated in some ways as normal objects. In particular, clicking once with the arrow tool selects the whole Live Paint group like an ordinary group, allowing you to move, scale or rotate it by dragging. Clicking on one of the objects in the Live Paint group with the direct select tool (white arrow) allows you to move that single object (but not to transform it in any other way) by dragging. When you move an object within a Live Paint Group, the fills automatically transform themselves to accommodate its new position. For example, in Figure 5.30, the final version of the design (in the bottom right-hand corner) was made simply by dragging the triangle to a new position.

A Live Paint group can be altered in other ways, using the ***Live Paint select tool***. This allows you to select the regions and their edges within a Live Paint group. (Remember that while you are live painting, these do not correspond to the actual objects in the group.) You can delete edges after selecting them; any fills will reconfigure themselves to the new arrangement, as if they had flowed through the gap where the edge had been removed.

Once you have finished with Live Paint, you can turn the group back into a conventional group of Illustrator objects. Simply select Expand from the Object>Live Paint sub-menu. Alternatively, selecting Release from this sub-menu gives you back your original objects, with a default stroke (0.5 pt black) and no fill.

Live Paint is especially useful for illustrators and animators who want to work in a way similar to the traditional method of creating outline drawings, usually in ink, and then colouring them in.

─TRY THIS─

Go back to your overlapping rectangles and experiment with moving each rectangle within the Live Paint group, observing how the fills and strokes accommodate your changes. Use the Live Paint select tool to select and delete some edges, again observing how the strokes change.

Expand any Live Paint group and move some of its constituent objects (you will have to ungroup, possibly more than once). This time, observe how the fills don't change. Release the group and see it return to its constituent objects.

DON'T FORGET

Modify existing gradient fills or apply them across several objects using the gradient tool.

Use the mesh tool to create complex two-dimensional blends of colour.

Apply brush strokes to existing paths using the Brushes panel.

Expand objects to turn the stroke into an independent filled shape which can be separated from the fill.

Make Live Paint groups from overlapping objects and fill regions using the Live Paint bucket instead of breaking them into individual objects using the Pathfinder panel.

When you select a region within a Live Paint group and move it, the fill reflows to accommodate the new arrangement of overlapping regions.

Expand a Live Paint group to turn it back into a group of conventional objects.

Effects, Filters and Styles

Vector graphics lend themselves to a style of working in which simple outlines are created and then decorated with stroke and fill, transformed and reshaped to produce a final drawing. In Illustrator, this approach can be taken a step further, by applying various *effects*. Very broadly speaking, there are two classes of effect that can be applied. First, there are shape distortions brought about by a systematic or random adjustment of anchor points. Second, there are "artistic" effects which alter the appearance of objects to look more like they were made with natural media. Figure 5.34 shows some examples of both kinds of effects applied to a simple hexagon.

These effects appear in two different places: on the Filter menu and on the Effect menu. There are important differences between the two. Filters permanently change an object. Effects are stored with the object as instructions to be obeyed when the object is displayed, but the object itself remains unchanged, so effects can be removed, or have their parameters reset, at any time. This is sometimes expressed by saying that effects change appearance but not structure. There is a way

Figure 5.34 *Effects applied to a simple shape*

of demonstrating the difference dramatically. The View>Outline and View>Preview commands allow you to switch between displaying the outlines of the shapes in your artwork and displaying them as they would appear when printed. If the first variation in Figure 5.34 had been produced by applying a filter (Filter>Distort>Pucker & Bloat...), in outline mode the object would have the same decorative shape as it does in preview mode and in the illustration shown here. But in fact it was produced by applying an effect (Effect>Distort & Transform>Pucker & Bloat...), so in outline mode the object would just be shown as a regular hexagon, exactly like the original shape (shown to its left). An effect is a property of the shape, like its stroke and fill.

Furthermore, some filters – mostly the "artistic" ones, that produce results like those shown on the lower row of Figure 5.34 – can only be applied to an object after it has been *rasterized*, that is, converted to a bitmap. (Use the command Object>Rasterize....) Once that has been done, the object can no longer be freely edited in the way we have been describing. It becomes frozen as a pattern of pixels. With effects, however, this does not happen. The rasterization is deferred until the object is actually displayed. Internally, it remains a vector object and it can still be edited.

In short, effects are superior to filters, which we will describe no further beyond pointing out that they are an older mechanism for achieving the same visual result as effects.

When you select an effect from one of the Effect menu's sub-menus, a dialogue box opens, in which you can set parameters for the effect, such as the amount of bloating or the frequency of zig-zags. Often these values are set with a slider. Most of these dialogues have a Preview checkbox, which allows you to see what happens when you alter a value. It is very much easier to assess the effect of a change by previewing it in this way than by trying to understand exactly how changing the value affects the algorithm used to achieve the effect, and what the result will look like.

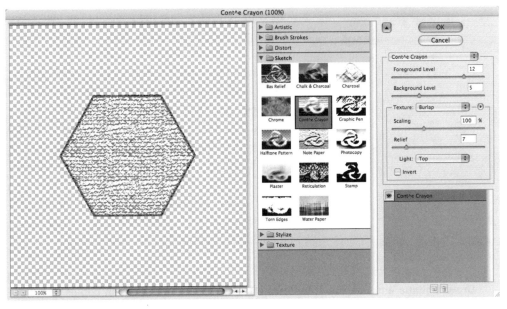

Figure 5.35 *The effect gallery*

The lower half of the **Effects** menu is headed **Photoshop Effects**. As this suggests, the effects you can apply are the same as some of Photoshop's filters. Most of them can be applied through the *effect gallery*, shown in Figure 5.35. (The effect gallery is identical to Photoshop's filter gallery, which is described in more detail in Chapter 4; it is implemented as a plug-in for Illustrator.) As you can see in Figure 5.35, the effects are arranged in groups, which you can collapse or expand. As well as displaying the controls for setting parameter values, the effect gallery provides a large preview of the effect applied to your object. Each available effect is shown as a small icon which is supposed to convey an impression of what that effect does; you apply an effect by clicking on the icon and then adjusting the parameters. Once you are happy with an effect, click OK.

---TRY THIS---

Draw two ellipses. Apply the pucker and bloat filter to one and the pucker and bloat effect to the other. Use outline view to see the difference between them.

Practise applying effects to simple shapes. Try all the available effects, including the Photoshop effects, and experiment with their parameters.

Experiment with applying two or more effects to the same object. Does it matter which order you apply the effects in?

The "lazy evaluation" mechanism, which allows objects to remain editable after effects have been applied to them, has been extended to transformations as well. The command **Effect>Distort & Transform>Transform...** brings up the dialogue box shown in Figure 5.36, which allows you to

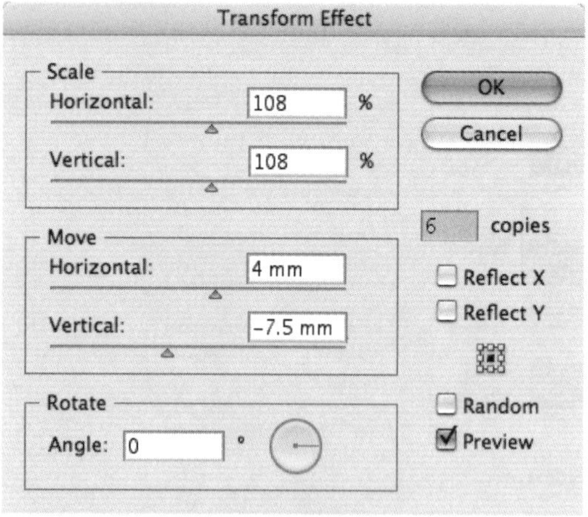

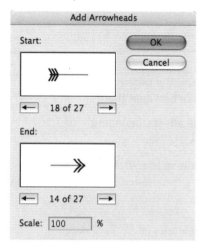

Figure 5.36 *Applying a transform effect*

apply movement, scaling and rotation to an object. You can even create several copies. Nevertheless, the object itself is not affected. For instance, if you apply a movement as a transform effect, the object won't actually move at all, as you can verify using the Info panel or the View>Outline command. It will just appear to have moved. Likewise, if you make six copies of an object there won't actually be six copies, but it will look as though there are. Furthermore, any changes you make to the object you started with will affect all the copies, so, for instance, you can set the fill colour for all copies at once, and always be sure that whenever you change the fill, every copy will be the same colour.

┌─ TRY THIS ───

Draw a shape and use the Transform effect to create half a dozen copies of it, each displaced by a small distance horizontally and vertically.

Apply a new stroke and fill to the object, and reshape it with the pencil tool. Note how the copies change at the same time. Check with the View>Outline command that your object has not been changed.

└───

Arrowheads

One specialized effect that you may need if you are drawing technical diagrams is that produced by Effect>Stylize>Add Arrowheads…. Normally, you would apply this effect to lines and curves, to turn them into arrows, such as you might find connecting states in a transition diagram. The dialogue box for adding arrowheads is shown in Figure 5.37. You can apply arrowheads to either or both of the start and end points of a path. Using the small left and right arrows below the two preview panes, you can cycle through 27 different styles. Not all of these are what you would immediately think of as arrowheads; some are arrow tails, while others, such as the pointing hands and flower shapes, stretch the notion of arrowhead to its limit. Some examples are shown in Figure 5.38.

The size of an arrowhead is proportional to the stroke weight of the line you add it to. This usually works well, but you can vary the size using the Scale field in the dialogue. (We did this with the arrowhead and tail on the circle in Figure 5.38.)

Figure 5.37 *Arrowhead settings*

There is one aspect of arrowheads which can be unsatisfactory. When you add an arrowhead, it is placed so that the centre of the object which represents the arrowhead is at the end point of the line you are adding it to. This means that the arrowhead projects beyond the end of the line, which makes it extremely difficult to place arrows so that, for instance, they just touch the edge of a circle, or to align them. (The two straight arrows at the left of Figure 5.38 are actually aligned on their centre points, but it doesn't look like it.)

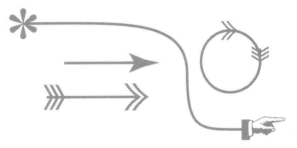

Figure 5.38 *Arrows*

One potential advantage of adding arrowheads using a filter instead of an effect is that the arrow, its head and its tail are automatically grouped. You can ungroup them in order to move the arrowhead along the arrow shaft if you need to do so. You cannot do this with the arrowhead effect, you have to adjust the length of the shaft instead.

---TRY THIS---

Draw two circles and a line connecting them. Practise adding different sorts of arrowhead to each end of the connecting line. Try to position the line so that each arrowhead just touches the outside of the circle it is next to.

Try using the arrowhead filter instead of the effect and experiment with moving the arrowheads instead of the line.

The Scribble Effect

Another effect that is somewhat different from the run-of-the-mill filters, transforms and distortions is the *scribble effect*. This makes vector artwork look as though it had been scribbled with a crayon. That's all it does, but it can be very useful for certain kinds of work. The effect provides considerable control over the precise appearance of the scribbled lines, as well as an extensive set of presets for common sets of parameter settings. Figure 5.39 shows some examples of scribbling applied to a simple shape with a gradient fill. (The original is at the top left.)

The Scribble... command can be found on the Effect>Stylize sub-menu. Its dialogue box is shown in Figure 5.40. The pop-up menu at the top can be used to select from a collection of presets; all but the last (bottom right) image in Figure 5.39 were created with presets from this list. Figure 5.40 shows the parameter values used to create this final image. As you can see, there are a fair number of parameters. They can be understood by imagining a crayon being scribbled back and forth to create an alternative version of the original artwork. The Angle parameter refers to the angle at which the crayon is moved across the page. The Stroke Width is, in effect, the size

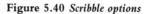

Figure 5.39 *Scribbling* 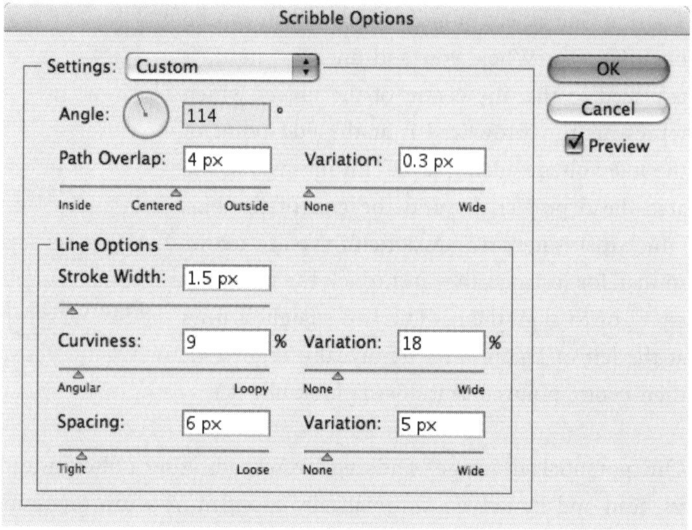   **Figure 5.40** *Scribble options*

of the crayon's point. (Note that scribbling is applied to the fill as well as to the original stroke.) The Path Overlap settings define how much the crayon goes over the lines, that is, the amount by which the scribbled fill goes over or falls short of the object's outline. Curviness defines whether the crayon moves back abruptly at the end of each scribble, or in a smoother curve. (You can see the variation of this parameter in some of the examples in Figure 5.39.) Spacing defines how close together the scribbled lines are. Both Curviness and Spacing can be subject to some randomness, by adjusting the associated Variation sliders, to produce a more natural-looking result. The way in which altering the various parameters affects the final result is most easily understood through experimentation.

Like many of the effects in Illustrator and Photoshop, the scribble effect is fun to play with, but more difficult to use effectively. If you ever need artwork with this sort of appearance, however, this is a well-implemented effect that is intuitively straightforward to use.

---TRY THIS---

Play with the Scribble effect. For instance, draw a polygon and apply all the presets scribbles to it.

Now try applying the effect to a similar polygon but with a very different stroke weight and fill from the first one. Observe what difference the fill and stroke settings for the shape make to the scribbled result.

Try to create a simple picture using the scribble effect to convey the impression of a young child's drawing.

3D Effects

The most startling of Illustrator's effects can be found on the Effect>3D sub-menu. Illustrator is a program for creating graphics in two dimensions, yet these special effects turn two-dimensional shapes into three-dimensional objects, which can be moved in space and rendered with different surface textures and lighting.

A short introduction to 3D graphics can be found in *Digital Multimedia*. Illustrator's 3D effects provide the lathing and extrusion constructions described in that book, and some simple rendering, as well as a means of applying rotational transformations (roll, pitch and yaw) to 2D and 3D objects. (Illustrator uses the term revolving for what we normally call lathing, and combines bevelling with extrusion, hence the commands on the 3D submenu are Extrude & Bevel..., Revolve... and Rotate....) Even this limited amount of three-dimensionality requires some ability to think in three dimensions, and it also places more demands on the processor than most operations in Illustrator, so if you aren't good at visualizing three dimensions or do not have a reasonably powerful computer with plenty of memory, you may prefer to skip this section.

Rotation in 3D

Rotation is the simplest 3D effect. It can be applied to two-dimensional artwork, as an extension to the rotate transform. Whereas the transform rotates objects around a single axis perpendicular to the paper (or screen), 3D rotation adds rotations around the other two axes. If you did this with a real flat object – for example, a shape made of coloured card that you had placed on a piece of paper – you would have to lift it so that it no longer lay flat on the paper, but Illustrator can make it look (more or less) as if an object is being rotated in 3D by applying a combination of transformations. Figure 5.41 shows a simple 2D object being rotated in three-dimensional space (the original object is in the top left-hand corner). You will notice that a lack of foreshortening produces unconvincing results.

The dialogue box opened by the Effect>3D>Rotate... command is shown in Figure 5.42. In the pop-up menu at the top you can select one of a set of preset rotations. As is usually the case with effects, the easy way to find out what each one does is by trying. If none of the presets is suitable, you can enter numerical values for the rotations about each of the axes (in degrees), or use the mouse to drag the cube at the top of the dialogue round to the required orientation.

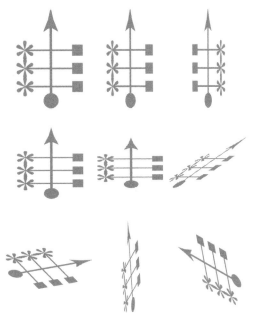

Figure 5.41 *Rotating a 2D object*

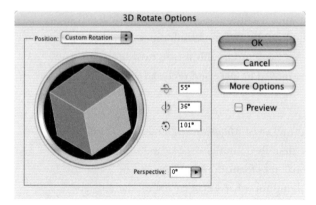

Figure 5.42 *The 3D rotation dialogue*

To give a better impression of spatial depth, you can apply a perspective transformation to rotated objects, using the field below and to the right of the cube to enter an angle, which represents the lens angle of a camera, supposedly capturing the 2D projection of the 3D scene. 3D rotation becomes more interesting when it is applied to the three-dimensional objects we will describe next. The controls shown in Figure 5.42 are incorporated in the dialogues for the remaining 3D effects.

---TRY THIS---

Draw a simple filled asymmetrical shape and practise rotating it in three dimensions. Observe what happens when you rotate it 90° in each dimension.

Make five copies of your original object, align them horizontally across the page and group them. Experiment with applying 3D rotations to the group. Try applying different perspective angles and assess the effects produced.

Extrusion

Applying 3D rotations to 2D objects does not really provide an illusion of three dimensions. In particular, if you rotate an object so that it is perpendicular to the plane of the document, it simply disappears – as you should have observed when doing the previous exercise – because it has no thickness. This is clearly unrealistic, but makes more sense when you consider that in fact there are no truly two-dimensional objects in our three-dimensional real world. You can make more substantial 3D objects by *extruding* 2D objects, as illustrated in Figure 5.43. As we explain

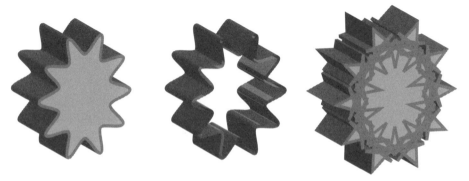

Figure 5.43 *Extrusion*

more fully in *Digital Multimedia,* this means extending a plane surface into the third dimension by sweeping it along a path. In Illustrator, you can only extend along a straight line perpendicular to the *x,y* plane, so your objects just grow outwards, as though they had been squeezed out of a shaped nozzle, as you can see in Figure 5.43.

You extrude a selected object using the Effect>3D>Extrude & Bevel... command, which opens the dialogue shown in Figure 5.44. As you can see, the top part of the dialogue is identical with the 3D rotation dialogue. This is because you can combine a rotation with the extrusion opera-

tion. In fact, you have to do so if you want to see anything three-dimensional, so one of the preset rotations is applied by default. Below this are two controls for the extrusion. The first, Extrude Depth, lets you set the depth, which is simply the distance through which your 2D object is extruded. The Cap control is used to choose whether or not the extruded object has a front face on it. If you do not cap it, only the outside edge is extruded, as in the second example in Figure 5.43. An extruded object is still an ordinary vector shape to which an (elaborate) effect has been applied, so you can go on editing the original shape, although you may need to use View>Outline to see what you are doing. You can continue to apply other effects to it: the right-hand example in Figure 5.43 shows a Zig Zag effect applied to our extruded object (after extrusion).

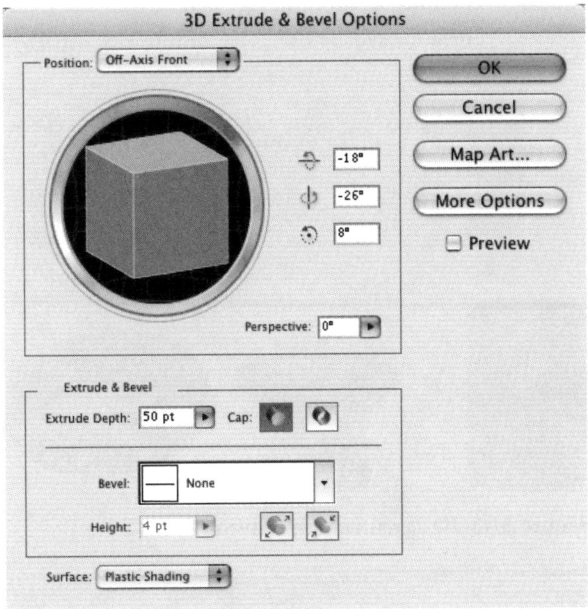

Figure 5.44 *The 3D extrusion dialogue*

By default an extruded object has hard edges. You can add a bevel using the next set of controls, which let you choose a bevel profile from a pop-up menu, set the size (height) of the bevel, and specify whether it should be inside or outside the main object.

──TRY THIS──

Practise extruding shapes made with the different shape tools; experiment with changing the extent of the extrusion, and applying different sorts of bevel. Apply different rotations to your extruded shapes to see how they move in space.

You can extrude type (see Chapter 8); just select it with the arrow tool and apply the effect. It is easier to use very large type (120 pt or more), otherwise you must use very small extrusions. Try creating a 3D logo from your initials.

Revolving

Revolving a path around an axis is an established way of creating 3D objects with rotational symmetry: cups and glasses, hats, cakes, and so on. With this effect we begin to move into real 3D modelling, and it can be a bit tricky to get things to work the way you want them to, unless you are already used to working in 3D.

Figure 5.45 shows three objects which were created by revolving, with the 2D shapes to which the effect was applied above them. Figure 5.46 shows the **Revolve** dialogue; it is similar to the **Extrude & Bevel** dialogue, in having the rotation controls at the top. Below the cube, there is a field for setting the angle of rotation; usually this should be left at 360° to make a closed object.

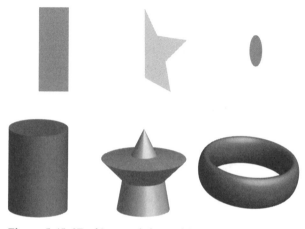

Smaller values will give you an object with a piece missing, such as a pie with a slice taken out of it. It is usual to begin with a shape that represents the outline of half of the object and rotate it about one edge, which will become the centre of the resulting object. As the example in the middle of Figure 5.45 shows, the result is not always what you might expect. You can choose whether to rotate about the left or right edge using the pop-up menu below the **Cap** buttons. Here you can also select an offset, if you wish to rotate about an axis that is outside your shape, so as to create a hollow object, such as the ring on the right of Figure 5.45. The original ellipse is the cross-section of the ring.

Figure 5.45 *3D objects made by revolving*

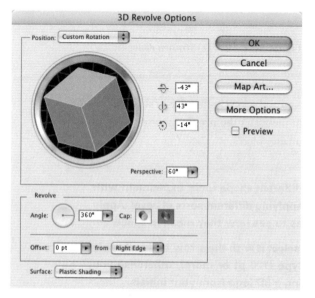

Figure 5.46 *The 3D revolve dialogue*

If the 2D shape you start with has a stroke, this will be used as a sort of skin around the 3D object. This is often not required, and it creates unnecessarily complicated surfaces, so for most purposes it is best to use a shape with its stroke set to none, and a fill that you want to use for the outside of your 3D object.

If you select several objects and revolve them, each one is revolved separately about its own axis, but if you group them, they are all revolved around a common axis. Each of these possibilities has its uses. In Figure 5.47, the tiny ellipse to the left of the large rectangle was grouped with the hat profile, so that when the Revolve effect was applied it produced the thin band around the crown; the two semi-circles were not grouped, but were selected with all the rest when the effect was applied. They were therefore rotated about their own axes, forming the bobble decorations. Notice that the rotation included in the effect was applied to all the selected objects together, so the decorations end up in the intended place.

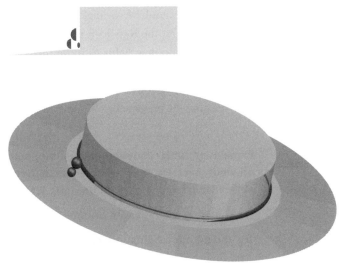

Figure 5.47 ***Making a hat***

> TRY THIS
>
> **Use the 3D Revolve effect to design a selection of interestingly shaped drinking vessels (glasses, goblets, etc.) and lamps.**
>
> **Try making a hat of your own, with some bobbles or other 3D decorations. Pay attention to the proportions, so that you make it reasonably realistic.**
>
> **Make an Edam cheese, complete with rind, with a slice taken out of it.**

Shading

So far, we have ignored the pop-up menu labelled Surface which appears at the bottom of the 3D effect dialogues. This menu is used to select a rendering algorithm. In increasing order of complexity, the options it offers are Wireframe, No Shading, Plastic Shading and Diffuse Shading. The names of the first two should be self-explanatory. Plastic Shading (the default option, which we have used in all these examples) creates a slightly shiny effect, while Diffuse Shading simulates a softer, diffused light. If you click on the More Options button in any 3D dialogue, the controls shown in Figure 5.48 are revealed as the dialogue box expands. These more advanced settings can be used for fine-tuning the shading algorithm, by adjusting the light intensity and other attributes. (The Wireframe and No Shading algorithms have no options;

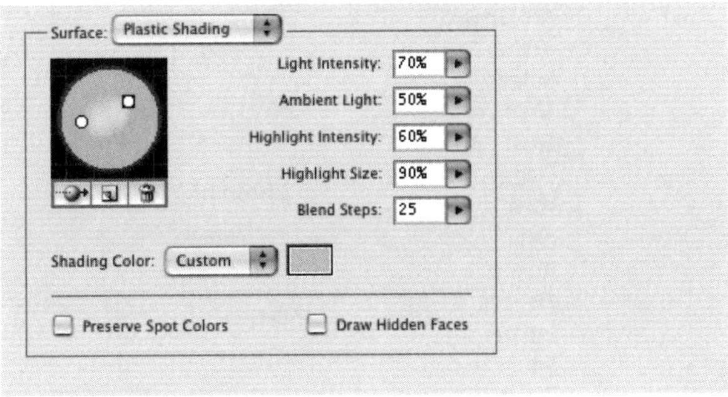

Figure 5.48 ***Adjusting shading and lighting***

Diffuse Shading does not have the highlight parameters shown here.) You can add additional light sources, by clicking on the New icon below the light sphere, and adjust their parameters independently. You can also drag lights to move them around. Unless you have very good 3D visualization skills and some experience of photographic lighting, you will have to rely on the preview to judge the effects of making changes in this part of the dialogue. Even on a powerful machine, updating the preview can be slow, so this process may be frustrating.

TRY THIS

Experiment with rendering and lighting some of the objects you created in the previous exercise. See what effect different shading algorithms have on an object's appearance, and on the time it takes to render.

Try changing the highlight parameters in a plastic shaded object.

Try adding more lights, moving them around and adjusting their intensity.

A shortcoming of Illustrator's 3D effects is that, because the lighting is applied as part of the effect, together with all the rotation, you cannot create a collection of 3D objects, arrange them in a scene with different rotations, then group them and apply the same lighting to the whole scene. However, Illustrator's shading algorithms have no pretensions to photo-realism, so this would probably not be a reasonable thing to attempt in this program.

Warping

Objects can be warped, as if they were drawn on some flexible material, like rubber sheet, which can be pulled and stretched in different directions. (Warping distortions were occasionally applied to text in pre-digital days by using rubber type instead of lead, and mechanically deforming it while printing.) Warp effects are applied by selecting an object and then choosing one of the commands from the Effect>Warp sub-menu, which is shown on the left of Figure 5.49.

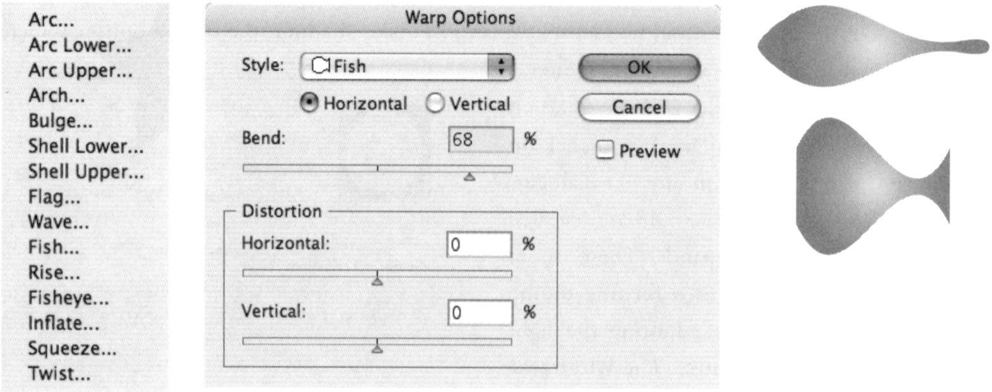

Figure 5.49 *Warp effects and their options*

Whichever effect you choose, the dialogue box shown in the middle of Figure 5.49 opens – the pop-up menu at the top will be set to the particular type of warp you selected, but you can change it if you wish. The Bend slider controls the amount and direction of the bending applied to the supposed rubber sheet. The other two controls allow you to add extra distortion on top of the fundamental warp, in either direction, or in both directions. At the right of Figure 5.49 you can see what happens if you warp a simple ellipse and a rectangle using a fish. Note that the warp is only applied to the object's shape, not to the gradient fill. A slightly more productive use of warp effects might be to create logos by squidging some text into a shape.

Warp effects, like the other effects on the Effect menu, alter the appearance of the objects they are applied to, but do not alter the structure, so the objects remain editable.

The warp effects only provide a limited collection of shapes. Arbitrary rubber-sheet distortions can be applied to objects using the commands on the Object>Envelope Distort sub-menu. However, this is of only limited utility. We will not describe envelope distortion here, but leave you to experiment with it yourself. It can be of value in creating interesting graphic elements out of more basic vector shapes - particularly ones which have already had some other effect applied to them – but you need a fair amount of experience to use warping to good effect.

---TRY THIS---

Practise applying warp effects to a simple object, such as a star or spiral. Experiment with each of the different warp shapes, and observe the effect of altering the bend and distortion parameters.

Experiment with applying warp effects to text and imported bitmaps.

Try using Object>Envelope Distort on a geometrical shape which you have already made more interesting by applying other effects.

The Appearance Panel

Applying strokes, fills, effects and transparency to an object all modify the way it is displayed, but without permanently affecting its shape. These aspects of appearance, which you can modify in a non-destructive manner, are collectively referred to as *appearance attributes*. The Appearance panel allows you to view and manipulate all of an object's appearance attributes.

Figure 5.50 shows the panel as it appeared when the object above it was selected. The object is actually a regular hexagon, and the Appearance panel shows how it has been altered. By double-clicking any of the attributes displayed in the panel, you can change any parameters it may have, so if, for instance, you wished to increase the amount of pucker and bloat distortion you could do so by double-clicking the first attribute, which would bring up the effect's dialogue box.

The **Appearance** panel can be used to edit the parameters of any effect that has already been applied to an object. For instance, if you have applied a 3D effect and you want to change the rotation applied to a shape, you can double-click the effect's entry in the **Appearance** panel to reopen the dialogue box. If you have applied a **Transform** effect and you want to make extra copies, you can do the same, and so on.

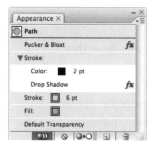

Figure 5.50 *Appearance attributes*

The **Appearance** panel lets you alter attributes in some ways that are not otherwise possible. In particular, you may have noticed that in Figure 5.50 the object has two strokes applied to it. Any number of strokes may be applied using the **Add New Stroke** command from the panel menu. Each successive one is laid over the existing ones. (One application for which this is more than merely diverting is drawing maps. You can make a symbol for a road by overlaying a thin white stroke on a thicker black one.) Less usefully you can also add multiple fills to an object. Notice also that the drop shadow effect is shown in a sub-list under the 2 pt stroke. This is because it is only applied to that stroke, as you can see by looking at the artwork. You can easily apply effects to individual attributes like this by selecting the relevant attribute in the **Appearance** panel and then applying the effect in the usual way, by choosing it from the **Effect** menu and setting its parameters. You can also drag effects around in the panel to reorder them (the order in which effects are applied usually alters the result), or to apply them to the entire object instead of a single attribute, or vice versa.

You can also use the **Appearance** panel to delete an appearance attribute, by selecting it and clicking on the dustbin icon at the bottom of the panel. The other buttons along the bottom of

the panel provide other functions on attributes. The leftmost, if selected, prevents any subsequently drawn shapes acquiring the appearance displayed in the panel. By default they do so, in the same way as they inherit the current fill and stroke. The next two buttons allow you to return an object to a state of nature: the first clears all appearance attributes, leaving the object unfilled and unstroked (presumably you would then go on to give it some new attributes); the second reduces it to a basic appearance, comprising just a single fill and stroke. The remaining button, despite looking like the standard **New** button, allows you to duplicate an attribute. This is most likely to be useful if you want another version of the attribute with different parameters.

—TRY THIS————————————————————————

Using the pencil or pen tool, sketch a map of the roads in your vicinity. Use the Appearance panel to apply a double stroke to each road. Try using different strokes to represent major and minor roads, and paths. Use the same approach to add other features, each with its own distinctive style, to your map.

Appearance attributes can be copied from one object to another. The established way of doing this is to select an object, choose the eyedropper from the **Tools** panel and click on any other object. In most applications, this would just sample the colour at the point you click, but in Illustrator, the stroke and fill colours and all other appearance attributes of the object clicked on will be transferred to the selection.

The **Appearance** panel offers an alternative way of copying attributes. Using this method, you select the object in the panel whose appearance attributes you wish to copy. A thumbnail of the selected object will appear in the top left corner of the panel – you can see such a thumbnail, with the word **Path** next to it, in the screenshot in Figure 5.50. If you drag this thumbnail out of the panel and on to any other object in the document, the selected object's appearance attributes are applied to any object you choose (but of course the result of applying the attributes to an object of a different shape will be different, and sometimes not easy to predict). This way, you transfer appearance attributes from a selected object to unselected ones; with the eyedropper you transfer them to a selected object from an unselected one.

┌─ TRY THIS ──

Draw a simple shape and experiment with applying a combination of effects to it until you achieve a pleasing result. Draw some more objects of different shapes and try transferring the first shape's attributes to them using both the methods we described: the eyedropper and the Appearance panel.

Some word processors allow you to define *styles*, which are named collections of text attributes, such as font, size, colour and justification. You define styles to capture a pattern of formatting which you may want to apply to several elements in a document that should all be identically formatted, such as all top-level section headings. In a similar way, Illustrator allows you to name a collection of appearance attributes and save it as a style.

The quickest way to create a style is by first drawing an object and applying the individual strokes, fills and effects you want. Then select the object and choose **New Graphic Style…** from the **Graphic Styles** panel menu. You name your new style in a dialogue, and it is then added to the **Graphic Styles** panel. You can apply the style by selecting one or more objects and then clicking on the swatch in the panel representing your chosen style. The set of appearance attributes that make up the style is then applied to the selection.

The default half dozen styles that you will find in the **Graphic Styles** panel are rather dull, but you can access several more style libraries, which are supplied with Illustrator, from the **Window>Graphic Style Libraries** sub-menu, or more conveniently from the **Graphic Styles** panel menu. Using library styles means your work may look like other people's, however.

┌─ TRY THIS ───┐

Create an object with an appearance that you like, or use the one from the previous exercise, and save the appearance as a style. Draw some more objects and apply your style to them.

Load each of the style libraries and practise applying library styles to your drawings. Note which of them you find appealing or likely to be useful.

└──┘

DON'T FORGET

Modify the appearance of objects by applying effects to them.

Commands on the Filter menu make permanent changes to artwork, those on the Effect menu leave the basic shapes unaltered and can be modified later. For this reason it is usually better to use effects than filters.

Most effects have parameters that can be set in simple dialogue boxes which appear when the effect is applied.

Photoshop effects are applied through the effects gallery, which provides a large preview of the result.

Transformations can be applied as effects.

Twenty-seven different types of arrowhead and tail can be added to lines.

The Scribble effect makes vector art look as if it was scribbled with a crayon.

The commands on the Effect>3D sub-menu can be used to rotate shapes in three dimensions, or to generate three-dimensional objects by extruding or revolving two-dimensional shapes.

Warp effects distort artwork as though it had been drawn on a rubber sheet that is pulled in different directions.

The Appearance panel is used to manage appearance attributes.

Double-clicking an attribute or effect in the Appearance panel allows you to change its value or parameters.

Apply multiple strokes, or apply effects to strokes instead of complete objects, using the Appearance panel.

Copy attributes from one object to another, either using the eyedropper or by dragging a selected object's thumbnail from the Appearance panel on to other objects in the document.

Save a collection of appearance attributes as a graphic style, which you can apply to other objects subsequently, using the Graphic Styles panel. Extra libraries of graphic styles are provided with Illustrator.

Symbols

Symbols and Instances

A symbol is a reusable piece of artwork. It is convenient to think of the symbol itself as being kept in the Symbols panel; your document can contain one or more *instances* of a symbol. (If you have worked with Flash, these concepts should be familiar to you.) You might like to imagine that an instance is a sort of image of the symbol that is projected onto the document through some cunning arrangement of mirrors and optical fibres (see Figure 5.51). In more technical terms, instances are references, or pointers, to the symbol. Either way, it is important to understand that each instance is connected to, or depends on, the symbol. If you change the symbol, every instance of it will alter to reflect the change. However, as you can see from the figure, you can apply different transformations and effects to each instance.

Symbols provide a convenient way of creating images and diagrams out of standard shapes. For instance, if you were creating a map, you would find it helpful to use a set of symbols for the various features of the landscape (castles, windmills, bridges, and so on). If you export your drawing to SWF or SVG format, as we describe later, using symbols helps keep the files small.

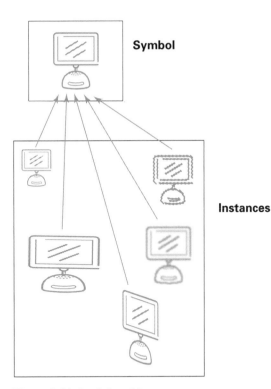

Creating a symbol is easy: create the artwork in the usual way, select it and drag it onto the Symbols panel, where it will appear as a thumbnail. (You can't do this if you have set the panels to auto-collapse. In that case, select the artwork and click the New icon on the Symbols panel.) A dialogue box will let you give the new symbol a name, and set its type to one of Movie Clip or Graphic. The distinction between the two types of symbol is only meaningful if you intend to export Illustrator artwork to use in Flash. The different types of symbol are described in Chapter 6. If you are not intending to export to Flash, it makes no difference which type you choose.

Figure 5.51 *Symbols and instances*

Unless you hold down shift while creating your new symbol, an instance of it will be left behind where the original artwork was. To create additional instances of the symbol, simply drag it from the Symbols panel to where you want the instance to be. You can subsequently select the instance in the usual way, and apply transformations and effects to it.

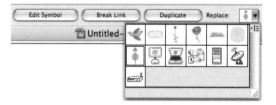

Figure 5.52 *Replacing a symbol*

You might want to change the symbol associated with a particular instance. For example, you might have placed a castle symbol in your map where you should have put a windmill. To make such a change, select the instance in the document and the symbol you require in the Symbols panel, then select Replace Symbol from the panel menu. Alternatively, use the Control panel. When an instance is selected, you will find that a thumbnail of the symbol appears in the Control panel, with a downward-pointing arrow next to it, labelled Replace. Clicking on this arrow causes a copy of the Symbols panel to fly out, as shown in Figure 5.52. To change the symbol for the selected instance, just click on a replacement in this panel. Either of these methods can be used to replace the symbol for several instances at once (provided that they are all selected) – even if they are not instances of the same symbol to begin with.

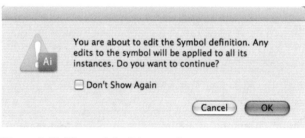

Figure 5.53 *The symbol editing warning*

Editing a symbol, and thus changing the appearance of all its instances, is also a simple process, although there are three different ways you can do it. The simplest is to double-click an instance of the symbol with the arrow tool. The dialogue box shown in Figure 5.53 will appear, warning you about what you are doing. If you click OK, all of the document except the instance of the symbol you are editing will be dimmed and you won't be able to select it. A red line will appear at the top of the document window to remind you what is going on. (This is an example of Illustrator's *isolation mode*, which we will describe more fully later.)

When you have finished editing, you click on the arrow labelled with the symbol's name, at the top left of the document window, to go back to editing the document. As the dialogue warned you, even though you only changed one instance, every instance of the symbol will be updated to reflect the changes, though any transformations and effects applied to specific instances will be unaffected – the new symbol will be transformed, filtered, or whatever, in just the same way the old version was. Figure 5.54 shows what happens when the old iMac symbol (one of the default set provided with Illustrator) used in Figure 5.51 is edited to make it look more like a newer model.

Alternatively, you can enter symbol editing mode by selecting an instance and clicking the Edit Symbol button on the Control panel, if you prefer. If you don't yet have an instance to edit, you can double-click a symbol in the Symbols panel. It will appear on its own in the document window, where you can edit it as described. When you subsequently create instances, they will look like the changed symbol.

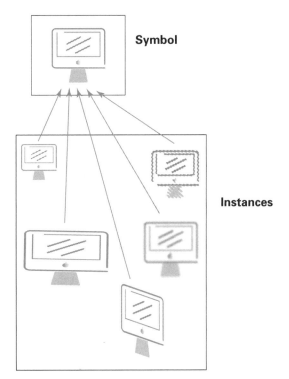

Figure 5.54 *Instances of an edited symbol*

You can delete a symbol in the expected way: just drag it to the dustbin at the bottom of the Symbols panel. But what happens to any instances of the symbol if you do this? When you delete a symbol of which instances still exist, the dialogue shown in Figure 5.55 appears. There are two options: Delete Instances, in which case all the instances disappear along with the symbol, or Expand Instances, which means the instances remain, but as ordinary objects (no longer instances of anything) which are capable of being edited independently and so on. In this case the instances are then said to be expanded.

Some ready-made symbols are provided with Illustrator. When you create a document, a small default set appears in the Symbols panel. You can access some other libraries of pre-defined symbols using the Window>Symbol Libraries sub-menu or the Symbol panel menu's Open Symbol Library sub-menu. When

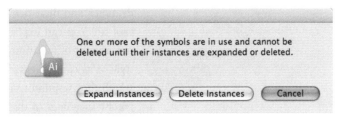

Figure 5.55 *Disposing of instances of a deleted symbol*

you choose a library from this sub-menu, its symbols appear in their own panel, from which you can drag instances. You cannot make any other changes to library symbols. Most of the library symbols are fairly crude examples of the sort of graphics you find in free clip art libraries.

---TRY THIS---

Create some symbols of the type used in some sort of diagram with which you are familiar (e.g., maps, circuit diagrams, state transition diagrams, etc.). Draw a diagram using instances of your symbols. Practise editing the symbols.

Symbol Sets and the Symbolism Tools

We have talked about using symbols for stylized diagrams, but they can also be used to create non-technical illustrations from repeated elements: clouds of butterflies, shoals of fish, forests of trees and flocks of birds, for example, can all be constructed out of instances of symbols. If you do this in a simple-minded or lazy way, it will be obvious that the resulting collection was made from identical elements. It is necessary to apply some apparently random variation to avoid an undesirable mechanical appearance; it will also often be necessary to use scaling for perspective. Using symbols may save you some work, but it still leaves you plenty to do.

Illustrator's **symbolism tools** are intended to mechanize the creation and touching up of groups of instances of symbols. They are used to introduce variations in size, orientation, position, spacing and shading among groups of instances of one or more symbols. To use these tools, you must begin by creating a **symbol set** using the **symbol sprayer** tool. Select a symbol in the Symbols panel, pick up the sprayer, and then drag it across the document. Instances of the symbol will be created along the track of the sprayer.

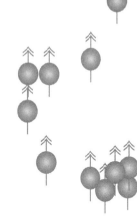

Figure 5.56 shows a simple example, using a crude symbol to show effect clearly. Double-clicking the symbol sprayer tool brings up the Symbolism Tools Options dialogue box shown in Figure 5.57, which is used to set options for all of the symbolism tools. If you use the default settings for the parameters in the lower pane of the dialogue box, the tool will behave rather like a paint spray: instances will be created within the region of the nozzle, as defined by the diameter, and their density will depend on how long you hold the tool still. You can explicitly control the density of the resulting set, the amount of variation of size, orientation, colour, transparency and style of its component instances, the size of the tools and the way in which they respond to movement. You can find a description of the precise meanings of these options in the Illustrator Help, but it will probably be easier to understand them through experimentation.

Figure 5.56 *A symbol set*

┌─ TRY THIS ───

Create a simple symbol, with an identifiable orientation and some colouring. Use the symbol sprayer to create a set of instances of your symbol.

Practise changing the parameters in the Symbolism Tools Options dialogue to alter the resulting set's density and distribution.

Try creating a more natural-looking symbol, such as a bird, butterfly or tree, and see whether you can create a convincing image of a group of these symbols.

└───

You can create symbol sets made up of instances of more than one symbol. Simply select another symbol in the Symbols panel, and spray again.

Once you have created a symbol set, you can refine it using the remaining seven symbolism tools. These allow you to modify the distribution (amount of variation) of the various properties of the component instances of the set (the same properties that you can adjust when you first use the symbol sprayer). To use one of these tools, you must first select the symbol set – it behaves as a single object as far as selection goes. If your symbol set includes instances of more than one symbol, but you want to modify only the instances of a single symbol, choose that symbol in the Symbols panel; the tool will then affect only the instances of that symbol. You then select one of the symbolism tools (they are all under the symbol sprayer tool in the Tools panel). If you want to change any of the tool's options, double-click the tool to get back to the dialogue in Figure 5.57. In particular, you can set the diameter, which determines the scope of the tool's effects. Once the options are set to your satisfaction, drag or hold the tool over the symbol set.

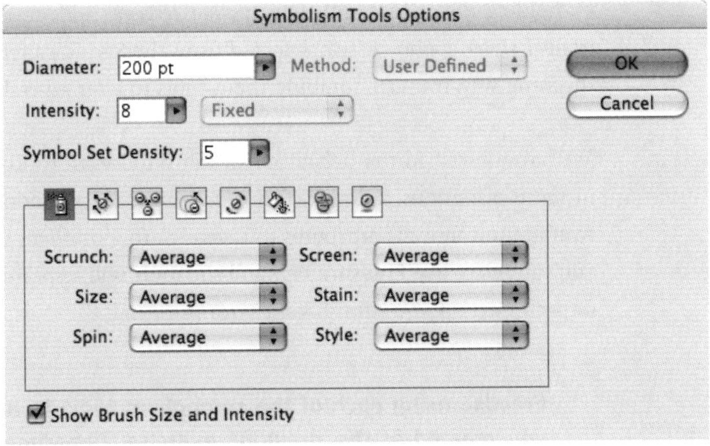

The *symbol shifter* moves instances: they follow it as you drag. The *symbol scruncher* increases or decreases the density: instances are scrunched up in the region of the tool, or pushed apart if you hold down [opt/alt] while using it. The *symbol sizer* makes instances bigger or, if you hold down [opt/alt], smaller. The *symbol spinner* changes instances' orientation: drag the tool round and they will follow it. The effect of these four tools is shown schematically in Figure 5.58.

Figure 5.57 *Setting options for symbolism tools*

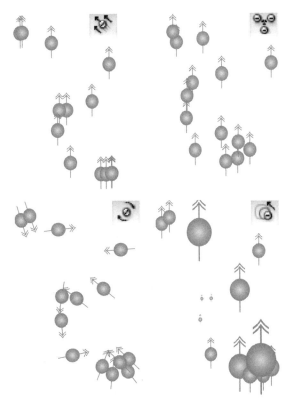

Figure 5.58 *A symbol set being shifted, scrunched, sized and spun (shown clockwise from top left)*

The *symbol stainer* changes their colour. You must set the fill colour before using this tool. If you then drag it over a symbol set, the fill colour will be laid over the instances' original colour; the intensity depends on how long you hold the tool over a particular region. You can remove stains by holding down [opt/alt]. The *symbol screener* adds transparency in a similar way. Finally, the *symbol styler* applies a style, selected from the Styles panel to instances, with intensity varying in the same way. You can combine these tools to alter several aspects of a symbol set.

We have described the behaviour of the symbolism tools with the Method set to User Defined in the tool options dialogue. You can also set it to Random to introduce random variations, or Average to cause the attributes to converge to a uniform value. If you are using a graphics tablet, you can select Use Pressure Pen and the tools will respond to pressure, increasing in the intensity of their effect if you press harder with the pen.

TRY THIS

Practise using each of the symbolism tools to alter the set of simple symbols you created in the previous exercise. Experiment with the effects of all the available options.

Use the symbol sprayer to create a scene using several different symbols from the Nature symbol library. Make use of the symbolism tools to create a realistic distribution of the elements of the scene. Add any other elements you need using other tools to complete the picture.

Symbols and 3D

The symbolism tools are labour-saving devices for creating compositions from repeated elements. Once you understand what symbols are, their use is straightforward. For many Illustrator users the importance of symbols will derive from the way in which they can be exported to Flash, which we will describe later. (This is especially valuable for animators.) More surprisingly, Illustrator's symbols have an important application in connection with the 3D effects we described earlier.

When you apply an Extrude & Bevel or Revolve effect, the surfaces of the resulting 3D objects are created from the stroke and fill of the 2D shape they are based on. You might want to have more elaborate designs on these surfaces, by mapping 2D artwork on to the surface. The only way of decorating 3D surfaces in this way in Illustrator is by using symbols.

Clicking on the Map Art... button in a 3D effect dialogue opens the sub-dialogue shown in Figure 5.59. You can do this when you apply the effect, or at a later time by double-clicking its entry in the Appearance panel. The forward and back controls at the top of the panel are used to iterate through the surfaces of the 3D object. To help you understand which surface is which – something that may not be obvious – the object is temporarily rendered as a wirefame in the

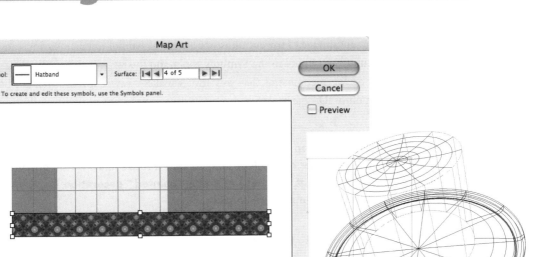

Figure 5.59 *Mapping a symbol onto the surface of a 3D object*

main document window, with the current surface highlighted in red, as shown in the inset in Figure 5.59. (Unfortunately this cannot be seen clearly in the greyscale reproduction.)

Using the pop-up menu at the top left, you can select any symbol in the **Symbols** panel, and it will be placed on the grid in the main part of the dialogue representing the current surface. (Dark parts of the grid represent hidden parts of the surface, light parts visible ones.) You can drag, resize and transform the symbol using the bounding box handles in the dialogue so that it fits the surface as you wish. The button labelled **Scale to Fit** provides a quick way of resizing the symbol so that it covers the entire surface you are applying it to. Figure 5.60 shows how a simple rectangle filled with a pattern can be mapped around the surface of a revolved object to make a spiffy hat band.

Because the mapped artwork is a symbol, you can alter it at any time by editing the symbol. (You may have to double-click the effect in the **Appearance** panel as if you were going to edit it, and click OK before the changes to the

Figure 5.60 *Wrapping a decorative band round a hat*

symbol appear on the 3D surface.) However, it is not a normal symbol instance, so you can only do so by double-clicking the symbol in the Symbols panel, and the resulting edit will change any instances there may be. We recommend that you always make a new copy of a symbol before using it for mapping onto 3D objects.

---TRY THIS---

> **Make a cylinder, and wrap some text around the outside of it by mapping a symbol. Make the cylinder more elaborate, so that it looks like a bottle of some sort, and put a label on it. Try putting some "painted" decoration on to the shades of the lamps you made previously.**

DON'T FORGET

> **Symbols are reusable pieces of artwork. Create a symbol by dragging some artwork to the Symbols panel.**
>
> **Any number of instances of a symbol may be placed in a document. Transformations and effects can be applied to each instance independently.**
>
> **Create instances by dragging a symbol from the Symbols panel into the document window. To change the symbol associated with an instance, use Replace Symbol from the Symbols panel menu.**
>
> **Edit a symbol by double-clicking an instance, selecting an instance and using the Edit Symbol button on the Control panel, or double-clicking the symbol in the Symbols panel. When you edit a symbol, every instance of it is changed.**
>
> **Make symbol sets by spraying symbols with the symbol sprayer tool.**
>
> **Use the symbolism tools to introduce variations of spacing, size, rotation and so on, into a symbol set.**
>
> **Symbols can be mapped to the surfaces of 3D objects created in Illustrator.**

Bitmaps

Illustrator is a vector drawing program, but bitmapped images are not entirely alien to it. However, it only allows you to work with them in limited ways, compared with the way in which you can work with vectors, and with the way in which true bitmapped image manipulation programs such as Photoshop allow you to work with bitmaps.

Combining Bitmaps and Vector Art

You can open files in most common bitmapped image formats, including JPEG, GIF, PNG and TIFF, just by using the File>Open... command in the usual way. When you do this, an Illustrator document is created which contains a single object comprising the bitmap from the file. If you open a photograph, it will probably appear huge in the Illustrator document, so you will usually have to scale it down. This is most easily done by dragging with the arrow tool while holding shift (to preserve the aspect ratio) and [opt/alt] (to scale it from the centre, which will be in the middle of the artboard).

You can draw in the new document in the usual way, to add vector elements. There are countless useful, interesting or fun ways in which bitmaps and vectors can be combined. Figure 5.61 shows just one example: we have added a slight touch of surrealism to a photograph by leaving our 3D hats on a deserted table. The original photograph was opened in Illustrator in the way just described, and reduced to a workable size. The hats were then copied and pasted from their original files, and their sizes and their effect parameters were adjusted to match the scene as well as possible. (Objects made with 3D effects are, of course, well-suited to placing into photographs, which are themselves already two-dimensional representations of three-dimensional scenes.) It was necessary to adjust the rotation of each hat so that it seemed to lie on a surface in the photograph, but this is not easy to achieve precisely. Ideally, you would want to match the way in which any 3D objects you introduced to a photograph were lit with the lighting in the bitmapped background. However, Illustrator doesn't really provide enough control over shading and lighting to do this well. In our example you might argue that the slightly odd lighting adds something to the effect we are trying to achieve, but for certain kinds of professional work this wouldn't be good enough. It is worth noting, though, that you couldn't make adjustments in context in this way if you placed the Illustrator files as smart objects in Photoshop instead. (See Chapter 4.)

Figure 5.61 *Adding vector objects to a bitmapped image*

Figure 5.62 *Using a clipping mask with a bitmapped image*

A different way of combining a bitmapped image with vector drawing is illustrated in Figure 5.62. What we have done here is create a ***clipping mask*** from a vector shape (a copy of the almond-shaped piece of the original design, which you can see in Figure 5.7). This only allows part of the image that we placed beneath it to show through, creating the effect of a photographic fill. (You can't use a bitmap as a fill in Illustrator the way you can in Flash. The closest you can get is by creating a pattern fill, but this produces a different kind of effect.)

Making clipping masks is very easy. The shape that you intend to use as a mask must be on top of the artwork that you want masked. The easiest way to make sure of this is by placing them on separate layers. (You can use a mask to clip any artwork, but it can be particularly effective with bitmaps.) You then select both the mask and the underlying artwork, and use the Object>Clipping Mask>Make command. The masking object disappears, so it doesn't matter what fill and stroke it had originally. For our illustration, we then pasted a copy of the complete original design over the masked image, and adjusted its colours and transparency to produce the final effect.

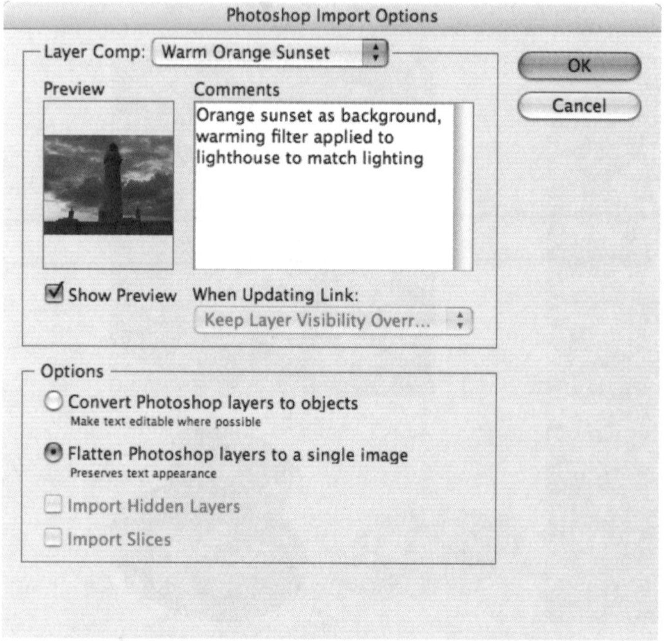

Illustrator treats Photoshop (PSD) files in a rather more sophisticated way than other bitmaps, with special options which provide a useful way of working between the two programs. When you open a Photoshop file in Illustrator, the dialogue box shown in Figure 5.63 appears, allowing you to select a layer comp (see Chapter 4) if the file has any, and offering you a choice about how the Photoshop layers are to be treated. If you choose to flatten the image, you will end up with a single indivisible object on one layer, as you do with other bitmapped images. However, if you choose Convert Photoshop layers to objects, each Photoshop layer will become a distinct object in Illustrator.

Figure 5.63 *Importing Photoshop layers*

Since objects can be manipulated independently, this effectively allows you to preserve the separation of artwork in an original layered Photoshop file, and continue working on the material relating to each layer separately within Illustrator. (See the section on layers in Illustrator below for information on how you can more easily manipulate the layers.)

---TRY THIS---

Open a photograph in Illustrator and explore different ways of adding vector artwork, such as a cartoon drawing, a decorative border, or some 3D objects.

Create a clipping mask from a vector shape to reveal only part of a bitmapped image, in order to create a decorative effect.

Open any layered Photoshop file and separate the layers. Apply clipping masks to different layers and see what result you get.

Importing Bitmaps

Instead of opening a bitmapped file, you can start by creating an ordinary Illustrator document, or opening an existing one, and incorporate bitmapped elements by copying and pasting selections from a file opened in Photoshop or some other image manipulation program. Only selections from a single layer can be pasted. You can also use drag and drop from most image applications.

The most flexible way of adding bitmapped images to an Illustrator document is provided by the File>Place… command. This allows you to add an image to a document, as pasting does, with the added option of either *embedding* the pixels in the Illustrator document, or just placing a *link*, or reference, to the image. Placing a link means that the Illustrator file remains smaller, but more importantly, it allows you to continue to edit the bitmapped image independently elsewhere, and have the updates reflected in the Illustrator file when you do so. Embedded images, on the other hand, become part of the Illustrator document. They are, as it were, frozen in the state they were in when you pasted them, and any changes subsequently made to the original bitmap will not show in the Illustrator file. (Bitmapped images files that you open in Illustrator, as described above, actually turn into Illustrator documents with the image you opened embedded in them. Pasting pixels also has the effect of embedding them. So in both these cases too, any subsequent editing of the original bitmap elsewhere will not affect the Illustrator file.)

When you select File>Place…, a standard file opening dialogue appears, with some checkboxes added at the bottom. In particular, one box is labelled Link. If you tick this box, a link to the file you choose to open will be placed in the document. If you don't, the file will be embedded. (Note that if you embed a Photoshop image, you are offered the dialogue shown in Figure 5.63, but not if you link to it.) In either case, you can then manipulate the bitmapped image almost as if you had pasted it in, with the exception that if you apply any filter to a linked image, it is replaced by an embedded version that has been filtered. This does not happen with effects, however.

Figure 5.64 *The* Links *panel*

For placed images, there are some useful extra possibilities, which are made available through the Links panel, shown in Figure 5.64 (even though some of them pertain to embedded images, too). This panel simply lists all images that have been added to a document using the Place... command, with a thumbnail showing the contents of each one. The panel menu's Panel Options... command allows you to change the size of these thumbnails. We have set it to the largest possible size here, to make the illustration clearer. Embedded images, such as the top two in Figure 5.64, are shown with the conventional image icon used by some Web browsers next to them. Linked images – there is only one here, at the bottom of the panel – have their file names. This makes it easy to remember or recognize which images are linked and which embedded.

Clicking an image's thumbnail in the Links panel selects it in the panel; note that this does not select the image in the document. Selecting an image by clicking it with the arrow tool in the document *does* select it in the Links panel too, though. Double-clicking a thumbnail in the panel, or selecting it and choosing Link Information... from the panel menu, causes a summary of the image's properties to be displayed. In the case of a linked file, this includes the path (useful if you want to edit the original file and have forgotten where it is), and some file metadata, including its size. For embedded images, information about the original file is not available since no link between the Illustrator document and the original of the image you embedded is maintained.

Four buttons along the bottom of the panel provide useful operations, which are applied to any image selected in the panel. The Relink button opens a file navigation dialogue so you can select a new image to take the place of the current one. At this point, you can choose whether to link or embed the replacement, regardless of how the current image was placed, although the default option will be to place the image in the same way as before. The Go To Link button selects the relevant image in the artwork and centres the document window around it. For documents with many placed images this is a quick and easy way of finding each one. Both of these buttons work for images that are either embedded or linked, despite the buttons' names. The remaining pair of buttons work only for links, however. The Update Link button causes any changes that have been made to the linked file on disk to be made in the version in the Illustrator document too. We said earlier that one of the advantages of using links is that you can continue to edit the original image file and changes will be propagated in the Illustrator document. This only happens automatically if you choose the appropriate value (Automatically) from the Update Links pop-up menu in the File Handling & Clipboard Preferences dialogue. Otherwise, you can elect to update links manually, and use Update Link when you need to. (The default is actually a compromise: Ask When Modified.) The last button, Edit Original, is used to open the linked file in its creator program (often Photoshop), so you can edit it there while working mainly in your Illustrator document.

Manipulating Bitmapped Images

Whether you link it, embed it, paste it or just open it, within Illustrator a bitmapped image is
treated as one single indivisible object. You can move it about, scale, rotate, skew and reflect it, and
align it with other objects, in the same way as any other object. If it is embedded, you can make it
into a symbol and create instances of it. But for as long as it remains a bitmap you cannot use the
free transform tool with modifier keys to distort it, or apply perspective to it. (You can make the
gestures, but nothing will happen.) You cannot select parts of it and, understandably, you cannot
apply a fill to it; you can't apply a stroke, either, which is not quite so reasonable.

Whereas transforming vector objects is done purely mathematically, transforming bitmaps requires
new pixels to be computed. This will generally lead to some loss of quality (see Chapter 4), so you
cannot manipulate bitmaps as nonchalantly as you do vectors. You should also bear in mind that
bitmaps have a fixed resolution associated with them, and if you finally export your artwork in
bitmapped form, as described at the end of the chapter, you may experience further loss of quality
if the resolution of imported elements does not match the resolution you choose for export.

You can apply most, but not all, effects to a bitmap. For instance, you can use the Effect>Distort
& Transform>Transform… command to apply transformations to its appearance without altering
the object itself, use the Transform>3D>Extrude & Bevel… command to add depth, making it
look as if the image is pasted on the front of a piece of board, or use the Effect>Stylize>Drop
Shadow effect for a more subtle kind of 3D appearance. Not surprisingly, all of the Photoshop
effects in the lower part of the Effects menu can be applied to bitmaps within Illustrator (without
altering the original image file). You cannot, though, apply any effect that relies on objects having
a stroke. For example, you can't add arrowheads – where would they go? Less obvious examples
of effects that can't be used with bitmaps include the Pucker & Bloat and Zig-Zag distortions, and
the Scribble effect.

Live Trace

A completely different way of dealing with bitmapped images is to convert them into vectors, or *vectorize* them, as it is often expressed. This means that instead of treating the bitmap as an indivisible object, it becomes a collection of vector shapes that you can edit individually like any other vector artwork. It also means that the image becomes resolution-independent, and can be scaled and transformed without the loss of quality characteristic of bitmapped images when you perform these operations.

Vectorization is sometimes also called *tracing*, because of its similarity to copying a picture by drawing over it on tracing paper and colouring it in. In both cases, the result is a collection of filled shapes that approximate the original image, to some degree of accuracy, but possess the characteristics of vector obects.

Illustrator has a powerful bitmap vectorizing facility, known as *Live Trace*. This is easy to use: simply open or place a bitmapped image in Illustrator, choose **Tracing Options...** from the **Object>Live Trace** sub-menu and set the parameters, select the bitmap and then choose **Make** from the same sub-menu. (If you have used the **Trace Bitmap** command in Flash, described in Chapter 6, the general procedure and parameters will be familiar, but you will find that the results are usually much better in Illustrator.)

Figure 5.65 shows the dialogue box used for setting Live Trace parameters. The **Preset** pop-up menu at the top left can be used for selecting one of several collections of settings, supplied as being suitable for common tracing jobs. The presets on this menu are shown to the left of Figure 5.65. Their names give a good general indication of the likely result of using them, but tick the **Preview** checkbox to determine what effect each setting will have on any specific image.

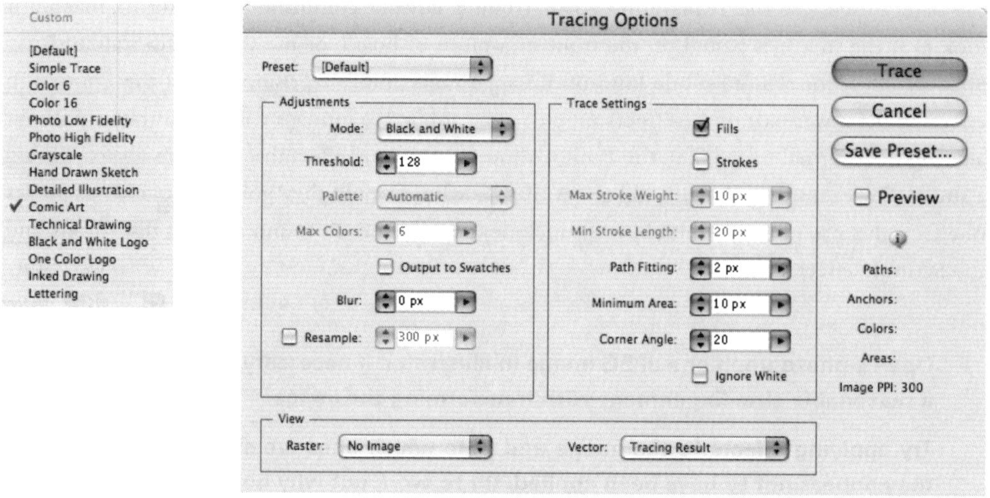

Figure 5.65 *Live Trace options*

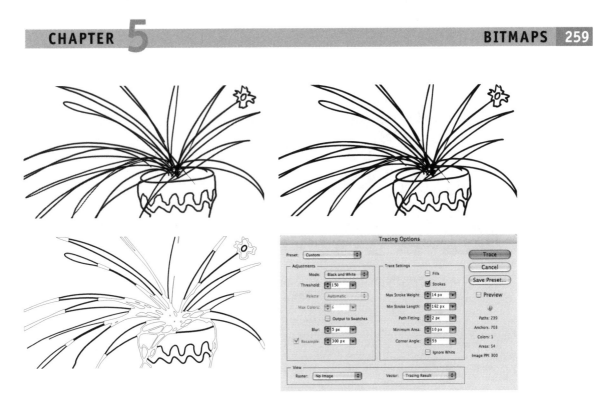

Figure 5.66 *Live tracing a bitmapped sketch*

If none of the presets seems to be appropriate, you can choose your own settings for many of the parameters that control the tracing. Although the meaning of each setting can be precisely specified, the actual effect that changes will have on the appearance of the traced artwork is not always easy to predict, especially in respect of the interactions of the different settings, so it is best simply to experiment. Two settings on the left side of the dialogue might need explanation. The Blur control is used to apply a Gaussian blur to the bitmap before doing the tracing; the value entered in the box is the blur radius. Blurring the artwork has the effect of smoothing it somewhat, so that the traced result will have fewer sharp edges. The Palette pop-up allows you to choose the colour palette (see Chapter 8) for the tracing. If you have any swatch libraries open, their names will appear here, and you can choose one to colour the traced image.

If you only need to trace using a preset, you can perform live tracing from the Control panel. Select the bitmap and a button labelled Live Trace will appear on the panel. Next to it is a downward-pointing arrow, which activates a pop-up menu listing the same presets that are shown in Figure 5.65. Just select one of these and click the Live Trace button.

Live Trace is particularly good for tracing hand-drawn sketches. Figure 5.66 shows an example: the original bitmap at top left – a quick sketch drawn using a graphics tablet in Photoshop – was traced with the Comic Art preset, giving the visually similar result shown at the top right, and then (starting with the bitmap again) with the settings shown at the bottom right, which produced a slightly more interesting and unpredictable result, shown at the bottom left.

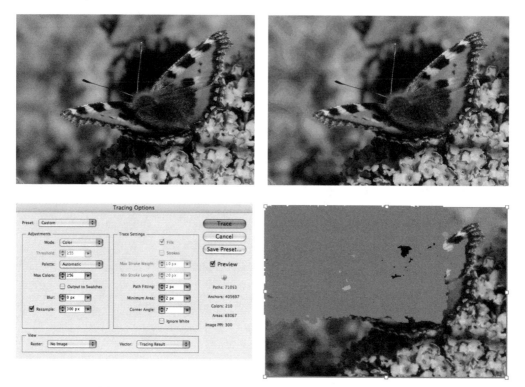

Figure 5.67 *Faithful tracing*

You can, however, trace any bitmap and the results can be extremely accurate. Figure 5.67 shows a detailed photograph and the result of tracing it using the values shown. (The original is the one at the top left.) Despite some posterization in the out-of-focus background areas, much of the fine detail from the original has been retained. In order to do this, Illustrator must create a vector image with a very great many anchor points and short paths. The screenshot at the bottom right of Figure 5.67 shows what happens if you select part of this tracing by dragging the arrow tool over it: there are so many anchor points and tiny paths that you cannot see any of the image. Selecting a specific filled area to alter would be extremely difficult. Furthermore, the file size goes up from under 5MB for the bitmapped original to over 11MB for the traced version. The vector image can, however, be arbitrarily scaled without loss of definition, unlike the bitmap.

┌─ TRY THIS ──┐

Create a simple bitmapped image, either by sketching in Photoshop or by scanning a hand-drawn picture or a simple object, such as your hand. Experiment with Live Tracing this image: try the different presets and then experiment with changing the values of the parameters, until you get a feel for how they affect the result.

Try tracing different sorts of images, including photographs.

└───┘

Having traced a bitmap, if you re-select it you can change the principal parameter values from the Control panel, or all of the values via the Tracing Options dialogue. This is why it's called "live" tracing – it remains editable until you expand it (see below). When a live trace is selected, two triangles appear on the Control panel. Holding down the mouse button with the cursor over one of these reveals a short pop-up menu that lets you select how to view the original bitmap and the traced result. You can, for example, show the original as a semi-transparent overlay, or the result as an outline. Either arrangement lets you compare the two easily.

Once you are happy with the result, selecting the Object>Live Trace>Expand command, or selecting the object and clicking the Expand button on the Control panel, will turn the traced bitmap into a group of vector objects, which you can then edit in exactly the same way as if they had been drawn in Illustrator from the start. (Don't forget that you will need to ungroup if you wish to separate the objects that the tracing has produced.) If you are confident that you will achieve the result you want, you can use the Object>Live Trace>Make and Expand command to combine the tracing and expansion in a single operation. Alternatively, if you want to give up on tracing, choosing Object>Live Trace>Release deletes the tracing, leaving the placed bitmap.

TRY THIS

Trace a bitmapped image. Practise using the Control panel to change the trace settings. Try to make a version with smooth paths and not many anchor points. Experiment with displaying the image and the result in different ways.

Expand the smoothly traced version and make some alterations to the resulting vector objects using Illustrator's ordinary tools.

Live Paint, which we described earlier, can be used in conjunction with Live Trace. Figure 5.33 was created in this way, by live painting the traced sketch in Figure 5.66. In such a case, the traced bitmap may have gaps where in fact you intended to create a continuous line. The Object>Live Paint>Gap Options... command opens a dialogue in which you can specify that gaps up to a specified size should be ignored – the fill will stop at them, even though the edge is not continuous. Options are provided for small, medium and large gaps, but you can specify an arbitrary width. The Object>Live Trace sub-menu has a Make and Convert to Live Paint command, which conveniently combines tracing with the creation of a Live Paint group which can then be coloured in, or you can click the Live Paint button on the Control panel to do the same thing.

TRY THIS

Trace a bitmapped image using one of the black and white presets. Use the Live Paint bucket to colour it in. You will find it easiest to use a fairly simple image and trace it coarsely, so that you end up with relatively large areas to fill.

DON'T FORGET

Bitmapped image files can be opened in Illustrator and have vector objects added to them.

Use clipping masks to create shapes filled with parts of an image.

Choose layer comps to import from a Photoshop file; either flatten layers or convert them to objects for editing independently in Illustrator.

Use the File>Place... command to add bitmapped images to an Illustrator document. You can embed the image or link to it.

Any further changes to the original of an embedded image will have no effect on the version placed in the Illustrator file. Changes to the original of a linked image may be propagated to update the version placed in the Illustrator file.

Use the Links panel to select, update and replace images, or edit linked files in the program they were created with.

A bitmapped image is a single indivisible object inside Illustrator. You can transform it and apply most effects to it. Symbols can be made from embedded images but not from linked images.

Use Live Trace to vectorize bitmaps; a wide range of settings is available.

Use Live Paint with Live Trace to vectorize artwork and colour it in quickly.

Shared Features

Illustrator is the oldest and most mature of the programs described in this book, so it is not surprising that some of the features that it shares with the others are more highly developed. It is often the case that enhancements that appear in one program make their way into others at a later date, so some of the features we describe here in the context of Illustrator may also appear in Photoshop, Flash or Dreamweaver in due course (where they have not done so already).

Selection

Illustrator has a *magic wand* tool, for making selections based on common attributes. In Photoshop, the magic wand selects pixels of a similar colour, but in Illustrator the magic wand tool selects objects with similar fill and stroke attributes. The Magic Wand panel, shown in Figure 5.68, is used to set the parameters determining which attributes are to be used as the basis of the selection, and what degree of similarity is required. (You may have to select Show Stroke Options and Show Transparency Options from the panel menu to see all the controls in this panel.) The way that magic wand selection works is best explained by a simple example. In Figure 5.69, the star and hexagon have the same fill and

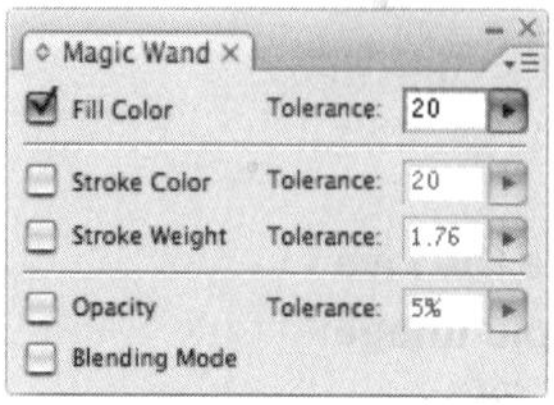

Figure 5.68 *The* Magic Wand *panel*

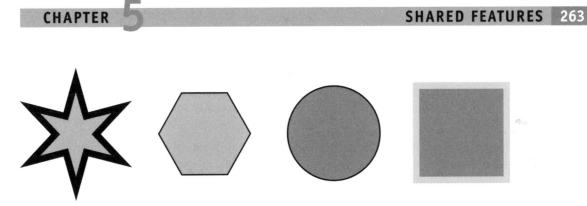

Figure 5.69 *Shapes to be selected by the magic wand*

stroke colour; the stroke weights are 5 pt and 1 pt, respectively. The circle and square have the same fill, but different stroke weights. The circle has the same stroke colour as the star and hexagon, but the square's stroke colour is different. Suppose you select the Fill Color checkbox in the Magic Wand panel, leaving the other checkboxes unselected. If you click on the star, both it and the hexagon will be selected, as they have the same fill. Similarly, if you click on either the circle or square, both will be selected. You will notice that there is a field labelled Tolerance next to the Fill Color checkbox. This is used to enter a threshold value; colours within tolerance will be considered to match, so you can select colours within a range.

The stroke options work in a similar way. Selecting only the Stroke Color checkbox allows you to select all objects with the same stroke colour, so in our example, if you had done so and clicked on the star, all the shapes would be selected except the square. (You can click anywhere in the object, you don't have to click the stroke.) If you just selected Stroke Weight, with a tolerance of 0 pt, clicking on the star would select it and the square. Increasing the tolerance above 5 pt would lead to all the shapes being selected whenever you clicked any of them. Criteria are combined in an obvious way, so if you select the Fill Color and Stroke Color checkboxes, you could select objects with the same coloured stroke and fill – the star and hexagon, for instance. As you can see from Figure 5.68, you can also use the magic wand to select on the basis of objects' transparency.

┌─ TRY THIS ───
│
│   **Download Figure 5.69 and practise using the magic wand to select combinations
│   of objects. Start by investigating the effect of ticking different checkboxes, then
│   choose values to select different pairs of shapes. Add some more shapes, with
│   different transparency settings, and investigate the use of transparency as a
│   selection criterion, both on its own and in conjunction with the others.**
│
└──

You can make selections on the basis of similarity using the commands on the Select > Same sub-menu. If you use these commands, you must first select an object (to determine what the other selected objects should be same as), then choose the appropriate sub-command. In this mode of selecting, there is no provision for using tolerance settings: if you select the same stroke weight, for example, only objects with exactly the same stroke weight as that of the current selection will be selected. On the other hand, this sub-menu provides some extra criteria: you can select all instances of the same symbol, or all objects to which the same style has been applied.

By making magic wand selections or using the Select>Same sub-menu, you can easily make global changes to a fill colour, for example: select all objects with that colour fill, then change the colour of all the selected objects in the Color panel. In the same way, you can make global changes to strokes and transparency.

Sophisticated selections of this sort are of most use in complex illustrations. The ability to remember selections is similarly over-powered for simple examples, but can be invaluable in images with many objects. If you have made a selection, using any of the available tools and commands, and you then choose the Select>Save Selection... command, a dialogue box appears, in which you can name the current selection. After you have done this, the name appears on the Select menu. Subsequently, if you choose the name from the menu, the same objects are selected again. You will appreciate the usefulness of this facility if you have ever made a complex selection, then had to deselect to perform some operation and then make the selection all over again. The Select>Edit Selection... command brings up a dialogue box in which you can remove selections from the menu. (The name of this command is confusing: the command doesn't actually edit any selection, it edits the contents of the Select menu.)

TRY THIS

Make a few magic wand selections from the document you created in the previous exercise, and store each of them in the Select menu. Reselect each of them by choosing their names from the menu. Investigate what happens if you delete one or more of the objects in a stored selection, or change its appearance attributes. Clear the Select menu when you have finished.

Colour

Illustrator's Swatches panel is shown in Figure 5.70. It differs from those of other programs in arranging some of the swatches in *colour groups*. There are three of these in the illustration, at the bottom of the panel. In the default view, where each swatch is shown as a thumbnail, each has a folder icon at its left end to indicate that it is a group. For convenience you can choose to display your swatches as a list, by selecting Small List View from the panel menu. In this view, folders are shown as collapsible sub-lists, as shown at the bottom of Figure 5.70.

Colour groups can be used to organize a collection of swatches or to tidy up the Swatches panel. You can create a colour group just by selecting several swatches (which you might have made previously by selecting colours in the Color panel and saving them as swatches) and then clicking the New Color Group icon at the bottom of the panel. Normally, you would only put swatches in the same colour group if they were related somehow, and you might often want to use the colours in a group in combination with each other and not with others. Illustrator provides several ways of making groups of related colours and using them to colour artwork.

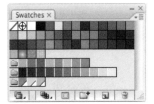

Most of these methods make use of rules of **colour harmony** to generate groups of colours which are supposed to work well together. These rules extend the notion of complementary colours, introduced in Chapter 8, by identifying other relationships between colours, usually on the basis of their relative positions on the **colour wheel**. You begin by choosing a **base colour**, and the rule tells you which colours you should combine it with. For instance, the analogous colours rule chooses the two colours that lie 30° to each side of the base colour, the split complement rule gives the analogous colours of the base colour's complement (which is diagonally opposite it on the colour wheel) and the triad rule gives two colours that are equidistant from the base colour around the rim of the colour wheel.

Figure 5.70 *The* Swatches *panel in thumbnail (top) and list view*

These harmony rules are essentially arbitrary, with little physical or physiological basis, and they are also somewhat culturally sensitive, but they are well established in the literature on colour theory and some people find them useful as a way of designing colour schemes. Illustrator's Color Guide panel, shown in Figure 5.71, provides a way of generating a colour group from a base colour, using any harmony rule you choose.

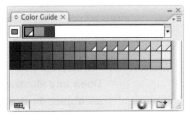

Figure 5.71 *The* Color Guide *panel*

In use it is simple. First, choose a base colour in any of the usual ways. (If you have anything selected in the document, you may well find that you have applied the colour you choose as either the stroke or fill. Unless you really do intend to do this, make sure that nothing in your document is selected before you choose the base colour.) Next, using the pop-up menu at the top of the Color Guide panel, choose a colour harmony rule that you like the look of, or which you feel is likely to meet your requirements. Figure 5.72 shows how the list of rules pops up with swatches of the colour group that each choice generates. The scroll bars can be used to move down to other more esoteric rules – the colour guide provides a total of 23 harmony rules for you to choose from. Each has a precise definition, but in most cases, trial and error will be the best approach.

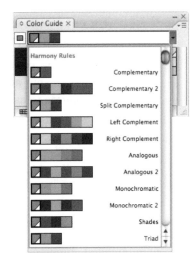

Figure 5.72 *Harmony rules*

When you choose a rule from the list, the corresponding colour group is transferred to the swatch row at the top of the panel. Below it, a collection of swatches based on the colours in the group is generated. There is one row for each colour in the group. For instance, in Figure 5.71, we chose the split complement rule, which gave us a colour group with three members, so there are three rows of swatches in the panel. Each row has one of the colours from the group in the middle, with tones and tints of it to left and right. The Color Guide Options... command on the panel menu brings up a simple dialogue that lets you set the number of variations in each row and the degree of change between them.

Thus, the Color Guide panel allows you to generate a set of colours derived from a base colour by applying tonal variations to the colours generated by a harmony rule. If you want to save the colour group generated by the rule to the Swatches panel, you can do so just by clicking the New Color Group button in the Color Guide panel. You can also select some of the variation swatches, by shift- or [cmd/ctl]-clicking, and save them as a colour group in the same way. You will then have a set of related colours in the Swatches panel to use in your artwork.

We should stress, however, that although Illustrator refers to rules for harmony, no such "rules" really exist, and at most the colour schemes which it generates should be considered as suggestions which you may or may not choose to adopt. You should always consider yourself free to choose any colour combinations which you feel will work well in the context of your work.

┌─ TRY THIS ───

Open any Illustrator file you have made that uses a range of colours and select an object. In the Color Guide panel, observe how the stroke or fill colour has been selected. Select different objects and swap the stroke and fill swatches in the Tools panel, and see how the Color Guide changes.

For one colour, look at the list of harmony rules, select any of the rules which seem to generate interesting or useful colour groups, and save them.

Choose one colour group you just saved and change all the stroke and fill colours in your artwork so that only colours from the group are used. Would it be accurate to say that the new colouring is harmonious?

──

The Live Color dialogue is used to manage colour groups and adjust the colours in them. It duplicates some of the functions of the Swatches and Color Guide panels and the colour picker (described in Chapter 8). It provides a convenient single dialogue for working with all the colours in a document, as opposed to the colour of the individual objects. You may, therefore, find it unnecessarily elaborate for simple jobs and it may not be appropriate for illustrations. Graphic designers should, however, appreciate the way in which the overall colour scheme of a design can be changed, and how Live Color makes it easy to experiment with colours.

There are many ways of reaching the Live Color dialogue. The Edit Colors button appears in several places: the Control panel (but only if the selected artwork has two or more colours), the Color Guide panel and the Swatches panel, if you click on the folder icon of a colour group. You can also double-click a colour group's folder icon in the Swatches panel to edit colours.

Whichever way you choose to open it, the Live Color dialogue should appear as shown in Figure 5.73. The colour group shown at the top left of the panel will depend on how you invoked the dialogue. If you started in the Color Guide or Swatches panel, the colour group from there will be shown; if you had selected some artwork and then clicked the button on the Control panel, a group called Artwork Colors, consisting of the stroke and fill colours of the selected objects, will appear.

The right half of the dialogue box contains a list of all the colour groups associated with the current document. This will be the same

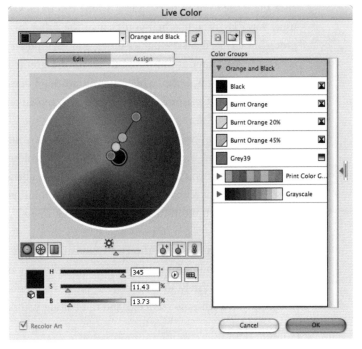

Figure 5.73 *The* Live Color *dialogue*

collection as you find in the Swatches panel. You can use the buttons above this list, at the top of the dialogue, to delete groups and add new ones. However, this is nothing new. It is the left half of the dialogue that introduces new possibilities.

There are two tabs near the top: Edit and Assign. In Figure 5.73, the Edit tab is active. Its purpose is to make changes to the colours in an existing colour group – the one displayed at the top of the Live Color dialogue. At any time, you can click on a colour group in the list in the right half of the dialogue to edit its colours instead.

As you can see in Figure 5.73, the Edit tab provides what is essentially an HSB colour picker, as described in Chapter 8. The coloured disk plots hue and saturation, and the slider just beneath it is used to adjust brightness. The three sliders at the bottom of the dialogue allow you to adjust colours by changing their components; you can set these sliders to RGB or CMYK instead of HSB, using a pop-up menu next to them.

The major difference between the Live Color picker and a standard HSB colour picker is the presence of several circles on the coloured disk, instead of the single circle normally found. These circles represent all the colours in the colour group you are editing. Clicking a colour swatch in the group causes the corresponding circle to be highlighted, and the sliders to be set to its value. You can then change the value by dragging the circle or moving the sliders. (You can also double-click the circle to open the standard Adobe colour picker, where you can change the value in the usual way.) By default, when you change the value for one colour, all the colour values in the group are changed: all the circles move, and they preserve their geometrical relationship, which represents the harmony rule used to create the group in the first place. So if you had a split-complement colour group, whenever you changed one of the colours, the others would adjust themselves so that the three remained a split complement trio.

If you aren't happy with the relationships between your colours that Illustrator's harmony rule has generated, click the chain link icon below the colour disk. This will uncouple the colours in the group, so that you can alter their values independently. It may very well be the case that, to preserve the visual relationship between your colours, you will have to modify the geometrical relationship, which means that you must unlink them.

In the bottom left corner of the Live Color dialogue is a checkbox labelled Recolor Art. If this is ticked, changes you make to colours are applied to any objects that are selected. The changes are previewed immediately so that you can judge their effect on the artwork. If Recolor Art is not ticked, the artwork is not affected, and the editing you do only changes the stored colour group.

TRY THIS

> **Select all the objects in the document you used for the previous exercise and open the Live Color dialogue. Make sure the Recolor Art checkbox is ticked, and adjust the colours in the Edit tab. See whether you think that changes you make while the colours are linked preserve the relationships among colours in the artwork. Try unlinking the colours and see whether you can do better by eye.**

Figure 5.74 shows the Assign tab of the Live Color dialogue, which is used to change the way the colours in a group are applied to selected objects. If you edit colours as we just described, the correspondence between the original colours in the artwork and the changed colours in the colour group stays the same. So, for instance, in a split complement, any object that was filled with the base colour would always be filled with whatever you changed the base of the trio to, and any objects filled with the complements would always be filled with the complements. When you are just altering the colour group consisting of the colours in the artwork, this is probably what you would want, but if you wanted to recolour the artwork using a different colour group, how would you map the old colours to the new ones? This is what you do in the Assign tab.

The left pane of the Assign tab contains two columns of colour swatches. The original ones from the selected artwork are in the wide left-hand column under Current Colors, and new ones from the colour group you have chosen to replace it are to the right of the current colours, under New. (The colour group might just be a version of the original colours that you altered in the Edit tab; you can still change the way in which old colours are mapped to new ones.) The idea is that each colour in the left column will be replaced by the colour in the same row in the right column. Where the new set contains fewer colours than the old one, some of the rows in the left column, such as

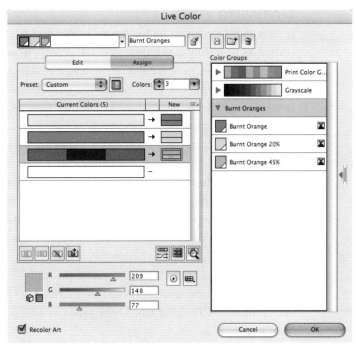

Figure 5.74 *Assigning colours*

the third row in Figure 5.74, will contain more than one swatch, indicating that more than one colour (three in this example) will be replaced by a single new colour.

You can change the mapping between old and new colours simply by dragging swatches in either column to a new position. As before, you must tick the Recolor Art checkbox to see the effect on the selected artwork. This allows you to experiment with different ways of replacing colours. Note that there is no undo facility within the Live Color dialogue, so you have to drag colours back to where they came from if you make a mistake. At any time you can select a new colour group from the pop-up menu at the top left of the dialogue, or from the list on the right, and the set of new colours, together with the associated mapping in your document, will change.

It takes a bit of practice to get used to manipulating colours in this way, and you can make a terrible mess of your artwork with it, especially if you don't understand much about colour, so we would advise you to treat Live Color as an advanced facility and approach it with caution.

---TRY THIS---

Make a simple geometrical design, such as a flag, and colour it using arbitrary colours. Use the Live Color dialogue to replace these colours with the members of a colour group. Use the Assign tab to experiment with assigning replacement colours to the artwork in different ways.

Drawing Aids

Even with all the effects and elaborate strokes and fills that Illustrator supplies, vector drawing remains an essentially algorithmic process that tends to produce artwork with a rather mechanical character. This can be a strength. It is admirably suited for technical illustration work and for designing layouts for Web pages, which you can subsequently use to guide the placement of page elements in a Web design application such as Dreamweaver. For such applications, and for graphic design work in which you want to bring out the mechanical character of the artwork instead of disguising it, Illustrator supplies tools for laying out objects systematically and precisely.

It should be emphasized that Illustrator is not a computer-aided design (CAD) tool, and although it can be used to produce high quality technical illustrations, it is not intended to be used for the production of blueprints or architectural drawings. There are, however, plug-ins that add some of the features of CAD tools, such as dimensioning and standard architects' symbols.

Guides

Illustrator has a layout grid and guides, as described in Chapter 2. The simple guides described in that chapter are sometimes called *ruler guides* to distinguish them from the other types of guide that Illustrator supports.

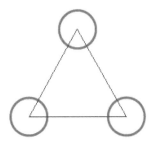

Figure 5.75 *An object guide*

Any object can be turned into a guide of arbitrary shape by selecting the object and choosing **Make Guides** from the **View>Guides** sub-menu. If, for instance, you wanted to position three objects at equal distances apart, you could draw an equilateral triangle with the polygon tool, convert it to a guide and use it to position the objects, as shown in Figure 5.75. Being a guide, the triangle does not appear on the final drawing. If you wished it to do so, you could click on the guide to select it, and then use the **View>Guides>Release Guides** command to turn it back into an ordinary object.

Objects will snap to a guide made from an object, just as they will to ruler guides. The **View>Snap to Point** command is used to turn snapping (to any type of guide) on and off. As well as causing objects to snap to guide lines, it will also make them snap to anchor points. More precisely, it will make the cursor snap to them. In the case of a triangular guide, for instance, turning this option on will make the part of an object you are dragging snap to the vertices of the triangle. (Drag by the centre to make the centres snap to the guides.)

> ─TRY THIS─
>
> **Draw a star shape and convert it to a guide. Use this guide to position smaller stars at equal distances around the circumference of a circle. Draw another star and position it at the exact centre of the circle.**

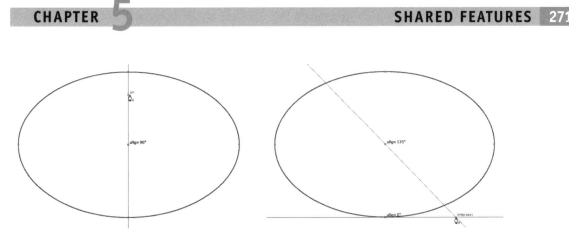

Figure 5.76 *Smart guides*

The most sophisticated guides are *smart guides*, which are a tremendous aid to drawing, although you might not think so at first, as they take a bit of getting used to. If you select View>Smart Guides, you will find that as you draw, thin blue lines with cryptic annotations start popping up all over the place. These are the smart guides and they are telling you where the cursor is in relation to objects in your drawing. (It is important to note, however, that smart guides do not work if View>Snap To Grid is selected.) For example, in the screenshot on the left of Figure 5.76 the smart guide shows that the cursor is on the vertical line running through the centre of the ellipse. If you diverge from the vertical, the guide disappears, so if you wanted to create another ellipse whose centre was directly above that of the ellipse, you would just have to follow the guide. The screenshot on the right of Figure 5.76 shows a more complicated example. Here the cursor is at the point where the horizontal line through the bottom of the ellipse intersects with the diagonal running through its centre.

Using the Edit>Preferences>Smart Guides & Slices... dialogue shown in Figure 5.77 (ignore the Slices Preferences) you can specify which angles smart guides should appear at, and other aspects of their display, including the Snapping Tolerance, that is, the distance from which objects should snap to the guides. The Display Options checkboxes near the top of the dialogue allow you to choose what the smart guides do; ticking Text Label Hints ensures that little text annotations appear to tell you when you are on a guide or a path, or at an anchor point or the centre of an object, or at the intersection of a guide and a path or two guides.

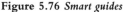

Figure 5.77 *Smart guides preferences*

Illustrator applies its own logic to determine when to show a smart guide. Potentially, every object has a collection of smart guides radiating from its centre and all its anchor points, but they don't necessarily appear whenever the cursor is over one. Only those associated with objects that Illustrator considers relevant do so. Sometimes it is necessary to pass the cursor over an anchor point to force the smart guides that you need to appear.

---TRY THIS---

Turn on smart guides and make sure that the preferences are set as shown in Figure 5.77. Draw a shape, select any drawing tool, and watch how the smart guides behave as you move the cursor around the window. Using the smart guides to determine the correct angles, draw eight other shapes lined up at the compass points relative to the centre of the first shape.

Alignment

Grids and guides provide a general mechanism for systematic layout. For the specific task of lining objects up with each other in rows and columns, the Align panel, shown in Figure 5.78, can be used. The general procedure is to select several objects and then click on one of the buttons in the panel. Their icons provide a good indication of what each button does. The aligning buttons on the top row, headed Align Objects, are particularly obvious: if you click on the first button, objects are moved so that their left edges line up, if you click on the second one, their centres are aligned vertically, and so on.

Figure 5.78 *The* Align *panel*

You may find it is helpful to group objects in order to place them in formation by alignment. For example, if you wanted to align twelve objects in three rows of three, you could start by aligning four of them horizontally to make a row and then grouping them, do the same with the second and third rows, and then finally vertically align the three groups.

If you just select all the objects that you want to line up, when you align on the left edge, they will all move to line up with the leftmost one in the selection, and so on for the other edges. When you align centres, the final centre position seems to be computed as the average of all the centres. In general, this is neither the centre of the bounding box of the selection nor the centre of any individual object. However, if you click on one of the objects after you have selected them, but before doing the alignment, it becomes a ***key object***, and is used as the basis of the alignment: left aligning will then align everything on the key object's left edge, and so on.

The buttons on the second row, labelled Distribute Objects, enable you to move objects so that they are equidistant from each other. The first button, for example, moves selected objects so that the vertical distance between the top of one and the top of the next is the same for all of them.

The other buttons let you space their centres and bottoms vertically, or the left and right edges and centres horizontally. If the objects are different sizes, this may not produce a pleasing arrangement. They may look better if the space between each object and its neighbour is the same. This arrangement can be achieved using the bottom pair of buttons, labelled Distribute Spacing. These are not visible by default; use the Show Options command in the panel menu to reveal them.

You can arrange objects so that they have a specific amount of space between them by entering a value in the box next to the buttons on the Distribute Spacing row. The default value here is Auto, which simply equalizes the spacing in the original arrangement of objects. If you want to set a specific value here, you must select a key object first. This object will be left in place, and the others will move to produce the desired spacing.

In the bottom right corner of the Align panel is a button labelled Artboard. If you click this, an object will be aligned to the artboard. For instance, to position a circle in the exact centre of the artboard, select it, click the Artboard button and then the horizontal and vertical alignment buttons. (It only makes sense to align a single object if the Artboard button is set.) The Artboard button's setting persists until you explicitly turn it off by clicking again.

---TRY THIS---

Draw nine circles and use the Align panel to arrange them in a regular 3 by 3 grid, like a noughts and crosses square. How would you place one object at the exact centre of another?

Draw five circles in random positions on the artboard and try using each of them as a key object for aligning and distributing space. Experiment with the Artboard button and observe how it affects the results.

As well as aligning whole objects you can align selected anchor points. Just select several anchor points using the direct select tool and use the controls on the Align panel as if you were aligning objects. The anchor points will line up or space themselves equally, and paths will grow or shrink to accommodate their new positions. This can be very useful. Figure 5.79 shows an example. Four lines were drawn haphazardly, and the Add Arrowheads effect was applied, to produce a set of arrows pointing roughly at the same place, as shown on the left. The anchor points at the arrowheads were all selected and right-aligned and their centres were vertically distributed. The same was then done to the other ends of the arrows, producing the neat equally-spaced version on the right. Note that some arrows therefore end up shorter than they were.

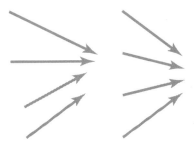

Figure 5.79 *Aligning anchor points*

You don't have to open the Align panel to use the Distribute Spacing buttons; they also appear on the Control panel whenever you have some objects selected, so many alignment tasks can be done from the Control panel.

┌─TRY THIS───

Draw a wavy freehand curve using the pencil tool, making sure it has plenty of anchor points. Select pairs of anchor points and align and distribute them, observing how the shape of the curve alters as you do so.

Try duplicating our example of aligned arrows in Figure 5.79: make sure that their heads all end at the same point and that their tails are neatly aligned.

Layers

The use of layers to organize your artwork is less compelling in Illustrator than in most of the other tools we describe in this book, because objects are already distinct entities, which can be selected independently, locked, hidden, or combined into groups. There is also a natural stacking order to objects – ones that you draw later are on top of ones you drew earlier – and you can bring objects to the front or send them to the back using the Object>Arrange sub-menu. Layers add an extra level of convenience, though, and they may provide a familiar way of working. Illustrator adds some new twists to the layer paradigm, suited to the nature of vector artwork.

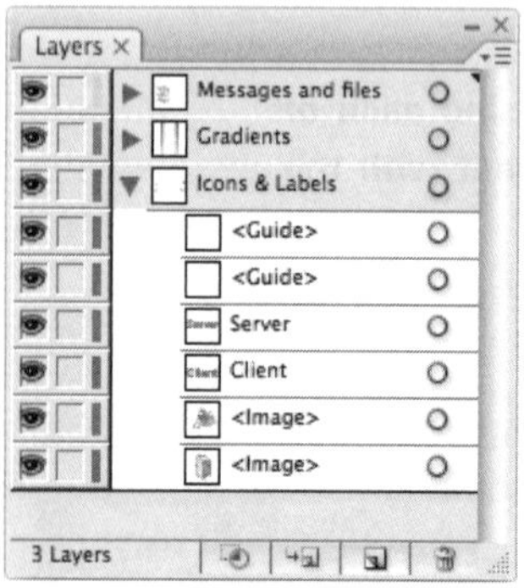

Figure 5.80 *The* Layers *panel*

Layers contain sub-layers, one for each object or group on the layer. Sub-layers containing groups contain their own sub-layers, and so on. Disclosure triangles expand and collapse layers in the Layers panel, shown in Figure 5.80. This panel provides the usual facilities for working with layers (as described in Chapter 2). You can add, delete and rename layers, hide and reveal them, and lock them to prevent any changes to their contents. The buttons down the right-hand side of the panel allow you to *target* a layer or sub-layer, which has the effect of selecting all the objects on that layer or sub-layer. This not only helps you find your way around crowded drawings, it enables you to apply effects to entire layers. This doesn't just mean applying them to all the objects presently on the layer (although it does that). It means that the effect will be applied to the layer from then on – any object you subsequently draw on that layer will immediately acquire any effects that have been applied to the layer. This works for other appearance attributes, too, so you can, in effect, set a default fill and stroke for each layer.

Note the difference between *targeting* a layer with its button, so you can apply appearance attributes to it, and *selecting* it, by clicking its name, so that you can draw on it. You can select a sub-layer corresponding to a group, and anything you draw will be added to the group.

You can drag objects from one layer to another, by selecting them and then dragging the small filled square at the extreme right of the Layers panel up or down to a new layer. Any appearance attributes attached to the object's original layer will be lost, and those attached to the new layer are applied instead. You can drag entire layers to new positions in the panel to change their stacking order in the conventional way, as described in Chapter 2. You can also drag a layer into another layer, where it appears as a sub-layer (although any objects it contains are not automatically grouped) and acquires any appearance attributes attached to the layer that now contains it.

---TRY THIS---

Create a document, and add three extra layers to it. For each of the four layers, use the commands in the Appearance panel menu to set a different fill and stroke. Draw several shapes on each layer. Select an object and then change its fill and stroke by moving it to a different layer.

Try dragging a layer into another layer, so that it becomes a sub-layer. Observe what happens to the objects on the layer that you dragged.

A common use of layers is to isolate parts of a picture so that you can work on it without risk of inadvertently selecting or altering other objects. You could do this by selecting everything else in the Layers palette and locking it. Illustrator provides a more convenient way of achieving the same result, provided that the artwork you want to isolate is either a group or a sub-layer within some other layer. You cannot apply this technique to entire top-level layers. If you want to apply it to one or more objects within a layer, select them and then use the Collect in New Layer command on the Layers panel menu to place them onto their own sub-layer.

Once you have grouped the objects you want to isolate or placed them on a sub-layer, you must then select them in the Layers panel. Selecting them in the document won't do, you must click on the entry in the panel for the sub-layer or group. Having done this, the command Enter Isolation Mode should become available on the panel menu. When you select this command, everything except the isolated objects is subtly dimmed in the document window. The dimming indicates that you cannot select or modify that material, so you are free to work on the isolated parts of the image without worrying about affecting anything else.

Figure 5.81 provides an example of a situation in which isolation mode is useful. The image on the left was actually drawn in Flash and exported to Illustrator. Flash only exports to an old version of the Illustrator file format, which does not support features such as symbols, and does not preserve layers, so the result is a complex image on a single layer. Fortunately, parts of the image are grouped, so it is possible to select the creature and work on it in isolation mode, as shown in the screenshot on the right, without worrying about changing the foliage and other parts of the background.

Figure 5.81 *Working in isolation mode*

When you have finished working on the isolated artwork, use the Exit Isolation Mode command on the Layers panel menu to go back to the normal mode of working, or click on the arrow that appears in the top left-hand corner of the document window in isolation mode. You should recognize that Illustrator automatically goes into isolation mode when you edit a symbol, as we described previously.

┌─TRY THIS──

Make a simple geometrical design by arranging differently coloured rectangles, in the style of a Mondrian painting. Select one of the rectangles and put it on a sub-layer of its own. Select several others and group them. Practise editing the sub-layer and the group in isolation mode. Try dragging a marquee over the design with the arrow tool, in isolation mode and in normal mode and notice the difference in what is selected. What happens if you draw some new objects while in isolation mode?

Type

The characters in outline fonts (PostScript Type 1, TrueType and OpenType fonts) are little vector drawings, so it is not surprising that vector graphics programs are good at manipulating text set using such fonts. That is not to say that Illustrator makes a good page layout program, but it does make it easy to incorporate type as a graphical element in designs. Having done so, you can then manipulate it like any other object, and apply colours, transformations and effects to it. Type remains editable, unless you explicitly render it, so you can change or correct the text at any time. Illustrator even incorporates a spelling checker (which is about as much use as any other) and a find and replace command.

Illustrator provides six different type tools, but the most basic, which normally appears in the Tools panel and is simply referred to as the type tool, automatically changes into one of the other type tools in an appropriate context. You can use this tool exclusively for most type creation tasks, the specialist tools are only needed in somewhat esoteric situations which we will not consider. You can create a line of text or a text frame as described in Chapter 8, by clicking with the type tool at a point where you want the text to begin, or by dragging out the frame, and starting to type. Typographical properties are controlled by the Character panel, and paragraph indentation and alignment can be specified in the Paragraph panel, both of which behave in the standard fashion described in Chapter 8. The most useful typographical controls appear in the Control panel when you have the type tool selected.

You can also use the type tool to fill absolutely any shape with text. Before you can do this you must first create a shape to fill. Then click on the outline of your chosen shape with the type tool. (The cursor changes shape when you hold the type tool over an outline to let you know that the tool will create type in the shape.) Any stroke and fill that you had applied to the shape are removed, and a text cursor appears at the top of the shape. You can then begin to type. Your text is automatically wrapped as you type, to fit within the shape. Figure 5.82 shows how text can be made to fill a triangle. If you need to stroke a shape which you have used as a container for text,

as we did here, just select the shape with the direct selection tool and set the stroke width and colour. If you use the ordinary selection tool it selects the type as well, and changing the stroke attributes would affect the type, but with poor results. (Normally, type does not have a stroke and adding one to it interferes with the appearance of the letters, as illustrated in Figure 5.83.)

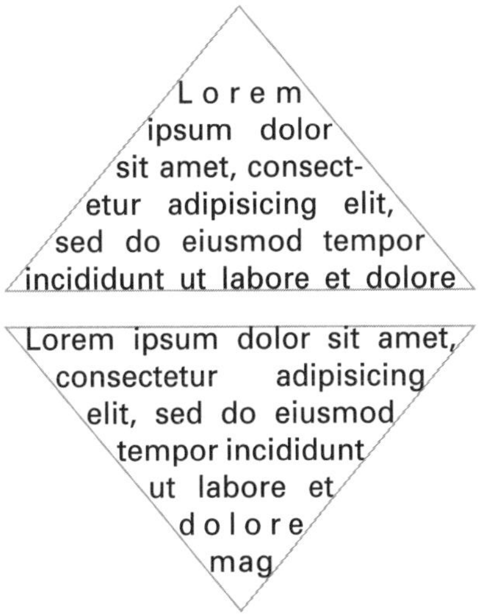

A shape that contains type can be transformed using the arrow tool like any other object, but the type in it will not be transformed. For instance, the lower triangle in Figure 5.82 was originally an exact copy of the top one. It was rotated through 180°; the text within the triangle has stayed the same way up, and adjusted itself to the new orientation of its container. Similarly, if we had scaled the triangle up or down, the text would have stayed the same size. Notice in the upside-down triangle that some extra text has been fitted in. When the text reflowed to fit the new shape, it no longer filled it because of the changed line breaks. On the other hand, if you use the free transform tool, or any of the specialized transformation tools or menu commands, the text will be transformed along with its container, unless you use the direct selection tool to select only the container. (Click the text, not the container's outline, otherwise you will just select a path segment or anchor point.) You can tell whether you have selected the text too, because if you have, the baselines will be shown in the highlight colour.

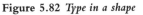

Figure 5.82 *Type in a shape*

Figure 5.83 *Stroked type*

In Figure 5.82 we justified the text, which emphasizes the shape of the container, but at the cost of some unsightly white space within the text. If you know something about typesetting, you can use the Type>Area Type Options… command to open a dialogue in which you can control many aspects of the way in which type is fitted into its container. In particular, you can set an inset spacing, to allow some space between the type and the edge of the containing shape.

┌─ TRY THIS ───┐

Draw some shapes and closed paths and fill each one with some text. Apply some transformations to the shapes in different ways, and see what happens to the text. Practise selecting the text and container independently with the direct selection tool.

Experiment with changing attributes of the type, such as alignment and justification, font and type size, and see how these changes interact with the shape that the type makes and how effectively it works.

└──┘

Another trick you can play on text in Illustrator is to set it along a path, as shown in Figure 5.84. Using the type tool, text can only be set along an open path; if you want to run it round a closed path, as we have done here, you must use the scissors tool to split the path at an anchor point, or use the *path type tool*. When you place the cursor over an open path with the type tool selected, it changes shape to indicate that you can set type on the path (a wiggly line appears through the standard I-beam text cursor). You click to set the starting point and type.

You can manipulate text on a path using the direct selection tool. If you select a path with type on it, three cursors appear in the text, one at each end and one in the middle. By dragging the cursors at the ends, you can alter the amount of space available for the text. If you drag the centre cursor, you can drag the text along the path. Any text that falls off the end disappears – remember that the path is open. You can make more space for the text by dragging the end cursor. If you drag the central cursor across the path, the text will flip over to the other side, changing its orientation as it does so, as in the example at the bottom of Figure 5.84. You can adjust the path's anchor points with the direct selection tool and the type will flow around the new path. As with shapes that you use to enclose text, a path that you set text along normally has its stroke removed. You can select the path with the direct selection tool and restore the stroke, if you wish.

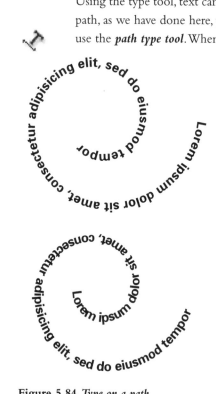

Figure 5.84 *Type on a path*

As well as the type tool and its variants, Illustrator supports a ***vertical type tool***, which has the same variants. It is primarily intended for use with scripts that are written vertically instead of horizontally. It can also be used to set type vertically for special effect.

You can select a block of type, or type on a path, like any other object and apply effects to it. Effects should always be used judiciously, but with text extra caution should be employed. A great deal of work goes into font design, and characters are made up of subtle features; most effects obliterate them, usually resulting in a mess. You must be particularly careful if you want the text to remain readable – it's a different matter if you just want to use it as a starting point for a design. Effects work best when applied to text at large sizes. The example at the top of Figure 5.85 shows some characters that have had the zig-zag effect applied to them. The text is set at 36 pt, with the zig-zag kept at a relatively low size of 2 px. The other two examples show two ways in which type can be give a three-dimensional appearance. The middle example has had a drop shadow effect applied to it, the bottom one has been extruded. These figures are intended to give some idea of the results of applying effects to type in Illustrator; they are definitely not meant to be taken as examples of good practice.

Figure 5.85 *Type effects*

Figure 5.86 *Type converted to shapes*

If you really want to play around with the appearance of text, you can convert it into a shape, so that it loses its textual identity and becomes just another collection of lines and curves. This is done by selecting the text with the arrow tool (not the type tool) and choosing Create Outlines from the Type menu. Having done so, you can distort it with the direct selection tool. Figure 5.86 started out as the typographer's nonsense word Lorem, set in the font Univers. The characters have been converted to outlines, and distorted by dragging anchor points.

Web Graphics

Illustrator's support for Web graphics falls into four areas: image maps, image slicing, bitmapped image export, and export to Web vector graphics formats. Image maps are rarely used on the Web nowadays, and image slicing is not considered good practice, so we will only describe the facilities for exporting images in formats suitable for use on the Web.

Exporting Bitmapped images

Images that are embedded in Web pages are stored in one of the three bitmapped formats that most Web browsers are capable of displaying – GIF, PNG or JPEG. (For more information about these file formats, see Chapter 8.) Vector artwork created in Illustrator can be converted into a bitmapped image and saved in any of these formats.

One way or another, the quality of your original vector image may be degraded when it is turned into a bitmap file small enough to download over the Internet. For most vector artwork, saving as GIF or PNG will entail the least loss of quality. Providing your artwork uses fewer than 256 colours, images can be saved as GIFs without loss of quality. PNG is a superior format in which images can be saved in full colour without loss of quality, but full support for PNG in browsers is not universal, and the format is therefore seldom encountered on the Web at present. The compression of JPEG files involves some loss of information. For photographic images, this loss is not usually perceptible, but the JPEG compression algorithm is poor at handling sharp edges, which are often found in vector graphics, together with areas of flat colour, which are efficiently compressed by GIF and PNG. As a result of these considerations, you should usually save Illustrator documents as GIFs, until such time as PNG is universally supported by Web browsers. Only use JPEG for complex images using gradients or embedded bitmaps.

Using the File>Save for Web & Devices… command, you can not only convert your artwork to a Web image format, you can preview the saved version and dynamically adjust the parameters that control its quality. The dialogue box for this command is shown in Figure 5.87. At the top are four tabs, which you use to select whether to view the original image, an optimized version, the two side by side (2-Up), or the original and three versions optimized with different settings (4-Up), as shown in the figure. (The chequerboard background on the previews indicates transparent areas.) You can thus easily compare the effect of different settings. Below each preview is a summary of its properties, including the size that the saved file will be, and an estimate of how long it will take to download over a slow Internet connection. You can use the pop-up menu above and to the right of the previews to choose a different bandwidth on which to base this estimate.

Controls for setting the various optimization parameters appear at the right of the dialogue box. Much of the time, it will be sufficient to choose one of the presets from the pop-up menu at the top. Each has a short descriptive name that summarizes the settings. Try the GIF presets first.

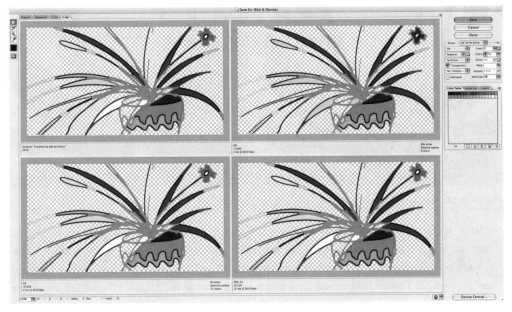

Figure 5.87 *Saving for the Web*

If you do not find any of the presets satisfactory, you can set all the parameters individually. The effects of the settings are described in Chapter 8.

Once you are satisfied with your settings and click OK you will be presented with a standard dialogue to finally save the file. This includes a pop-up menu labelled Format. You should select Images Only from this menu; the other options only apply if you are slicing your image or making an image map – heritage options left over from an earlier era of Web graphics

---
TRY THIS

Open several different images you have created in Illustrator, some plain and simple, others with complex fills and strokes. For each one, select File>Save for Web & Devices.... Switch to 4-up view and apply different GIF and PNG settings. Examine the previews carefully. Choose the version you think is the best (considering quality and file size) and save it.

Try using the JPEG previews on the same images. Can you obtain JPEG files that are as small as the GIFs without loss of image quality?

As well as previewing the appearance of a Web image file when you save it, it is possible to preview artwork for the Web as you draw, as though it was a bitmap, using pixel preview mode. What this means is that the artwork is always shown as if it had been rendered at screen resolution. This usually only makes a difference if you zoom in. Normally, the vectors would be

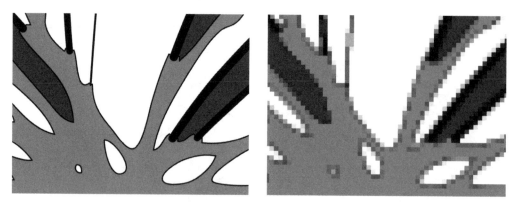

Figure 5.88 *Normal (left) and pixel (right) previews*

rendered at the new magnification when you zoomed, so they would remain as smooth as ever; if you are using a pixel preview, however, the pixels are magnified, showing the jagged edges normally associated with bitmapped images. The View>Pixel Preview command toggles the pixel view on and off. Figure 5.88 shows part of an image blown up 1200%, on the left using the normal preview mode, on the right using pixel preview mode.

---TRY THIS---

Create a document with several shapes, including some with gradient fills and others with brush strokes applied to them. Switch to pixel preview and zoom in to examine the effect of converting the shapes to bitmaps for Web graphics.

Web Vector Graphics

Until recently, vector graphics have had to be rendered as bitmaps in order to be added to Web pages. There are now two vector formats which can be displayed one way or another by most browsers, however, and Illustrator can export artwork in both of these formats.

SVG (Scalable Vector Graphics) is an XML–based language for vector graphics, defined by a World Wide Web Consortium Recommendation. It was designed by a committee including among its members representatives from most of the major companies involved in computer graphics, but its most influential proponent at the time of writing is Adobe. Most modern browsers support the display of SVG images natively to some extent. The exception is Internet Explorer, but plug-ins are available which allow SVG to be displayed in that browser too.

SVG is a highly capable format with roots in PostScript, the established industry standard for vector graphics in print media. It is extensible and can be manipulated by scripts via a Document Object Model, like other elements of Web pages. Being XML, SVG is text-based, which means that SVG files can be written by hand using a text editor or easily generated by scripts, if you are good at that sort of thing. Text files can also be transmitted over networks with less risk of corruption than binary data. The drawback is that they are more bulky than binary files.

You can export a file from Illustrator as SVG, using the File>Save for Web & Devices... command. There are no presets for the SVG format, but you can select SVG from the file format pop-up menu. (This is below and to the left of the presets pop-up.) Various options then become active, but unless you are an SVG expert, just accept the defaults and save the file in the usual way.

TRY THIS

Open a fairly complex Illustrator document, or create a new one, perhaps by painting with the paintbrush tool. Export it as SVG and again as a GIF. Open each image in a Web browser and compare the quality. (If you have an old browser, or only have Internet Explorer, you will need to install a plug-in.)

Although SVG is a W3C standard, which integrates well with other Web technologies and had a lot of support from Adobe, it has not yet achieved widespread popularity, and SVG images are rarely seen on the Web. By far the majority of vector graphics on Web pages use the SWF (Flash movie) format. SWF files can only be displayed by a plug-in, so you cannot entirely rely on every user being able to see them, but the SWF format has become extremely popular and is currently very widely used. Adobe claim that more than 90% of desktop devices can play Flash movies. SWF is a compact format, in which vector objects are represented as binary data. SWF was designed for Flash, so it is often used for interactive animations, but it can equally well be used as a format for still vector graphics.

We describe in Chapter 6 how Illustrator files can be imported into Flash. This is valuable if you want to use Illustrator's superior vector drawing tools to prepare artwork to use in a Flash movie that you assemble in Flash itself, and export as SWF from there. This will usually be the best way to make complex animations, and is essential if you wish to add interactivity. For single images or simple animations, you can export a SWF file directly from Illustrator. There are two ways of doing this. You can select SWF as the format in the Save for Web & Devices dialogue. A slightly cryptic set of relevant options appears, as shown in Figure 5.89.

The pop-up menu immediately below the file format selection is used to choose the earliest version of the Flash Player plug-in you wish to be able to display your SWF. Earlier versions do not have all the capabilities of the latest one, but they may be more widely installed. Choosing the version one less than the current one usually gives you the greatest chance of being playable on the largest number of users' systems, but if you need the latest features you will have to choose the latest player version.

Figure 5.89 *SWF options*

The next pop-up menu offers two choices: AI File to SWF File and AI Layers to SWF Frames. (AI stands for Adobe Illustrator in this context.) The first option is appropriate if you simply want to save your Illustrator artwork in a vector form that can be displayed by the Flash plug-in. The second is explicitly for creating Flash animations using Illustrator's drawing tools. As the menu entry indicates, each layer in your Illustrator artwork becomes a frame of animation. Thus you can make animations by drawing the content of each frame on a separate layer in Illustrator. In many cases, you can copy objects to a new layer and make small changes instead of drawing each frame from scratch. When you save layers as frames, you can set a frame rate for the animation to be played back at, in the box labelled Frame Rate. You can also tick the checkbox labelled Loop, if you want the animation to start again and play continuously after it reaches the end.

The remaining options in the dialogue can be left with their default values until you have learned more about Flash.

As an alternative to using the Save for Web & Devices dialogue, you can use the File>Export command and select Flash (swf) from the pop-up menu labelled Format on Mac OS and Save As Type on Windows at the bottom of the file save dialogue. After you have selected the destination, a dialogue presents the settings for SWF export in a more expansive form. It also offers some additional possibilities. In particular, you can choose to export AI Layers to SWF Files and AI Layers to SWF Symbols as well as exporting to a single file or sending layers to frames. The first of these options lets you split layers (which may still ultimately end up as frames) into separate files, in cases where that provides a more convenient way of organizing them for subsequent processing. The final option turns the layers into Flash symbols, which are reusable objects like Illustrator's symbols. For a fuller explanation of symbols in Flash see Chapter 6.

If you use the File>Export... route to make SWF files, you can click on a button labelled Advanced to see even more options. Most of these relate to embedded bitmaps, but surprisingly, the frame rate is one of the advanced options, too. For single images and simple animations, we would advise you to stick with the basic options provided by the Save for Web & Devices... dialogue. If you are a Flash expert, you will probably usually find it more productive to import Illustrator artwork into Flash and embellish it and export the SWF from there.

┌─TRY THIS─────────────────────────────────

Repeat the previous exercise, but save as SWF instead of SVG.

Create a simple animation by drawing an object, then pasting it into several layers at slightly different positions in Illustrator. (If you have done some animation before, make a more elaborate animation.) Export the layers as frames in a SWF file and preview your animation in a Web browser.

DON'T FORGET

Use the magic wand and the Select>Same sub-menu to select items with the same or similar stroke and fill attributes.

Use colour groups to organize swatches.

Create colour groups using colour harmony rules in the Color Guide panel.

Use the Live Color dialogue to adjust the colours in a colour group and apply them to selected artwork.

Convert objects to guides and use smart guides to help arrange objects.

Use the Align panel or the buttons on the Control panel to align and distribute objects. Use the direct select tool to select anchor points for alignment using the Align panel.

Organize objects in layers and sub-layers. Target layers and set layer attributes. Drag selected artwork from one layer to another in the Layers panel.

Use isolation mode to avoid accidentally selecting or changing objects.

You can set type in shapes or along paths. Apply effects to type or convert it to outlines and modify it, but exercise discretion in doing this.

Export bitmapped images, SVG and SWF files using the Save for Web & Devices dialogue.

WHAT ELSE?

We have been able to describe most of Illustrator in this chapter, because there are only a few basic concepts in vector graphics, and once you understand about paths, shapes, strokes and fills, most of the tools that work with them are simple. You will find that we have omitted some refinements and details, but these should soon make sense to you once you have grasped the basics.

Among the more esoteric tools we have omitted are the liquify (sic) tools, which apply local distortions to parts of objects, and the graph tools, which are used to create various types of charts from data. (It is highly debatable whether Illustrator is the best program for such tasks.) There are also some advanced operations you can perform on paths, if you are happy thinking about vector artwork in terms of paths, but these are less important than they used to be, with the introduction of more intuitive ways of working, such as Live Paint.

A theoretically interesting feature is the ability to create different versions of an image on the basis of sets of data that control certain aspects of its appearance. However, to take full advantage of this type of data-driven graphics requires the use of programming to generate the data sets.

Flash

In This Chapter

Flash began life as a program for creating vector graphics animations, often with interactive features, to be played over the Internet. Over the years, it has grown into a tool for building "media-rich" Web applications, incorporating bitmapped and vector graphics, sound and video as well as animation. Interactivity is provided by a scripting language, ActionScript, which resembles JavaScript. ActionScript too has evolved over the years; it is now capable of performing elaborate computation in response to events, manipulating graphics and interface elements and exchanging data with remote servers. It is thus misleading to see Flash simply as an animation program with some interactive features – although it is still a very popular tool for that purpose – since ActionScript allows it to be used to build sophisticated front-ends to all sorts of distributed systems. Web developers who find the technologies defined by World Wide Web Consortium standards restrictive use Flash to create more expressive and dynamic Web interfaces, although this comes at the cost of abandoning Web standards, and in practice it has often led to poor accessibility. An adequate description of ActionScript would require a complete book in itself, however – and you would need a fair amount of programming knowledge to understand it – so in this chapter we have just concentrated on using Flash without scripting.

Flash movies can be embedded in Web pages. Web browsers must use a plug-in or ActiveX control to play them when the page is displayed. The Flash plug-in and control are distributed with almost all browsers and are freely available for all major platforms (Linux, Mac OS X and twenty-first century versions of Windows). It is estimated that one or other Flash plug-in is installed on 98% of desktop computers in "advanced economies" and on slightly fewer in the developing world. Many Flash movies are destined for the Web, but they can also be exported as *projectors*, which play in isolation. Flash movies are also becoming widely used on mobile devices, such as phones and PDAs, which implement a restricted player known as **Flash Lite**. Adobe have also created the **AIR** (*Adobe Integrated Runtime*) environment, which allows applications built from a mixture of Flash and Web-standard content to be run on the desktop.

The diversity of outputs from Flash, and the range of possible destinations, implies a diversity of ways of using the program, with varying emphases on drawing, arranging imported media in time, animation and scripting. Even without knowledge of ActionScript you can create rich time-based media that can be exported in a compact form, embedded in Web pages and streamed over the Internet or played on a mobile device.

Before we begin to describe Flash, we should warn you that the program has always suffered from usability problems and continues to do so. Although the latest version is an integrated part of Adobe's various Creative Suite packages, there are still interface inconsistencies between Flash and the longer-established Adobe applications, such as Photoshop and Illustrator. To take a typical example, Flash has an **Align** panel, which uses the same icons as the **Align** panel in Photoshop and Illustrator, but it has different options – not worse, but different – which can be confusing if you move between the programs. Similarly, Flash's **View** menu is near the left end of the menu bar, next to the **Edit** menu, whereas the corresponding menu in Photoshop and Illustrator is to the right, next to the **Window** menu. Generally, the menu structure seems to have a different logic behind it, so you often cannot find menu commands in Flash where you might expect them. Tools that have the same icon as those in other programs don't necessarily work in the same way. More seriously, Flash is sometimes very particular about the exact order in which you carry out certain operations, and things can go wrong if you deviate from this order. Some users describe Flash as "cranky", and it can certainly seem that way. The quantity of Flash content in existence shows that it is possible to overcome its crankiness, but it can lead to frustration.

Basic Concepts

Documents and Movies

A *Flash document* is the file in which you assemble and organize various media elements, which may include animation, still images, video and sound. You also attach scripts to these elements in the Flash document. The document is what you work on in Flash, but it is not the finished product that people will see. This usually takes the form of a *Flash movie*, often also called a *SWF file*, which is published from Flash and can be embedded in a Web page or played by the stand-alone player. (Although they are referred to as movies, they do not necessarily contain moving pictures; a Flash movie may consist of a single frame.) The document defines the appearance and behaviour of the movie; you can edit documents, but not movies (except by importing them into a document). Flash documents have the extension .fla; Flash movies use .swf as their extension.

Flash can also export *animated GIFs*, *QuickTime* and *WMV* movies, and sequences of still images in a variety of file formats. Most of these additional export formats cause some features, especially interactivity, to be lost, and are primarily of use to animators, for exchanging animations between Flash and other programs or for preparing them for video distribution.

Documents are usually created using the **File>New...** command. This causes the dialogue box shown in Figure 6.1 to be displayed; choose the type of document you want from the list on the left. Frequently the first choice, **Flash File (ActionScript 3.0)**, will be correct: it creates a new document for you to work in, and allows you to use the most recent version of ActionScript. Even if you aren't going to do any scripting, some features you may use will have scripts hidden within them, and some of these rely on ActionScript 3.0. If it is important that your published movie be compatible with older versions of the Flash plug-in, you should use the second option, **Flash File (ActionScript 2.0)**. We will look at some of the other possibilities briefly later on.

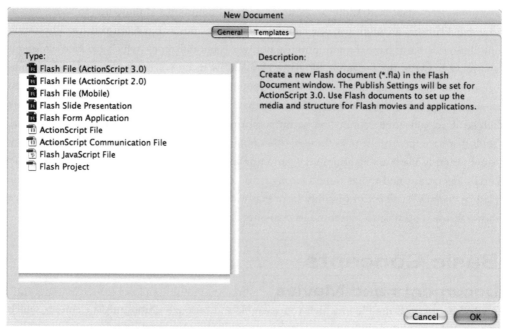

Figure 6.1 *Creating a new Flash document*

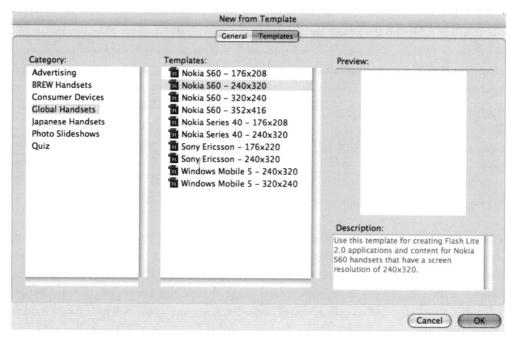

Figure 6.2 *Creating a document from a template*

The new document dialogue has two tabs; if you click on **Templates** instead of the one labelled **General**, the dialogue shows you a list of categories, within each of which there is a list of *templates*, as shown in Figure 6.2. Choosing a template creates a new document whose size is determined by the template and which may include some scripts and graphic elements appropriate to the sort of movie you are making. The templates are specially useful when you are creating movies for mobile devices. Selecting a template from the categories for different sorts of handsets or devices sets up your document correctly, so that the stage is the right size to fit on the device's screen, and the **Publish** settings (see below) are set up to target the Flash Lite player. This imposes certain restrictions on what you can do with Flash, as we will explain later.

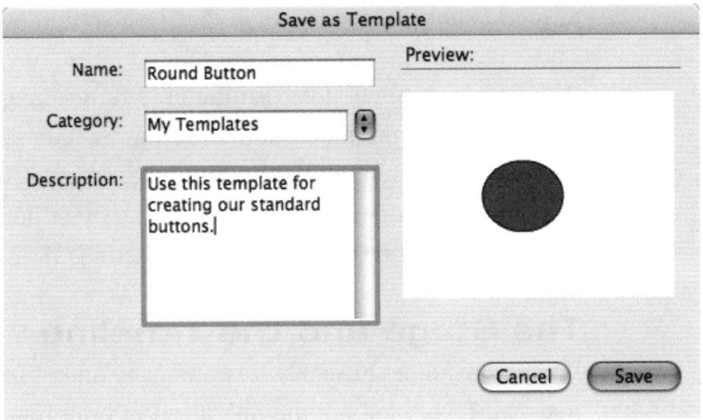

The remaining categories of template are for specialized types of Flash movie, as implied by their names. You can also save your own movies as templates, using the **File>Save as Template...** command. You would normally use this command to save a skeleton that you wanted to reuse to create a collection of similar documents. When you save a template, you are prompted to give it a name (which will be displayed in the new document dialogue in future), and

Figure 6.3 *Saving a template*

to assign it to a category – you can either select an existing category from the pop-up menu, or type the name of a new category, as shown in Figure 6.3. You can also enter a short description.

If you haven't disabled the Welcome screen, as we recommended in Chapter 2, you can create common types of document from that screen when the program starts up. If you wish, you can also instruct Flash to create a new document on each start-up, by setting the appropriate option in the general **Preferences**.

When you have finished working on your Flash document, you will usually need to create a Flash movie from it. Movies may be created using the **File>Export>Export Movie...** command. (Note that **File>Save** and **File>Save As...** save the document, not a movie. Similarly, **File>Open** and the **File>Open Recent** sub-menu also work with documents, not with movies.) Make sure that the format is set to **Flash Movie** when you choose the destination in the usual file-saving dialogue. After you click the **Save** button, a second dialogue box appears, which allows you to set various parameters of the saved movie. It is usually safe to use the defaults. An exported movie normally plays in a continuous loop (unless you have explicitly prevented it from doing so). That is, when it reaches the final frame, it immediately goes back to the beginning and plays again.

When you have finished work on a Flash document, you will often want to export a movie and embed it in a Web page. The File>Publish command will export a movie together with the necessary HTML code to embed it, in a single step. Using this command results in the creation of two files: the Flash movie itself and an HTML file, which can be opened in a browser where it will display the movie. An HTML file created in this way contains nothing but the markup needed for the Flash movie, so if you want to add more content to the Web page you will need to edit the HTML, for example in Dreamweaver. (See Chapter 7.) The File>Publish Settings... command can be used to set parameters for the SWF and HTML files, and to select other formats for export and to set appropriate parameters for them. Note that by default Flash will include any layers you have hidden when exporting the final movie; to avoid this happening it is important to turn off Export hidden layers in the Flash section of the Publish Settings... dialogue.

Web designers should note that the HTML document generated by Flash is not valid. You may prefer to export the movie and write the markup yourself, although you will need to use one of several slightly dubious tricks that have been devised to get round the different requirements of Internet Explorer and other browsers. If you don't care about validation, it is safe to leave everything under HTML in the Publish Settings dialogue set to the default values to begin with.

The Stage and the Timeline

What distinguishes Flash movies from many other forms of interactive multimedia is that they are *time-based*. They are not the only form of time-based interactive media, but they have become the most widely used. Flash movies consist of one or more *frames* which – except where there is only a single frame – are displayed in succession, unless a script interferes with this sequence. This is in contrast to hypermedia – in particular, Web pages – where the page remains static until the user does something, such as clicking on a link. (Of course, Web pages can contain time-based media, but we are talking about the fundamental structural principle here.) Because of this, Flash has to provide a means of arranging elements in time. Anything that is displayed on a screen is inevitably arranged in space, too, so Flash also needs a way of arranging elements spatially.

The two most important components of the Flash interface are its *timeline* and a window called the *stage*, which perform these two functions. The timeline shows the sequence of frames. The stage is where you create or assemble the elements of each frame. Sometimes, the stage is referred to as the document window in the Flash manual, by analogy with other programs, but this is not really accurate. The stage only displays part of the document at a time (a very small part in the case of a long movie); it is the timeline which actually shows all of the document, by providing a spatial view of the temporal succession of frames making up the movie. The stage only displays the contents of the frame which is currently selected in the timeline. In the default workspaces, the timeline and stage are docked together, as shown in Figure 6.4, but the panel menu in the top right corner of the timeline has a Placement sub-menu, with commands which can be used

Figure 6.4 *The timeline and the stage*

to position the timeline on the other sides of the stage. (You will often want to see as many frames as possible, so it usually makes most sense to dock the timeline to the top or bottom, but for a document with just a few frames and many layers, using one of the sides for the timeline may give you more space to work on the stage.) By choosing Undock from Document, the timeline can be separated from the stage and will then behave as a dockable panel. If you are working with two monitors, for example, you can thus drag the timeline to one of them, leaving the stage on the other, which will give you a more convenient working layout. Finally, by clicking on the icon at the top left corner of the stage, you can hide or reveal the timeline.

As you can see in Figure 6.4, a numerical scale runs along the top of the timeline, indicating frame numbers. Each frame is represented by a narrow column below this scale. Where a frame has something in it, as the first 40 frames do in Figure 6.4, its colour and the icons that appear in the timeline provide information about its content, as we will explain later. Empty frames are shown blank, as every frame beyond the 40th is in Figure 6.4. Every fifth blank frame is shaded, simply to make it easier to match them to the frame numbers in the scale.

A Flash document is composed of layers. Each layer extends through time across all the frames. In the timeline, layers are stacked vertically, with the foremost at the top. So in Figure 6.4 there are four layers, whose names are shown on the left of the timeline. The timeline is thus a two-dimensional view of the document, with time (measured in number of frames) running from left to right and layers ordered from top to bottom. You can add new layers by clicking on the Insert Layer icon at the left of the row of icons below the layer names. Double-click a layer's name to change it. For complex documents, you can create *layer folders* to group layers together. Click the Insert Layer Folder icon and then drag layers into the folder. You can hide or show a layer or layer folder by clicking in the column below the eye icon. Clicking on the eye icon itself shows or hides all the layers. Similarly, you can lock and unlock layers by clicking below the padlock icon. In Figure 6.4, all but one of the layers have been locked, to prevent accidental changes.

Figure 6.4 also shows how the stage extends beyond the visible area of the frame. The additional area, known as the *pasteboard*, is shown in light grey. In this example, only the contents of the pale rectangle, with foliage and the nose of the creature, will be visible in this frame when the exported movie is played. By placing objects on the pasteboard like this, you can arrange for them to move into or out of the frame as a movie plays, as we will show later. (You could think of this in terms of actors and scenery coming on to the stage from the wings, or exiting into the wings.) You can also see in Figure 6.4 that, if more than one document is open, tabs are used to keep all the documents in a single window. You move between open documents by clicking on the tabs. (If you undock the timeline from the stage, the tabs appear on the stage.)

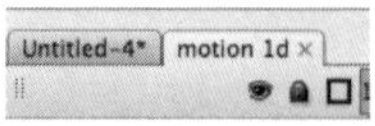

The timeline and the stage work in conjunction with one another. The current frame is always the one that is displayed on the stage. You can set a new current frame by dragging the marker attached to the vertical red bar at the top of the timeline through the frame numbers. Having set the current frame, you create or modify its contents on the stage. Flash's drawing tools, which are described in the next section, may be used for these operations, but you can also import frames from a file created in some other program.

A newly created document contains just a single empty frame on one layer, so its timeline looks like Figure 6.5. By default, the pixel dimensions of a new document are set to the rather unusual value of 550 by 400 pixels, and the frame rate — that is, the speed at which any movie you export will play back — to 12 frames per second, a reasonable value for many types of animation. You can change the pixel dimensions and frame rate by using the Modify>Document... command. (Clicking on the button labelled Make Default in this dialogue will cause all subsequently created movies to use the new values you have specified.) Once you have created a document there are many things you can do to it, but at heart Flash is a program for creating vector-based animation, so we will start by describing how to do that.

Figure 6.5 *The timeline of a new document*

Flash can be used in several different ways to create animation. The most traditional method is to create each frame individually by drawing it or importing an image from a file. The completed animation is a sequence of frames, each one differing to some extent from the preceding one. The illusion of movement is created by persistence of vision when the frames of the sequence are displayed in rapid succession. Other methods only require you to create certain frames, known as *keyframes*, and use some of Flash's special animation features to generate the rest of the frames automatically. If you intend to create the artwork in Flash itself you will need to do some drawing in at least some frames. Hence we must begin by looking at Flash's drawing tools.

TRY THIS

Create a new Flash document and add some layers to it. Change the pixel dimensions and frame rate to new values.

Look at the Publish Settings. Try selecting some additional formats and see what options become available. For the time being, turn off Export hidden layers under the Flash tab, to avoid any "draft" layers being exported.

DON'T FORGET

Flash was originally a program for creating animation with interactivity, but it has evolved; now it is also a tool for building media-rich Web applications.

Objects are organized in a Flash document, then the result is exported as a Flash movie to be embedded in a Web page or played on a mobile device.

A Flash movie (or SWF) is composed of one or more frames. Movies can also be exported as a sequence of still images or as video.

Documents can be created from scratch or from a template.

The timeline shows the sequence of frames over time, from left to right.

The stage is a window in which individual frames can be created and edited.

Flash documents are composed of layers, which are displayed in the timeline.

Artwork

As well as providing drawing facilities, Flash also allows you to import different kinds of artwork from other applications. Since Flash is able to import Illustrator files, we would recommend that, if possible, you do any vector drawing in Illustrator, which is an excellent vector graphics application, instead of in Flash, which is not. Sometimes, though, it is necessary or more convenient to edit imported artwork in Flash, so you need to know how to do so, and if you don't have Illustrator, you will need to do your vector drawing in Flash itself. You can also import scanned drawings and *vectorize* them in Flash; we describe how to do this later on.

Drawing

Flash is a ***vector graphics*** application. This means that a picture (that is, the contents of a frame) consists of a collection of shapes, each of which is made up of simple lines or ***strokes*** and which may be filled with a colour or a more complex pattern. You create pictures on the stage, using drawing tools. If you have used another vector drawing program, such as Illustrator (see Chapter 5) or Freehand, the principles behind Flash's drawing tools will be familiar. There are, however, some crucial differences between Flash and other vector graphics programs.

Lines and Shapes

The simplest thing you can draw is a line. For most people, the easiest way to draw a line is with the ***pencil tool***, which is selected by clicking on its icon in the Tools panel. Lines are drawn by dragging the tool across the stage using the mouse, or a pressure-sensitive pen on a graphics tablet. Flash inserts a straight line or ***Bézier path*** (see Chapter 8) that approximates the motion of the cursor. The style of approximation is determined by the option you choose for the pencil tool.

Figure 6.6
Options for the pencil tool

In general, whenever a tool is selected, a set of options becomes available. Some of these appear in the Properties panel, which serves much the same function as the Options bar in Photoshop and Illustrator. However, others appear as buttons and pop-up menus in a small panel at the bottom of the Tools panel. For the pencil tool, two options are set in this way, with the controls shown in Figure 6.6. We will describe the function of the round button at the top later. The pop-up menu below it provides three options to control the smoothing applied to the lines you draw. If you select Straighten, your movements will be approximated by straight lines or, if they are obviously curved, by segments of circles or ellipses. Furthermore, if your drawing looks like a triangle, rectangle, square, ellipse or circle it will be converted to a precise version of the shape it approximates. (Some options, which can be set in the Drawing pane of the Preferences dialogue, control how good an approximation must be before Flash will turn a curve into a line or substitute a geometric shape.) If you select Smooth instead of Straighten, ***Bézier curves*** with few control points will be used to approximate the line. Finally, if you select Ink, the movements will be followed closely, using curves with many control points – generally, this will produce a somewhat ragged line if you are trying to draw with a mouse. No matter which smoothing option you select, holding down the shift key while you are dragging will force the pencil to draw a straight line that is either horizontal or vertical.

The ***line tool*** and ***pen tool*** provide alternatives to the pencil tool for drawing lines and curves. The line tool can only create shapes made out of straight lines. After selecting it, you click at the point where you wish one end of the first line to be and then drag with the mouse button held down; the line appears to be pulled out of the starting point, so that you can easily see what its final appearance will be. When you let go of the mouse, the line is fixed with its other end at the point where the mouse button was released. If you immediately press and drag again, you can add a second line joined to the first. In this way, polygonal shapes can be drawn quickly. Holding the shift key while dragging constrains the lines to be at multiples of 45° to the horizontal.

The pen tool in Flash behaves in a standard fashion, as described in Chapter 8. It can be used to draw straight lines, by clicking at successive end points, or Bézier curves, by dragging away from the end points towards control points. It is the most flexible curve-drawing tool in Flash's **Tools** panel, but the least intuitive if you do not have any prior experience of vector drawing.

TRY THIS

Create a new document and practise drawing lines on the stage with each of the pencil, line and pen tools. Try drawing a rectangular shape, a curvy line and a simple face, selecting the appropriate tool or combination of tools for each.

Stroke and Fill

Any stroke (a line or curve) has a specific weight (thickness) and colour; you can also choose whether to draw it as a solid line or in some other style. These various stroke properties can be set using the **Properties** panel whenever a drawing tool is selected. The properties available for the pencil tool are shown in Figure 6.7. At the top is a pop-up menu, from which the stroke style is chosen; the default set of styles includes a hairline, solid line, dashes, dots and rough wavy lines. To the left of this pop-up is a field for entering the weight of the stroke. Units of pixels are used. A value between 0 and 200 may be entered, or a slider control, activated by clicking on the small triangle to the right of the text field, can be used to vary the width. (You cannot alter the stroke weight if you choose **hairline** as the style.) You also can set a **Smoothing** value between 0 and 100 to specify the amount of smoothing applied to lines that are drawn with the **Smooth** option selected in the **Tools** panel. If you click the **Custom...** button on the right of the **Properties** panel, an additional **Stroke Style** dialogue opens, providing a wider range of style options. The colour of the stroke may be set in several different ways, which we will describe shortly.

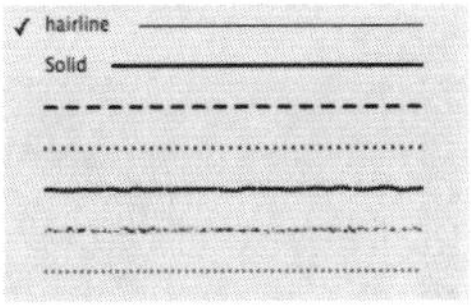

When you draw a line, the values that were last set in the **Properties** panel are used to determine its weight, colour, style and so on. You can alter its appearance at any time by selecting the line (see the section on selection below) and changing these values. An alternative quick way of

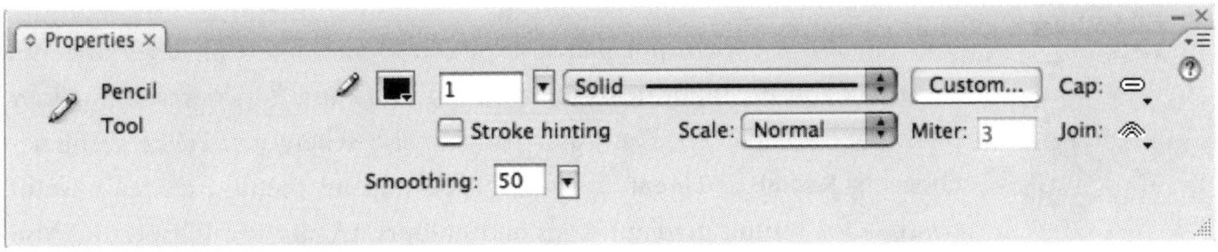

Figure 6.7 *Properties for the pencil tool*

changing strokes is to use the **ink bottle** tool from the Tools panel. When you click on a line using this tool, the values currently set in the Properties panel are applied to it.

If you draw a closed shape with the pencil, line or pen tool, it is initially left unfilled. To colour it in, you first set a **fill** colour, and then select the **paint bucket** from the Tools panel and click inside the shape. The paint bucket fills any area with a line drawn round it. It provides an option

(in the usual place at the bottom of the Tools panel) for determining how well joined up the line needs to be. By default, it ignores small gaps, but you can tell it to ignore bigger ones, or insist that the boundary be properly closed.

There are several different ways to select the stroke and fill colour. Near the bottom of the Tools panel there are two colour swatches, indicating the current stroke and fill. The stroke swatch has a pencil above it, the fill has a paint bucket. If you hold down the mouse over either of these swatches, a colour palette, as shown in Figure 6.8, pops up. You can click on one of the colours in the palette to choose one of the default colours, or on the white icon with a red stroke through it (at the top right of the palette) to choose no colour. You can also choose one of the gradients at the bottom of the panel, which allows you to do things like drawing a rainbow-coloured line,

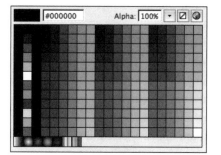

or applying a gradient fill. Alternatively, you can type a hexadecimal colour value in the text field at the top left of the palette. Finally, by clicking on the icon in the top right-hand corner of the palette, you can open the system colour picker and choose any colour you want. The term **alpha** is used in Flash to mean transparency. By typing a percentage in the Alpha field, you can make fills or strokes partially transparent.

Figure 6.8 *Setting a colour*

When you have the pencil, line or pen tool selected, a swatch with attached colour palette also becomes available in the Properties panel. (It can be seen in Figure 6.7.) This is used in the same way as above, to set the stroke colour. When you select the paint bucket, the same control appears in the Properties panel for setting the fill colour. When you select certain other drawing tools, which we will describe shortly, swatches for both stroke and fill appear in the Properties panel.

You can also use the Color panel, shown in Figure 6.9. It includes swatches for stroke and fill, input fields for entering R, G and B values, and a colour picker (see Chapter 8). The Color panel is also where you create gradients; choosing Radial or Linear from the Type pop-up menu activates a set of controls for setting gradient stops and colours. (Again, see Chapter 8.) You can also create **bitmap fills** in this panel, to paint with bitmapped textures.

Figure 6.9 *The* Color *panel*

The *eyedropper tool* can be used to apply the stroke or fill used for one object to another. If you click on a line with the eyedropper, the stroke weight and colour are set to those of the line you clicked on. The values are shown in the Properties panel and the colour is set in the Color panel and in the stroke swatch in the Tools panel. At the same time, the tool changes into the ink bottle, so if you then click on another line its stroke will be set to match the values you sampled with the eyedropper. If you use the eyedropper to sample a fill, by clicking inside a filled area, the fill colour values are set to match the sampled area and the tool changes into the paint bucket, so you can transfer that fill to other objects.

Shapes

Like most drawing programs, Flash provides a *rectangle tool* for drawing rectangles and squares, the latter being drawn if the shift key is held down while you draw. You simply select the tool and drag out the shape. The *oval tool* (which at first will be in the concealed sub-menu under the rectangle tool) makes elliptical shapes, including circles. Holding down the shift key forces a circle to be drawn; otherwise an ellipse is produced which fits inside the invisible rectangle whose opposite corners are at the start and end of the drag. (When you try this, you will see that it is more intuitive than it may sound.)

The Properties panel lets you set the stroke and fill values for shapes when either of these tools is selected; by default it will simply use the last settings chosen. Other options for each tool are also available, as Figure 6.10 shows. For the rectangle, there is an interesting option which allows you to draw rectangles with rounded corners, by setting corner radii using the controls in the lower part of the panel. For the oval tool, there is an unusual option for drawing ovals with slices cut out; in this case you have to specify the angle of the slice with the Start angle and End angle controls. The Inner radius setting allows you to specify a hole in the middle of the oval, so this tool can generate toroidal shapes. Some of these possibilities are illustrated in Figure 6.11.

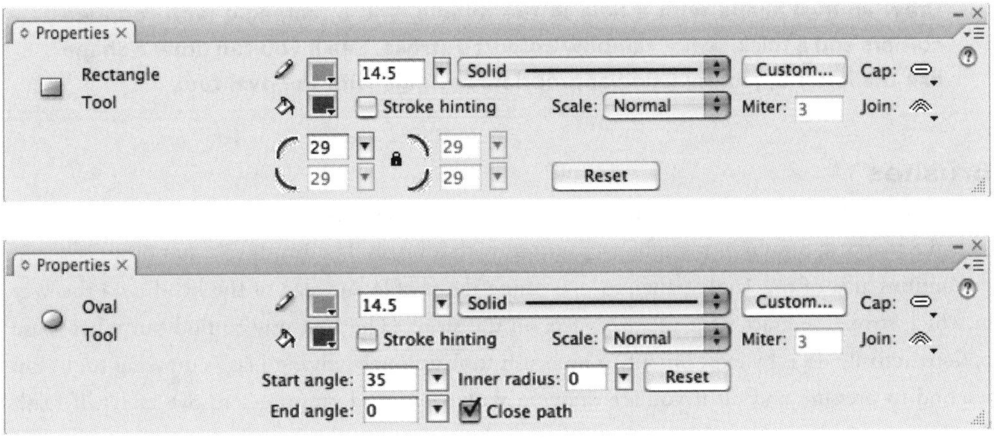

Figure 6.10 *Setting properties of rectangles (top) and ovals (bottom)*

Flash also has a second, similar pair of shape tools, the ***rectangle primitive*** and ***oval primitive*** tools (also found under the rectangle tool in the Tools panel). These are used in the same way as their non-primitive counterparts, but the parameters of the shapes that they produce can be changed later, whereas with the basic tools, values such as the radius of a rectangle's corners are fixed forever when you draw it. (The need for two separate pairs of tools is something of a mystery.)

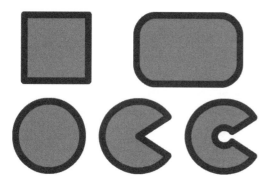

Figure 6.11 *Shapes drawn with the rectangle and oval tools*

Finally, there is a ***polystar tool***, for drawing stars and regular polygons. In a further anomaly, options such as the number of sides of the polygon are not set in the Properties panel, but in a dialogue launched by clicking on a button labelled Options... in the Properties panel. The dialogue allows you to set the style of polygon or star you require, the number of sides and so on.

The precise geometrical shapes that you can draw with these tools may not be of much use for most cartoons and animation, but they are often used to create user interface elements such as buttons, as we will see later.

TRY THIS

Practise drawing lines and shapes using the pencil tool. Use a range of different colours, styles and stroke weights. Using the eyedropper tool as we described, transfer the properties of some of your lines and shapes to other ones.

Draw a rectangular shape, each of whose sides has a different line style and colour. Add a gradient fill. (You may need to adjust the gap-closing option for the paint bucket if your drawing is not accurate.)

Draw an oval shape with a hole in the middle, and a rectangle with rounded corners and a thick, wavy, rainbow-coloured stroke. See if you can draw a shape like the letter C, just by using appropriate settings with the oval tool.

Brushes

At the opposite extreme to the formal geometry of rectangles and ovals, the ***brush tool*** allows you to make marks in a fashion resembling painting with a brush. The brush tool has options, set in the options area of the Tools panel, to determine the profile and size of the brush and the way in which strokes interact with other objects on the stage. (The best way to find out what these options actually do is by experiment.) The brush tool, uniquely among Flash's drawing tools, can respond to pressure and tilt if you are drawing with a pen and pressure-sensitive tablet. If Flash detects that a driver for a graphics tablet is installed on your computer, extra options appear when

you select the brush tool. If you click on the teardrop-shaped icon in the tool's options, the width of the stroke will vary according to the pressure you apply with the pen; click on the tilt-sensitivity icon, and the angle of the brush strokes will vary with the angle of the pen. Figure 6.12 shows some types of marks that can be made with Flash's paintbrush.

The brush tool is probably the most appealing way for people trained in the use of traditional art materials to draw in Flash, especially if a pressure-sensitive tablet is being used, although it doesn't simulate art materials at all well – the marks it makes usually look more like those made with a felt-tip marker pen than with a paint brush. Flash's brush tool is very basic, compared to Photoshop's or Illustrator's brushes. In particular, there is only a choice of eight different preset sizes and nine different preset tip shapes, which is very limiting.

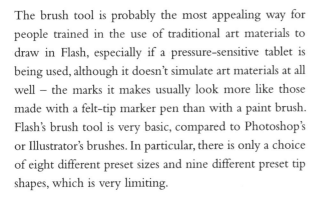

Figure 6.12 *Painting with the paintbrush tool*

The apparent simplicity of the brush can be misleading: despite appearances, "brush strokes" are actually fills. If you were to draw a ring with the brush, for example, you would not have produced a circular line with a heavy stroke, but a filled band, whose outline was in fact a pair of concentric circles. The stroke is invisible when you use the brush tool; all you see is the fill of the shape. On the left of Figure 6.13 is a flower drawn with a calligraphic brush. On the right, we have made the stroke visible instead of the fill, to demonstrate the way in which each apparent brush stroke is constructed as a shape. Because brush strokes are fills and not strokes, when you have the brush selected you set the colour of the "line" you are drawing by setting the fill in the Properties panel or elsewhere, not the stroke. (Contrast this with the way that calligraphic effects are applied to strokes in Illustrator.)

Figure 6.13 *"Brush strokes" are fills*

┌─ TRY THIS ───

Practise drawing with the brush tool, using different sized brushes and experimenting with pressure- and tilt-sensitivity if you have a graphics tablet. Try drawing a simple face or animal – or a cartoon – with the brush, using different colours for the eyes, mouth, hair and other details.

Selection

Even if you avoid drawing in Flash by importing artwork from another program, you will some-times need to be able to select parts of a drawing so that you can move or transform them. When we come to animating in Flash, for example, you will see that one way to make animation is by moving or transforming selected shapes or parts of shapes. Flash provides a ***selection tool***, whose icon is the conventional black arrow. When you have selected something with this tool, you can move or transform it, or change its stroke and fill using the controls in the **Properties** panel. Flash's way of selecting and manipulating objects is not conventional, however. It has some unex-pected features, which can be confusing for people familiar with other media tools programs.

Crucially, the way in which objects behave when they are selected depends on which ***drawing mode*** was in force when they were created. The default drawing mode – and therefore the one you are likely to experience first – is ***merge drawing***. In this mode, whenever you draw something it interacts with anything that is already on the stage. Objects that are drawn in this way exhibit three distinctive characteristics. First, strokes and fills can be selected independently. Second, by default only individual segments of a compound path are selected. Third, where shapes overlap, they are split into separate pieces. This can lead to much confusion and frustration at times.

Consider the filled oval shown at the left of Figure 6.14. Clicking inside the shape with the arrow tool does not, as you might expect, select the entire filled ellipse. Instead, it just selects the fill. Once it has been selected, the fill can be manipulated independently of the enclosing stroke that is apparently its boundary; for example, it can be dragged out of it, as shown. If you want to select an entire shape that was made in merge drawing mode – that is, the fill and stroke together – you must double-click in the fill.

Where an object is drawn from separate strokes, as, for example, you might draw a triangle with the line or polystar tool, clicking on a line only selects the part drawn with an individual stroke. With freehand lines, you may find that when you click on a line a much smaller part of it is selected than you expect. Double-clicking a line selects all the lines connected to it, so in the example of a triangle, double-clicking any one side of the triangle would select all three sides (but double-clicking inside the triangle would select its fill as well).

Things become more complicated when shapes overlap, because in Flash, when a line crosses a shape, it divides that shape into segments which will be selected separately by the arrow tool. The line is also divided into segments at the points where it crosses the shapes. After moving the fill of our ellipse we end up in just this situation: the elliptical line that was the stroke crosses the oval fill. If we now click on the line and drag it, only the visible segment moves. The original oval line has been split. The same thing happens again in the new position. The small segment at the top can therefore be selected and dragged independently, as shown at the right of Figure 6.14.

Figure 6.14 *Selection of line and fill for objects drawn in merge drawing mode*

In order to select the areas or lines you need, you can hold down the shift key while clicking or double-clicking. If you do so and click on an unselected object it will be added to the selection; if you shift-click on an already selected object, it will be removed from the selection.

The arrow tool can also be used to select several objects or parts of objects at a time. If you hold down the mouse button and drag with the arrow tool, a selection rectangle is pulled out. Any object inside the rectangle becomes selected when you release the mouse button. If the objects were drawn in merge drawing mode, where an edge of the selection rectangle passes through an object, both strokes and fills are split along the edge, and only the parts that lie within the rectangle will be selected. This is another potential surprise if you are used to the behaviour of selection tools in other programs, but it is consistent with the way Flash treats overlapping shapes made in merge drawing mode.

Selections can also be made with the *lasso tool*. If this tool is used without modifiers, it will produce a freehand outline and anything inside the outline will be selected. Again, if the objects were drawn in merge drawing mode, both strokes and fills will be split wherever the selection outline intersects the objects. If you select the lasso tool and then click the polygon mode button at the bottom of the Tools panel, the lasso behaves like the line tool, enabling you to draw polygonal selection areas. In this case, you must double-click to close the selection polygon; for standard lasso selections it is sufficient to let go of the mouse button.

---TRY THIS---

> **Draw some shapes or a simple scene or object of your choice, using both strokes and fills (in the default merge drawing mode). Experiment with altering parts of the drawing by making selections with the arrow and lasso tools and then changing line characteristics, fill colours and the arrangement of the shapes.**

Merge drawing mode may not seem odd if you have never used any other vector drawing program, although the way that selection splits objects and strokes can be very disconcerting. If you have used another vector drawing program, however, you will probably think that the objects you draw – ellipses, rectangles, and so on – should retain their identities. For instance, in Figure 6.14, you would expect that you could select the entire filled ellipse and drag it as a single object. You can indeeed do this in Flash, but only if it was drawn in *object drawing* mode.

If you look back at Figure 6.6, you will see that, as well as the smoothing options, there is a small round button in the options area of the Tools panel. This appears when any drawing tool is selected, and it is used to switch between the default merge drawing mode and object drawing mode. To use object drawing mode you must explicitly turn object drawing on by clicking this button – but don't forget to turn it off again if you wish to return to merge drawing mode. Any shape which was drawn in object drawing mode can be selected with a single click using the arrow tool, and it does not split any object it intersects. Furthermore, if a selection rectangle intersects an object, it selects all of it, without splitting it into pieces. This is often much more useful. (If you import artwork from Illustrator, as we shall describe shortly, the objects behave more or less as if they had been created in object drawing mode. That is, they continue to behave roughly in the same way that they did in Illustrator.)

The brush tool is, by its nature, a special case. You can use it in either object or merge drawing mode, which affects how the brush marks interact with other objects. However, even in object drawing mode, if a single brush stroke (i.e. one that you make in a single drag) overlaps itself, the partial strokes merge, so you can, for example, paint an area by scribbling with the paintbrush.

It is possible to convert objects from merge drawing mode to object drawing mode. Select one or more objects, and choose the Union command from the Modify>Combine Objects sub-menu. They will then be treated as a single object and won't affect objects that they intersect. Conversely, if you select an object, and then choose Modify>Break Apart, its fill and stroke will become separately selectable, and will interact with any objects they overlap, as if they had originally been created in merge drawing mode.

---TRY THIS---

Practise using all of Flash's drawing tools in object drawing mode. What is the effect of drawing shapes in merge drawing mode on top of shapes made in object drawing mode and vice versa? Experiment further with selection.

The Modify>Combine Objects sub-menu has several commands besides Union. Draw several overlapping shapes in object drawing mode and experiment with using the different available Combine Objects commands.

You can use the Edit>Cut and Edit>Copy commands to move or copy any selected objects to the clipboard, in the usual way. Flash provides two different commands for pasting: Edit>Paste in Place and Edit>Paste in Center, depending on where you want the pasted object to be placed: in its original position or in the middle of the stage.

If you select several objects, you can group them together, using the Modify>Group command. As long as they remain grouped, the objects can be manipulated as a single entity. In particular, the group can be moved as a whole, and transformed in the various ways we will describe in the next section. If you need to work with the individual members of the group again, you can use the Modify>Ungroup command to separate them out.

Transformations and Reshaping

Once you have selected an object on the stage you can transform it in various ways. Broadly speaking, there are two approaches you can take to transformation: either you can do it by hand and eye, manipulating objects directly on the stage, or you can do it numerically, by entering values in the Info and Transform panels. The first approach may feel more natural for artists and designers; the second provides greater accuracy.

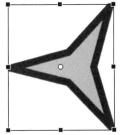

The simplest form of transformation is movement. This is done by selecting the object or objects to be moved with the arrow tool and then dragging; holding down [opt/alt] while dragging causes the objects to be copied, as you might expect. Note that, although a bounding box appears round an object drawn in object mode when you select it, you still have to drag inside the object itself to move it. If it has no fill, you have to drag the stroked outline.

Figure 6.15 *The free transform bounding box*

Other transformations are performed using the *free transform* tool. This can be used like the arrow tool to select and move an object, but it has extra capabilities. When you select anything with the free transform tool, a bounding box with handles at the corners and half way along each side appears, as shown in Figure 6.15. If you place the cursor directly over one of the handles, it changes to a double arrow to indicate that you can scale the object by dragging. If you are over

one of the handles in the middle of a side, you can scale in the direction perpendicular to the side, as illustrated in the middle of the top row of Figure 6.16; if you are over one of the corner handles, you can scale in both directions at once by dragging diagonally. If you hold down the shift key while dragging a corner, the object's proportions are maintained as its size changes.

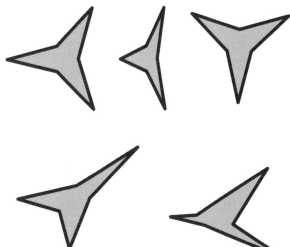

If you hold the free transform tool near, but not actually over, one of the corner handles, the cursor turns into a circular arrow; this indicates that you can rotate the object by dragging it, as illustrated at the top right of Figure 6.16. (The corner handles can actually be dragged in more or less any direction to make the object rotate,

Figure 6.16 *Free transformations*

but moving them as if you were actually pulling the object round to its new position produces the most intuitive feedback.) By default, the object is rotated around its centre point, but you can move the centre of rotation by dragging the circular icon – visible near the middle of the shape in Figure 6.15 – to a different position.

The free transform tool can also be used for performing skewing transformations. When you move the tool near to a side of a bounding box, but not over any handle, the cursor turns into a pair of parallel arrows, and you can skew the object by dragging parallel to the side. Finally, by holding down [cmd/ctl] while dragging a corner handle, you can distort the bounding box and its contents. Some effects of skewing and distortion are illustrated at the bottom of Figure 6.16.

The Modify>Transform sub-menu offers alternative ways of invoking the scaling and rotation tools. It also provides some further useful transforms, including reflections in the horizontal and vertical axes (Flip Vertical and Flip Horizontal respectively).

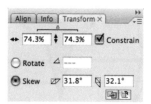

Figure 6.17 *The* Info *panel*

If you know the exact coordinates to which you want to move an object, you can select the object and enter the values in the X and Y fields at the top right of the Info panel, shown in Figure 6.17. (Note that the X and Y values in the bottom right of the Info panel show the current cursor coordinates.) Click in the appropriate square in the little grid to the left of the X and Y fields to choose whether to set the coordinates of the top left corner or of the centre of the object. Similarly, if you know the exact size to which you need to scale an object, you can enter the width and height in the W and H fields.

Figure 6.18 *The* Transform *panel*

The Transform panel, shown in Figure 6.18, offers a numerical way of applying scaling, rotation and skew transforms to selected objects. The two fields at the top of the panel are for entering percentage factors by which to scale the object horizontally and vertically (indicated by the tiny double-headed arrows). By selecting the checkbox marked Constrain before you enter any values, you can ensure that the scaling is uniform – that is, that the height and width are scaled by the same proportion. In this case, you only need to enter one of the values as the other is automatically set to match it.

The remaining three fields are for providing values, in degrees, for a rotation or skewing. Use the radio buttons to select either rotation and skew – they cannot be applied at the same time. (But separate amounts of horizontal and vertical skewing can be applied at the same time.) Rotations are measured clockwise, so use negative values if you want to rotate objects anti-clockwise. In the bottom right corner of the panel there are two easily overlooked buttons. The one on the right

resets all transforms, so long as the object is still selected – clicking it returns the object to its original state. The left-hand button is used to copy the object while transforming it.

┌─ TRY THIS ───┐

Draw a simple asymmetrical object and practise using the free transform tool to alter its scale, position on the stage and angles of rotation and skew. Try moving the circle that marks the centre of rotation, and see what effect it has on the different transformations. What happens if you drag the handle in the middle of a side all the way through the object and out the other side?

Try performing the same transformations using the Info and Transform panels and the commands on the Modify>Transform sub-menu.

Now draw several objects, group them together, and experiment with applying transformations to the whole group.

└───┘

Alignment

A different way of moving objects is by aligning them with each other. The Align panel, shown in Figure 6.19, provides a means of laying out objects in various ways. This has many uses – for example, when laying out controls in a movie that provides interactivity via buttons. When you click on one of the icons in the Align panel, all currently selected objects are moved in the way indicated. Most of the icons are self-explanatory. For example, clicking on the icon at the left of the top row causes all the selected objects to be aligned

Figure 6.19 *The* Align *panel*

along their left edges – the selected object that is originally furthest to the left is used to set the position to which the others are aligned. Similarly, objects can be aligned along their right, top and bottom edges, or centred vertically or horizontally. They can also be distributed (using the second row of buttons) so that the distance between corresponding edges is the same. Unless the objects are all the same size, this often produces unexpected results. More often, what you want to do is distribute the objects so that there is an equal amount of space between each of them. This is what the two icons labelled Space in the bottom right of the panel do. Selecting the button at the far right of the panel, labelled To Stage, causes the alignment or distribution to be performed relative to the stage. For example, if you select this option and then click the left align icon, all the objects will be lined up on the left-hand edge of the stage.

You can also use the Align panel to scale objects so that they are all the same size. This is done with the Match size buttons in the bottom left of the panel, which match the selected objects' horizontal or vertical dimensions, or both. In each case, the size is set to match the largest selected object. Again, you can select To Stage, in order to make objects as tall or as wide as the stage.

┌─ TRY THIS ───┐

Draw nine different objects and try out all the different ways of aligning and distributing them on the stage. Finally, arrange them in an evenly spaced three by three grid, centred on the stage.

└───┘

In addition to these facilities for transforming and arranging entire objects, Flash has a ***subselection tool*** which can be used to adjust anchor points of curves, as described in Chapter 8.

Graphic Symbols

A ***symbol*** is an element that can be stored and used repeatedly in a movie. There are three types of symbol, but to start with we will only consider the simplest type: graphic symbols. These are graphic objects which can be used many times when you need several copies of the same object. Consider Figure 6.20, for example. Here we have four creatures on the stage; the largest looks like a parent of the other three. All four are, in fact, copies – or, more accurately, ***instances*** – of a single graphic symbol. As you can see, the instances are not identical copies of the symbol; they differ in size and proportions, but they are obviously based on the same artwork.

There are two ways of creating a symbol: either select some existing artwork on the stage and choose the Modify>Convert to Symbol... command, or use the Insert>New Symbol... command, and then create the symbol from scratch. You can use whichever is best suited to what you are working on. If you like to see your symbol in context while you are drawing it, use the first method, but if you like to create all your elements before assembling them, use the second.

According to which command you use, one of the almost identical simple dialogues shown in Figure 6.21 will appear. For now, ignore the other options, select the Graphic radio button and give your symbol a unique name. If you are converting existing artwork to a symbol, you can also set its ***registration point***, using the little grid below the name field. This is used as the basis for measuring and positioning objects relative to the symbol.

When you create a new, empty symbol, you are returned to the timeline and stage when you dismiss the dialogue box, but the timeline header now shows the name of your symbol, and no frames from the main movie are visible – the timeline looks the same as it does when you create a new movie, with a single keyframe on one layer. For the simple graphic symbols we are considering at this point, you just draw your new symbol on the stage. When you have finished, you can return to working on the main document by choosing Edit>Edit Document.

Figure 6.20 *Instances of a graphic symbol*

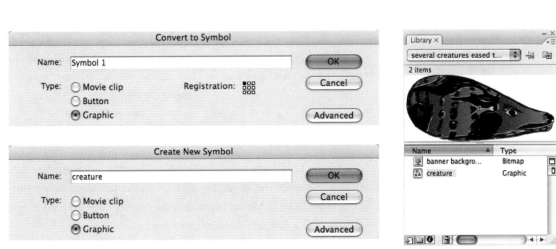

Figure 6.21 *Creating a symbol*

Figure 6.22 *The* Library *panel*

When you create a symbol, it is added to the document's ***library***, which you can browse in the Library panel, shown in Figure 6.22. The bottom part of this panel contains a scrolling list of all the symbols you have created in your document. In this little example there are only two symbols: our creature, and a bitmapped image that was imported for use as the background. More elaborate documents will usually have many more symbols in their libraries; to help keep them organized you can create folders within the library, nested to an arbitrary depth. When you click on a symbol's name, a preview of its appearance is shown at the top of the Library panel. To open a folder within the library you must double-click the folder icon.

To use a symbol you drag it from the Library panel onto the stage. This will add an instance of it to your animation. You are not limited to creating instances of your symbol in the main movie: you can create instances of symbols within other symbols, allowing you to build up symbols hierarchically. For example, you could make a bicycle symbol containing wheel symbols and then create instances of the bicycle to make a bicycle race animation.

Each instance starts out as an exact copy of the symbol, but it can be scaled, rotated and so on independently, without altering the original symbol or any other instance of it in any way. No matter what drawing mode the symbol was created in, an instance is selected as an indivisible object when you click on it with the arrow or free transform tool, and transformations are applied to the instance as a whole.

When you select an instance, the Properties panel tells you what symbol it is an instance of, and what type of symbol that is. As Figure 6.23 illustrates, it also tells you the dimensions and location of the instance. On the right-hand side of the panel are some controls for applying colour effects to the instance. Using the pop-up menu labelled Color, you can select Brightness, to make it darker or lighter, Alpha, to apply transparency, or Tint, to apply a colour tint over the instance.

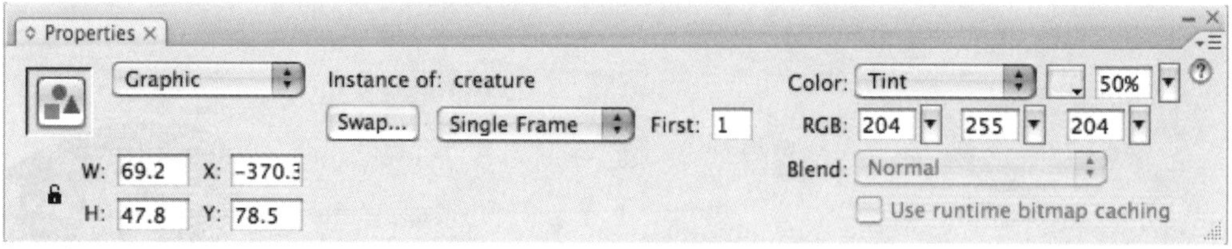

Figure 6.23 *Properties of an instance*

When you select an option under the Color pop-up menu, appropriate controls appear beneath it, which let you provide suitable values for the effect. Figure 6.23 shows the controls for Tint. The default option for Color is None, which doesn't mean that the instance has no colour, but that it just has the same brightness, alpha and tint as the original symbol.

┌─ TRY THIS ───┐

Create a graphic symbol representing a tree. In the main document, draw a simple landscape, and make a wood using instances of your tree symbol. Change the size and other properties of the instances, so that the perspective looks correct and there is some variation in the trees' appearance.

└───┘

You may wonder why you need symbols and instances when you could easily copy and paste objects instead. A full answer must wait until we have considered animation and the other types of symbol, but one advantage is that if you edit a symbol, the changes are propagated to all the instances of it. There are several ways of editing symbols. The most straightforward is by double-clicking it in the Library panel, or selecting an instance on the stage and using the Edit>Edit Symbols command. This causes the symbol to appear alone on the stage, where you can edit it like any other artwork. While you are doing so, the symbol's name is shown in the bar at the top

left of the stage. When you have finished editing, clicking on the blue left arrow will return you to the full stage and timeline.

If you prefer to see the symbol in context while you are editing it, you can double-click an instance on the stage, instead of in the Library panel, or use the Edit>Edit in Place command. This will cause everything on the stage except the instance to be dimmed, while still remaining visible. Even though you appear to be working on a single instance, it is important to remember that it is the symbol itself that you are editing, and the changes you make will affect all its instances. If several instances are present on the stage, you will therefore see them all change. As before, when you have finished editing the symbol, click on the blue left arrow at the top left of the stage.

┌─ TRY THIS ───┐

Edit the tree symbol you used in the previous example to change its appearance significantly. Observe how all the instances change too. Try editing the symbol both in isolation and in place, to see which method you prefer.

└───┘

A second advantage of using symbols is that they help reduce the size of exported movies. Only a single copy of the symbol is actually included in a movie. Each instance is recorded as a reference to the symbol together with a small amount of information about its position and any transformations or colour effects that have been applied to it. Because Flash movies are so often delivered over the Internet, keeping them small so that they require less bandwidth is always a good idea.

Importing Artwork

Although Flash's drawing tools have some additional features beyond those described in the preceding sections, they are not as powerful as those provided by dedicated vector drawing tools such as Illustrator and, as noted, they have quirks which may interfere with the productivity of someone used to other applications. Also, Flash does not provide any means at all of creating bitmapped images. It is common, therefore, to use other graphics applications in conjunction with Flash and we would advise you to do so wherever possible.

A range of different file formats can be imported into Flash, using the File>Import>Import to Stage... and File>Import>Import to Library... commands. As you might expect from these commands' names, if you import to the stage, the imported artwork is placed directly in the document, but if you import to the library it is turned into a symbol, which you can drag to the stage to create instances when you wish. The exact range of formats available for import depends on the platform on which you are using Flash and whether or not you have installed QuickTime.

Illustrator Files

Illustrator files are the most important type of vector graphics that you can import. Although Flash and Illustrator are both vector applications, they differ in significant ways, so it is neces-

sary to map Illustrator's concepts and objects to Flash's when importing. The dialogue shown in Figure 6.24, which appears when you select an Illustrator file to import, provides considerable flexibility in the way this mapping is performed.

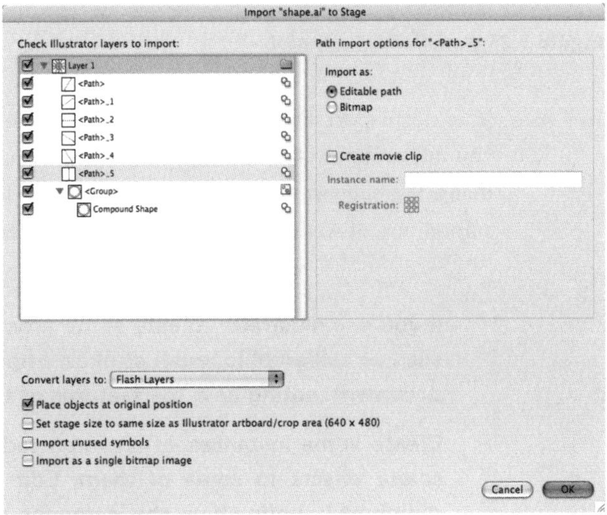

The imported file's structure is shown on the left of the dialogue, as it would be in Illustrator's Layers panel, so you can see the layers, the objects on each layer and the way they have been grouped. Below this are several options controlling how the original layers are to be treated in Flash. By default, Illustrator layers are mapped to Flash layers,

Figure 6.24 *Importing an Illustrator file*

but you can opt to merge them down to a single Flash layer, or, as we will describe in more detail later, you can choose to place each layer in a separate keyframe. Finer control over each of the Illustrator objects is provided. If you select any shape, group or layer in the left of the dialogue, a set of options appears to the right, allowing you to determine exactly how that object should be imported. In particular, you can choose to turn an object into a bitmap or into a movie clip – a type of symbol that we will describe shortly. (If you are importing from a complex Illustrator file you will see a very long list on the left of the dialogue, with everything checked by default. Unchecking the checkbox for each layer will deselect everything listed under that layer, so that you can then more easily check only the objects you actually want to import.)

Illustrator has its own symbols, as described in Chapter 5. When you import an Illustrator file containing symbols, they are turned into Flash symbols. If you wish, you can turn any Illustrator symbol into a bitmap during this process. Imported symbols appear in the **Library** panel; you will see an **Assets** folder with the filename of the file you imported from, and a sub-folder within that labelled **Illustrator symbols**. The sub-folder contains the symbols themselves.

If you import artwork from an Illustrator file you cannot subsequently edit that artwork in Illustrator and have the changes reflected in your Flash document. However, if you have imported

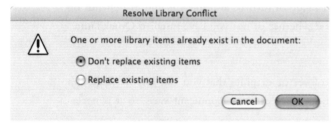

Figure 6.25 *Re-importing a symbol*

it as an Illustrator symbol – and providing you have not edited the symbol in Flash – you can edit the original Illustrator file and re-import it. The dialogue shown in Figure 6.25 will then appear. If you choose to **Replace existing items**, the symbol, and all instances of it, will be updated with the new version.

You can export Flash documents to Illustrator files, using the File>Export>Export Image… command; choose **Adobe Illustrator** as the format. However, no version of Illustrator more recent than 6.0 is supported, and some information is lost, such as the identity of symbols, so this is not a good way of working. It is better to edit in Illustrator and re-import to the library if necessary.

─TRY THIS─

If you use Illustrator, create some artwork that uses features lacking in Flash, such as calligraphic brush strokes. Import the result into the library of a Flash document, noting how the features of the Illustrator file are treated.

Create some instances of an imported symbol and apply transformations or colour effects to some of them. Edit the original artwork in Illustrator and re-import it, noting how the instances are updated when you do so.

Bitmapped Images

As we have stressed, Flash is fundamentally based on vector graphics. Flash documents can, however, incorporate bitmapped images. The nature of bitmaps and their differences from vectors means that they cannot be so readily manipulated without loss of quality. They also tend to increase the size of exported movies and they can slow down animations significantly. Nevertheless, the greater expressiveness and range of textures in bitmapped art means that it is often worthwhile combining bitmaps with vector graphics in Flash. In particular, bitmapped images can often be used effectively as static backgrounds, and ActionScript can be used to control the display of a set of bitmapped images as a slide show. Additionally, Flash can convert bitmaps into vector drawings, which can be an effective way of creating animations.

A range of bitmapped formats, including JPEG, GIF and PNG, can be imported into Flash. The range is extended if QuickTime is installed. In particular, using QuickTime, TIFF files can be imported, which is useful for scanned images. There is no support for Camera RAW files.

When completed Flash movies are exported as SWF files, all images are converted to JPEGs. This means that any files – such as compressed digital photographs – that originated in JPEG form will be recompressed, with an inevitable loss of quality. For that reason, uncompressed or losslessly compressed bitmapped formats are to be preferred when they are available.

The greatest flexibility is provided for importing Photoshop files, so in most cases the best way to work with bitmaps of all sorts is by opening or creating them in Photoshop, saving as PSD files and importing those into Flash.

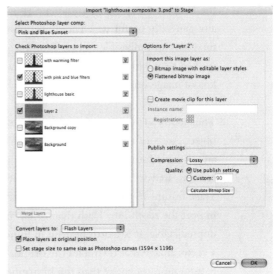

The import dialogue for Photoshop files, shown in Figure 6.26, is similar to that for Illustrator files. It lets you choose which layers to import and whether to convert them to Flash layers or keyframes, or to flatten them into a single layer. Additional options are available for each individual layer. If the Photoshop file contains layer comps, as the one in Figure 6.26 does, you can choose one of them from the pop-up menu at the top of the import dialogue and the corresponding set of layers will be checked for importing, as shown. (See Chapter 4 – the file being imported here is the one illustrated in Figure 4.21.) There is also a handy option (at the bottom of the dialogue box) to set the size of the Flash document to match the Photoshop image.

Figure 6.26 *Importing a Photoshop file*

This means that you can start by creating a background in Photoshop, import it into Flash and ensure that the stage is the right size to accommodate it before you proceed any further.

The layers of an imported bitmap appear in the Library panel, in their own folder, even if you import them to the stage. If you explicitly import to the library, a graphic symbol is also created for the entire image.

If you import a Photoshop file that consists of just a single layer, the import dialogue is by-passed and the image is imported as a single symbol. This is what happens if you import files in other bitmapped formats, such as JPEG. In that case, it is possible to edit the symbol in an external program, usually Photoshop. When you select such a bitmap in the Library panel, the Edit with... command becomes available in the panel menu. If you select this, you can choose an application in which to edit the image. On saving, the changes are propagated to the Flash symbol. For files that Flash can identify as Photoshop files, a special Edit with Photoshop command is also provided, which causes the image to be opened in the correct program straight away.

---TRY THIS---

If you have a copy of Photoshop, open a photograph, make some modifications to it and save it as a PSD file. Import the result into Flash. Repeat the experiment with a multi-layered Photoshop file with layer comps. In both cases, examine the Library panel to see what symbols have been created.

Flash is emphatically not a bitmapped image editing program. By selecting a bitmap and using the Modify>Break Apart command you can make a bitmap editable to some extent, but not in any generally useful way. Therefore, when you import a bitmap image, you can normally only treat it as an indivisible object. Transformations – moving, scaling, rotation or skewing – may be applied to it, although you should be aware that in general this cannot be done without some loss of image quality.

The Modify>Trace Bitmap command can be applied to a selected bitmap to convert it to a vector object. Areas of roughly the same colour are turned into filled vector shapes. Various parameters are available for controlling the fidelity with which the bitmap is traced. As with other aspects of creating artwork, this job can be done much better and more easily in Illustrator, using its Live Trace feature. If you wish to use vectorized bitmaps, it is better to do the tracing in Illustrator and import the result into Flash than to try and use Flash's tracing command, which is awkward and unpredictable. It is worth bearing in mind, though, that if you trace a bitmap faithfully to obtain a vector image that resembles the original closely, it is highly likely that the vectorized result will require more memory than the bitmapped original.

DON'T FORGET

Flash is fundamentally a vector graphics application.

Draw lines with the pencil, line or pen tools.

Set the colour, weight and style of strokes in the Properties panel; set extra options for the pencil at the bottom of the Tools panel.

Set the colour of fills and strokes in the Properties panel, Tools panel or Color panel.

In Flash, Alpha means transparency. Fills and strokes can be semi-transparent.

Pick up strokes and fills from existing shapes with the eyedropper and transfer them to other objects with the ink bottle or paint bucket, respectively.

Use the rectangle, oval and polystar tools for drawing geometrical shapes.

Use the brush tool for more natural looking marks. Brush marks are actually filled shapes, with invisible strokes. Turn on options in the Tools panel for sensitivity to pressure and tilt if you use a graphics tablet and pen.

In merge drawing mode – the default – shapes and lines are split where they overlap and stroke and fill can be selected separately.

In object drawing mode, objects don't interact when they overlap and can be selected as a whole. Use the round button near the bottom of the Tools panel to turn object drawing mode on and off.

Use the black arrow tool to select objects or lines. Use the lasso tool to draw a freehand selection; turn on polygon mode to use the lasso like the line tool.

Use the free transform tool or the commands on the Modify>Transform command to move, scale, rotate or skew objects.

Objects can be aligned or uniformly distributed vertically and horizontally using the Align panel.

A symbol is an element that can be stored in the library and used repeatedly. You can turn existing artwork into a symbol using Modify>Convert to Symbol... or create a new symbol before you have done the drawing.

To create an instance of a symbol, drag it from the Library panel onto the stage. Editing a symbol alters all the instances of it.

Instances can be individually transformed or have colour effects applied. Editing an instance does not affect other instances of the same symbol.

Artwork created in other programs, including Illustrator and Photoshop, can be imported to the stage or the library.

Animation

The preceding descriptions of drawing and importing artwork into Flash should have provided enough information for you to create images for single frames. We can now turn to the subject of combining frames into an animation, transferring our attention from the stage to the timeline.

You will recall from the beginning of the chapter that the timeline provides a spatial representation of a sequence of frames. Layers are stacked vertically and frames are arranged horizontally. That is, time runs from left to right, with the scale at the top of the timeline measuring time in frames. The relationship between this and elapsed time in seconds is determined by the movie's frame rate, which can be set in the Modify>Document... dialogue or in the Properties panel when nothing is selected in the timeline or on the stage. A value between about 24 and 30 will produce high-quality animation as smooth as film or TV, but many computers may not be able to play back movies at that rate, especially if the frames are large in size. Values around 12 are more commonly used for Flash animations, especially if they are destined for the Web. This rate is often used in animation generally (traditionally, this is animating on "2s" – i.e. holding each image for two frames out of the 24, 25 or 30 frames per second required for film or TV). It is sufficient to produce a convincing illusion of movement, but it may sometimes appear jerky, depending on the animator's skill. Lower rates can also be used if stylized motion is adequate.

Animating One Frame at a Time

Traditional animators working on film or videotape create every frame of their animations by photographing each frame independently. Almost any materials can be used, but most traditional animation is made from drawings or paintings on paper or cel, or from manipulation of a group of three-dimensional models on a miniature stage set. Flash allows you to work in a similar way, by adding frames to the timeline and filling them one at a time by drawing on the stage or importing graphics. When you work in this way, creating your animation one frame at a time, each frame must be a *keyframe* – by definition, in Flash a keyframe is a frame whose contents you create explicitly. Shortly, we will see how the contents of other frames can be computed automatically. In most animation, each frame will differ from the one preceding it only in a small way – that is how the illusion of continuous movement is created.

Frame-at-a-time animation is simple but time-consuming. Let's assume that you are starting from scratch with a new movie containing a single, initially empty, keyframe. Its timeline will look like Figure 6.4: the little circle in the middle of the grey rectangle for the frame in the timeline indicates that it is a keyframe. By clicking it in the timeline you select this keyframe (the rectangle will turn black when it is selected). You can then create an image that will be the first frame of your animation. The image is created on the stage using the tools and techniques described in the previous section.

Once the first frame is complete, you click on the next frame position in the timeline and select Insert>Timeline>Keyframe. This creates a new keyframe which, by default, will contain a copy of the frame to its left. This enables you to make adjustments to the contents of the frame so that objects appear to move, fade in or out, or otherwise change. Alternatively, you can start over with an empty keyframe; the command Insert>Timeline>Blank Keyframe is provided for this purpose. Once each frame is complete, you add another new keyframe after it, and so on.

Traditional animators sometimes use a device known as a lightbox to help them draw successive frames of an animation. The frames are drawn on thin sheets of paper, sometimes called *onion skins*, which are laid on the surface of the box, which contains a light bulb. The top of the box has a translucent inset that allows the light to pass through. This makes it possible to place a completed drawing on the top of the lightbox, put a fresh sheet of paper on top of it and see the details of the drawing below through it. Hence, elements of the first frame can be copied by tracing and the relative positions of objects in the successive frames can be seen. Flash provides a similar facility. By clicking on the Onion Skin icon below the timeline, a faded version of adjacent keyframes is shown beneath the current frame on the stage. By default, the two preceding and following frames are shown, if they exist. The extent of onion-skinning can be altered by dragging the markers above the timeline which show where it begins and ends. Generally, using more than one or two onion-skinned frames is confusing. Probably the closest you can get in Flash to a digital equivalent of traditional hand-drawn animation is by turning on onion-skinning, inserting blank keyframes and painting each frame with the brush tool.

Animation is about creating movement from still images, so you need to be able to test your work in motion at frequent intervals. This can be done by using the Control>Test Movie command, but since you will be doing this a lot, you will probably find it worth using the keyboard shortcut [ctl enter/cmd return]. This opens a movie created from the current document in the Flash Player, running inside Flash. For quickly checking the animation, you can play through it on the stage instead (though some features which we will describe later are disabled when you do so), using Control>Play or by simply pressing enter/return. You can also scrub through an animation by dragging the *current frame indicator* – the red box above the frame numbers in the timeline.

┌─ TRY THIS ──
│
│ **Create a short animated sequence one frame at a time. If you are good at drawing,**
│ **use the brush tool to draw every frame in a blank keyframe, as described. If not,**
│ **make a simple drawing on the stage in frame 1 using shape tools, and let every**
│ **new keyframe be a copy of the preceding one, which you change progressively**
│ **or add additional shapes to in succeeding frames. (For example, animate a trail**
│ **of bubbles or a bunch of floating balloons.) Experiment with onion-skinning.**
│ **Try playing your animation through in the timeline and also use Test Movie to**
│ **preview it in the Player. Pay attention to speed and pacing.**
└──

It should be stressed that although Flash provides a mechanism for creating animation quickly, with its tools for moving and transforming objects, and its onion-skinning facilities, and so on, it can't make you into an animator. In other words, Flash can't tell you how to change your images from one frame to the next so that a convincing or expressive illusion of motion is created. Just about anyone can produce bouncing logos, but if you want to produce more ambitious animation you will have to spend more time observing how things move and how to represent motion than you will need to spend mastering Flash.

If you prefer to make your images outside Flash and import them, there are several ways of creating animation sequences. Conceptually the simplest is to create each frame in a separate file. If the files are named following a consistent convention, so that each one includes a sequence number in its name, Flash will recognize the sequence and import it into successive frames on the timeline. (For reasons which should be obvious, you can only use Import to Stage... for importing any files which you wish to be placed as keyframes on the timeline; it should really say "import to timeline".) Various formats can be used for the file names. The most reliable consists of inserting a sequence number, padded with an appropriate number of leading zeros before the file extension (this is important – if you forget the zeros the frames will not be in the correct order unless you have fewer than ten), as in anim001.gif, anim002.gif, anim003.gif, and so on.

To import such a **numbered file sequence**, choose the File>Import>Import to Stage... command and then, in the navigation dialogue that appears, select just the first member of the sequence and click Import. Flash will display the dialogue shown in Figure 6.27 to tell you that it thinks the file

This file appears to be part of a sequence of images. Do you want to import all of the images in the sequence?

Cancel   No   Yes

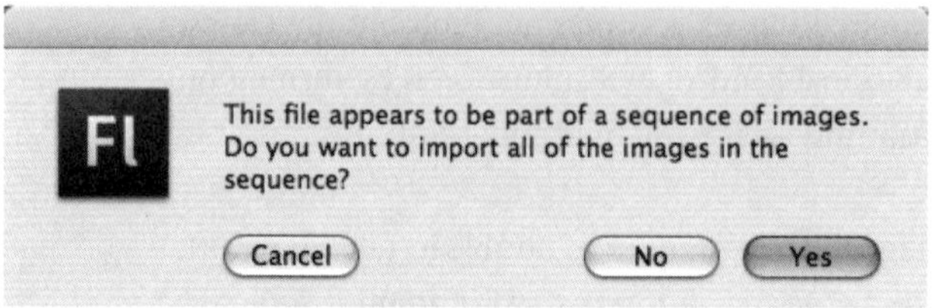

Figure 6.27 *Importing a numbered file sequence*

is the first in a sequence and to ask whether you want it to import all of the images. If you click Yes, each file will be imported into a new keyframe. (If you click No, it will import only the first image in the sequence.) Note that if there are any gaps in the numbering of the sequence, Flash will stop importing at the end of a consecutive run of numbers. (For example, if you have a sequence of 49 images called anim001.gif to anim050.gif, with anim010.gif missing, only the first nine images will be imported if you select anim001.gif.)

As well as a sequence of image files, Flash can import the frames of an animated GIF; it will automatically place each frame of the GIF as a keyframe on the timeline. It can also import the layers of an Illustrator or Photoshop file as a sequence of keyframes, using the dialogue we described when discussing how to import still artwork. You must ensure that you select Keyframes from the pop-up menu labelled Convert layers to... in the import dialogue. You can, however, select any layers that you want from the original file. (Both Photoshop and Illustrator provide facilities for building animations on layers for this purpose.)

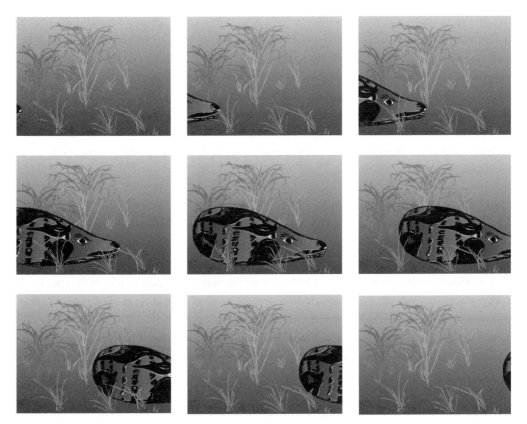

Figure 6.28 *Some of the frames from a simple example of motion tweening*

Motion Tweening

For certain types of animation and motion graphics, it is possible to draw only certain keyframes and use Flash's interpolation – or *tweening* – facilities to insert additional frames by moving elements of the keyframes in easily specified ways. Flash offers more than one kind of tweening. In the simplest case – a basic *motion tween* – a keyframe is created, containing an instance of a graphic symbol. A second keyframe is created at some point further along in the timeline as a copy of the first keyframe, and, with the second keyframe selected, the object is moved to a new position. Flash is then instructed to tween the motion between the two keyframes. (The details of how this is accomplished will be described shortly.) When the movie is exported and played, all the frames between the two keyframes are constructed automatically, and the object appears to move in a straight line between its positions in the two keyframes. This is demonstrated in Figure 6.28, though this only shows a few frames of the final movie, of course, not all of them.

In Flash, motion tweening encompasses much more than just interpolating the position of an object on the stage. An object's size and angle of rotation can also be changed using motion tweening; so can its colour, brightness and transparency. Filters, which may be applied to symbols, can also be tweened. By using a sequence of keyframes placed at different intervals, the object can be made to change direction and speed. By using layers, a whole collection of objects can be made to move independently. In addition to motion tweening, Flash supports **shape tweening**, or morphing as it is more commonly known, whereby one shape can be transformed into a different one. (We discuss shape tweening later on.) By combining the various types of tweening that Flash provides, animations can be produced in a range of styles, but they usually retain a mechanical feeling. The only reliable way of producing realistic or expressive motion is a frame at a time – and then only if you have some talent for animation. Tweening can, however, be profitably used in motion graphics.

Creating Motion Tweens

All tweening requires two (or more) keyframes to be created explicitly; the intermediate frames between each pair of keyframes are interpolated by computation from them. Conceptually the process is simple: you draw the keyframes at the beginning and the end of the sequence and tell Flash to tween them. However, Flash is rather particular about the order in which the necessary operations are carried out, and, although there are several ways of creating motion tweening that will work eventually, Flash can sometimes behave in a confusing fashion if you do not follow the procedures described below precisely, at least until you understand what is going on. In particular, we advise you to avoid the use of the Insert>Timeline>Create Motion Tween command, even though this may seem to you to be an obvious choice.

Tweening can only be applied to instances of graphic (or movie clip) symbols, not to artwork that has not been converted into a symbol. Furthermore, each instance that you want to tween must be on a separate layer. For the moment, assume that there is only a single object to be tweened.

Begin by creating a symbol. Now insert a keyframe at the point in the timeline where you want the motion to begin (if there isn't a keyframe there already), select it in the timeline, and place an instance of your symbol in that frame, by dragging it from the Library panel on to the stage. Next, click in the timeline at the point where you want the tweening to end and insert a keyframe there, using the Insert>Timeline>Keyframe command. You will see the symbol instance appear in the new keyframe. With this end keyframe selected, move the instance, apply transformations to it, or use the Properties panel to change its brightness, colour or transparency (alpha). You can make as many changes to the instance as you wish. To take a simple example, a combination of moving and scaling an object can be used to make it seem to move closer or further away. Now click in the timeline to select any frame *between* the start and end keyframes. Finally, go to the Properties panel and select Motion from the pop-up menu labelled Tween. The frames in the timeline should turn mauve in colour, and an arrow should appear between the start and end keyframes, as shown in Figure 6.29.

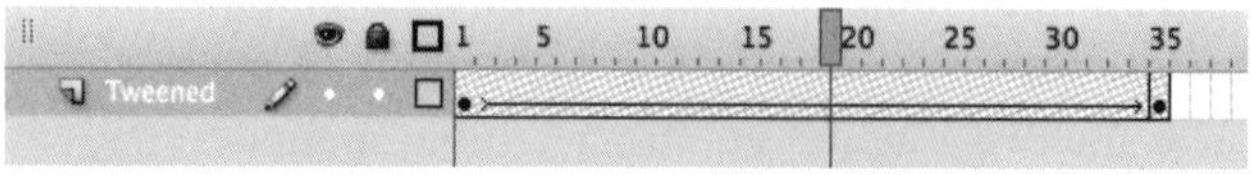

Figure 6.29 *Motion tweening shown in the timeline*

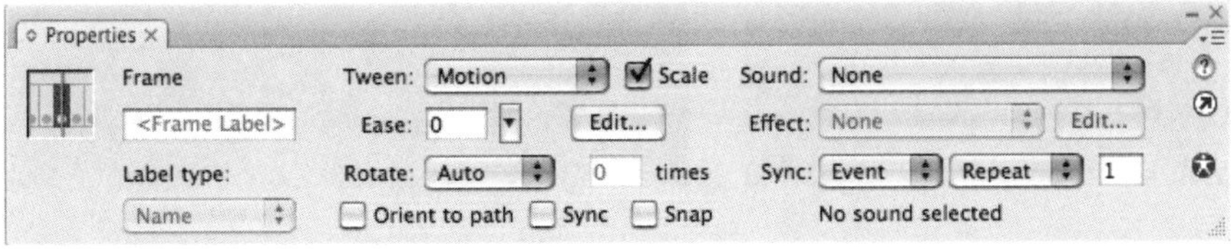

Figure 6.30 *Properties of a tweened frame*

(Note that the end keyframe does not change colour, however.) If this arrow has a solid line, as in Figure 6.29, all is well. If the arrow is shown with a dotted line instead of a solid one, however, the tween has not been applied correctly, and you will have to backtrack and do it again.

Figure 6.30 shows the **Properties** panel with a tweened frame selected. The left part of the panel is mostly concerned with scripting, while the right contains controls dealing with sound, which we will consider later. The controls in the middle affect the tweening. As we already noted, the **Tween** pop-up shows that motion tweening has been applied. The checkbox to its right, labelled **Scale**, must be selected if you have changed the size of the instance in the end keyframe and want the scaling to be tweened – otherwise only the position is tweened, and the size will change abruptly when the movie reaches the final keyframe. Similarly, if you want an object to rotate during the tweening, it is essential to select a suitable value from the **Rotate** pop-up. Selecting **CW** or **CCW** (that is, clockwise or counter-clockwise) ensures that the object will rotate an exact number of times in the chosen direction; you specify how many rotations you want by entering a value in the field to the right of the **Rotate** pop-up. (An object that rotates an exact number of times will end up in the same orientation in the final keyframe as it was in the first.) Choosing **Auto** from this pop-up is appropriate for partial rotations; the object's orientation will then be tweened between the values in the start and end keyframes, rotating in whichever direction is nearer. If you select **None**, the object is not rotated during tweening, so any rotation you may have applied in the final keyframe will happen suddenly when the movie reaches that frame.

┌─TRY THIS──┐

Create a new movie, draw a shape in the first frame and convert it to a symbol. Create a keyframe at frame 25, move the object to a new position, and tween the motion. Test the resulting movie.

Experiment with tweening all the other tweenable properties of your object. Observe the effect of selecting the Scale option in the Properties panel for the tweened frames, and the effects of the different rotation options.

└──┘

An animation consisting of a single motion tween is not likely to be very interesting. To make a more engaging animation you can place several symbol instances on separate layers and tween each one independently. Figure 6.31 illustrates this, using the example already seen in Figure 6.20.

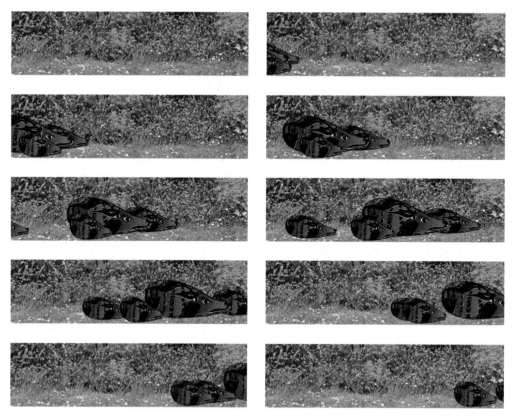

Figure 6.31 *Motion tweening on several layers (every 20th frame)*

(The figure only shows every 20th frame.) Instances of the same symbol used in Figure 6.28 have been placed on separate layers, and scaled differently. They were also placed at different distances from the edge of the frame in both the start and end keyframes, as shown in Figure 6.32. When the position of these instances is tweened, they therefore move at different speeds, since they have to cover different distances in the same number of frames. This means that their spatial relationship changes as the movie plays, which adds some variety of movement and starts to suggest a certain independence among the smaller creatures. Compared to Figure 6.28, we have made the movie wider and narrower and used many more frames, in order to accommodate the extra motion. We also used a bitmapped background to provide some additional interest. Only position was tweened in this example – a true motion tween.

You can quite easily create successive tweens on the same layer. Having created a motion tween in the manner described earlier, just add another keyframe further along the timeline. Select this new keyframe and move or alter the instance being tweened again, then select any frame between your new keyframe and the preceding one, and set the tweening to **Motion**, as before. This way, tweened objects can be made to change direction, for example.

Figure 6.32 *Start and end positions for the motion tweening*

In Flash, *frames*, as distinct from keyframes, do not contain any content of their own – their content is calculated when the movie is displayed. If you add frames after a keyframe, using the Insert>Timeline>Frame command, the contents of the keyframe will be held for all the following frames, up to any following keyframe. This is how you can keep an object in the same place for several frames, or add a static background to an animation, as we did in the example in Figure 6.31.

In the timeline, frames are plain, without a small dot (which indicates a keyframe) or an arrow (which indicates tweening).

---TRY THIS---

Make the animation you created in the previous exercise more elaborate by placing several instances of your symbol on separate layers and tweening their motion and other properties independently. Add a static background layer.

Easing

As we have described it so far, the movie shown in Figures 6.31 and 6.32 is still a very poor piece of animation. Each creature moves at its own constant rate in a straight line across the frame. They look as though they are being pulled on strings. To achieve a better effect it is necessary to change their speed during the course of the animation. One way to do this is by adding extra keyframes and building up the motion from tweened sections, as we mentioned earlier, but the transitions at the keyframes will tend to be too abrupt if this method is employed. The Ease slider – found under the disclosure triangle to the right of the Ease field in the Properties panel when a tweened frame is selected – can be used to make movement start or stop gradually, instead of suddenly. If this is used in conjunction with intermediate keyframes, it can produce reasonable motion, but the result is still fairly crude.

Better control over the rate of change of tweened properties is available, though. Clicking on the button labelled Edit... to the right of the Ease field brings up a *custom easing* dialogue, illustrated in Figure 6.33. The diagonal line in the Custom Ease In/Ease Out dialogue box represents the way the property being tweened varies with time. It is a plot of the value of the tweened property (to be more precise, the difference between its value and the value it had at the beginning of the tweening) against the number of frames of tweening, so its slope is the property's rate of change.

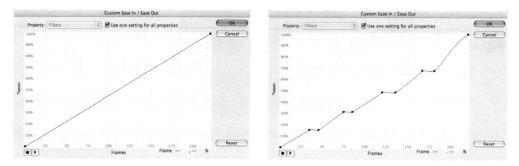

Figure 6.33 *Custom easing*

If you haven't applied any easing yet, the relationship starts out purely linear, as shown in the screenshot on the left of Figure 6.33. To start with, the object moves in a straight line, or rotates, fades, or changes in whatever way you have set, at a uniform rate.

To change this relationship, you alter the shape of the line. This is done by manually adjusting the direction lines of Bézier control points. (See Chapter 8.) There are control points at the start and end of the curve to begin with, marked with little square black handles. Dragging their direction lines transforms the initial straight line (representing uniform velocity) into a variety of smooth curves, representing different rates of change. You can add extra control points by clicking anywhere on the curve. These points can then be dragged up or down, and their direction lines can be adjusted as well, so that a rich variety of curves – and hence of accelerations and speeds – can be achieved, as shown on the right of Figure 6.33. Dragging a handle right into the point itself converts it to a corner point. Two consecutive corner points will be connected by a straight line. If you make part of the curve horizontal in this way, the object will stand still during the corresponding frames. Dragging a control point so that the line slopes downwards makes the object go backwards. If you make a mess of the curve, clicking the **Reset** button at the bottom right sets it back to a straight line, so you can start again. The process does sound rather complicated in explanation, but in practice it is quite straightforward, though it is likely to require some practice before you can be sure of achieving the results you want.

You can preview the effect of your changes by clicking the triangular play button in the bottom left-hand corner of the **Custom Ease In/Ease Out** dialogue. The easing illustrated on the right of Figure 6.33 was applied to the tween for the small fat creature in the movie shown in Figure 6.31; you can see several sections where the curve is altered to make the creature pause as if catching its breath from time to time.

Figure 6.34 shows some simple custom easing curves for objects with the easing slider set to +100 (easing out) and –100 (easing in). You should now be able to appreciate how these curves correspond to the way this control makes movement start and stop gradually.

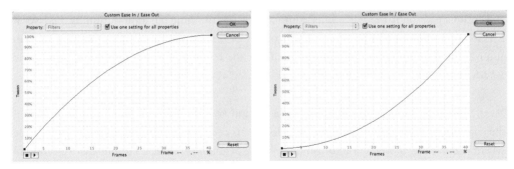

Figure 6.34 *Simple easing out (left) and in (right)*

By default, if you have tweened several properties at once, such as position, size and rotation, the same easing curve is applied to all of them. However, the Property pop-up menu at the top of the custom easing dialogue can be used to apply different curves to each property, so that, for instance, the size of an object could change at a different rate from its position. Select a property from the menu and create a curve, as described. It will only be applied to the selected property.

TRY THIS

Create a simple animation in which a single object moves across the stage using motion tweening. Experiment with applying custom easing to the motion. Start by adding a single control point to the curve and dragging it to different positions until you understand what effect the shape of the curve has on the motion. Then add extra control points to produce more complicated variations of pace.

Use custom easing in an appropriate way to improve the layered animation you made in the previous exercise.

Motion Guides

It is not always adequate to move objects in a straight line, even with variations of speed. You can, of course, use lots of keyframes and combine simple linear movements with rotation and scaling to produce more interesting motion, but there is a simpler and more effective way. Flash lets you create a path, known as a *motion guide*, for objects to follow when they are motion tweened. The procedure is as follows.

First, create some tweened motion as before. Then select the layer on which the tweened object has been placed and either click on the Add Guide Layer icon at the bottom left of the timeline, or use the Insert>Timeline>Motion Guide command. A new layer, with the motion guide icon beside its name, is created above the selected layer, which is right-indented below it, as shown in Figure 6.35. Select the guide layer

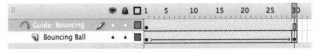

Figure 6.35 *A motion guide layer in the timeline*

and create a path on it; the guide layer automatically has the same duration in time as the layer it is attached to. You can use the pencil or pen, or any of the shape tools to create the path. You can also paste in a path that you have created in Illustrator, but you will have to select it and use the Modify>Break Apart command to allow it to be used as a motion guide.

Next, you select the starting keyframe of the motion tween, and on the tweened layer (not on the guide layer) move your symbol instance so that its centre is at the point on the motion guide where you want its movement to begin (usually the beginning). Then, go to the final keyframe of the tween and move the instance so that its centre is at the end of the motion guide, or at some other point where you want it to stop. It is essential that the centre of the tweened object be on the path, otherwise the motion guide will have no effect.

When you play the movie, the tweened object will follow the path defined by the motion guide. If you preview it in the timeline, you will still see the motion guide, unless you have hidden its layer, but when you export the movie and play it, the guide will not show.

By default, the object retains its orientation as it moves, rather like a cork bobbing up and down. If you wish it to seem to follow the path, like a vehicle on an undulating road, for example, select any tweened frame and check the box labelled Orient to path in the Properties panel. It takes some practice to produce any realistic sort of movement in this way. It can therefore be easier to piece together short sequences of linear motion with rotation, or to animate a frame at a time.

Figure 6.36 *Motion along a guide*

Figure 6.36 shows an example of a motion guide in use. The ball on the top layer follows the path that has been sketched as a motion guide, so that it appears to bounce. Some rotation has also been applied to the ball for added realism, but if nothing more is done the motion will be unrealistic – not so much because the motion guide is not an exact representation of the path of a bouncing ball (it isn't, but animation is more concerned with conveying the impression of how something moves than with its actual motion) – but because the ball will move along the path at

a constant rate, which is definitely not what bouncing balls do. To create a more realistic impression of a bouncing ball it is necessary to combine movement along a path with custom easing, to make the ball slow down at the top of the bounce and accelerate on the way back down. Figure 6.37 shows the easing curve used for the position property to achieve this in our example. Note how the easing curve does not resemble the motion guide. This is because the curve plots the total displacement along the path, not the height of the ball, as the

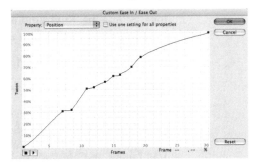

Figure 6.37 *Custom easing for the ball's position*

motion path does. It can be quite tricky trying to match points on the path – for example the tops of the bounces – with points on the easing curve. A scale of frames is supplied along the bottom of the **Custom Ease In/Ease Out** dialogue box, which provides some assistance.

A slightly surprising aspect of using motion guides is that if you create a new layer directly below a tweened layer which has a motion guide associated with it, the new layer also becomes associated with the motion guide. This can cause chaos if done by accident. To detach a layer from a motion guide, select the layer, choose the **Modify>Timeline>Layer Properties…** command and select the **Normal** radio button under **Type**, instead of **Guided**.

TRY THIS

> **Create a simple animation using motion tweening and a motion guide, to make an asymmetrical object trace a spiral course on the stage. (Draw the spiral by hand with the pencil, or import one drawn in Illustrator.) Experiment with the Orient to path option to see how it affects the object's movements. Add some custom easing and tween the object's size so that it speeds up, shrinks and vanishes as it reaches the centre of the spiral.**
>
> **Try to duplicate our example of a bouncing ball. Design a ball with a pattern, so you can see it rotate as it moves. Design a suitable motion path and make the ball enter from one side of the frame as though it had been kicked high in the air by a player beyond the frame's edge. Observe how the ball moves before you apply any easing. Now add custom easing to try to simulate realistic motion. How difficult is it to achieve a successful result by these means?**

For animation, a frame rate of 12 frames per second is usually sufficient to create an illusion of smooth motion. Frame rate can be changed in the Properties panel, but slower rates will generally result in jerky movement.

Animate one frame at a time by adding keyframes to the timeline and creating their content on the stage.

Insert>Timeline>Keyframe adds a keyframe whose contents are a copy of the previous frame, which you can then modify.

Insert>Timeline>Blank Keyframe adds a blank keyframe.

Turn on onion-skinning to see adjacent frames overlaid on one another.

Use Control>Play to watch your animation on the stage, or Control>Test Movie [ctl enter/cmd return] to play it in a Flash Player.

Use File>Import>Import to Stage to import numbered image sequences if you have created the content of your frames in another program. Discontinuity in the numbering of the image files will mean only some are imported.

Animated GIFs can be imported; each frame will be automatically converted to a keyframe.

Layered Photoshop or Illustrator files can be imported; selected layers will be converted to keyframes if you choose the correct option in the dialogue.

Use motion tweening to automatically interpolate the position, size, rotation, brightness, colour and transparency of an instance of a symbol. Each instance to be tweened must be placed on a separate layer. Successive motion tweens of the same instance may be created on the same layer.

To create a motion tween, drag a symbol to a keyframe at the start of the tween, create another keyframe at the end and move the instance or change its properties. Then select a frame in between the start and end and set the Tween pop-up to Motion in the Properties panel.

Unlike keyframes, tweened frames have no content; they are generated automatically when the movie is played back.

Use custom easing to vary the rate of change during the tween. Different tweened properties can be eased independently.

Use a motion guide on a guide layer to make an object move along a path that isn't a straight line. Any path may be drawn with the usual tools, or imported from Illustrator.

To detach a layer from a guide layer, use the Modify>Timeline>Layer Properties… command and select the Normal radio button under Type, instead of Guided.

Editing Animations

You will often need to make changes to an animation which require you to select and manipulate frames in the timeline. On each layer in the timeline, a keyframe is shown as a verticle rectangle with a small circle in it; if the keyframe has any content, the circle is filled; if it is a blank keyframe, the circle is just a hollow outline. (A frame that is not a keyframe has a rectangular marker instead of a circle.) Clicking on a keyframe in the timeline selects that frame on that layer (the keyframe turns black if it is selected correctly), and any objects in that keyframe will be automatically selected on the stage. Other keyframes and layers can be added to the selection by shift-clicking to select a contiguous block of keyframes on the same or an adjacent layer, or [cmd/ctl]-clicking to add non-contiguous frames or layers to the selection. Don't be tempted to try and select a block of frames by dragging over them. Dragging frames in the timeline moves them. When you click in the timeline, the current frame indicator (the red bar) moves to the frame you clicked in, so if you have several frames selected, it is the one you selected last that will be set as the current frame and displayed on the stage. Dragging the current frame indicator, or clicking in the numbers at the top of the timeline, deselects any existing selection, but it does not automatically select the new current frame. You must always explicitly click in a keyframe to select it.

Clicking on a layer's name selects all the frames in that layer. Clicking in any frame on a layer selects the layer itself, so that any operations such as adding a new frame will affect that layer. Thus, the Insert>Timeline>Keyframe and similar commands only add frames to the selected layer, not to the entire timeline, so you can end up with different numbers of frames on different layers.

Once selected, frames can be copied, cut and pasted. Don't be tempted to use Edit>Copy and so on for copying and pasting frames; these commands work on the graphical objects contained in the frames, not on the frames themselves. Use the commands Edit>Timeline>Copy Frames, Edit>Timeline>Cut Frames and Edit>Timeline>Paste Frames or their keyboard shortcuts. Similarly, use Edit>Timeline>Remove Frames to delete frames from the timeline. Pressing the delete key will remove the contents of the selected frames; it does not remove frames from the timeline. It is possible to select one or more frames in a tweened sequence, but because the tweened frames are computed by Flash, you cannot edit their contents on the stage. If you try to copy and paste tweened frames, you will break the tween. That is, you will get a keyframe at the beginning of the pasted frames which matches the first keyframe of the original tween (whether that was included in the original selection or not), followed by a set of frames without interpolation. A broken tween is indicated by a dotted arrow in the timeline. To repair it, add a keyframe at the end of the pasted sequence and reposition the object in the start and end keyframes.

─TRY THIS──

Open or create an animation that includes layers and tweening and practise selecting frames and layers, until you completely understand how selection works. Try duplicating part of the animation by copying and pasting frames.

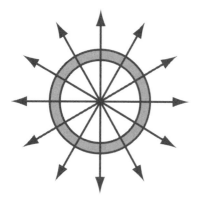

Figure 6.38 *A rotating symbol*

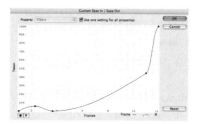

Figure 6.39 *Custom easing of the rotation*

As well as copying and pasting graphic objects (using `Edit>Copy` and so on) and frames (using `Edit>Timeline>Copy Frames` and so on) in the usual way, Flash allows you to copy and paste the motion tweening applied to one object to another object. This can be most easily understood through an example.

Figure 6.38 shows a symbol that might be a sort of ancient cog wheel. We can make this rotate in a uniform manner by tweening its angle of rotation. The spokes are 30° apart and tweening occurs over 12 frames, so by setting the angle in the ending keyframe to 11/12 of 30° we ensure that when the animation plays in a loop, the transition from the final frame to the first will make the same rotation as the transitions between all the frames within the animation. In other words, the cog will appear to rotate at a uniform speed forever.

However, this looks more like a cog that should move in a jerkier way, like part of a watch or a complicated mechanism. To make it do so, the custom easing shown in Figure 6.39 was applied. The idea of the cog as part of a mechanism suggests that it ought to be driving another one, so we added a second instance of the symbol (along with a background gradient), as shown in Figure 6.41.

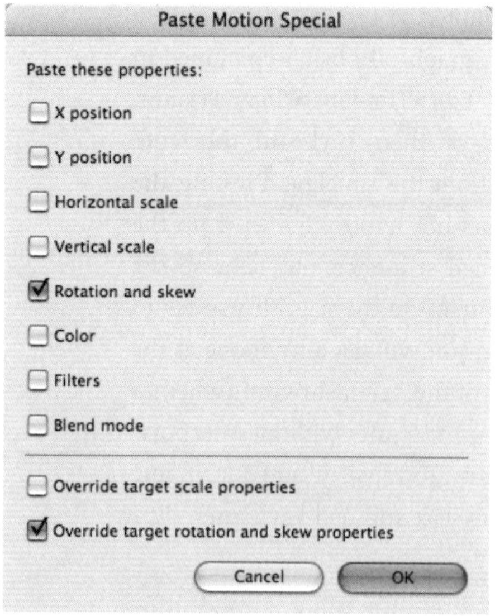

In order to make it look as if the two cogs are interacting, the large one must move in the same way as the smaller one. To make it do so, the motion of the first cog was copied and pasted on to the second. This was simply done by selecting the frames in the timeline corresponding to the movement of the first instance on the layer containing it. (In this case, that means all of the frames on the first cog's layer.) The `Edit>Timeline>Copy Motion` command was then used to copy the motion of the cog to the clipboard.

The second instance of the cog was on its own layer, of course, with a keyframe at the beginning and no tweening. The instance was selected in this keyframe on the stage and the `Edit>Timeline>Paste Motion Special...` command was used. This command opens a dialogue box, in which check-boxes are used to select aspects of the motion to be copied, as shown in Figure 6.40. We only wanted to make the big cog

Figure 6.40 *Selecting which aspects of the motion to paste*

Figure 6.41 *Two instances with the same motion*

rotate in the same way as the smaller one does, so all the other options were unchecked. If we had wanted the second cog to take on all the properties of the first, we could have just used the Edit>Timeline>Paste Motion command, which pastes all the aspects of the motion. In this case, that would have made both cogs the same size, which was not what we intended, so the Paste Motion Special… command is needed here.

When the dialogue was dismissed, a motion tween was automatically created in the layer for the second, larger cog, which matched the motion tween for the smaller one, including its custom easing, so when the movie is played the two move in synchronization.

The result was a pleasant motion graphic, but it might have been better if the two cogs rotated in opposite directions, to look as if one was driving the other. The Modify>Timeline>Reverse Frames command reverses selected frames, so that they run backwards. By selecting the frames on one layer and applying this command, one of the cogs was made to rotate backwards. But there is a problem with using Reverse Frames in this context. When motion tweened frames are reversed, the custom easing is lost, so the backward-spinning cog moved smoothly instead of jerking in time with the other one. This actually looked all right, but it wasn't what was intended.

Fortunately, there is a way of fixing matters; you can copy and paste easing curves themselves. The easing curve is copied to the clipboard if you use the keyboard shortcut for copying, [ctl/cmd]-C while the Custom Ease In/Ease Out dialogue is open. (You can't use a menu command, because the menu bar is disabled while the dialogue is active.) If you then use the pasting shortcut ([ctl/cmd]-V) the next time the dialogue is open, the curve is pasted. In other words, the easing curve becomes a copy of the first one. This solves our problem: the easing curve from the tween of the first cog was copied, a tweened frame on the second cog's layer was selected, the Custom Ease In/Ease Out dialogue was opened again and the curve was pasted into it. The result was a movie in which the two cogs moved jerkily in opposite directions in perfect synch with each other.

---TRY THIS---

Create a graphic symbol and add several instances of it to different layers. (If you are good at drawing create something like a windmill, a bicycle or even a human or animal character.) Animate one of the instances using motion tweening with custom easing to alter its position, size and colour, or some other suitable combination of properties. Give the object or character some distinctive motion, then try copying its motion to other instances. Observe the effect of using the Paste Motion command, and the Paste Motion Special... command with different options.

Try reversing the motion of one of the instances. Copy and paste an easing curve to restore custom easing to the reversed motion.

Timeline Effects and Transitions

Selecting, cutting, copying and pasting frames in Flash is roughly equivalent to trimming and assembling short video clips in a video editing program such as Premiere. In video it is common to use *transitions*, such as dissolves and wipes, as an alternative to straight cuts for moving from one scene to another. Flash also has its transitions. They are one type of *timeline effect*. Most of the timeline effects are simple time-based visual effects, such as expansion, contraction and other transformations (which could be achieved with motion tweening), explosion and blurring over time, as well as fades (in and out) and wipes, which can be used as transitions. You can apply timeline effects to most sorts of object, including graphic objects, symbol instances and bitmaps.

To add an effect or transition you select an object on the stage and then choose the effect you want from one of the sub-menus found under the Insert>Timeline Effects own sub-menu. A dialogue box showing a preview of the chosen effect opens, with controls at the left for changing any parameters that alter its behaviour. Most effects have an easing slider that allows you to vary the pace at which the effect changes over time, but there is no provision for custom easing. This is not a serious omission in the case of effects, though, as simple easing in or out is usually all that is needed. Figure 6.42 shows an example dialogue for setting the parameters of an effect.

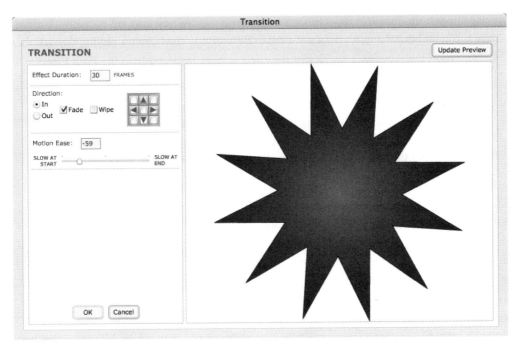

Figure 6.42 *Setting parameters for a timeline effect*

Generally, the quickest way to find out what changing a parameter's value does is by experiment. You can click on the **Update Preview** button to get an impression of the changed effect, and then test the movie in the usual way to see what the effect looks like in context. You can change the parameters later on; make sure that you have selected the object to which you previously applied the effect, then click on the **Edit...** button in the **Properties** panel. (It will have the name of the effect next to it.) This will open the effect's dialogue again.

What actually happens when you apply an effect to an object can be somewhat unpredictable; timeline effects are among Flash's less well implemented features and they do not always behave as you might hope or expect. When you apply an effect to an object, you will generally find that the layer containing the frame(s) to which you applied the effect is altered, and the layer's name is changed to the name of the effect, even if you only applied the effect to a small part of the layer. There should be a set of additional frames created for the duration of the effect, which will therefore extend the duration of the affected layer (but not of any other layers).

In order to create an effect, the original object is turned into a new symbol (or possibly several symbols) and tweening is applied to it. This means that once an effect has been applied, it is no longer a simple matter to edit the original object, for example to change its colour. You will find that both a new symbol labelled with the effect's name and an effects folder have been added to the Library. It is important to note that some effects cannot be seen if you try to preview by playing through the timeline; this can be very confusing when you first try to apply timeline effects. If you find that the effect does not seem to be working when you try playing through the timeline, export the movie and check that the effect is working properly in the Flash Player.

---TRY THIS---

> **Experiment with applying each of the timeline effects to a simple shape, such as a star, to see what each one does. Look at the timeline and Library after you have applied each effect and note what has changed. Try previewing your effects in the timeline, and exporting the movie for viewing in the Flash Player.**

Many of the timeline effects are redundant – because you can achieve the same result using motion tweening – and some are just gimmicks, though there might be an occasional use for them. The transitions, though, are frequently useful. A very common application of transitions is in constructing slide shows from a set of bitmapped still images. A cross-fade effect is achieved by applying a fade-out to one image so that it overlaps a fade-in applied to the next. In detail, the procedure is as follows.

Import a bitmapped image to the stage in the first keyframe of a new movie. Make sure that you set the document dimensions to match the image if they don't already, by selecting the radio button labelled Contents under the dimensions boxes in the document properties dialogue, which you invoke with the Modify>Document command. Add sufficient frames to allow the viewer time to look at this first image, and then add a keyframe after the last of these new frames. In this keyframe, select the bitmap on the stage, and choose the Transition effect from the Insert>Timeline Effects>Transform/Transition sub-menu. Deselect the Wipe checkbox (we only want to fade the image) and set the duration to somewhere between 20 and 30 frames. Preview the movie: you should see the image held for a while and then fade out. Adjust the time and easing on the fade out until you are happy with it. Lock the layer for safety once you have got the fade-out right.

Add a second layer to your document and insert a keyframe on this layer at the same position in the timeline as the keyframe from which your fade-out starts on the first layer. Import a second image into this keyframe on the new layer. Select it on the stage and apply the Transition effect again. This time, fade in, but use the same duration as for the fade-out. Once again, experiment with easing – it may or may not be appropriate to match the easing on the fade-out.

The next step is counter-intuitive. The new image should be held for several frames after it has faded in, but because of the way the effect has now wrapped the image into a symbol you can't simply add frames. Instead, insert a blank keyframe after the fade-in and import the image again (or place it on the stage from the library). Then add frames sufficient to give time for viewing the new image, and create a fade-out just as you did for the first image. Preview the movie again.

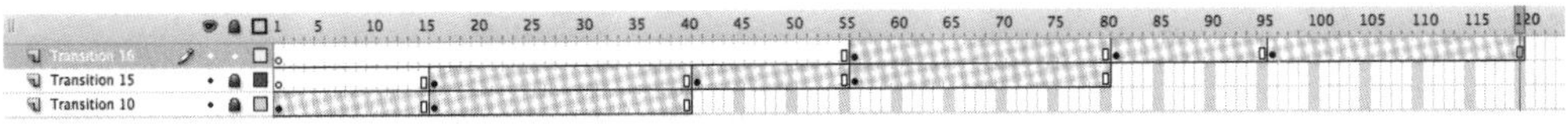

Figure 6.43 *Timeline for a slide show with cross-dissolves*

Continue in this way, adding new images on new layers, with the fade-in for each new image overlapping the fade-out of the previous image. Figure 6.43 shows the sort of timeline that will build up as you proceed. You can see that the layers have been automatically numbered and named with the not-very-helpful label "Transition". For each image after the first one, there is a new layer with a set of blank frames, followed by a fade-in, some frames during which the image is held and then a fade-out. Notice that the fades last longer than the time the image is held for. This is typical: fades and dissolves can be quite slow, but people don't want to look at the same image for very long. You should experiment with the timing, however, to determine for yourself how long you want to hold each image. It will depend on the audience your slide show is aimed at (whether for adults or children, for example), and on the complexity of your images, and on whether they contain any text (which requires additional time to read).

┌─ TRY THIS ───

Follow the instructions just given to create a slide show from a set of bitmapped images, using cross-dissolves between each image.

Try making a similar slide show using wipes instead of dissolves, so that one image reveals the next, but this time use just two layers, cross-dissolving back and forth between them.

Try making a slide show where the slides contain a significant amount of text. Make sure that you allow sufficient time for the text to be read, but not so long that the audience gets impatient.

───

Animated Symbols

Now that we have described Flash's approach to animation, we can reveal that symbols can themselves be animations. This is why you see an empty timeline as well as an empty stage when you create a new symbol: it holds the frames of the symbol. A complete animated sequence can be turned into a symbol. This means that when you make an instance of such a symbol, you get a copy of the whole animation, which you can scale and transform (just as we did with instances of single-frame graphic symbols) and which plays in the same way as the original animation. This provides a very economical way of creating more complex animations with repeated elements.

Figure 6.44 shows a simple example. We began by creating a "pulsar", that is, a star whose brightness fades up and down periodically. This was done using the Insert>New Symbol... command, which, as we described earlier, provides a blank stage and timeline on which to create a symbol. In earlier examples, we have just drawn on the stage to create a symbol for use as a graphic object,

Figure 6.44 *Instances of an animated symbol*

and have ignored the timeline, but we can use the timeline while creating a symbol in just the same way as when we are creating a whole movie. In this case, we drew a star and filled it with a gradient, then tweened its brightness down over the course of 30 frames and up again over the next 30. (Just a few selected frames from the sequence are shown in Figure 6.44.)

We then returned to the main timeline, created a layer for the background and drew a dark rectangle on it. We added a second layer on top of the background and dragged three instances of the animated pulsar symbol onto it, positioning and scaling them to different sizes. Despite the fact that the pulsar animation has a duration in itself, both layers in the main timeline still consist of just a single keyframe at this point.

However, our animated pulsar actually takes 60 frames to go from maximum brightness to minimum and back up to maximum. Therefore, if we want the movie to pulse smoothly as it plays in a loop, its length must be an exact multiple of 60. We added frames (not keyframes) to both layers to extend the movie to 60 frames.

We could have achieved the same effect in this case by copying and pasting the motion from a single pulsar animation that had not been made into a symbol, but the use of symbols has several advantages. First, we can edit the symbol – for example, to change the fill of the star or the easing on the pulsation – and all its instances will be updated. Second, when the SWF is exported, only one copy of the symbol is needed, so the file is smaller and will take less time to download. And finally, in just the same way as we described earlier for instances of graphic symbols that were not animated, instances of animated symbols can have certain transformations and effects applied to them, for example to alter their size, colour or transparency (alpha). This means that certain types of variation of an original animation sequence can be created quickly and easily.

┌─TRY THIS──────────────────────────────────────

Make an animation by creating a graphic symbol with multiple frames, animated either by tweening or a frame at a time. Place several instances of your symbol on the main timeline, with some transformation or effects applied. Make sure that your animation plays in a complete loop.

Having all the instances move in synch is a bit dull. Try adding the instances to distinct layers, at different keyframes. What implications does this have for the length of the movie and the appearance of the symbol?

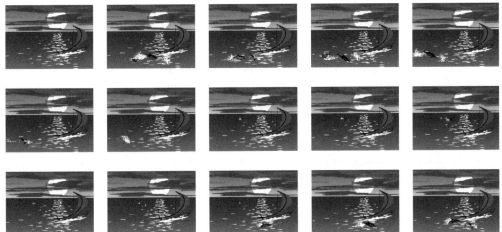

Figure 6.45 *Timeline and selected frames from an animation with nested symbols*

Animated sequences can contain other animated sequences, which can be combined with tweening and frame-at-a-time animation to make elaborate movies. Figure 6.45 is an example, in which various techniques, including frame-at-a-time animation, motion tweening and shape tweening (see below) have been combined. Symbols within symbols are used to make the groups of dolphins that jump out of the water. Each leaping dolphin is an instance of the same symbol, shown in Figure 6.46, which was drawn by hand in Flash, one frame at a time. Two groups were created as symbols, one with two instances of the dolphin, the other with three, with the instances offset in the timeline so that the dolphins leap out after each other. Finally, three instances of one group and one of the other were placed at different keyframes in the main timeline, scaled and positioned so that the boat appeared to be surrounded by a school of leaping dolphins.

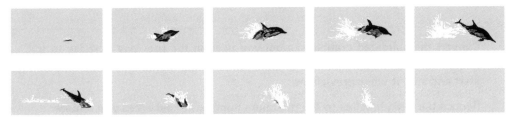

Figure 6.46 *Some frames of the animated dolphin symbol*

Looking back at Figure 6.21, you will see that as well as graphic symbols you can create symbols of type **Button** or **Movie Clip**. You can also change the type of an existing symbol by selecting it in the **Library** panel, clicking on the info button at the bottom of the panel, and selecting the appropriate radio button in the dialogue that appears (another version of the ones in Figure 6.21). **Button** is a special sort of symbol, used to control movies in response to users' input. They are not strictly necessary any more. Movie clip symbols are similar to the graphic symbols we have used so far: they are reusable pieces of animation. There are some important differences between movie clips and graphic symbols, though. A movie clip is a completely self-contained movie-within-a-movie, with its own timeline. It can be controlled – stopped, started, and so on – independently of the main movie and other clips.

To see what we mean by this, consider the simple pulsar animation again. Suppose that we cut the length of the main movie's timeline down to 30 frames. When the movie was played in a loop, the stars would dim, but then jump straight back to their full brightness when the movie looped back from frame 30 to frame 1. However, if the pulsar had been a movie clip symbol, the stars would have pulsed regularly, irrespective of the length of the main movie. The timeline of a movie clip symbol is not affected by a jump from the last to first frame. In fact, the movie would work – the stars would pulsate regularly – even if the main movie only had one frame, comprising a keyframe with the three instances of the movie clip symbol on top of the background. What is more, if you used the **Control>Stop** command to halt the movie while you were previewing it, if the pulsars were instances of a graphic symbol, everything would freeze, but if they were instances of a movie clip symbol, they would carry on pulsating, because the **Stop** command only stops the main timeline, not the independent timelines of the clips. This may be a little difficult to understand from a description, but it will become clear when you experiment with using the two different kinds of symbol for animation (or other self-contained movies) yourself.

The biggest and most significant difference between graphic symbols and movie clip symbols is that movie clip instances can be controlled by scripts, which respond to events, such as mouse clicks and key presses. This opens up a huge range of possibilities for interactivity, including animations that respond to mouse movements and others that use the laws of physics to create realistic motion dynamically. The full realization of the possibilities of controlling clips by scripting needs a good understanding of programming, and we cannot convey that in this book, so we will have to leave it as a tantalizing possibility for you to explore elsewhere.

---TRY THIS---

Convert the animated graphic symbol you used in the previous exercise to a movie clip symbol, and see how this affects the movie's behaviour when you start and stop it while previewing.

Reduce the main timeline to the minimum number of keyframes you require.

Figure 6.47 *Applying a filter*

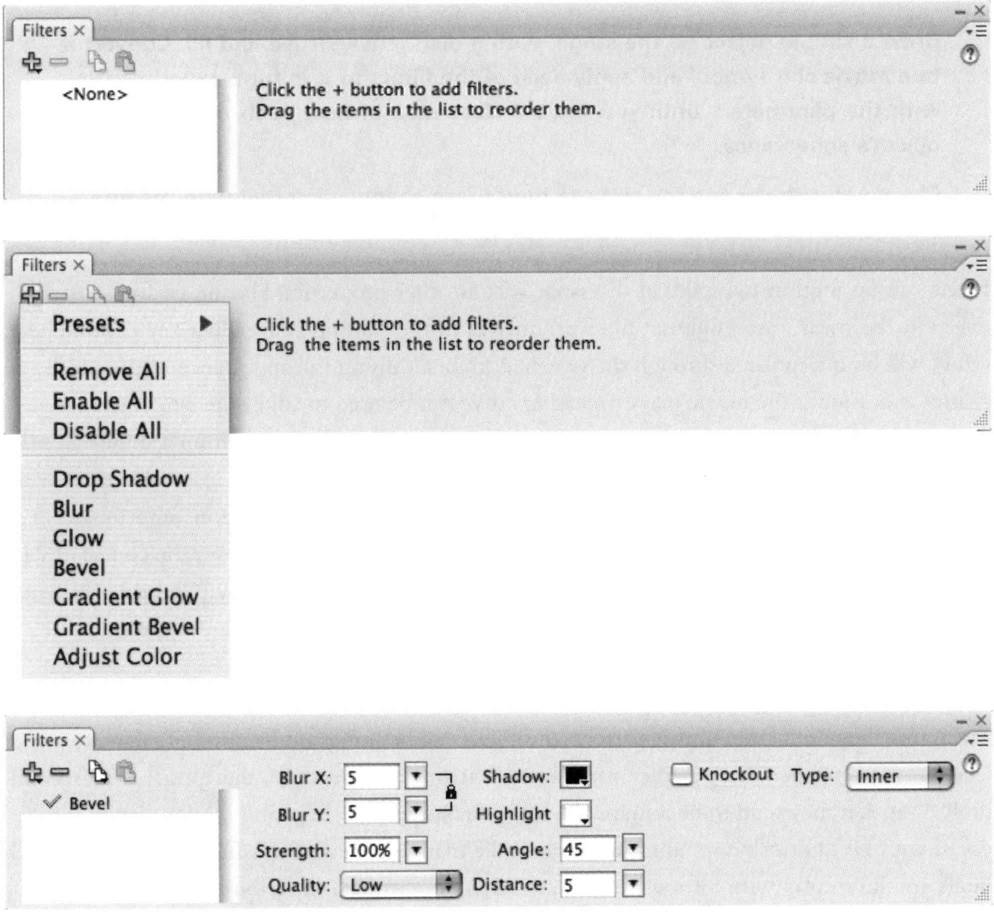

Tweening Filters

Flash provides a small collection of *filters*, which you can apply to movie clip instances, text objects or buttons, but not to any other sort of object. The available filters are similar to Photoshop's layer effects, described in Chapter 4. They include drop shadow, blur, several types of glow, bevel and a colour adjustment (yet another way of changing the colour of an object).

To apply a filter, use the Filters panel, which is conveniently docked with the Properties panel in the default workspace. On the stage, select an object of one of the types that can take filters. Initially, you will just see a + button with an attached pop-up menu in the Filters panel. If you click on the button and pop up the menu, you can select one of the available filters to add. At that point, the rest of the tab will show controls for setting the values of the available parameters for the chosen filter. Figure 6.47 shows the process. As you can see from the middle illustration, there are seven filters, most of which will be familiar if you have used Photoshop.

┌─TRY THIS───┐

Draw a simple object on the stage, with a distinctive stroke and fill. Convert it to a movie clip symbol and apply each of the filters to it in turn, experimenting with the parameters until you have a clear idea of how each one affects the object's appearance.

Change the stroke and fill, and see how these changes interact with the filters.
└──┘

Filters can be motion tweened, in the same way as other properties. Having created a motion tween in the usual way, simply set filter parameters in the starting and ending keyframes. These values will be interpolated through the tweened frames, causing the appearance of the object to change over time as the movie plays. An easing curve can be used to adjust the rate of change, just as it can for any other tweened properties. Figure 6.48 shows a few frames from a simple animation made in this way. Tweened filters were applied to a bitmapped image, in combination with tweened rotation. (The effect does not show up well in greyscale reproduction, unfortunately.) A glow, colour change and gradient glow were all applied and then removed over the course of 240 frames to make a gradually changing decorative element that loops smoothly. (Compare this with the methods used to make a similar animation in Photoshop, as described in Chapter 4.)

Applying and tweening filters is very easy. There are just two problems with tweened filters. The first is that they noticeably impair performance. This can be mitigated by choosing **Low** from the **Quality** pop-up when setting filter parameters, but this also degrades the quality. The second problem is that they tend to encourage the sort of pointless and irritating motion graphics associated with DVD dsitributors' animated logos. Like many of Photoshop's filters, Flash's animated filters are fun to play with for a while, but are often best avoided in serious work.

Figure 6.48 *Selected frames from an animation made by tweening filters*

┌─TRY THIS───┐

See whether, by combining some filters applied to a suitably coloured circle with some other layers and tweens, you can create an animated dawn or sunset.
└──┘

Shape Tweening

Motion tweening is an efficient way of animating, both in terms of the effort needed on the part of the animator and the computational power needed to play it back. *Shape tweening* provides an alternative type of interpolation, but it is power-hungry and can be much more difficult to use.

Shape tweening is a process of transformation, that is, turning one shape into another – for instance, a moon into a star, or Dr Jekyll into Mr Hyde. This type of transformation is often referred to as **morphing**, and is popular in films based on special effects, to the extent that "shape shifting" has become something of a cliché. However, shape tweening can also be used more subtly to create interesting graphic effects. Shape tweening was used to make the spray and the ripples on the surface of the water in the animation shown in Figure 6.45, for example.

Whereas you can only apply motion tweening to instances of symbols, you can only apply shape tweening to objects that are *not* instances of symbols. This can be difficult to remember at first, but it does make sense if you think about what shape tweening is doing. If you want to apply shape tweening to imported bitmaps, you must first break them apart using the Modify>Break Apart command; the results are likely to be highly unpredictable, though.

Creating shape tweening is similar to the procedure for creating motion tweening that we described earlier. You start by drawing something in a keyframe where you want the tweening to begin, but don't make it into a symbol. Next, create a new keyframe at the point in the timeline where you want the tweening to end and draw the final image. Note that for shape tweening – unlike motion tweening – you will often not want the original image from your first frame to appear in the final frame. The purpose of shape tweening is transformation. This means that you may well want to insert a blank keyframe at the end point of your tween, so that you can draw a new image in it. (But it doesn't matter if you insert an ordinary keyframe by mistake; you can always delete its contents.) Alternatively, if you wish to create the final frame of the tween by altering your original drawing, you will need a keyframe that is a copy of your starting frame.

Once you have created the artwork in the starting and ending keyframes, select any of the tweened frames in between them and choose Shape from the Tween pop-up menu in the Properties panel. You can set an easing value for shape tweening just as you can for motion tweening, but there is no custom easing facility. You can also choose between Distributive and Angular blending. The former is smoother, while the latter preserves corners and straight lines in the intermediate frames. It is worth experimenting to see the different effects of the two – sometimes they behave just the same as each other, but at other times they create quite different effects, depending on the artwork being tweened.

Students just beginning to learn animation are often set a simple exercise in which they are asked to transform a circle in the bottom left corner of the frame to a star in the top right over the course of 24 frames drawn on paper (or something very similar). You can cheat using shape tweening, as shown in Figure 6.49, but you'll stand a better chance of becoming a real animator if you do it by hand, one frame at a time; you will also get a more original result, and quite possibly a better one. Flash's shape tweening has a very mechanized feel to it.

Figure 6.49 *Shape tweening*

Like "motion tweening", "shape tweening" is a rather misleading name, since it is not only the shape that is transformed; all aspects of the initial drawing, including its colours, size and position, can be changed. In Figure 6.49, for instance, the original object was not moved and altered to produce the last frame; a completely new shape was drawn in the final position. The shape tweening interpolates the movement of the object as well as the morphing. So, if all you want to do is create a gradual blend of colours, for example, it is more efficient to use motion tweening of the tint than to use shape tweening on identical, but differently coloured, shapes.

┌─TRY THIS───

Make an animation using shape tweening to turn a three-pointed star into a five-pointed one, then a 12- and finally a 20-pointed star. Try changing the colours, position and number of objects being morphed by shape tweening. For instance, try turning one red star into four blue ones.

The appearance of the intermediate frames produced by shape tweening is not, except in simple cases, readily predictable, and can sometimes be very surprising. This is especially the case if you draw more than one shape on the tweened layer or transform a single shape into several different ones. You can produce interesting effects serendipitously by experimenting with such unpredictable transformations, but if you need to retain control over the results you may prefer to use *shape hints* to control the morphing to some extent.

Shape hints provide a means of identifying points that you wish to correspond in the initial and final images. With the keyframe at the beginning of the tween selected, choose the Modify>Shape>Add Shape Hint command. A small red circle labelled a appears at the centre of the object being tweened; drag this circle to a point which you wish to constrain. Now select the final keyframe in the tween. The labelled circle appears again, and so you drag it to the point you wish to correspond to the one you designated in the first keyframe. When the tweening is applied, the corresponding points will be translated in as direct a manner as possible. You can go back to

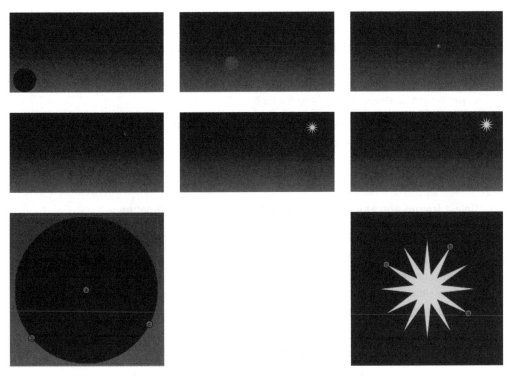

Figure 6.50 *Using shape hints*

the starting keyframe and add additional shape hints in the same way as the first one. Figure 6.50 shows the effect of constraining shape tweening in this way while turning the circle into a star. By mapping the centre of the circle and two points on its rim to somewhere other than the obvious corresponding points of the star, we have forced the shape to turn itself inside out while being morphed, which creates a more dramatic transformation during the course of the animation.

We recommend that you test the effect of shape hints as you go along, since they are by no means as predictable as you might think at first. Over-constraining, by adding too many shape hints, can have disastrous effects. If you find you need to remove a shape hint, just drag its circle off the stage. Don't expect shape hints to do too much for you. If you need to control any type of tweened change closely – motion as well as morphing – it is better to add additional keyframes and create the tweened animation in stages.

You should remember that shape tweening is a computationally intensive process, and that all tweened frames have to be computed at the time the movie is played back. If you become enchanted with morphing and try to base an entire animation on it, with many independently shape-tweened layers, you will find that even the most powerful computers will struggle to play back your movie smoothly. Shape tweening should therefore be used judiciously.

Try adding shape hints to the transformation of a five-pointed star into a 12-pointed one. (This will be easier if you make the stars quite large.) For example, try mapping points of the first star to opposing points of the last one, instead of corresponding ones. What happens if a shape hint marker is moved away from the shape in the final frame?

Experiment further with shape tweening, including using several independently tweened layers, and assess the results.

DON'T FORGET

Select frames and keyframes by clicking on them in the timeline.

Drag the red bar through the timeline to set a new current frame; this does not automatically select the frame, however.

Use the commands on the Edit>Timeline sub-menu to cut, copy, paste and delete frames. Using the delete key or Edit>Cut, etc. will delete frames' contents, but not the frames themselves.

Copy and paste motion tweening and easing curves to make several objects' tweened properties change over time in the same way.

Use timeline effects to create transitions, such as dissolves. Preview effects in the Flash Player if they do not show up when playing through the timeline.

Create movie clip symbols and graphic symbols with more than one frame as reusable animations within a movie.

You can set the colour (tint), alpha, size, etc. of instances of animated symbols independently, in the same way as for still graphic symbols.

Movie clip symbols have their own independent timelines and can be controlled by scripts; instances of movie clip symbols can be added to a single keyframe in the main timeline. For animated graphic symbol instances you need to create sufficient frames in the main timeline for the duration of the animation.

Apply filters to movie clip instances, button instances or text objects to produce graphic effects such as glows and drop shadows. Tween the filter settings using motion tweening, to produce easy motion graphics.

Use shape tweening to morph one shape into another. Shape tweening cannot be applied to symbols, but otherwise is applied in almost the same way as motion tweening. Test the results – they can be unpredictable.

Shape tweening is computationally intensive; use it with discretion.

Use shape hints for more control over morphing.

Sound and Video

As you will have realized from looking at contemporary Web sites, Flash movies don't have to be silent and they don't have to consist purely of drawn or imported vector and bitmapped graphics. You can add a synchronized soundtrack to provide backing music or dialogue and you can add "spot sounds" – sound effects that play at specified points in the movie. You can combine animation with imported video, or you can just use a Flash movie as a video player.

Sound

Adding sound is a two-stage process. First, a sound must be imported into the movie's library. Flash can import sounds in several different formats: MP3 files can be used on any platform, AIFF on Macs and WAV on Windows; if you have QuickTime installed, WAV files can be used on Macs, too, and several other formats are then supported, including Sun AU files and QuickTime movies consisting only of a soundtrack. Flash cannot record sounds directly, though, it can only import them from a file already on disk. This is done in the same way as importing artwork, using the File>Import>Import to Library… command.

Any sound that you have imported appears in the Library panel, alongside the symbols and any other imported items. If you select a sound in the Library panel, the preview area of the panel shows its waveform, as shown in Figure 6.51. Sampling rates of 11, 22 and 44kHz are supported, in 8- or 16-bits. If your sound was recorded at a different sampling rate, for example, at the 48kHz used by DAT, it will be automatically resampled by Flash, which might cause a deterioration of quality. Try to avoid mixing sampling rates if you possibly can. Sound files can occupy a large amount of space, and if your movie is intended to be played over the Internet, you may well find it is necessary to compromise on quality and use a lower sampling rate than the 44kHz used by audio CDs, in order to reduce the movie's bandwidth requirement.

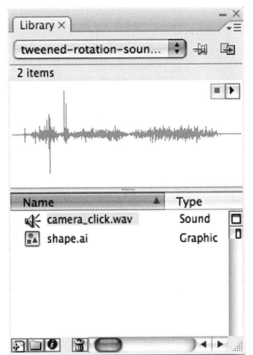

Figure 6.51 *An imported sound*

To use a sound in a document once you have imported it, you should first create a new layer to hold it. (This isn't strictly necessary, but it is more convenient and is strongly recommended.) Insert a keyframe in the new layer at the point where you want the sound to begin playing. With this keyframe selected in the timeline, the Properties panel can be used to choose a sound to add to the layer:

Figure 6.52 *Sound on a layer in the timeline*

the pop-up menu labelled Sound at the top right of the Properties panel contains entries for every sound you have imported. To add a sound, just select it from this pop-up menu. When you do so, a miniature waveform will appear in the timeline, on the layer on which you selected the keyframe, as shown in Figure 6.52. (Note the considerable differences between the method for adding sound to a Flash movie and the methods for adding artwork, and between the ways the presence of these different media is indicated in the timeline.) You can add several layers with sounds to a movie: they are treated like channels in a conventional audio device and are mixed down when the movie is exported.

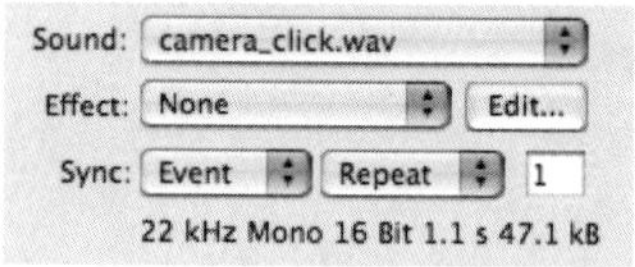

Sounds can be synchronized with the movie's playback in one of two ways. *Event sounds* start to play when the keyframe at which the sound was added is displayed, and they continue to play until they reach the end of their duration or for a specified number of repetitions, irrespective of how the playback of the movie proceeds. For example, an event sound will continue to play even if the movie is stopped, in the same way as a movie clip.

Stream sounds are synchronized to the main movie: if the main movie stops, the sound stops too; if frames are being displayed more slowly than the movie's specified frame rate – because it is being streamed over a slow network connection or played on a slow machine, for example – picture frames are dropped to ensure that the relationship between sound and picture set on the timeline is maintained (you may well have observed this happening on the Web). Stream sounds behave like still images in that they are only played during static frames following the keyframe in which they first appear. If a subsequent keyframe with a different sound, or no sound, is added to the sound layer, the first sound stops. Stream sounds are suitable for synchronized soundtracks, while event sounds are useful for providing ambient sound and spot effects. Use the pop-up menu labelled Sync on the Properties panel to choose whether a sound is an event or stream sound.

If you want to use an event sound, you first add the sound to your movie, as described above, and then select Event from the Sync pop-up menu. You can choose Repeat or Loop from the adjoining pop-up menu to specify that the sound should repeat a specific number of times, which you type into the box next to the pop-up, or forever (Loop). If you just want the sound to play once, select Repeat and leave the count set to 1.

If, on the other hand, you want the sound to be synchronized to the playing of the animation, choose Stream from the Sync pop-up menu. (It is not advisable to set a number of loops in this case.) This will be appropriate for dialogue or a music track that has been fitted to the picture.

Using **Stream** may lead to dropped frames in the animation, but this is usually less intrusive than either a loss of synchronization (for example, between speech and a character's lip movements in a cartoon-style animation) or interruptions to the audio. However, it is not entirely acceptable, so it is worthwhile keeping the bandwidth requirements of the movie as low as possible.

What if you want a sound to stop at a certain frame? This is easily achieved. Create a keyframe in the layer containing the sound at the point where you want it to stop, and select that keyframe. In the **Properties** panel, select the sound from the pop-up menu and select **Stop** from the **Sync** pop-up menu. The sound will stop at that keyframe, even if it is an event sound.

TRY THIS

Practise adding sounds to movies. Import several sounds from disk and add them as both event sounds and stream sounds to one or more of the movies you have made for earlier exercises. (You can find free sound effects and music on the Web if you do not have the facilities to record your own.) Note the differences in behaviour between the two types of sound.

Try creating a chorus effect by adding the same sound to several layers, offset by a few frames. Try making all the sound stop at a fixed point before the end of the movie.

Flash has a basic sound editing facility, but it is so rudimentary that it is hardly worth learning about. If you need to prepare or modify a sound, use a dedicated application, such as Soundbooth, or one of the many free or cheap audio capture and editing utilities that are available.

By default, when you export a movie as a SWF file, any sounds in it are compressed as **MP3** audio. Since this is the most compact sound format available for SWFs, and it achieves a quality that is generally felt to be acceptable, it is usually sensible to stick with this default. If you wish to change the format, or adjust the detailed settings, you can do so via a number of routes. To change the settings for all the sounds in a movie, first choose **Publish Settings...** from the **File** menu, then click on the **Flash** tab, and finally click the **Set** button next to either **Audio Stream** or **Audio Event**. The dialogue box shown in Figure 6.53 will appear. If you understand audio compression, you can set different parameters, or choose an alternative format, using the various pop-up menus in the dialogue.

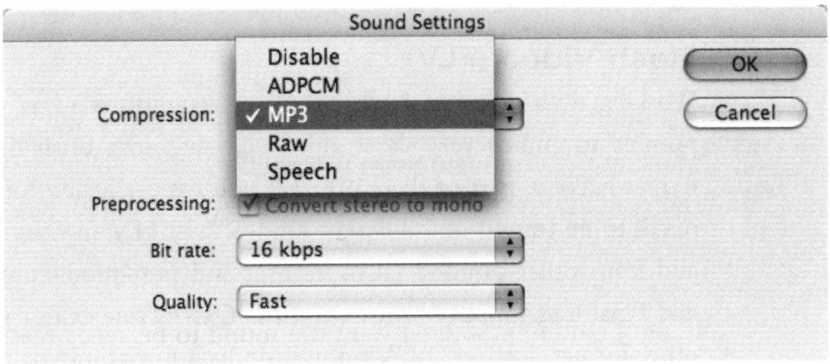

Figure 6.53 *Setting sound properties for a movie*

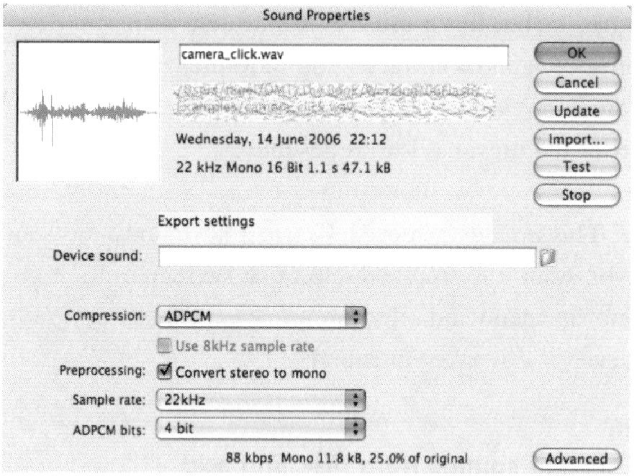

Figure 6.54 *Setting an individual sound's properties*

You can also set the export settings of individual sounds, by double-clicking them in the Library panel. This opens the Sound Properties dialogue shown in Figure 6.54. Details of the sound you double-clicked and its waveform are displayed in the upper part of the dialogue. Normally, Compression is set to Default, which picks up the values set in the Publish Settings dialogue but, if you choose a different method from the Compression pop-up menu, you can enter values for the parameters corresponding to your chosen method, as shown here.

Sound should be used judiciously on the Web. Many people find it intrusive and irritating and others may be working in environments such as shared offices where sound may annoy their colleagues. You should always provide a means of turning sound off (and back on), if you can, and think about how to convey your message without using sound. (For the first 35 years of motion picture history, films had no embedded sound at all; they succeeded in telling stories and conveying information by other means.)

Video

One of the more surprising recent developments in Flash is the way its enhanced support for video has led to it becoming the most widely used video format on the Web. For applications such as video sharing, Flash's animation and most of its interactive features are irrelevant: video in Flash's own *FLV* (*Flash Video*) format may be streamed and viewed in a Web browser using the Flash Player plug-in. The success of Flash video is due to the high proportion of computers and other devices on which the Flash Player is installed, more than any compelling technical advantages of the format. Indeed, the quality of Flash video is generally inferior to that of the other popular Web video formats, Windows Media and QuickTime.

Flash Video (FLV)

Working with video in Flash is not so straightforward as working with sound. Although it is possible to embed very short video clips within a Flash movie (see below), so that the video frames become part of the SWF that you export, video for streaming or progressive download needs to be treated in a different kind of way. FLV movies can be exported from Premiere Pro, and from other popular video editing and post-production programs, including After Effects and Final Cut Pro, by way of the *FLV QuickTime export plug-in*. Alternatively, video in some other format, such as DV, Windows Media, QuickTime or AVI, can be imported into Flash and converted into FLV in the process. Finally, the *Flash Video Encoder* is a separate program that can be used to convert video from other formats to FLV. It allows batch processing, so you can queue a set of files for conversion, specify the settings you want to use, and then set the conversion going. The Flash Video Encoder can be run on a machine that does not have Flash installed, so if you do a lot of converion to FLV you can set up a machine as a dedicated video converter. Video conversion is a computationally intensive task, so this would be worthwhile if you intend to do much of it.

Streaming, Progressive Download and Embedding

There are three ways in which video can be incorporated in a Flash movie. *Streamed* Flash video depends on the use of the *Flash Media Server* to deliver the data stream. In this mode, frames are played as soon as they are delivered to the user's machine. Because of this, a video stream can begin playing almost immediately. There is no need for the movie to be downloaded in its entirety and played from the local disk, so streamed video places less of a burden on the user's machine. This is the best way of delivering video for most purposes, and the only way of delivering live Flash video, but the Flash Media Server is a relatively expensive program, and entails the use – and additional expense – of a dedicated server or some hosting supplier.

Progressive download is a low-end substitute for streaming. In this mode, the movie is downloaded and played off disk, but it starts playing as early as possible, that is, at the point where the time taken to download the rest of the movie will not exceed the time taken to play the whole movie. While the first part of the movie plays, the remainder is downloaded, so that by the time it is needed, it is on the user's disk. (For more information on streaming and progressive downloading, please see *Web Design: A Complete Introduction* or *Digital Multimedia*.)

The third option for using video in Flash is *embedding*: in this case the video becomes part of the SWF file that is exported from Flash. This provides interesting possibilities for mixing live-action (but not live broadcast) video with animation, but it causes the SWF file to become large, since video is a sequence of bitmapped images, albeit compressed. It is also necessary for the frame rate of the Flash movie to match the frame rate of the video. A movie with embedded video cannot start playing until the entire movie has been downloaded, so this method will lead to the longest delays for the user. It is recommended that only video clips of no longer than ten seconds in duration be embedded.

To import a video clip into a Flash document, you first create and select a layer and then choose Import Video... from the File>Import sub-menu. This command starts the video import "wizard", a series of dialogues which guide you through the process. Figure 6.55 shows the sequence used to import video for progressive download. Provided that you understand the different possibilities for Flash video, the video import wizard should be largely self-explanatory. The first dialogue just asks you where the video file is. There are two possibilities. If the file is on your local disk,

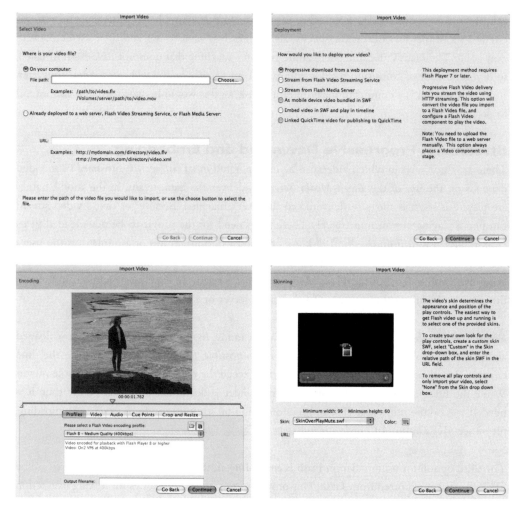

Figure 6.55 *Using the video import wizard for progressive download*

you can use the Choose... button to open a system file-opening dialogue and browse to the file, or if you prefer, you can enter the pathname by hand in the box. If it has already been uploaded to a server, you can enter a URL instead. In that case, though, the video must be in FLV format. Local files can be in any format recognized by Flash: if you have QuickTime installed on your system (Windows or Mac), you can import any QuickTime, AVI, DV or MPEG movie; if you are using Windows and only have DirectX, you can import AVI, MPEG or Windows Media files. Video in these formats will be re-encoded as FLV when they are imported.

If you choose a video file on your disk, the next dialogue will ask you how you want to use it. As you can see from Figure 6.55, there are more possibilities than the three major ones that we have described, but the others can usually be ignored, and may be greyed out.

If you choose the first option, **Progressive download from a web server**, unless the video is already in FLV format the next dialogue offers you the chance to set parameters for the encoding process, which turns it into FLV. (If you have selected an FLV file, this dialogue is skipped.) Unless you understand video compression quite well, the best thing to do here is choose one of the profiles from the pop-up menu. The prefix to each profile indicates the earliest version of the Flash player needed to play video encoded using it, and the figure in brackets at the end tells you the data rate of the resulting FLV video. For instance, the profile we have chosen here, **Flash 8 – Medium Quality (400kbps)**, needs Flash Player 8 or higher, and 400 kilobits per second of bandwidth (i.e. it is not suitable for dial-up connections). The middle part of the profile's name gives a rough, somewhat optimistic, indication of the picture quality.

If you know about video compression, you can click on the **Video** tab in the bottom part of the dialogue, and choose the parameters for the encoding in detail. Similarly, if your video has a soundtrack, and you understand about audio compression, the **Audio** tab provides an opportunity to set parameters for encoding the soundtrack.

You can also do some basic video editing in this dialogue. You can trim unwanted material off the beginning and end by dragging the markers attached to the bottom of the bar below the video preview to the desired positions (to set **In** and **Out** points). Alternatively, click on the **Crop and Resize** tab and set the **In point** and **Out point** using timecode values in the **Trim** pane. In this tab, shown in Figure 6.56, you can also crop and resize the video. In the **Crop** pane you can set values for the top, right, bottom and left of the picture, either numerically or using the sliders, to reduce the amount of picture to be shown. As you do so, a dashed outline shows you the area to which you have cropped the picture. In the **Resize** pane you can set the width and

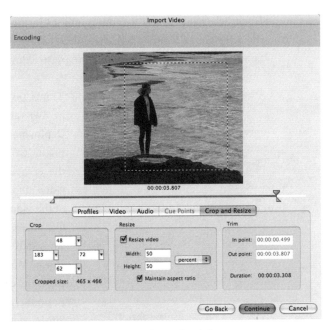

Figure 6.56 *Trimming, cropping and resizing*

height, either as pixel values or percentages; this resizes the whole picture, rather than cropping it. You may often need to resize full-frame video to maintain quality at low data rates.

After you click **Continue**, the video import wizard offers you a final choice, concerning the appearance of the playback controls that will be added to your movie to allow the user to start and stop it or control the sound. The pop-up menu labelled Skin is used to choose a style, or *skin*, for the controls. The skins' names are built up out of pieces that indicate which controls are present and where. For instance, SkinOverPlayMute has play and mute controls superimposed over the movie, whereas SkinUnderPlaySeekStop has play and stop buttons, and a slider to go to a particular place in the video, placed below the movie. When you select a skin, the preview in the dialogue shows you what it will look like and indicates the minimum height and width your movie must have to accommodate the controls. In this dialogue you can also choose a colour for the controls: the default is a rather nasty shade of blue. Using an alpha value less than 100 makes the controls translucent, which is often quite attractive. When you have finished with this dialogue, a final one appears, which gives you detailed instructions about where to put the FLV file on your server relative to the SWF file, to ensure that it will be found and downloaded when somebody views the movie. When you click Finish at this point, the encoding process begins. It may take some considerable time, depending on the speed of your computer. When it has finished you will see the playback controls in a keyframe on the timeline. The video itself occupies no space on the timeline, because it is external to the movie.

If you select one of the streaming options in the second phase of the import wizard (shown at the top right of Figure 6.55), the video must be in FLV format, and the wizard proceeds in the same way as it does if you choose progressive download for an FLV file.

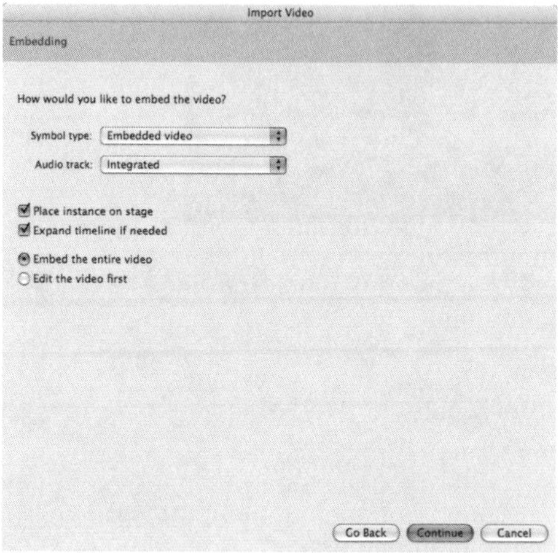

Figure 6.57 *Choosing options for embedded video*

Things go slightly differently if you choose Embed video in SWF and play in timeline in the import wizard's Deployment dialogue. An extra dialogue, shown in Figure 6.57, allows you to choose what form you want the embedded video to take. If you choose Embedded video under the Symbol type pop-up menu, the frames of the video are placed in the timeline; they behave rather like an imported sequence of stills, although, since they are video, there are some technical differences. If you choose Movie clip instead, the video is made into a movie clip symbol, which means that it can be controlled by ActionScript. If you choose Graphic, the video is made into a graphic symbol, so you can use it repeatedly by creating instances, but you cannot control it by scripting.

Video is always imported into the library. Ticking the checkbox labelled Place instance on stage causes an instance to be created automatically. Since each frame of video becomes a frame in the timeline, it may be necessary to add frames to accommodate the full length of the video. However, this is done for you if you select Expand timeline if needed. If you select the radio button labelled

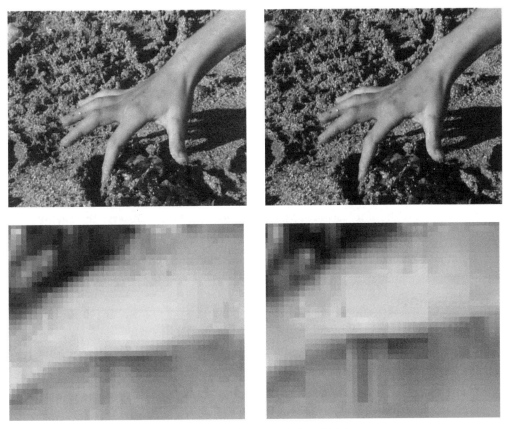

Figure 6.58 *A DV frame (left) and its compressed FLV equivalent (right)*

Edit the video first, another dialogue follows this one, in which you can perform slightly more elaborate editing. In particular, in addition to trimming and cropping, you can splice several clips together. Flash is not a video editing program, though, and we would not advise you to use it as one, except as a last resort.

After you have set the embedding options, the sequence continues in the same way as we described for progressive download, allowing you to set the encoding options, giving you a summary of what will be done, and then performing the encoding. Once this process is completed, the video frames will be available on the timeline, and you can add animation on top of them if you like.

Whenever video is encoded for playing over the Internet, it must be compressed. The software components that perform compression and decompression are called *codecs*. Many different codecs are used by video editing programs, employing different compression algorithms. The *On2 VP6* codec is used by default for encoding Flash video; it is claimed to produce high-quality video at low bit rates, suitable for use on the Web. The quality and data rate depend on the profile used in compression. Figure 6.58 shows a frame of original DV compared to the same frame compressed as FLV using the Flash 8 - Medium Quality (400kbps) profile, with a detail from each frame, blown up to four times natural size, below. In neither case is the quality great (DV is already compressed) but the visible square blocks of pixels (compression artefacts) in the FLV version are more noticeable. When the movie is reduced to quarter-frame size the quality is acceptable, but it remains inferior to other Web video formats.

---TRY THIS---

If you have the facilities, shoot some short video clips (or use our samples from the support site) and import them into your computer. Practise importing them both as embedded files and for progressive download into a Flash movie.

Experiment with compression settings for embedded video. Observe the quality of the resulting playback, and the bandwidth requirements.

Try mixing embedded video with drawn animation and spot sounds.

DON'T FORGET

Import sound files in common formats into the Library.

Create new layers for sounds. Add a sound at a keyframe by selecting it from the Sound pop-up in the Properties panel.

Event sounds start to play when the keyframe is reached and continue to play until they reach their end. Use them for spot effects.

Stream sounds are synchronized to the movie. Use them for soundtracks. The picture may play jerkily when movies with synchronized sound are played over slow connections. Sound files can be large.

Use the Sync pop-up to choose between event and stream sounds.

Flash Video (FLV) files can be exported from popular video editing programs, or created by importing video in some other format into Flash.

Streamed video uses the Flash Media Server to deliver frames which are played as soon as they arrive on the user's machine.

Progressively downloaded video is downloaded to the user's machine and starts playing as early in the download as possible.

Embedded video becomes part of the SWF file; it should only be used for very short clips.

Use the Video Import Wizard to import video, select streaming, progressive download or embedding, and set parameters for encoding as FLV.

Flash Video is highly compressed, with consequent loss of picture quality.

WHAT ELSE?

We have completely omitted any description of the ActionScript language and how it can be used to provide interactivity and to create Web applications in Flash. This is both because ActionScript requires a book in itself to describe it fully, and because it needs programming experience to understand and use it.

The current incarnation of Flash's scripting language, ActionScript 3.0, is a powerful language that incorporates many ideas from other contemporary programming languages, making it much more capable of handling complex tasks than the simple scripting language provided in early versions of Flash. This power has come at the price of lost simplicity. Scripts are no longer simple actions, and they cannot be attached to a frame, movie clip or button to respond to events, in a way that was easily grasped even by people with no programming experience. Instead, to do something as simple as making a button that starts a movie when it is pressed requires knowledge of object-oriented programming concepts such as methods and event handlers, and an understanding of the event handling model implemented by Flash. While these are not hard to understand, they do require some background in programming, and are not likely to hold much interest for designers and animators. We could not teach enough within the space of this chapter to enable you to do any useful scripting, so you must seek elsewhere in order to learn.

There are ways of using scripting without actually doing any. You can start your movie with a template that includes scripts. Try the slide show template to get a taste of what is possible. You can also use Flash components, which are reusable elements that have interactivity built in to them. You have seen a component in the shape of the controller that is added to a movie when you import video. Most available components are controls that respond to user input, and while they minimize the need for scripting, they do not eliminate it entirely, since you must do something with any input from the user, which requires extra programming.

One other topic that we only touched on very briefly is the use of Flash on mobile devices. As well as providing templates for many models of mobile phone and PDA, Flash is integrated with Adobe Device Central, a program that simulates such devices, allowing you to preview how they will look and behave. When you create Flash movies for mobile devices, you must use a restricted version of ActionScript, which resembles early versions of the Flash scripting language, so if you want to do scripting but don't feel competent to tackle ActionScript 3.0, working for mobile devices may offer a way of getting started.

Dreamweaver

In This Chapter

Web pages and sites, accessibility and validation

Dreamweaver's user interface and preferences

Page layout and simple formatting

Creating and using CSS rules for typography and layout

Adding images, Flash, tables and forms

Using behaviours and the Spry framework for interactivity

Setting up and updating sites

Using templates

Dreamweaver is a tool for Web site design and management. Web pages can be created and laid out; links, tables, forms, images and multimedia content can be added. JavaScript actions can be used to incorporate dynamic behaviour and interaction. Pages can be combined into a site, whose structure can be displayed and modified. The program includes a built-in FTP client which can be used to upload sites – and changes to sites – to a server. Unlike the other programs described in this book, Dreamweaver does not provide tools and facilities for creating and manipulating media elements, such as images, within the application, but relies on other programs to do this. Its purpose is to combine elements into a form that can be displayed in a Web browser.

Dreamweaver can also be used as an environment for developing *Web applications* which incorporate *server-side scripts* interacting with databases to generate pages' contents dynamically. We will mostly pass over this aspect of the program in this book, however, since this type of Web development relies on extensive technical knowledge that we do not expect most of our readers will possess. Instead, we will describe Dreamweaver's facilities for creating Web pages, concentrating on page layout and formatting, and for managing sites. (We will not discuss the extensive facilities for extending and customization of Dreamweaver itself; our descriptions are confined to the program as it is installed out of the box.)

Dreamweaver is something of an odd man out among the programs described in this book. Most obviously, it presents a different user interface, with panels that behave and look unlike those we described in Chapter 2, which are used in all the other programs. More subtly, Dreamweaver is unnecessary, in a way that the other programs in this book are not. If you want to edit bitmapped images, you will need Photoshop, or another program that does the same job. Similarly, for creating and editing vector graphics, you will need Illustrator or an equivalent vector graphics application, and for making Flash movies, Flash is really the only possibility. But Web pages can be created in any text editor, without the use of any Web "authoring" program at all. However, Dreamweaver remains a popular program that is widely used.

Dreamweaver also differs from other media tools in the way that it has developed. The basic technologies of bitmapped images and vector graphics are well established and stable, so new releases of Photoshop, for example, bring new ways of working and additional features, but they rarely invalidate what has gone before. Web technology, however, is changing rapidly. So, too, are people's ideas about the best ways of using the technology. Dreamweaver must try to keep up with these changes, as well as expanding its set of features. One result of this is that Dreamweaver still includes a comparatively large number of features that are no longer relevant to contemporary thinking about Web design, but are retained for compatibility with old projects.

We will deliberately avoid describing these out-of-date features, in order to encourage you to work within Web standards, using a modern approach to Web design. This does mean that, when using Dreamweaver, you will see some features that are not mentioned in this book – specifically those related to frames and table-based layouts, and some aspects of dynamic behaviour. These may simply be ignored.

Fundamentals

Web Pages and Sites

Web pages are documents marked up using a **markup language** that provides a set of **tags**, which indicate the logical structure of the page. Tags are also used to include images and other multimedia elements, such as Flash movies, in Web pages, and to implement **links** between pages, which may be followed in the manner of cross-references in a book. Each tag identifies an element of the document, such as a paragraph, heading, table, list or embedded image. A tag can also set the values of **attributes**, which are named properties of the element it represents. For example, when an image is embedded in a page, an attribute is used to identify the location of the file containing the image data. Almost all Web pages are marked up using some version of the **Hypertext Markup Language (HTML)**. The most recent version of HTML is **XHTML 1.1**. (The X refers to the fact that it is defined using XML.) Where no confusion results, we will use HTML as a synonym for XHTML.

As well as HTML markup, Web pages may include **style sheets** written in the **Cascading Style Sheets** language (CSS), which specify the visual formatting of document elements, and scripts written in **JavaScript**, which provide interactivity and dynamic behaviour. Style sheets and scripts are often placed in the **head** of the document – an invisible element used to contain elements that are not actually displayed. Every Web page contains such a head element and a **body** element, which holds the page's content, consisting of text marked up with tags.

Some Web design packages attempt to conceal the tags entirely, presenting a desktop publishing interface to HTML documents. Dreamweaver, however, assumes that you have some knowledge of HTML and CSS; you may find it difficult to work with if you don't. For example, you can select elements using their tags, and sometimes you need to know which tags are used for certain purposes. Dreamweaver also makes it easy for you to edit tags and style sheets if you know how.

Teaching you HTML, CSS and JavaScript is beyond the scope of this book. If you need more information on these topics, consult our book *Web Design: A Complete Introduction* (John Wiley & Sons Ltd., 2006). Within Dreamweaver, the Reference panel gives access to detailed specifications of HTML and CSS elements, mostly based on the content of some well-respected books published by O'Reilly and Associates. This does not provide any tutorial material, though.

A collection of Web pages is usually organized into a ***Web site***. During development, all the documents making up a site are normally kept in a single folder on the Web designer's machine. Dreamweaver always assumes that these documents are part of a site, so before you can proceed you need to know how to create sites.

Creating Sites

When you select the Site>New Site... command to define a new site, a dialogue box with two tabs, marked Basic and Advanced, opens. If you click on the Basic tab, the dialogue becomes a "wizard" which guides you through the process of setting up a site by asking you a series of questions, which you can answer by filling in text fields or making selections from pop-up menus. After you have answered one set of questions, you move on to the next, which may be determined by your answers to earlier questions – for example, you will only be asked for the address of an ***FTP server*** if you have indicated that your site will be uploaded by FTP.

To create a test site, it is sufficient to enter a name for the site in the first screen, leaving the URL field blank, as shown in the first screen in Figure 7.1. Then answer No when asked whether you want to use a server technology, and choose Edit local copies on my machine, selecting a folder to hold them in the next screen, also shown in Figure 7.1; finally, choose None when asked how you connect to your server. We will return to the topic of sites later in the chapter, and explain how to use the Advanced tab to set more options.

┌─TRY THIS───
│
│   **Create a site called something like Test Site to hold pages for the practice**
│   **exercises in this chapter.**
│
└──

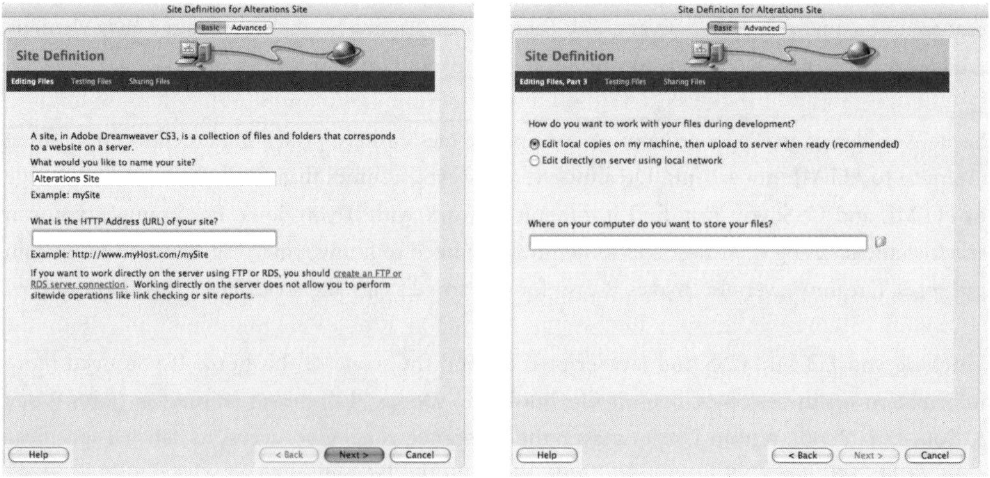

Figure 7.1 *Stages in creating a new site*

Accessibility

Web pages should not present barriers to people who, for whatever reason, have difficulties using the normal interfaces provided by browsers. Examples of such barriers include the use of images to convey information that isn't provided any other way, thus making the page inaccessible to blind people and others who rely on screen readers; using text fixed at a small size or that has low contrast with its background, causing problems for anyone with less than perfect vision; using colours that cannot be distinguished by people with defective colour vision for important page elements, including text; including forms or other controls on a page that cannot be operated by keyboard alone, and therefore cannot be used by people suffering from repetitive strain injuries or other physical problems that make it impossible for them to use a mouse or pointing device; and using rapidly flashing elements, which can cause seizures in susceptible people. These are just a few of the ways in which Web pages can fail to be *accessible*; in total, these potential barriers affect a very large number of Web users worldwide.

All recent versions of HTML and XHTML include features that can be used to enhance the accessibility of Web pages. However, Web designers and developers must use these features correctly. For instance, the img element that is used to embed images must (in XHTML) have an alt attribute whose value is a textual alternative to the image, that conveys the same information as the picture. This alt attribute must be present if the markup is to be valid. However, that doesn't mean that browsers won't display the page without the attribute. (Although, strictly speaking, if the page was XHTML they should not display it, in practice all conventional browsers will happily overlook the omission of an alt attribute.) It is up to the Web designer to insert that attribute and give it an appropriate value.

Dreamweaver will help, as much as it can, to ensure that the pages you create using the program are accessible. For instance, if you set the preferences appropriately, you will always be prompted for an alt attribute's value whenever you insert an image. However, there is no way that any program can determine whether the text you provide is an adequate alternative to the image – that is something that you have to ensure for yourself.

Web accessibility is not a simple subject, but it is an important one. You can find more information about it in Chapter 9 of *Web Design: A Complete Introduction*, or in Joe Clark's book, *Building Accessible Websites* (New Riders: 2003).

User Interface

It is unfortunate that the user interface to Dreamweaver has not been brought into line with those of the other Adobe CS3 programs. Although it is fundamentally the same, with menus, dialogues and panels, there are significant differences that make it harder than one would like to switch between Dreamweaver and other programs.

Panels

Panels in Dreamweaver share many characteristics with panels in the other programs, as described in Chapter 2, but they are not identical. Panels can be combined into panel groups, which can be combined into docks on either side of the workspace, but docks cannot be collapsed into icons, and the controls for hiding and revealing groups in a dock, and for moving groups about, are slightly different from those in the CS3 standard panels.

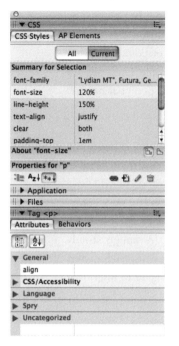

Figure 7.2 *Docked panel groups*

Figure 7.2 shows a docked set of panel groups in Dreamweaver. Groups can be hidden or displayed by clicking on the disclosure triangle to the left of the group's title. Here, the **CSS** and **Tag Inspector** groups are shown in full. Notice that the title of the latter, which would just appear as **Tag Inspector** if it were closed down, changes when the group is displayed (by clicking on the triangle) to indicate something about the contents of the panel. The closed panel groups (**Application** and **Files**) don't occupy much screen space, although they are wider than the collapsed icons of the other programs, but any panel can be accessed with a single mouse click. Notice that disclosure triangles are also used within panels to hide and display sub-panels. For instance, in the **Tag Inspector** shown here, there are five sub-panels.

If a panel group contains more than one panel, as most do, the individual panels are shown as tabs; you can bring each one to the front by clicking its tab. You can drag an individual panel by its tab out of its set, and either add it to another panel group, by dropping it when the outline of the group is highlighted, or make it into a single-panel group of its own, by dropping it onto the dock when there is a highlight between existing groups. You can also just drop it away from the dock, to get a floating panel group, which you can position wherever you want on the screen. Floated panel groups can be combined into stacks, like the standard CS3 panel groups. These behave like floating docks.

To move an entire panel group out of or into a dock, you must drag on the dotted area to the left of the disclosure triangle, called the **gripper**. If you drag by the plain area above the group's title, it won't join a dock, but will just float on top of it. You can tell if this is going to happen, because the panel group will remain solid and move as you drag it. If you drag by the gripper, the panel group stays where it is while you drag and a translucent copy follows the cursor.

A dock can be resized by dragging its bottom right corner; a panel group in a dock can be resized by dragging the bar that separates it from its neighbour. As one open panel is dragged larger, other open ones shrink to accommodate the expansion within the same overall size.

Each panel has a panel menu, which pops up when you click on the icon at the right-hand end of the title bar. Although the icon looks slightly different from the one used for the same purpose in other programs, the panel menu functions in the same way, to provide commands that are related to the operations provided by the panel. There is a sub-menu on each panel menu, Group … with, where the … is replaced by the panel's name. This lets you recombine your panels without having to master the dragging and dropping manipulations.

The Window>Workspace Layout sub-menu is used to manage different arrangements of panel groups; select Default from the sub-menu to put everything back neatly where it started.

> ┌─TRY THIS──
> **Practise working with panels, panel groups and docks in Dreamweaver, as you did in other programs in Chapter 2. Make sure you know how to hide and reveal panel groups and individual panels and how to combine panels into groups.**

The Insert Bar

There is no Tools panel in Dreamweaver. The nature of Web page design does not lend itself to an approach based on using tools. Instead, there is an ***Insert bar***, which is docked at the top of the workspace by default. You can drag it by the gripper and add it to any other dock or stack if you like, but its default position is convenient.

Figure 7.3 *The* Insert *bar as tabs (top) and as menu (bottom)*

The usual layout of the Insert bar is illustrated at the top of Figure 7.3. Although it appears to be a tabbed group, you can't separate the tabs; you can only move the bar as a whole. Each tab has a set of icons representing objects of some sort, such as images, links or elements of forms, that you might want to add to a Web page. You do this by clicking on the appropriate icon, which opens a dialogue box in which you set parameters specific to the object you are inserting. Some of the icons in the Insert bar, such as the sixth one from the left in Figure 7.3, have a downward-pointing arrowhead beside them. Clicking on this arrowhead reveals a drop-down menu with variations on the basic object, as shown in Figure 7.4,

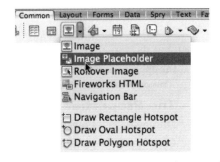

Figure 7.4 *Drop-down menu on the* Insert *bar*

Figure 7.5 *Customizing the favourite objects*

from which you can choose one to insert. We will describe specific instances of this procedure as we go along. You can also drag an icon from the Insert bar into the document window, and drop it. You can't drop objects at arbitrary positions on the page this way, you can only insert them within text – dragging an icon is just a shortcut for moving the cursor and inserting the object.

If you don't like the tabbed Insert bar, you can select Show as Menu from the panel menu, to change its appearance to the form shown at the bottom of Figure 7.3. The categories that were previously tabs become entries on the pop-up menu at the left. (This menu also has the command for going back to the tabbed version of the bar.)

The Insert bar includes a category labelled Favorites, which you can use to hold the objects that you need most often. On the assumption that every Web designer will have his or her own favourites, this category starts out empty. To add objects to it, you must [ctl-click/right-click] on an empty part of the Insert bar in any category, and select Customize Favorites... from the context menu. (This is one of those rare occasions when you can only perform an action using a context menu.) The dialogue box shown in Figure 7.5 will open. You have probably seen similar dialogues before. You add an item to the collection of favourites by double-clicking it in the list on the left. It then moves over to the list on the right, which contains the current set of favourites. You can remove items from this right-hand list by selecting them and then clicking the dustbin icon above the list. You can use the up and down triangles to change the order of items, and use the appropriately named button at the bottom to add separators between groups of items.

The Properties Panel

Dreamweaver's *Properties panel* (also known as the *Property Inspector*) is its equivalent of the Control panel or Options bar in other programs. Since there are no tools, its only function is to display the properties of whatever you have currently selected, and to allow you to change them.

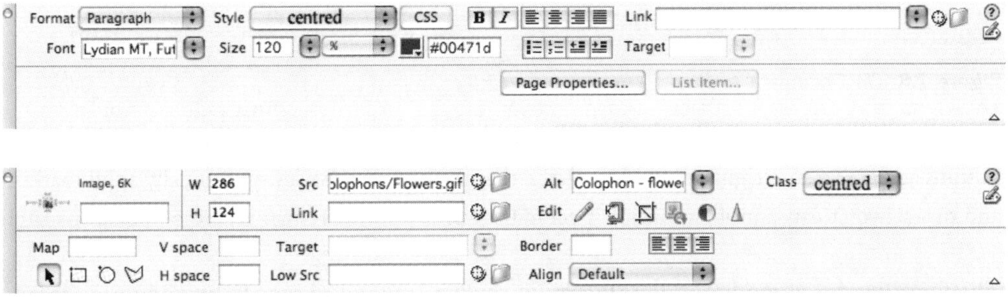

Figure 7.6 *The* Properties *panel with text (top) and an image (bottom) selected*

The Properties panel is context-sensitive and changes depending on the type of thing you have selected. Figure 7.6 shows the Properties panel with some text selected and with an image selected. The panel is divided into two horizontally, with the lower half holding less frequently used options. You can hide these by clicking on the upward-pointing arrowhead in the bottom right corner of the panel, but unless you are very short of screen space this is not necessary. In many contexts, the Properties panel provides buttons which give you access to dialogues and other panels for setting values, instead of providing the controls itself. For instance, in the upper screenshot in Figure 7.6, clicking the button labelled CSS would cause the CSS Styles panel to open so you could edit any style sheet rules applied to the current selection.

The Properties panel is not a true panel. It cannot be added to a panel group or dock. Normally, it is positioned at the bottom of the workspace, but you can drag it by the grey area at its left-hand end to any position you like.

┌─ TRY THIS ──┐

Identify the Insert bar and Properties panel. You can't practise using them until you know how to create documents, but familiarize yourself with their appearance. Create your own favourites for the Insert bar – it doesn't matter if you don't know what they are, just practise adding objects to the favourites.

└───┘

The Document Window

You will spend most of your time in Dreamweaver adding content to individual Web pages in the document window. Because a site is made up of several pages it is often convenient to have several open at once. The document window uses tabs to avoid having lots of windows open. (See Figure 7.7.) You can click on the tabs to switch between open documents.

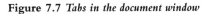

Figure 7.7 *Tabs in the document window*

Unlike other CS3 programs, Dreamweaver uses *toolbars*, of the type more often found in office applications than media tools, to provide access to some common functions. By default, the only one that is displayed is the Document toolbar, shown in Figure 7.8. The buttons at the right of

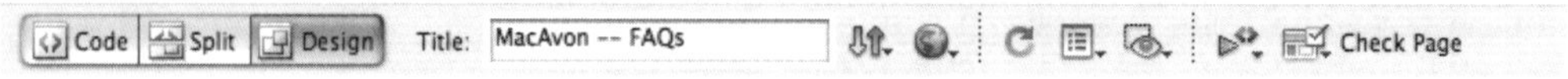

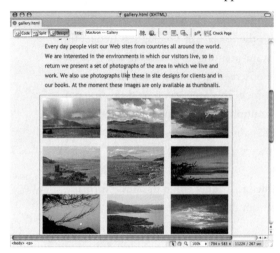

Figure 7.8 *The* Document *toolbar*

the toolbar are used to perform common operations on Web pages. In particular, the pair of buttons at the extreme right are used to check that the document uses syntactically valid markup and that it won't cause problems with specific browsers. We will return to these operations later.

The three buttons at the left of the Document toolbar are used to specify how the page should be displayed in the document window proper. In *design view*, illustrated in Figure 7.9, the page is shown more or less as it will appear in most browsers. Clicking on the left-most button switches the window to *code view*, in which the actual marked-up source document is displayed, as shown in Figure 7.10. In this view, Dreamweaver becomes a text editor with special features, including syntax colouring, for dealing with documents in the various programming and scripting languages used on the Web. This view is therefore only useful to Web designers and developers who understand these languages and are comfortable working on the raw source documents without seeing how they will appear in a browser. The middle button provides a compromise option, the *split view*, in which the code and design views of the same document are combined in the window, as in Figure 7.11. This should make it easy to edit the code directly while seeing the displayed result at the same time. However, as you can see in the illustration, the horizontal split of the window does not leave much room for either view, making it awkward to work in this way.

Figure 7.9 *Design view*

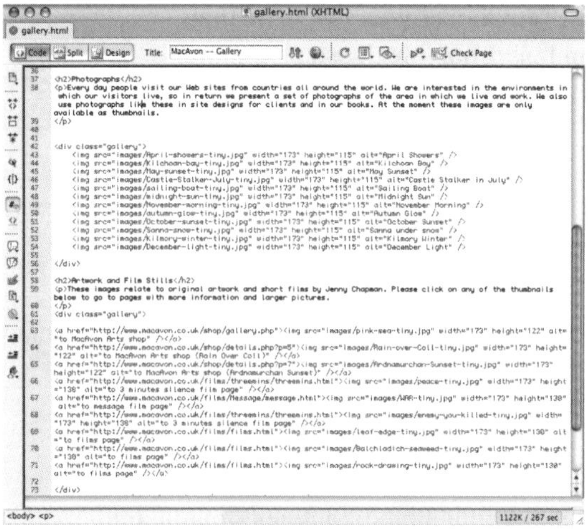

Figure 7.10 *Code view*

The two buttons at the extreme right-hand end of the Document toolbar are especially important. The first is used to *validate* the code of the document in the window – that is, to check that it conforms to the syntax rules of the language it is written in. (Validity is a formal property, concerned with the official definition of the language.) The other button in this group is concerned with the practical question of whether your page, valid or not, is going to cause any problems with popular browsers. Both of these buttons have drop-down menus attached to them from which you can choose what to check, as shown in Figure 7.12. You will notice that there is a **Check Accessibility** command, but even for a totally accessible page this will produce an enormously long list of issues that you have to check manually, so it is not much help.

To the left of these buttons for checking pages is a trio of buttons that control aspects of the display in the document window. The first is a refresh button. This is sometimes needed if you have made changes to the document in code view or using an external editor, in order to force the update of the design view to match the current state of the code. The next two buttons have drop-down menus, shown in Figure 7.13, which you can use to determine what you want to see displayed in the document window in addition to the visible content of the document itself.

Two final buttons appear to the left of the middle group. The first provides various operations on files, including transferring them to and from a remote server. We will return to these file operations later. The left-most button has a drop-down menu of browsers attached to it, from which you can choose one. (The **Preview in Browser** pane of the **Preferences** dialogue allows you to specify the set of browsers that should appear in this menu.) You can also nominate a primary and secondary browser, which can then be accessed rapidly using function keys. By selecting a browser from this drop-down menu, you can preview the current document in that browser.

It would be nice if this facility was redundant, so that all you had to worry about was validity of the code, but each browser has its own peculiarities, and for the foreseeable future it will remain necessary to test Web pages in as many browsers as possible. You need to be aware that Internet Explorer 6 is the most idiosyncratic of commonly-used browsers. It is also, at the time of writing, still the most

Figure 7.11 *Split view*

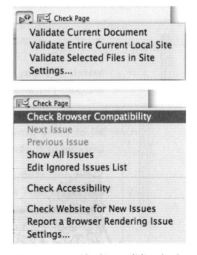

Figure 7.12 *Checking validity (top) and browser compatibility (bottom)*

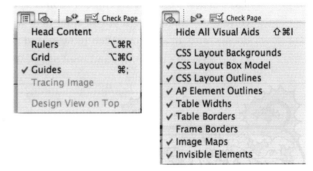

Figure 7.13 *View options and visual aids*

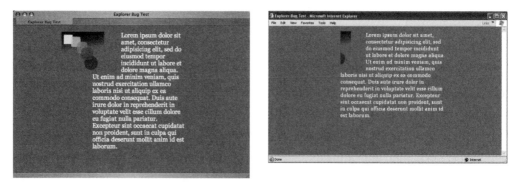

Figure 7.14 *A Web page rendered in a standards-compliant browser (left) and Internet Explorer (right)*

widely used, so it is essential to test Web pages in Explorer 6, which is not standards-compliant. Figure 7.14 shows the sort of problem you may discover by doing so. (The document shown is valid XHTML, so the browser compatibility check does not detect any problems with it.) Note that if you are using Dreamweaver on a Macintosh system, you will not be able to do this from within the application, even if you have a virtual Windows system running on your Mac.

TRY THIS

Install as many different browsers on your computer as you can get hold of, including Internet Explorer 6, if you can.

Use the Preview in Browser pane of the Preferences dialogue to ensure that all of these browsers will be available to you in the drop-down menu on the Document toolbar.

View any Web sites which you visit regularly on all the browsers you have installed. Note any differences in the sites' appearances in different browsers. Pay particular attention to pages that fail in some way – causing error messages, crashing your browser, or displaying jumbled text and images, especially when you blow the pages up.

The last feature of the Document toolbar is a text field in which you can type a *title* for the current document. The text you enter here will appear in the title bar of the window when the document is opened in a Web browser and will be the name by which the page is identified in the browser's history list and bookmarks. When creating real sites it is therefore important to choose the title carefully.

The Document toolbar is not the only toolbar provided in Dreamweaver, but it is probably the most useful and is the only one displayed by default. The View>Toolbars sub-menu lets you display others. You will notice that, in this context, the Insert bar is considered to be a toolbar, and can be hidden by un-ticking its entry on the View>Toolbars sub-menu. Figure 7.15 shows all the available toolbars displayed at the top of the document window. In addition to the Document toolbar (now the middle row), there is a Standard toolbar below it, similar to that used by many applications such as word processors to provide quick access to common File and Edit menu commands. As well as the usual buttons, this bottom toolbar can be used to open

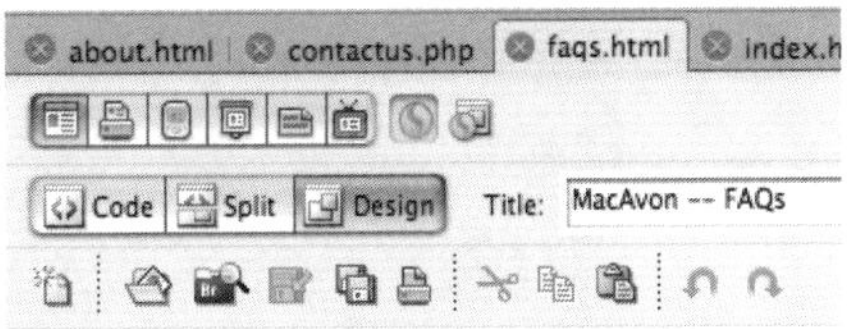

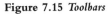

Figure 7.15 *Toolbars*

Bridge (described in Chapter 3) to browse for images and other media files. Finally, the Style Rendering toolbar appears at the top, above the Document toolbar; it is used to control how style sheet formatting is previewed in the document window. The default setting is usually correct.

Along the bottom of the document window, some information and additional controls are displayed, as shown in Figure 7.16. At the extreme left, the *tag structure* of the insertion point is displayed. We will explain how to use this to select precise elements shortly. Over on the extreme right, a box shows the document's size in bytes and an estimate of the time it will take to download. (The speed of the connection used for this estimate is set as a preference.) A pop-up menu immediately to the left of this information allows you to set the dimensions of the document window to one of several sizes commonly used by Web browsers on monitors with different resolutions. To the left of that is a pop-up menu that you can use to set the magnification of the window, to values from 6% (to get a view of a large page all at once) to 6400% (for precise positioning). Finally, there are Dreamweaver's only three tools: an arrow tool for making selections, a hand tool for dragging the document in the window, and a magnifier tool. Make sure that the arrow tool is selected here when you need to make selections. (Since the other tools are redundant, you can always keep the arrow selected.)

```
<body> <ul.qlist> <li> <a>                    ▶ ✋ ⊖  100%  ▼  791 x 504 ▼  58K / 14 sec
```

Figure 7.16 *The bottom of the document window*

┌─**TRY THIS**───┐

Open any HTML document using the File>Open... command. (If you do not have any HTML documents of your own, you can download some samples from www.digitalmediatools.org.) Place the cursor in different places and note the tag structure displayed.

Practice switching the document window between its different modes. Can you see any correspondence between the code and the way it is displayed in design mode?

Check the validity of the code in the HTML document you are displaying, check it for browser compatibility and preview it in any browsers you have installed on your computer.

└───┘

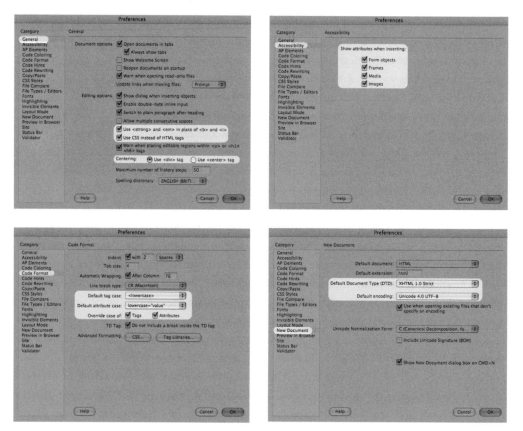

Figure 7.17 *Recommended preference settings*

Preferences

We don't usually tell you how to set a program's preferences, but as we explained earlier, Dreamweaver retains some old features that can interfere with its producing code that is accessible and complies with standards. By setting some preferences in the right way, you can help minimize the possibility of producing bad markup.

The relevant settings are in four different categories within the Preferences dialogue: General, Accessibility, Code Format and New Document. The specific settings you need are highlighted in Figure 7.17. The only one of these settings that may be controversial is the choice of Default Document Type (DTD) in the New Document category.

A DTD is a formal definition of the syntax of a markup language, such as XHMTL. When you specify a DTD in a document you are asserting that the document will conform to the rules of the language whose DTD you specify. So, by specifying the XHTML DTD, you are saying that the document should only contain valid XHTML. When you look at the settings for this preference, you will see that there are six possible DTDs, as well as **None**. (Never use **None**. If a DTD is not present, Internet Explorer 6 will go into "quirks mode", in which it emulates the bugs in earlier versions of Explorer when it displays your page. This is likely to result in an even worse mess than it would make otherwise.) As its name implies, **XHTML 1.0 Strict** is a DTD that imposes more rigorous restrictions than the alternative **XHTML 1.0 Transitional**. By using the strict DTD, which we recommend, you will be prevented from using features that may interfere with accessibility and do not conform to current thinking on the best way to mark up Web pages.

This leaves a possible choice between XHTML and HTML 4. Although there are those who disagree vociferously, we believe that it is better to use the forward-looking XHTML than the older HTML 4, which will one day become obsolete. (However, if you understand the statement that XHTML served with the MIME type **text/html** is parsed by browsers as malformed HTML 4, and think that it matters, you will probably want to use **HTML 4 Strict** as your DTD.) You may even like to use **XHTML 1.1**, but this can cause problems with some browsers. **XHTML Mobile** is only for Web pages intended specially for viewing on mobile devices. If you work mainly on such pages, then this would be an appropriate choice here.

The DTD that you specify in your preferences will normally be used whenever you create a new page, but you can choose a different one later if you have reason to.

DON'T FORGET

Dreamweaver is a tool for Web page design and Web site management.

Web pages are documents marked up using HTML and styled using CSS. They can incorporate scripts written in JavaScript.

Create sites with the Site>New Site... command, and set the location of the local site folder.

Web pages should be accessible.

Dreamweaver's panels are slightly different from those in other CS3 programs, but they can be grouped and docked in a similar way.

The Insert bar is used to add objects to a Web page.

The Properties panel is context-sensitive and lets you see and change properties of the currently selected element.

The document window can display a page in design, code or split view.

Toolbars provide quick access to useful operations.

Set up the preferences to help ensure that the code that Dreamweaver generates conforms to the latest standards and Web design best practice.

Formatting Web Pages

Dreamweaver is unnecessarily powerful for simply formatting text and images using HTML. Some word processors, including Microsoft Word and the Writer module of OpenOffice.org, can export documents as HTML, allowing you to format simple Web pages using their standard features. There is also a range of page construction programs and services (often offered over the Web) ranging from simple utilities that allow novices to build pages in ten minutes by filling in templates, to sophisticated text editors with HTML and CSS editing modes, such as TextMate, UltraEdit or emacs, and dedicated Web page editors, such as TopStyle and SEEdit, which provide experts with complete control over page markup. Any of these might be adequate if simple formatting is all you need to do. Nevertheless, Dreamweaver also performs these tasks well and it makes sense to use it to do so if they are being done as part of a larger site design project.

Structure and Appearance

Dreamweaver takes the established conventions of word processors as its starting point for text formatting. Text is entered by clicking at an appropriate place in the document to place the insertion point and then typing. Text is wrapped as it approaches the right-hand edge of the document window. A new paragraph is started by pressing [return/enter]. You can select text by dragging over it, or by using other mouse or keyboard operations that you will be familiar with, such as double-clicking to select a word, or using shift and the arrow keys to select characters adjacent to the cursor. Menu commands and the Properties panel can then be used to apply formatting to the selected text. You might think, therefore, that you are in the familiar world of WYSIWYG editing, and that what you see in the document window is what you will get when you look at the page in a Web browser. Things are not that simple, though.

The formatting of Web pages has two distinct aspects. First, there is the *structure* of the page, that is, how it is divided into paragraphs, headings, lists, emphasized words, and so on. Second, there is the *appearance* of those structural elements – for example, the fonts used for headings, the style of bullets used for points in a list, the margins applied to paragraphs, the position of blocks of text and images on the page, and so on. In modern Web design practice, structure and appearance are kept separate. HTML tags are used to mark up the structural elements, and CSS rules are used to define their appearance. (For a more detailed account of this distinction, and a thorough description of XHTML and CSS, see *Web Design: A Complete Introduction*.)

Dreamweaver blurs the distinction between structure and markup to some extent, owing to its origins in a time when they were less cleanly separated. Mostly, you apply tags, thereby defining structure, using the Properties panel, the Insert bar and some menu commands, and specify appearance by defining rules in the CSS Styles panel, although some simple CSS styling can be applied directly from the Properties panel. If you set up your preferences as we recommend, some menu commands which would otherwise be used for specifying appearance via markup will be disabled, but there are still some cases where inappropriate markup may be created. We will mention some of these as we go along, so that you can avoid them.

You can approach the formatting of a single page by entering the text, applying markup as you go, and then defining style sheet rules to give the page the appearance you desire. When you are constructing an entire site, though, you will generally want to apply consistent styling to all its pages. This can be done by using an external style sheet, which is kept in a separate file, and referred to from each page. Dreamweaver lets you choose whether style sheet rules should be used only in the current document, or kept in an external style sheet for use across a whole site. It also lets you attach an external style sheet to the current document, thereby importing all the styling you have defined in that style sheet.

Layout

In contemporary Web design, CSS is used to control the layout of Web pages. Many sites make use of layouts based on columns. For instance, a popular layout for blog pages uses three columns: a large central column for the text of the blog's entries, a left column for links to categories and monthly archives, and a right column for a search box, RSS feed link, contact details and other administrative links. Other popular layouts use just two columns, and both two- and three-column layouts may include a header region at the top and a footer at the bottom. Of course, there are many, many other options for laying out a Web page, and CSS provides complete control over the positioning of elements, but the popular columnar layouts are useful in many contexts, so Dreamweaver provides ready-made page skeletons and style sheets for several variations on the multi-column idea. When you use the File>New command to create a new document, the dialogue shown in Figure 7.18 opens. This allows you to choose one of Dreamweaver's standard layouts to serve as a starting point for your Web page.

The new file dialogue can do a lot more than this, because simple HTML files are not the only type of document that Dreamweaver can create. In the left-most column of the dialogue, you can choose between five general types of document. For now, we will only consider blank pages. When you choose this category, the next column shows you the different sorts of page that Dreamweaver distinguishes. Most of these are only of interest to Web developers who understand the server-side technologies used to create pages dynamically. In this book, we will not deal with these matters, so we are primarily concerned with creating HTML pages, which means selecting the first category in this column, as we have done in Figure 7.18.

The third column then gives you the list of available layouts. When you choose one of these, a diagram showing what the layout will look like appears at the right-hand side of the dialogue box, together with a summary of the layout's properties.

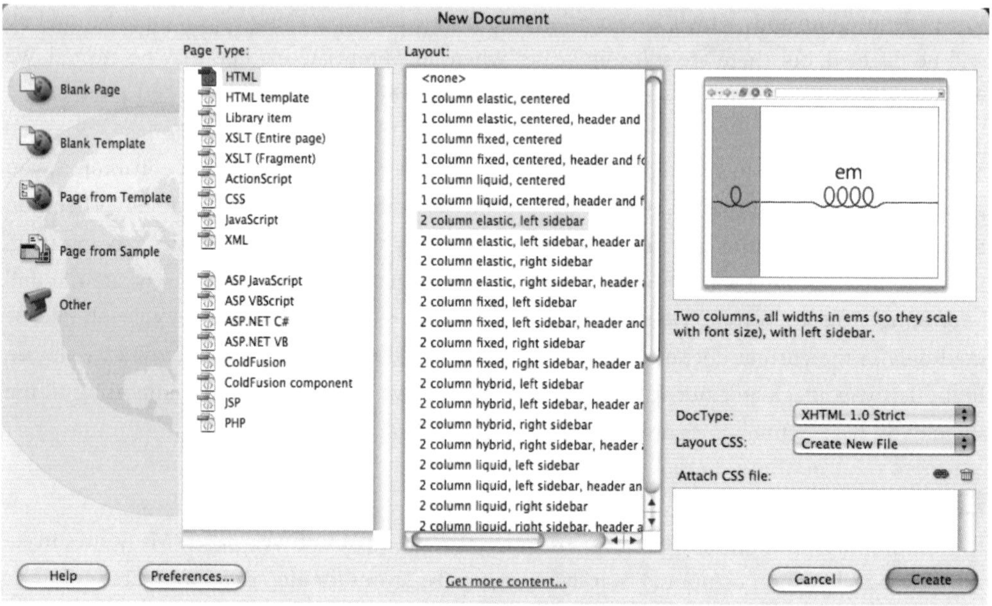

Figure 7.18 *Choosing a layout for a new document*

We don't have space in this book to go into the full details, but using CSS for layout leads to three kinds of column. **Fixed columns** are always the same width, no matter what the user does with their browser. **Elastic columns** scale with the font size in the browser. That is, if a user increases the font size, perhaps because they cannot read small print, elastic columns will get wider, so that the text will fit within the column in the same way. (With a fixed column, the text would have to reflow as the characters got bigger, in order to fit in the same width.) **Liquid columns** also change size, but in their case the change occurs when the browser window is resized. A liquid column's width is expressed as a percentage of the window's width, so if a user makes their browser window narrower, liquid columns will shrink, so that they still fill the same proportion of the window. (Again, there is much more on this subject in *Web Design: A Complete Introduction*.)

The full list of layouts offered in the new file dialogue includes one-, two- and three-column layouts based on fixed, elastic and liquid columns. Some use one type of column exclusively, while others, designated "hybrid" in the list, use a mixture. Where a layout's name refers to a "sidebar" it means that one of the columns is significantly narrower than the others. Some of the layouts also include header and footer regions.

The pop-up menu immediately below the layout's preview lets you choose the DTD for the document you are creating. The DTD you set as a preference will be used by default. You can also choose where Dreamweaver should put the CSS rules defining the layout. **Add to Head** will incorporate them in the new document; **Create New File** will put them in a separate, newly created, external style sheet; Link to Existing File allows you to reuse an existing external style sheet. If you do this, you must click the chain link above the text field labelled Attach CSS File, and browse for the style sheet. The rules in the style sheet will be used for the layout, but it is sensible to choose a layout that matches the style sheet, otherwise the dummy content that Dreamweaver puts in the newly-created file will not be formatted appropriately. You can also attach a style sheet that doesn't have rules that control layout in it, just typography and other aspects of appearance. This is done in the same way as attaching a layout style sheet, but you select one of the other options for the layout rules.

If you have chosen to create a new style sheet for the layout, you will be prompted for a location to save it. This should be within the folder you designated when you created the site. The new document itself is not automatically saved at this point. As with new documents in any other program, it appears in the document window, but you must explicitly use the File > Save As... command to save it to disk.

If you choose <none> for the layout, the document window shows a blank page. Some standardized pieces of HTML appear in the head of the document, but you don't normally see these in design view. Within the limits of CSS's layout capabilities, you can create whatever layout you desire on such a blank page. If you do choose one of the available layouts, some dummy content appears in the new file, which allows you to see where the different parts of the page are. Figure 7.19 shows an example. You will delete this content in order to add your own.

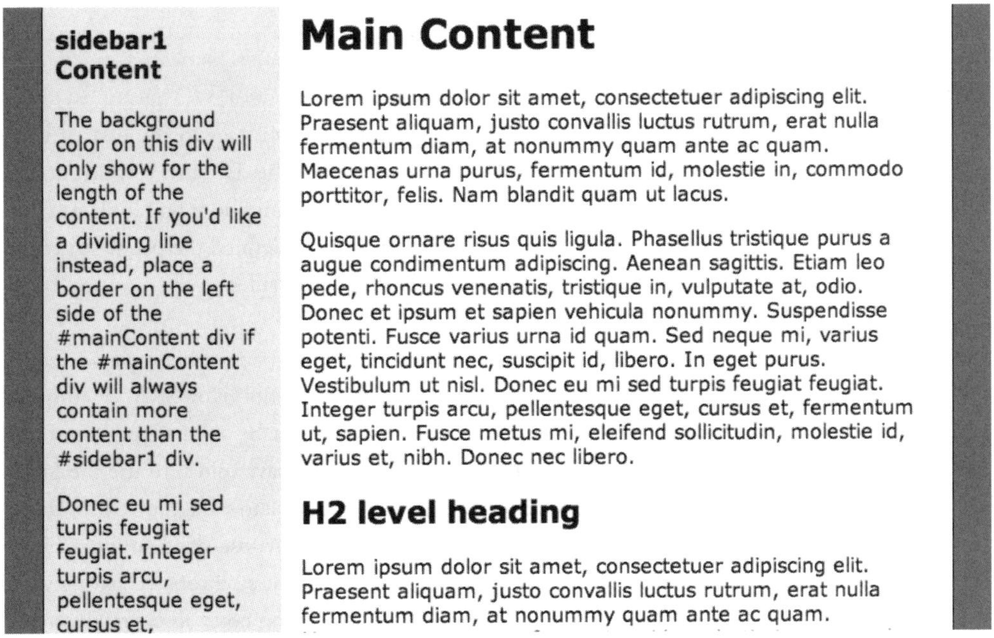

sidebar1 Content

The background color on this div will only show for the length of the content. If you'd like a dividing line instead, place a border on the left side of the #mainContent div if the #mainContent div will always contain more content than the #sidebar1 div.

Donec eu mi sed turpis feugiat feugiat. Integer turpis arcu, pellentesque eget, cursus et,

Main Content

Lorem ipsum dolor sit amet, consectetuer adipiscing elit. Praesent aliquam, justo convallis luctus rutrum, erat nulla fermentum diam, at nonummy quam ante ac quam. Maecenas urna purus, fermentum id, molestie in, commodo porttitor, felis. Nam blandit quam ut lacus.

Quisque ornare risus quis ligula. Phasellus tristique purus a augue condimentum adipiscing. Aenean sagittis. Etiam leo pede, rhoncus venenatis, tristique in, vulputate at, odio. Donec et ipsum et sapien vehicula nonummy. Suspendisse potenti. Fusce varius urna id quam. Sed neque mi, varius eget, tincidunt nec, suscipit id, libero. In eget purus. Vestibulum ut nisl. Donec eu mi sed turpis feugiat feugiat. Integer turpis arcu, pellentesque eget, cursus et, fermentum ut, sapien. Fusce metus mi, eleifend sollicitudin, molestie id, varius et, nibh. Donec nec libero.

H2 level heading

Lorem ipsum dolor sit amet, consectetuer adipiscing elit. Praesent aliquam, justo convallis luctus rutrum, erat nulla fermentum diam, at nonummy quam ante ac quam.

Figure 7.19 *Dummy content in a newly created page*

You could go further and base your page on one of the "professionally designed" samples provided with Dreamweaver. To do this you would select **Page from Sample** at the left of the new file dialogue, and then choose a category and a sample, as before. However, we do not recommend this route: most, if not all, of these samples appear to use table-based layouts, which, as we will explain later, are not considered good practice in modern Web design.

When you are more experienced at Web design and have learned about CSS, you may find it easiest to start a site by creating a site-wide style sheet that defines the different formatting rules that you want to use in all the pages. There are several sample style sheets that you can use as a starting point if you take this approach. Choosing **Page from Sample** at the left of the new file dialogue, and then selecting **CSS Style Sheet** in the next column, will allow you to browse the sample style sheets provided. If one of them seems to fit the job, you can select it in the right-hand column. CSS style sheets always open in code view, but you can edit them using the **CSS Styles** panel, in the way we will describe for editing the styles attached to an HTML page.

TRY THIS

Open the new file dialogue using File>New... and look at the previews for all the layouts provided. Create new documents based on several different layouts. If you have the time and patience, try them all, but otherwise make sure to include some with fixed, elastic and liquid columns, and some hybrid layouts. For each layout you try, preview the document in your default browser and observe what happens when you change the font size or make the browser window narrower or wider.

Simple Formatting

You can use the **Properties** panel and menu commands to add HTML tags to the text of your pages as you type, but in design view it will not be obvious that this is what you are doing. Dreamweaver will apply some default styling to elements such as headings, so it will look as if you are formatting them as you go along, but in fact you have only really defined the page's structure. However, you will be able to apply styling properly by defining CSS rules.

Having said that, there are some buttons that appear on the **Properties** panel while text is selected which set attributes that do control appearance. These attributes are not allowed in documents conforming to the **XHTML 1.0 Strict DTD**, so the documents will not be valid if you use them, but this does not stop Dreamweaver inserting them, even when you have told it to use the Strict DTD. Also, if you use the buttons that control indentation to indent plain paragraphs, they do so using tags which, while valid, are not being used for their correct purpose of identifying block quotations. This is another practice that should always be avoided. (These buttons do have a valid use in the context of lists, as we will describe shortly.) Other formatting controls correctly create a CSS rule for you, though. We will only consider these.

Figure 7.20 *Text properties*

Figure 7.20 shows the state of the Properties panel when some text has been selected in the document window. The controls that you should avoid using have been dimmed.

Paragraphs and Headings

There aren't very many structural elements in the text on Web pages, so the marking-up that can be done using the Properties panel (or the equivalent commands on the Text menu) is limited to a few types of paragraph.

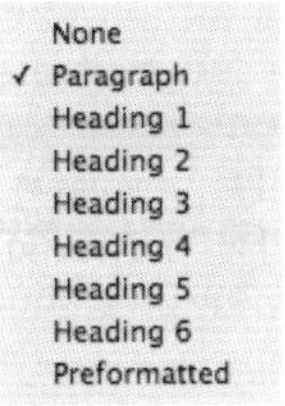

The Format pop-up menu at the left of the panel, shown in Figure 7.21, can be used to distinguish different types of paragraph. Most paragraphs are just HTML p elements, which can be obtained by selecting Paragraph from this menu. Although the format is set to None when you start a blank document, as soon as you press [return/enter], it changes to Paragraph, which is applied to the text you have just typed, so that this amounts to the default format, as you would probably expect. If you want a different type of paragraph, you can either change the format before you type it, or place the cursor in the paragraph and then select a different format. As you can see from Figure 7.21, most of the formats are headings. The exception is Preformatted, which means that spaces and line breaks will be retained when the page is displayed. This is intended for including code (such as program source code) in a page, which is a specialized requirement. Don't try to use preformatted blocks to lay out text using spaces. It won't work very well, if at all, and there are always better ways.

Figure 7.21
Block formats

HTML provides a generous allowance of six levels of heading. You should always use the different levels to express hierarchy in your page. That is, use Heading 1 as the top-level heading, usually describing the whole page, Heading 2 for sub-headings, and Heading 3 for sub-sub-headings within each sub-heading. Most people are unlikely to need further levels, but if you do, they are available. Do not choose the heading level on the basis of its default appearance. That is, don't use a level 3 heading at the top of a page, just because default level 1 headings are huge and ugly, and don't jump from level 1 to level 3 because you want a bigger difference in appearance than level 2 provides. You can always change the appearance of your headings using a style sheet. Remember that at the moment you are just marking up the structure of the page, as much for the benefit of programs such as screen readers or search engines as for browsers.

To make this description more concrete, consider the extremely simple Web page shown in Figure 7.22. This will evolve into the home page of a little example site: a small online gallery

Welcome

Welcome to my personal online gallery and shop, Alterations, where you can view and buy high quality reproductions of my art work. Our digital prints are made with archival quality materials under my personal supervision, and every effort is made to reproduce the striking colours and character of the originals.

I hope that these works may prove inspiring to you, my visitors. If I can feel that selling a single print has improved somebody's life, all my efforts will have been worthwhile.

Dereq Ffisq

Enter the gallery and shop.

Figure 7.22 *Paragraphs*

that sells "fine art" prints. (Neither the artwork nor the artist should be taken seriously; this is just an imaginary example.) The version shown in Figure 7.22 is what is obtained by simply typing the text into Dreamweaver. Each paragraph is styled identically, using the defaults in the browser that was used to display it. The paragraphs are HTML p elements. You can see this by placing the cursor in any paragraph. The tag structure display in the bottom left corner of the document window will show that the current element (the one containing the cursor) is a p within the

`<body> <p>` body element, which contains all the displayed content of the page.

Welcome

Welcome to my personal online gallery and quality reproductions of my art work. Our under my personal supervision, and every

Figure 7.23 *A level 1 heading*

There is no meaningful structure in this document, since all the paragraphs are marked up in the same way. Looking at it, though, you would probably think that the word Welcome at the top should be a heading. Because it's the topmost heading on the page, it must be a Heading 1, in terms of the options available on the Properties panel. If we place the cursor on that line, and select Heading 1 from the Format pop-up, the heading changes its appearance as shown in Figure 7.23. It looks awful, but we can change that later. More importantly, if you now place the cursor on this line, the tag

`<body> <h1>` structure display will show that you are in an h1 element. This means that any program, including a Web browser, that processes the page can recognize the heading, and that any formatting we subsequently define for level 1 headings will be applied to this one, as well as to any others on the page – or anywhere in the entire site if we use a single style sheet for all the pages in it.

Emphasis

There are two options for emphasizing words and phrases. The I and B buttons on the Properties panel appear to set selected text in italics and boldface, respectively, like the equivalent controls in a word processor do. However, if you set up the preferences as we recommend, they will actually mark up the selected text as being emphasized and strongly emphasized, respectively. The difference is subtle: italic and boldface are properties of the text's appearance; emphasis and strong emphasis are structural properties, which may be expressed in different ways – for example,

Welcome to my personal online gallery and shop, Alterations, where you can view and buy *high quality reproductions* of my art work. Our **digital prints** are made with *archival quality materials* under my personal supervision, and every effort is made to reproduce the *striking colours* and character of the originals.

Figure 7.24 *Emphasis*

by setting the type in different sizes. (In fact, you can define a style sheet rule to set text marked as italic in upright bold text, or whatever you like, but this is clearly perverse. Appearance is separate from structure, but it should not contradict it.)

It is widely believed that people looking at Web pages don't read every word, but skim the text looking for the important bits. To help them, we could add some emphasis to our welcome page. To do so, it is only necessary to select the text – by dragging over it, for example – and click the I or B button. Figure 7.24 shows the result, although we must again emphasize that all we have done is mark up some of the text as being emphasized: the appearance shown here is just the browser's default for such text, and we will change it later. Once again, placing the cursor in the text causes the tag structure display to reveal how it has been marked up: emphasized text becomes an em element, strongly emphasized text is a strong element.

`<body> <p> <em>`

┌─ TRY THIS ───┐

Start thinking about making a small Web site about somebody who is important to you. This could be a partner or family member, a film star, musician or sports personality, a pet, or even yourself.

Create a new blank HTML page, and write a few paragraphs introducing your subject, suitable for the home page of your site. Give the whole page a heading, and divide the text into short sections, each with its own sub-heading. Mark up the headings appropriately, and apply emphasis to bring out some key words and phrases. Remember that you will change the actual appearance later.

└──┘

Font Properties

The formatting we have described so far is all extremely limited, of course, compared to the sort of formatting you will be used to from word processing. You can do very much more with CSS, but even if you stick to the Properties panel you can change the font, size and colour of selected text. None of these work quite as you probably expect, though.

Font Size

Consider font size first. Figure 7.25 shows the relevant part of the Properties panel. To begin with, the field labelled Size will have the value None in it; using this setting means that the text will be set at the default size as determined by the user's browser preferences. Note that the default size for headings is usually

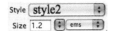

Figure 7.25 *Size controls*

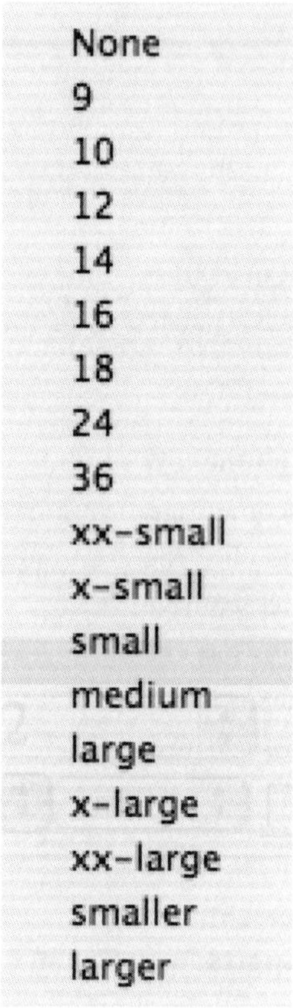

None
9
10
12
14
16
18
24
36
xx-small
x-small
small
medium
large
x-large
xx-large
smaller
larger

Figure 7.26 *Font sizes*

bigger than that for ordinary paragraphs, so the meaning of a value of None here depends on the element that contains the selection. There is much to be said for leaving the value alone so that users will see text at the size that suits them, but the ratios between the sizes of different headings are not well chosen, so for those at least you will probably want to set sizes explicitly. You may also want to use font size as a design feature.

The pop-up menu attached to the Size box provides some common values that you can use. These are shown in Figure 7.26. As well as common numerical values, there are some relative sizes at the bottom of the list. These are used to set the selected type's size relative to the browser default or the size of surrounding text. So, large is a bit bigger than the default, x-large is a bit bigger still, and so on. The values larger and smaller increase or decrease the size one step compared to the surrounding type's size, so, for example, if you had set some type to large, and then made a selection within it and selected larger, the result would be x-large. The ratio between these values is determined by the browser. Careful designers will prefer to set type sizes for themselves. To do this you can enter a number in the field. This activates the pop-up menu to its right, from which you can choose the units. Figure 7.27 shows the available choices. Most of these, such as in and cm, are not normally used for specifying font sizes, but CSS does permit it, so Dreamweaver provides them as options. Graphic designers will probably assume that pt (points) are the most suitable units for specifying type size, but in fact this is not usually the best option, as we explain below.

Specifications of font properties for a Web page can only be considered as suggestions, because the ultimate choice of what size type is used lies with the user and their browser. Most browsers allow the user to increase or decrease the size of type, no matter how the page's designer has specified it. (The exception is Internet Explorer, which does not allow the scaling of type speci-

pixels
points
in
cm
mm
picas
✓ ems
exs
%

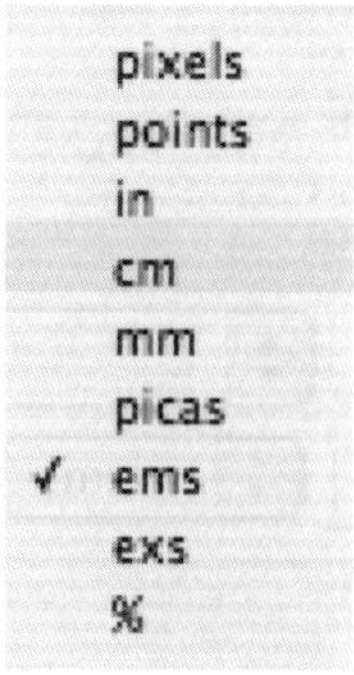

Figure 7.27 *Type size units*

fied in px units.) In other words, you cannot rely on the size that you specify actually being used, so you cannot base other page dimensions on it. It's far better to accept that the user is the one who should specify the size at which they want to read most type, and then specify special type treatments using multiples of that size. You can do this by specifying sizes in *em* units. One em is equal to the size of the font, so in a 16 pt font, 1 em equals 16 pt. When you specify the size in ems, the em is taken from the current font, so, for example, setting the size of selected text to 1.2 em will make it 20% bigger than any text that surrounds it. In the same way, you can, if you find it more natural, use % as the units. For example, setting the size of selected text to 120% has the same effect as setting it to 1.2 em.

If you must set font sizes using absolute units – in particular, points – remember that you are not designing for print. Sizes that are conventional in book design are much too small for easy reading on the Web. We would advise never using any size less than 14 pt, and then only if you have good reason not to rely on the browser's default.

Returning to the business of actually setting the size of some selected text, you will see several things happen when you do so. First, of course, the size of the selected text shown in design view will change as you specified. Second, a new value will appear in the field labelled **Style** on the **Properties** panel. For instance, in Figure 7.25, when we changed the size of some text to 1.2 em, the name style2 appeared here, replacing the **None** that was there before. Third, if you look at the tag structure display in the bottom left corner of the document window, you will see that, unless you had selected an entire paragraph, the selected text has been marked up as a **span** element. Fourth, the name of the selected element (span or paragraph of some sort) is shown in the tag structure display with a dot and the same name that appears in the **Style** field after its name. What's this about?

`<body> <p> <span.style2>`

When you set the font size, Dreamweaver does what it should: it defines a CSS rule and applies it to the selected text. In order to do this, that text must be marked up with some tag. The **span** element exists simply to delimit runs of characters so that you can apply styling to them. So Dreamweaver adds this element if you haven't selected a whole paragraph. (Again, we assume that you have set your preferences as we recommend. If the tag structure display shows a **font** element, go back and check that you have ticked **Use CSS instead of HTML tags** in the **General Preferences**.)

Dreamweaver adds a **class** attribute to the **span** so that the CSS rule that sets the font size can be applied to it. (We will explain a little more about this in the next section.) The value of the **class** attribute is, in our example, style2, which Dreamweaver also uses in the same way that word processors use style names, to identify the particular typographic properties that you have applied. (In general, you can apply a combination of properties, including the font and colour, as well as the size.) This means that if you want to set some other text in the same style, you can choose it from the **Style** pop-up menu in the **Properties** panel, instead of explicitly setting the values again. Near the bottom of this menu, you will find a command **Rename**.... This can be used to give a style a more meaningful name than the style1, style2, and so on, that Dreamweaver uses. Note that you are not allowed to include spaces in style names.

Colour

Changing the colour of selected text can be done in a similar way to changing its size. Figure 7.28 shows the text colour controls on the **Properties** panel, and illustrates what happens when you click on the colour swatch. You can select a colour from the palette that pops up,

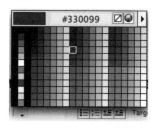

Figure 7.28 *Text colour controls*

or click on the colour picker button to select from the full range of available colours as described in Chapter 8. You can also enter a hexadecimal colour code – a standard way of writing down colour values for the Web – in the field provided, as shown at the top of Figure 7.28. (The code is made by concatenating the base-16 representations of each of the red, green and blue components, but you don't really need to understand how the hexadecimal values are constructed.) Whether you type it explicitly or select the colour some other way, the hexadecimal code is displayed in the panel, preceded by a # sign. If necessary, a span element will be inserted and a new style will be defined for the coloured text. (If you had already changed the size, however, no additional span will be inserted, and a new style will only be created if the existing one was applied elsewhere, otherwise the style will be modified.)

When using coloured text you should always ensure that there is good tonal contrast between the text and its background. Don't, for instance, use pale grey text on a white background. When you use coloured backgrounds (see below), remember that some people cannot tell certain colours apart, most commonly red and green. You should try to avoid potentially problematical combinations, but if you always use high tonal contrast any difficulties will be minimized.

TRY THIS

Set the top-level heading on the page you made in the previous exercise to a suitable size and colour. Try using different units for the size, and preview the effect in different browsers. See what happens if you use the browser's controls to change the font size, or set the default to different values.

Set a sub-heading to the same colour as the main heading, and to a size between that of the heading and the rest of the text. Change the name of the resulting style to sub-heading, and apply it to all the other sub-headings on the page.

Font Family

Based on your experience with word processors or the other programs described in this book, you might expect that the pop-up menu labelled Font on the Properties panel would feature a list of all the fonts installed on your computer, from which you could choose one in which to set the selected text. Instead, you will find something quite different there, as Figure 7.29 shows. The actual entries you will see may be different from the ones shown, but you will certainly see a menu containing lists of fonts. For the most part, the fonts on these lists are likely to come from a very limited set, including Arial, Helvetica, Times New Roman, Georgia and Verdana.

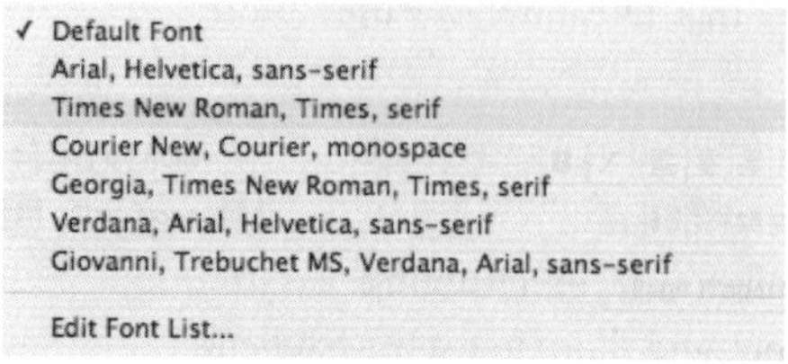

Figure 7.29 *Choosing fonts*

The sad truth is that you cannot specify fonts to be used on a Web page, simply because you have no way of knowing what fonts any user may have installed. Font data is not embedded in Web pages, and browsers do not download fonts; the text is displayed using fonts installed on the user's machine. Therefore, although you can specify the font you would prefer to be used, you have no guarantee that it actually will be. Hence, CSS allows you to specify a list of fonts, in decreasing order of preference. A browser will use the first font on the list which is available to it.

In case none of the named fonts that you specify is installed, you can use *generic fonts*. One of the names serif, sans-serif, cursive, fantasy and monospace is typically placed last in a font list. If none of the explicitly named fonts can be found, then the system font that falls into the category implied by the generic name is used. Even here, there is no guarantee about what will be displayed, because some browsers allow users to specify which fonts are used. It is quite possible that when you set the font to serif some people will see type in Verdana (a sans serif font).

Despite all this, it is worth putting the fonts you really want to use at the head of the font lists you specify. Although few ordinary computer users will have the sort of vast font library that graphic designers are used to having at their disposal, most people have more than the few fonts that come with their system. Office software and the programs described in this book bring a host of fonts with them, for example. Taking a more pessimistic view, some people will indeed only have the system fonts, and the intersection between the fonts on the major platforms consists of only a handful of fonts, essentially the ones that appear in the default font lists in Dreamweaver. When you want to specify fonts, we advise making up a font list with the font you really want to see at the beginning, no matter how esoteric it is, possibly followed by a similar but more common font, then one of the standard system fonts that is vaguely similar to what you want, and finally the appropriate generic font.

For instance, our imaginary artist seems to be the sort of person who would set his name in a fancy handwriting font. For this purpose, Bickham Script would be ideal, but it is not likely that many people will have it installed. Apple Chancery would be an acceptable substitute, and it is installed on all Macs; for Windows users, Zapf Chancery is similar and quite widely installed. In case none of these is available, the generic font cursive should ensure display using some hand-writing font in most cases.

Figure 7.30 shows the effect of using this font list to set the "signature" near the bottom of our page, and how the displayed text changes when fonts on the list are not available. Notice that the size changes as well as the appearance of the characters. If we had been setting a more extended piece of text, this could have made it reflow, so it is always worth bearing in mind that any layout you see on your machine may not match what some users see when they visit the completed page on the Web.

Dereq Ffisq

Dereq Ffisq

Dereq Ffisq

Figure 7.30
Substituting fonts

Figure 7.31 *Defining font lists*

To create the necessary new font list, the command Edit Font List... is selected from the bottom of the pop-up menu of font lists. The dialogue box shown in Figure 7.31 is then displayed and new lists can be constructed from the set of available fonts – either by selecting fonts from the list on the right or by typing their names into the box below it, and clicking the left-pointing arrows to move them to the list on the left. The interface provided for this purpose is poor, with the list of installed fonts occupying the small pane at the bottom right, which cannot be resized. The order in which the fonts are displayed does not make finding particular ones easy. (It's often faster to type the whole list into the text box yourself, separating the font names by commas.) If you have font management software installed, it may be worthwhile activating limited sets of fonts for each Dreamweaver project you work on, so that this interface becomes more manageable.

Once you have defined a list that includes the fonts you want to use, you apply it in the same way as you apply colour or size changes, by first selecting text and then choosing the list from the pop-up menu in the Properties panel. A span element is inserted if necessary, and a new style and associated CSS rule are created.

---TRY THIS---

Select some text on your Web page and apply one of Dreamweaver's font lists to it. Preview the page in different browsers.

Define a font list of your own, with the intention of setting your selected text in a special font that you like. Add suitable substitute fonts to the list in case your chosen font is not available. Apply this font list and preview the page. If you are able to do so on your computer, deactivate the fonts on the list, one by one, and preview the effect. (You may need to quit and restart your Web browser before you see the effects of deactivating fonts.)

Backgrounds

Web pages are not printed on paper, so there is no particular reason to use a white background unless you want to. In Dreamweaver, you can set a background colour for the current page using the Modify>Page Properties... command, or the Page Properties... button on the Properties panel. Either of these will cause the dialogue shown in Figure 7.32 to appear. Here you can set

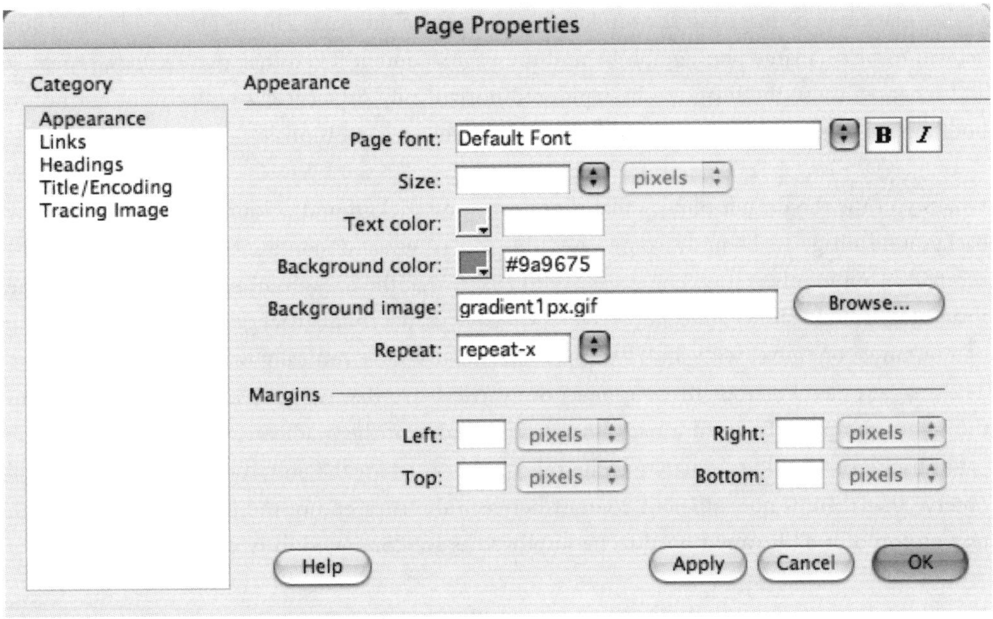

Figure 7.32 *Page background properties*

many properties that will apply to the entire page, but for now we will only be concerned with the Background color and Background image fields.

The Background color is set in the same way as the text colour we described earlier, using the pop-up swatch palette or colour picker, or by typing a hexadecimal colour value. The choice of an appropriate background colour will depend on the purpose and general appearance of the site, but you should always remember to provide sufficient tonal contrast between the background and any text or images that appear on top of it.

Using an image as background is a little more complicated. The problem is that an image has fixed dimensions, but a Web page can be any size, depending on how big the user makes their browser window. If the image is bigger than the page, it will simply be clipped, but what if it is smaller?

By default, the image will be *tiled* by the browser. This means that multiple copies of the image will be arranged across and down the page, like tiles on a bathroom wall, to fill the available space. For this to be successful, the image must be designed so that it makes an attractive pattern when arranged in this way. Textures that merge seamlessly at the edges of the tiles usually work best. You can create suitable images uses Photoshop's pattern maker, as we describe in Chapter 4.

You can modify the tiling behaviour using the Repeat setting in the Page Properties dialogue. If you set this to repeat, the background image will be tiled. If you set it to no-repeat, a single copy of the image will be placed in the top left-hand corner of the page. This might be suitable if you wanted to place a large photograph behind the page's content. The other two settings, repeat-x and repeat-y cause the image to be replicated horizontally or vertically, respectively, but not in both directions at once. This is only likely to be useful very occasionally.

Unless you use the default tiling – that is, repeat – the background colour may show where the background image is absent. In some cases, this sort of visual discontinuity at the edges may be acceptable, but in others it will be necessary to ensure that the background colour blends into the image. Figure 7.33 shows an example. Here, we have used a simple background image consisting of a rectangle one pixel wide and 200 pixels tall, filled with a vertically oriented linear gradient. The image is tiled horizontally (x-repeat) not vertically, so that we get a band of gradient across the top of the page. To avoid a hard line at the bottom of the gradient, we made sure that the page's background colour exactly matched the colour used for the end of the gradient. (You will observe that there is not sufficient contrast between the dark end of the gradient and the black text on top of it. This would need to be improved as we continued to work on this page.)

You must always remember that not everyone will see a background image. Some users disable the display of images in their browsers, and it is also possible that network problems will cause a page to load without its images, including its background image. It is therefore essential that you always specify a background colour yourself – even when using a background image – to ensure that your text colour will have sufficient contrast with its background in all cases. If you fail to do this, the text will be displayed on the browser's default background (usually white, but in some cases a colour determined by users' preferences), where it may be entirely illegible.

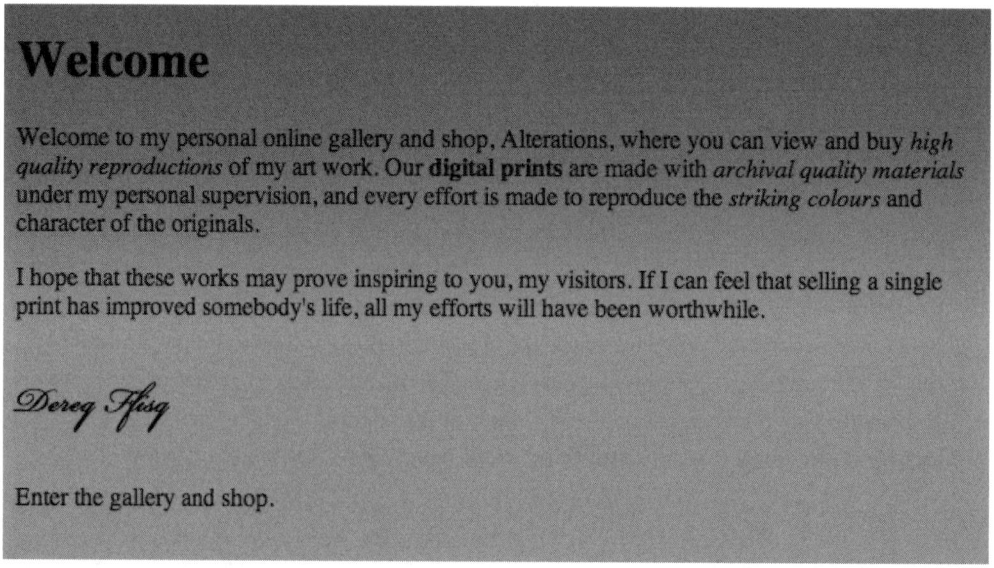

Figure 7.33 *Using a background image and colour*

┌─ TRY THIS ───

Use a fairly small image as a background for your Web page. Try each of the repeat settings, previewing in one or more browsers to see how they work.

Design background images suitable for each of the different repeat options and apply them to your page. In each case, set a suitable background colour.

If you work with Photoshop, design a pattern and use it as a tiled background.
└──

Links

Looking back to Figure 7.20, you will see that the Properties panel includes a field labelled Link. This is used to insert links into documents that refer to other pages in the site or elsewhere on the Web. It is a simple process. First, you must select in your document the text that you want people to be able to click on when the page is displayed in a browser. Links to files within the same site can then be added by clicking on the folder icon and navigating to the file. The file open dialogue that is displayed has an extra pop-up menu which allows you to choose between using a URL for the link which is relative to the document containing it or one that is relative to the root of the site. Usually it is safer and more convenient to use URLs relative to the document. When you have selected the file to link to, click the Choose button, and the file's relative URL will appear in the Link box.

If you browse to a file that is not within the local site (i.e. a file that is neither in the folder you specified when you created the site, nor in a sub-folder within it), you will be warned that the file may be inaccessible when the site is published, and Dreamweaver will offer to copy the file into the site folder for you. It will almost always be a mistake to add a relative link to a file outside the site folder, so you should copy any such files when you link to them.

For links to pages on other sites, an absolute URL, consisting of a domain name and path, can be entered by hand in the Link box. Be sure to include the http:// prefix. Although Web browsers nowadays allow you to omit this when you type a URL in their address field, it must be present when you include an absolute URL in a link inside a document. Don't use the field labelled Target to specify a frame or a new window for the link to open in. The target attribute which would be inserted if you do is not permitted in strict XHTML, and the practice of opening windows when links are clicked should be avoided on accessibility grounds (even though it is commonly done at present).

┌─ TRY THIS ───

Create some extra pages for your site – they can just be empty files at this stage. Add some links from the home page to these new pages, and some other links to pages on other sites. Preview the home page, and try following the links.
└──

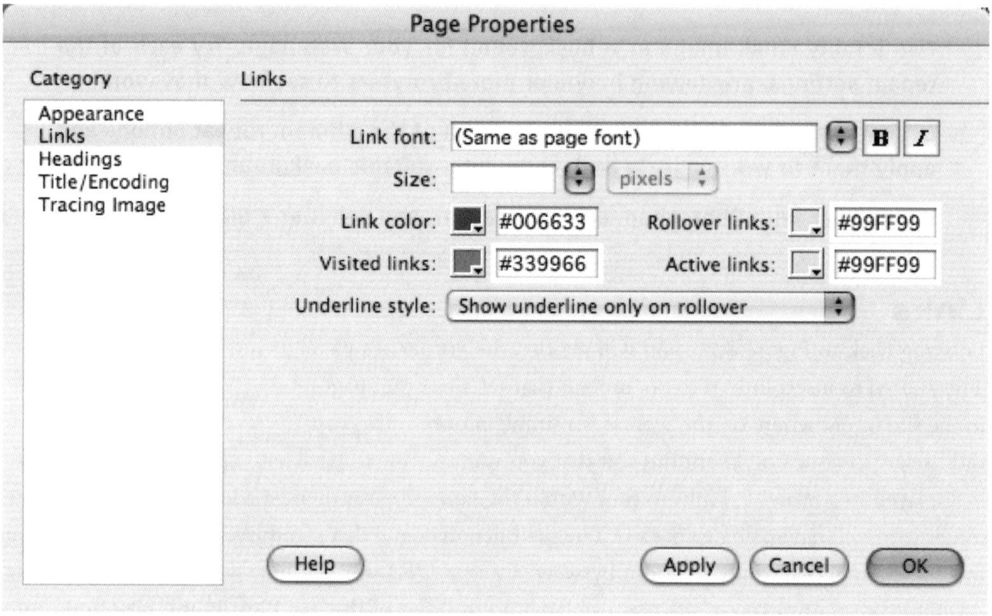

Figure 7.34 *Styling links*

Since the beginning of the World Wide Web, links have been displayed in blue underlined text by default, and this continues to be how they are shown unless you specify otherwise. You can write CSS rules to apply arbitrary styling to links in all their possible states, but most simple cases can be dealt with using the Links category in the Page Properties dialogue, shown in Figure 7.34.

To begin with, you can set the typographic properties of links: the font, size and any bold or italic styling. These settings will apply to all links, so make sure that the font and size will fit with the text surrounding them. (Or contrast with it if that's what you want to do, but this is harder to do well unless you have a lot of experience with typesetting.)

Unlike other elements, links have different states, and you can use different styling to distinguish between them. A link may have been visited recently, or the cursor may be over it, with or without the mouse button being depressed, or none of these may be the case. These states which a link may be in are referred to in CSS as visited, active, hover and link, respectively, although Dreamweaver uses the familiar term *rollover* for the hover state. In the Page Properties dialogue, you can set different colours for links in each of these states. You can also use the pop-up menu at the bottom of the dialogue box to specify how underlining should be used on links: always, never, only on rollover, or in any state except rollover. On accessibility grounds it is advisable always to use underlining to help identify links, if only on rollover, and you should always ensure that if you do use different colours for different states, your chosen colours have good tonal contrast with one another. (If you have difficulty assessing tonal contrast, put your screen into greyscale and look at the text without colour.) It is becoming customary to use a more subdued tint of the link colour for visited links, so that they are evidently both links, but the visited ones are less insistent. Since in most cases the active state does not last very long, it is not important to distinguish it.

To achieve more complex rollover effects, or to use different styling for links in different contexts, it is necessary to create CSS rules explicitly, as we will describe later.

TRY THIS

Define the styling of links for your page. Try different combinations of colours for the four link states, making sure the colours are tonally well distinguished from one another, and experiment with the different underlining options. When you preview each attempt, roll over and click on the links. (You may need to clear your browser's cache to make visited links revert to their normal state.)

Try setting links in a different font or size from the rest of the text on the page and assess the results.

Lists

HTML allows for three types of lists. The two most common and useful of these, *unordered* and *ordered* lists, can be marked up directly from the Properties panel. (The third type, *definition lists*, can be added from the Text>List sub-menu, but we will not describe them in detail.) The names "unordered" and "ordered" lists are possibly misleading, because all lists are ordered. The two types would be better called bullet lists and numbered lists. (Even then, the distinction is redundant because CSS can be used to generate either bullets or numbers for any type of list.) Lists of either of these two types are made up of *list items*.

You can either make a list as you insert text, or you can type some text and then turn it into a list. In the first case, click on the numbered list or unnumbered list button in the Properties panel and start typing the first item. Press [return/enter] at the end of the item, then type the second, and so on. When the list is complete, press [return/enter] twice. If you have already typed the text for the list items, just select it all and click the button for the type of list you want. Each paragraph you had typed will become a separate list item.

To make lists within lists you need to use the indent button. Previously, we told you not to use this for indenting paragraphs, but it functions differently when used for lists. Clicking this button when you start a new item causes that item to be indented an extra amount, and a new list is begun. You can change its type using one of the list buttons. Lists within lists use a different style of bullet or number from the enclosing list, by default. When you have finished the inner list, you can click the outdent button to go back to the outer list.

┌─ TRY THIS ───┐

Practise making lists of items. Try numbered and bullet lists. What happens if you select the items in a bullet list and click the numbered list button? What if you only select some of the items and then click the numbered list button?

Make some nested lists, with bullets within bullets, numbers within numbers and a mixture of nested bullets and numbered items.

└───┘

One use of lists that is becoming increasingly common is, at first sight, a little surprising. Most sites with more than a few pages have a ***navbar*** (short for "navigation bar") on every page. The navbar comprises links to the most important pages on the site, or to all the pages if it is a small site, allowing users to go directly to them from any other page. No current version of HTML has an element specifically for navbars, despite their ubiquity, but it is generally agreed that a navbar should be considered as a list of links, and marked up accordingly. As well as being logical, this markup is good for accessibility, because devices such as screen readers can treat lists in a special way. However, Dreamweaver also provides a method of creating navbars from images, which we will look at briefly later on.

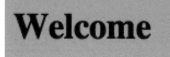

Figure 7.35 *A navbar*

To create a navbar, you can type the text of each link on a separate line, select each one in turn and use the Link field to add the actual link, in the way that we described earlier, and then select the whole lot and turn it into a bulleted list. When you preview the page in a browser, the navbar items will pick up whatever styling you have defined for links. Figure 7.35 shows a crude example. Notice that the entry for Home is not a link. This is because this is the home page, and it is neither necessary nor desirable to have a link to the page you are on – such a link could do nothing, but it might confuse some visitors to the site into thinking that clicking on it will take them somewhere else.

Looking at Figure 7.35, you will probably protest that you have never seen any navbar that looked like that, and if you had, you wouldn't be impressed. Quite right, but we will soon apply some CSS that will transform its appearance into something more familiar and attractive.

┌─ TRY THIS ───┐

Add a navbar to your Web page. You can simply link to the dummy pages you made earlier, but the exercise would be more useful and realistic if you thought about the site's structure. What pages will your site need and how will they be organized? Your navbar should reflect that organization.

└───┘

DON'T FORGET

Structure, expressed in markup, and appearance, defined by style sheets, are separate aspects of Web pages.

Create pages with one, two or three columns by choosing a standard layout for a blank HTML page in the New File dialogue.

Columns can be fixed, elastic or liquid.

Use the Properties panel to apply basic markup and formatting, including headings and emphasis.

Setting the font size (using absolute or relative units) or type colour creates a CSS style, which is applied to selected text.

You cannot know which fonts any visitor to a site will have available on their machine, so you must create font lists, which specify fonts to be used in displaying your text, in decreasing order of preference.

Use generic font names at the end of font lists, in case no font you have specified is available. Always provide alternatives for unusual fonts.

Set background colours and images in the Page Properties dialogue. Background images may be tiled. Always specify a suitable background colour, even if you are using a background image.

Create links by selecting the link text and using the Link field in the Properties panel. Set link styles for the whole page in the Page Properties dialogue.

Use the list buttons in the Properties panel to create bulleted and numbered lists. Use bulleted lists of links as navbars.

Using CSS

We have described how to create simple CSS rules implicitly, by applying formatting commands to selected text, but to use CSS systematically and to achieve a greater range of typographical effects, it is necessary to create style sheets explicitly. Before we look at how Dreamweaver handles CSS, we must review how style sheets are used to control the appearance of HTML documents.

A style sheet comprises a collection of *rules*, which specify the formatting to be applied to certain parts of the document. Many aspects of the document's appearance can be controlled, including fonts and type size, background and foreground colours, margins, alignment and positioning. A rule consists of a *selector*, which determines what the formatting defined in the rule will be applied to, and some *declarations*, which set the values of *properties*, such as font-size and color, which control the presentation of the selected elements.

CSS provides several different kinds of selector. The simplest consists of an element name, and is used to define the format of every element of that particular type, for example, every level 1 header (h1), list item (li) or piece of emphasized text (em). (Dreamweaver calls these "tags", though technically the tag is the actual characters used in the markup, such as <h1>.) Another kind of selector defines the layout for a particular *class* or subset of elements. (These select elements whose class attribute has a particular value.) For example, you might define a class of decorative headers, which you wanted to be set in a special way while still being marked up as level 1 headers. The rules created implicitly by applying formatting to selected text use selectors of this sort. The remaining sorts of selector let you specify formatting for an individual named document element (technically, one with an id attribute), or for elements that occur in a particular context, such as italicized text within a level 1 header. Rules with such *contextual selectors* are invaluable for avoiding superfluous markup, but Dreamweaver provides no assistance with formulating these selectors. You need to know how to write them by hand if you wish to take advantage of them.

As we mentioned previously, CSS rules can be included in the head of a document (an element containing information relating to the document that is not itself displayed), or they can be kept in a separate style sheet file, which can be referred to from different documents, to maintain consistent styling across a site. Dreamweaver can manage rules in both these types of location.

Displaying and Editing Rules

Dreamweaver has a CSS Styles panel, which is used to display and edit the declarations in CSS rules. (So it should be called the CSS Rules panel.) It uses a tabular format to show the property values, which may be easier to work with than the raw CSS syntax. (You can always edit the actual CSS in code view if you prefer.) Rules can get complicated, and some property values may be long, so you might find it worthwhile undocking the CSS Styles panel, or at least closing down any other panels it is docked with, and dragging it out wider than usual when you are working on CSS.

The CSS Styles panel can display a lot of information in a relatively small space, but this makes it more complicated than most panels. It has two distinct modes, All and Current; within each one there are different ways of displaying information about the rules and altering property values. To make it easier to see what is going on, we will begin by using the panel to look at some of the styling we applied earlier using the Properties panel.

You will recall that we applied a special font and size to the "signature" at the bottom of our page. Figure 7.36 shows what the CSS Styles panel would look like in Current mode if the text of the signature was selected. At the top is a summary of all the CSS properties that have been explicitly set by rules applied to this text. In this case, these are font-family and font-size, the CSS names for the font properties that we used for the signature. You can see that the font list, size and units match those we selected in the **Properties** panel earlier on.

If you select a property in this summary by clicking it, as we have done here with **font-size**, the middle pane of the panel tells you where that property was defined. This information is redun-

dant in the present case, but in complex style sheets it can be useful as it may not be immediately apparent which rules are being applied, and which file they are defined in.

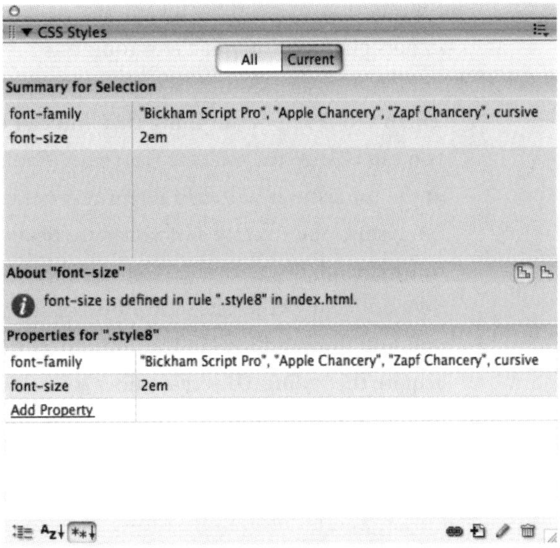

In this simple case, the properties of the selected text are simply repeated at the bottom of the panel. In more complicated cases, where more than one rule applies to the selection, the summary will show the values of all properties that have been set by some rule, whereas the bottom pane of the panel (the **Properties** pane) will only show the properties that have been set by the rule that provided the value for the property that you have selected in the summary.

If you want to concentrate on the style sheet, without being concerned with the document's contents, click on the button labelled **All** to change the **CSS Styles** panel's mode so that it displays all the rules. In this mode, the panel's arrangement is simpler. There are just two panes; the top one lists all the selectors of your rules, and the lower one shows you the properties set by whichever rule you have selected in the top pane, as Figure 7.37 illustrates. Note that the selectors for class styles, including those created implicitly by Dreamweaver, begin with a full stop (period).

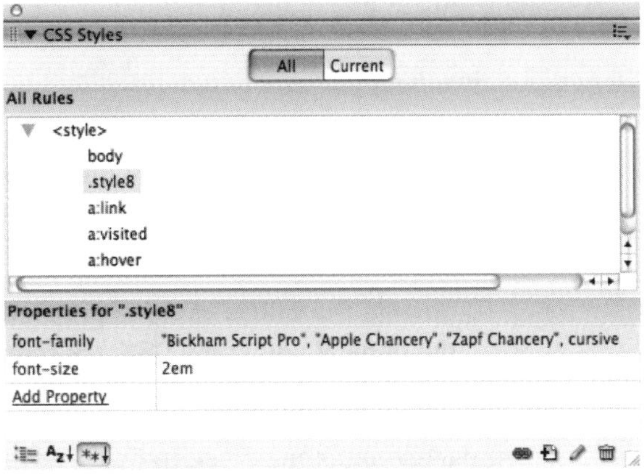

The **CSS Styles** panel isn't just there for displaying CSS rules, it allows you to change them, too. If you click on a property in the bottom pane, a suitable control will appear to allow you to change its value, as in our example in Figure 7.38.

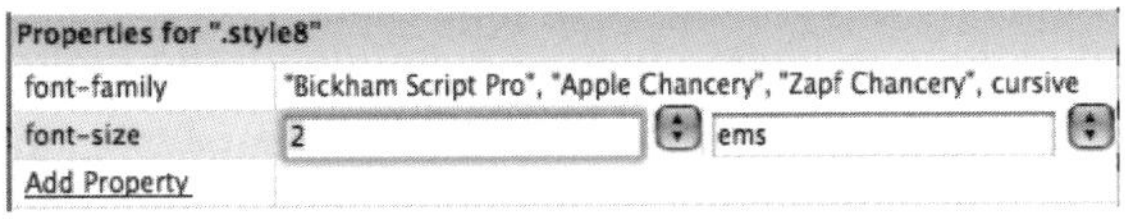

Figure 7.36 *The* CSS Styles *panel in* Current *mode*

Figure 7.37 *The* CSS Styles *panel in* All *mode*

Figure 7.38 *Changing a property's value*

Here, we clicked the font-size property, which produced controls allowing us to type a new font size, or select one of the values provided by the pop-up menu (these are the same values as the menu on the Properties panel provides), and change the units. The controls that appear when you edit a property depend on the type of value. For instance, if you click a colour, the palette of colour swatches pops up; if you click a font list, the menu of font lists that are currently defined appears, and so on. This means that it is easy to set a value of the right type, and difficult or impossible to set one of the wrong type.

There is one important thing that you can do in All mode which you can't do in Current mode; you can change the selector for a rule. If you select a rule, and then click its selector a second time in the top pane, it will turn into a text field, into which you can type a new selector. (That is, you can change the selector as if you were renaming a file on the desktop or in Bridge.) But you need to be careful. If you change the name of a class selector (one that begins with a .) Dreamweaver does not change the class attributes of any elements to which the rule applied, so those elements will lose their styling. If there are other elements whose class matches the new name, they will acquire the styling. (But remember to include the . at the beginning of the selector.) This may be exactly what you want to do, but it may come as a surprise if you thought you could just change the name of the rule to something more memorable. If that is what you want to do, you should use the Rename… command on the Style pop-up menu in the Properties panel.

It could be argued that the CSS Styles panel provides too many ways of doing things. We have not described everything about it, but you should be able to use it for finding out what styling is being applied to your page, and for making changes to it.

┌─TRY THIS──┐
Familiarize yourself with the CSS Styles panel by selecting text in different parts of the Web page you have been building and looking at the values displayed in the panel. Include some links, styled text and unstyled text in your experiments. What happens if you select a mixture of styled and unstyled text?

Change the values of some properties and see how it affects the appearance of the page. If you know CSS, try changing a selector.
└───┘

At the bottom of the Properties pane of the CSS Styles panel, in the column used for property names, the words Add Property appear, as you can see in Figures 7.36 to 7.38. As you might guess, this is used to extend a rule, by providing values for additional properties. By doing so, you are specifying extra formatting to be applied to any elements that the rule matches. If you click on Add Property, as if you were editing a property, the words are replaced by a text field, with a pop-up menu attached to it, as shown in Figure 7.39. If you know what all the CSS properties are, you can type a property name in the text box; if you are not sure, you can select one from the pop-up menu. The full menu is extremely long and unwieldy, but despite this it does not actually include all of the properties defined in the CSS 2.1 standard. (Note that if you type a name that is not available in this menu — even if you enter a legitimate property name — Dreamweaver will ignore it.) Once you have selected or entered a property, an appropriate control appears for you to set its value. In some cases, this will just be a text field; in others, a pop-up menu or other helpful control is available.

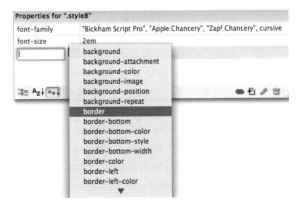

Figure 7.39 *Adding a property*

To show how the **CSS Styles** panel can be used for changing the formatting of parts of a document, let us suppose that we have decided that the signature at the bottom of our page should appear over on the right, as shown in Figure 7.40. (Compare this version with Figure 7.33.) It seems sensible to begin by replacing the meaningless class name that Dreamweaver generated with something more appropriate and memorable. Since we want to go on applying the font characteristics we have defined to the same text, we use the **Rename...** command on the **Style** pop-up menu to change the style name to **signature**, as we explained previously. In the **CSS Styles** panel, the corresponding selector shows up as .**signature**.

We could add the necessary properties in either mode of the **CSS Styles** panel. If it was only displaying CSS for the current selection, we would have to select the text of the signature before proceeding; if it was displaying all the rules in the document, we would select the .**signature** selector in the top pane. In either case, the properties for the rule would appear at the bottom of the panel.

Teaching you CSS is beyond the scope of this chapter. There are many books on the subject that you can read, and we will have to assume that you have done so. If you are unsure about the effect of any property you can select **O'Reilly CSS Reference** as the **Book** in the **Reference** panel, and look up the property's details by selecting it from the (long) **Style** pop-up menu that appears.

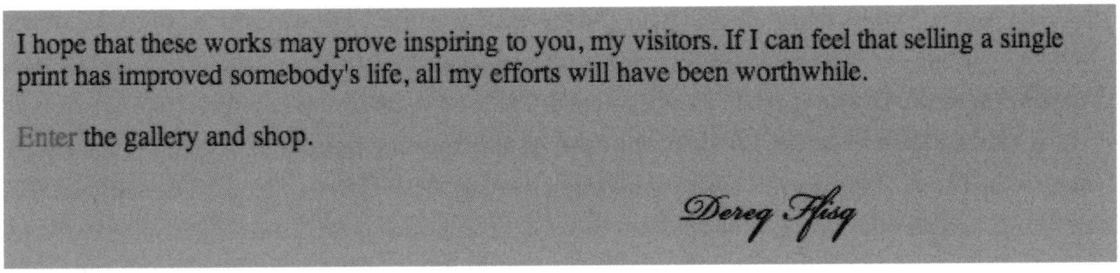

> I hope that these works may prove inspiring to you, my visitors. If I can feel that selling a single print has improved somebody's life, all my efforts will have been worthwhile.
>
> Enter the gallery and shop.
>
> *Dereq Ffisq*

Figure 7.40 *Floating the signature*

You will discover that, to achieve the effect we want, the float property should be set to right. This will move the signature (or anything with the signature style applied to it) to the right margin. At present, the rule makes no mention of this property, so we use Add Property, as just described, to add it to the rule. Because float is permitted only a few values, a pop-up menu appears when we add the property, and right can be selected from it. The signature will then move flush to the right edge of the page, but it would look more as if someone had signed the text above if we pull it back a little way, as it is in Figure 7.40. This was done by adding the margin-right property and setting it to a suitable value. The positioning of the element is best judged by eye, so setting the right margin in the CSS Styles panel can be done with the document window in design view. The value can be changed, as we described earlier, by clicking it and entering a different number; the design view will be updated to reflect the change straight away.

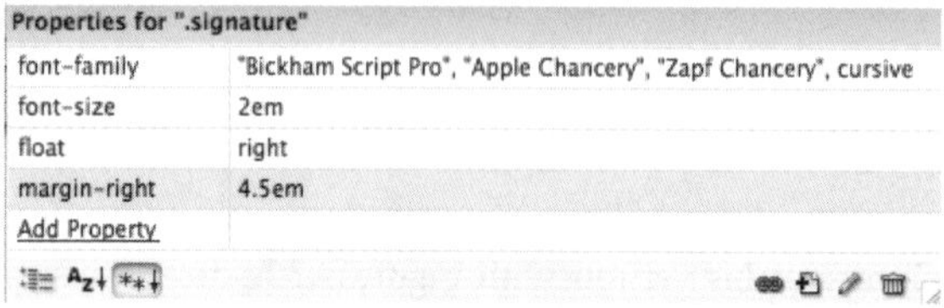

Properties for ".signature"	
font-family	"Bickham Script Pro", "Apple Chancery", "Zapf Chancery", cursive
font-size	2em
float	right
margin-right	4.5em
Add Property	

Figure 7.41 *CSS properties to float the signature*

Figure 7.41 shows the CSS Styles panel after the new properties have been added and their values set to produce the result in Figure 7.40.

─TRY THIS────────────────────────────

Place a short line of text near the right edge of your page. Try changing the distance between the text and the edge until you find a pleasing arrangement.

Look up the border and padding properties in the Reference panel; add a narrow frame around your floated text, with a small space separating it from the text on all sides.

Creating CSS Rules

So far, we have created rules implicitly by applying styling with the Properties panel and then extending or changing them in the CSS Styles panel. When you become confident about using rules to apply formatting, you will find it quicker to create rules from scratch. Doing this also makes it easier to work systematically, and create a collection of rules that define the styling of a whole page or an entire site.

You can create a new rule by clicking on the New icon at the bottom right of the CSS Styles panel, or by using the Text>CSS Styles>New... menu command. In either case the dialogue box shown in Figure 7.42 will open. The radio buttons are used to choose which type of selector will be used in the rule you create. The first option, Class, creates the same sort of rule we have seen being created implicitly when formatting is applied using the Properties panel. The selector will be a class name, and the rule will be applied to any elements whose class attribute's value matches the name. (In the raw CSS created for the rule, the selector will have a . at the beginning, but you can leave it out here.)

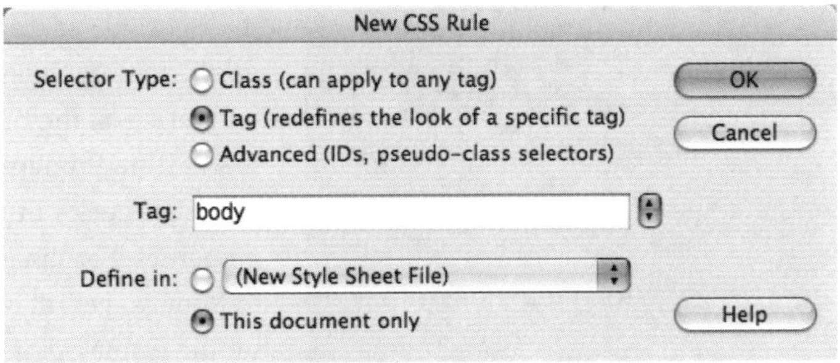

Dreamweaver treats rules of this type as *styles* – named collections of formatting properties, resembling the styles that you use in page layout programs or word processors. This type of rule fits in most readily with the pseudo-WYSIWYG editing style that is encouraged by Dreamweaver's design view. You can apply a style by selecting some text (or some other

Figure 7.42 *Creating a new rule*

type of object) and choosing the style's name from the pop-up menu in the **Properties** panel. This will actually add the appropriate class attribute to the selected element, but it will look as if you had applied the style to the selection. For example, we need to apply special styling to our navbar, to stop it looking like a bullet list. We could begin by making a new CSS rule, choosing **Class** as the type, and giving it a suitable name – navbar, for instance. After clicking **OK** in the **New CSS Rule** dialogue, a new elaborate dialogue opens, in which we can define all the properties we want declared in our new rule.

The list on the left of the dialogue is used to select subsets of the available CSS properties. (Figure 7.43 shows the subset related to typography.) Choosing an element from the list causes

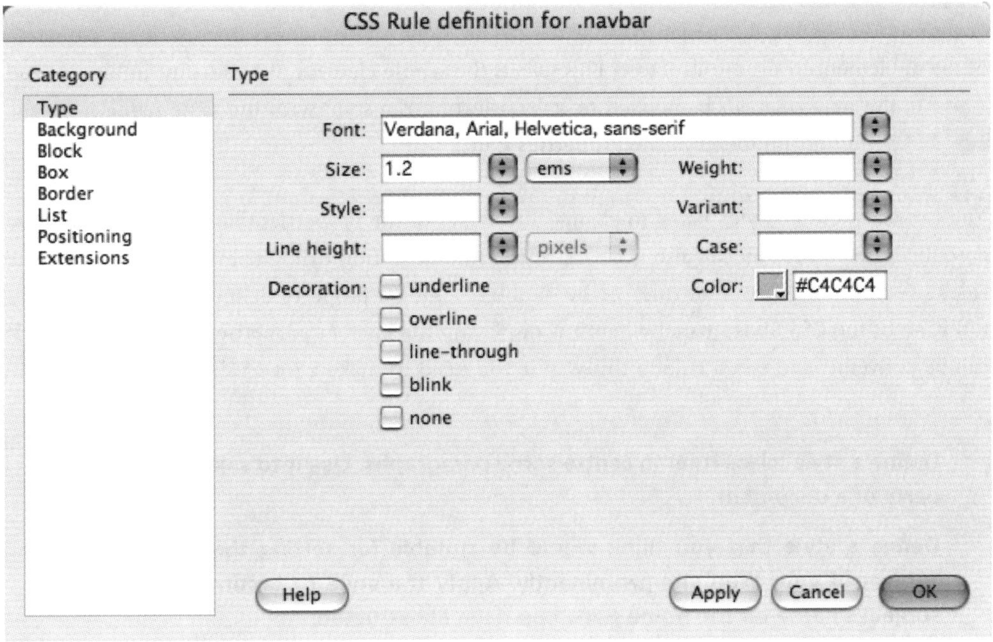

Figure 7.43 *Defining properties in a rule*

Figure 7.44 *Navbar with a rule applied to it*

the right side of the box to display input elements for setting up the corresponding style parameters. We can choose a font list and set all the other type properties that you have already seen in the Properties panel and the CSS Styles panel. The other categories in this dialogue allow you to set most CSS properties. For instance, in the List category, we set the Type to None, to get rid of the bullets, and in the Block category, we set the display property to block, because we don't want the navbar to look like a list, and also set the whitespace property to nowrap, to prevent items being split across lines. As before, we will not attempt to describe the effect of any properties, which you can find described in the Reference panel or in any good book on CSS. Figure 7.44 shows the effect of these settings, and those shown in Figure 7.43 on our navbar. As you can see, we have made some improvement to its appearance, but we still have a long way to go before it is acceptable.

Once you have set all the properties you need and dismissed the dialogue, you will see your new rule in the CSS Styles panel, but it will not yet have been applied to anything in the document. You need to select an element to apply the rule to. This is often most easily done using the tag structure display in the bottom left corner of the document window. For instance, we would want to apply our navbar style to the list of links that we have used for the navbar itself. Instead of dragging over the list, it is easier to place the cursor anywhere in it, and then click on the name of the ul element in the tag structure. This selects the whole element, without any ambiguity, and the new rule can be applied to it by selecting the style with the same name from the Style pop-up menu in the Properties panel.

`<body> <ul> <li> <a>`

`<body> <ul.navbar>`

You can use the CSS Styles panel to change any values of the properties that a rule defines, as we described previously. You can also get back to the rule definition dialogue by double-clicking the rule's selector in the list of all rules, or by double-clicking a property defined by the rule in the top pane of the CSS Styles panel when it is displaying the current properties for the selection. It can be convenient to edit a rule in this way, if you need to make a lot of changes at once.

┌─ TRY THIS ───

Define a style (class rule) to centre some paragraphs. Use it to selectively centre parts of a document.

Define a style that you think would be suitable for setting the name of the subject of your Web site prominently. Apply the style to occurrences of your subject's name on the home page you have constructed.

The second option for creating a new rule shown in Figure 7.42 is Tag. This is the choice to use for a style that defines the layout of some document element wherever it appears, unless a specific style has been applied to it. You should use tag selectors to redefine the appearance of headings, emphasized text, and other elements that ought to have a consistent appearance throughout a page or site. The text field at the bottom of the box is used to enter the name of the element, or you can choose an element name from the pop-up menu to the right of the text field. Once you have selected an element and clicked OK, the dialogue box from Figure 7.43 appears for you to set the properties in the same way as you would for a rule with a class selector.

Properties that you wish to apply to everything – for example, a page-wide font – can be set in a rule for the body element. Such a rule can be defined like any other rule with a tag selector, but one is also created when you set the page properties in the Page Properties dialogue. Having two ways of setting these properties is confusing. We recommend that you use one method consistently, and don't set up the page in the Page Properties dialogue and then edit the resulting rule in the CSS Styles panel, or vice versa.

┌─TRY THIS──
│ **Use any CSS properties you think appropriate to define rules to set em and**
│ **strong elements in distinctive ways that communicate emphasis.**
│
│ **Improve your level 1 and 2 headers by redefining their appearance.**
└──

The final type of selector that is available when you define rules, Advanced, will be of most interest to anyone who understands CSS already. Although the dialogue only mentions IDs and pseudo-classes; the Advanced option can also be used for contextual selectors, which help avoid unnecessary markup and the excessive proliferation of classes. For instance, although we previously defined a rule that set the colour of the navbar (or rather of everything belonging to the class navbar), in Figure 7.44 the links are the same colour as ordinary links, because the rule for link colours, being more specific, overrides the rule for the navbar and its contents. We could define a new class and assign all the links within the navbar to it, but CSS already allows us to use a selector for links within the navbar: .navbar a:link. So, by choosing the selector type Advanced, and entering .navbar a:link, we can define the appearance of navbar links without the need for an extra class, and hence without bloating the markup with extra class attributes.

In a similar way, we can also define a new rule for rollover in the navbar, as Figure 7.45 illustrates. When you click on the Advanced button, the Selector field is automatically filled in with a selector that would match whatever is

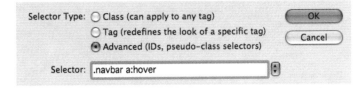

Figure 7.45 *Using a contextual selector*

Figure 7.46 *The styled navbar*

selected in the document window. Usually this will be a good starting point, but you may have to alter it slightly. In our example we had to add the :hover part of the selector by hand.

To complete the redefinition of the styling of the navbar links, we also need to define a rule for visited links within the navbar. Finally, we also need a rule for the list items themselves, which changes their display property to inline. To get a bit of space between the navbar links, we also added a right margin to these elements. The result of these new rules is shown in Figure 7.46.

---TRY THIS---

Use the method outlined above to lay out the navbar which you created earlier horizontally, in a suitable font. Without changing the markup at all, edit the CSS rules you just used, so that the navbar is displayed at the left of the page, with the links above each other. If you are not sure which properties to use to achieve the desired results, consult a book on CSS before you start.

When you create a rule, you can choose whether to add the definition to a style sheet file which you will then be able to use in other documents, or just define it in the current document. If you select the Define in: radio button and leave the pop-up menu set as it is in Figure 7.42, you will be prompted to save the style sheet file. If there are already some style sheet files in your site, you can choose one of them from the menu and add your new style to it. Otherwise, select the button labelled This document only, and the rule will be added to a style element in the current document's head. It will then not be able to affect the appearance of any other document in the site.

Using external style sheet files is strongly recommended, because it makes it easy to impose a consistent style on an entire Web site. You can add rules to a site-wide style sheet as you create them. When you add new pages to a site, you will want to incorporate any rules that you have already defined. This means that you must attach the style sheet or style sheets in which they have been saved. You can do this is by clicking the link button at the bottom of the CSS Styles panel. The dialogue shown in Figure 7.47 will open.

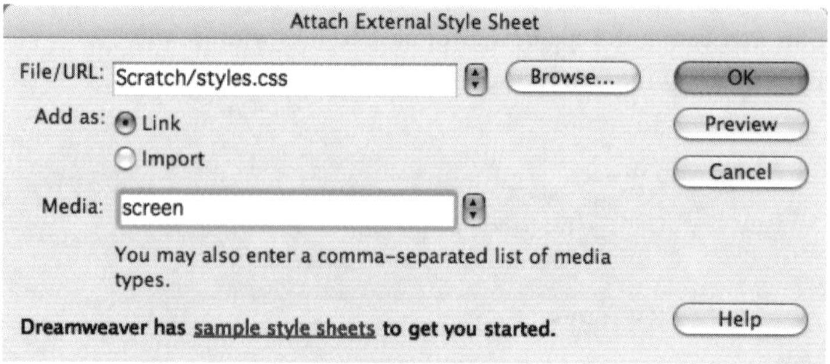

Figure 7.47 *Attaching an external style sheet*

You can use the **Browse...** button to navigate to the style sheet you are attaching, if it does not appear in the pop-up menu of recently used style sheets.

Dreamweaver provides some sample style sheets to get you started. If you click on the underlined message at the bottom of the dialogue shown in Figure 7.47, which reminds you about the sample style sheets, you will see the dialogue shown in Figure 7.48, where you can browse these samples. If one of them seems suit-

Figure 7.48 *Browsing the sample style sheets*

able, you can check how your document would look if you attached it, by clicking the **Preview** button; if you like the result, you can click **OK** to go ahead. If you are uncertain about things like colour schemes, or how to use CSS, it can be a good idea to start with one of these style sheets and tweak it by editing rules in the **CSS Styles** panel to get a unique style sheet of your own.

Returning to the dialogue shown in Figure 7.47, the pair of radio buttons labelled **Add as**: lets you choose the form of HTML markup that is used to refer to the style sheet from the document. **Link** is the simpler method. (It creates a **link** element, which is how the HTML standards recommend that external style sheets should be referenced.) **Import** produces messier code (a CSS @import directive is included in a **style** element within the document). Some Web designers prefer it, on the grounds that certain old browsers which claim to support CSS, but actually do so very badly, will ignore it and not attempt to interpret the style sheet. However, this is an increasingly irrelevant consideration these days, and the **Import** option should usually be reserved for its intended use of including one style sheet within another.

The field labelled **Media** is intended to let you specify which media (screen, print, aural, etc.) your style sheet should be used for. In principle, for example, an aural style sheet can be used to specify how a screenreader should read the document – where it should pause, or use emphasis, and so on. In practice, this facility is not widely implemented. Most designers only create the style sheets needed to display their pages in conventional graphical Web browsers. For these, **screen** is the appropriate value to choose. If you choose one of the other values, you can use the **View>Style Rendering** sub-menu, or the buttons on the **Style Rendering** toolbar, to select which media should be simulated in the document window preview.

If you click the Preview button before dismissing the Attach External Style Sheet dialogue, Dreamweaver will show you what the page in the document window will look like when the rules in the style sheet file you have attached are applied to it. This gives you a chance to cancel if there is a problem.

If you have created some rules in a document and you decide you should move them out into an external style sheet, you can do so by selecting the rules in the CSS Styles panel (shift-click or [cmd/ctl]-click to select several, in the usual way) and choosing the Move CSS Rules… command from the panel menu. A dialogue is displayed, allowing you to select an existing style sheet file, or create a new one. The same method can be used to move rules from one style sheet file to another.

---TRY THIS---

Move all the CSS rules you have created so far into an external style sheet file.

Add some marked-up content, including an appropriately modified copy of the navbar, to one or more of the dummy pages you created earlier. Attach the style sheet to the pages. Is the formatting consistent with the home page?

CSS and Layout

CSS can be used to control the position of elements on the page, as well as their appearance. The standard layouts that we mentioned when we described how to create new HTML documents use CSS to arrange columns, headers and footers. These layouts serve well for many Web sites, and newcomers to Web design would be well advised to use them wherever possible. Sometimes, though, it may be necessary to lay out elements in arrangements that don't fit the formula of three or fewer columns, possibly with a header and footer.

As long as you use fixed layouts, where all the dimensions are specified in absolute units, such as pixels, it is very easy to create arbitrary layouts. The trouble is that layouts made from fixed-width elements do not usually behave very gracefully when the text or window is resized. Liquid and elastic layouts are to be preferred, but getting them right is more difficult.

Absolutely Positioned Elements

If you are used to page layout software, such as InDesign, or even if you have just used text blocks in Photoshop or Illustrator, you may well feel that the natural way to lay out pages is by drawing frames where you want them, and then adding content to them. So, for instance, if you wanted to place a sidebar down the right side of a page, you would expect to be able to draw out a rectangle in the desired position and then add the sidebar's contents to it. You can indeed do this in Dreamweaver, but because the Web is very different from print media, there are other ways of achieving the same result that may be more effective.

Although Dreamweaver does not have a **Tools** panel, there is an item in the **Layout** category of the **Insert** bar which behaves like a tool; you click to select it and then drag it in the document window. This "tool" is referred to by the inelegant name of the **Draw AP Div** button, because what it creates in the document is a div element that is *absolutely positioned (AP)*. A div element is a container for other elements, most often used to group together parts of a page, such as a sidebar or footer. Hence, AP div elements appear to be a natural way of implementing layouts.

Figure 7.49 shows an AP div as it appears when you have just dragged it out or selected it in the document window in design view. The little square *selection handle* attached to the top left corner appears when you click anywhere within the boundary of the element. You can click this handle to select the element itself. When you do so, the resizing handles appear at the corners and in the middle of each side. You can drag these handles to change the size of the element, or drag the square selection handle to move it to a different position. When an AP div is not selected, you will just see a thin black outline around it, instead of the thick blue outline with handles shown here.

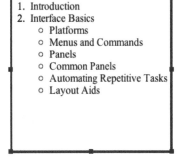

Figure 7.49 *An AP* div *element*

You can add content to an AP div either by clicking within its boundaries and then typing, or by adding embedded objects, in the way we will describe in the next section. Indeed, there is little point in creating the AP div element unless you do so – in themselves, AP div elements are invisible, and serve only as containers for other things. You can apply markup and formatting within the element in exactly the same way as you do in the main document. Here, for example, we have made a nested list. We could now put this list anywhere we wanted on the page simply by dragging the AP div that contains it.

It is possible to nest AP div elements within other AP div elements, which provides one way of creating elaborate layouts. It is also possible to stack AP div elements on top of each other, somewhat in the manner of layers, which provides another. Because both of these possibilities exist, it is not clear what should happen if you draw out a new AP div inside another. Should it be nested inside it, or stacked on top of it? In other words, should it push aside anything already inside the existing div, or overlay it? The answer will depend on whether you have ticked the checkbox labelled **Nesting** in the **AP Elements** category of 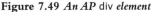 Dreamweaver's **Preferences**. If you do, the new element will be placed inside the old; if not, it will be stacked on top of it, unless you hold down [opt/alt] while you drag it out.

The **AP Elements** panel provides a few facilities for managing AP elements. It vaguely resembles a **Layers** panel in other programs, allowing you to show and hide AP elements, and rearrange their stacking order. Where you have nested elements, the nesting hierarchy is shown in the panel.

Since AP elements are not layers, these facilities are not very useful. It can sometimes be helpful to be able to click an element's name in the panel to select it – for example, if it is hard to get at in the document window. At the top of the panel is a checkbox labelled **Prevent overlaps**. If this is ticked, you will not be able to create AP div elements that overlap each other. This may be a useful constraint for some designs, but there is no technical problem with overlapping elements: if you want to use them, clear this checkbox.

┌─ **TRY THIS** ──
│
│ **Create a new blank HTML document and drag out an AP div element. Add some text to the element. Practise selecting, moving and resizing it.**
│
│ **Place the cursor outside the AP div, and add some text to the document. See how it interacts with the AP div.**
│
│ **Draw some more AP divs, including overlapping and nested ones. In each case, see how they interact with the contents of the others. Use the AP Elements panel to select each one, and to change the stacking order where they overlap.**
│
└──

If you select an AP div element, the tag structure display in the bottom left-hand corner of the `<body> <div#apDiv1>` document window will show it as a div with a # sign after it, followed by a name. The same name will appear in the **AP Elements** panel. Dreamweaver generates the names automatically; they are of the form apDiv1, apDiv2, and so on.

If you look at the **Properties** panel with an AP div element selected, you will see its name `<body> <div#apDiv1>` displayed in the panel, and here you can change it to something more meaningful. You will also find some properties that you can set, as shown in Figure 7.50. These include the left (**L**) and top (**T**) coordinates of the element, which together define the position of the element's top left-hand corner, its width (**W**) and height (**H**), and its z-index, which is its position in the front-to-back stacking order. (It's easier to change this value indirectly by dragging in the **AP Elements** panel.) You can set a background colour and image for the element, in the same way that you do for the whole document, and assign the element to a class, thereby applying to it any CSS rules defined with that class as their selector.

You will rarely need to use the properties in the bottom part of the panel, with the possible exception of **Overflow**. This determines what happens if the contents of an AP div element become too big to fit in it – for instance, if the font size is increased. The possibilities are **visible**,

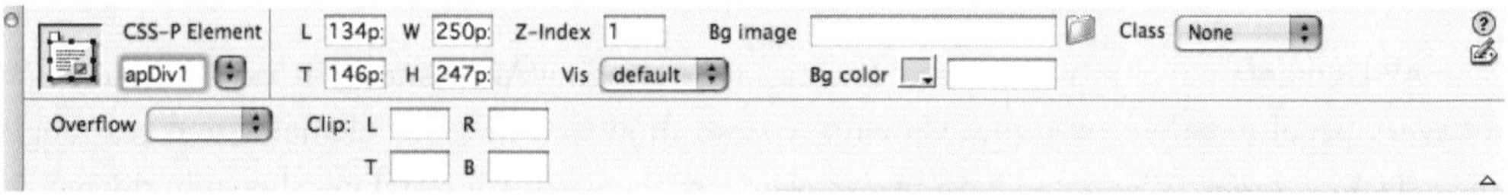

Figure 7.50 *Properties of an AP* div *element*

which allows overmatter to spill out of the element (usually ruining the appearance and layout of the page), hidden, which just conceals overmatter, scroll, which fits out the element with scroll bars, making it behave rather like a frame, and auto, which causes scroll bars to appear only if they are needed. The last of these is usually the best option. Hiding the overflow can be used to good effect in some CSS techniques involving image replacement, but this is a bit advanced for newcomers to Dreamweaver and CSS.

If instead of looking at the Properties panel, you look at the CSS Styles panel when an AP div element is selected, you will see something like Figure 7.51. Most importantly, the position property has been set to the value absolute. This is what makes the AP div element behave in the way it does. Without this, it would be part of the main text flow in the body of the document. The coordinates of the top left corner and the height and width are shown here – the values for these properties are set indirectly when you drag out the element or set its position and size numerically in the Properties panel. Similarly, the z-index is here again, too.

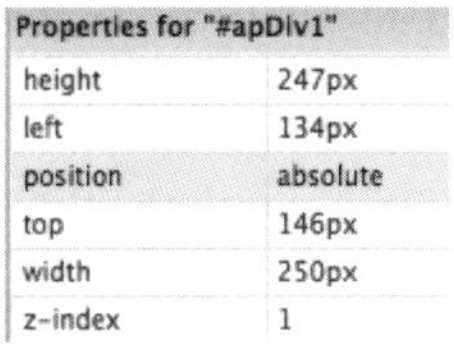

Properties for "#apDiv1"	
height	247px
left	134px
position	absolute
top	146px
width	250px
z-index	1

Figure 7.51 *CSS properties of an AP* div *element*

You can edit these CSS properties like any others. In particular, you can change the units of the width and height, to ems or %, so that the element will behave in an elastic or liquid fashion, instead of being fixed. Where you have a layout made from several div elements, you must make sure that you use compatible units for their coordinates and dimensions, otherwise the layout may break when the font size is changed or the browser window is resized. We go into more detail on this subject in Chapter 10 of *Web Design: A Complete Introduction*.

If you set the position property to static (or delete it entirely – the effect is the same), the element can be *floated* to the left or right of the main flow. That is, it will be pushed as far to the left or right as possible, while other text is wrapped round it. Figure 7.52 shows a div element that has been floated to the left. (We also put a shaded background on it, so you can see its extent.) Many useful layouts can be created using floated elements in conjunction with margins and padding. The possibilities are extensive, and once again we must refer you to a good book on Web design or CSS for further details.

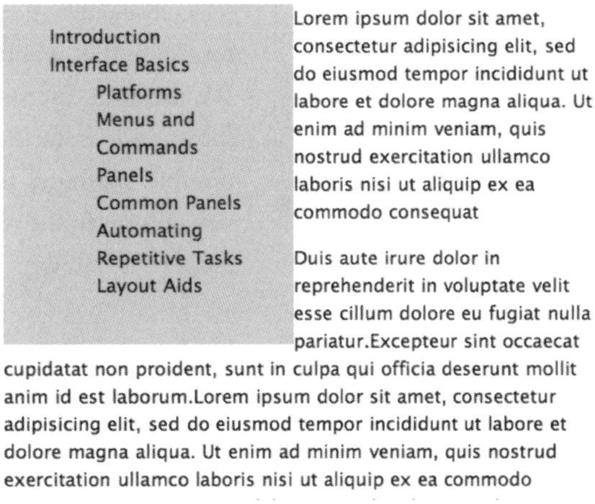

Introduction
Interface Basics
Platforms
Menus and
Commands
Panels
Common Panels
Automating
Repetitive Tasks
Layout Aids

Lorem ipsum dolor sit amet, consectetur adipisicing elit, sed do eiusmod tempor incididunt ut labore et dolore magna aliqua. Ut enim ad minim veniam, quis nostrud exercitation ullamco laboris nisi ut aliquip ex ea commodo consequat

Duis aute irure dolor in reprehenderit in voluptate velit esse cillum dolore eu fugiat nulla pariatur.Excepteur sint occaecat cupidatat non proident, sunt in culpa qui officia deserunt mollit anim id est laborum.Lorem ipsum dolor sit amet, consectetur adipisicing elit, sed do eiusmod tempor incididunt ut labore et dolore magna aliqua. Ut enim ad minim veniam, quis nostrud exercitation ullamco laboris nisi ut aliquip ex ea commodo

Figure 7.52 *A floated element*

The ease with which you can create AP div elements encourages the notion that they should be used like frames in a page layout program: if you want to place a block of text, an image or other embedded object somewhere on the page, you may feel that you can draw out an AP div where you want it, and add the content to it. But these elements are not like layout frames; they actually form part of the markup, and excessive use of them can lead to bloated pages that take longer to load than they need to, and which can become hard to maintain, a condition known to Web designers as *divitis*. In fact, many div elements are redundant. For instance, for Figure 7.49, we created an AP div and added a numbered list to it. We could just as well have set the position and size of the list itself (the ol element) and dispensed with the div, because any element can have its position property set to absolute. Dreamweaver doesn't make it as easy to do this as to draw out the AP div, but it is possible, and results in better code.

You need to know a little more about how AP elements work to appreciate what is required to turn any element into an AP one. We have mentioned that the position property must be set to absolute. If you select this property in the CSS Styles panel in Current mode, and look at the middle pane, you will see that it is defined in a rule with #apDiv1, or whatever the name of the AP element is, as its selector. Selectors beginning with a # sign cause the rule to be applied to a single element, which has the name as the value of its id attribute. Dreamweaver recognizes any element that has an id attribute that is matched by a rule that sets position to absolute as an AP element. So to make any element into an AP element, you need to give it an id attribute and create a rule that sets the position property.

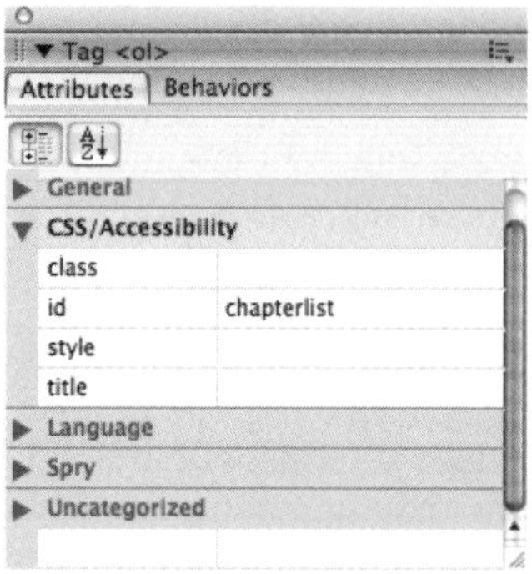

Figure 7.53 *The tag inspector*

You can set an id attribute by editing the code, but a simpler way, if you are not comfortable editing HTML, is by using the Tag Inspector. This panel's heading consists of the word Tag followed by the currently selected element's name in angle brackets, so if you select an ol element, for example, it will be labelled Tag <ol>. It is divided into two sub-panels. We are only interested in the one labelled Attributes. As Figure 7.53 shows, this is further divided into categories, within which all of the possible attributes for the element are listed. To set an attribute's value, you enter it in the appropriate box, in much the same way as you set CSS properties' values.

Suppose that we wanted to turn the numbered list that we put into an AP div in Figure 7.49 into an AP element itself, instead of using the div. To begin with, the list is inserted into the document, as we described previously. It will be placed in the normal flow of text on the page. Next, the ol element is selected. This is most easily done by placing the cursor somewhere in the list, and then clicking on ol in the tag structure display. The Tag Inspector will be headed Tag <ol> at this point. The CSS/Accessibility category of attributes is revealed, and a name is entered for the id. This name must be unique (within the document), so that it identifies this element and only this element. (Validating the document will detect any clashes between id values.)

To finish turning the list into an AP element, it is necessary to create a suitable CSS rule. If you click the **New Rule** button on the **CSS Styles** panel while the ol element is selected, and choose **Advanced** for the selector type, the selector will helpfully be set to the id value you just gave to the element, with the necessary # sign in front of it. In the **CSS Rule Definition** dialogue, you can set the position property to absolute in the **Positioning** category. Here you can also set the position and dimensions of the element, but you don't need to be particular about the values you use to begin with. Once you have created the rule, the list will start to behave like the AP div we described earlier: it will have a selection handle and when selected it will have resizing handles, so you can move it into position and set it to the correct size by dragging in the document window. The element will also appear in the **AP Elements** panel.

This technique is useful for positioning navbars and other lists of links. It can also be applied to images and other embedded objects, and to individual paragraphs. Remember that AP elements do not have to use absolute units, they can be made elastic or liquid.

Absolute positioning and the creative use of float and margin properties have superseded earlier techniques for page layout. In particular, it should never be necessary to use a table to lay out a page, and the practice is strongly discouraged on the grounds of both accessibility and semantic considerations. Tables should be reserved for their intended use, that is, displaying tabular data in rows and columns.

Frames are also problematic, because they break the one-to-one relationship between URLs and Web pages. Pages made out of frames have several URLs associated with them, which makes it very hard to bookmark them effectively. Frames therefore present accessibility and usability problems, so their use should be avoided, although there may be a few rare cases where frames provide the best way of organizing a site.

Unfortunately, Dreamweaver makes it easy to use table-based layouts and frames, because the program dates from a time when there were no alternatives. You simply have to ignore most of the facilities for using these features.

┌─ TRY THIS ───

Follow the procedure described in the preceding paragraphs to create and position a list absolutely without using an AP div element.

Verify that you can move and resize the list in the same way. Select the list using the AP element selection handle, and then select the list element using the tag structure display. Note what happens to the Properties panel.

└──

> **DON'T FORGET**
>
> **A CSS style sheet comprises a collection of rules, each of which consists of a selector and some declarations, which give values to properties controlling layout and appearance.**
>
> **Use the CSS Styles panel to examine rules and edit them by changing properties' values.**
>
> **Create CSS rules using the New Rule button in the CSS Styles panel. Choose a selector type (class, tag or advanced) and then use the Rule Definition dialogue to build the declarations by setting values for properties.**
>
> **Use class selectors to define styles, tag selectors to redefine the appearance of elements of a certain type, and id and contextual selectors for absolute positioning and advanced CSS techniques.**
>
> **Link to external style sheets to impose a standard style on a whole site.**
>
> **Drag out AP div elements by hand to lay out Web pages in an intuitive way.**
>
> **Make any element into an AP element by giving it a unique id attribute and defining a rule that sets its position property to absolute.**
>
> **Table-based layouts should be reserved for displaying genuine tabular data.**
>
> **Avoid using frames: they cause usability and accessibility problems.**

Page Content

Most Web pages include some images, and many also include embedded Flash animations, tables and data entry forms. You can add objects of these types using the icons and menus on the Insert bar, as we described earlier. Dreamweaver also provides an Insert menu with sub-menus, if you prefer to use menu commands. (Both the menu and the Insert bar are also used for adding other sorts of object to the document; anything that is not marked-up text is inserted in these ways.) Once the initial click, command or drag and drop action has been made, a file open dialogue is displayed, allowing you to choose the object to be inserted. When this has been done, the Properties panel changes to allow you to set attributes for the inserted object.

Images

Bitmapped images are the most commonly used type of embedded object. As we explain in Chapter 8, Web browsers can only display images in one of three bitmapped formats: GIF, JPEG and PNG. You can insert images in any of these formats. Dreamweaver also allows you to insert Photoshop (PSD) images, converting them to a Web format and optimizing them at the time, as described in Chapter 8. Dreamweaver is not fully integrated with the other CS3 programs, so you cannot do the same with Illustrator files.

Inserting an image does not actually embed image data in the document. It inserts an img element, which contains a pointer to the location of the actual image file. This works best if the image file is located within the site. That is, the image file should be in the directory you set as the local root when you created the site, or one of its sub-directories. If it is not, when you select the file in the open dialogue, you will be asked whether you want to copy it into the site. You should do so in almost every case.

HTML treats embedded images as if they were text characters, so there are only some places in a document where they can legitimately be inserted. (In technical terms, img is an inline element.) In particular, you can insert an image inside a paragraph, but not between paragraphs. However, Dreamweaver will let you insert an image at the cursor, no matter where it is, and it does not automatically wrap a paragraph around it, so it is possible to create pages that are not valid HTML by inserting images carelessly, for example, by placing the cursor right at the beginning of the document. Be careful to make sure that your image is either inside a paragraph, or in a div element, and don't omit to validate your pages.

Unlike the background images that we described earlier, every inserted image occupies its own space on a page, and pushes text and other content out of the way. In Figure 7.54, for example, we have inserted a banner image at the top of our page. The original content is now pushed down. If we had used the same image as a background, with repeat set to none, it would have appeared in the same place, but the navbar would have been overlaid on top of it. Sometimes this may be what you want to do, but generally images will be treated as page elements in their own right.

Web designers cannot call on all the compositing effects, such as alpha channels and clipping paths, that print designers are used to, so images can only be used in fairly unimaginative ways on Web pages. In Figure 7.54, we have again used a gradient whose end colour matches the page background, in order to make the image blend into the page. (More often, images have hard, rectangular edges, which limits the design possibilities.) In Figure 7.54, everything above the navbar, including the text, is part of the image. This is a commonly used technique: the text in

Figure 7.54 *An image embedded in a Web page*

the image has been rendered as a bitmap, so there is no possibility of users substituting a different font. For logos, where the font is an integral part of the branding, this is justifiable, but in general such *GIF text* should be avoided, because it presents accessibility problems (users who cannot read small print are unable to make it bigger), it may make the page less visible to search engines, and it will increase the size of pages, and thus the time it takes them to load.

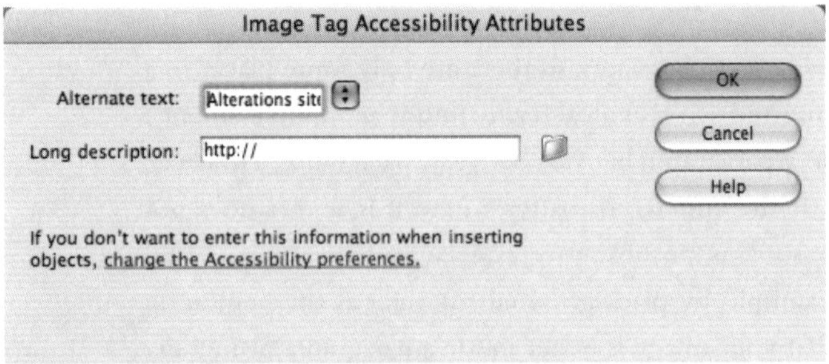

Figure 7.55 *Accessibility attributes for an image*

If you have followed our advice about setting preferences, and have ticked all the checkboxes in the **Accessibility** category, the dialogue box shown in Figure 7.55 will open after you have selected an image file. It allows you to enter values in two fields for attributes of the **img** (image) element which may assist users with accessibility problems.

The first of these fields, **Alternate text**, is the more important: it lets you provide a short textual alternative which will stand in for the image in situations where the image itself will not be seen. The most compelling such situation is when a blind person using screen reader software visits the page. The textual alternative will then be read out to them. If this text is absent, most screen readers will read the entire URL of the image file, which is not only useless, but also time-consuming and irritating for the user. Where GIF text has been used, the alternative text should match the rendered text, so that it can be read by screen readers. For other images, textual alternatives should try to provide the same information as the image, or describe what it is, not what it looks like. Writing good alternative text is not easy.

The second value requested in the accessibility attributes dialogue (**Long description**) is less important. Theoretically, HTML provides a way to link an image to a separate document with a long description of it, for cases where the short alternative text is not enough. Most contemporary Web browsers don't know what to do with long descriptions, even when they are being used in conjunction with a screen reader, so it is not really worth doing this. If you feel a long description would be helpful, just add an ordinary link to it, so everybody can use it.

Figure 7.56 shows the basic properties displayed in the **Properties** panel when you select an inserted image. (Most of the extra properties available when the lower half of the panel is revealed should be set using CSS instead of the attributes that would be inserted if you set them here.)

Figure 7.56 *Image properties*

The text field next to the thumbnail of the inserted image at the extreme left of the Properties panel can be used to provide an id value for the img element, which can subsequently be used to identify it in scripts and style sheets. (If you want to use absolute positioning with an image, you can set the id here instead of in the Tag Inspector.) The Src text field is filled in automatically with a relative URL identifying the image file. This can be changed later either by typing a new URL into the field or by clicking on the folder icon to its right and navigating to a new image file. The field labelled Alt holds the image's short textual alternative. You can edit it here if you are not satisfied with what you entered when inserting the image.

The W and H fields can be used to set the width and height of the image — that is, the width and height at which it is displayed by the browser. In general, these should never be set to anything other than the natural width and height of the image. Using other values means that the Web browser will have to resize the image, a task which Web browsers generally do badly. If an image is the wrong size for the page, create a version that is the correct size by resizing it in Photoshop.

You can control aspects of the positioning of images using CSS rules. The Class pop-up menu at the right of the Properties panel lets you apply a rule with a class selector to an image. (There is an inconsistency in the interface here, as this is behaving exactly like the identical pop-up menu that is labelled Style in the Properties panel when text is selected.) You can float an image, or alter the way it aligns with the surrounding text, and apply margins, borders and padding to it, for example. In Figure 7.54, we used CSS to set the margins on the image to zero, forcing it into the top left corner of the page and overriding the small margin we had added to the page body.

In Figure 7.56 you can see that the Properties panel has a Link field for images, as it does for text. Adding a link to an image means that clicking anywhere on the image causes the link to be followed. (In HTML terms, it puts the image inside the a element forming the link.)

─TRY THIS─

Practise adding images to an HTML document that also contains several paragraphs of text. Try setting the width and height to values other than the natural ones of the images. Do you agree that the browsers make a poor job of resizing the images?

Define a CSS rule to float objects to the right, and apply it to your images.

Editing Images

Dreamweaver is intended for putting together Web pages and sites, not for preparing the content that goes on those pages. It does, however, provide some very basic image editing facilities. More importantly, it makes it fairly simple to use image editing programs such as Photoshop to make changes to images that have already been inserted in HTML documents.

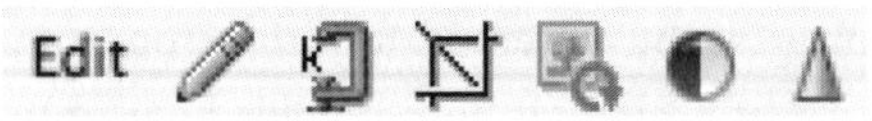

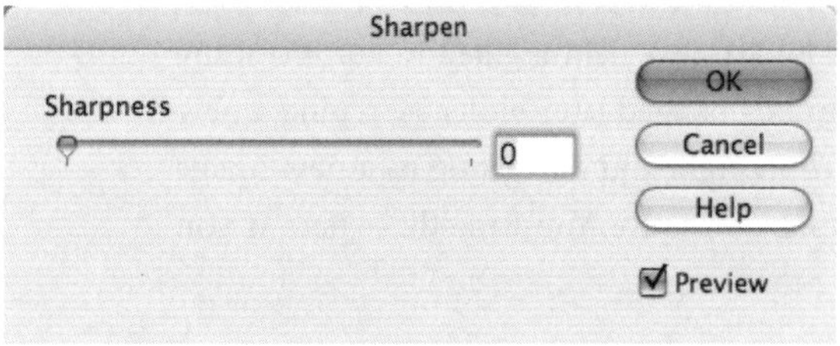

Figure 7.57 *The image sharpening dialogue*

The image editing functions are invoked by the set of buttons labelled Edit that appear below the Alt field in the Properties panel. Reading from left to right, these buttons are used to edit the selected image in an external image editor, to optimize, crop, resample, adjust its brightness and contrast and sharpen it. (The button for editing will not always look like a pencil, as we will explain shortly.) We described the adjustments as basic, but it would be more accurate to call them crude. For example, Figure 7.57 shows the dialogue box used for sharpening an image in Dreamweaver. The degree of control is inadequate, and the results are extremely poor, compared to what you can achieve with unsharp masking in Photoshop, as described in Chapter 4. The crop tool is adequate, but the other adjustments should only be used if really you have no alternative.

Hence, the ability to open an image in an external editor is valuable. You must nominate external editors for JPEG, GIF and PNG files. Most likely you will want to use Photoshop or Fireworks for all of these, but you can use different editors for each type if you prefer. The File Types/ Editors category in the Preferences dialogue, shown in Figure 7.58, is used to set the editor for all types of files, not just image files. You select a file type in the left-hand column of the bottom pane, and then add editors for it in the right-hand column, by clicking the + sign and browsing for the application you want to be used. You can nominate one editor as the default by selecting it and clicking the button labelled Make Primary. For images in Web graphics formats, Fireworks is already set as the default editor, and because Fireworks and Dreamweaver were developed together (by Macromedia), integration between the two is particularly smooth. If you are a Photoshop user, though, you will find it better to use that; Photoshop is included in the list of editors for JPEG, GIF and PNG, so you just need to make it the default.

You can edit an embedded image using the default editor for files of that type by double-clicking the image in the document window, or by selecting it and clicking the Edit button on the Properties panel. This will have the appearance of the icon for the editor – in particular, if you have set Photoshop as the default editor, you will see the Photoshop icon here. (If you want to edit the file with an editor other than the default, [right-click/ctl-click] the image and choose an editor from the Edit With sub-menu of the context menu.) The external editor will open the image file, and you can make changes. When you have finished, save and close the file. Back in Dreamweaver, the image in the document will be updated with your changes unless the original image was a Photoshop (PSD) file: Dreamweaver treats these as a special case. When you insert a Photoshop image, as described in Chapter 8, Dreamweaver keeps track of the location of the original PSD file. If you then select the embedded image, which will have been converted to

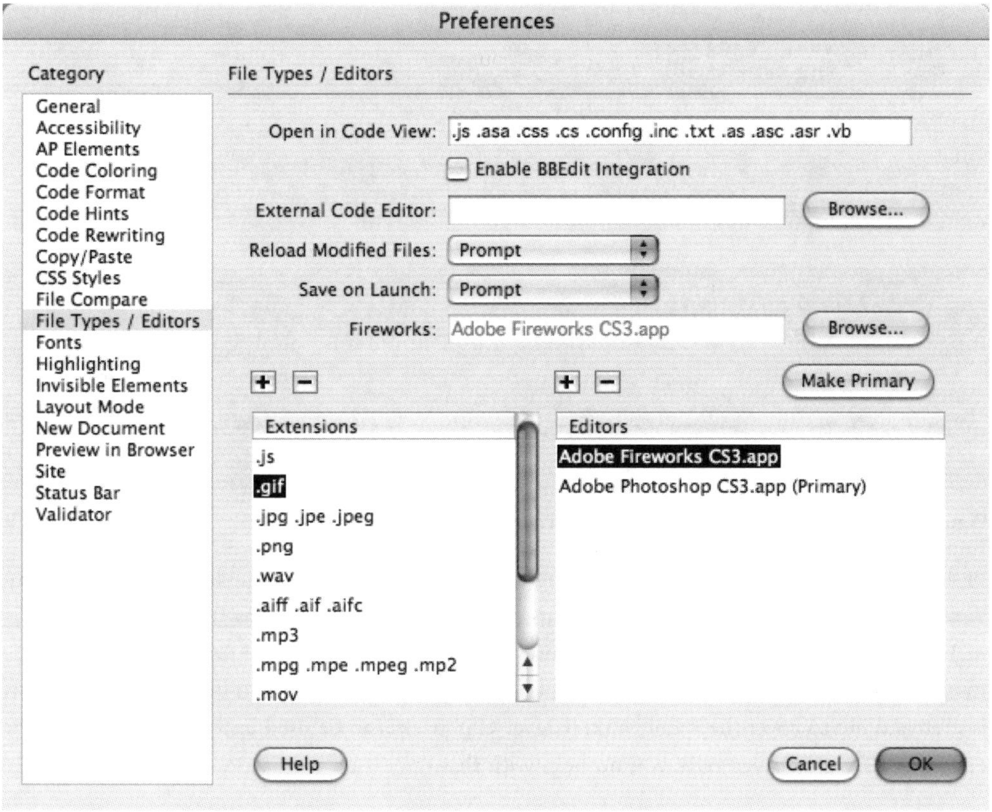

Figure 7.58 *Setting external editors*

JPEG, GIF or PNG during import, and click the edit button (which will have the appearance of the Photoshop icon) on the Properties panel, Photoshop will open the original PSD file for you to edit. However, when you save and close the file in Photoshop, the embedded image is not automatically updated in your document – you must re-import it explicitly.

┌─TRY THIS───┐

Set up default editors for all the Web graphics file formats. (Use Photoshop for all of them unless you have a good reason not to do so.)

Try editing any JPEG, GIF or PNG files that you have embedded in your pages.

└───┘

Image Navbars

We previously described using a list of links as a navbar, and applying CSS rules to control its appearance and make the links change theirs on rollover. This is the preferred way to make navbars, but it limits the possibilities for original design, and many Web designers prefer to use images for their navbar links. This makes it possible to use special fonts without running the risk

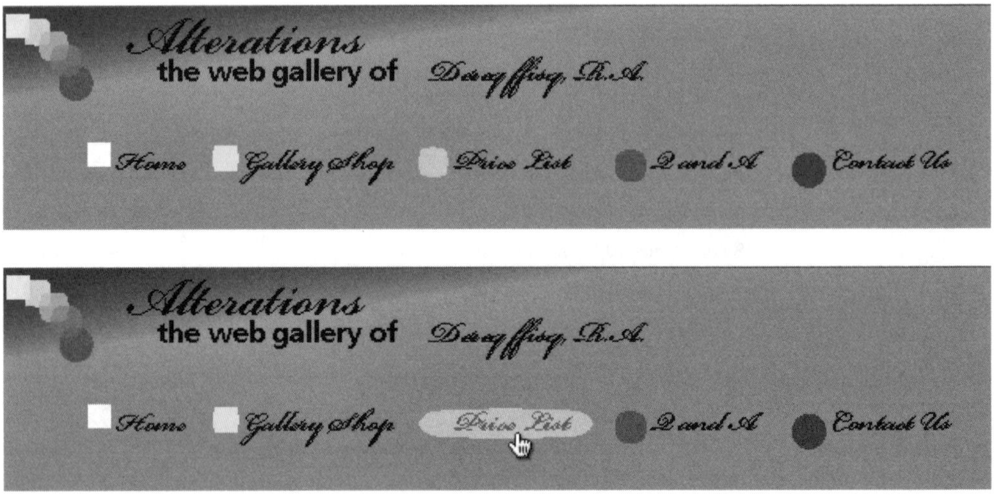

Figure 7.59 *An image-based navbar with rollover effect*

of their being substituted, and to apply typographic and visual effects to the links, or to use purely visual iconic links. If images are used in this way, rollover effects, such as the crude one shown in Figure 7.59, are usually created using JavaScript to replace one image with another – in this case, the link text with the small icon next to it is replaced by a modified image where the icon is stretched out to cover the whole link. (Clever CSS tricks can be used instead to achieve similar effects, but Dreamweaver gives you no help with that.)

We don't recommend the use of navbars made up of images, for reasons that we will explain at the end of this section, but we recognize that many Web designers – and their clients – like image-based navbars, so we will tell you how to make them, even though we think you shouldn't.

Dreamweaver makes inserting an image-based navbar fairly simple, but first you must create all the images you are going to need. There may be as many as four for each link in the navbar, corresponding to the four states that Dreamweaver recognizes: up, over, down and over-while-down.

The up state is the normal one; this is how the link appears most of the time. The other important state is over. A link goes into the over state when the cursor rolls over it; this is the same as the rollover state we met when defining link colours earlier. The down state is not much used, it is entered when a link has been clicked, so there is usually no time for it to be seen. Normally, clicking causes a new page to be loaded, and even if that has the same navbar, it will be reset. You can, however, specify that a particular link should be loaded in its down state; this can be useful for indicating to the user which page they are actually on. Normally, you would make over-while-down the same as the down state, so that there is no visual feedback when a user rolls over a link that is down, suggesting that nothing will happen if they click.

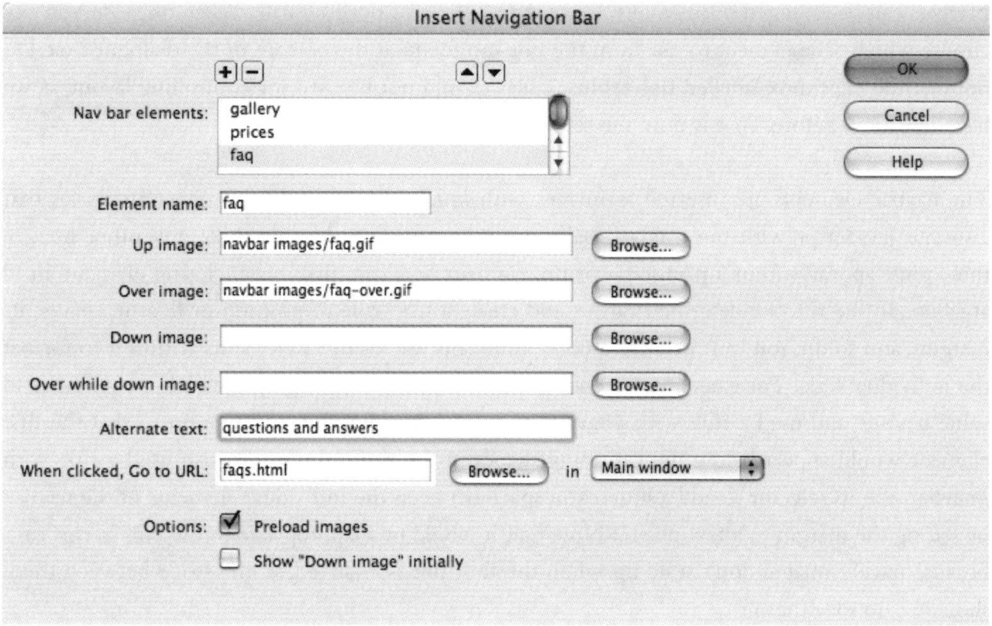

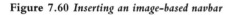

Figure 7.60 *Inserting an image-based navbar*

Once you have prepared as many images as you need for each link, you can insert the navbar. (Dreamweaver only permits one image-based navbar on each page.) There is a navbar button on the menu that drops down from the image icon on the **Insert** bar, or you can use the **Insert>Image Objects>Navigation Bar** command. The dialogue box shown in Figure 7.60 opens. Its operation is fairly intuitive. The small pane at the top lists the elements as you add them. Use the + button to add each new element (the first is already there for you). Give it a name in the box labelled **Element name**, and then use the browse buttons to locate the images for each of the states you are going to use.

It is essential that you add a textual alternative for each element, by entering it in the box labelled **Alternate text**. Otherwise, these links, which are fundamental to navigating the site, will not be available to anyone using a screen reader or text-only browser, or in the event that network problems prevent the images loading.

The link destination is entered in the last text field. Don't change the **in** pop-up to anything other than **Main window**. Ticking the checkbox labelled **Preload images** will cause the browser to load all the images for all the states in advance, so that they are in its cache when they are needed. If you don't tick this box, users with slow connections will not see the rollover images as soon as they move the cursor over the link, but will see a "broken image" icon instead. If you are distinguishing the **down** state, the box labelled **Show "Down image"** initially should be selected for the navbar element that corresponds to the current page.

Navbars can be arranged horizontally across the page, or vertically, usually down one side. You can choose which arrangement to use from the pop-up menu at the bottom of the dialogue box. Do not tick the checkbox labelled Use tables: tables should not be used for controlling layout, as we have remarked before. That is now the job of CSS.

The navbar elements are inserted as images with links attached and some extra attributes that associate JavaScript with the link to make the rollover effects happen. Like any other images, these must appear within a paragraph or div element. You can give this enclosing element an id attribute, in the way we described earlier, and create a CSS rule to position or float it, change its margins, and so on. You can then use a contextual selector for the a elements within it to format the individual links. For example, we enclosed our navbar in a paragraph, which we gave the id value navbar, and used a rule with #navbar as its selector to set the left margin so that the first element would appear below the cascading shapes in the page banner. We also used a rule with #navbar a as its selector to add a little extra space between the individual elements of the navbar, by setting the margin to a few pixels. (Note that it would be inappropriate to use ems in this case, because navbar images don't scale up when the font size is changed, so the space between them shouldn't do so, either.)

If you need to change the navbar later on, use the Modify>Navigation Bar command to get back to the dialogue shown in Figure 7.60.

This is all quite simple, and if you pay more attention to the design of the images than we did in our simple example, attractive and functional navbars can be created in this way. You have doubtless seen many of them on the Web. So what can be wrong with it? Nothing that can't be overcome with some additional care, but simply inserting a navbar in the way we've just described and doing nothing more can lead to problems.

First and foremost is the accessibility problem that results from using images as text, which many navbars do. People who have trouble reading small print (and there are many of them) can't make it bigger. This also applies to icons used as links — some people may find it hard to distinguish between them if they are too small. It is possible to use CSS to set the size of the images in em units, which will make them scale up with the font, but this is an extra step and since you have no way of knowing what font size the user will have set, there is no guarantee that the em sizes you calculate will be the images' natural dimensions. At least if you provide the alternative text for the images, screen reader users will have no problems with an image-based navbar, but if you omit it, you will leave them without any site-wide navigation.

Second, the rollover effect relies on JavaScript. It has been estimated that something between 10 and 15% of Web users disable JavaScript in their browsers, because they feel that it has been abused by advertisers to produce unwelcome pop-up and pop-under windows, and because of perceived security risks. These users will not see any rollovers. Some mobile devices used for Web browsing do not support JavaScript, so rollovers will not work for people using these devices either. The links should still function correctly, but users will not see the visual feedback you intended, and you will have wasted your time creating the rollover images. Few users disable CSS support however, and mobile devices mostly make an effort to implement CSS, so rollovers implemented using CSS, as we described earlier, are more likely to be seen. If you want to use fancy images in your navbar, you can still do so while using CSS to implement the rollover effects, though the technique is too advanced to describe here.

These drawbacks, as well as an inevitable increase in the bandwidth requirements, are inherent in the use of images in navbars. The final problem lies in Dreamweaver's implementation. If you use XHTML 1.1, XHTML 1.0 Strict or HTML 4.01 Strict as the DTD, inserting a navbar will cause your page to be invalid. Dreamweaver includes several attributes that are not allowed by any of those DTDs. This is indefensibly shoddy. It means that if you want your pages to validate, you must either use a transitional DTD, or clean up the code by hand. (Dreamweaver's find and replace command can be used to do this relatively easily.) None of these reasons means that you should never use image-based navbars, but you should consider alternatives first.

TRY THIS

Make a copy of the home page of your site, and replace the navbar you made previously with one that uses images as the links. Prepare suitable images for at least the up and over states, and insert the navbar, making sure to provide textual alternatives for all the links.

Preview the page in several browsers, making sure the rollovers work. Now disable JavaScript in a browser. Is the navbar still usable? Try validating the page in Dreamweaver.

Flash Movies and Video

Flash movies (SWF files – see Chapter 6) are embedded in the same way as images. The Flash icon can be found on the Media menu in the Common tab of the Insert bar. (It is possible that some other icon will appear in its place, in which case you simply need to reveal the drop-down menu and select Flash.) Click on the icon (or on Flash) then navigate to the SWF file you want to embed. It will be inserted at the cursor. Like images, Flash movies cannot appear between paragraphs.

Figure 7.61 shows the properties that can be set in the Properties panel when an embedded Flash movie is selected. These properties are a mixture of parameters to the Flash player and attributes of the elements used to embed the movie.

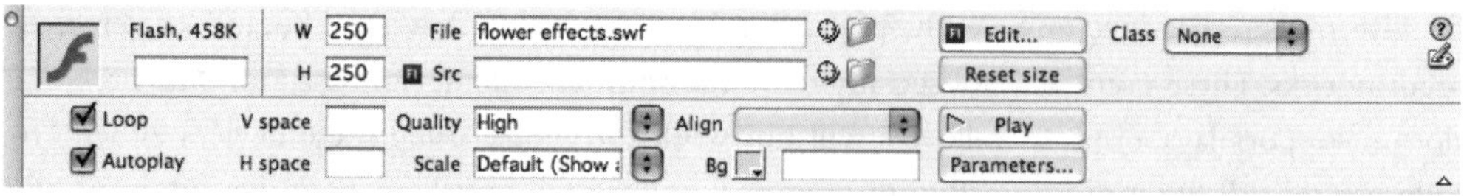

Figure 7.61 *Flash movie properties*

As with other elements, these presentational attributes should not be used; CSS can be used instead – use the **Class** pop-up to assign a CSS style to the movie. You should ignore the **V space**, **H space** and **Align** controls. The unlabelled box in the top left-hand corner is for giving the movie a name; this is mostly needed for scripting purposes. The **Play** button can be used to preview the movie within Dreamweaver's document window.

The **Loop** and **Autoplay** checkboxes are used to determine whether the movie should play continuously, and whether it should start spontaneously when the page loads, respectively. For strict accessibility you should deselect **Autoplay**, but this is not often done in practice. However, you should be aware that users with cognitive difficulties may be confused by time-based media that start without warning. As we note in Chapter 6, there are no playback controls provided by default for Flash movies, but it is simple to incorporate them within the movie itself.

The **Quality** and **Scale** values are used for the corresponding Flash Player parameters. If you need to set others, click the button labelled **Parameters**... to open a dialogue in which you can add name/value pairs for the **param** element.

As with navbars, if you try to validate a page containing a Flash movie, you will find that it fails, no matter which DTD you are using. This is due to a fundamental problem with the way Web browsers deal with Flash and other types of media that they cannot display themselves. A full account of the problem is given in *Web Design: A Complete Introduction*. Briefly, two different elements are needed to ensure that a Flash movie will play both in Internet Explorer on Windows, and in any other browser. One of these, the **embed** element, has never been part of any HTML standard. (It isn't just our insistence on using strict DTDs that causes pages with embedded Flash to fail to validate.) Because Internet Explorer does not correctly implement the **object** element, which is the standard way of embedding media, it is necessary to use **embed** as well as **object**, thereby causing the code to become invalid. Dreamweaver makes matters worse by automatically including JavaScript code to check for versions of the Flash Player, and doing so in a way that causes another error.

The only way to get round this problem is to use JavaScript to write a different **object** element dynamically when the page is loaded in Internet Explorer. Dreamweaver does not support this admittedly dubious approach, so unless you can write the necessary code yourself, you will have to live with invalid pages when you use Flash content.

─TRY THIS─

Use Dreamweaver to create a page to display a Flash movie – ideally one that you created yourself. Add extra material to the page to show off and/or explain the movie. Compare the page you created in this way with the page created by publishing the movie from Flash.

Simple Flash movies are not the only sort of content created in Flash that you can embed in your Web pages using Dreamweaver, as you can see from the pop-down menu on the Media menu in the Common tab of the Insert bar. We won't discuss Flash buttons, text or paper, because these are (quite rightly) rarely used. Flash video, which we describe in Chapter 6, is, however, an increasingly important format for delivering video over the Web. You must use Flash itself, or the standalone video encoder, to prepare video in FLV format. You can then easily add it to a Web page in Dreamweaver.

When you click the Flash Video button, the dialogue shown in Figure 7.62 opens. You choose the video file by navigating to it in the usual way, and as with other elements, Dreamweaver will offer to copy it to your site folder if it isn't there already. The difference between progressive download and streaming is explained in Chapter 6; you can only use streaming if you have the Flash Streaming Server (which you may well not have), otherwise you must settle for progressive download. You choose which option to use with the Video type pop-up menu at the top of the dialogue.

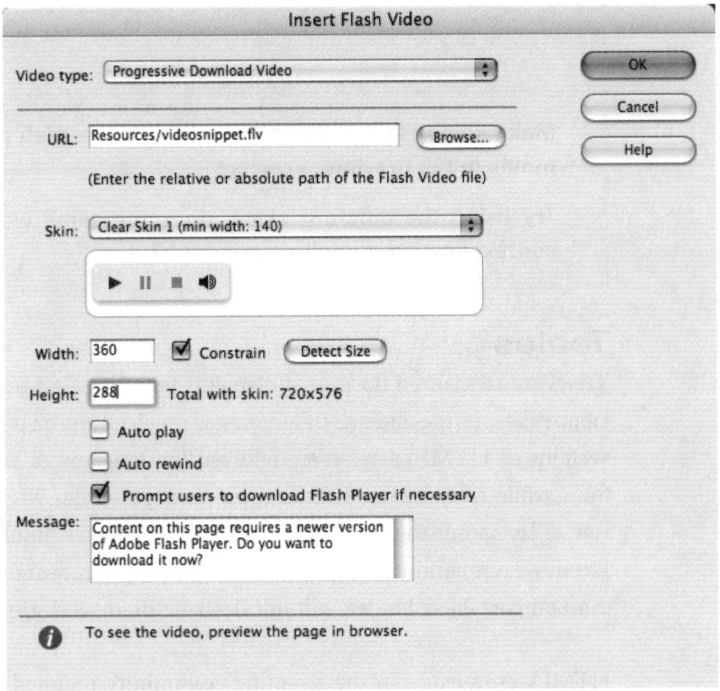

Figure 7.62 *Embedding Flash Video*

Dreamweaver will insert a Flash video player component in your page. The Skin pop-up menu lets you choose its appearance: the display below it shows you what the controls will look like. You can set the width and height of the player, or by clicking on the button labelled Detect Size, you can let Dreamweaver discover the movie's natural dimensions. If the video originated on DV and has not been resized, this will be much too big for display on most Web pages, and you should therefore set a smaller size, preserving the aspect ratio by checking the Constrain box.

The checkboxes at the bottom of the dialogue should be self-explanatory. The message to be displayed if the user does not have a sufficiently recent version of the Flash Player installed can be customized, although the default is simple and to the point.

The HTML code used to embed the video player component is the same as that used to embed a Flash movie. That is, it uses invalid markup.

Flash Video is not the only Web video format, but it is the only one that Dreamweaver supports adequately. Plugin and ActiveX objects are available on the same drop-down menu that includes Flash. These are used for embedding other video formats, such as QuickTime and Windows Media: Plugin inserts code that works with browsers that use the plug-in mechanism for playing media; ActiveX is for Internet Explorer on Windows, which uses Microsoft's ActiveX controls. However, there is no easy way to insert code (albeit invalid) that works in both types of browser, the way you can for Flash and Flash Video.

---TRY THIS---

Make some Flash video and embed it in a Web page, as you did with a Flash movie in the previous exercise.

Try using the different skins; do some skins work better than others in the context of your overall page design?

Tables

Tables are specialized document elements which should be used for just one purpose: to display tabular data. In the absence of any better mechanism for positioning elements on a page in early versions of HTML, they were abducted by designers as a way of simulating a layout grid, and for a while table layouts were a staple of page design. Style sheets now provide a much better way of laying out page elements in HTML and tables should no longer be used for that purpose. Dreamweaver continues to provide elaborate support for table layouts, presumably so that old sites can be maintained, but we will not describe them, and strongly advise you to avoid their use.

HTML's provenance in the scientific community required the inclusion of tables from an early stage. The elements concerned with tables are among HTML's most complicated features and laying out tables by writing HTML by hand is a thankless task.

An easier way to create a table is by clicking the Table icon in the Common or Layout category on Dreamweaver's Insert bar. The dialogue box shown in Figure 7.63 is displayed, in which you can set the basic parameters of the table: the number of rows and columns, the width of the rules separating cells, the padding between each cell's contents and the separator, and the space between cells. You can also specify which row and/or column – if any – should be considered to be headers.

These will be marked up using a different element from the data cells (th instead of td); normally they would be formatted differently, using CSS rules for the relevant element types. At the bottom of the dialogue, you can specify some extra values to help make your table more accessible. Caption is used to identify the table, much as the figure captions in a book are used. Don't use the Align caption pop-up menu to specify the caption's alignment – Dreamweaver will generate invalid markup for strict DTDs if you do. Use CSS instead. For large or complicated tables, you can also provide a summary of the table's purpose and structure. This is helpful to people using screen readers, who will not be able to see the spatial relationships between the table's cells which are used to communicate the structure to sighted people.

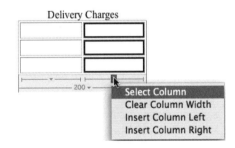

Figure 7.63 *Setting up a table*

When you dismiss the Table dialogue, an empty table is inserted into the document. If you have Table Widths and Table Borders ticked in the View>Visual Aids sub-menu, when the table is selected you will be shown the current widths of the columns, as illustrated in Figure 7.64. The tiny downward-pointing triangles have menus attached, as the figure shows, which can be used to perform simple operations on the columns or on the table as a whole.

Figure 7.64 *A selected table*

An entire table is selected by clicking on its top left corner – the cursor turns into a white arrow with a table icon attached. A row or column can be selected by clicking just outside the table, to the left of or above the row or column in question – the cursor then turns into a thick black arrow. Selecting in this way can be tricky, because the selection is only possible when the cursor is within a very small area. For columns and the entire table, it is easier to click somewhere inside the table and use the commands on the menus attached to the table widths. Individual cells are selected by clicking inside them; a rectangular collection of cells can be selected by dragging over them, or by shift-clicking. With a cell or range of cells selected, you can use the Modify>Table sub-menu to split a cell vertically or horizontally, or merge a selection into a single cell. You can also delete the row or column containing the selection, or insert a row or column after it. The easiest way to alter the width of columns or the height of rows is by dragging the bars separating them from their neighbours. You can also resize the whole table by dragging the outside borders. You enter information into the table by placing the insertion point in a cell and then typing or, if you wish to insert images and other types of embedded content, using the Insert bar. You can use the arrow keys to move between cells; tab and shift-tab take you to the next or previous cell, respectively, as in a spreadsheet.

The Properties panel can be used to make some changes to a table or selected cells. In particular, you can set text properties that will affect the contents of selected cells in the same way as you format text in other contexts, as we described near the beginning of this chapter. It is also possible to assign tables to a class and apply CSS styling to them via class rules. The CSS for formatting tables can get complex. Once again, you should consult a good book on CSS before attempting any non-trivial table formatting.

---TRY THIS---

Create a table that looks like an English-language calendar's display of the days in a month, with days of the week as headings across the top and the individual dates arranged in a grid. Fill the table with the days of the month in which you are doing this exercise. Merge cells for the unoccupied days at the beginning and end of the month to create a single blank at each end.

Forms

HTML *forms* provide the basic method of gathering information from users to pass on to server-side scripts for such purposes as product registration, surveys and buying goods. Forms normally work in conjunction with a CGI script or its equivalent. Server-side computation lies beyond the scope of this book, so we will only briefly survey Dreamweaver's facilities for constructing forms. Bear in mind that this is only part of the construction of a complete Web application.

The Insert bar provides a simple and intuitive method of creating forms and adding input elements to them. The Forms category of the Insert bar, shown in Figure 7.65, includes icons representing forms and the various elements which HTML allows you to place inside them to be filled in by the user. (Not all the icons are entirely perspicuous – use the tool tips to find out what they are.) The properties appropriate to each type of element are set using the Properties panel, which as usual changes its appearance to correspond to the selected element. If you understand how form elements work and interact with server-side scripts you will find building forms in Dreamweaver very simple. (If you don't, you may be better off avoiding the use of forms.)

Figure 7.65 *Form elements*

Figure 7.66 *Form properties*

Before you can add any controls or input elements, you must insert a form to hold them. (If you try to insert an input element before you have inserted the form, Dreamweaver offers to insert the form for you.) Figure 7.66 shows the **Properties** panel when a form element is selected. It has a text field at the left in which you can enter a name for the form. The field to the right, labelled **Action**, should be filled in with the URL of the script to which the data entered into the form should be sent for processing. If the script is part of your site you can navigate to it in the usual way instead of entering the URL. The **Method** pop-up menu at the bottom is used to select the HTTP method, **GET** or **POST**, for sending the data. (**POST** is usually preferable, unless you need to allow form data to be passed as part of a URL – for instance, as the destination of a link.)

When you insert an input element or control within a form, the dialogue shown in Figure 7.67 will appear, if you have set the accessibility preferences as we recommended. It allows you to attach a label to the element, in such a way that screen readers will be able to associate the label and element. If you just add a label as ordinary text, proximity enables sighted users to understand which label goes with which element, but screen readers cannot do this and need some extra help. By specifying the label in this dialogue, you provide that help. The **Style** option shown here is the most flexible way of associating the label and element, and is usually recommended. Although setting the **Access key** and **Tab index** values is intended as a further aid to accessibility, it may also lead to confusion with modern screen readers, so accessibility experts often recommend against using these.

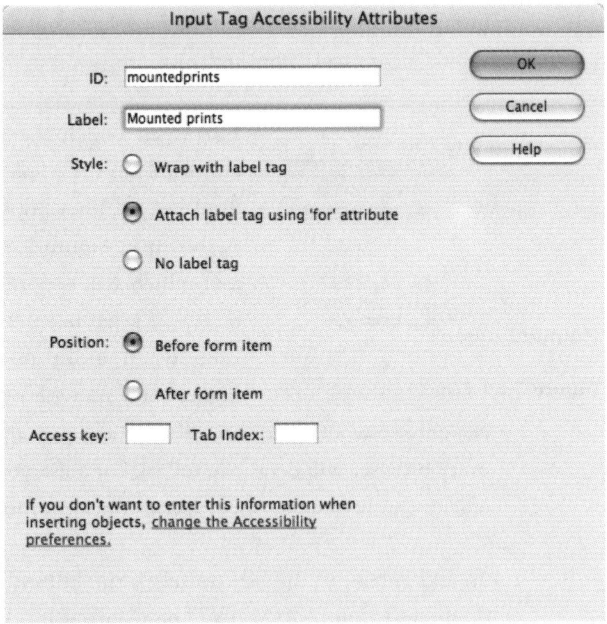

Figure 7.67 *Accessibility attributes for an input element*

The upper screenshot in Figure 7.68 shows the **Properties** panel when a *checkbox* is selected. It has a name, which can be set in the text field at the left. The name entered here will be used as the variable for the data associated with the element when values are sent to the server. The **Checked value** field is used to set the value assigned to the correspondingly named variable when the data is sent, so in this example, if the checkbox is ticked, a variable **opt-out** will be sent with

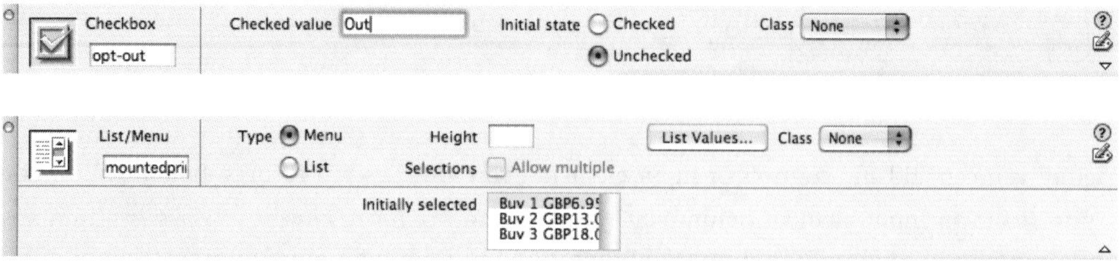

Figure 7.68 *Properties of a checkbox (top) and a list/menu (bottom)*

the value Out. The Initial state radio buttons are used to specify whether the checkbox should appear ticked (Checked) or empty (Unchecked) when it is first displayed.

Most form controls have very similar properties, which, for the most part, we will leave you to explore for yourself. Controls which do not accept a single value present some complications. For instance, several **radio buttons** may share the same name; this has the effect of linking them into a group, such that only one may be selected at a time. The initial state of all but one (the default) should be set to Unchecked.

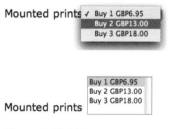

Figure 7.69 *Lists*

Lists from which the user can pick a value are the most complicated control. They are implemented as HTML **select** elements, which may be displayed as either pop-up menus, or as a list in a small scrolling window, as shown in Figure 7.69. In either case, it is necessary to provide all the text which will appear, and, for each entry, specify the value that should be sent if it has been chosen from the list. The **Properties** panel's appearance when a list is selected is shown in the lower screenshot in Figure 7.68. As with other form controls, you must provide a name. You can choose whether to show the list as a pop-up menu or not (though there is no guarantee that every browser will do as you tell it). For a list, you can set the height, which determines how many entries can be seen at once, and also permit more than one entry to be selected at a time.

To add entries to the list, you click the button labelled List Values..., which opens the dialogue shown in Figure 7.70. You add new entries by clicking the + button and typing the text you want in the left column. After tabbing across to the right column, you can enter the value that should be sent when that entry is selected. When you have set the values, you can choose which one should be the initial selection by clicking it in the small scrolling list that appears at the bottom of the **Properties** panel, as you can see in Figure 7.68.

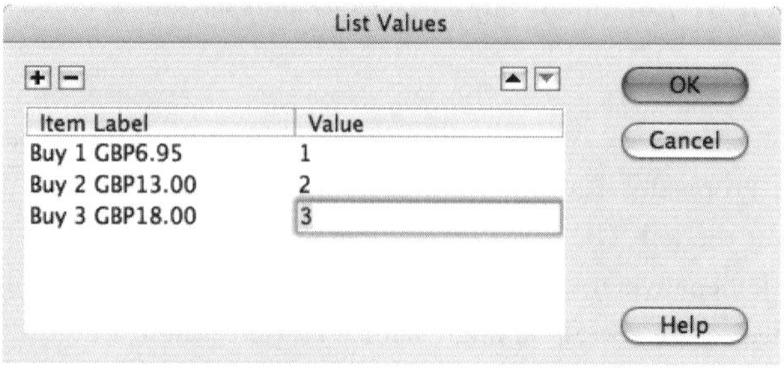

Figure 7.70 *Providing list values*

Every form needs a submit button, which the user must click in order to send the data they have entered to the server for processing. You use the button object for this purpose. In the Properties panel you can select whether to use it as a submit button or a reset button, which clears the form.

TRY THIS

Create a new page for your site, containing a form, such as a registration form or a survey. Use as many different types of form element as possible.

Set the action to http://www.digitalmediatools.org/Book/Resources/ Dreamweaver/dumpvars.php. When you submit the form (providing you are connected to the Internet) you will see the variables sent from the form and their values.

DON'T FORGET

Add images, Flash movies and video, tables and forms using the Insert bar.

Insert bitmapped images in GIF, JPEG or PNG formats, or import and convert Photoshop files.

Always provide a textual alternative for an image.

Edit embedded images in external programs that you have nominated; changes made to inserted GIF, JPEG or PNG files will be automatically applied.

Photoshop files are an exception: if you edit a PSD file you have already imported, you must re-import it afterwards.

You can insert navbars that use images as links, but be aware of a range of potential problems.

Always provide textual alternatives for image-based navbars, without exception. Without this text, some users will be unable to navigate the site.

Embed Flash movies (SWFs) in the same way as images.

Include Flash Video (FLV files) by embedding a video player component that will load and play your video.

Only use tables for displaying tabular data.

Set the basic parameters of a table when you insert it. Adjust column widths and split or merge cells subsequently. Use CSS to style borders and so on.

Use forms to gather input from users and send it to a server-side script for processing.

Insert a form, set the Action attribute to point to the script and then add input elements, such as checkboxes, text fields and lists.

JavaScript

Web pages that consist only of styled text and images are *static* – they don't do anything once they have been loaded into the browser. In contrast, pages with *dynamic* elements respond to events such as mouse clicks and rollovers, by changing in some way. Apart from CSS rollovers, implementing dynamic page elements requires *scripting*. That is, a small program must be written which is executed in the browser when some event occurs, and causes some elements of the page to be changed. Scripts are written in a relatively simple language called *JavaScript*.

As we explained in connection with image-based navbars, relying on JavaScript may cause problems, because a significant number of people disable it or use devices that do not support it. Hence, it is important that you make sure that your page can be used – links can be followed, forms can be submitted, and so on – even if the scripts don't work. Furthermore, in the past there have been considerable incompatibilities between different browsers' support for JavaScript. With the arrival of a standard *Document Object Model*, which specifies how scripts can access and change elements of the page, these incompatibilities are becoming less of a problem. Nevertheless, it is important to test pages that use JavaScript in as many browsers as possible.

The code for responding to events and updating the page is usually fairly trivial, but any kind of programming requires practice and skills which many designers lack. Dreamweaver provides ready-made code for certain commonly used types of interaction, concealing the scripts almost entirely. If you have no programming experience, you can still add dynamic behaviour to your pages by using these scripts. They fall into two classes, which were added to Dreamweaver at different times. We will describe them in the order they were developed.

Behaviours

The older class consists of a set of pre-built parameterized scripts, called *behaviours*, which you can attach to elements of a page to perform some *action*, such as replacing one image with another, or hiding a part of the page. Each behaviour has some *parameters*, such as the URLs of an image and its replacement, for which you specify values when adding the behaviour. You also select an *event*, such as a mouse click or rollover, that should trigger the behaviour. Whenever that event occurs, the action will be performed in response.

Behaviours are fairly crude, and many of them either cause actions that are not recommended nowadays, such as opening a pop-up window, or are ineffective, such as trying to detect the type of browser being used. Others, such as page elements that move across the screen, have become clichés that hark back to the days when "Dynamic HTML" was in vogue.

We have already seen an example of the use of behaviours, when we looked at image-based navbars. The underlying image swap effect is available on its own, as one of the image objects on

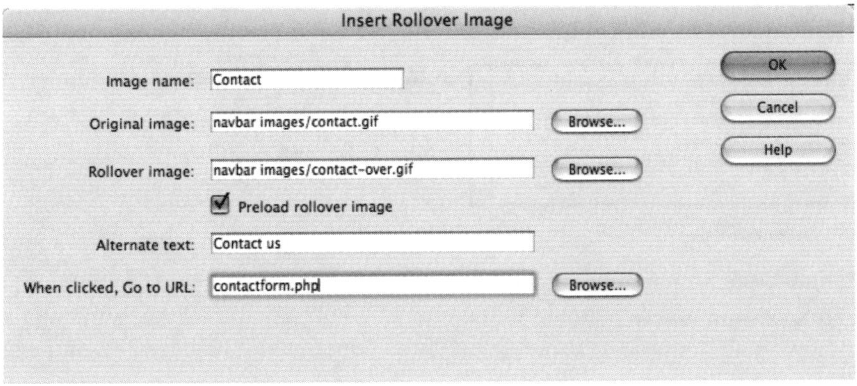

Figure 7.71 *Making an image rollover*

the Insert bar. (Look back at Figure 7.4.) When you click on this icon, the dialogue box shown in Figure 7.71 will appear. You choose two images, one for the normal state and one for the rollover state. (There is no provision for a down state.) You can add a URL, so that the image functions as a link, and you must provide a textual alternative.

The Behaviors Panel

Rollovers and image-based navbars are special cases of interactivity, in which the element involved in the behaviour and the event that triggers the action are pre-determined. This makes it possible to use the Insert bar to add these behaviours. In the more general case, you need to select the element and event, as well as setting parameters for the behaviour; this cannot be done just by clicking an icon on the Insert bar. Most behaviours are therefore added using a longer sequence of operations. First, an element is selected; second, a behaviour is added to the selected element, and its parameters are set using the Behaviors panel; finally, if the default is not suitable, the event that should trigger the action is specified. You can add any number of behaviours to an element, although you are rarely likely to need more than one.

The Behaviors panel is docked with the Attributes panel in the Tag Inspector, so when you select an element its name is incorporated into the title bar to show you which element the behaviour is being attached to. The panel resembles the top pane of the navigation bar dialogues: +, − and up and down triangle buttons are used to add, delete and rearrange elements of a scrolling list of behaviours. Clicking on the + button causes a menu to drop down, displaying all the available behaviours (as illustrated in Figure 7.72). Any behaviours which cannot legally be attached to the currently selected document element are greyed out.

Figure 7.72 *Choosing a behaviour*

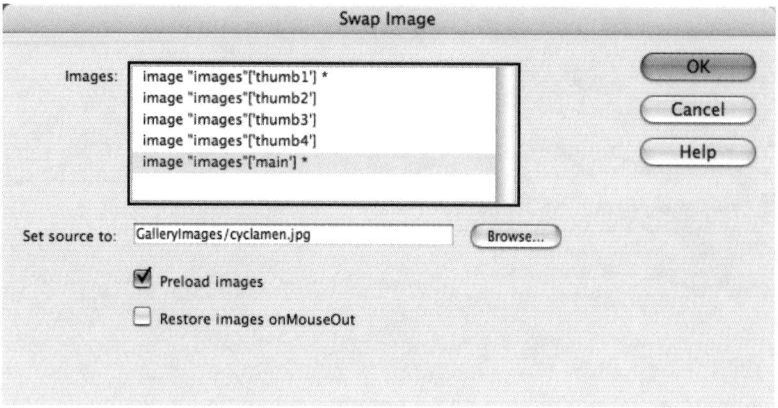

Swap Image

Images:	image "images"['thumb1'] *	OK
	image "images"['thumb2']	Cancel
	image "images"['thumb3']	Help
	image "images"['thumb4']	
	image "images"['main'] *	

Set source to: GalleryImages/cyclamen.jpg   Browse...

☑ Preload images

☐ Restore images onMouseOut

Figure 7.73 *Setting the parameters of a behaviour*

Note the presence of the ~Deprecated sub-menu. This contains behaviours that you should not use; they are only there for compatibility with pages made in earlier versions of Dreamweaver.

Selecting a behaviour from the list causes a dialogue to be displayed, in which you enter the appropriate parameters. Figure 7.73 shows an example. As with all the behaviours provided with Dreamweaver, the meaning of the parameters is fairly self-evident. However, in case of doubt, every parameter dialogue for a behaviour has a **Help** button, which causes a detailed explanation of its usage to be displayed in Adobe Help Viewer.

Once you have provided the behaviour's parameters, it is added to the list in the **Behaviors** panel. This list has two columns: the right-hand column lists all the behaviours attached to the selected document element; the left-hand column shows the event which will trigger the behaviour listed next to it. A default event, which is usually the most sensible, is initially chosen. If this is not, in fact, the event you wish to use to trigger the behaviour, you can select the behaviour and, as you can see in Figure 7.74, the entry in the events column acquires a pop-up menu from which you can select an alternative event. Most events can be associated with most types of element, although a few, such as **onFocus** and **onBlur**, can only be associated with form controls and links. The entries in the menu of events that begin with <A> will cause Dreamweaver to put a dummy link around the selected element to receive an event which otherwise it could not. This is not likely to be something you need to do unless you expect visitors to your site to be using very old browsers.

Figure 7.74 *Choosing the event*

Space does not allow us to describe all the available behaviours; in any case, since new behaviours can be added, no such description could be complete, so we will restrict ourselves to describing

Figure 7.75 *An image gallery*

a single example showing how behaviours can be used to create a page that reacts to user input in a useful way. The Dreamweaver Help facility should provide adequate assistance in using the others, but bear in mind our earlier remarks about their usefulness, or lack of it.

The Swap Image behaviour is the basis of rollovers, but you can use it explicitly to achieve different related effects. In particular, you can make the image that is swapped different from the one that receives the event, to create a so-called "remote rollover", where moving the cursor over one image causes a different one (somewhere else on the page) to change. Alternatively, you can associate the behaviour with the onClick event, so that clicking an image causes another one to change. We will do this to create the image gallery illustrated in Figure 7.75. (We did tell you not to take Dereq Ffisq's artwork seriously....)

In order to be swapped, an image must have a name, which you give it by typing in the text field at the left of the Properties panel while it is selected. Once this is done, creating the effect is simple.

The image which is to serve as the control is selected and the Behaviors panel is used in the way just described to add a behaviour to it, in this case Swap Image. The parameters dialogue is the one shown in Figure 7.73. The list at the top shows the names of all the images on the page; you must select one of these to be replaced by clicking on its name in the list. The field labelled Set source to is filled in with the URL of a replacement image. Normally, this will be within the site, so you can use the Browse... button to navigate to it.

When the behaviour is triggered, the image selected is replaced by one contained in the chosen URL. If the Preload Images checkbox is ticked, the images will be downloaded with the page to ensure a smooth swap. If Restore Image onMouseOut is selected, the original image will be restored when the mouse moves away from the control. This is desirable if you are using the default mouseOver event to trigger the swap; otherwise, you may prefer to deselect this option, as we did in the present example.

The intention is that when a user clicks on one of the four small images down the left side of the page, the large image to the right will be replaced by a full-sized version of the thumbnail that was clicked. We prepared the four large images, all at the same size so they could be swapped without resizing or distortion, and, for each one, we also saved a scaled-down version to act as the thumbnail. The thumbnails were added to the page in the usual way, and the large version of the first image was added in the right column, and given the name main. All we then had to do was select each thumbnail in turn, and attach the Swap Image behaviour to it, with the event set to onClick. In each case, main was selected in the parameters dialogue and the URL was set to point to the full-sized image corresponding to the selected thumbnail.

┌─ TRY THIS ───┐

Make your own image gallery for your site, using Swap Image behaviours.

By attaching a behaviour to the body element triggered by the onKeyPress event, make the gallery revert to displaying the first image whenever the user presses a key. (The easiest way to select the body is by clicking its name in the tag structure display at the bottom of the document window.)

└──┘

The Spry Framework

Dreamweaver's newer mechanism for adding interactivity is based on a JavaScript library known as the *Spry framework*. There are three facets to this framework. *Spry effects* can be used to add simple visual effects to elements of a page, such as making them fade in or out. *Spry widgets* are user interface elements that go beyond the simple form elements provided by HTML, and more closely resemble some of the interface elements found in desktop applications. ***XML data sets*** are used to display data in the form of XML on the page. The data is retrieved from the server, where it may be generated dynamically by a script.

The technique of using JavaScript to retrieve and display XML data dynamically is referred to as *AJAX* (which stands for Asynchronous JavaScript and XML). The term's meaning is often extended to include any use of JavaScript to provide sophisticated interactivity, so Spry widgets and effects might also be included.

It should be apparent that over-use of effects can easily become tiresome, and that using non-standard interface elements is likely to confuse some visitors to your Web site. Retrieving data dynamically and using it to rewrite the page can also be confusing and lead to usability problems, such as an inability to bookmark a particular state of a page. Furthermore, AJAX has potential security problems, so for all of these reasons it should be used judiciously.

Unlike behaviours, which are copied into the HTML document when you add them, the JavaScript code for the Spry framework is kept in external files, which are referenced from the document. The first time you use a Spry effect, widget or XML data set, Dreamweaver will copy the relevant part of the Spry framework into your site.

XML data sets can only be used effectively as part of a Web application which includes server-side computation. Otherwise, they are largely redundant, and add unnecessary complications. An account of Web applications is beyond the scope of this book, so we will confine our description of the Spry framework to its effects and widgets.

Spry Effects

Spry effects are easy to use, but also easy to abuse. Before you make part of your page shake when the cursor rolls over it, you should ask yourself whether users are going to thank you for having done so. In fact, we would be hard pressed to find a compelling use for Spry effects, so we must resort to a somewhat contrived example.

Looking back at the image gallery in Figure 7.75, you can see that the thumbnail for the image currently being displayed is redundant – clicking it won't have any effect. Perhaps it would be a good idea to make it disappear, and perhaps it would be nice for it to fade out instead of just vanishing. One of the Spry effects, Appear/Fade can be used to achieve this.

Spry effects are applied as behaviours, using the procedure described earlier. They can be found on the Effects sub-menu of the pop-up menu used for adding behaviours. They are mostly time-based transitions, such as you might use in video editing, so they include a parameter that sets their duration, that is, the time it takes for the effect to occur. Figure 7.76 shows the parameter dialogue for the Appear/Fade effect. The other effects use similar dialogues.

Appear/Fade
Blind
Grow/Shrink
Highlight
Shake
Slide
Squish

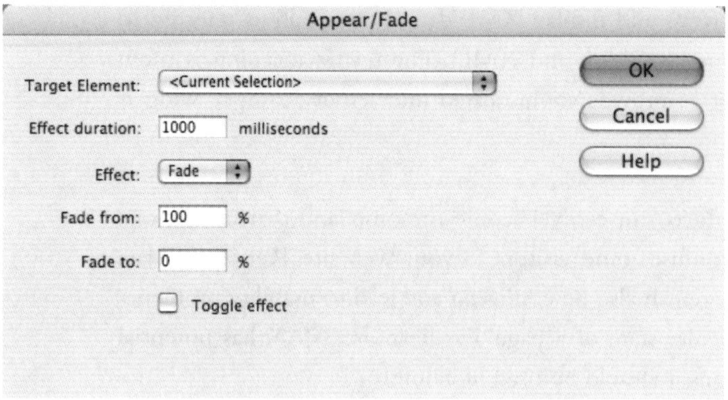

Appear/Fade

Target Element: <Current Selection>   OK

Effect duration: 1000   milliseconds   Cancel

Effect: Fade   Help

Fade from: 100   %

Fade to: 0   %

☐ Toggle effect

Figure 7.76 *Setting parameters for the* Appear/Fade *effect*

Remember that the element that you have selected will be the trigger for the effect. You still have to choose which element will be faded, and this is done with the Target Element pop-up menu at the top of the dialogue, which lists the values of the id attributes of any elements on the page which it would make sense to fade in or out. The default option is the current selection. For our example, this happens to be what we want. We therefore select each thumbnail in turn and apply the effect, with onClick as the event, so that any thumbnail will fade away when a user clicks on it.

The duration and intensity of the effect can be set, and you can choose whether to fade the target element in (Appear) or out (Fade) using the pop-up menu. If the Toggle event checkbox at the bottom of the dialogue is ticked, the first event will cause the chosen effect, the next will cause its opposite, and so on: alternate events will cause the target element to fade in and out.

This is easy, but less than useful. If we make a thumbnail fade when it is clicked, it will be out of the way while the corresponding image is displayed, but unless we do something more it will never come back. Toggling the effect is not appropriate in this case. We want the thumbnail to fade back in when any other thumbnail is clicked and fades out.

To do this, we attach three extra behaviours to each thumbnail, which make all the others fade in. In theory, this should work. When you click on the second thumbnail, for instance, it will fade out. If you then click on the first thumbnail, it will make the second fade back in again. Unfortunately, because of the way this effect works, it also makes the third and fourth vanish momentarily, before fading in. There appears to be no way to avoid this, which illustrates the pitfalls of using a general-purpose JavaScript framework, instead of writing your own scripts.

─TRY THIS─

Create a Web page with a mixture of textual elements and images. Experiment with applying Spry effects using various elements as the trigger and target, and using different events to invoke the effect. Try to think of useful ways of employing these effects.

Try adding Spry effects to the image gallery you created for the previous exercise, to make it more interesting.

Spry Widgets

The Spry widgets can be sub-divided into two classes: validation widgets and interaction widgets. The widgets in the first class are used to ensure that input entered into a form is valid, according to some criterion set by the form's designer. For instance, if a text field is supposed to hold an email address, you can use a validation widget instead of a plain text field, and stipulate that the text entered should have the form of a valid email address. The interaction widgets are used to provide user interface elements that plain HTML pages cannot offer, such as a set of tabbed panels (resembling a panel set in an Adobe CS3 application). These widgets are not just simple parameterized scripts, like behaviours. They consist of some HTML markup for creating the necessary page elements, some CSS for controlling their appearance, and some JavaScript for performing actions in response to events.

We will begin by describing validation widgets, which are the simpler type but illustrate some features which they share with the more elaborate interaction widgets.

Widgets are added using the Insert bar. The validation widgets can be found in both the Spry and Forms categories; the latter is more convenient if you mix them with ordinary form controls. There are four widgets, for text fields, text areas, checkboxes and select 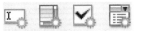 elements (lists or menus). You add them in the usual way, by clicking on their icons. (You cannot add widgets to a new document before you have saved it – Dreamweaver needs to know the document's location so it can determine where to copy the Spry library files.)

Because a validation widget incorporates a form control, the accessibility attributes dialogue from Figure 7.67 will be displayed when you insert one. Once the accessibility attributes have been set, the widget will be added to the document at the cursor. Figure 7.77 shows the way a text field widget, with a label, looks in the document window. As you can see, it has a flag attached to the top left corner which clearly distinguishes it from an ordinary text field. This flag is only visible when the widget is selected or the cursor is over it.

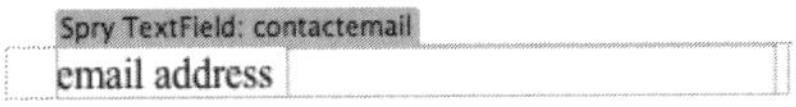

Spry TextField: contactemail

email address

Figure 7.77 *A text field widget in the document window*

The Properties panel is used to give the field a name (which is displayed in the flag) and to set its validity criteria. Figure 7.78 shows how you would set up a Spry text field that was to contain an email address.

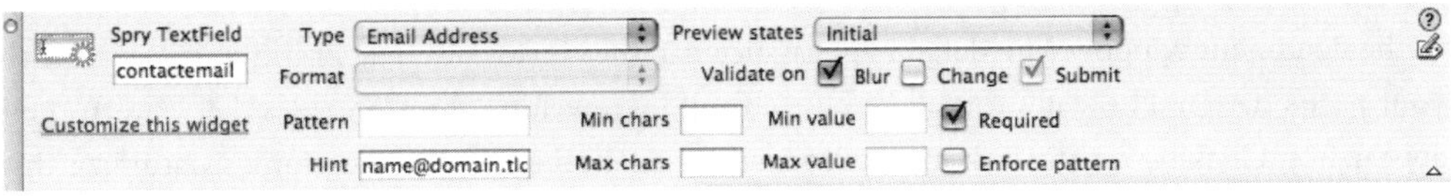

Spry TextField	Type	Email Address	Preview states	Initial		
contactemail	Format		Validate on ☑ Blur ☐ Change ☑ Submit			
Customize this widget	Pattern		Min chars	Min value	☑ Required	
	Hint	name@domain.tld	Max chars	Max value	☐ Enforce pattern	

Figure 7.78 *Setting up validation of an email address*

The **Type** pop-up menu provides a list of typical sorts of value that you might expect a user to enter. Choosing **Email Address** from this list makes Dreamweaver insert Spry code which checks that the text entered has the form of a valid email address – that is, that it contains a single @ character and a . with at least one character before and after it. (Note that this is not adequate to guarantee that the email address is real, or even feasible.) Similar checks can be inserted for URLs, IP addresses, dates, and so on. For some types, the **Format** pop-up can be used to choose a more specific type. For instance, if you choose **Date** as the type, you can choose whether to use North American, European or ISO formats, with two or four digits for the year. In the field labelled **Hint** at the bottom of the **Properties** panel you can enter a sample of the sort of value (for instance, name@domain.tld for an email address) to indicate to the user what is required.

The validation code will be executed in the browser, so there is a choice about when it should run. You can use the row of checkboxes labelled **Validate on**, at the right of the **Properties** panel, to specify the event or events that will trigger validation. If you only tick **Submit**, users will be able to enter invalid data in all the fields of a form as they go through it, and will only be told about invalid entries when they click the **Submit** button. Ticking **Blur** means that they will be informed as soon as the cursor moves out of the field being validated, while ticking **Change** means that validation will occur whenever a change is made to the data. This is usually too severe, because it does not allow fields to be in a partially filled-in state, unless that satisfies the validity criterion. The choice of whether to validate on **Submit** or **Blur** will depend on the nature of the form and the likelihood of people making errors or deliberately entering invalid data.

You can specify additional constraints on some types of data. For any type of textual input, you can specify a minimum and maximum number of characters, while for fields containing numbers you can specify minimum and maximum numerical values. You can also tick the **Required** box for fields that cannot be omitted. The checkbox labelled **Enforce pattern** causes the pattern to be checked during typing, and invalid characters to be rejected. For example, if you had set the type of a field to **Integer**, only digits could be entered in it.

A text field validation widget can be in one of four possible states: **Initial**, when the page first loads; **Required**, when a value that has been specified as required has not been entered; **Invalid Format**, when data that does not satisfy the validation criterion has been entered; and **Valid**, when valid data has been entered. You can see how a widget will appear in each of these states by selecting it from the pop-up menu labelled **Preview states**. The widget will be shown in the chosen state in the document window. The default appearance is rather lurid, and may not fit in too well with your page's design. The states can all be customized by rewriting the CSS rules that govern their appearance. Clicking on the link in the **Properties** panel consisting of the words **Customize this widget** doesn't actually let you customize the widget, but it does open the Help Viewer at a page describing the relevant rules. If you understand CSS, you will be able to change these rules, as we described previously, to give the widget a more suitable appearance.

The other validation widgets behave in a similar way, but with different, less elaborate, validation conditions, and fewer possible states. Each widget contains a conventional form control within it, so as well as setting up the validation, you must select the control and set its properties, just as you would if you were using the bare control in a form. For instance, if you insert a Spry **Select** widget, you must click on the list inside it and add the list values in the way we described previously.

If you are building a complete Web application, and are using Spry validation widgets for the user interface, it is important to understand that the client-side validation that they provide is no substitute for validating the data on the server. JavaScript validation checks can help users, by alerting them to errors before the form is submitted, and they can help prevent robots and mischievous users from submitting the form with nonsensical data, but it is always possible for somebody to turn off JavaScript in their browser, or to generate requests using some other program. In that case, the validation code will not be executed, and malformed data could be sent to the server, where it could cause trouble, unless the script on the server checks it.

---TRY THIS---

Redo the form you made at the end of the previous section, using Spry validation widgets wherever possible. Set appropriate validation conditions. Test the form by entering both invalid and valid data. Try using different settings for the Validate on conditions, and see how they affect the user's experience.

There are four types of interaction widget in all: **Menu Bar**, **Tabbed Panels**, **Accordion** and **Collapsible Panel**. The first of these, **Menu Bar**, is used for adding navbars with sub-navbars. The other three widget types are used to present information in a minimum of space, by allowing users to hide some of it. We will describe the **Tabbed Panels**  widget in some detail, since the other two information-hiding widgets resemble it. We will describe the **Menu Bar** widget more briefly, and leave you to investigate it fully for yourself.

Figure 7.79 shows a typical use of the **Tabbed Panels** widget. We have three sets of information about an image to present: the image itself, some details about the formats it is available in, and a form to add it to a shopping basket. If we were to put all this information on a single page, it would be long and tedious and would require scrolling. If we split the information over three pages, there would be a page refresh whenever the user moved between the three sets of information. By using a set of tabbed panels, however, we can confine the page to the size of a typical browser window, while avoiding page refreshes.

A **Tabbed Panels** widget is added from the **Spry** category of objects on the **Insert** bar. When it is first added to a document, it appears as shown in Figure 7.80. Like the validation widgets we described before, interaction widgets feature a blue flag, which you can use to select the widget as a whole.

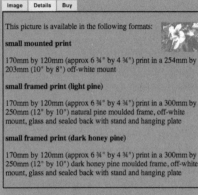

Figure 7.79 *Tabbed panels*

If you click in one of the tabs, which are initially labelled Tab 1 and Tab 2, and look at the tag structure display, you will see that the tabs are marked up as list items, and their appearance is due to some fancy CSS which comes as part of the widget. As a consequence of this way of doing things, you can change the label on any tab just by altering the text, as you would for any other list item. Similarly, the content of each tab is wrapped in a div element, so you can just replace the Content 1 placeholder with the material you want to display in the first tab, and apply markup and styling to it in the normal way. For the example in Figure 7.79, we added a level 1 heading, some text and an image, and created some CSS rules to lay them out as we wanted.

To add content to another tab you must bring it to the front: move the cursor over the tab heading (the label Tab 2 in a newly inserted Tabbed Panels widget). An eye icon will appear at the right of the tab. Clicking on this will bring the content area of the panel for this tab to the front, 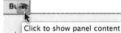 so you can add material to it as you did to the first panel.

Adding extra panels is done in the Properties panel, which is shown in Figure 7.81. Make sure that you have the whole widget selected, not just one of the individual panels, or you won't see the relevant properties. The process for adding panels should be familiar. The scrolling list in the middle of the Properties panel shows you all the tabs. The + button just above it is used to add a new tab and panel; the − button removes the selected panel, and the up and down triangles can be used to reorder the tabs. As an alternative to using the eye icon, you can bring a panel to the front by selecting it in this list.

The Default panel pop-up menu to the right also lists all the tabs' labels; select one to be displayed when the page is first loaded into a browser. Note that, if a user bookmarks the page containing the tabbed panels, this default panel will be displayed when they go back to the bookmarked page, no matter which panel was in front when the bookmark was created. This is a character- istic problem of pages that use JavaScript to control what is displayed: it is impossible to bookmark a particular state of the page.

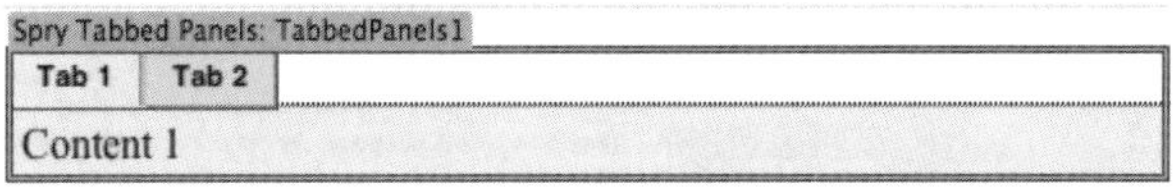

Figure 7.80 *Initial state of tabbed panels*

Unlike behaviours, Spry interaction widgets degrade gracefully when JavaScript is disabled or not supported. In the case of tabbed panels, the panels are displayed one above the other. A user without JavaScript will have to scroll, but all the information will be available to them, and they will be able to use any form controls on any panel.

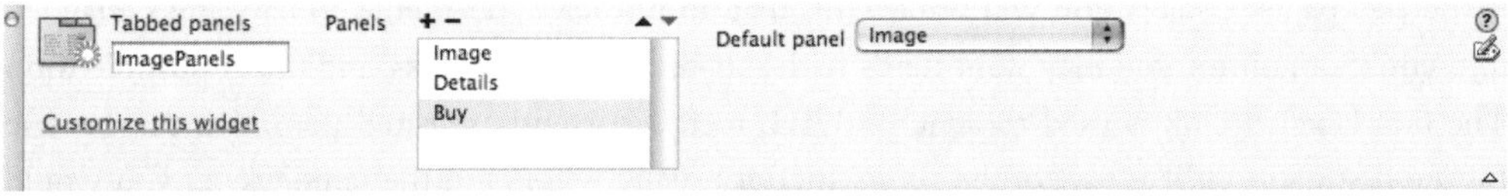

Figure 7.81 *Properties of a* Tabbed Panels *widget*

─TRY THIS───

Think about how you could effectively use a set of tabbed panels on your Web site, perhaps by combining content from several pages into one. Create a new page that uses tabbed panels in this way.

Investigate for yourself the accordion and collapsible panel widgets. Once you have mastered tabbed panels, you should find these easy. Try redoing the page you just made with tabbed panels using an accordion instead.

The Menu Bar widget is not vastly different from the other interaction widgets in the way it is inserted into a document and customized. The appearance in the document window of a partly built menu bar is illustrated in Figure 7.82. Each entry in the bar may have a sub-menu attached to it, and each of the entries in a sub-menu may have a sub-sub-menu attached to it. No further levels of menu hierarchy are possible, but usability considerations suggest that this is a good thing.

The Properties panel with this Menu Bar widget selected is shown in Figure 7.83. Instead of the single list pane that we saw in the case of the Tabbed Panels widget, there are three list panes, one for each level of the menu. They work in the same way, though, with the + and − buttons being used to add and remove items,

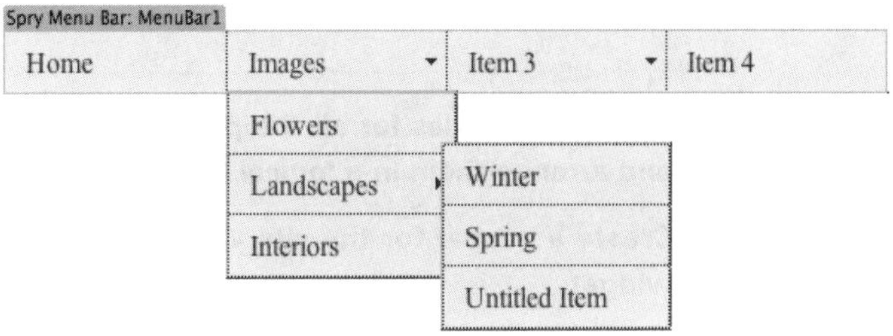

Figure 7.82 *A* Menu Bar *widget*

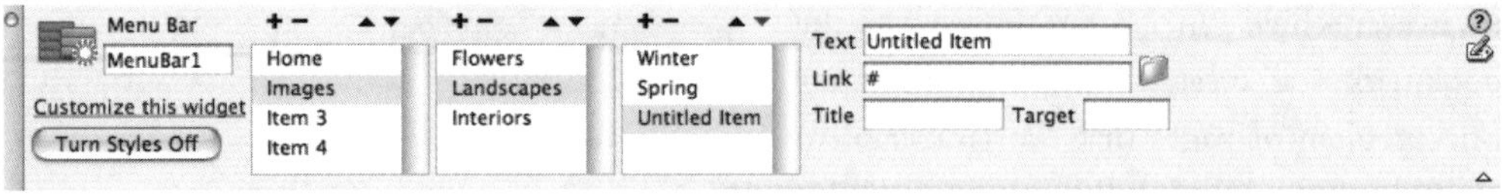

Figure 7.83 *Properties of a* Menu Bar *widget*

and the up and down triangles used to change their order. If you want to add a sub-menu or a sub-sub-menu, you select the menu item it is to be attached to, and add a new item in the pane to its right.

You set the text of each item by entering it in the field labelled Text at the top right of the Properties panel. Usually, you will want items that do not have sub-menus to have links attached to them. (Sometimes, you may want items with sub-menus to have links, and this is possible too.) The box labelled Link is used to attach a URL to the currently selected item. You can browse for the destination if it is part of the site (which it usually will be) in the same way as you would when attaching a link to some text. The Title box can be used to add a title attribute to the link. On most browsers, the text of this attribute will pop up as a tool tip when the cursor is over the item; screen readers may read the title, which should provide enough information for a user to decide whether the link is worth following. Do not use the box labelled Target.

Menu bars are marked up as nested lists, in accordance with current ideas about the best markup for navbars. This means that you don't have to restrict yourself to plain textual entries in the menus. You can use small images (providing you specify a textual alternative) or apply extra styling with CSS. You can even apply a Swap Image behaviour to an image inside a menu, but we don't recommend it.

For anything more elaborate than simple text, you will need to insert the item's content in the document window. To make it easier to see what you are doing, you can turn off the menu bar styling – so that the items are displayed as a plain list – by clicking the button labelled Turn Styles Off. This only affects the display in the document window, it doesn't alter the way the menu appears in a browser.

TRY THIS

Write down titles for all the pages that you think should be in your Web site, and arrange them in a logical hierarchical order.

Create a navbar for the site which reflects this hierarchy, using the Menu Bar widget.

Create dummy pages, add links to the navbar menu and copy it to each of the pages. Preview the site, and use the menu to navigate around it.

Spry widgets are a considerable improvement over the old behaviours as a means of adding JavaScript-based interaction to pages. They should be used with some caution, though. The Spry framework is relatively new – it was only made widely available with the release of Dreamweaver CS3. It may well contain bugs. Sites that use Spry should therefore be tested extensively.

DON'T FORGET

JavaScript can be used to make pages respond to events such as mouse clicks and rollovers.

Use JavaScript judiciously – a significant number of users disable it in their browsers, and some mobile devices do not support it.

Behaviours are fairly crude pre-built parameterized scripts that cause some action to occur when a specified event happens.

Select an element, add a behaviour in the Behaviors panel, set parameters and choose an event to trigger the action.

Use the Swap Image behaviour to create remote rollovers and image galleries.

The Spry framework is a JavaScript library that provides effects, interaction widgets and XML data sets.

Add Spry effects in the same way as behaviours. The time-based effects include a duration parameter.

Use validation widgets to ensure that values entered into text fields, text areas, checkboxes and select elements are valid. Client-side validation is not a substitute for server-side validation.

Add a widget using the Insert bar. Select widgets using the blue flag attached to their top left corner.

Set validation criteria in the Properties panel.

Use the Tabbed Panels, Accordion and Collapsible Panel widgets to present information in a compact form.

Add content to the tab and panel of a Tabbed Panels widget in the usual way.

Click on the eye icon in a tab to bring its panel to the front for adding content.

Add extra panels in the Properties panel.

Use the menu bar widget to add hierarchical navigation menus to pages.

Add menu items and sub-menus in the Properties panel.

Set the text of plain menu entries in the Properties panel, or add content to the list items making up the menu for more elaborate entries.

Sites

Web pages are rarely created in isolation. The concept of a Web site as a collection of related pages is a familiar one. A Web site can easily grow to include a hundred or many more individual pages. Keeping track of changes, ensuring that all the links between pages remain valid and, where appropriate, maintaining a consistent style throughout the site can become major problems for large sites. Dreamweaver provides various site management tools to help.

Local and Remote Sites

Most Web sites are not developed on the machine which ultimately hosts them. Instead, they are built on a designer's machine and **uploaded** to a server when they are ready. Similarly, updates will be performed and tested away from the server and then uploaded. Dreamweaver incorporates this model of site development in its facilities for site management. The first step in constructing a site is to create a **local site**, which you use to keep track of the files on the machine where the site is being developed. The local site can be associated with a **remote site** – usually on a different machine, and quite possibly in a completely different geographical location – from which the files are served to the Internet.

We showed how to set up a local site using the Site Wizard at the very beginning of this chapter. You will remember that you created a site by selecting the Site>New Site... menu command, which opened the Site Wizard. Previously, we only gave the site a name and selected the local folder. You could also specify the remote location and connection details by working through the wizard, but if you understand the questions you can just as easily go straight to the **Advanced** tab of the dialogue and enter the necessary data directly. You can bring up this dialogue for a site you have already defined, in order to add to or change the information, using the Site>Manage Sites... command. In the dialogue box that opens, select the site whose details you want to edit from the list displayed, and click Edit....

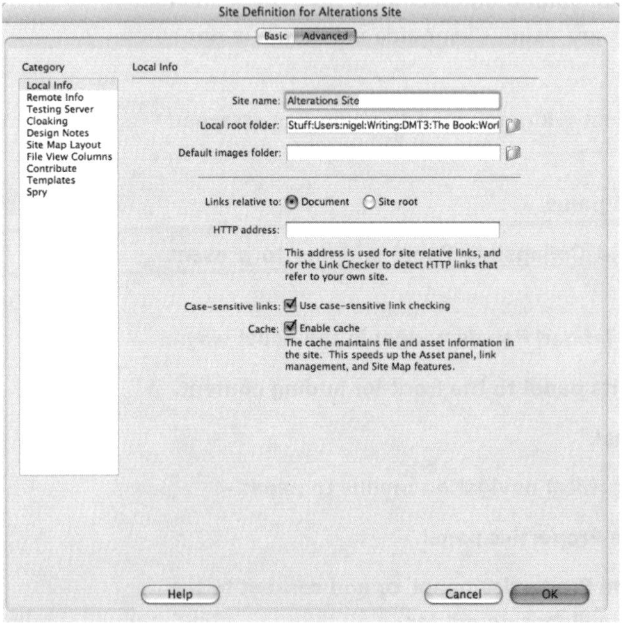

In Advanced mode, the dialogue is arranged into several categories, in the same way as the Page Properties or CSS Rule Definition dialogues. It may look intimidating at first, but you only really need to deal with two

Figure 7.84 *Local site information*

of the categories for most ordinary sites. The Local Info category, shown in Figure 7.84, is where you set the information for the local folder, which we previously provided via the Site Wizard. You can give the site a name to help you identify it when you are working on several sites, and select or create the folder to hold all the site's files locally while you work on them. Leave the Document radio button selected as the value for Links relative to, unless you know what you're doing and have a good reason to use URLs relative to the site's root. The HTTP address field is used to enter the URL where the site will be kept when it is uploaded. It is not necessary to specify this URL (you might not even know it when you create the local site), but if you do so, Dreamweaver can check links more effectively. You should check the box labelled Case-sensitive links if you know that the server where your site will be held distinguishes between upper-case and lower-case in URLs. (Unix systems do.) Creating a local cache speeds up some site management operations, but like all caching technology it can cause problems, so you may find it better to leave this box unchecked. If you do let Dreamweaver use a cache, you will find that after certain operations it will warn you that the cache is being rebuilt. This is normal and no cause for alarm.

Entering the Local Info is sufficient to create a local site, and this is all you need to do before you start working on HTML documents. You can also set up the details of the remote site at the same time, or add them later using the Site>Define Sites... command to return to the dialogue.

The Remote Info category initially contains only a pop-up menu from which you can select the server access mode. The initial value is None, which you could use during development if you did not yet know the details of where the site was to be hosted. The alternatives are Local/Network for sites that are served over a local area network, FTP for sites that are held on a remote machine and updated using the FTP protocol to transfer files from the local site, WebDAV, RDS and (on Windows only) Microsoft Visual SourceSafe. Each of these last three is for sites that are accessed by the corresponding protocols for collaborative working.

FTP is the most common case for sites hosted on the Internet, but it is relatively complex to set up. If you select FTP from the Access pop-up menu, fields are displayed in which you can enter the information needed to connect to the remote host. (See Figure 7.85.)

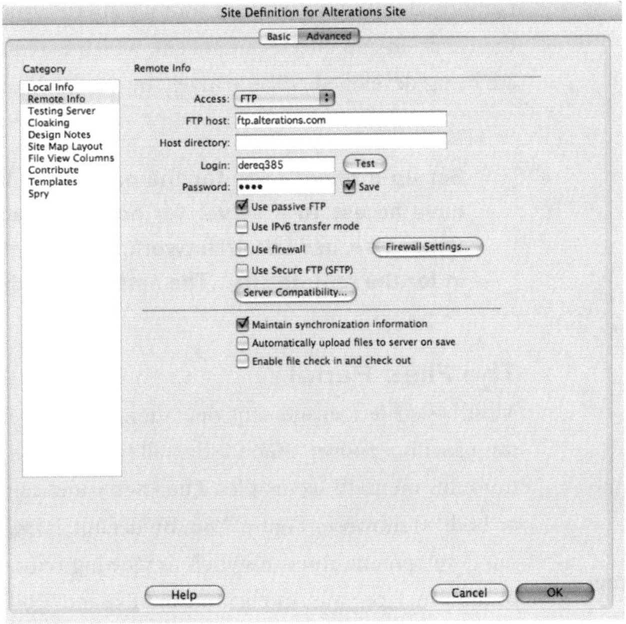

Figure 7.85 *Remote site information for FTP access*

The values for FTP Host (its URL), Host directory, Login and Password depend on the way the server has been set up. You can usually leave the Directory field blank. Ticking the Save checkbox next to the password field means that you will not have to type the password every time Dreamweaver connects to the server. This is convenient, but may be a security risk on a shared machine. When you have filled in these fields, click the Test button, and Dreamweaver will attempt to connect to the server, using the values you have supplied. If the attempt is unsuccessful, you probably entered some value incorrectly.

If you maintain the server yourself, you will have had to create the domain and user, and set the password; the directory will often be determined by the server's global configuration. If the site is to be served from a Web hosting provider, or a client's own servers, you will need to obtain the necessary information from the site administrator. Similarly, you should consult whoever is in charge of your network administration to see which values to tick in the four checkboxes below the password.

If you select a value other than FTP for the access method, you will only have to enter a subset of these values, or their equivalent. The three checkboxes at the bottom of the dialogue, below the line, are common to all the possible access methods. If you tick Maintain synchronization information, Dreamweaver will store information that enables it to only upload changed files, to save time when the site is updated. The option Automatically upload ... on save means that changes you have made will be propagated to the server immediately whenever you save a file. This is a fairly reckless way to proceed, and we advise against ticking this checkbox. The last box enables the check-in and check-out system, which is required to prevent conflicting updates when sites are being developed collaboratively by a team. We will say a little more about this system shortly.

┌─TRY THIS───

Set up a remote site for the pages you have developed in this chapter. If you have access to a server for hosting Web sites, use FTP as the access mode. Otherwise, use Local/Network, having set up a folder on your machine to stand in for the remote site. (The settings for this access mode are trivial.)

└──

The Files Panel

Most basic site management operations can be carried out in the Files panel. At the top left of this panel is a pop-up menu listing all the sites you have defined in Dreamweaver. You select a site from this menu to see its files. The Files panel can be configured to show local files, remote files or both, as shown in Figure 7.86. By default, it only shows local files, which is convenient during site development. You can switch to viewing remote files using the pop-up menu at the top right of the panel, or you can click on the Expand/Collapse view button to see local and remote sites side by side. When you do this, the panel jumps out from its docked position and occupies the centre of the screen. This view is most convenient when you are updating a site.

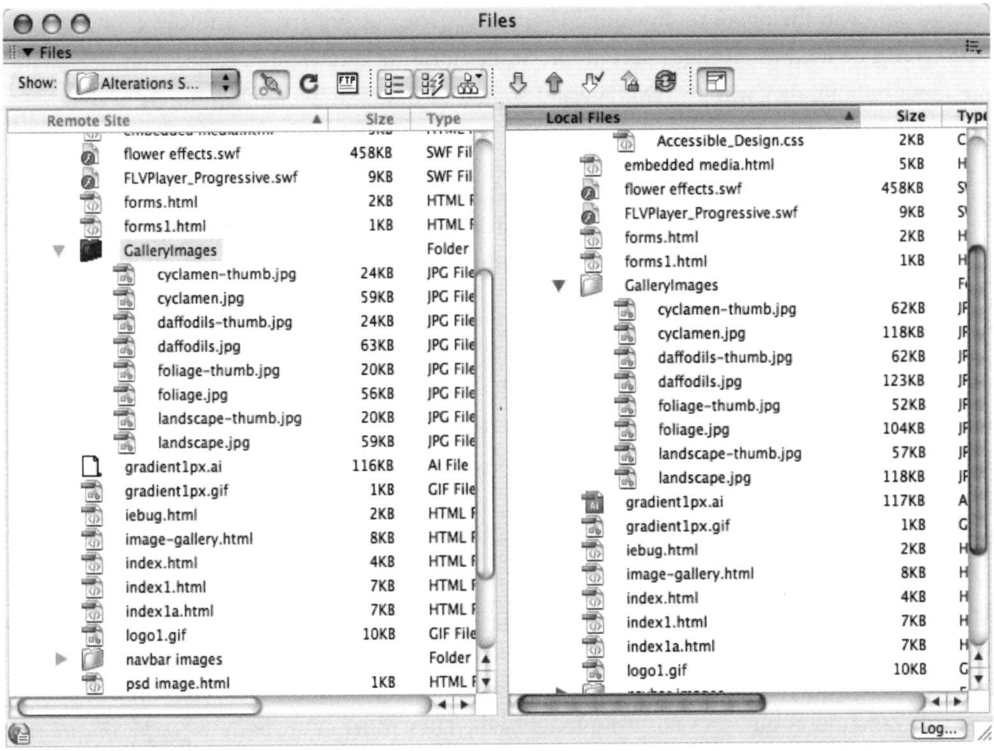

Remote Site	▲	Size	Type		Local Files	▲	Size	Typ
					Accessible_Design.css		2KB	C
flower effects.swf		458KB	SWF Fil		embedded media.html		5KB	H
FLVPlayer_Progressive.swf		9KB	SWF Fil		flower effects.swf		458KB	S\
forms.html		2KB	HTML F		FLVPlayer_Progressive.swf		9KB	S\
forms1.html		1KB	HTML F		forms.html		2KB	H
▼ GalleryImages			Folder		forms1.html		1KB	H
cyclamen-thumb.jpg		24KB	JPG File		▼ GalleryImages			F
cyclamen.jpg		59KB	JPG File		cyclamen-thumb.jpg		62KB	JF
daffodils-thumb.jpg		24KB	JPG File		cyclamen.jpg		118KB	JF
daffodils.jpg		63KB	JPG File		daffodils-thumb.jpg		62KB	JF
foliage-thumb.jpg		20KB	JPG File		daffodils.jpg		123KB	JF
foliage.jpg		56KB	JPG File		foliage-thumb.jpg		52KB	JF
landscape-thumb.jpg		20KB	JPG File		foliage.jpg		104KB	JF
landscape.jpg		59KB	JPG File		landscape-thumb.jpg		57KB	JF
gradient1px.ai		116KB	AI File		landscape.jpg		118KB	JF
gradient1px.gif		1KB	GIF File		gradient1px.ai		117KB	A
iebug.html		2KB	HTML F		gradient1px.gif		1KB	G
image-gallery.html		8KB	HTML F		iebug.html		2KB	H
index.html		4KB	HTML F		image-gallery.html		8KB	H
index1.html		7KB	HTML F		index.html		4KB	H
index1a.html		7KB	HTML F		index1.html		7KB	H
logo1.gif		10KB	GIF File		index1a.html		7KB	H
▶ navbar images			Folder		logo1.gif		10KB	G
psd image.html		1KB	HTML F					

Figure 7.86 *The* Files *panel*

You can only see files on the remote site if you are connected to it. The button resembling a disconnected plug in the toolbar at the top of the panel is used to make connections. When Dreamweaver is connected to the remote site, the remote files are displayed. The button changes to look as if it had been plugged in. Clicking on it in this state closes the connection.

The files in each site are shown in a list; folders can be expanded by clicking on the small triangles beside their names, in the familiar way. Information about the size, type and modification date of each file is shown. The panes can be resized by dragging the bar that separates them.

Many people like to use the Files panel as a control centre for work on a site. If you double-click a file's name in the Files panel it will open in the document window. You can add files and folders to the site using the commands on the File sub-menu of the Files panel menu. The newly created folder or file is placed in the same folder as the file currently selected in the Files panel.

Files can be deleted from either the local site or the remote site by simply selecting them and pressing delete, and they can be moved between folders by dragging and dropping. When this is done, Dreamweaver offers to scan the site and update any links to the file that has been moved, to reflect its new location. Drag and drop can also be used to copy files from the local to the remote site or in the opposite direction. Alternatively, the Put (up arrow) and Get (down arrow) buttons can be used to transfer selected files to the local or remote sites, respectively. When you use these buttons, files will be automatically copied to the corresponding position in the folder hierarchy in the other site.

┌─ TRY THIS ───

Organize your local site into folders if it is not organized that way already. Practise using the Files panel to move and copy files between folders. Put some or all of the files on the remote site.

Many Web sites are created and maintained by teams of designers and developers working together. Allowing more than one member of a team to make independent updates to the same site is potentially a recipe for chaos, but it is not practical to expect every update to be done by the same team member. Dreamweaver incorporates a simple check-in/check-out system to prevent more than one person working on the same file at once.

The system must be enabled in the Remote Info pane of the New Site dialogue in Advanced mode, which we described earlier. (See Figure 7.85.) If you tick the Check in/out checkbox, you must provide a Check out name for yourself; this name will be displayed in the Files panel of anybody working on the site, to show who has checked out any files that are being modified. You may also provide your email address, which will be displayed as an underlined link in their Files panel, so that they can easily send you messages. If you want to check files out automatically when you open them, you must not only tick the Check out files when opening checkbox; you must ensure that you always open files from the Files panel. Using the File>Open... command instead will by-pass the checking out process.

With the check-in/check-out system enabled, you can use the Check Out and Check In buttons on the Files panel instead of Get and Put. If you select a file from the remote site and click the Check Out button it is locked so that nobody else can work on it – they will see a red mark indicating that it has been checked out, and your check-out name to show who has done so. After working on the file, you can check it in again, making it available to other people to work on. The modified version of the file is put back on the remote site and your local copy is locked – so now you can make no further changes without checking it out again.

More sophisticated support for collaborative working on Web sites is provided by the *WebDAV* (Web-based Distributed Authoring and Versioning) protocol, **RDS** (Remote Development Services) and Microsoft's Visual SourceSafe system. All of these are systems for facilitating collaborative Web site development; they are more secure than Dreamweaver's built-in check-out system.

WebDAV is an open standard, implemented in several Web server programs, including Apache. RDS is part of Adobe's ColdFusion application server, Visual SourceSafe is a Microsoft proprietary system – only available on Windows – which requires a client to be installed on the local machine, as well as software on the server. If you wish to use any of these systems, you specify them in the **Server Access** pop-up menu in the **Remote Info** category of the **New Site** dialogue. A button labelled **Settings…** appears, and clicking on it opens a dialogue box in which you can enter the appropriate server address, password and other information required to use the system you have chosen. After that, the **Check Out** and **Check In** buttons use the protocol you have specified instead of Dreamweaver's own less robust system.

TRY THIS

If it is feasible in your work environment, set up your site for collaborative working and give some other people access to it. (It would be adequate to use network access over a local area network.)

Enable the check-out/check-in system as described, and experiment with working on the site at the same time as other people.

As we mentioned when describing the document window, there is a drop-down menu of file operations on the **Document** toolbar. The buttons on this menu can be used to transfer the document which is currently open in the document window to the server, or check it in. You can also retrieve or check out a more recent version of the file. Working directly with remote files like this can be convenient when making small updates, but it carries obvious risks; for major changes it is safer to save files locally and check them thoroughly before uploading. A useful little extra command on this menu is **Locate in Site**, which causes the open file to be selected in the **Files** panel.

Synchronization

Most Web sites will need to be updated from time to time, and some need updating frequently. In a typical update, some pages will be changed, others may be removed and new ones inserted. This work will be done on the designer's machine, that is, in the local site. It is only necessary to upload files that have changed during the update. When more than one person is working on a site, it may be the case that some files on the remote site have been changed more recently than those on the local site, and it will be necessary to download them to bring the local collection up to date. Keeping track of which pages have been changed is tedious – the sort of job best left to computers. You can quickly tell which files on the local site are newer than ones on the remote site, or vice versa, using the **Select Newer Local** and **Select Newer Remote** commands, which can be found on the **Edit** sub-menu of the **Files** panel menu. (Using these commands will cause a connection to be opened to the remote site if it is not already connected.)

Most likely, as well as finding out which files are out of synch between the local and remote sites, you will want to *synchronize* the two, so that they both contain the most recent versions of the same files. To do this, click the **Synchronize** button on the **Files** panel. When you do so, the dialogue shown in Figure 7.87 asks you whether you wish to synchronize the entire site, or just selected files and folders, and in which direction you wish files to be transferred. When you click

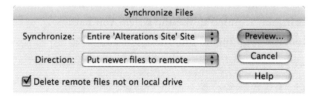

Figure 7.87 *Synchronization options*

on **Preview**, the sites are scanned, a process which may take some time for large sites. After the scan is complete, a window, such as the one shown in Figure 7.88, is displayed showing you which files will be transferred. The icon that appears in the **Action** column next to each file's path name indicates what will be done with that file. In a situation where you were working on your own and only changing files on the local site, you would see **Put** icons next to all the files you had changed (as you can see for almost all the files shown in Figure 7.88). Files that have not been changed do not appear in the list, because they should be left where they are.

You can select any file in the list and use one of the buttons at the bottom of the dialogue box to change the operation that Dreamweaver will perform when it actually does the synchronization. In particular, you can tell it to ignore some files. Here, we have chosen not to upload the file gradient1px.ai. The comment in the final (**Status**) column tells us this.

After you have scutinized the preview and marked any files that you want ignored you click **OK** and the sites are brought up to date. There is no way to by-pass the previewing step and

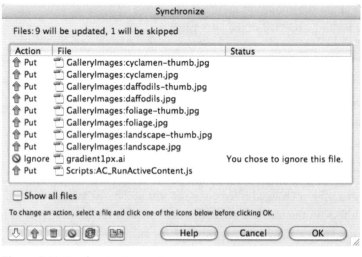

Figure 7.88 *Synchronization preview*

synchnronize immediately, which is probably a good thing. The FTP client in Dreamweaver is surprisingly slow compared to some dedicated FTP programs, so the synchronization may take an appreciable amount of time.

It's quite likely that there will be certain types of file that you would never want uploaded to the remote site, but which you would want to keep within the local site. For example, if you used Photoshop or Illustrator to prepare graphics which you exported as JPEGs or GIFs, you would probably find it convenient to keep the original Illustrator or Photoshop files with the rest of the site, but you wouldn't want to upload them. You could tell Dreamweaver to ignore them whenever you synchronized the site, as we just described, but you can also tell it to ignore all files of a particular type. This exclusion of file types is called *cloaking*.

Cloaking can be set up when you create the site, or at a later date, using the Site>Manage Sites… command. There is a dedicated Cloaking category in the Advanced pane of the dialogue, as shown in Figure 7.89. Cloaking needs to be enabled, by ticking the checkbox. You can then enter a set of file extensions in the text field at the bottom of the dialogue, to exclude those file types from synchronization operations. Here we have excluded Photoshop and Illustrator files, and Flash documents.

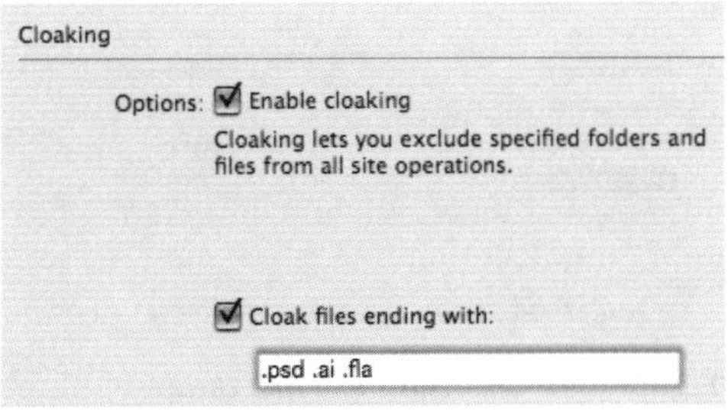

Figure 7.89 *Cloaking*

If you organize your work by folders, you can cloak certain folders as well as – or instead of – specific file types. Select the folder in the Files panel and use the Site>Cloaking>Cloak command on the panel menu. (This command does not appear on the main Site menu.) For cloaked folders, this command turns into Uncloak, as you would expect. You cannot cloak individual files, only folders or all files with a specific extension.

> ┌─TRY THIS──────────────────────────────
> **Make some changes to your local site and then synchronize the remote site with the local one, excluding any files you don't want uploaded.**
>
> **Enable cloaking and exclude any file types or folders you don't want to upload. Make some more changes and synchronize the site again.**

Link Checking

In most conventionally organized Web sites, it should be possible to reach any page of the site by following links. Files that cannot be reached are said to be *orphaned*. Files usually become orphaned due to a mistake, and so it is helpful to be able to track them down. It is even more helpful to be able to identify *broken links* – that is, links which have relative URLs that do not point to any file in the site. Again, these often occur as the result of simple errors made by the site designer. The command Site>Check Links Sitewide causes Dreamweaver to find orphaned files and broken links for you. It will also find and display any *external links* – ones which point outside the site. These are not checked automatically by Dreamweaver, even if you are online, so you must follow them yourself to verify that they are working. (There are utilities and Web-based services available which will verify links for you, including external ones.)

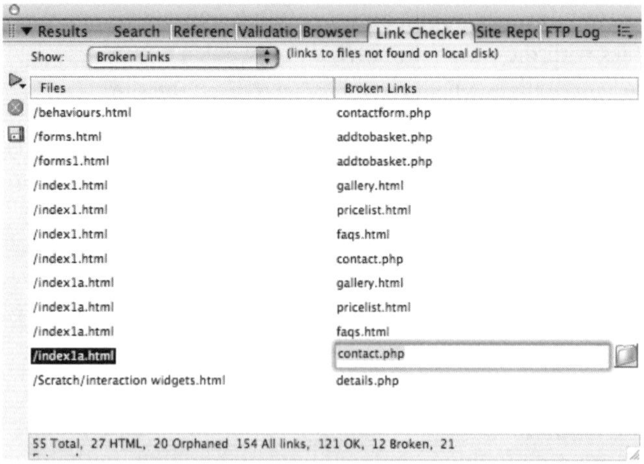

Figure 7.90 *The results of a link check*

After Dreamweaver has checked a site's links, the Results panel opens, to show what it found in its Link Checker pane, as shown in Figure 7.90. The pop-up menu at the top, labelled Show, allows you to see broken links, orphaned files or external links. If you choose to display broken links you can fix them directly in this pane. Simply select the link destination (in the right-hand column, as shown for the file **contact.php** in Figure 7.90) and then either type in the correct name in its place or use the folder button that appears on the right to navigate to the correct file.

If you have a file open in the document window, you can check that particular file for broken links, orphans and external links by simply using the menu command File>Check Links.

┌─ TRY THIS ───┐
│ **Check all the links in your site. If no errors are found, move or rename some files** │
│ **(but don't let Dreamweaver update links when you do so) and check again. Fix** │
│ **any broken links that you find in either case.** │
└───┘

Assets and Templates

In most non-trivial Web sites, certain elements are used repeatedly to establish a uniform style. For example, a company logo or a standard navigation bar may appear in the same position on every page; a particular background image may be attached to all the pages, or a standard disclaimer may be included on every page from which files may be downloaded, and so on. There is already an element of reusability in a Web site, since images and so on are included by reference: if you keep a single copy of each image so that you always use the same URL wherever it is used, any changes made to an image will appear on every page that uses it.

The Assets Panel

Dreamweaver uses its Assets panel, shown in Figure 7.91, to help you keep track of all the images, movies and other reusable items in your site, including any colours you have used and the URLs attached to all the links in the site. The panel lists every such asset. It is divided into categories for each of the types of object you might use. The row of buttons down the left-hand side allows you to select a category to display. (Use the tooltips if you are not sure what the icons represent.) When you select an asset, it is displayed in the preview area at the top of the panel. You can add it to a

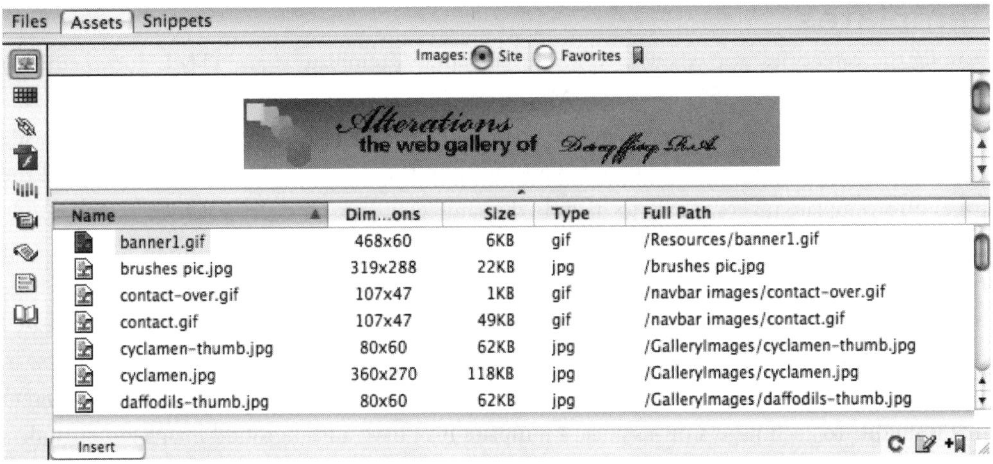

Figure 7.91 *The* Assets *panel showing images*

document at the insertion point by dragging it from the panel or clicking on the Insert button, and you can start up an application to edit it by double-clicking it or clicking on the Edit icon in the bottom right corner of the Assets panel. You can build up a collection of favourite assets, for those images and so on which you use frequently, by selecting an asset and clicking the Add to Favorites icon (to the right of the Edit icon). You can display either favourite assets or all the assets of the site – within a category, such as images – using the radio buttons at the top of the panel.

The Assets panel does not always get updated when you add new assets to the site, so you may need to click the Refresh button at the bottom to get a view of all the assets currently available.

Bridge, which we described in Chapter 3, can be especially useful for constructing Web sites. It provides an alternative to the Assets panel for browsing a site's assets, but it has more powerful facilities for organizing and searching assets and for tagging them with metadata. You can drag files in appropriate formats directly from Bridge into the document window in Dreamweaver, or add them to an open document using the File>Place>In Dreamweaver command available in Bridge. For image files, this will have the same effect as inserting them using the Insert bar. In particular, if you add a Photoshop file this way, the optimization dialogue (as described in Chapter 8) will appear. If you place an HTML file, it will be added as a link (with the file name as the link text) at the cursor in the open document in Dreamweaver.

┌─ TRY THIS ───┐
│   │
│   **Open the Assets panel and refresh it to show all the assets for your site. Examine** │
│   **the assets in each category. Add some images to a page using the Assets panel** │
│   **instead of the Insert bar. Compare using the Assets panel with using Bridge to** │
│   **manage and insert assets.** │
│   │
└───┘

Templates

Among the categories of assets you will find ***templates***. A template is an HTML document that can be used as the basis of many pages. Most Web sites have a unified appearance – that is, the pages resemble each other, which conveys a sense of the site as a single entity. Using site-wide style sheets helps impose uniformity on typography and some elements of layout. Basing all the pages on a template makes it easy to include the same elements on every page.

A template will usually contain some ***locked regions***, which cannot normally be edited in any page based on the template, and some ***editable regions***, which can be changed in every document based on the template. The locked regions will contain those page elements that you want to appear in an identical form on every page of the site, while the editable regions are available for the content that is unique to each page. For instance, a template may have a background image and include a navigation bar and a company logo, which should appear in the same position on every page in the site. These would be made into locked regions. Editable regions would be provided to contain the text and images of each individual document.

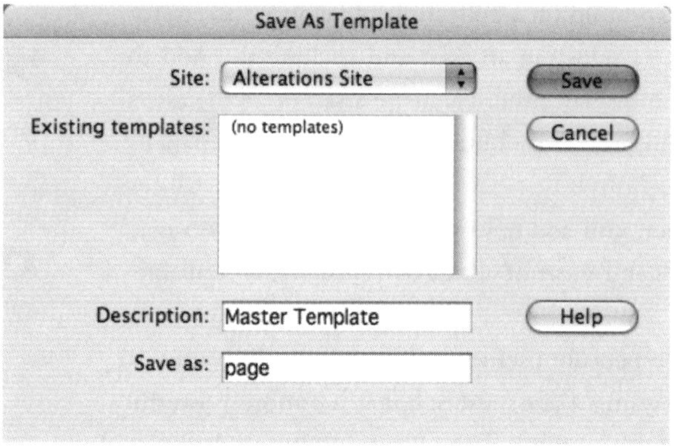

Figure 7.92 *Saving a template*

The most straightforward way to create a template is to make a document in the normal way, as if you were creating an ordinary page, and use the File>Save as Template… command to save it as a template. When you do so, you won't see the normal file-saving dialogue. Instead, the dialogue shown in Figure 7.92 appears. You can give the template a name (don't give it an extension, .dwt will be added automatically) and add a short description to remind yourself what the template should be used for. You can also choose a site to use the template in, from the pop-up menu at the top.

When you click Save in this dialogue, a prompt appears asking you whether you want Dreamweaver to update the links in the template. You will almost certainly want the links to be updated. This is because the destination of links that use relative URLs depends on the location of the file the link appears in – that's what makes them relative. When you base a new document on a template, it is therefore necessary to make sure that all the relative URLs on links in the template are rewritten to make them work within the new document. Dreamweaver does this by assuming that URLs in templates are relative to the location of the template itself. Therefore, when you turn a document into a template, the links must be updated to reflect the template's location and not just copied from the original document.

Template files are stored in a special Templates folder within the local site. You don't usually need to think about this, because you can open templates from the Assets panel, but you should be aware that the Templates folder is there. Don't move templates out of this folder, or they won't work any more.

When you are working on a template, Dreamweaver displays the string <<Template>> prominently in the document window's title bar to remind you of the fact.   `<<Template>> page.dwt (XHTML)`

When you first save a file as a template, all of it is locked, so you must add some editable regions. The Common category of the Insert bar includes a Templates menu, where you will find an Editable Region button. When you click this, an editable region is created at the cursor. You are prompted for a name for it. The region is not an HTML element itself, and it can be within any element. For instance, in Figure 7.93, we have added two editable regions to a template. The one on the left, labelled MainContent, was placed in the body of the document, the other, labelled RightBar, is inside a div element that has been floated to the right to make a sidebar. Note that the div itself is outside the region. This means that when a document is created from the template, content can be placed within the sidebar, but the container itself cannot be modified or deleted.

To create a document based on a template, use the normal File>New command but choose Page from Template at the left of the dialogue box. The next column will then show you a list of all the sites you have presently defined in Dreamweaver; when you select one of these, a list of all the templates for that site appears to its right. You can choose a template from the list to serve as the basis of your new document. Ticking the checkbox labelled Update page when template changes ensures that any alterations you make to the locked regions by editing the template file will propagate into the new document based on it. This is usually the most convenient arrangement.

The new document then opens as a copy of the template, showing all its locked and editable regions. You can now replace the place holders in the editable regions with content specific to your document. You will not be able to edit the locked parts of the document. On the other hand, if you edit the template (double-click its name in the templates category of the Assets panel),

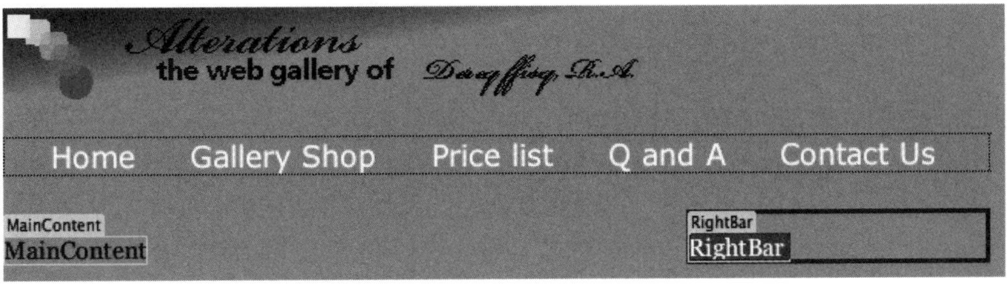

Figure 7.93 *Editable regions in a template*

any changes will be propagated to all the documents based on it. (You will be asked whether you wish to update all pages that use the template whenever you save it.) Thus, if you build your site from one or more templates, making global changes, such as swapping the site logo for a new version, can be done just by editing the template.

Templates can be even more useful if you nest them, that is, if you create templates which are themselves based on templates. For example, if only some pages in a site feature a sidebar, you could make a template for the whole site with no sidebar. For example, in Figure 7.93, the RightBar region could be omitted. This reduced template could be saved as PageWithNoSidebar. For any pages that did need a sidebar, a new template, PageWithSidebar, could be made, based on PageWithNoSidebar, with the addition of the RightBar region. Pages with and without sidebars could be created from PageWithNoSidebar and PageWithSidebar, respectively. This sounds rather complex in explanation, but is really quite straightforward in practice.

Creating a nested template is done by combining the procedure for creating a document based on a template with the procedure for saving a document as a template. That is, you make a new document, selecting Page from Template in the New File dialogue and choosing the base template. You then add new locked and editable regions, and use the File>Save as Template… command to save the nested template. This can then be used as the basis of new documents, or even new templates. Changes to either the base template or the nested template will be propagated to all documents based on the nested template, as you would hope.

TRY THIS

Create a template with an image in the top left corner of the page, a standard heading, and some areas to hold different text on each page. Create some pages based on the template.

Change the image in the template and verify that the image in each file created from it changes too.

Rebuild your Web site using templates to maintain the elements of layout and design which are common to all the pages. Where you have pages which share some additional common features, use nested templates.

DON'T FORGET

Select the server access mode and then set up connection details for a remote site. For FTP, provide the host's URL, the site's root directory and the login name and password for connecting.

Use the Files panel to manage files and folders on the local and remote sites.

Enable Check in/out to prevent conflicts when sites are being developed and maintained by more than one person.

Synchronize the local and remote sites so that they contain identical files.

Use the link checker to find broken links, orphaned files and external links.

Use the Assets panel or Bridge to keep track of all the images, movies and reusable items on the site.

Base documents on templates to include the same elements on every page.

Templates contain locked regions, which cannot be changed, and editable regions, to contain content that is unique for each page.

Use nested templates as the basis of subsets of the site.

WHAT ELSE?

We explained right at the beginning of this chapter that Dreamweaver has a lot of features that we have not described, because they are no longer considered good practice in Web design. This means that, as you look around at the menu commands and buttons on the Insert bar, you will see some things that are not mentioned in this book. As you learn more about Web technologies, you may find that some additional features become useful to you, but you can go a long way just using basic markup and the CSS Styles panel.

Dreamweaver aspires to be a tool for Web application development, as well as Web design. If you are using server-side technologies such as ASP or ColdFusion, you may find that Dreamweaver helps you integrate server-side computation with page design, but these features go well beyond the scope of this book.

If you are a Web developer, and understand HTML, CSS, JavaScript and some languages used for server-side computation, sooner or later you are likely to become frustrated working in design view or find yourself dissatisfied with the code that Dreamweaver generates. You will want to write the code yourself. Dreamweaver's code view serves as a powerful code editor for the languages used on the Web. It provides useful facilities, including syntax colouring and auto-completion. We have not described the code editor, because if you know enough to make use of it, you should have no difficulty with it.

Shared Concepts

W e noted in Chapter 2 that most media tools have many interface features in common. In that chapter we looked at the general characteristics of the programs and their user interfaces as a whole. In this chapter, we will look at some panels, tools and dialogues that appear in three or more programs in more or less the same guise. These features all share the common characteristic of requiring a certain amount of background knowledge in order to understand them properly, so unlike most of this book, in this chapter we include some theory to support the practical instruction.

Colour

Almost all images use colour, and media tools that work on images – both still and moving – provide facilities for choosing, applying and adjusting colours. To understand these facilities and get the most out of them, it is necessary to know something about colour theory.

Colour Models and Modes

Colour theory gets remarkably complicated if you go into it in any detail, but fortunately it is quite easy to grasp enough of the essentials to understand what's going on when you use digital media tools to work with colour in your media files.

RGB Colour

In a bitmapped image, the colour of each pixel may be represented by three values giving the amount of red, green and blue light which must be mixed together to produce the required colour. In vector graphics, colours used as part of the objects' descriptions, to be applied when they are displayed, can be represented in the same way, using three values. We say that any image whose colours are stored in this fashion is represented in the *RGB colour model*. Usually, each of the three values occupies one byte, that is, 8 bits, giving a total of 24 bits for each pixel. An image that uses three bytes to represent colour values is therefore said to be in *24-bit colour*, or to have a *bit depth* of 24. Other bit depths are sometimes encountered, but at present 24 is the most common.

CMYK Colour

If you take beams of light of any two of the RGB model's three *primary colours*, red, green and blue, and combine them you will obtain a third colour. Red added to green gives yellow, red added to blue makes a bluish red called magenta, and green added to blue produces a pale greenish blue called cyan. (Don't confuse adding coloured light like this with adding coloured pigments, which mix with quite different results.) These three new colours, yellow, magenta and cyan are called *secondary colours* in the RGB model. (Again, if you are familiar with working with real art materials, try not to get confused. When mixing pigments, yellow, magenta and cyan are referred to as the primary colours.) An alternative way of looking at these secondary colours is that they are what you get when you take white light (which is the sum of all three of red, green and blue) and remove one of the primaries. For example, if you remove the red from white light (leaving green and blue) you get cyan, which is called the ***complementary colour*** of red. Magenta is the complementary colour of green, and yellow that of blue. The RGB secondary colours form the basis of an alternative colour model, ***CMYK colour***, which is available as an alternative to RGB in programs like Photoshop and Illustrator. CMYK is used extensively in the print industry.

The ***colour mode*** of an image in Photoshop or Illustrator is the model used to represent colours in that image. So if the colour mode is set to **RGB Color**, colour values will be interpreted using the RGB colour model; if it is set to **CMYK Color**, the CMYK model will be used. The range of colours that can be represented in CMYK is not the same as the range that can be represented in RGB, so if you have to change the colour mode of an image – for example, if you are supplied with a CMYK original image that you wish to embed in a Web page, and therefore have to convert to RGB – the colours may shift.

Illustrator only supports the RGB and CMYK colour modes; Flash can only deal with RGB, and the colour specifications used in CSS and generated by Dreamweaver are likewise restricted to RGB colour. Photoshop, though, supports some additional colour modes, as we mentioned in Chapter 4, but only one of these is likely to be of interest for multimedia or Web design work.

Indexed Colour

In indexed colour, instead of storing three 8-bit numbers for each pixel, only one number is used. (In principle this number may be any size, but is usually 8 bits in practice.) This number is not interpreted as the pixel's colour itself, but as an index into a ***colour table***, containing full 24-bit colour values. The colour of the pixel is the value at the entry in the table corresponding to the stored index value as illustrated in Figure 8.1. (This works exactly like "painting by numbers".) The colour table must contain entries for all the colours used in the image, known as the image's ***colour palette***. If 8 bits are used for index values, only 256 different colours can appear in the colour table. If an image containing more than 256 colours is converted to indexed colour, it follows that some colours will have to be left out

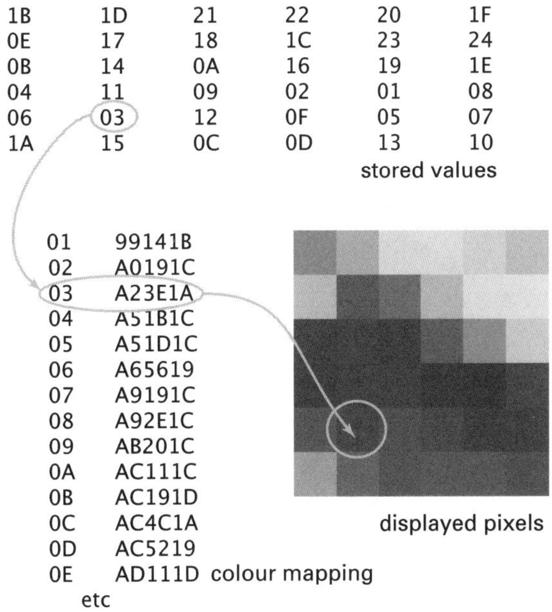

1B	1D	21	22	20	1F
0E	17	18	1C	23	24
0B	14	0A	16	19	1E
04	11	09	02	01	08
06	(03)	12	0F	05	07
1A	15	0C	0D	13	10

stored values

01	99141B
02	A0191C
03	A23E1A
04	A51B1C
05	A51D1C
06	A65619
07	A9191C
08	A92E1C
09	AB201C
0A	AC111C
0B	AC191D
0C	AC4C1A
0D	AC5219
0E	AD111D

etc

colour mapping

displayed pixels

Figure 8.1 *Indexed colour*

and replaced with others. This can produce undesirable artefacts in the resulting image. The reason for putting up with this shortcoming of indexed colour is that the number of bytes needed to store the image is cut by nearly a factor of three, which substantially reduces image file sizes. GIF files are stored using indexed colour, and so are 8-bit PNG files.

Before support for 24-bit colours in video hardware became more or less universal, some low-end computers were restricted to displaying only 256 colours at one time. Such machines used indexed colour in the hardware to help them overcome this limitation. Owing to limitations in the way this was implemented, it was possible that the same image could end up being displayed using a different set of colours on different platforms. To avoid this, a set of 216 colours was identified which could be guaranteed to display the same on all machines. These 216 colours are referred to as the ***Web-safe palette***. Many Web design guides still advise you to stick to the Web-safe palette colours for images destined for the Web, but this advice is now out of date.

You will see references to Web-safe colours in different contexts when you are choosing colours. Colour pickers may warn you if you select a colour that is not in the Web-safe palette, which is still one of the standard swatch libraries available in all the programs we describe. It should be understood, though, that it is only certain old systems that are so limited in their ability to display colours that only the Web-safe colours can be relied on. As it would be unreasonable for anybody with such a system to expect to be able to view contemporary high-quality graphics, it is foolish to confine yourself to the Web-safe palette for most images. (The Web-safe colours are an uninspiring and very limited collection.) Despite the number of places it crops up, you can safely regard the Web-safe palette as a relic of earlier times that is no longer of any importance.

The HSB Colour Model

A popular way of thinking about the relationships between different colours is to arrange them around the rim of a circle, known as the ***colour wheel***. The wheel is constructed by arranging the primaries equally spaced around it, with the secondaries in between them such that each one is opposite its complementary primary. This basic colour wheel is illustrated in diagrammatic form in Figure 8.2. It can be extended by including tertiary colours, which you get by mixing secondaries, and so on. However, colour is a continuous phenomenon, so the colour wheel should really have a continuous gradation of intermediate colours all the way around the rim.

The colour wheel has been used as the basis of various theories of colour harmony, which some people find useful when they are designing colour schemes for Web pages and so on.

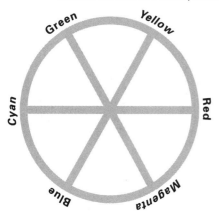

Figure 8.2 *The colour wheel*

It lies behind Illustrator's Live Color facilities, described in Chapter 5. It also forms the basis of an alternative colour model, which is commonly referred to as the **HSB model**, with the H standing for **hue**, S for **saturation** and B for **brightness**. (Brightness is sometimes also referred to as lightness, while some authorities prefer to call brightness the **value**, and therefore refer to the HSV model – it's all the same model, though.) In this model, instead of trying to describe a colour by saying how to mix it out of red, green and blue light, we use a description that more closely resembles the way we usually think about colour when mixing pigments. The first component of this description is the colour's hue, which is equated with its position around the rim of the colour wheel. The hue is what you might think of as the pure colour, just as though it had come straight out of a tube of paint.

Fully saturated colours are pure hues, not mixed with anything else. In the HSB model, therefore, a fully saturated colour will have a value for hue which relates to the precise colour it is, and values for both saturation and brightness set to 100%. When saturation and brightness are reduced below 100%, the colour behaves as though reducing saturation added white to the pure hue, producing a lighter **tint**, and reducing brightness added black to the pure hue, producing a darker **tone**. This colour model is designed to work in a way analagous to mixing pigments, and to be intuitively obvious to people familiar with traditional art materials.

Saturation can be added to the graphical representation of colour in the colour wheel by filling in the wheel's disk, as shown in Figure 8.3. Pure white is placed at the centre, representing any totally unsaturated colour, and the fully saturated hues are left around the rim. The space in between is filled with a graduation of tints. Any hue can be specified as an angle, giving the anti-clockwise rotation required to reach it from pure red, which is arbitrarily taken to be at 0°.

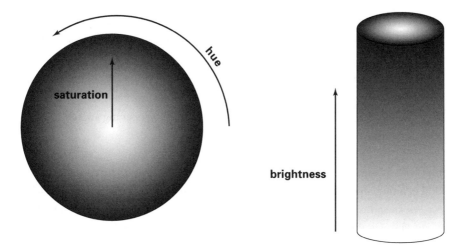

Figure 8.3 *The HSB colour model*

Saturation is specified as the distance from the centre, expressed as a fraction of the circle's radius. The circle on the left of Figure 8.3 shows how these two components are represented.

But what about brightness? In order to incorporate this into the geometrical representation a third dimension is needed, which is not available on two-dimensional monitors. Instead, a circle as just described is considered to be a slice through a cylinder, as shown on the right of Figure 8.3, which increases in lightness from the bottom, where it is completely black, to the top, where colours have their full intensity.

There is no HSB colour mode, since HSB is just a way of visualizing colours in any colour model. It provides a popular way of choosing and adjusting colours.

Picking Colours

You often need to choose a colour in any media tool, to apply it using some painting or drawing tool, to set it as the current foreground or background colour, to use in a CSS rule, or as the basis of a selection. A range of methods are available for picking a colour, varying in complexity.

Swatches

The simplest method is to choose a colour from a set of *swatches*, small square samples arranged on a panel, as illustrated in Figure 8.4. The Swatches panel, which is present in Photoshop, Illustrator and – in trivially different form – Flash, serves two purposes. Its primary use is to store colours that are used repeatedly in a document. (In Dreamweaver, the Colors category in the Assets panel is used for this purpose.) This function is extended to allow sets of swatches to be shared between projects, and for standard swatch libraries to be made available.

When you create a new document in Photoshop, Illustrator or Flash, a default set of colours is displayed in the Swatches panel. You can add your own colours (chosen by one of the methods described below) to the Swatches panel in any program and delete colours from it. You can also replace the default set with some other swatch library, or add another library. In Photoshop and Illustrator, the library's names are included in the Swatches panel menu, in Flash the panel menu has Add Colors... and Replace Colors... commands, which you use for opening swatch libraries from disk.

Photoshop comes with a large number of swatch libraries, mostly corresponding to standard sets of colours used in printing, the so-called colour books. Illustrator also has many swatch libraries, including colour books and other libraries arranged thematically (and a bit arbitrarily), such as the Cool and Bright libraries. Illustrator displays these libraries in separate panels, instead of incorporating them into the main Swatches panel. As the example in Figure 8.4 shows, these panels have the same form as the Swatches panel itself. You can drag individual swatches from a library

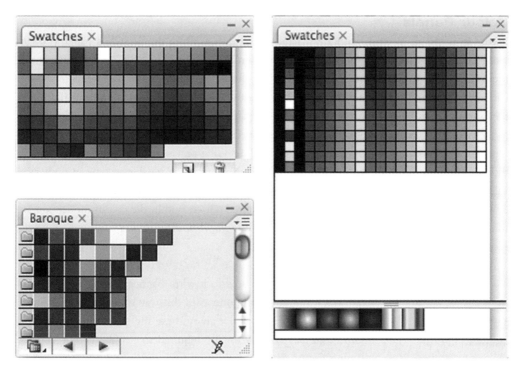

Figure 8.4 *The Swatches panel in Photoshop (top left) and Flash (right) and a swatch library in Illustrator*

into the Swatches panel. In all three programs (Photoshop, Illustrator and Flash) you can also save a set of swatches as a library and reopen it later. If you are using a specific set of colours across a particular project, it is a good idea to save it as a swatch library. Sets of swatches which have been saved in Photoshop using the Save Swatches for Exchange… command on the Swatches panel menu can be opened in Illustrator, and vice versa.

Illustrator adds extra convenience to swatches, by letting you create colour groups, which are sets of swatches. You can see that the Baroque swatch library, shown bottom left in Figure 8.4, is made up of groups, each having a folder icon at its left end. You can drag an entire group to the Swatches panel using this folder icon. We described some of Illustrator's other unique colour facilities in Chapter 5.

---TRY THIS---

Practise setting foreground, background, stroke, fill and text colours, as appropriate, by using swatches from the default sets in all your programs.

Explore the swatch libraries supplied with Illustrator and Photoshop. Practise adding swatches from a library to the Swatches panel and deleting swatches from the panel. Save a library of your own swatches using Save Swatches for Exchange… and open it in another document.

Colour Panels

If you do not wish to work with a restricted set of colours using the **Swatches** panel, you can specify colours explicitly in the **Color** panel, shown from Photoshop and Flash in Figure 8.5. Illustrator's **Color** panel is almost identical to Photoshop's, except for the two swatches in the top left corner. In Photoshop, these represent the foreground and background colours; in Illustrator, they show the stroke and fill colours. The swatch pairs are identical in appearance and function to the two swatches at the bottom of the **Tools** panel in these programs. You click on one or the other to set the corresponding colour. To set a colour value precisely, you can use the sliders in the middle of the panel or the numeric entry fields. You will only be able to type in numerical values if you know them, which means having some numerical colour specification to hand, but by using the sliders it is possible to produce any desired colour within the colour model you are using: the chosen swatch in the top left corner of the panel updates to show the colour corresponding to the sliders' positions as you move them.

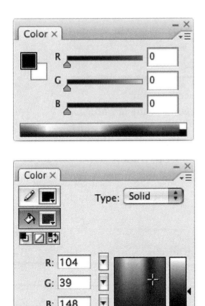

Figure 8.5 *The* Color *panel in Photoshop (top) and Flash (bottom)*

Although you can get used to it with practice, mixing colours from red, green and blue components in this way is not entirely intuitive. Moving the sliders does not always have the effect you expect, and some trial and error is usually required to get the colour you are aiming for. As we noted above, many people find the HSB colour model more comfortable. You can select **HSB Sliders** from the **Color** panel menu to change the **R**, **G** and **B** sliders shown in Figure 8.5 to **H**, **S** and **B** and use them to adjust hue, saturation and brightness.

Flash's **Color** panel, also shown in Figure 8.5, provides a similar interface to Photoshop's and Illustrator's. The sliders are concealed under the triangles to the right of the colour component numbers, but they function in just the same way as in the other programs. There are significant small differences, though: in Flash, clicking on either of the stroke or fill colour icons causes a palette of colour swatches to pop up, from which you can choose a colour, as you do from the **Swatches** panel. (In fact, this pop-up palette effectively is the **Swatches** panel, and any changes you make, such as deleting a colour from the **Swatches** panel, are reflected in the pop-up palette.) The **Color** panel has an additional field and slider, labelled **Alpha**, for adjusting the opacity of the colour. (In Photoshop, opacity is a property of layers, while in Illustrator opacity adjustment is made independently in the **Transparency** panel.) Similarly, in Flash the Color panel is where you define gradient fills, but in Illustrator this is done in a separate panel, as we will describe later.

In Dreamweaver, there is no Color panel, but when you click on a colour swatch in the Properties panel, to set the colour of some text for example, a palette of swatches pops up, as in Flash.

┌─TRY THIS───┐

Practise setting foreground, background, fill and stroke colours by adjusting the sliders in the Color panel. Choose a colour in an image and try to match it using the Color panel sliders. Try RGB and HSB sliders. Do you find one of the colour models easier than the other to use for this purpose?

└──┘

Sampling Colours

If you want to match a colour that is already present on screen, use an *eyedropper tool* to sample colours. The basic operation of the eyedropper is the same in all programs: clicking with this tool samples the colour of the pixel where you click. However, eyedroppers can be used in different contexts and behave slightly differently in some programs.

The eyedropper that you will find in the Tools panel in Photoshop, Illustrator and Flash is selected like any other tool. In Photoshop, clicking anywhere in the document sets the foreground colour; [opt/alt]-clicking sets the background colour. There is a pop-up menu in the Options bar that allows you to specify how the sample is taken. The default, Point Sample, uses the colour of the pixel where you click. The other options specify the size of a square in pixels; the sampled colour is then the average colour within a square of that size surrounding the pixel you click on.

In Illustrator, the eyedropper sets the fill and stroke colours to match the object you click on, and it applies these attributes to any object that is currently selected. In fact, in Illustrator, the eyedropper samples other appearance attributes, too, including transparency, stroke width and style, and various text attributes. Double-click the eyedropper in the Tools panel to specify which attributes are sampled and applied. Illustrator's eyedropper can sample colours from anywhere on the screen. If you click with the tool and keep the mouse button held down, you can move the cursor anywhere on the screen, and when you let it go the colour will be sampled and used as the fill colour.

Flash's eyedropper behaves in a broadly similar way: if you click the fill of an object, it samples the fill colour and then changes into the paint bucket tool, so you can apply it to another object. If you click the stroke, it samples the width, style and colour of the stroke, and changes to the ink bottle tool. In other words, in each program, the eyedropper samples attributes so that they can be used for other objects as if you had set them explicitly.

The Tools panel is not the only place where you can find an eyedropper, though. In Photoshop and Illustrator there is an area at the bottom of the Color panel, called a *colour ramp*, filled with a spectrum of colours, as you can see in Figure 8.5. When you hover the cursor over the ramp it turns into an eyedropper, to indicate that you can select a colour by clicking. The eyedropper also appears when the cursor is over the Swatches panel, again indicating that clicking will sample the colour under the cursor. As we described in Chapter 4, an eyedropper is also used in the Color Range and Replace Colors dialogues to sample a colour to use for making a selection.

Finally, when you use the Swatches panel in Flash, or a pop-up palette of swatches in Flash or Dreamweaver, the cursor changes to an eyedropper, as it does in Photoshop and Illustrator, but this eyedropper can be moved anywhere on the screen to sample the colour of any pixel.

┌─ TRY THIS ───┐

Practise using the eyedropper tools in all programs to sample colours. In Photoshop, set the foreground and background colours to values sampled from a photograph. In Illustrator and Flash, draw some objects, set the stroke and fill of one of them and copy it to the others. In Dreamweaver, set the colour of some text to match a colour from your desktop image or pattern. Make sure that you understand what is being sampled by the eyedropper in each program, and how the sampled values are used.

└───┘

Colour Pickers

The most elaborate way of choosing colours is by using a *colour picker*, which presents the colours that can be represented in the chosen colour model in a graphical form. Both Windows and Mac OS X have system colour pickers, which can be accessed from most programs, and these are used by Flash and Dreamweaver for picking colours. Adobe have created their own, platform-independent colour picker, and this is used in Photoshop and Illustrator.

The Apple system colour picker can be presented in several different ways. Three of them are shown in Figure 8.6. The leftmost display is an HSB picker. Because monitor screens are two-dimensional, the HSB model must be displayed as a disk, representing hue and saturation for a particular value of brightness, together with a separate slider representing the brightness cylinder. As the brightness changes when the slider is moved, the hue and saturation in the corresponding slice through the cylinder are displayed in the circle. A user chooses a colour by clicking; the hue and saturation can be deduced from the coordinates of the click. The position of the slider provides the third component of the HSB value for the selected colour.

The other views of the colour picker are more easily understood. The middle one illustrated just consists of sliders, like the Color panel. The pop-up menu can be used to select which set of sliders (i.e. which colour model) is used. The right-hand view in Figure 8.6 is the crayon picker, which is more entertaining than useful. Its mode of operation should be evident. As well as these three,

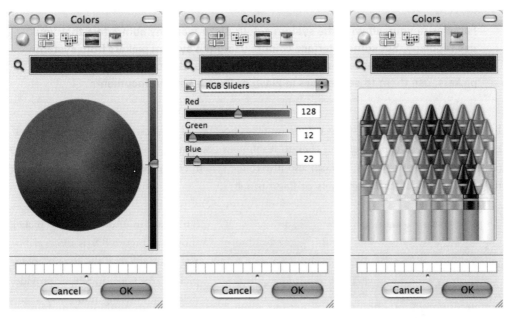

Figure 8.6 *The Mac OS X system colour picker*

you can also display swatches of named colours from certain standard palettes, or you can choose colours from an image of a spectrum. Thus, the colour picker duplicates the function of all the other available methods of choosing colours, but in a single dialogue. You switch between the different displays using the icons at the top of the dialogue.

In contrast, the standard Windows colour picker, shown in Figure 8.7, presents different methods of selecting colours in a single dialogue. On the left is a set of swatches for a very limited range of colours. On the right is an HSB picker, except that, unlike the Apple picker, hue and saturation are arranged along two perpendicular axes, giving a square instead of a circle, which distorts the colours' distribution somewhat. Colours are picked in the usual way, by moving the brightness slider and clicking to set the hue and saturation components. Alternatively, numerical values can be entered, either in HSB or RGB. As with the Apple colour picker, it is possible to save colours that you use frequently, and have their swatches shown in the Windows colour picker whenever you invoke it.

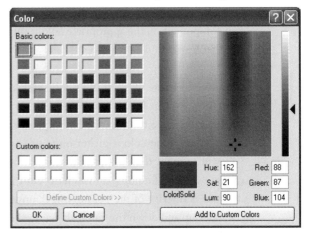

Figure 8.7 *The Windows XP system colour picker*

TRY THIS

Familiarize yourself with the system colour pickers on any computers that you use regularly. Set some interface colours using the system pickers from system preference dialogues or control panels. When you understand the system colour pickers, use them to set colours in Flash or Dreamweaver documents.

In Flash and Dreamweaver, when colour swatches pop up (as we described earlier) there is a button above them which you can click to reach your computer's system colour picker if none of the swatches is satisfactory. You can also invoke the system colour picker by [opt/alt]-clicking the fill or stroke swatch in the Tools or Color panels.

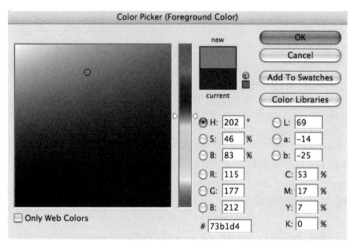

Figure 8.8 *The Adobe colour picker*

The standard Adobe colour picker, shown in Figure 8.8, is more elaborate than either of the system colour pickers. As you can see, it provides fields for entering numerical values for HSB, RGB and (for print) CMYK components, as well as the hexadecimal values used for colours in HTML. Each of the components of the HSB and RGB colour models has a radio button next to it. When you click one of these buttons, the slider in the middle of the colour picker is used to control the component you have selected, while the large coloured square at the left plots the values of the other two components in the appropriate colour model. So if you select brightness (**B**), the picker works like the Windows colour picker.

An interesting way of using the Adobe picker comes from selecting hue to be controlled by the slider, as shown in Figure 8.8. When you do this, the square on the left can be considered as a vertical radial slice through the HSB cylinder, with the centre of the cylinder on the left. If you look at the Adobe colour picker on your monitor in colour with the H radio button selected, you will see that the colours running up the left edge are shades of grey, which is what you should expect to find on the cylinder's centre line. The thin vertical rectangle in the middle of the dialogue is the rim of the colour wheel, unwrapped into a continuous colour ramp. By moving the slider up and down this ramp, the vertical slice is rotated around inside the cylinder. You select a colour by first moving the slider to set the hue, then clicking a point inside the large square to set the saturation (distance from the left edge) and the brightness (distance from the bottom).

We will explain the significance of the checkbox labelled Only Web Colors when we describe optimizing images for the Web at the end of this chapter.

It might seem, at first sight, that colour pickers are an overly complicated means of carrying out the simple job of choosing a colour, but you will find as you work with them that they are really quite simple. Once you have grasped the principles of the colour models, it should become clear how the controls in the pickers can be used to obtain exactly the colour you want.

The Adobe colour picker can be reached in Photoshop and Illustrator via the simpler Color panels, where clicking (in Photoshop) or double-clicking (in Illustrator) on one of the swatches causes the picker to be displayed. Similarly, clicking or double-clicking one of the swatches at the bottom of the Tools panel opens the colour picker; the colour you set in the picker is used for the foreground, background, stroke or fill, according to which swatch you clicked.

┌─ TRY THIS ──┐
│   │
│   **Practise selecting colours using the Adobe colour picker in Illustrator and** │
│   **Photoshop. Observe how selecting each of the H, S, B and R, G, B radio buttons** │
│   **changes the way the colour space is displayed and how the slider control works.** │
│   **Which option makes it easiest to find a particular colour you have in mind?** │
│   │
└──┘

Gradients

Filling objects or selected areas with a ***gradient***, in which colours gradually blend into each other, can produce some pleasing results. Gradients are created in the same way in Photoshop, Illustrator and Flash, although they are applied slightly differently. Since HTML and CSS don't support gradients, you cannot use them in Dreamweaver. It is easiest to understand gradients in the context of vector graphics, where a gradient behaves as a special type of fill, so we will start by describing how gradients work in Illustrator.

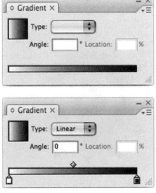

You can create and apply gradient fills using the Gradient panel. Its initial appearance is shown at the top of Figure 8.9. Clicking on the swatch at the top left activates it, applying a gradient fill to any selected objects and adding some controls to the panel, as shown at the bottom of Figure 8.9. At first the panel shows a default gradient, with a constant rate of variation from white to black. You can change many aspects of the gradient. Selecting Radial from the Type pop-up menu makes the gradient blend outwards from the centre of the filled object, instead of linearly from left to right. The two stars in Figure 8.10 show uniform linear (upper star) and radial (lower star) gradient fills applied to an object. (They may not look very uniform, but that is the result of an optical illusion.)

Figure 8.9 *The* Gradient *panel in Illustrator*

Figure 8.10 *Linear (top)
and radial (bottom) gradients*

Gradients do not have to fade between black and white. The markers below the bar are known as ***gradient stops***. The colour of the gradient is interpolated between the stops. By clicking the gradient stop at the left end of the bar you can select a colour for the start of the gradient, using the Color panel, in the usual way. (You may have to choose RGB from the Color panel menu to get access to colours other than greys.) Similarly, by clicking the gradient stop at the right-hand end you can set the ending colour for the gradient. You could possibly create a primitive sunset effect by setting the starting colour to red and the ending colour to yellow. Any object filled with this gradient would show a continuous blend of colours from red through a range of oranges to yellow. This wouldn't be too impressive if you applied it to a rectangle that was supposed to represent the sky, because the gradient would run from left to right, instead of from top to bottom. The field labelled Angle in the Gradient panel can be used to make the gradient run in a different direction. Setting it to -90° would make the colours blend from yellow at the bottom to red at the top. A value of -75° produces a less obviously artificial result. (The Angle field is disabled for radial gradients, where it doesn't make sense.)

You won't always want the mid-point of the gradient to lie exactly halfway between the two ends. For a sunset, for example, you might want more red than yellow, with the red fading up to the orange colour in the middle of the colour range quite slowly and then rapidly turning yellow. Dragging the diamond-shaped marker above the gradient bar moves the mid-point to achieve such effects. You can also drag the gradient stops inwards from the ends of the bar if you want bands of solid colour at each end of the gradient. You can exert still more control by adding extra colours. Clicking underneath the gradient bar causes a new gradient stop to appear. A new mid-point diamond also appears between the new stop and its neighbour. You can set a colour for any stop you add, so you could create bands of different reds, oranges and yellows for a spectacular sunset effect. The stars in Figure 8.11 show linear and radial fills with several intermediate colours applied to an object. (The colours are alternately black and white for better reproduction. Again, there is an optical illusion here: there isn't really a solid white ring at the outside of the lower star.)

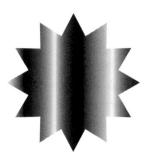

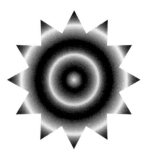

Figure 8.11 *Gradients with
intermediate stops*

When you drag a stop, the box labelled Location at the right of the panel shows its position as a percentage of the full extent of the gradient. If you drag a mid-point marker, the location is shown as a percentage of the distance between the neighbouring stops.

Creating and applying gradients in Flash is done in almost exactly the same way as it is in Illustrator, but there is no separate **Gradient** panel. Instead, you choose **Linear** or **Radial** from the **Type** pop-up menu at the top of the **Color** panel. This is a convenient arrangement, since you can choose the colours for the gradient stops in the same panel. When you select one of the gradient types as a fill, a gradient ramp with stops below it appears, as shown in Figure 8.12, which you use to set the colours of the gradient in the same way as in Illustrator. However, gradients in Flash are more limited; they have no mid-point diamonds and therefore always change at a uniform rate between the gradient stops.

Figure 8.12 *Creating a gradient in Flash's* Color *panel*

As in Illustrator, a gradient set in Flash will be applied to any selected objects and saved as the current fill, which will then be applied to any objects you draw subsequently, until you set a new fill. In both Illustrator and Flash, gradients can be saved as swatches and applied from the **Swatches** panel, in the same way as solid colours.

TRY THIS

Practise creating and applying gradient fills to shapes in Illustrator and Flash. Begin by applying the default grey gradient to any shape, then change the colours at each end of the gradient, and try moving the mid-point. Next, add extra colours and adjust the positions of all the gradient stops. Try both linear and radial gradients.

Photoshop approaches gradients in a different way, because there can be no concept of a fill in bitmapped images. Instead, you use gradients to paint pixels. They are applied using the *gradient tool* from the **Tools** panel.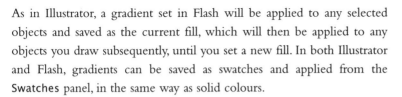

Photoshop has five different sorts of gradient. As well as the two types of gradient found in Illustrator and Flash – linear and radial – Photoshop also provides *angular* gradients, in which the blend sweeps round a circle, *reflected* gradients, which are like linear gradients, but reflected to form a symmetrical blend, and *diamond* gradients, which are similar to radial gradients, but form a diamond pattern instead of a circle. Figure 8.13 illustrates these types more clearly than any description can.

Figure 8.13 *Linear, radial, angular, reflected and diamond gradients*

The basic procedure for using Photoshop's gradient tool is as follows: select the tool and select the type of gradient you require using one of the buttons on the **Options** bar. (The buttons look just like miniature versions of the pictures in Figure 8.13; each button selects the type of gradient it resembles.) Next, select a preset gradient from the drop-down palette on the **Options** bar, set the blending mode and opacity, and then drag across the image with the tool to create the gradient itself. The role of the line you drag out depends on the type of gradient you are making.

For a linear gradient it defines the line along which the colours blend, with the line's end points defining the start and end points of the gradient. Beyond the ends, a solid fill of the ending colour is applied. For a radial gradient, the line defines the radius of a circle; the starting point of your line acts as its centre, and is coloured with the starting colour for the gradient, the end point of the line defines the extent of the circle, beyond which the solid fill of the ending colour is used. For an angular gradient, the line is also the radius of a circle, but the gradient wipes round the circle, so the starting and ending colours appear on either side of the line. (You can see this clearly in the example in the middle of Figure 8.13.) If you choose a reflected gradient, the line is used in the same way as it is for a linear gradient, except that the resulting gradient is reflected about the starting point. In the fourth example in Figure 8.13, for instance, the gradient tool was only dragged from the middle of the filled area to the right edge. Finally, for a diamond gradient, the line serves as a radius, as it does with a radial gradient, but the blended colours are arranged to form the diamond shape.

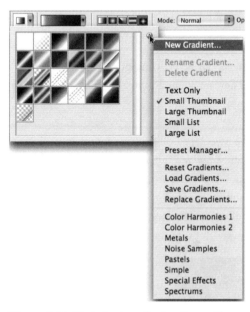

Figure 8.14 *Photoshop's gradient options with fly-out menu of additional presets*

In Photoshop a gradient will fill any selected area in the current layer, or the entire layer if no selection is active.

Using the fly-out menu on the palette of gradients that drops down from the **Options** bar (shown in Figure 8.14) you can load additional preset gradients. Some of these, such as those in the **Metals** category, are quite useful and attractive. Nevertheless, this selection of preset gradients provided with Photoshop may well not be adequate for your needs, but it is easy to adapt them to make new ones. With the gradient tool selected in the **Tools** panel, click on the gradient swatch on the **Options** bar instead of the triangle next to it that controls the drop-down palette. The **Gradient Editor** window, shown in Figure 8.15, will open. The top panel duplicates the drop-down palette from the **Options** bar. The lower half of the window is used to modify the gradient. By now, it should look familiar to you, with a gradient ramp and stops below it that allow you to set colours. (In Photoshop, you can go straight to the colour picker by double-clicking any colour stop.) Photoshop's Gradient Editor has an extra facility beyond those found in Illustrator and Flash. As well as the colour stops below the gradient ramp, there are opacity stops above it, allowing you to set and blend the transparency as well as the colour.

When you are happy with your gradient you can click the New button and it will be saved and added to the gradient palette for future use. Any gradient that you have created can be applied as any of the five different types.

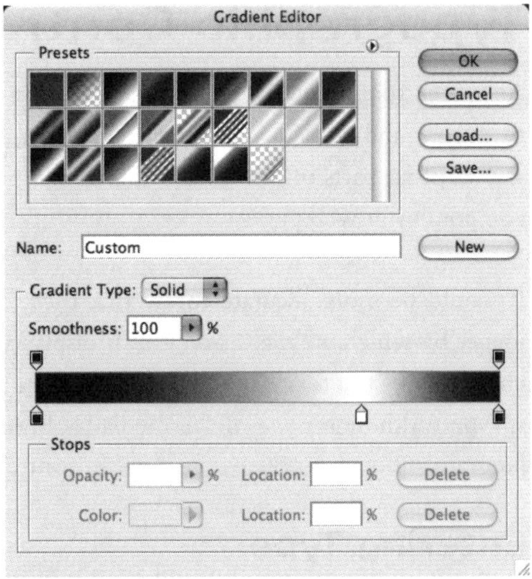

Figure 8.15 *The Gradient Editor in Photoshop*

─TRY THIS─

In Photoshop, create a new image, and add five layers to it, each filled with a different type of gradient, but all based on the same preset gradient.

Open the Gradient Editor and practise adjusting the colours, opacity and rate of change of a gradient. Add new stops to produce a more complex effect. Create a pleasing new gradient and apply it as each of the five different gradient types.

DON'T FORGET

Images for display on screen use the RGB colour model. Indexed colour may be employed to reduce file sizes.

The HSB colour model, based on the colour wheel, provides a more intuitive way of visualizing colour values.

Colours can be selected from a set of swatches, or chosen by clicking, using sliders, or specifying numeric values in the Color panel.

The eyedropper tool is used to sample colours from an image or elsewhere on the screen.

Colour pickers provide an interface for choosing colours with a choice of colour model. Flash and Dreamweaver use the system colour pickers, Illustrator and Photoshop use Adobe's own.

Objects or areas can be filled with linear or radial gradients, which are created by setting gradient stops in the Gradient panel or editor.

Typographic Controls

All media tools allow you to work with text in some way. Graphics programs let you add text to images and treat it as a graphic element, applying effects and manipulating it in the same way as other parts of the image. Web design programs are based around text, which is a primary component of Web pages.

It would be more accurate to say that these applications allow you to add *type* to your documents, by which we mean text as it is displayed with layout and font properties, not just the bare characters of the text. (Text and *Text* are the same, considered as text, but different, considered as type.) Although none of the media tools described in this book is a fully-fledged page layout program, all of them offer considerable control over the layout and appearance of type.

Entering Type

T In Photoshop, Illustrator and Flash, you use the *type tool* from the Tools panel to add type. You use it in one of two ways: either you click at a point in the document window and start typing, or you drag out a rectangle. In the first case, text is entered starting from the point at which you clicked, and formatted according to the settings you have chosen, as described below. To start a new line you must explicitly press return. We will call text entered in this way a *text block*. In the second case, the rectangle you dragged out is treated as a *text frame* and the text you type is laid out within it, with lines wrapping as they do in a word processor. You only need to press return to start a new paragraph. If the text overflows a text frame it is hidden, whereas a text block can flow right over the whole image. In Photoshop, you need to confirm or cancel, using the tick or cross mark on the Options bar, when you have finished entering text. In Illustrator and Flash you can just select a different tool.

If you resize a text frame, the text in it stays the same size and reflows to fit the altered frame, but if you resize a text block, the type itself changes size. You can perform other free transformations on both types of text. (See the chapters describing the individual applications for a description of free transformations in each program.) While you are entering text, the cursor changes to the familiar I-beam shape. You can then use it to make selections by dragging over characters; selection shortcuts, such as double-clicking to select a word, usually work as you expect.

As is often the case, Flash does things in a slightly different way. It recognizes three different kinds of text: *static* text is any text that you enter while you are creating a document; *dynamic* text is created by scripts while the movie runs; *input* text is for users to enter input when the movie runs. Since we are not concerned with scripting in this book, only static text is of any interest here. You must choose the kind of text you require from a pop-up menu in the Properties panel when the type tool is selected.

With Static Text selected, if you just click on the stage with the type tool, a text block is created, as in Photoshop and Illustrator, which gets longer as you type and grows downwards when you add explicit new lines. Text frames in Flash are not quite the same as they are in the other programs, though. You cannot drag out an unconstrained text frame; no matter how far down you drag, you end up with a rectangle one line deep, but the width is determined by how far you drag sideways. When lines wrap, the text frame automatically grows downwards, it never overflows. Drag handles on the corners can be used to make the frame wider or narrower, leaving the text the same size. The height adjusts itself to accommodate all the text in the frame.

In all three programs that have a free transform tool, both text frames and text blocks can be transformed with it. The text will be transformed along with its container; for instance, if you scale up a text frame in Illustrator, the text in it will get bigger. In Illustrator and Flash, you can use the arrow tool to transform a container without affecting the text in it. (In Photoshop transformations are applied to entire layers, including text layers. The distinction between transforming text and transforming its container therefore does not exist.)

Text blocks in Flash have a single round drag handle in the top right-hand corner. Text frames have a large hollow handle in this position. You can turn a text block into a text frame by double-clicking the special drag handle in the top right corner. Conversely, if you drag this handle on a text block, it turns into a text frame.

TRY THIS

In Photoshop, Illustrator and Flash practise typing lines of text and dragging out text frames and filling them with text. Make text frames overflow and resize them to accommodate the overflow.

Try applying scaling and other transformations to text blocks and frames. Note the differences between the different applications.

Dreamweaver approaches text in a quite different way. Text is central to HTML, and much of CSS is concerned with its formatting. As we explained in Chapter 7, you can enter text just by typing, as if you were using a word processor.

Formatting Type

The appearance of type has two separate aspects: the appearance of individual characters – the font they are set in, the type size, any kerning that is applied, and so on – and the layout of paragraphs – indentations, justification, and so on. Separate panels or sub-menus are used to control these two distinct aspects. Although different applications provide varying degrees of control, most of the values that you can set are standard, despite the different ways in which type is created. Most simple formatting operations can be carried out using controls on the Options bar (or **Properties** panel in Flash). For more esoteric type properties, Photoshop and Illustrator have separate **Character** and **Paragraph** panels. Illustrator and Flash have **Type** menus, which provide an alternative way of setting properties, as well as some extra commands.

Character properties, however chosen, are applied to any text that is selected; if none is selected, they are applied to any characters you type subsequently. This is just like the way a word processor works. Paragraph properties are similarly applied to any paragraphs you have selected, the paragraph containing the insertion point, or any paragraphs you type after setting the properties at the beginning of a new paragraph.

In Dreamweaver, the formatting that we describe below is all applied through CSS rules. Because of the fundamental difference in approach, text formatting in Dreamweaver is described separately in Chapter 7, and we will not consider it in this chapter.

Character Formatting

The fundamental properties governing the appearance of characters are the font from which they are taken, the size at which they are set and their colour. Every program that deals with type lets you choose these properties. These properties are among those that can be applied using the **Options** bar in Photoshop and Illustrator, and the **Properties** panel in Flash. Figure 8.16 shows the appearance of the relevant panel when text is being entered. You will see that despite some cosmetic differences, all three programs provide versions of the same controls.

In each program the font is chosen from a pop-up menu, which displays the name of the chosen font (Myriad Pro in Figure 8.16). Where fonts are grouped into a family with different weights and styles – for example, for the font Humana Sans, we have Light, Light Italic, Medium, Medium Italic, Bold and Bold Italic – Photoshop and Illustrator show the family in the font name field at the left and let you choose among the variants from the menu attached to the field to its right. Flash just shows you all the font files installed on your system, but allows you to apply an italic or bold style to any font using the two buttons labelled **B** and **I**.

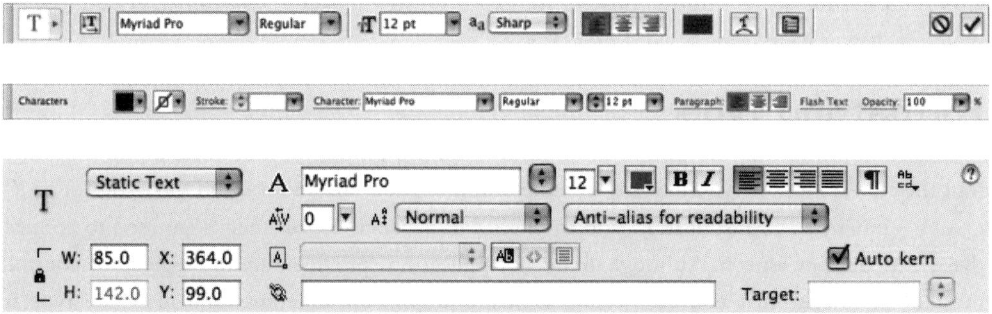

Figure 8.16 *Basic type controls in Photoshop (top), Illustrator (middle) and Flash (bottom)*

The field to the right of the font fields is used to enter the chosen size. The standard unit for type size is the *point* (pt); 1 pt is equal to 1/72 inch, which is just under 0.3528 mm. A point is thus also equal to the size of one pixel at the nominal resolution used for graphics to be displayed on a monitor. You can type a value, choose from a pop-up menu of preferred sizes in Photoshop or Illustrator, or set the size using a slider control that pops up next to the size field in Flash.

You can also choose the colour of type. Clicking on the colour swatch among the type controls brings up some means of choosing the colour, although it is different in all three applications. In Photoshop the colour picker is displayed, while in Flash a colour palette pops up from this swatch, with a button to bring up the colour picker if the colour you want is not in the palette. In Illustrator, clicking the swatch causes a copy of the **Swatches** panel to pop up, whereas **shift**-clicking it causes the **Color** panel to appear instead.

In Illustrator, uniquely, you can set the opacity of selected characters, if you want them to be partially transparent.

┌─ TRY THIS ───

In each of Photoshop, Illustrator and Flash, create a document, drag out a text frame and type a couple of paragraphs. Practise selecting words using the type tool, and changing the font, size and colour of selected words. Explore the range of fonts available to you in each program.

Typography does not end with the choice of font and type size. In Photoshop and Illustrator, more elaborate control requires the use of the **Character** panel. (Illustrator provides a quick way of accessing this panel. Clicking on the underlined word **Character** next to the font name causes a copy of the panel to pop up below the **Options** bar.) The **Character** panel is virtually identical in these programs. Illustrator's is shown in Figure 8.17. Photoshop's panel has a few minor extra options that we will not describe. The fields at the top of the panel duplicate those on the **Options** bar, allowing you to set the font and size in the **Character** panel if you prefer.

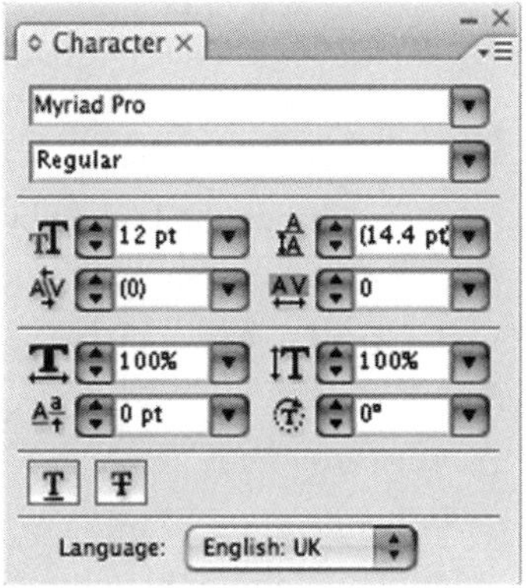

Figure 8.17 *The* Character *panel in Illustrator*

Kerning is the technique of moving certain pairs of letters, such as AV, closer together to maintain an illusion of uniform spacing. Fonts usually come with tables that specify which pairs of letters should be kerned and by how much. Ticking the checkbox labelled **Auto Kern** in Flash's **Properties** panel instructs the program to use this information; in Photoshop and Illustrator, kerning tables are used by default. You can set precise values for kerning any pair of letters, by moving the text insertion point between them and entering a value in the field with an icon denoting kerning next to it, or by picking a value from the attached pop-up menu in Photoshop and Illustrator, or by dragging a slider in Flash. Negative values will move the letters closer together, positive ones will push them apart. To revert to using the font's own kerning information in Illustrator or Photoshop, choose **Auto** or **Metrics**, respectively, from the pop-up menu by the kerning icon. Alternatively, you can turn kerning off by selecting 0.

An operation related to kerning is *tracking*, sometimes referred to as *letter spacing*, which means increasing or decreasing the spacing between all the letters by a fixed proportion. When you are typesetting text intended primarily for reading continuously, it is usually a bad idea to alter the tracking, except possibly for headings. When text is used as a graphic element, though, tracking it is perfectly legitimate and it is widely used in graphic design. You can enter a value to be applied to selected characters using the appropriate field in the **Character** panel in Photoshop or Illustrator, but Flash does not support tracking.

These advanced typographical controls become more important when type is used as an element of a graphic design than they are in mundane text documents. Careful adjustment of kerning and tracking can make the difference between a perfect title, headline or logo and one that doesn't look quite right.

TRY THIS

Type a short heading above the paragraphs you set in the last exercise. Practise changing the tracking of the heading. Try to make the heading fit the width of the text frame by increasing the tracking.

Type pairs of letters, including some using mixed cases, such as AV, VW, Wa, Yv, fl, and so on. Experiment with the effect of adjusting the kerning on the appearance of the letter pairs. Try changing all the kerned pairs to some different fonts. Does changing the font alter the visual effect of the kerning?

Text is normally set on evenly-spaced baselines; the distance between consecutive baselines is called the *leading*. A default value proportional to the type size is normally used, but you can change the leading by entering a new value in points. For text to be displayed on a screen, the default leading, which is based on printing practice, is usually too small and you will often find it beneficial to use a higher value. In Photoshop and Illustrator the leading is considered to be a property of selected characters and is set in the **Character** panel. This allows you to use different leading for different lines in a paragraph. In Flash, the leading is applied to an entire paragraph, and is set in the dialogue box shown in Figure 8.18 that pops up when you click the **Edit Format Options** button

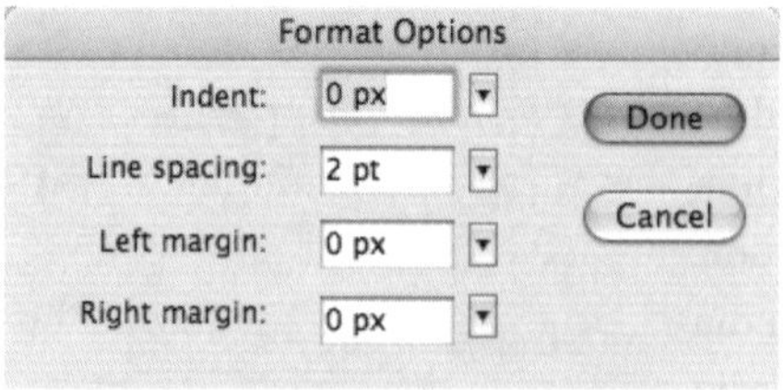

Format Options		
Indent:	0 px ▾	Done
Line spacing:	2 pt ▾	
Left margin:	0 px ▾	Cancel
Right margin:	0 px ▾	

Figure 8.18 *Setting leading and other options in Flash*

in the Properties panel. Here, you set a value for the spacing between the lines, which is added to the type size. The other programs follow conventional practice and use a value of leading that includes the type itself. So, to put 12 pt type on baselines 14 pt apart, in Photoshop and Illustrator you would set the leading to 14 pt, but in Flash you would set the line spacing to 2 pt.

You can also temporarily shift the baseline, which has the effect of raising or lowering characters; this is normally used for setting superscripts and subscripts. Flash just lets you choose between Normal, Superscript and Subscript, while Photoshop and Illustrator let you set a value for the shift, positive to move characters upwards, negative to move them down. Finally, Photoshop and Illustrator will let you stretch and shrink characters vertically and horizontally, by entering values in the appropriate fields.

┌─ TRY THIS ───┐

Adjust the leading of lines in paragraphs that are set in different type sizes and different fonts. Experiment with setting the leading to zero, and increasing it to a high value. Judge the effects of different leading, font and type size combinations on readability. Add subscripts and superscripts to some letters.

└──┘

Paragraph Formatting

Paragraphs can be set *left-aligned*, with the words lined up at the left margin but with ragged edges at the right, *right-aligned*, with them lined up on the right margin but ragged at the left, *justified*, when they are lined up on both margins, with extra space being inserted between words to allow this to happen, or *centred*, with both margins ragged and the text arranged symmetrically about its centre line. Whereas text in printed books is usually justified, text on monitors does not always justify well and left alignment may be more successful. Figure 8.19 shows the four basic paragraph alignment styles, with the icon used to represent each style on the Paragraph panels in

Tue velis nit wis nim nonsequatue facidunt pratet esequat iril del-iquam zzriusto dipis eliquam, consecte enit la amconsecte coreet wismolummy nim diamet, quis diam vel et nullamet amconulputem do-lore magnim dolutate er se volorer in ut.	Tue velis nit wis nim nonsequatue facidunt pratet esequat iril del-iquam zzriusto dipis eliquam, consecte enit la amconsecte coreet wismolummy nim diamet, quis diam vel et nullamet amconulputem do-lore magnim dolutate er se volorer in ut.	Tue velis nit wis nim nonsequatue facidunt pratet esequat iril del-iquam zzriusto dipis eliquam, consecte enit la amconsecte coreet wismolummy nim diamet, quis diam vel et nullamet amconulputem do-lore magnim dolutate er se volorer in ut.	Tue velis nit wis nim nonsequatue facidunt pratet esequat iril del-iquam zzriusto dipis eliquam, consecte enit la amconsecte coreet wismolummy nim diamet, quis diam vel et nullamet amconulputem do-lore magnim dolutate er se volorer in ut.

Figure 8.19 *Left-aligned, centred, right-aligned and justified paragraphs*

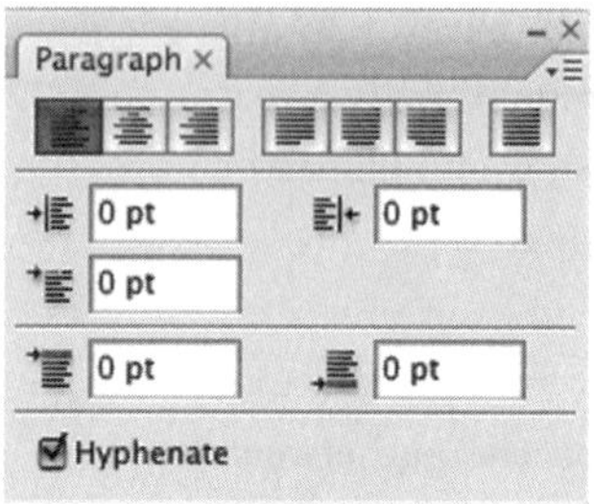

Photoshop and Illustrator shown below each example. The Paragraph panels in Photoshop and Illustrator are identical, and shown in Figure 8.20. In Flash, paragraph alignment is set in the Properties panel, like other typographical properties. (Refer back to Figure 8.16.)

Figure 8.20 *The* Paragraph *panel in Photoshop and Illustrator*

If you are typing in a text frame, paragraphs automatically align themselves in the way you specify. If you are typing a text line (i.e. if you clicked with the type tool instead of dragging out a frame) the alignment mode you choose affects the way the lines of type grow relative to the point where you started to type. Left-aligned and justified text grows away from the insertion point to the right, as you would expect, whereas right-aligned text leaves the insertion point always in the same place, pushing text you have already typed to the left, and centred text grows equally in both directions.

---TRY THIS-------------------

Apply each of the different alignment options to the heading and paragraphs you typed previously. Experiment with combinations of alignments, such as a centred heading over justified text. Consider whether different alignment options may be appropriate for different kinds of text.

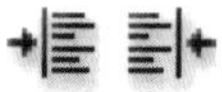

It is possible to add margins to the left and right sides of paragraphs. These can be used simply to provide some space between the words and the edges of the enclosing text frame (the option only makes sense in a frame), in the way that margins are used in books and other printed matter, or to indent whole paragraphs. You can also set an indentation for the first line – one convention for typesetting paragraphs uses an indent on the first line of each paragraph.

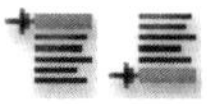

An alternative convention for distinguishing paragraphs is to leave some extra space between them. Flash does not offer a way of doing this, apart from inserting a blank line, but the Paragraph panel in Photoshop and Illustrator has fields for specifying extra space above and below paragraphs – the bottom pair of fields in Figure 8.20. (The distinction between the icons for space above a paragraph and first line indent is subtle. Hover the cursor over the icon and wait for the tool tip if you are in doubt.)

---TRY THIS-------------------

Use Illustrator or Photoshop (or Flash if you really want) to create an interesting poster with several different blocks of text. For example, a poster for a concert would include the date, venue, performers and highlights from the program. Use any combination of typographic controls (and colour) to produce a pleasing and readable composition.

Over the years, typographic features from Adobe's page layout program InDesign have found their way into Photoshop and Illustrator. For many users of these programs, most of the typographical innovations will go more or less unnoticed – if they use text blocks, the text may look a bit better than it would in Word. For designers who incorporate text into their images, however, there are some extra opportunities to take control over the fine detail of typography.

Two different algorithms for paragraph layout are available; the *Adobe Single-Line Composer* and the *Adobe Every-line Composer*. The single-line composer uses the simple-minded line breaking algorithm employed by word processors: words are added to a line until no more will fit, and then a new line is started and the spaces on the full line are adjusted to even out the inter-word gaps. The every-line composer takes a more sophisticated approach of determining the optimal line breaks by considering an entire paragraph at a time. This tends to produce more even and pleasing spacing. The every-line composer is used by default for text blocks, but as it doesn't make sense for single text lines, the single-line composer is used for these. You can choose one or the other explicitly from the `Paragraph` panel menu.

The `Paragraph` panel menu is also used to fine-tune the parameters of justification and hyphenation and to select hanging punctuation (i.e. where punctuation marks at the end of lines of justified text are allowed to extend beyond the end of the line, which paradoxically gives the text a more even appearance). The `Character` panel menu is used to select certain character treatments, such as small caps.

TRY THIS

Create a text frame in one of these applications, and fill it with a few paragraphs of text. Select a paragraph and experiment with using the different composers, and with changing the hyphenation and justification parameter values. Try doing this in conjunction with different paragraph alignments.

The fanciest typographic features are only available with *OpenType* fonts. In Photoshop these features are chosen from the `OpenType` sub-menu of the `Character` panel menu, but in Illustrator a neat `OpenType` panel is available, as shown in Figure 8.21. The available options include standard and extended ligatures, swash capitals, alternative glyphs and positioning options. Not all options make sense for every font: swash capitals are only generally available for italic and calligraphic fonts, for example.

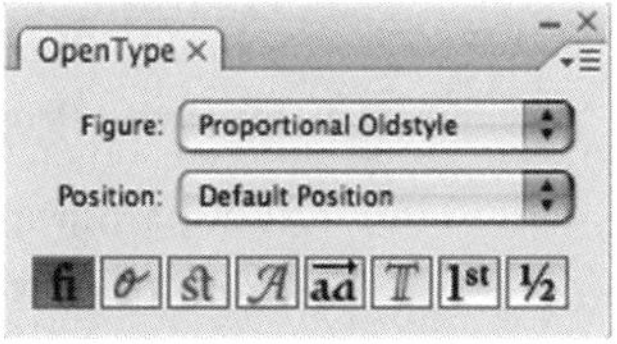

Figure 8.21 *Illustrator's* OpenType *panel*

Illustrator also provides character and paragraph styles, similar to InDesign's. The concept will probably be familiar from word processing applications: a style is a named collection of attributes, which can be applied to selected text. By defining styles for structural elements of your document, you ensure that it is consistently laid out. This facility is invaluable for lengthy structured documents, but its utility in the context of Illustrator – which is primarily concerned with graphics and can only handle single-page documents – is debatable. You can import styles from one document into another, so styles can be used to maintain a consistent appearance for the text elements of a collection of documents. However, this seems to be a specialized requirement, so we will not describe the facilities for using styles in any detail. Styles are available through the Character Styles and Paragraph Styles panels, whose use should be evident if you have ever used any style-based word processing or page layout software.

DON'T FORGET

Just click with the type tool and start typing to make a text block.

Drag out a text frame with the type tool, then enter text inside it.

In Flash, choose Static Text in the Properties panel before entering text.

Use the free transform tool to resize text boxes and frames together with the text inside them. In Illustrator and Photoshop use the arrow tool to resize the text box or frame without affecting the text.

The appearance of type has two separate aspects: the appearance of characters and the layout of paragraphs.

In Dreamweaver all text formatting should be applied through CSS rules.

Character properties are applied to selected text, or to text typed subsequently if none is selected.

Set the font, type size and colour in the Options bar or the Character panel in Photoshop or Illustrator, or in the Properties panel in Flash.

Kerning and tracking values control the spaces between characters and must be set in the Character panel.

Leading is the space between consecutive baselines. Set leading in the Character panel in Photoshop or Illustrator, or by using the Edit Format Options dialogue from the Properties panel in Flash.

Set paragraph alignment (left-aligned, centred, right-aligned or justified) and margins in the Paragraph panel in Photoshop or Illustrator or the Properties panel in Flash.

Advanced typographical controls, including some that take advantage of OpenType fonts, are available in Photoshop and Illustrator.

Bézier Curves

Bézier curves are a mainstay of vector drawing. They are used to construct smooth, flowing paths and outlines, which cannot be represented efficiently in vector form using any other type of curve. Their most obvious use is for drawing irregular smooth shapes in vector applications, including Illustrator and Flash. Bézier curves are also used in Photoshop, for constructing clipping paths, masks and selections, as well as for creating vector shapes that can be combined with bitmapped images.

So what is a Bézier curve? There is a precise mathematical answer to that question, but it isn't much help when it comes to drawing them. Figure 8.22 shows some examples, but this does not immediately convey the essential properties that unify all these curves. This will emerge by considering how to draw them.

Figure 8.22 *Some Bézier curves*

Without exception, programs that use Bézier curves provide a pen tool for precise curve drawing. Most also provide some means of automatically approximating a path dragged out by the mouse or a pressure-sensitive pen by fitting curves to it – Illustrator and Flash have their pencil tools, Photoshop its freeform pen. These are convenient, but to really understand Bézier curves you need to use the pen. Once you have mastered it, you will find it to be a precise and flexible tool, even though it is used in quite a different way from a real pen.

To draw a curve, start by making sure that the stroke is set to a suitable width and colour, and that the fill is set to none. Even if you intend to make a closed curve and fill it, having it filled while you are drawing will be confusing. Select the pen tool, move the cursor to the point where you want the curve to begin, press the mouse button and keep it pressed. The cursor changes to an arrowhead shape and a small square appears where the curve will begin. Now drag the mouse in the direction you want the curve to start heading. You will see two lines emanating from the start point, one following the cursor, the other going the same distance in the opposite direction, as shown in Figure 8.23(a). These are called **direction lines**. The length of the direction lines will determine the amount of bulge the curve eventually exhibits. When you become practised with the pen tool, you will be able to judge how far to extend the initial line. To begin with,

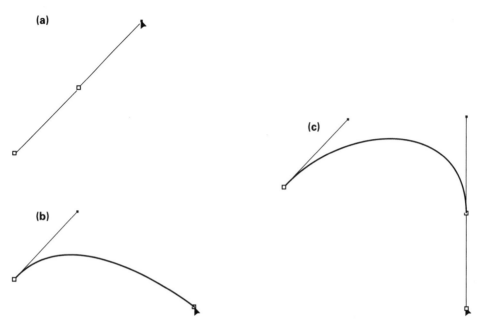

Figure 8.23 *Drawing a curve with the pen tool*

try pulling it a distance equal to about one third of the distance between the start point and the place you intend to put the end point. You don't need to get it exactly right, because you can adjust the shape of the curve later.

When you are happy with the first direction line, release the mouse button. Move the cursor to where you want the curve to finish and press the button. Again, a point appears and the cursor changes to an arrowhead. At the same time, a curve is drawn between the start point and this new end point, as in Figure 8.23(b). You will see that the direction line away from the curve at the start point disappears, leaving just the one which the curve follows. You now drag out the direction line at the end point, just as you did at the start point. This time, you can see the curve that you are drawing, as in Figure 8.23(c). As you drag the direction line, the curve will change shape. When it is satisfactory, release the mouse button and [cmd/ctl]-click away from the curve.

Many different curves can be produced by this procedure, depending on the direction and length of the two direction lines. As Figure 8.22 shows, not all of them are likely to be very useful. Broadly speaking, two shapes of Bézier curve can be built which are likely to be effective. The first curve in Figure 8.22 is an example of what is called a **C-curve**: it has a single bulging segment. The second example is an **S-curve**, with two bulges on opposite sides. (The other two examples in Figure 8.22 are C- and S-curves that have crossed their legs, as it were.) You draw C-curves by pulling the direction line at the end point to the opposite side of the curve from that at the start point. For S-curves you drag the direction lines to the same side of the curve (see Figure 8.24).

The shape of a curve is defined by its two end points, the direction line that goes away from the start point (the line you drag out when starting the curve) and the direction line that goes towards the end point (the line that is a reflection of the one you drag out at the end). You could think of the curve as setting off along the first direction line, then being pulled smoothly round by some force so that it runs into the end point along its direction line.

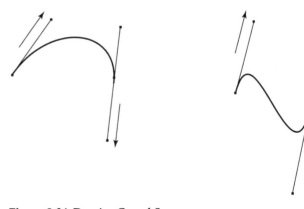

Figure 8.24 *Drawing C- and S-curves*

Usually, paths are built by combining several segments, each of which is a Bézier curve. The main advantage that Bézier curves have over arcs of circles, parabolas, and other candidates for building paths is that adjacent segments can be made to join up completely smoothly. This is the reason for the apparently superfluous second direction line; it ensures that curve segments will join smoothly. If, having drawn a curve as described above, instead of deselecting the curve you go on to add a third point by dragging with the pen again, the new segment you create will join smoothly to the first, because the direction line going into the end point of the first segment makes a straight line with the direction line going out of the start point of the next segment. Since these two points are the same, we just need the two to form a single line, the same length on each side of the meeting point. You can carry on in this way to create long smooth curves, built out of Bézier segments. If you end by clicking over the point where you started, you will make a closed curve that can be filled to make a shape.

Figure 8.25 *A corner point*

The points where segments meet – the points where you start to drag with the pen – are called ***anchor points***. The anchor points we have been describing so far are called ***smooth points***. Sometimes you want a path to make an abrupt corner (as in Figure 8.25) instead of being continuously smooth throughout; the point at such a corner is called a ***corner point***.

The account of how direction lines determine the shape of a curve tells us that, in order to make a corner point instead of a smooth point, we need to make sure that the direction lines do *not* coincide as they do normally. You need to split apart the two lines that appear when the pen is dragged. To do this you begin by drawing a segment as before, but once you have the curve the shape you want, instead of releasing the mouse button you press [opt/alt]. This leaves the direction line that determines the way the segment enters the anchor point alone, but allows you to drag the other direction line – the one that determines how the next segment leaves the anchor point – independently. In the case of Figure 8.25, we dragged the line so that it was on the same side of the curve as the incoming one, as shown in Figure 8.26. You can then continue as before to set the other end of the new segment.

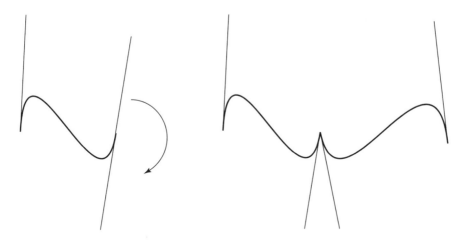

Figure 8.26 *Making a corner point*

The pen tool can also be used to draw straight lines – simply click once at each end without dragging. Polygons can be constructed by clicking at each of the vertices in turn. Mixing straight lines and curves is a little more complicated, because the gestures needed to make a curve preclude the ones needed to make straight lines, so an extra step is needed. If you want to draw a curved segment and follow it with a straight one, first draw the curve, then immediately click on its end point. You can then click somewhere else to complete the line. To follow a straight line with a curve, you do roughly the same. After you have clicked to set the end point of the line, place the pen over it again and hold down the mouse button. One direction line will appear, which you can drag to set the starting direction of the following curve. You complete the curve by dragging away from its end point in the usual way.

┌─ TRY THIS ──┐

Try to reproduce Figure 8.25 by following the procedure we have described in the text and illustrated in Figure 8.26.

Draw a square just using the pen tool. Practise making different shapes built out of a combination of straight lines and curves.

└──┘

Part of the attraction of curves built out of Bézier segments is that it is easy to reshape them if they prove unsatisfactory. It is possible to add new anchor points to a curve, or delete existing ones. Smooth points can be converted to corner points, and vice versa. Anchor points can be moved and the direction and length of direction lines can be adjusted.

In Illustrator, if you select a path you can reshape it with the pen tool. (Paths are always selected while you are drawing them.) The pen's behaviour changes once a path is selected, to allow you to add, delete or convert anchor points, depending on where you position it.

If you click with the pen on a part of a curve between anchor points, a new anchor point is added and its direction lines are displayed. You can then use the direct selection tool (see below) to move the direction lines to shape the curve around this new anchor point. On the other hand, if you click on an existing anchor point it will be deleted, and the curve will take on a new shape dictated by the remaining points. The cursor provides an indication of what will happen when you click: it changes from a plain pen into one with a small + sign below it when you are able to add an anchor point. Similarly, a – sign appears when you can delete an anchor point.

Converting between corner points and smooth points is somewhat more involved. When the pen tool is over an anchor point, press [opt/alt]. The cursor changes into an angle sign to show that the pen is now behaving as a point conversion tool. If you click on a smooth point, it will be turned into a corner point, but one without direction lines – the incoming curves approach the point in straight lines. To turn the smooth point into a corner point of the usual sort, with independent direction lines, you must drag one of its handles with the point conversion tool instead of just clicking. Similarly, to convert a corner point into a smooth point, you must drag away from the corner point, to create a pair of direction lines.

If you don't like the pen changing its behaviour in this way, you can disable the behaviour by ticking the checkbox labelled Disable Auto Add/Delete in Illustrator's general Preferences, and select the add anchor point, delete anchor point and convert anchor point tools explicitly from the Tools panel. Their icons look the same as the cursor does when the pen changes its behaviour automatically. They pop out from beneath the pen tool in the Tools panel if you hold down the mouse button.

In Flash the ordinary pen does not change its behaviour in the manner just described, you must always use the dedicated tools for adding, deleting and converting anchor points.

TRY THIS

Take one of the paths combining lines and curves that you made in the previous exercise or draw a new one. Practise reshaping it in Illustrator and Flash by adding and removing anchor points, and converting corner points into smooth points and vice versa.

In both Illustrator and Flash, the direct selection tool, which looks like a hollow arrow, is used primarily for adjusting individual anchor points. If you click on a path with this tool, the path is selected and all of its anchor points are shown as hollow circles. The direct selection tool can then be used to drag anchor points to a new position, in the same way that the ordinary selection tool is used to drag entire objects. When you move an anchor point, the curves that meet at that point are automatically reshaped. Whether the anchor point is smooth or a corner, the direction and length of the direction lines remains the same as it is dragged. This means that smooth points remain smooth and corner points stay as corners, with the curves that meet going in and out at the same angles; the curves reshape to accommodate the new position of the anchor point.

You can also use the direct selection tool for changing the length and trajectory of direction lines. These become visible as soon as you click on an anchor point. Once they appear, you can drag their ends to change the shape of the curve, just as you would when drawing it originally. The lines at corner points can be dragged independently; those at smooth points move together, to maintain their symmetrical relationship. Holding down [opt/alt] while you drag a line at a smooth point separates it from its companion, giving you another way of converting the smooth point to a corner.

The reshaping tools (but not the ordinary pen) can be used on any path or shape, whether or not it was drawn with the pen. If you prefer to draw with the pencil tool, you can still subsequently make precise adjustments with the pen and the direct selection tool. You can even use these tools to make adjustments to marks made with brush tools. In Flash, the marks made with the brush tool are actually outlines constructed of Bézier curves, whose shape can be altered like any other

---TRY THIS---

> **In Illustrator and Flash, practise reshaping paths by adjusting the direction lines at anchor points, both smooth and corner points. Practise adjusting drawings made with the pencil tool in Illustrator, and with the brush tool in Flash, using the direct selection tool in each program. Observe what sort of effects may be achieved by this means.**

Bézier shape. In Illustrator, brush strokes are paths with a special type of stroke applied, so the path can be reshaped like any other sort of stroked curve. We describe the nature and use of the brush tools in Illustrator and Flash in more detail in Chapter 5 and Chapter 6, respectively.

Accurate use of the pen requires practice. There are several pitfalls that most beginners encounter when learning to draw with the pen, but these can be avoided with care. Make sure you have selected the stroke and fill values you require before you start drawing. If your curve disappears when you deselect it, check that the stroke isn't set to none. If your curve spontaneously closes itself and fills with colour when you don't want it to, make sure the fill is set to none. It is also very easy to forget to [cmd/ctl]-click away from a path when you have finished with it. If you then use the pen tool again, thinking that you will start a new path, the old path will be connected to the new point you start at. Finally, don't forget the difference between the pen tool and the pencil tool; the pen tool is not intended to simulate a real pen, so don't try to drag the tool along the curve or line you want to draw. You can only drag the direction lines.

DON'T FORGET

Use the pen tool for drawing Bézier curves.

Before you start drawing set the stroke to a suitable value and the fill to none.

Drag out direction lines at the start and end points: a curve will be drawn between the two points, its form determined by the direction and length of the direction lines.

Add extra path segments by dragging out more direction lines.

Make corner points by holding down [opt/alt] and dragging one direction line away from its partner.

Draw straight lines with the pen by simply clicking at the start and end points. Always [cmd/ctl-click away from a path when you have finished drawing.

Add and remove anchor points and convert smooth points to corner points using the pen tool on a selected path (or the pen variants in Flash).

Use the direct selection tool to select and adjust individual anchor points, or to alter the shape of marks made with the brush tool in Illustrator or Flash.

Web Graphics

In Photoshop and Illustrator, the `File>Save for Web & Devices…` menu command brings up an almost identical dialogue (see Chapter 4 and Chapter 5), which invokes a mini-application for optimizing images for use on the World Wide Web. In Dreamweaver, a similar but different dialogue for the same purpose appears when you add a Photoshop image to a document.

The basic operation of these dialogues is described in the chapters devoted to the individual programs. For most purposes, that is all you need to know, but if you specialize in building Web sites you may want to take advantage of the extra options that are available for more effective optimization. Before describing some additional details of the way images can be optimized, we must first review some of the characteristics that image files must have if they are to be successfully deployed on Web pages.

Web Image Files

The fundamental requirement for images that are to be used in Web pages is that they be in a form that can be displayed by Web browsers, and that they be of a suitable size for transmitting over the Internet in a reasonable time. In practice, a "reasonable time" must be less than the time it takes for someone to get bored waiting for images to download. Although broadband access is becoming increasingly widespread it is not universal, downloads are never instantaneous, and Web designers often use many images on a single page. Since people get bored quickly in front of a computer that doesn't appear to be doing anything, file sizes must be kept down. This immediately rules out using files in the native format of image manipulation programs, such as Photoshop, and the formats for interchange between such programs (for example, TIFF) because these use large file sizes to keep the image in a form that is readily editable – for instance, layers are usually kept separately, each requiring as many bytes as the entire image would if it was flattened.

Unfortunately, vector graphics are rarely used on the Web, and bitmapped images inherently occupy a lot of bytes – usually three for each pixel, although this may be reduced to one by the use of indexed colour. To reduce their space requirements (and hence the bandwidth needed to download them rapidly), compression algorithms are employed. The range of available techniques can be broadly divided into two categories: *lossless* and *lossy*. Any lossless compression algorithm has the property that if it is used to compress an image, and then its inverse decompression algorithm is used to restore it to full size, the resulting image is identical, bit for bit, with the original. Lossless compression algorithms work by cleverly encoding the image data so that it occupies fewer bits, by taking advantage of redundancy in the uncompressed representation. In contrast, lossy algorithms work by discarding information, so that if an image is compressed and then decompressed the result will usually be different from the original. Naturally, it is not just any data that is discarded. On the basis of studies of human image perception, the algorithms are designed to ensure that only visually insignificant information is discarded. The most widely used lossy image compression algorithm was developed by the Joint Photographic Experts Group (JPEG), after whom it is named. JPEG compression can be controlled by a quality setting which determines how much data is lost, allowing you to trade off image size against quality.

Indexed Colour

As we explained near the beginning of this chapter, the principle of indexed colour is used in some image files to reduce their size. A palette containing all the colours in the image is stored with the file and each pixel is represented as an 8-bit value which serves as an index into the palette. Using indexed colour reduces the space occupied by an image by a factor of almost three compared with the alternative, sometimes called *direct colour*, of storing 24-bit values in the bitmap. (Almost three because the palette itself occupies some space.) This reduction comes at a price, though. Many images, especially photographs, contain very many more than 256 colours. A crude approach to reducing them to indexed colour is to create the palette from the most common colours in the image, and map all the other colours to their nearest matches in the palette. The result is often an unsightly *posterization* of the image – areas of similar colours merge, as in a cheaply printed poster, to produce bands and hard-edged shapes instead of tonal gradations. The alternative is to *dither* the missing colours. Blocks of any colour that is not in the palette are replaced by patterns made up of dots of several colours that are, in the hope that optical mixing will produce the illusion of the missing colour. Dithering can result in a blurring of the image, though, and the dot patterns are visible on close inspection. Also, dithering can be done well or badly. Photoshop and Illustrator do a fair job, but Web browsers do a poor one.

File Formats

Of the hundreds of graphics file formats in use, only two are routinely understood by Web browsers: GIF and JPEG. These share some characteristics – both are bitmapped formats which employ some form of compression to reduce the size of images – but they differ in many important respects, making each one suitable for different types of image used in different situations.

GIF (Graphics Interchange Format) was developed by Compuserve and used extensively on its bulletin board systems before the Internet superseded such services. It is quite an elderly format in computing terms, better matched to the capabilities of MS-DOS systems with 8-bit graphics cards than contemporary Macs and PCs. It continues to flourish, though, and still serves admirably for purposes, such as logos and buttons, where its limitations become a virtue. Additionally, it has some special features that otherwise superior formats lack, as we will see.

GIFs are losslessly compressed using an algorithm known by the initials of its originators, *LZW*. The LZW compression algorithm is patented. Any image manipulation software that reads or writes GIF files must implement LZW, and so requires a licence. LZW compression works best on images that contain areas of flat colour; it copes less well with tonal gradations, soft edges and noise. This means that GIF is not generally suitable for photographic images, but makes it useful as a bitmapped format for images that were originally created as vector graphics.

GIF uses indexed colour, with up to 256 entries in the colour table. So although the data compression is lossless, information is necessarily discarded when 24-bit artwork is saved in GIF format. The loss of colours may often be more intrusive than the artefacts that result from lossy compression. It does, of course, substantially reduce file sizes. The format is flexible enough to use the minimum number of bits per pixel required by the colour table, so for images with few colours additional worthwhile savings are made. For instance, an image that only used 16 different colours would require only four bits for each pixel and would therefore be half the size of an image that used all the available 256 colours.

The GIF format does have a couple of special tricks up its sleeve which give it a considerable advantage over JPEG in certain situations. The first is transparency. One colour in the palette can be designated transparent. That is, when the image is displayed (on a Web page, for example), wherever that colour value would appear, anything beneath it shows through. Transparency can be used to create the appearance of irregularly shaped images and objects that float above a background. The use of a designated transparent colour means that a pixel is either fully transparent or opaque, there is no provision for partial transparency and blending.

GIF's second trick is that a single GIF file may contain a whole animation sequence, as described in Chapter 4. For this reason in particular, GIFs are still very widely used on the Web.

Finally, GIFs may be *interlaced*. Normally, images are displayed from the top downwards as data arrives in the browser. If a GIF is interlaced, then the data is reordered, so that it can be displayed in a series of bands, rather like a Venetian blind, the gaps between the bands being filled in one at a time as more data arrives. This is sometimes claimed to be a more agreeable way for users to see an image built up if they are using a slow connection to the Internet.

PNG (Portable Network Graphics) was developed as an alternative to GIF. PNG uses a different, but still lossless, compression algorithm, which is not patented, so there are no licence fees for using the algorithm. PNG also improves on GIF in other ways, most significantly by providing for up to 48-bit colour and an alpha channel, which allows for partial transparency and compositing. The PNG format has been standardized and is endorsed by the World Wide Web Consortium, but it has not yet managed to supersede GIF on the Web, partly because of flawed and incomplete support in the most popular Web browser, and it has now largely fallen into disuse, except among die-hard Open Source supporters. (PNG files are used for other purposes, though. For instance, the icons used in the user interfaces of Photoshop and the other digital media tools programs are stored in PNG format.) Although Photoshop and Illustrator support the export of PNG files from the **Save for Web & Devices** dialogue, we will not describe them in any detail.

Pedantically speaking, there is no such thing as a ***JPEG*** file – JPEG defined a compression algorithm but their standard did not provide a file format. Images compressed using the JPEG algorithm can be stored in a variety of file formats. What are (almost) universally referred to as JPEG files are technically JFIF (JPEG File Interchange Format) files. These files always use 24-bit colour, with no form of transparency.

It is the use of lossy compression that distinguishes JPEG images from GIF and PNG. By intent, JPEG compression was designed to work with photographs and images with similar characteristics of continuous variation of tone and colour – the very sort of images that lossless algorithms do not compress effectively. It is routinely claimed that it is possible to reduce the size of such an image by a factor of between 20 and 25 without appreciable loss of quality, making JPEG a more or less automatic choice for presenting photographs, video stills and scanned images on Web pages. By sacrificing some quality, it is possible to achieve even higher compression ratios.

JPEG's effectiveness at compressing continuous tone images is offset by its poor handling of areas of flat colour and, above all, sharp edges. The data that is discarded during JPEG compression is associated with rapid colour changes, so sharp edges tend to become blurred. In particular, text becomes less readable, so images that include text should be stored in some format that uses lossless compression if it is necessary to maintain legibility.

JPEGs cannot be interlaced, but an extension to the JPEG standard, which is widely supported, allows for them to be stored in such a way that they can be displayed progressively by a Web browser as the data is received from a server. This means that the image is displayed as a series of progressively better approximations. At first, a crude version corresponding to a very low quality setting is shown. As more data arrives, the displayed image becomes gradually better, until, when the whole file has been received, it is shown at the quality at which it was prepared. Progressive display is somewhat slower than the alternative of storing the image so that it will be displayed at full quality from the top down as it arrives, but it has the advantage that the user can soon get an idea of what the image looks like – and move on if they aren't interested.

Optimizing for the Web

As the preceding description implies, preparing an image for use on the Web requires a suitable file format to be chosen, and various properties appropriate to the chosen format – the quality of JPEG compression, whether a GIF is to be interlaced, and so on – have to be set. If indexed colour is to be used, it may be necessary to tinker with the colour palette to minimize the adverse effects of dithering. The process of setting these properties in order to produce a file of acceptable quality that will download in a time appropriate for the Web page it will be used on, subject to assumptions about the typical connection speed available, is referred to, somewhat imprecisely, as *image optimization*.

You may find it helpful at this point to review the basic features of the Save for Web & Devices dialogue, as described in Chapters 4 and 5. As we explained there, for simple situations, all you need to do is choose one of the presets, check the previewed version of the image and click Save, but sometimes more fine-tuning is needed. The dialogue provides plenty of opportunities for honing the optimization process.

One refinement of the preview in this dialogue that we did not mention previously concerns the reproduction of colour on different platforms. When working with colour images for the Web, you should be aware that the colour displayed for a particular value stored in an image will be perceptibly brighter on a Macintosh than on a Windows system. In other words, if you create images on a Mac – still the preferred platform of many designers – they will look dull when they are displayed on a PC – the preferred platform of most domestic and business users. You can preview the appearance of an image on different platforms using the pop-up menu to the right of the image previews. (It functions like and resembles a panel menu.) Choose Standard Windows Color if you are using a Mac and want to see what the image will look like on Windows, or Standard Macintosh Color if you are in the inverse situation.

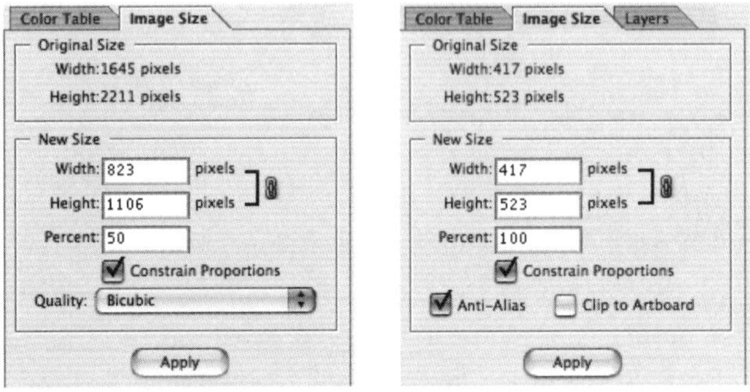

Figure 8.27 *Resizing during optimization in Photoshop (left) and Illustrator (right)*

You can choose to resize an image during the optimization process if necessary – it may be that the only way you can make a file small enough is by shrinking the image. The Image Size tab in the lower right of the dialogue box is attached to a simple image resizing dialogue, as Figure 8.27 shows. This dialogue is a simplified version of Photoshop's Image Size dialogue, and allows you to set a new size, either using absolute dimensions for the height and width, or as a percentage. (This tab may be concealed by the Color Table, which we will describe later.) In Photoshop, the Quality pop-up is used to choose the interpolation method to be used during the resampling from the same set of options as the full Photoshop resizing dialogue described in Chapter 4. In Illustrator, there is no question of interpolation because the resizing is done on the vector original. Instead, you can choose whether to anti-alias the image and whether to clip it to the artboard, that is, to use the entire area of the artboard instead of just the bounding box of the art work itself. When you have chosen your settings, you must explicitly click the **Apply** button to change the image's size, otherwise nothing will happen.

To the left of the tabbed image previews is what you might call a mini-toolbox. This holds four tools: a hand tool, for moving the image around when the pane is too small to show all of it at once at your chosen magnification; a magnifier, for zooming in (click with the tool) and out ([opt/alt]-click with it); an eyedropper for sampling colours; and a slice selection tool. Image slicing is not an operation that can be recommended, so we will ignore this last tool.

Whichever tool you have selected, a continuously updated read-out of the colour under the cursor is shown at the bottom of the window. The red, green and blue components are given, together with an alpha value for images that use partial transparency; these are followed by a hexadecimal value, made by combining the red, green and blue components into a 24-bit value, expressed to base 16. Last, for file formats using indexed colour, comes the index into the palette used for the colour under the cursor.

R: 204   G: 207   B: 195   Alpha: 255   Hex: CCCFC3   Index: 208

Each of the presets available in the pop-up menu below the **Done** button represents a collection of values for the individual settings that are controlled by the input elements below it. If, after looking at the preview of the optimized version of the image, none of the presets seems to be good enough, you will have to set parameters by hand. You choose the file format from the unlabelled pop-up menu at the top left of this group of controls. The options which become available depend on the format you choose. We will consider the options for each of the Web image file formats in turn. We will not deal with the options for the WBMP format (available in Photoshop) as this is not a Web image format, nor for SWF in Illustrator, which is described in Chapter 5.

GIF Settings

The options for GIFs, shown in Figure 8.28, are the most extensive. The first option you can set (reading the panel in rows from left to right) is a value between 0 and 100 for the amount of lossiness to be applied when the image is compressed. This is surprising, in view of the fact that GIF files are always losslessly compressed. However, it has become common practice to optionally discard some information before applying the LZW compression, to increase its effectiveness. This information can never be retrieved, making the combined process lossy. Applying small amounts of

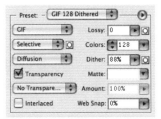

Figure 8.28 *GIF options*

lossiness (less than 10) can reduce file sizes by a worthwhile amount, without any appreciable loss of image quality, but using high values results in unsightly artefacts. The value can be typed directly in the **Lossy** field, or set using the slider which pops up when you hold down the mouse button with the cursor over the triangle to the right of the field.

The second row of options in the dialogue is used for selecting the colour palette. The pop-up menu on the left is used to choose the method by which the palette is to be built. The basic set of choices is between Perceptual, Selective, Adaptive (which all cause the palette to be constructed dynamically from the colours in the original image) and Restrictive (Web) (which uses the fixed Web-safe set of colours). Some other fixed palettes are provided as additional choices: the Mac OS and Windows system palettes, and black and white (1-bit colour) and greyscale.

The three methods of constructing the palette dynamically give different priorities to the colours in the image. The perceptual method bases its priorities on the sensitivity of the human eye to different colours, favouring those we are most aware of. The selective algorithm (the default) favours areas of flat colour and Web-safe colours; it is designed with GIF compression and Web browsers in mind. The adaptive method prioritizes the image's most common colours.

The next field, labelled Colors is for choosing the size of the palette. The pop-up menu attached to this field lets you select powers of two for the number of colours – these values all fit in an exact number of bits, so there is little or no advantage in choosing any other number, but you can type in a value or use the increment and decrement arrows if you like. (Notice that the GIF presets only go up to 128 colours, since it is widely believed that the extra 128 available in a 256-colour palette provide little extra quality, but you should test this for yourself.)

The next pair of settings is concerned with dithering colours that are not in the palette. The pop-up menu on the left lets you choose an algorithm for constructing the patterns of dots used to replace missing colours. This refers to dithering introduced during the optimization of the image. Dithering may also occur when the image is previewed in a browser on any system with limited colour abilities. Browsers often make a poor job of dithering, so it is important to try and avoid the need for browser dither by doing it beforehand. (By selecting Browser Dither from the pop-up menu just above and to the right of the previews you can see what kind of result browser dithering could produce.) The first option, No Dither makes no attempt to dither, leaving it up to the browser, which may result in posterization. Pattern dither resembles the traditional half-tone screening used in printing to produce many colours from the limited number of process inks. For Web images it usually produces too noticeable a pattern. The options Diffusion and Noise introduce randomness, which makes the dithering less obvious. For Diffusion only, a percentage value can be set in the box on the right to control the amount of dither that is applied.

┌─TRY THIS──┐

Open a photograph in Photoshop and a vector drawing in Illustrator, and select the File>Save for Web & Devices... command. Choose one of the GIF presets and then modify it by choosing different colour palettes and dithering options. Use the 2-up view to judge the effect on your images.

└──┘

The next pair of options deals with transparent areas of the image. Selecting the Transparency checkbox causes the transparent areas of the image to be assigned a colour which is used to denote transparency in the GIF. In other words, areas of the image that are transparent in Photoshop or Illustrator will remain transparent and allow the background to show through when the saved GIF file is embedded in a Web page. Alternatively, you can select a colour in the Matte field, which will be used to fill the transparent areas. Actually, there is a little more to it than that. Aliasing of edges can result in pixels that are partially transparent (before saving), which can produce a halo effect if the image is placed on a background such as a Web page. Matting causes these partially transparent pixels to be blended with the matte colour. If you select both a matte colour and transparency, the matte colour is blended with the partially transparent pixels, while fully transparent pixels are left alone. If you know what the background colour of the Web page containing the image will be and choose the same colour for a matte with transparency, this will avoid the halo. The options provided on the Matte pop-up menu are None, if you do not want to use any matte colour, Eyedropper Color, which causes the matte colour to be taken from the most recent selection made with the eyedropper tool in the mini-toolbox, White, Black and Other…, which causes the colour picker to be displayed. In Photoshop, there are also options for using the foreground and background colours.

---TRY THIS---

Make a copy of a photograph or some scanned artwork, and use the eraser in Photoshop, with anti-aliasing turned on, to create some transparent areas and a transparent, irregular edge to the image. Go back to the Save for Web & Devices dialogue, select GIF for the file type, and preview the image in a browser. Experiment with setting different matte colours and preview the results.

On the bottom row of options for GIF optimization are, first, a checkbox that is used to select interlacing, and second, a field for setting the extent to which you will allow colours to be automatically replaced by the nearest value in the Web-safe palette so as to avoid dithering. The value is expressed as a percentage; higher values allow more colours to be replaced in this way. We usually say that colours "snap to" the Web-safe palette. Unless you have a special reason for doing so, don't make your colours snap to the Web-safe palette, as it will probably ruin your image.

JPEG Settings

The fundamentally different nature of JPEG images means that the optimization settings available when this format is chosen are not quite like those for the other formats. There is a field for specifying a matte colour, but since JPEGs do not support transparency this is always used to fill in transparent areas with a matte colour – if you select None, white will be used by default. There is a checkbox for stipulating progressive download, which is similar to interlacing, as we described earlier. Otherwise, the JPEG options derive from the JPEG format's distinctive characteristics.

The most important of these is the quality setting used in applying lossy compression. This represents a trade-off between image quality – the extent to which, after compression and decompression the appearance of the original image is preserved – and file size. Higher quality means larger file size. However, the quality setting is really just a parameter to the compression process that determines how much data is discarded. The effect this will have on the perceived image quality depends on the content of the image itself; some images will still be entirely acceptable at low quality settings that would thoroughly degrade other images. It is particularly useful to have the 2-up and 4-up previews available so that you can immediately judge the effect of changing settings before you save the file.

There are three ways of setting the quality. The simplest is to use the pop-up menu at the left to choose between Low, Medium, High, Very High and Maximum. High is good enough for many photographs intended for Web pages, and Medium can often be used without much loss of quality. Finer gradations may make little visible difference, but you can set a precise value in the Quality field; a slider is attached to the triangle by this field for setting the value non-numerically.

Above the Quality field is a checkbox intriguingly labelled Optimized – but the whole process under consideration is optimization. What this option refers to is a means of adding extra compression to the JPEG file, using an optional feature of the standard. However, this means that not all browsers will be able to render the image, so it should not be used if compatibility is important.

Below the Quality field is another field equipped with a slider for setting an amount of Gaussian blur (see Chapter 4) to be applied before compression. Blurring reduces the impact of the artefacts produced by high levels of JPEG compression. Using this option obviously implies that the image may appear blurred to some extent, so don't use it unless you are using a low quality setting and the preview suggests that a bit of blur really will improve the final result.

TRY THIS

Using a photograph as the image to be optimized, in Photoshop select JPEG as the file format and then adjust the quality from the lowest to the highest available values. For every value, compare the optimized and original images. Try adding Gaussian blur, and see what effect it has, both for high and low quality settings. Repeat the exercise using different photographs with different visual characteristics (landscapes, interiors and portraits, for example).

Try exporting a vector drawing from Illustrator as a JPEG, using the Save for Web & Devices… dialogue. How does the result compare with the photographs you just exported? Do the various settings have the same effect?

JPEG files may include ICC (International Colour Consortium) *colour profiles*, which are used by colour management software, such as Apple's ColorSync, to ensure that colours are reproduced accurately. A colour profile captures features of the device on which the image was made, and a Web browser that understands colour profiles can compensate when it displays the image on a device with different characteristics. The checkbox labelled ICC Profile should be selected if you wish to embed a colour profile in your JPEG. Note, though, that this can only be done if the image has already been saved in the application's native format with a profile.

If you find yourself using the same combination of settings many times, you can save them as a preset, to be added to those already available in the Settings pop-up menu. This is done by choosing Save Settings... from the small pop-up menu to the right of the Presets pop-up. You are presented with a file-saving dialogue, since presets are actually kept in files, but all you really need to do is provide a name for your settings. Afterwards, that name appears in the Settings pop-up menu. If you ever decide you don't need it, you can remove it using the Delete Settings command in the same menu. This removes the currently selected preset.

All JPEG files – including photographs in JPEG format downloaded from digital cameras – will already have had lossy compression applied to them, and you may not know what settings were used. If you need to compress these files further for use on Web pages, as is often the case with large photographs, the quality of the result will depend not only on your new settings, but also on how much the original file was compressed. Each time a JPEG is compressed again, more of the original image information is lost and the image is visually degraded further. This is one of the reasons that you cannot depend upon using the same settings every time, but need to use the previews to judge the best settings for each image.

If it is essential that you constrain your image to a certain file size, or if you really don't want to be bothered with the decisions involved in choosing a format and setting the parameters, there is a quick but rather crude alternative. On the pop-up menu by the Settings presets menu is a command Optimize to File Size.... Selecting this command produces the dialogue box shown in Figure 8.29. You simply set the size you want the file to be, tell the application whether to take your current settings as a starting point, or do the job entirely automatically, including the choice of file format, and then let it do its best to optimize your image so that it is reduced to the size you desire. This is certainly a quick way of carrying out the task, but it does mean relinquishing control over the various trade-offs to a program (that is, to a set of decisions made by a programmer).

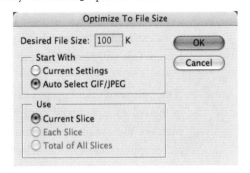

Figure 8.29 *Optimizing to a specific file size*

─TRY THIS─

Find some settings for JPEG and GIF compression that you feel offer a good compromise between file size and quality, and save them as presets. Try applying these presets to other images with a range of visual characteristics.

Use the Optimize to File Size... dialogue to reduce your images to several different file sizes, ranging from 5% to 50% of their original size. Evaluate the quality of the resulting images. See if you can do better by selecting optimization parameters yourself using Save for Web & Devices.

Editing the Palette

When you are saving your image in GIF format that uses indexed colour it is sometimes desirable to change the colour palette from the one which is automatically constructed by the application. This can be done using the Color Table tabbed pane in the lower right of the Save for Web & Devices dialogue. (As you can see in Figure 8.30, the Color Table is normally docked with the Image Size pane, which we described previously.) Here, you can add extra colours, delete existing ones, or change the values that palette indices are mapped to.

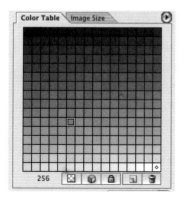

Figure 8.30 *Editing the colour table*

Adding a colour that was left out when a palette was created automatically is perhaps the operation you will be most likely to want to perform. It is sometimes the case that a colour has great visual significance while only appearing in a very small area of the image, so that it gets overlooked by the automatic colour reduction algorithms. To add such a colour to the palette by hand, you simply select it – the easiest way is usually by sampling it from the image with the eyedropper – and click the New button below the colour table swatches. If your palette has been constructed dynamically, that is, using one of the perceptual, selective or adaptive methods, the new colour will replace the nearest colour to it that is already in the palette. If the palette has fewer than the maximum 256 entries and you wish to add the colour as an extra entry in the palette, you can hold down the [cmd/ctl] key while you click on the button. This will convert the palette to a custom one and no colour will be replaced.

If the palette fills right up you can delete colours. Select a colour, either by clicking on its swatch in the colour table or by using the eyedropper, and then click on the dustbin icon below the swatches. You can also edit colours. If you double-click a swatch in the colour table, the colour picker appears and you can select a new value. The effect is to change the colour stored in the location in the palette occupied by the colour you double-clicked. This means that every pixel in an image whose value is the index of that location will change colour. This is a rather drastic operation, and Photoshop has better ways of replacing colours, as we described in Chapter 4.

─TRY THIS─

> **In Photoshop, open an image that uses a wide range of colours. Using the Save for Web & Devices dialogue, select GIF and set the number of colours to a low value. Try editing the Color Table to add missing colours from the original image and see whether the optimized image is improved.**

Saving the Optimized File

The final step in optimization is to save the file to disk. While you are doing so, you are offered the opportunity to save an HTML file that embeds the image as well as the optimized image file itself. This is only really useful if you have built an entire Web page by slicing an image, since the HTML to put the slices together must be quite elaborate. We would never recommend creating Web pages in this way. For the more sensible case, when you just want to save the image, it is necessary to prevent the HTML being created. Clicking Save in the Save for Web & Devices dialogue takes you to an extended file-saving dialogue. Below the usual text field for entering a file name is a pop-up menu labelled Format on Mac OS systems, or Save As Type on Windows. From this, you should choose Images Only and ignore the remaining options.

Devices

The command Save for Web & Devices… also allows you to save files for "devices", that is, mobile phones and PDAs. *Device Central* is a program, included with Adobe's Creative Suites, that can be used to preview the appearance of images and time-based media on mobile devices. Clicking on the button labelled Device Central… in the bottom right corner of the Save for Web & Devices dialogue will cause Device Central to open and preview the image you are currently working on. (If you are creating work specially for mobile devices, Device Central can be used to set up documents so that they are the right size from the beginning. In the case of Flash movies, starting from Device Central will also ensure that the Publish settings are appropriate for the capabilities of your chosen device.)

Figure 8.31 shows a typical image preview. The operation of Device Central should be largely self-explanatory. With the Emulator tab selected, as it always will be if you come from the Save for Web & Devices dialogue, you choose a device from the list on the left, and set parameters for the way you want the image to be used (for example, as a full screen image, or as an incoming call indicator), the level of back-lighting and ambient light levels, and so on. In Figure 8.31 we have shown our image as an incoming call indicator under outdoor light. (As you can see, we have made a poor choice of image for this particular job.) The Device Profiles tab can be used for displaying the capabilities and characteristics of each available device.

In Photoshop there is a Device Central… button available in the new file dialogue box. (See Figure 4.8 in Chapter 4.) Clicking this button will dismiss the dialogue and open Device Central

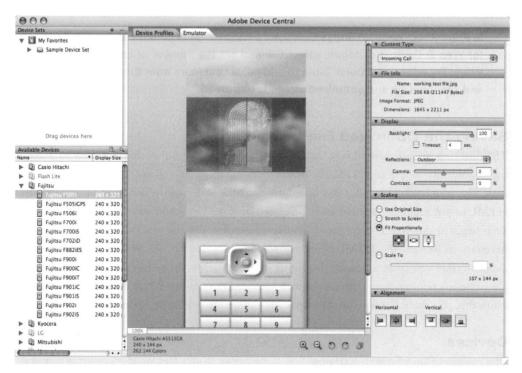

Figure 8.31 *Previewing an image in Device Central*

with its New Document tab displayed, as shown in Figure 8.32. Here you can choose a device and set options for the kind of document you want to create. When you click the Create button, you are returned to Photoshop, with a matching new document to work on.

In Illustrator, the Device Central... button only appears if you select Mobile and Devices from the New Document Profile pop-up menu. In Flash, you must select Flash File (Mobile) in the General tab of the new file dialogue if you wish to set up your document in Device Central.

Alternatively, you can start up Device Central explicitly, and choose an application – Photoshop, Illustrator or Flash – from the File > New Document In sub-menu. You can choose a device and so on in the same way as above, and then click Create to work on it in the chosen program.

┌─ TRY THIS ───

Open a selection of images and preview their appearance in a range of mobile devices by opening Device Central from the Save for Web & Devices dialogue.

Practise creating images and Flash movies for mobile devices by setting up documents in Device Central. Take note of the characteristics (resolution, colour mode, etc.) that have been set.

└──

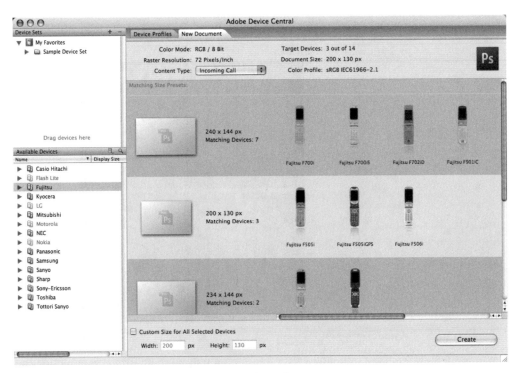

Figure 8.32 *Setting up a new document in Device Central*

Optimizing in Dreamweaver

So far, we have considered the optimization of an image for the Web to be something you do in the program in which you created the image, in order to export a version suitable for the Web. If you are a Web designer who is not familiar with graphics programs, you may well prefer to perform the optimization when you import the image into Dreamweaver. This can be done, but only for Photoshop files.

If you add an image to an HTML document, in the manner described in Chapter 7, and select a Photoshop (PSD) file, the dialogue shown in Figure 8.33 will appear. Despite differences in appearance, this dialogue duplicates most of the essential functions of Photoshop and Illustrator's **Save for Web & Devices** dialogues that we have been describing so far.

Like those dialogues, this provides you with a preview of one or more versions of the image you are importing, optimized for the Web, in the sense we explained earlier. By default, a single view of the original image is shown. If you tick the **Preview** checkbox at the top of the dialogue box, a preview of the optimized version will be shown instead. As in Photoshop and Illustrator, you can compare the effect of different optimization settings by splitting the preview to show two or four different previews. In Dreamweaver, the layout of the previews is controlled by the

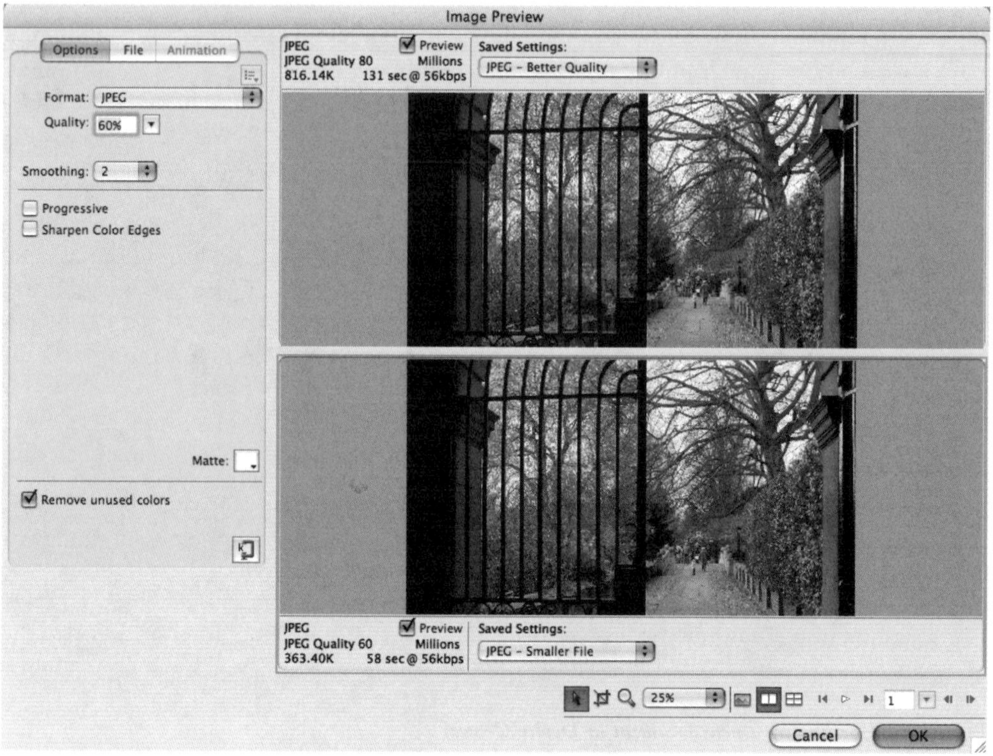

Figure 8.33 *Optimizing a Photoshop file while importing it into Dreamweaver*

buttons next to the magnification pop-up below them. (Although the two-up button indicates a vertical split, as Figure 8.33 shows, it actually causes the preview to split horizontally.) For each version, there is a copy of the **Preview** checkbox. If it is checked, you can choose a preset from the **Saved Settings** pop-up. A summary of the properties of the optimized file appears. As in the other programs, in many cases choosing one of these collections of settings may be all that you need to do.

If you are not happy with any of the presets, you can set parameters by hand in the **Options** pane of the panel on the left. The available parameters match those we have described. If you choose GIF as the format, you will be able to edit the colour palette.

If you need to optimize the image to a specific file size, click on the icon in the shape of a G-clamp, and enter the desired size in the simple dialogue that appears.

The **File** pane of the left-hand panel can be used to scale the incoming image, in the same way as you would resize an image you were saving from Photoshop. Here, you can also crop the image, by entering values for the coordinates of the top left corner, and the width and height. You will also notice that there is a crop tool available under the previews (to the right of the arrow tool), which you can use to crop the image by eye.

When you click OK, an optimized file in your chosen format is saved. By default, the file will be saved into the root folder of the site containing the HTML file into which you are inserting it. You can choose another location in the usual way, but if it does not lie within the site, a warning will be given and Dreamweaver will offer to copy the file into the site, as with any other image. After you have saved the optimized image, a simple dialogue appears in which you can – and should – provide alt text for the image. You can also provide a URL for the longdesc attribute if that is appropriate.

Dreamweaver gives you a second chance to adjust the optimization settings for any image. With an image selected, click on the G-clamp icon in the Properties panel to reopen the optimization dialogue and alter any settings you wish to.

┌─ TRY THIS ───
│ **Save a photograph from Photoshop as a PSD file and import it into an HTML**
│ **document in Dreamweaver. Experiment with the optimization settings as you**
│ **did when saving Web graphics from Photoshop and Illustrator. Notice the**
│ **correspondences between the controls and settings in the different programs.**
└──

DON'T FORGET

Web images must be in JPEG or GIF (or PNG) format, and should be optimized to reduce file size and bandwidth requirements.

GIF files are losslessly compressed and use indexed colour (a maximum of 256 colours). Dithering can be used to avoid posterization.

JPEG files are lossily compressed and are the most suitable format for images with continuously varying tone, such as photographs. Greater compression of JPEGs produces smaller file sizes but lower quality images.

Preview optimized images and set options appropriate to each file type in the Save for Web & Devices dialogue in Photoshop and Illustrator.

Edit the Color Table to improve the colour fidelity of GIF images.

Use Device Central to preview images and Flash movies for mobile devices.

In Dreamweaver, optimize Photoshop (PSD) files as you import them into HTML documents.

Index